THE
DELUSIONS
OF CROWDS

Also by William J. Bernstein

Rational Expectations:
Asset Allocation for Investing Adults

Masters of the Word:
How Media Shaped History

The Investor's Manifesto:
Preparing for Prosperity, Armageddon, and Everything in Between

A Splendid Exchange:
How Trade Shaped the World from Prehistory to Today

The Birth of Plenty:
How the Prosperity of the Modern World Was Created

The Four Pillars of Investing:
Lessons for Building a Winning Portfolio

The Intelligent Asset Allocator:
How to Build Your Portfolio to Maximize Returns and Minimize Risk

THE
DELUSIONS
OF CROWDS

Why People GO MAD in GROUPS

WILLIAM J. BERNSTEIN

Grove Press
New York

Published simultaneously in Canada
Printed in the United States of America

First Grove Atlantic hardcover edition: February 2021
First Grove Atlantic paperback edition: February 2022

Library of Congress Cataloging-in-Publication data is available for this title.

ISBN 978-0-8021-5710-2
eISBN 978-0-8021-5711-9

Grove Press
an imprint of Grove Atlantic
154 West 14th Street
New York, NY 10011

Distributed by Publishers Group West

groveatlantic.com

22 23 24 25   10 9 8 7 6 5 4 3 2 1

To Kate, Johanna, and Max

CONTENTS

THE
DELUSIONS
OF CROWDS

PRELUDE

Nearly two centuries ago, a young Scotsman named Charles Mackay simultaneously attacked the subjects of God and Mammon in memorable style. Born in 1814, he enjoyed a distinguished literary career as a popular poet, writer of ballads, and American Civil War correspondent and editor for British newspapers. But posterity remembers him best for his 1841 authorship, at the tender age of twenty-seven, of *Memoirs of Extraordinary Popular Delusions*, which narrated multiple historical episodes of mass mania, several of which had to do with either religion or money.[1] It has been in print ever since.

Mackay chronicled the end-times delusions that supposedly gripped Europe as it approached the year A.D. 1000, as well as the remarkable religious madness of the Crusades. The book's best known chapters, though, detail the financial mass delusions of the Dutch tulipmania of the 1630s and the twin stock market bubbles in Paris and London in 1719–1720. These episodes, which constitute the first three chapters, are what propelled the book to its long-lasting fame.* Successive financial manias followed the book's publication with such frequency, regularity, and global impact that, nearly two centuries after it was written, the book is still required reading among finance professionals.[2]

Mackay was certainly not the first to intuit the contagious nature of human irrationality. Consider, for example, this passage from Herodotus:

> When [Darius] was king of Persia, he summoned the Greeks who happened to be present at his court, and asked them what they would take to eat the dead bodies of their fathers. They replied that they would not do it for any money in the world. Later, in the presence of

---

* The book was subsequently renamed *Memoirs of Extraordinary Popular Delusions and the Madness of Crowds*, and hereafter is referred to simply as *Extraordinary Popular Delusions*.

the Greeks, and through an interpreter, so that they could understand
what was said, he asked some Indians, of the tribe called Callatiae,
who do in fact eat their parents' dead bodies, what they would take
to burn them. They uttered a cry of horror and forbade him to mention such a dreadful thing. One can see by this what custom can do,
and Pindar, in my opinion, was right when he called it "king of all."[3]

The Greeks, after all, were antiquity's intellectuals, and Darius must have
been tickled to box their rhetorical ears. His unspoken messages to the
Greeks: You may be the most learned among humankind, but you are just
as irrational as the rest of us; you are simply better at rationalizing just
why, despite all evidence to the contrary, you are still right.

While the ancients and Mackay were well acquainted with human
irrationality and popular manias, they could not know their precise biological, evolutionary, and psychosocial wellsprings. Mackay, for example,
must have asked himself exactly why groups of people, from time to time,
chase the same ludicrously overpriced investments en masse.

Today, we have a much better idea of how this happens. In the first
place, financial economists have discovered that human beings intuitively
seek out outcomes with very high but very rare payoffs, such as lottery
tickets, that on average lose money but tantalize their buyers with the
chimera of unimaginable wealth. In addition, over the past several decades, neuroscientists have uncovered the basic anatomic and psychological mechanism behind both greed and fear: the so-called limbic system,
which lies close by the vertical plane that divides the brain between its
right and left hemispheres. One symmetrically placed pair of the limbic
system's structures, the nuclei accumbens (singular: nucleus accumbens),
lie approximately behind each eye, while another pair, the amygdalae
(singular: amygdala), sit just under the temples.

Using functional magnetic resonance imaging (fMRI), researchers
have found that the nuclei accumbens fire not only with reward, but even
more intensely with its anticipation, be it culinary, sexual, social, or financial. In contrast, the amygdalae fire with disgust, fear, and revulsion. If,
for example, you adore your aunt Flo's lasagna, your nuclei accumbens
and their connections will fire ever more rapidly on the way over to her
house, and likely peak just as the aroma wafts from the serving dish. But
as soon as the first bite is taken, their firing rate decreases, and if your

aunt informs you upon arrival that she's burned the dish, they will almost completely cease firing.[4]

The benefit of an active anticipatory circuitry seems obvious; Mother Nature favors those who anticipate and strive, whereas the enjoyment of satiation, once achieved, offers little evolutionary advantage. And few things likely stimulate the nuclei accumbens as does the knowledge that some of those around us are becoming effortlessly wealthy. As economic historian Charles Kindleberger observed, "There is nothing so disturbing to one's well-being and judgment as to see a friend get rich."[5]

Novelists and historians have known for centuries that people do not deploy the powerful human intellect to dispassionately analyze the world, but rather to rationalize how the facts conform to their emotionally derived preconceptions. Journalist David Halberstam's magisterial *The Best and the Brightest* illustrated how the nation's most brilliant policy makers deluded themselves about American military involvement in Vietnam, a tendency once again evident; our recent foreign adventures suggest that we have not successfully climbed that particular learning curve.[6]

Over the past several decades, psychologists have accumulated experimental data that dissect the human preference of rationalization over rationality. When presented with facts and data that contradict our deeply held beliefs, we generally do not reconsider and alter those beliefs appropriately. More often than not, we avoid contrary facts and data, and when we cannot avoid them, our erroneous assessments will occasionally even harden and, yet more amazingly, make us more likely to proselytize them. In short, human "rationality" constitutes a fragile lid perilously balanced on the bubbling cauldron of artifice and self-delusion so lucidly illustrated by Mackay.

Mackay's own behavior demonstrated just how susceptible even the most rational and well-informed observers can be to a financial mania. Shortly after he published *Extraordinary Popular Delusions* in 1841, England experienced a financial mania that revolved around the great high-tech industry of the time, the railroad, which was even larger than the twin bubbles that swept Paris and London in 1719–1720. Investors, greedy for stocks, underwrote the increase in England's track mileage from two thousand in 1843 to five thousand in 1848, and thousands of more miles were planned but never built when shares finally went bust. If anyone should have foreseen the collapse, it was Mackay.

He did not. During that mania, he served as the editor of the *Glasgow Argus*, where he covered the ongoing railroad construction with a notable lack of skepticism and when he published the second edition of *Extraordinary Popular Delusions* in 1852, he gave it only a brief footnote.

Financial manias can be thought of as a tragedy like *Hamlet* or *Macbeth*, with sharply defined characters, a familiar narrative arc, and well-rehearsed lines. Four dramatis personae control the narrative: the talented yet unscrupulous promoters of schemes; the gullible public who buys into them; the press that breathlessly fans the excitement; and last, the politicians who simultaneously thrust their hands into the till and avert their eyes from the flaming pyre of corruption.

The promoters follow a classical Shakespearean tragic path and are consequently the most fascinating of the actors. Most begin as brilliant, hardworking visionaries who intuit before others the riches that a new technology will bestow upon society. In the process of bringing their visions to fruition, they grow rich and powerful and, in a capitalist society that judges men by their wealth, become their nation's lions. When the speculation runs its course and bursts, they wind up disgraced and bankrupt and usually, but not always, narrowly escape the jailer.

The public proves easy pickings for the blandishments of the heroic, charismatic promoters. Competent investing requires a rare combination of mathematical ability, technological expertise, and, most critically, a working knowledge of economic history. Alas, people greatly prefer stories to data and facts; when faced with such a daunting task, humans default into narrative mode, and perhaps the most pleasing story of all is one that involves the effortless wealth to be had from buying into a new technology.

The press falls prey to the promoters in the same way as the public. Few things corrode journalistic excellence as the ease of writing about the revolutionary ventures of brilliant businessmen, who with alarming frequency grace magazine covers, first as heroes, then as accused felons.

Finally, financial manias sweep into their ambit politicians, whose reputations and popularity are enhanced by the economic prosperity that temporarily results from speculative excess, and who not infrequently get caught raiding the cookie jar.

The narrative arc of financial manias does not vary much either. Most speculative episodes combine two factors: exciting new technologies that foretell prosperity for all, and easy credit. Today in the United States, only about 10 percent of the money supply consists of actual circulating bills and coins; the rest exists as credit that can be created, within limits, at will by the banking system. That, in turn, depends upon how optimistic banks, mortgage companies, and other lenders are that they will be repaid. This process is such a counterintuitive and shocking notion that it bears repeating: banks print money. Indeed, they are as manic-depressive as the public they serve, and in the midst of the euphoria of a bubble, banks often fan the flames of speculation by "making money" with abandon, as occurred most spectacularly in the run-up to the 2007–2009 financial crisis.

Four characteristic subplots accompany a bubble. First and foremost, financial speculation begins to dominate all but the most mundane social interactions; whenever and wherever people meet, they talk not of the weather, family, or sports, but rather of stocks and real estate. Next, otherwise sensible professionals quit reliable, good-paying jobs to speculate in the aforementioned assets. Further, skepticism is often met with vehemence; while there are always some folks old enough, and with memories long enough, to have seen the play before and to know how it ends, their warnings are met with scorn and ridicule, which over the past several decades has been usually capped with these five words: "You just don't get it." Finally, normally sedate observers begin to make outlandish financial forecasts. Asset prices are predicted to not merely move 10, 20, or 30 percent up or down in a given year, but rather will double, triple, or add a zero.

Beyond its three chapters on financial manias, *Extraordinary Popular Delusions* also contained three long chapters on religious manias: one each on biblical prophecy, the Crusades, and the pursuit of witches. While religious and financial manias might seem to have little in common, the underlying forces that give them rise are identical: the desire to improve one's well-being in this life or the next. And the factors that amplify the contagion of financial and religious mass delusions are also similar: the hardwired human propensity to imitate, to fabricate and consume compelling narratives, and to seek status.

Religious manias seem a near constant feature of human history, a fairly recent example of which was the Solar Temple tragedy. On the evening of October 4, 1994, residents of the Swiss village of Cheiry were startled by flames coming from a farmhouse perched above the town, where firefighters encountered a bizarre, ghastly sight: twenty-two bodies, most wearing red, black, or white capes, with a few women wearing golden ones. All but three of the victims had been shot, and in addition, ten had plastic bags over their heads. Most were found lying in a circle, their heads pointed outward; shell casings and empty champagne bottles littered the floor.

This was only the beginning; over the next two and a half years, dozens more murder/suicide victims were discovered in Switzerland and Canada, a total of seventy-four dead, all sect members or their children; all of the deaths that followed those at Cheiry occurred within a few days of either an equinox or solstice.

Two men led the sect: a mysterious, charming, and attractive forty-six-year-old Belgian physician named Luc Jouret, who had fled conspiracy and weapons charges in Canada in 1993; and a seventy-year-old French-Canadian named Joseph Di Mambro. Among the eventual victims were the wife and son of Jean Vuarnet, a revered 1960 French Olympic ski gold medalist who later licensed his famous name to an international sunglass manufacturer. Before his death, the young Vuarnet told a reporter, "The theme of the passage from life to death came up again and again. Jouret explained that there was nothing to fear—quite the contrary. I began to feel close to sacrifice."[7]

The last Solar Temple victims were discovered on March 24, 1997; two days later, police in Rancho Santa Fe, near San Diego, found the bodies of thirty-nine members of another end-times group, the Heaven's Gate religious sect, who had also died around the same equinox and believed that after death they would be transported off the planet by a spacecraft hidden in the tail of Comet Hale-Bopp.[8]

The Solar Temple and the Heaven's Gate religious sects are just two examples in a long list of well known modern apocalyptic end-times groups: Jim Jones's Peoples Temple, whose mass-suicide/murders in Guyana in 1978 took the lives of 918; the Branch Davidians, whose standoff with clueless federal authorities in Waco, Texas, killed 86 in 1993; and the murderous Japanese Aum Shinrikyo doomsday group, who perpetrated the 1995 Tokyo subway nerve gas attack. What's striking about all these groups is that so many of their members, like Jouret and Vuarnet, were highly educated and accomplished.

Nor are end-times mass delusions peculiar to the modern world; medieval Europe produced a bumper crop of spectacular, if less well remembered, episodes. Modern neuropsychological research sheds some light on why groups of otherwise sane, intelligent, and well-adjusted people delude themselves that the world is going to end in a particular way and, oftentimes on a particular date. Humans understand the world through narratives; however much we flatter ourselves about our individual rationality, a good story, no matter how analytically deficient, lingers in the mind, resonates emotionally, and persuades more than the most dispositive facts or data.

More recently, psychologists have begun to appreciate just how effectively arresting narratives corrode our analytical ability. Perhaps the most compelling of all stories is the end-times narrative; if we understand our existence in narrative, then we all want to know its denouement. The end-times story is solidly embedded in many of the world's religions, and especially in all three Abrahamic ones, so pervasive that it has become nearly invisible, lurking behind many of every day's headlines and tweets, and so old that it goes at least as far back as, and likely further than, the dawn of civilization.

Not only does the hunger to know "the rest of the story" gnaw deeply into our consciousness; end-times narratives possess yet another irresistible attraction: the promise of delivery from a human existence famously labeled by Thomas Hobbes as "solitary, poor, nasty, brutish, and short" and pervaded with a corruption that favors the wealthy and powerful at the expense of the righteous. Few narratives comfort as well as one that promises the return of a savior who will turn over the table and set things right. This yearning for mankind's fresh start is deeply embedded in the Bible, most especially in the books of Ezekiel, Daniel, and Revelation, which have supplied the blueprints for several bloody end-times movements.

The nascent field of evolutionary psychology provides a convincing mechanism for the spread of mass manias. Within the space of approximately ten thousand years after the first tribes crossed over from Siberia into North America at the end of the last Ice Age, humans had established themselves from the subarctic to the Great Plains to the tropical Amazon Basin. Biological evolution could not have proceeded rapidly enough to favor the very specific skills needed to survive in such varied environments; it would have taken far too long, for example, to have evolved a genetically derived talent for kayak-making on the subarctic coast, then a talent for buffalo-hunting on the Great Plains, followed by one for making poison blowguns in the Amazon. (The most rapid known human evolutionary adaptations—the development of adult lactose tolerance among northern Europeans and high-altitude tolerance in Tibetans—are estimated to have taken 3,000 to 10,000 years.)[9]

Rather than hardwire into our genes a distinct ability for making kayaks, hunting buffalo, or fashioning poison blowguns, evolution instead encoded the general-purpose skill of imitation. Given a large enough population and enough trial and error, someone will eventually figure out how to build, for example, a serviceable kayak, and the rest can accurately imitate the process.[10]

We imitate more than other animal species; as soon as someone creates a useful innovation, others quickly adopt it. Yet our propensity to imitate also serves to amplify maladaptive behaviors, primary among which are delusional beliefs. Admittedly, in a modern postindustrial society, the imitative acquisition of skills does improve our economic potential, but it does far less to promote survival than it did, say, in the premodern era in the subarctic, Great Plains, or Amazon Basin. Thus, in the modern world, the tradeoff between imitating adaptive and maladaptive behaviors has become less favorable than it had been in the past, and we are now stuck with a late-Pleistocene imitative predisposition that has become increasingly costly in the modern age, one of the most expensive and dangerous being the spread of the belief that the world will soon end.

Not only do people respond more to narratives than to facts and data, but preliminary studies demonstrate that the more compelling the story, the more it erodes our critical-thinking skills.[11] This research suggests, in addition, an inherent conflict of interest between the suppliers and consumers of opinion: the former wish to convince and will devise the most compelling narratives possible, whereas the latter, if they are rational, should intentionally avoid those narratives and rely only on data, facts, and analytical discipline.

Closely related to our preference for compelling narratives is the human tendency for self-deception. Since humans are adept at detecting the "tells" that others are lying, the ability to deceive oneself eliminates the tells, and so makes one a better deceiver.[12] Throughout history, relatively few of the protagonists of religious mass delusions were the con men they seemed to skeptical outsiders, but rather the sincerely self-deceived victims of their own delusions.

Beginning about 150 years ago, Protestant Christianity evolved a doctrine, technically known as "dispensational premillennialism" (for short, "dispensationalism"), which its modern advocates have honed into the world's most compelling end-times narrative. Although its precise content varies depending on the theological flavor, the basic narrative predicts that the Jews return to Israel, rebuild the Jerusalem Temple, and there resume sacrifices. The Roman Empire then reassembles itself in the form of a ten-member confederation under the leadership of a charismatic, brilliant, and handsome individual who turns out to be the Antichrist, the earthly manifestation of the Devil, who enters into a seven-year alliance with the Jews. After three and a half years, the Antichrist betrays the Jews and thus precipitates an invasion of Israel not only by the Russians, but also by two hundred million Chinese, who travel over the Himalayas to get there.

A cataclysmic nuclear war ensues: Armageddon, along with other horrors, collectively known as the Tribulation. At the end of the seven-year period, Christ returns to defeat the Antichrist and establish the millennium. Along the way, billions die. Christians who have found Jesus are conveniently saved from Armageddon and the Tribulation by being transported up into heaven—the Rapture—which occurs right before the trouble starts. The Jews come off somewhat less well; a third of them convert to Christianity and proselytize the rest of humanity and so survive the Tribulation. The other two-thirds are out of luck.

The current polarization of American society cannot be fully understood without a working knowledge of the above dispensationalist narrative, which strikes the majority of well-educated citizens with a secular orientation as bizarre. In contrast, for a significant minority of Americans, this sequence of prophesized events is as familiar as *Romeo and Juliet* or *The Godfather*, and the appeal of televangelists such as Jerry Falwell, Jim Bakker, and Jimmy Swaggart rest solidly on their dispensationalist credentials.

Several reasons dictate concern about the prevalence of the dispensationalist end-times narrative. The centrality of Israel, and particularly the rebuilding of the Temple, to this belief system has profoundly affected U.S. Middle East policy. Uncritical American support for Israel's expansion of

West Bank settlement and its apparent abandonment of a two-state solution can be traced directly to the advocacy of evangelicals, so-called Christian Zionists, who now exert far more influence than Jewish Zionists. Indeed, the opening and closing benedictions at the May 2018 dedication of the new U.S. Embassy in Jerusalem were given by two dispensationalist ministers. One of them, Robert Jeffress, once claimed that Hitler had helped plan the Jew's return to Israel; and the other, John Hagee, had deemed Hurricane Katrina God's punishment for New Orleans's sinfulness.[13]

Even a mild degree of fatalism about the inevitability of Armageddon in the nuclear age is dangerous. A 2010 Pew Foundation poll found that more than a third of Americans believe that Jesus will return in their life-time, and most of those believe in the Rapture.[14] One such American was Ronald Reagan, who could discourse knowledgably about dispensational theology with the likes of Jerry Falwell. In the same vein, evangelicals, most of whom are dispensationalists, make up nearly a quarter of the U.S. military; their influence is particularly prominent at the Air Force Academy, whose service branch operates most of the U.S. nuclear arsenal.[15] In 1964, when Daniel Ellsberg and his boss at RAND, who had both just audited the U.S. nuclear chain of command, screened *Dr. Strangelove*, a movie about a psychotic SAC general fixated on the fluoridation of drinking water—an obsession shared even today by a few dispensationalists—who triggers the Third World War, they remarked that the film could well have been a documentary.[16]

Throughout history, Christians have labeled Jews as the Antichrist, the very concept of which is explosive. Even today, for a few extremist evangelicals, applying that label to someone, or to any group, justifies their murder.

Finally, dispensationalism alone can and does occasionally trigger mass death, as occurred in 1993 at Waco, Texas, when the Branch David-ian sect, led by the Book of Revelation–obsessed David Koresh, collided with federal officials with no understanding of his belief system.

Given that the roots of apocalypticism are found in both the New and Old Testaments, and likely have earlier roots in Fertile Crescent polythe-ism, it is not surprising that the doomsday scripts of both extremist Israeli Jews and the Islamic State have more than a passing resemblance to that of Christian dispensationalists, differing only in who plays the heroes and who plays the heavies. Today's Muslim apocalypticists almost uniformly consider Jews to be the Antichrist, and the remarkable ability of the Islamic State to attract recruits from around the world to the killing fields of Syria and Iraq rested in no small part on an end-times narrative drawn directly from the hadith, the sayings of Muhammad.

If we are to comprehend how social epidemics such as financial bubbles and violent end-times apocalyptic manias originate and propagate, it is equally instructive to understand those circumstances in which they do not occur. Our modern understanding of how crowds can at times behave wisely began in the fall of 1906, when the pioneering polymath (and cousin of Charles Darwin) Francis Galton attended the annual West of England Fat Stock and Poultry Exhibition in Plymouth. There, he performed an experiment in which a large group of people acted with surprising rationality. Approximately eight hundred participants purchased tickets for an ox-weighing contest at sixpence each, with prizes awarded for the most accurate guesses of the weight of the dressed animal, that is, minus its head and internal organs. Amazingly, the median guess, 1,207 pounds, was less than one percent off the actual weight, 1,198 pounds. The *average* estimate was 1,197 pounds; Galton did not report this nearly dead-on number in his first *Nature* article because he felt that the median value, the one exactly in the middle of the estimates, was more theoretically appealing than the more accurate average.[17]

Galton's conclusion about the accuracy of collective wisdom has since been repeatedly confirmed.[18] More recently, *New Yorker* writer James Surowiecki summarized this concept in his bestseller *The Wisdom of Crowds*, in which he laid out three requirements for effective crowd wisdom: independent individual analysis, diversity of individual experience and expertise, and an effective method for individuals to aggregate their opinions.[19]

So what qualifies, for our purposes, as a "crowd"—the wise ones of Francis Galton and James Surowiecki, or the unwise ones of Luc Jouret, Joseph Di Mambro, and David Koresh?

What separates delusional crowds from wise ones is the extent of their members' interactions with each other. It's doubtful that all, or even most, of Galton's eight hundred contestants ever physically gathered into a single group. A key, and usually overlooked, feature of his experiment is that it involved the *dressed* weight of the ox. Contestants had to fill out an entry card with their address so that the winners could be notified, and since the result would not become known until the ox was later butchered, this would have discouraged the contestants from congregating before completing their card.

A few years ago finance professional Joel Greenblatt performed a clever variation on the Galton experiment with a class of Harlem school-children, to whom he showed a jar that contained 1,776 jelly beans. Once again, the average of their guesses, when submitted in silence on index cards, was remarkably accurate: 1,771 jelly beans. Greenblatt then had each student verbalize their guesses, which destroyed the accuracy of their aggregate judgment—the new, "open" estimates averaged out to just 850 jelly beans.[20]

Thus, the more a group interacts, the more it behaves like a real crowd, and the less accurate its assessments become. Occasionally, crowd interaction becomes so intense that madness results. As put most succinctly by Friedrich Nietzsche, "Madness is rare in the individual—but with groups, parties, peoples, and ages it is the rule."[21] Mackay also recognized this; perhaps the most famous line in *Extraordinary Popular Delusions* is "Men, it is said, think in herds; it will be seen that they go mad in herds, while they only recover their senses more slowly, and one by one."[22]

Accordingly, the accuracy of a group's aggregate judgment rests on the participants *not* behaving like a crowd. It also, as Surowiecki points out, depends upon the diversity of the group; the more points of view a group brings to bear on an estimate, the more accurate that estimate is liable to be.

Diversity of opinion also benefits the individual as well; as put by F. Scott Fitzgerald, "The test of a first-rate intelligence is the ability to hold two opposing ideas in mind at the same time and still retain the ability to function."[23] Over the past three decades, psychologist Philip Tetlock has examined the forecasting accuracy of hundreds of well-regarded experts; he found that those who took into account a wide variety of often con-tradictory viewpoints performed better than those who viewed the world through a single theoretical lens.[24] In plain English: beware the ideologue and the true believer, whether in politics, in religion, or in finance.

While Surowiecki's book on crowds describes how group decisions can succeed, mine will describe how they can fail, and what happens when they do. In the most extreme cases, not only do crowds go mad, but as occurred several times in the twentieth century, entire nations do so as well.

Mackay didn't get everything right, nor was his compilation even original; he may have derived inspiration, or even more, from a volume published four years prior by one Richard Davenport, *Sketches of Imposture, Deception, and Credulity*, which covered many of the same areas, although not in nearly as much detail.[25] And while Mackay's lurid description of the tulipmania, for example, introduced the term into the modern lexicon, it also earned the scorn of modern observers, who point out that it was hardly the society-wide phenomenon he described.[26]

Further, Mackay's chapter, subject, and chronological organization is chaotic; chapters on crowd behavior (e.g., financial bubbles, the Crusades) are interspersed with ones on fads (hair length, beards, and duels) and health and scientific dead ends (magnetization, alchemy).[27]

That said, Mackay's errors, disorganization, and possible lack of originality pale before the fact that he realized, as well as any observer of that era might have, just how often our social nature interferes with our rationality.

I first read *Extraordinary Popular Delusions* more than a quarter century ago, and while the financial manias described in the first three chapters fascinated me, I thought them irrelevant to the relatively well-behaved capital markets of the early 1990s. I was wrong: over the next several years, as the dot-com bubble progressed, Mackay's descriptions of financial madness came to life before my amazed eyes.

Two decades later, the Islamic State and its predecessors proved so remarkably adept at proselytizing believers around the world that they attracted thousands from safe, prosperous Western countries to the killing fields of Iraq and Syria. They did so, in large part, by peddling an end-times narrative remarkably similar to that believed by large numbers of Christians, a subject also dealt with in some detail by Mackay.

As someone who was already greatly influenced by *Extraordinary Popular Delusions*, the rise of the Islamic State rang a loud and clear bell. If ever there was a modern manifestation of a religious mania, this was it; the time was ripe to examine the history of mass delusions, from the medieval period to the present day, through the prism of the remarkable recent advances in the neurosciences.

I chose to ignore several types of episodes covered in great detail by Mackay, especially fashion and health crazes. Some readers may also wonder why, in today's fraught and polarized political atmosphere, I also chose not to explicitly cover political episodes. In order to keep the title to a manageable length, and because of the personal resonance of financial and religious mass manias, I confined this book to those two areas. The reader will, however, encounter no great difficulty connecting the episodes described in the coming pages, as well as their underlying psychology, to manias of all types, particularly to the totalitarianism of the last century and the viral conspiracy theories of this one.

Easily the most important geopolitical event of the new century was the 9/11 attacks on the Twin Towers and Pentagon, a catastrophe that amplified an already well-established modern Islamic apocalypticism re-awakened by Western political and cultural dominance and the 1979 Soviet invasion of Afghanistan. Arguably the most important transformation in American cultural and political life in the last century was the rise of evan-gelical Protestantism, which presents profound risks for American policy in the Middle East and for the command and control of strategic weapons. The rise of both Muslim fundamentalism and Protestant evangelicism can be easily understood in the context of prior religious manias.

In more general terms, this book will provide a psychological frame-work for understanding just why humanity occasionally suffers from mass manias of all types. Manifestly, man is the ape that imitates, tells stories, seeks status, morally condemns others, and yearns for the good old days, all of which guarantee a human future studded with religious and financial mass manias.

Anyone who writes about mass delusions quickly bumps up against a highly inconvenient sociological fact. Like Darius's Greeks and Callatiae, every single one of us is a creature of our societal norms, and occasionally one society's sacrament is another's desecration. Many, if not most, of the world's theologies, for example, tend to view the others' belief systems as heretical, even among closely related sects. *Especially* among closely related sects—Freud's famous "narcissism of small differences." As the old joke goes, a delusion shared by hundreds of people is called a "cult," whereas one shared by millions is called a "religion."

A significant number of Americans believe in the literal truth of the Book of Revelation: that the world will suffer, sooner rather than later, a world-ending cataclysm. While less fundamentalist Christians and non-Christians might consider that end-times narrative delusional, such institutional delusions are only rarely acutely harmful to either their believers or to the rest of the world. Quite the contrary, in fact—all successful societies depend to a certain degree on shared delusions. Whatever American society's flaws, our greatest strength is our belief in the rule of law and equality under the law; likewise, our economy functions reasonably well because almost all of us believe that money made of paper and of even more ethereal electronic transactions represents real assets and obligations. But at base, such beneficial common beliefs are not much more than society-wide con games: they're true only so long as most people believe in them—the so-called Tinker Bell Principle. I've chosen, thus, to focus on mass delusions that go bad: "Extraordinarily Harmful Mass Delusions and the Madness of Crowds," if you will.

The stories flow in approximate chronological order, starting with medieval end-times manias not covered by Mackay and ending with the most spectacular recent example of the same phenomenon—the rise of the Islamic State in the Middle East. In between, the steady stream of financial and religious manias over the past several centuries appear in the order in which they occurred, along with the relevant neuroscience.

Our journey into the dark heart of human mass delusions begins in medieval Europe, where an obscure Cistercian monk, inspired by the Bible's apocalyptic books, developed a theology that sparked a series of grisly Protestant end-times revolts.

1

JOACHIM'S CHILDREN

Tiger got to hunt,
Bird got to fly;
Man got to sit and wonder, "Why, why, why?"
Tiger got to sleep,
Bird got to land;
Man got to tell himself he understand.

— Kurt Vonnegut[1]

In the late twelfth century, the kings and queens of Europe undertook the arduous journey to a monastery in the remote Calabrian hills to bask in the legendary wisdom of a nearly forgotten Cistercian abbot named Joachim of Fiore. Passing through on his way to the Third Crusade in 1190–1191, Richard the Lionheart sought his vision of the future.[2]

The quiet intellectual abbot was fond of numbers and historical analogies, and what attracted Europe's rulers to his monastery was his organization of human history into three ages that foretold a coming golden era. Joachim, unfortunately, had unwittingly lit a prophetic fuse. His vision of the future spoke eloquently to the downtrodden poor and stirred revolution in their hearts, and over the following centuries, his initially peaceful schema would mutate into a bloody end-times theology that engulfed wide swaths of Europe.

Understanding how this happened invokes the Bible's three major end-times narratives: the Old Testament books of Ezekiel and Daniel, and the New Testament's last book, Revelation. While these three books may seem obscure to modern secular readers, they help to explain the cultural polarization between Christian evangelicals and the rest of American society that has become so evident the past several election cycles. For the former, the contents of these three books are as familiar as the stories of the American Revolution and Civil War; for the latter, they are largely terra incognita. Further, even evangelicals are often unaware of the ancient Near East history behind these narratives, particularly the complex interplay among the Egyptians, Philistines, Assyrians, Babylonians, Persians, and the two Jewish kingdoms, Israel and Judah.

Ezekiel, Daniel, and Revelation provide the backdrop to a series of end-times religious mass delusions that were in many ways similar to the tragedy at Cheiry. Such manias have been a nearly constant feature of the Abrahamic religions since their births, most prominently involving the town of Münster in the sixteenth century, the Millerite phenomenon in the mid-nineteenth century United States, and the repetitious and widespread predictions of imminent end-times that followed the establishment of the modern state of Israel.

Religious manias tend to play out in the worst of times, during which mankind desires delivery from its troubles and a return to the Good Old Days, a mythical bygone era of peace, harmony, and prosperity. One of the earliest surviving Greek poems, Hesiod's "Works and Days," from around 700 B.C., expresses this well. Greece at that time was desperately poor, and the author scratched out a hard living on a farm in Boeotia, just northwest of Athens, which he described as "bad in winter, sultry in summer, and good at no time."[3] Things, Hesiod imagined, must have been better in years past. First came the gods on Olympus, who made a "golden race of mortal men" who

> lived like gods without sorrow of heart, remote and free from toil and grief: miserable age rested not on them; but with legs and arms never failing they made merry with feasting beyond the reach of all evils. When they died, it was as though they were overcome with sleep, and they had all good things; for the fruitful earth unforced bare them fruit abundantly and without stint. They dwelt in ease and peace upon their lands with many good things, rich in flocks and loved by the blessed gods.[4]

The next generation was "made of silver and less noble by far." They were still blessed, but had sinned and failed to offer sacrifices to the gods, and were followed by a third generation of men whose armor, houses, and tools were of bronze. The gods, for some reason, gave the fourth generation a better draw than the third; half died in battle, but the other half lived as demigods. The fifth generation, Hesiod's, was "a race of iron, and men never rest from labor and sorrow by day, and from perishing by night; and the gods shall lay sore trouble upon them." Their children, Hesiod predicted, would fall even further short—venal, foulmouthed, and, worst of all, disinclined to support their parents in their dotage.[5] Hesiod had stolen a more than two millennia march on Thomas Hobbes's *Leviathan*: life was indeed solitary, poor, nasty, brutish, and short.

The misery of Hesiod's day, bleak as it was, was at least intrinsic to the local land and culture—the poverty of the soil, the venality of man, and the aggression of neighboring city-states. A Greek city's hostile neighbors, after all, shared the same religion and culture, and while they often enslaved their defeated neighbors, before the Peloponnesian War they generally did not put them to the sword.

Around the same time as Hesiod, several hundred miles away, the Hebrews' troubles were of a more existential sort, and they gave rise, eventually, to the most common current-day end-times narratives, which promised a happier human existence in the next world, at least for those who kept the faith and survived the transition.

How the Jews came to settle the Holy Land remains a mystery, as historians question both the existence of Moses and the Exodus from Egypt. What is beyond dispute is that the Israelites had an easier time subjugating the Canaanites, Palestine's culturally more advanced but less aggressive original inhabitants, than they had with the ferocious "Sea Peoples" who followed. The latter, a mysterious race, plagued Egypt and possibly extinguished several western Mediterranean civilizations, including the Mycenaean. Not long after the supposed Exodus, a local branch of the Sea Peoples, the Philistines, established a beachhead in the area between the modern Gaza Strip and Tel Aviv and began to push inland.

The Philistine threat served to unite the small and disparate Israelite tribes. They eventually settled on Saul, a sometime mercenary of the Philistines, as their leader. He defeated his former employers and so brought about the beginnings of unity among the Hebrews. Upon his death not long after 1000 B.C., one of his lieutenants, David, who had also served the Philistines, succeeded him. A more militarily talented and charismatic leader, he brought under his dominion not only the northern and southern states,

Israel and Judah, respectively, but also conquered as his own personal possession a heavily fortified town, Jerusalem, held by the Canaanites.

Under David, the Jewish domain reached its maximum geographical extent, reaching as far north as Damascus. What is today called the "Davidic Kingdom" was not a unified state, but rather consisted of three separate components: Judah and Israel, whose individual kingships David separately occupied, and Jerusalem, his personal property.

His son Solomon held this confederation together. An ambitious builder, he erected a series of palaces, forts, and places of worship, most notably Jerusalem's First Temple. He also enthusiastically practiced marital

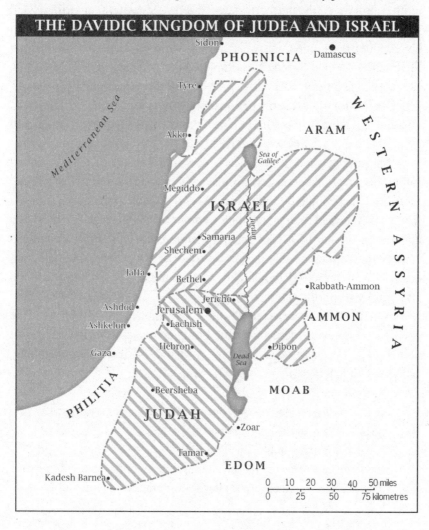

diplomacy; he betrothed a pharaoh's daughter and maintained, at least according to I Kings, seven hundred other wives and three hundred concubines. One of his forts, at Megiddo, would later become better known by its Greek name: Armageddon.

Solomon's edifice complex, and particularly the huge labor corvées necessary for his building schemes, bred resentment, and when he died in 931 B.C., his son Rehoboam refused to travel north to Israel's capital, Shechem, for his coronation, and so Israel left the confederation.[6]

The north-south schism proved fatal to Jewish independence when the Assyrians became the region's preeminent military machine. By the ninth century B.C., the northern state, Israel, was paying them tribute, and when Tiglath-Pileser III gained the Assyrian crown in 745 B.C., he hurled his conquering legions westward and carved Israel up. His successors, Shalmaneser V and Sargon II, completed the conquest by 721 B.C., and, as recorded in Sargon's Annals, "27,290 men who dwelt in it I carried off, fifty chariots for my royal army from among them I selected. . . . That city I restored and more than before I made it great; men of the lands, conquered by my hands, in it I made to dwell."[7]

Sargon deported the northern elites to the banks of the Tigris and Euphrates; they disappeared into history's mists as the ten "lost tribes," most likely assimilated into the local Mesopotamian population. The Assyrians then turned their sights on the southern state, Judah, and mounted an abortive assault in 701 B.C., and then unaccountably left it alone for a century thereafter, possibly as a buffer state between them and the Egyptians. This hiatus saved Judah, and the Jewish people, from the oblivion suffered by its northern branch.

When the Assyrians fell to the Babylonians around 605 B.C., the Jews faced an even more fearsome conquering force in the person of their king, Nebuchadnezzar, who in 597 B.C. conquered Jerusalem and, according to II Kings,

> . . . Jehoiachin the king of Judah went out to the king of Babylon, he, and his mother, and his servants, and his princes, and his officers: and the king of Babylon took him in the eighth year of his reign.
>
> And he carried out thence all the treasures of the house of the LORD, and the treasures of the king's house, and cut in pieces all the

vessels of gold which Solomon king of Israel had made in the temple
of the LORD, as the LORD had said.

And he carried away all Jerusalem, and all the princes, and all
the mighty men of valour, even ten thousand captives, and all the
craftsmen and smiths: none remained, save the poorest sort of the
people of the land.[8]

Worse was to come. Around 587 B.C., Zedekiah, the puppet installed by the
Babylonians, rebelled. In response, the Babylonians breached Jerusalem's
wall and poured through it. The king fled but was caught near Jericho,
where the Babylonians "slew the sons of Zedekiah before his eyes, and
put out the eyes of Zedekiah, and bound him with fetters of brass, and
carried him to Babylon."[9]

The Judeans must have known, given the experience of their vanished
northern neighbors, that Nebuchadnezzar threatened their culture and very
existence with extinction, and so they sought a drastic solution that their
Greek near-contemporary, Hesiod, whose culture was not existentially
threatened, did not seek: a miraculous cataclysm that would deliver them
from oblivion.

Among the exiles carried off to the banks of the Euphrates along
with Jehoiachin in 597 B.C. was a Temple-trained priest named Ezekiel.
His book, written either by him or by others in his name, opens five years
later, around 592 B.C., with his vision of the heavens opening to reveal a
chariot carrying the Lord drawn by four phantasmagorical winged creatures, each with four faces: human, lion, ox, and eagle.

Whoever wrote this first major apocalyptic book of the Bible did so
over the decades during which conditions in the Holy Land deteriorated.
As described in II Kings, the Babylonians had exiled Judah's royalty,
priests, and wealthy, but left behind a large underclass. Initially, the elites
sent to Babylon were optimistic about their prospects for a quick return,
but the destruction of Jerusalem and the First Temple in 587 B.C. drove
their evolving narrative in an apocalyptic direction.

Ezekiel's author turned his story away from the impieties of Judah
that had brought about its conquest and toward the return of the Lord and
the reestablishment of the Jewish nation. He spun a narrative that would
grow ever more resonant over the millennia: the corruption of man, the

wrath of God, His return, and, later, that of His son to reestablish His kingdom and condemn the faithless to eternal damnation.

Ezekiel's book proceeds through three parts: first, the appointment of Ezekiel as a prophet (someone who relays messages from God); second, the restoration of the Davidic kingdom and the destruction not only of its real enemies, but also of a mythical one, the fearsome Gog, ruler of the land of Magog; and third, the splendors of the new Temple and of a resurgent and greatly enlarged Jewish nation. (Later books of the Bible confuse the issue of who and what were Gog and Magog, since either can be interpreted as individuals or places.)

Ezekiel also describes how, following the reestablishment of the old Davidic kingdom, the Israelites will suffer an invasion by this mythical marauder, who they then defeat, the first substantive biblical mention of a character who would eventually evolve into the New Testament Antichrist, one of modern Protestant apocalypticism's leading actors.[10] This three-act process of prophetic verification with wondrous and frightening visions, the vanquishing of evil forces, and the glories of the new world became the foundation of many subsequent end-times narratives.

The second major apocalyptic Old Testament book, Daniel, purportedly plays out contemporaneously with Ezekiel. It opens with the conquest of Jerusalem, exile to Babylon, and Nebuchadnezzar's patronage of four clever Hebrews—Shadrach, Meshach, Abednego, and Daniel—who "in all matters of wisdom and understanding, that the king enquired of them, he found them ten times better than all the magicians and astrologers that were in his realm."[11]

Nebuchadnezzar, it seems, had a dream that he just barely recalled. He knew only that it was of great portent, but otherwise lacked detail. When told by his court's soothsayers that their repertoires did not include dream recovery, he ordered not only their murder, but also that of all of the kingdom's wise men, the four Hebrews included.

Luckily for Daniel, the Lord revealed to him the royal dream's content: a frightening apparition with a gold head, a silver chest and arms, a bronze stomach and thighs, iron calves, and feet of iron and clay (hence the modern phrase "feet of clay"). A stone shatters the beast's feet; the stone then grows ever larger, first into a mountain, and then fills the entire earth.[12]

The gold/silver/bronze/iron motif of Daniel's beast matches that of Hesiod's ages; this was likely not a coincidence, since Persian texts from the same period also describe four historical ages named according to these four metals.[13]

The Lord also interpreted the dream for Daniel, who passes it on to Nebuchadnezzar; the beast's head is the king himself, the silver and bronze parts lesser future kingdoms, and the iron and clay feet a great amalgamated empire that would easily rupture because of the incompatibility of its two elements. Finally, the Lord takes over rulership: "In the days of these kings shall the God of heaven set up a kingdom, which shall never be destroyed; and the kingdom shall not be left to other people, but it shall break in pieces and consume all these kingdoms, and it shall stand for ever."[14]

Daniel was not written during the Babylonian exile, as it implicitly claimed, but rather in the second century B.C. In the more than three centuries between the time of Nebuchadnezzar and the book's actual composition, much had happened: King Cyrus had conquered the Babylonians and allowed the return to Palestine of the Jews, who built the Second Temple, only to find themselves reconquered by Alexander in 332 B.C. To any literate Judean during Greek rule, the narrative's prophecy seemed clear: the iron and clay feet of Nebuchadnezzar's beast represented the weakness of the Greek Ptolemaic and Seleucid empires—the successor states of Alexander the Great's conquests—and their eventual destruction. Daniel's authors and editors likely made it appear to have been written three centuries earlier than it actually was to enhance its prophetic credibility.

The Greeks presented the Jews with yet another existential threat. In 167 B.C., Antiochus IV Epiphanes, the ruler of the Seleucid Greek empire in the Levant, appointed as the Jewish high priest one Menelaus, who favored a radical reformation of religious practices and whose agenda included the abolition of sacrifices and Mosaic law. He converted the Second Temple into a secular space and desecrated it with a statue of Zeus.

The conflict among reformist priests, traditional Jews, and Antiochus spiraled out of control; between 167 and 164 B.C. Antiochus's forces plundered the Temple, destroyed the sacred scrolls, and punished by death any observance of the Sabbath, circumcision, and the offering of sacrifices. He also pillaged Jerusalem; murdered, enslaved, and deported thousands of its inhabitants; razed the city's walls; and garrisoned Greek troops in the city.

Nor was this all: The Jews were required to worship idols on the Temple's site and offer pigs in sacrifice. The eventual explosion, the 164 B.C. rebellion led by the traditionalist Maccabee brothers, resulted first in the elimination of these abominations, and finally in an independent Judean state that would last until the Roman conquest in 63 B.C.

Daniel's first half ends with its hero sent to the lion's den for worshipping the Lord and his miraculous survival under His protection. In its second half Daniel is now himself the dreamer of an apparition he professes not to understand, but in fact is simply a variation of Nebuchadnezzar's dream. Four phantasmagorical beasts, each more awe-inspiring than the last, emerge from the sea: a lion with plucked wings; a bear with ribs between its teeth; a leopard with four heads and four wings; and a final one that defied taxonomy, "dreadful and terrible," with iron teeth and horns that increased in number as he watched, one of which had eyes and a mouth that spoke "great things." The Lord appears, flames issue from his throne, and He vanquishes this fourth beast, who, just as in Nebuchadnezzar's dream, represents the Seleucid Empire. Over the succeeding reigns of Cyrus and his successors, Darius and Belshazzar, Daniel has further dreams in which the conquest of Persia by Alexander and the breakup of his empire are told in allegorical form. The book's final chapter describes a divine judgment in which the dead are resurrected, some to enjoy "everlasting life," while others are condemned "to shame and everlasting contempt" under the permanent rule of the Lord.[15]

The Bible's third great apocalyptic book, Revelation, was written sometime around A.D. 95 by a man identified in the text as "John," the humble recipient of its contents from God. The author was probably not John the Apostle, who would have been about ninety years old at the time, but rather a more pedestrian prophet who lived, likely as a prisoner, on the island of Patmos in Asia Minor. His work would eventually become codified by most Christian sects as the last book of the Bible.

If they are honest, most modern readers, even those with deep religious backgrounds, find Revelation a difficult text to absorb, dense and nearly uninterpretable. According to one of the book's foremost historians, R. H. Charles,

> From the earliest ages of the Church it has been universally admitted
> that the Apocalypse [Revelation] is the most difficult book of the en-
> tire Bible. . . . And not only is it the cursory reader that is bewildered
> but also the serious student, as the history of the interpretation of the
> Apocalypse clearly shows.[16]

Revelation reads as a disorganized jumble of images even more phantasmagorical than Daniel's dreams, to which it bears more than a passing,
and probably not coincidental, resemblance.

Because of this, a meaningful grasp of the book requires specialist
historical knowledge of not only the eastern Roman Empire, but also of
the Macabbean period. Charles's detailed literary analysis of the book
suggested that John of Patmos likely died just before he completed it,
and that its difficulty likely results from the incompetent editing of his
unfinished original draft; even among learned academics, a near total lack
of agreement about its narrative structure reigns, a difficulty that has, over
the past several centuries, produced no end of mischief and mayhem.[17]

Revelation consists of twenty-two chapters; the first three comprise
introductory letters from John to seven churches in the eastern part of
the Roman Empire. The next two chapters describe the Lord's throne
surrounded by twenty-four elders and four worshipful beasts, and the appearance of a scroll closed with seven seals that can only be opened by a
descendant of David, king of the Jews. A slain lamb with seven horns and
seven eyes, felt by biblical scholars to represent Jesus, fills that bill and,
one by one, undoes the seals.

Chapters 6 through 8 describe what happens next: the first four seals
issue forth horses colored white, red, black, and pale, signifying, respectively, war, international conflict, famine, and plague. The fifth produces
martyred souls beneath an altar, signifying persecution, and the sixth an
earthquake. There then follows an interlude in which 144,000 Jews are
"sealed" (marked on their foreheads with the Lord's name; 12,000 from
each of the twelve tribes). The seventh, and last, seal is introduced by eight
angels; the first seven carry trumpets, and an eighth lays waste to the world.

The next three chapters yield an equally bewildering tableau: the
sounding of the seven trumpets by angels, whose devastation essentially
recapitulates the seven seals, with an intermission between the sixth and

seventh in which John is ordered to eat a small book by an angel who then instructs him to design the new Jerusalem and Temple.

The book's second half features a great red dragon with seven heads, seven crowns, and ten horns, identified as Satan, who unsuccessfully attempts to devour a newborn, the son of God, as an allegorical Mary is about to give him birth.*

This was followed by yet more phantasms: another beast with seven heads, ten crowns, and ten horns that produces the usual mayhem; a third compound beast with only two horns that does the same; the return of the "lamb" (Jesus) who exercised command over the host of 144,000 Jews; the pouring out of seven bowls (or vials, depending on the version), which yield calamities analogous to those of the seals and trumpets; and, finally, a horrendous female figure, the Great Whore of Babylon, interpreted by scholars as either the Roman Empire or an apostate Jerusalem.

In chapters 19 and 20, an angel casts the dragon/Satan into the Lake of Fire for a thousand years, and martyrs are resurrected. After the thousand years Satan returns and recruits a vast army, "the number of whom is as the sand of the sea," including Gog from Magog for a final battle, at the end of which Satan is tossed back into the fire lake forever. The Last Judgment separates the just from the wicked, the latter of whom get sealed up with Satan into the fire lake along with, for good measure, "death and hell." The last two chapters describe the glory of the New Jerusalem of immense size, ". . . twelve thousand furlongs. The length and the breadth and the height of it are equal," and Christ's promise that he shall shortly return.[18]

Revelation's basic narrative seems to be that Jesus returns to earth and does battle with evil and eventually casts it into a fiery eternity, extracts the righteous into heaven, condemns the rest, and destroys the world. The precise details, however, are a matter of interpretation. Further, it almost certainly shares a common origin with the similar Old Testament end-times narratives, particularly the book of Daniel, which it closely resembles. Indeed, the structure and content of both Daniel and Revelation are hardly unique to Christianity and Judaism; philosopher and theological historian Mirceau Eliade has identified many themes common in religions around the world and in many eras; one of the most persistent is of the

---

* Another interpretation is that the mother represents the Jewish people and the infant the newborn Christian community.

world ending in fire that spares the righteous, which he speculated was of Persian/Zoroastrian origin.[19]

Ambiguous in the extreme, Revelation allows for an infinity of interpretations, most critically, just how "a thousand years" should be understood, when in human history that millennium lies, and so precisely when the end-times itself occurs. In theological lingo, the study of such questions is known as "eschatology": the final disposition of mankind in the end-time.

Revelation's opacity and ambiguity only amplified its influence, since they open the way to a wide range of allegorical interpretations about when and how the world ends. In the words of religious historian Robert Wright,

> Ambiguity, selective retention, and misleading paraphrasal combine to give believers great influence on the meaning of their religion. But for raw semantic power, none of these tools rivals the deft deployment of metaphor and allegory. In a single stroke, this can obliterate a text's literal meaning and replace it with something radically different.[20]

According to an international survey in 2010, fully 35 percent of Americans today believe that the Bible represents the literal word of God, and a similar percentage think that Jesus will return to earth in their lifetimes.[21] It seems reasonable to assume that the further one travels back in time, the more universal such beliefs must have been.

From Christianity's earliest days, theologians postulated three different chronologies of Christ's return. The first is that the Church had already established the millennium, and that Christ would return at its end. In theological terms, this time sequence is called "postmillennialism," involving either a present or future millennial period, followed by the Last Judgment and Jesus's return. The second, premillennialism, implies that Jesus returns *before* the millennium, followed by the Last Judgment; in other words, not only Jesus's return and the Last Judgment, but also the millennium itself all lie in the future. The last possibility was that the millennium is merely an allegorical concept, and does not exist in reality, so called "amillennialism."[22] Of these three interpretations, premillennialism supplies the most compelling narrative, and almost from the moment of Revelation's completion, its ambiguity and mankind's hunger for a resonant

traditional story ending have spawned a constant stream of premillennial-
ist end-times stories.

The most prominent Christian theologian of the late Roman Empire,
Saint Augustine of Hippo, resisted that temptation and swore off any
attempt to calculate the occurrence of the end-times: "In vain therefore
do we try to reckon and set limits to the years that remain for this world,
when we hear from the Mouth of Truth that it is not ours to know this,"
and, more colloquially, "relax your fingers and give them a rest."[23] Augustine's reticence would remain the Church's dominant eschatological
stance until Joachim's theological heirs, impatient for the end-times,
came on the scene.

Humans understand the world largely through narratives, and while end-
times prophecies are perhaps the most compelling ever told, they have a
less than stellar predictive track record. Research on forecasting shows
just how miserable humans are at predicting the future, and that merely
observing the historical "base rate" of past events almost always predicts
the future far better than narrative-based reasoning. Obviously, the base
rate frequency for the end of time has thus far been zero.

Given the zero accuracy of end-times predictions, just why are we
so swayed by these compelling narratives? And, more generally, why is
narrative-based reasoning so faulty? Psychologists have demonstrated
that people are "cognitive misers" who avoid rigorous analysis in favor
of heuristics—simple mental shortcuts—and that a compelling narrative
is the most powerful heuristic of all.*

Over the course of the twentieth century, neuroscientists discovered
that there are two different types of human thought processes: fast-moving
emotional responses located in our deeply placed and evolutionarily ancient
limbic system, our so-called "reptilian brain," and much slower conscious
reasoning that arises from the evolutionarily newer cortex that overlies
the limbic system. In 2000, psychologists Keith Stanovich and Richard

---

* Strictly speaking, a heuristic is a story we tell ourselves as a mental shortcut that bypasses
more rigorous analysis, whereas a story told to us by others is often aimed at altering our
own heuristics.

West applied labels to these two apparatuses, System 1 and System 2, respectively, a prosaic taxonomy we've been stuck with since.[24]

From an evolutionary perspective, the primacy of System 1 over System 2 makes sense; for hundreds of millions of years, long before humans evolved their impressive System 2, the fast-moving System 1 drove the animal kingdom's behavioral responses to the hiss of the snake or the dimly perceived footfall of the predator, so it's not surprising that the slower human System 2, likely less than a hundred thousand years old, operates in the thrall of the far more ancient apparatus. Put more simply, our faster emotional machinery leads, and our slower "reason" follows. In a state of nature, the benefits of the dominance of System 1, which reacts to sensory information of danger even before it reaches consciousness, is obvious, but in a relatively safe postindustrial world where the dangers have a longer time horizon, System 1 dominance often incurs great costs.

Narratives powerfully engage our brain's fast-moving, emotionally driven System 1 and so make an end run around analytical thinking. Most of the time, we employ narratives toward useful ends: the deployment of scary stories about an unhealthy diet and smoking to encourage changes in mealtime behavior and tobacco consumption, of sermons and fables about honesty and hard work that improve societal function, and so forth. On the downside, by overwhelming our System 2 and discouraging logical thought, narratives can get us into analytical trouble.

Thus, the more we depend on narratives, and the less on hard data, the more we are distracted away from the real world. Ever lost yourself so deeply in a novel that you became oblivious to the world around you? Ever heard a radio broadcast so hypnotizing that you sat in your driveway for ten minutes so you didn't miss the end? In the world of psychology, this is called "transportation." Psychologist Richard Gerrig defines a narrative as a device that temporarily mentally transports the listener or reader away from their immediate surroundings; when it ends, they return to their surroundings "somewhat changed by the journey."[25]

In other words, a work of fiction or nonfiction, movie, stage performance, or painting temporarily transports the reader, viewer, or listener away from the real world and returns him or her to it a slightly different person. As put by Emily Dickinson,

There is no Frigate like a Book
To take us Lands away
Nor any Coursers like a Page
Of prancing Poetry –
This Traverse may the poorest take
Without oppress of Toll –
How frugal is the Chariot
That bears the Human Soul.[26]

Over the past several decades, researchers have demonstrated how easily people's grasp of simple facts becomes corroded with fictional data, even when clearly labeled as such. In a classic experiment performed by Paul Rozin and his colleagues at the University of Pennsylvania, subjects were told that two newly bought identical glass bottles contained sucrose, and that both bottles were being used for the first time. They were then told that brand-new labels had then been attached, one declaring "sucrose," the other "cyanide." The experimenters firmly told them, "Remember, sugar is in both bottles."

The sugar from both bottles was then stirred into some water-containing cups; the subjects were asked to rate how much they would like to drink from each cup, then asked to take a sip from both: forty-one of fifty subjects chose the cup containing sucrose from the bottle labeled "sucrose," an effect that persisted even when the subjects applied the labels themselves.[27]

This study, and others like it, demonstrates that humans cannot segregate the worlds of fiction and fact—in other words, that they cannot cleanly "toggle" between the literary and real worlds. Witness the 1975 release of the movie *Jaws. Time* magazine reported that summer:

> Formerly bold swimmers now huddle in groups a few yards offshore, bathers stunned with sun hover nervously at water's edge and at the hint of a dorsal fin retreat to the beach. "Ya want to get jawed?" shouted one kid to another in the Santa Monica, Calif., surf. Even the lowly dogfish, the spaniel of the seas but a shark just the same, is suspected of homicidal intentions. "Kill it, kill it," urged a Long Island angler to his companion dangling a 2-ft.-long, almost toothless fish from his rod, "before it grows up to kill us all."[28]

The effect was intentional; the producers had delayed the film's release to coincide with the summer season. As one of them said, "There is no way that a bather who has seen or heard of the movie won't think of a great white shark when he puts his toe in the ocean."[29]

In the 1970s, psychologists Clayton Lewis and John Anderson looked at the effect of identifiably false assertions on the verification of well-established facts. In the simplest example, subjects were told historically accurate statements about George Washington being the first president, crossing the Delaware, and wearing a wig. When given statements labeled as false—that Washington wrote *The Adventures of Tom Sawyer* or is still alive today, for example—the subjects took longer to verify the true statements and made progressively more errors in doing so with each additional false statement.[30]

Gerrig described other experiments, often rather detailed and arcane, demonstrating that the more closely a fiction adheres to historical fact, the harder it is for the reader to later separate the narrative fiction from fact. He cited as one example the Sherlock Holmes mysteries, whose historical and geographic settings are generally accurate. Although the Arthur Conan Doyle reader may initially be able to cleanly separate the fictional nineteenth-century London from the actual historical London, Gerrig found Doyle's portrayal of nineteenth-century London so realistic that even its fictional components intruded into his real-world mental picture of the city.[31]

In other words, literature, movies, and art can blur fact and fiction. As Gerrig put it: "Immersion in narratives brings about isolation from the facts of the real world."[32]

Other researchers go further and suggest that compelling fictional narratives corrode the analytical process itself. Two psychologists at Ohio State University, Melanie Green and Timothy Brock, extended Gerrig's analysis. They began by observing that narratives manifestly earn more public attention than rhetorical arguments:

> Novels, films, soap operas, music lyrics, stories in newspapers, magazines, TV, and radio command far more waking attention than do advertisements, sermons, editorials, billboards, and so forth. The power of narratives to change beliefs has never been doubted and has always been feared.[33]

Green and Brock quantified "transportation" according to several measures: the reader's ability to visualize the narrative's scene and place him or her in it, the degree of mental and emotional involvement, the perception of the narrative as relevant, the desire to know the ending, and the feeling that "the events in the narrative have changed my life." Contrariwise, an awareness of the things going on in the room, wandering attention, and the ease with which the narrative was later forgotten lowered the "transportation score."

They had subjects read a heartrending true story about the fatal stabbing of a small girl named Katie by a psychiatric patient, "Murder in the Mall," presented in one of two formats. The first was a "nonfiction" version in a two-column, small-print style configured to look like a newspaper report; the second, a "fiction" version resembling a literary magazine, was headed by a bold-font warning, "The events in Murder in the Mall comprise a short story, the *Fiction Feature*, as published in Akron Best Fiction, an Ohio fiction magazine, in December 1993. Resemblance to real persons and places is of course coincidental."

Green and Brock then split their subjects into two groups according to the above-discussed transport scores, low and high, and asked them about beliefs pertaining to the story. In each case, the highly transported subjects were more likely than those who were less transported to be sympathetic toward Katie, the little girl in the tale, and believe that the world was unjust, that mall attacks were common, and that the freedom of psychiatric patients should be restricted. Remarkably, clearly labeling the story as fictional did not lessen the degree to which it affected their beliefs: the effects of transport were the same for the nonfiction and fiction formats.

They next asked the subjects to engage in elementary analysis of the text, such as the "Pinocchio" and "fourth grade practice" identification tests, in which they were asked to circle words and phrases that, respectively, rang false or that a fourth grader might not understand. The results were equally dramatic: In both cases, the high-transport group identified fewer than half the items found by the low-transport group. These data were consistent with the hypothesis that, in the authors' words, "transported individuals are less likely to doubt, to question, or to engage in disbelieving processing. Transportation increased the perception of authenticity."[34] In other words, a high degree of narrative transportation impairs one's critical facilities.

Green and Brock, in noting that the labeling of narratives as true or fiction had no effect on how well they transported their readers, remarked:

> Once a reader is rolling along with a compelling narrative, the source has diminishing influence. In this fashion the belief positions implied by the story might be adopted regardless of whether they corresponded with reality. Thus, narratives might need to be used to advantage by low-credible sources or by speakers who lack cogent arguments.[35]

Thus, the deeper the reader or listener enters into the story, the more they suspend disbelief, and thus the less attention they pay to whether it is in reality true or false. While reverse causation is possible—that less analytical people may be more likely to be transported—it makes more sense that transportation impairs analytical ability, and that the more compelling the narrative, the more carried away its consumers become.

Put another way, a good story usually trumps the most ironclad fact. The Republican primary debate held on September 16, 2015, provided a compelling example of this. When asked about the safety of vaccines, Ben Carson, a renowned neurosurgeon, briefly summarized the overwhelming data that demonstrated the absence of correlation between vaccination and autism. Donald Trump responded that "autism has become an epidemic" and then related the story of the "beautiful child" of an employee who developed autism after a vaccination. Most observers scored the interchange in Trump's favor; wrote one journalist, "Trump knows what he's doing, because a story like the one he told is more affecting and persuasive than just presenting the facts."[36] If you want to convince someone, target their System 1 with narrative, not their System 2 with facts and data.

Music stimulates System 1 even more strongly than does narration. Auditory information passes via the inner ear's hair cells to the acoustic nerve, then through relays from the lower to the upper brainstem, and thence to the thalamus, which distributes information about sound to both System 1 and System 2.

The paired thalami sit on top of the brainstem; they can be thought of as the brain's primary relay stations for sensory information coming from below. Critically, the thalami connect directly with System 1, particularly the nuclei accumbens and amygdalae, which mediate, respectively, pleasure and disgust.[37] The thalami also send information about sound to

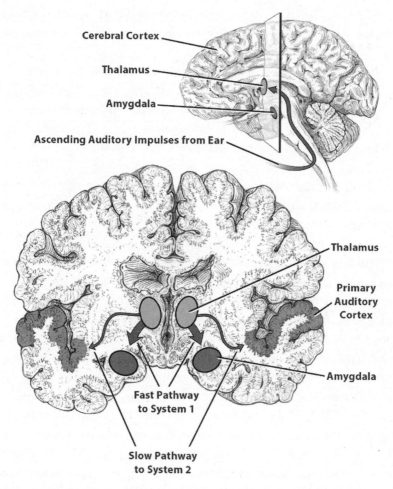

Figure 1-1.   Schematic diagram of auditory information flow to Systems 1 and 2

the auditory part of System 2, which consists of a part of the temporal lobe known as Heschl's gyrus, and the cortical association areas beyond it. These interpret sound and make us consciously aware of it; critically, these connections to System 2 are more indirect and thus slower than the connections to System 1.

The more direct pathway from the thalami to System 1 means that even before a thrilling tune reaches our consciousness via System 2, it can send chills up our spines by activating the nuclei accumbens; conversely, when we hear the dark minor key that accompanies a film's villain or the hero's impending doom, our amygdalae fire almost instantaneously.

Music can thus be thought of as the evolutionarily ancient superhighway to our emotions. Since music can bypass our System 2 so effectively, its persuasiveness has been well appreciated since ancient times; melody may well have predated syntactically complex human speech. Mothers spontaneously sing to their infants, and around the world nearly all religious ceremonies and patriotic events involve music.

George Orwell beautifully describes the appeal of music to the irrational in *Animal Farm* when the pig Major (the allegorical Marx or Lenin) exhorts his followers to revolt against Farmer Jones with a song from his childhood, *Beasts of England*:

> The singing of this song threw the animals into the wildest excitement. Almost before Major had reached the end, they had begun singing it for themselves. Even the stupidest of them had already picked up the tune and a few of the words, and as for the clever ones, such as the pigs and dogs, they had the entire song by heart within a few minutes. And then, after a few preliminary tries, the whole farm burst out into Beasts of England in tremendous unison. The cows lowed it, the dogs whined it, the sheep bleated it, the horses whinnied it, the ducks quacked it. They were so delighted with the song that they sang it right through five times in succession, and might have continued singing it all night if they had not been interrupted.[38]

Perhaps the best known example of real-world musical persuasion is Leni Riefenstahl's *Triumph of the Will*, her documentary portrayal of the 1934 Nazi Party Congress in Nuremberg. The film, which masterfully weaves video of the event with music by Richard Wagner and the Nazi composer Herbert Windt, remarkably contains no verbal narration beyond snippets of the speeches of Hitler and other Nazi leaders. *Triumph of the Will* so impressed Hollywood filmmakers that when the U.S. entered the war, Frank Capra modeled his *Why We Fight* movie series after it.

Music lay largely dormant as a political tool until the mid-1980s, when American political campaigns enthusiastically embraced melody in campaign advertising: sprightly uplifting tunes in a major key for the ad's candidate, and in foreboding dark, minor keys (or less frequently, circus-clown riffs) for the opponent.

A classic of the genre is a thirty-second clip run by the 2004 George W. Bush presidential campaign entitled "Wolves," which began with a voice-over, accompanied by dark and brooding music, that accused the congressional Democrats of defunding counterterrorism operations in a dangerous world, symbolized by a video of a pack of wolves crouched in a meadow.* Observed musicologist and communications academic Paul Christiansen:

> Although the imagery and voice-over lend meaning to the ad, they are only handmaidens to the music, which conveys most of the emotional affect. And it is not just any music—it is music that one might find in a horror film: a low, rumbling drone, primal drums, shrill dissonance, uncanny timbres, and more.[39]

The end-times narrative compels for yet another reason: the human hunger for tragedy. Ambulances clustered around a crumpled vehicle on the road's shoulder will slow traffic, whereas an intact abandoned car in the same position will not. The headline "Dozens of Miners Killed in Explosion" sells newspapers, whereas one that reads "Things Gradually Getting Better" does not. As famously put by Tolstoy at the beginning of *Anna Karenina*, "All happy families are alike; each unhappy family is unhappy in its own way."[40] The path to a successful novel rarely runs through successful marriages and harmonious siblings.

Humans attend more to bad news than to good news. This seems to be a patently obvious feature of human nature, and so psychologists have had a field day experimentally verifying our preoccupation with tragedy and individual bad fortune. In one study, subjects bet on a football game and returned a week later to settle up and review the game with the researchers. Those with losing bets spent far longer discussing the game than the winners.[41] The human preference for bad news is so widespread that "bad is stronger than good" has become one of the basic precepts of experimental psychology; in evolutionary terms, a focus on negative

---

* The clip may be viewed at https://www.youtube.com/watch?v=_s71-Q2XBZg.

outcomes confers a genetic advantage by making humans attend more to environmental risk.[42]

Like many evolutionarily driven psychological phenomena, the compelling nature of bad news has proved dysfunctional in the digital era. One study, for example, found that fake news stories, which are generally lurid and sensationalistic, are 70 percent more likely to be retweeted than real ones. Bots, the researchers noted, did not accelerate the spread of false news—humans on keyboards and cell phones did. The "three degrees of Alex Jones" phenomenon on YouTube has become a grim joke among media academics: Only three clicks will separate a video on replacing your lawnmower's spark plug and Mr. Jones raging that the Sandy Hook school-massacre was a "hoax."[43]

Given the human attraction to negative news, the Book of Revelation's staying power is not surprising.

One of the first Christian theologians to construct the path to the end-times was Joachim of Fiore. Born in 1135 in Calabria, Italy's toe, he, as had his father, trained and worked as a notary before making a pilgrimage in his late twenties to the Holy Land, where he apparently underwent a spiritual crisis. He returned from the Holy Land to Sicily and subsisted as a hermit in the shadow of the Mount Etna volcano, then recrossed the Strait of Messina to wander as a preacher in Calabria. At some point, he buried himself in scripture and was ordained at the Benedictine monastery in Corazzo. He must also have been politically adept, for he garnered the encouragement and support of Pope Lucius III, became abbot at the monastery, and successfully converted it to the Cistercian order.[44] Subsequently, he consulted with and obtained the ideological sanction of two more popes.

Numbers captivated him, especially seven and twelve: the seven ages of Augustine, the seven days of creation, and the seven seals and vials of Revelation; and the twelve apostles and twelve tribes of Israel. Better yet, twelve could be broken down into seven and five, which represented the seven churches of Asia Minor and the five senses. Surely, he thought, such powerful numerology could be applied to biblical interpretation to expose not merely history or morality, but also to predict the future.

He was also fond of the number three. The Holy Trinity, he thought, was the key: it divided history into three ages: that of the Father, from

Abraham to the birth of Christ; that of the Son, from Christ to Joachim's era; and a final era encompassing both the present and future of the Holy Spirit, to be ushered in by an angel with a sword.

Inclined toward mathematics, Joachim also organized scripture into geometric schema in which he arranged history into, among other shapes, interlocking circles and trees with historical "side shoots," which he described in the *Book of Figures*.[45]

The modern reader may scoff at such unscientific numerology—"number mysticism," in the words of mathematician Eric Temple Bell—but medieval theologians had an excuse. The Greek mathematician Pythagoras's brilliance in deriving natural laws from pure mathematics shone down the millennia. "Everything is a number," he is supposed to have said, and until Francis Bacon invented the observationally based scientific method, numbers held pride of place in natural philosophy, as science was known in those days, and ofttimes in theology as well.[46]

We are all, in the language of psychology, pattern-seeking primates. This is hardly a new concept: Around 1620, Bacon observed that humankind "is of its own nature prone to suppose the existence of more order and regularity in the world than it finds."[47] That is, we are hardwired to detect relationships where often none exist, a tendency science writer Michael Shermer has labeled "patternicity." Joachim's fanciful numerological schemas certainly qualify as such.[48]

Evolutionary natural selection provides a ready explanation for our tendency to hallucinate patterns. In the distant human past, the penalty was high indeed for missing a clue about a serious threat, such as a vague hiss or a flash of yellow-and-black stripes in the peripheral vision, while the cost of hearing snakes or seeing tigers everywhere, while considerable, does not compare with that of getting snakebit or eaten. Evolution thus favors the overinterpretation of data, not just in humans but in any organism with a functioning nervous system.[49]

The Bible is a long book, about 783,000 words, in more than 2,000 standard print pages that describe a myriad of players and plays and thus provide a treasure trove for those who seek patterns and connections, especially for the mathematically inclined Joachim, whose historical schema concluded in a Third Age of joy, freedom, and plenty, in which the truth of God would be directly available to all believers, without ecclesiastical intermediation, a happy state of affairs that would endure until the Last Judgment.[50]

Joachim was no revolutionary or charismatic prophet who stirred the masses with messages from God, but rather a wonky interpreter of scripture. Moreover, he had been coy about the precise details of the Third Age, with its nebulous perfection of human nature and proto-communism that would vanquish all human vices, particularly the desire to possess material goods. In a vague foreshadowing of Marx, "To each will be given in such a manner that he will rejoice less on his own account than because his neighbor has received something. He will count a thing less as his own than as given to others through him."[51] So mild was his vision, which would transpire gradually on earth with no discernible intervention from Revelation's fearsome phantasms, that three successive popes endorsed it. The future Third Age, Joachim thought, would eventually correct the flaws in the contemporary Second Age, but its oppressed feudal masses were not as patient as Joachim. They had more proactive measures in mind.

Joachim's math, because it both carried popular appeal and lent itself to all sorts of biblical schemes and number mysticism, has endured, in one form or another, until the present day. Prime among his activist heirs, for example, was a spiritual faction of the newly ascendant Franciscans, who were repelled by the materialism of their increasingly successful order. For them, the math was simple: Matthew 1:17 clearly stated that fourteen generations lay between Abraham and David, fourteen generations between David and the Babylonian exile, and fourteen generations from the exile to the birth of Christ. This First Age thus lasted forty-two generations, each generation thirty years in length—1,260 years in all. The current Second Age would be of the same length and so would end in A.D. 1260, when the millennial Third Age would commence.

As the medieval period progressed, the economic growth following the erosion of feudalism and the rise of trade and the money economy led to extremes of income inequality that produced a plethora of virulently anti-Semitic end-times narratives. One of them, the German-language *The Book of a Hundred Chapters*, appeared at around the same time as Martin Luther's heresies.

It opened with the Archangel Michael relaying a message from God to its anonymous author: humankind had so angered the Almighty that He was on the brink of wreaking fearsome destruction, but He had decided on a reprieve. God wished the author to gather the faithful to await the arrival of the "Emperor from the Black Forest" who would deliver a bloody Revelation-style end-times, as well as abundant food and wine. The faithful, drawn largely from the suffering poor, would pitch in with widespread murder, particularly of the aristocracy and clergy. The *Book*'s Messiah did not turn his cheek, but rather prescribed the murder of twenty-three hundred clergy per day for four and a half years.[52]

Revulsion at the Church's manifest corruption was nothing new: Long before Martin Luther, and long before Joachim, the profligacy and carnal sins of the clergy, and particularly of the pope, had appalled Christendom. Luther was simply the right man at the right time in the right place. Gutenberg's printing press, invented roughly seven decades before, had brought down the cost of reproducing a pamphlet or book by a factor of approximately thirty, and printers in Luther's Wittenberg, who could turn out type not only in the Latin alphabet but also in the Greek and Hebrew ones, stood at the forefront of the new technology.

To accomplish his reformation, Luther needed the support of the aristocracy, and so he rigorously confined his dissent to the theological and eschewed the political. The great reformer took counsel from the biblical books of Romans and 1 Peter that Caesar's laws still had to be obeyed: "Submit yourselves to every ordinance of man for the Lord's sake."[53]

While Luther thus had little patience for those who sought social reform, those who did deployed his methods. Not only had Luther destroyed the powerful church monopoly on scriptural interpretation, but he had also demonstrated for all to see the might of the printing press. When challenged about how little preaching he did, he replied, "We do that with our books."[54]

In the early sixteenth century, poor crops, a rapacious aristocracy, and Lutheran zeal combined to ignite bloody popular revolt. Legend has it that on June 23, 1523, six years after Luther nailed his ninety-five theses to the door of the Wittenberg Castle Church, the countess of Lupfen-Stühlingen in Swabia, just north of modern central Switzerland, ordered twelve hundred peasants intent on harvesting their hay to instead collect snail shells on which to mount her presumably large supply of thread. The countess's acute need for these shells so angered her peasants that it triggered an uprising that spread across much of German-speaking Europe over the following two years.[55]

In 1524–1525, peasant armies fought a series of battles, collectively known as the German Peasants' War (colloquially, the War of Snails), against *landsknechts*, mercenaries hired by the local aristocrats. These encounters more often than not resulted in the wholesale slaughter of approximately one hundred thousand of the poorly trained and armed rebels.

Throughout most of this episode, social, and not religious, concerns drove the German rebels, loosely known as the Swabian League, but the revolt's bloody denouement was largely the work of a millennialist priest named Thomas Müntzer and his deluded, frenzied followers.

In March 1525, the rebels met at the Swabian town of Memmingen and formulated a dozen demands, the Twelve Articles, and printed at least twenty-five thousand copies. Only the first demand was overtly theological: Each city could elect its own preacher, who would "preach the gospel simply," which presumably excluded the Latin Catholic Mass. The next ten demands were more economic than religious: among them, how preachers were to be paid, the abolition of serfdom, reductions in rent, the right to hunt and fish, and the return of recently privatized communal lands. The last article humbly observed that were any of the preceding eleven demands later proven contrary to scripture, they were null and void.[56]

Nonetheless, Müntzer, who acquired a leadership position late in the revolt, had read and interpreted at least one of Joachim's treatises. Little is known about Müntzer's origins. The best guess is that he was born to an artisan family in Stolberg, just outside Aachen, at the modern juncture of Belgium, Germany, and the Netherlands. His educational background is likewise blurred; he left few academic traces, and some have said his father's life ended on the gallows at the hands of a corrupt nobleman and so left the son with an antiauthoritarian, apocalyptic streak. All that is known is that he was ordained, which did not require a university education, around 1514, though his writings suggest advanced academic training.

Three years later, Luther's dissent exploded at Wittenberg, and Müntzer journeyed there to drink in the revolutionary fervor. He likely met Luther and even preached from his pulpit; he certainly met Luther's brilliant colleague, Philip Melanchthon. At first, Müntzer fought side by side with the Wittenberg faction against the pope's partisans, and in 1520 Luther recommended him to fill in at Zwickau for the preacher Johannes Sylvius Egranus, who had gone off to study with a list of humanist scholars that included Erasmus of Rotterdam.

In Zwickau, Müntzer gave full vent to his theologically intolerant impulses and millennialist fervor. As did Luther, he labeled Catholic priests and monks "monstrosities" and "flesh-tearing harpies," and also began to preach that salvation could be had with direct communication with God, independent of scripture.[57] This was too much even for Luther and for Egranus, the latter of whom had by then returned to Zwickau and demoted Müntzer to one of the town's smaller churches. There, Müntzer may have come under the influence of the "Zwickau prophets," laymen who shared his mystic belief in the importance of dreams and the irrelevance of holy writ for salvation.

Müntzer's inflammatory sermons and tracts led to his expulsions, first from Zwickau, and then from Prague and multiple other locations; eventually, he landed in the Saxon town of Allstedt. Along the way he developed his own apocalyptic end-times themes. In 1524, he preached a famous sermon to Duke Johann of Saxony that centered on the Book of Daniel's narrative of Nebuchadnezzar's dream. On the off chance the Duke had missed the allusion, he informed him that the Church in Rome, and those noblemen who supported it, had taken the place of Daniel's doomed Greek Seleucid Empire. As frosting on the millennialist cake, Müntzer made it plain that the dreams of prophets, often lay men with no formal religious training, held primacy over the interpretation of scripture, and that they were all now living in the Last Days. Most alarmingly of all, Müntzer declared himself the new Daniel, and that his followers, "the elect," who understood the immediacy of the Apocalypse, were present not merely to observe, but to actively bring it about.

After Münzter's sermon, the Duke departed in angry silence, and Müntzer continued to inflame the tenuous situation in Allstedt by publishing further anticlerical tracts. Eventually, the Duke had enough and shut down Müntzer's printing press and summoned the preacher to his castle at Weimar for interrogation. Fearing for his life, Müntzer departed Allstedt and, several turbulent stops later, shared command of the rebel forces at the disastrous Battle of Frankenhausen, the climax of the Peasants' War.

By this point, Müntzer had convinced himself and many of his followers that God had chosen him to bring about the Apocalypse, and he had mustered not just his dreams, but multiple scriptural passages as well to buttress his authority. He seemed especially impressed by Matthew 24, in which Jesus forecast the destruction of the Temple, followed by a global catastrophe featuring famine, plague, war, earthquakes, among other calamities. God had also armed Müntzer with the Sword of Gideon, with

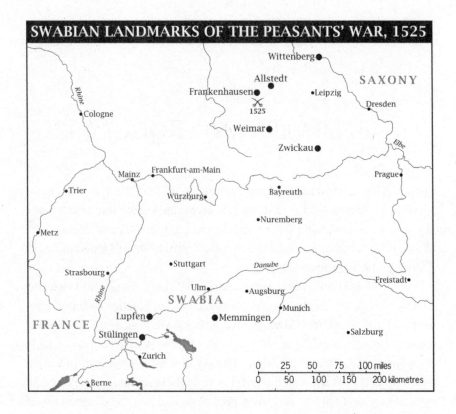

SWABIAN LANDMARKS OF THE PEASANTS' WAR, 1525

which he and his host would prevail against the vastly superior noblemen's army and, according to one observer, "catch all the bullets of the enemy in the sleeve of his coat."[58]

Thus encouraged, on May 14, 1525, the rebels rushed toward the *landsknechts* who, at the cost of a half dozen casualties, slaughtered about 90 percent of the attacking force, approximately six thousand souls.[59] Müntzer fled the battlefield in haste and was quickly captured and brought before the noblemen who, after a lengthy interrogation, had him beheaded.[60]

The violent deaths of Müntzer and his followers would prove the mere curtain-raiser for a bloody apocalypticism that, borne on the prosperous Baltic maritime trade routes, would sweep through northwestern Europe during the following decade.

2

BELIEVERS AND ROGUES

Such was the fevered and delirious atmosphere in the Westphalian city of Münster in February 1534 that residents reported seeing three suns in the sky, easily recognized in that era as the same portent seen after the death of Julius Caesar that foretold the Second Triumvirate of Octavian, Mark Anthony, and Lepidus.

This vision particularly energized a new Protestant sect known as the Anabaptists, who rejected the traditional Catholic practice of infant baptism, and instead rebaptized new converts into the faith as adults. A Catholic named Hermann von Kerssenbrock, who had observed the events of 1534 as a young boy, later recorded that "The sky seemed to gape open, splitting into long cracks from which terrifying fires flickered out. . . . [Peasants] saw the city as if ablaze, and when they rushed to investigate, they found that the flames had not only been harmless to the city but had disappeared altogether."[1]

The young von Kerssenbrock wondered at the madness of the street scene, and described the Anabaptists as

> . . . so deranged, so unbalanced, so driven by frenzy that they also surpassed the Furies described in poetry. They rushed about in the marketplace in quite a shameless manner, some with their hair streaming, some with clothing loose and flowing, some with their wimples blowing in the wind. Some lifted themselves up in crazy dances as if about to fly with the help of their mania. Some collapsed face down on the ground, forming the shape of the cross by sticking out their arms. . . . Some lay in the soft mud, rolling themselves over and over. Some fell to their knees and bellowed. Some howled with gleaming eyes. Some frothed at the lips. Some made threats while shaking their heads and gnashing their teeth, and some ostentatiously

uttered lamentations while striking their breasts. Some cried, some laughed. We, on the other hand, did not so much laugh at their crazed madness as grieve.[2]

Less than a decade after Thomas Müntzer's short-lived, bloody, and inept revolt, another cohort of Joachim's children would execute their fevered visions of the end-times with far greater competence in the town of Münster. There, between 1533 and 1535, the so-called Anabaptist Madness consumed the municipality before it too succumbed to a final assault by the powers that be.

Following the disastrous German Peasants' War, the focal point of the evolving crowd madness moved north, to what is today western Germany and Holland. This area had for decades enjoyed the increasing prosperity of the Hanseatic League, a loose confederation of trading states that stretched along the Baltic and North Seas, roughly from today's Estonia to Flanders. In contrast to the Peasants' War, which mainly sprang from social discontent, the folk rebellion in Germany and Holland was driven by a new religious doctrine, Anabaptism.

In the late eighth century, Charlemagne had conquered Münster, east of modern Holland and south of Emden, and dispatched a missionary named Ludger to proselytize the region and forcibly convert its inhabitants to Christianity. There, on the bank of the river Aa, Ludger built a monastery (*monasterium*, in Latin), from which the town derived its name. As Münster grew prosperous within the Hanseatic economy, its opulent cathedral and numerous grand churches heightened the outward appearance of municipal prosperity.

Münster's ecclesiastical splendor came at a cost: Church tithes necessary to support it fell hard on the backs of the faithful, the clergy themselves paid no taxes, and the land cultivated by the monks and the looms worked by the nuns competed with local farmers and cloth producers. Such ecclesiastical rapacity was hardly unique to the town; all over Europe, the Church's behavior fanned the flames of religious strife and public anger.[3]

Anabaptism itself had its origins in a series of arcane theological discussions a decade earlier in Zurich, where a Catholic priest named Ulrich Zwingli established a reformed church in 1519. Zwingli had participated in a series of formal doctrinal disputes sponsored by the town council, of which

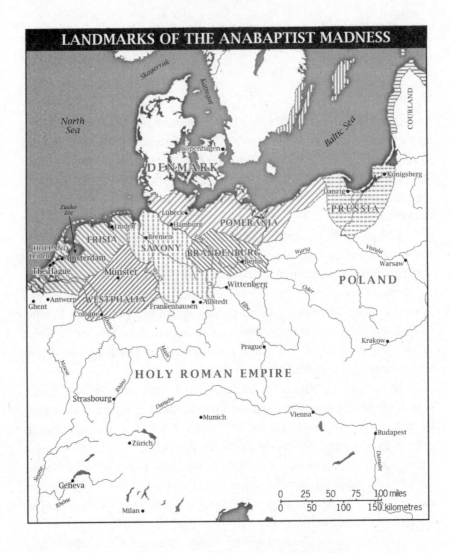

LANDMARKS OF THE ANABAPTIST MADNESS

he was declared the winner. One of the issues discussed before the council concerned the timing of baptism. ("Anabaptism" derives from the Latin, *anabaptismus*, "rebaptisim" or "second baptism.") Logically, only an adult acting of his or her free will can give meaningful obedience to Christ, as described in the gospels of the New Testament. Despite this, infant baptism became well established by the third century, and was near universal and unquestioned Church practice by the time of Luther and Zwingli.

One of Zwingli's opponents in the city council disputations, a merchant named Conrad Grebel, opposed infant baptism—"child washing," as his theological descendants would later disparage it. Following the disputations, Grebel rebaptized one of his friends, George Blaurock, and the two of them then began baptizing anew other adults.

At the time, not much was made of this. Zwingli himself remarked that little theological daylight separated him and Grebel, save for "unimportant outward things, such as these, whether infants or adults should be baptized and whether a Christian may be a magistrate."[4]

But the Anabaptist fuse had been lit, or, more accurately, two fuses: one leading through the Baltics and Low Countries (modern Netherlands and Belgium and the estuaries of the Rhine, Ems, Scheldt, and Meuse rivers), and the other through Münster. Both the Münster and Baltic/Low Countries fuses burned separately until 1534, when they would combine in Münster to ignite one of history's most tumultuous mass delusions.

Melchior Hoffman, a German fur trader who plied the profitable routes among the Hanseatic cities, lit the Baltic/Low Country fuse. A decade younger than Luther, he gained the Wittenberg professor's approval around 1523 and spread his reformist heresies as he traveled. A few years later, Hoffman took the Book of Revelation to heart, departed from Luther's teachings, and began to preach the imminence of an apocalyptic battle between the forces of good and evil.

As have apocalypticists before and since, he enthusiastically applied home-brewed eschatological math. Hoffman calculated that Christ died in A.D. 33, and the apostolic period lasted one hundred years, until A.D. 133. For the sins of the Judeans, he believed, mankind received a punishment of three and a half years, which was increased by a factor of twenty during the Babylonian period, and by a another twenty-fold for the falling away of the Church from Christ, i.e., 1,400 years. Therefore, the apocalypse would occur in 1533 (133 + 1,400), a prediction that precipitated riots and mayhem in multiple Baltic trading cities, including Lübeck, Stockholm, and some Danish ports, a trail of chaos that earned him expulsion from each.[5]

By its nature, Anabaptism was an appealing but decentralized theology whose adherents were unified by little else than the belief in adult baptism. Eventually, Anabaptist communities sprung up all over western Europe, particularly along the Hanseatic trade routes. Hoffman's apocalyptic brand of Anabaptism met its greatest success in the Low Countries, especially in Emden, the largest city in East Frisia, a coastal area of Germany just east of the modern Dutch border.

The Habsburgs had inherited the Low Countries from the Burgundians in the late fifteenth century. During this period, their cities had become among the most prosperous on the Continent, and their inhabitants, empowered by Luther's destruction of the Church monopoly on scriptural interpretation and Gutenberg's printing press, congregated in small, unofficial groups, called conventicles, which became hotbeds for a wide variety of religious sects.

Around 1530, Hoffman passed through Strasbourg, then a beehive of Reformation activity. The city was home to, among other doctrines, the mild Swiss version of Anabaptism, which he grafted onto his apocalyptic creed. In 1531, echoing Revelation, he decided that Strasbourg would be where Revelation's 144,000 holy messengers would assemble and prevail against a great siege of the city by the forces of evil. Petitioning the Strasbourg city council to establish his own church earned him one more exile, whereupon he returned to the Low Countries and rebaptized large numbers of adults, three hundred alone at a single sitting in Emden's main church.[6]

In December 1531, authorities of the Holy Roman Empire, the Low Country's ostensible rulers, captured one of Hoffman's disciples, Jan Volkerts, who had rebaptized fifty converts in Amsterdam. They all but invited him to escape, but he chose martyrdom instead and was beheaded along with nine followers. In response, Hoffman lowered the sect's profile by forbidding adult baptism.[7] In 1533, Hoffman unwisely returned to Strasbourg, where a synod convicted him of relatively minor heresies and imprisoned him in a series of abysmal prison cells. He greeted his grim new surroundings with equanimity; since the Apocalypse was imminent, he wasn't going to be there long, a sunny assumption that proved incorrect. He survived imprisonment for a decade, during which burghers on the street below occasionally heard him softly chant psalms and endlessly repeat "Woe ye godless scribes of Strasbourg."[8]

Upon Hoffman's incarceration, one of his followers, a baker named Jan Matthys, turned up in Amsterdam, declared himself the prophet Enoch, and, to the joy of the faithful, resumed adult baptism. Enoch was one of only two Old Testament characters taken by God to heaven while alive, the other being Elijah, whose identity Hoffman had already appropriated. Further, some Anabaptists cited Revelation 11:3–12 as proof that Enoch and Elijah were the two unnamed witnesses who ascend to heaven. As 1533 passed into 1534, Low Country believers were forced to postpone the apocalypse to 1535 and moved its venue north from Strasbourg to the more religiously tolerant town of Münster.

In March 1534, at least three thousand Amsterdam Anabaptists attempted to reach Münster by sailing across the Zuider Zee. They were blocked by Habsburg troops, whose response to the attempt was considered mild for that era: they executed only about a hundred heretics and let go the rest as innocent dupes. The next day several "apostles" brandished swords and paraded through Amsterdam's streets to warn of a Judgment Day just before Easter; they were caught and killed. By that year, the Habsburg authorities in The Hague had deployed "flying columns" to round up Low Country Anabaptists, who were tortured and presented with the choice between recantation and execution.[9]

On a frigid night in February 1535, a group of Anabaptists ran naked through Amsterdam and shouted "Woe to the godless!" Public nakedness symbolized to the faithful innocence before God, and was also common in Münster; the men who refused to put on clothes were executed, and the women who refused were drowned. (The sword and naked walkers left the Dutch language with two new words, zwaardlopers and naaklopers.)

Anabaptist insurrections broke out in numerous other Dutch cities as well, which brought more executions. By mid-1535 as many as 20 percent of Amsterdam's population may have undergone adult baptism. Many, if not most, of the anointed were outsiders, refugees from spiraling repression and resistance that included several large-scale pitched battles. On May 11, armed Anabaptists occupied the city's main market, and before being arrested cried out, "Whoever loves God, join us!" Three days later, the authorities tore out the hearts of eleven of the ringleaders; that summer, the authorities cut off the tongue of an Anabaptist leader because he used it to preach; his right hand because he had used it to baptize, and finally, his head.[10]

Even for the era, the suppression of the Anabaptists was brutal, certainly more than that applied to the followers of Luther and Zwingli; that these last two groups abrogated the Church monopoly on scriptural interpretation was bad enough, but at least they respected private property and the authority of secular governments. The Anabaptists did neither; in most cases they advocated the confiscation of concentrated wealth—particularly the Church's—and denied the legitimacy of existing governments. The Anabaptists compounded their sedition with belief in an imminent End and, in many cases, actions that might hasten it.

Numerous as the Dutch Anabaptists were, the Habsburgs had far too tight a grip on Holland for them to succeed; they needed softer political ground, which meant, in practice, a city not under the thumb of the Habsburgs. They found it in Münster, where the second fuse to the Anabaptist Madness would be lit.

Many of the Hanseatic towns, such as Danzig and Lübeck, were so-called "free cities," essentially independent of the distant and increasingly impotent Holy Roman Emperor, and so owed only a nominal fealty to him. Most of these nearly independent municipalities were ruled by a local nobleman, in Münster's case a "prince-bishop," chosen by the local cathedral but confirmed by the pope, often at a steep price, and who often ruled more as a feudal master than as an ecclesiastical figure who combined both civil and clerical authority.

In 1525, Münster's prince-bishop, Frederick von Wiede, frightened by the Peasants War, devolved power to a town council of twenty-four members that included two co-mayors. Less than a decade later, the council, which, unlike the Low Country governments, was largely free of Habsburg influence, would become the wedge with which the Anabaptists effected their frenzied, violent mayhem.[11]

Most historians assign Anabaptism's beachhead in Münster to one Bernard Rothmann, born around 1495 to a blacksmith who, along with his ancestors, had stood accused of witchcraft. Young Bernard was described as having a "fickle and clownish temperament," and being too poor for schooling, found himself under the tutelage of his uncle, a vicar at St. Maurice's Church in Münster, where he became a choirboy and eventually made a living singing. By the time puberty cut short his vocal career, he had earned the wherewithal to study at Mainz, where he earned a master's degree. In 1529 he returned to St. Maurice's.[12]

Sometime around 1530 Rothmann, by now a persuasive preacher, acquired the financial support of wealthy cloth merchant, guild leader, and city council member Bernard Knipperdolling, who first converted to Lutheranism and subsequently, under Rothmann's influence, became a secret Anabaptist. Knipperdolling printed Rothmann's tracts, which fanned Anabaptism's flames, not only in Münster but also in the Low Countries.

The modern understanding of the Anabaptist Madness owes much to two observers, the aforementioned Hermann von Kerssenbrock, and Heinrich Gresbeck, the latter an Anabaptist-convert carpenter who remained through most of the episode and played a small but critical role in its end. Both von Kerssenbrock and Gresbeck left detailed written accounts that, when interpreted in the light of their respective biases, seem credible.[13]

Von Kerssenbrock described how, initially, Rothmann faithfully taught Catholic doctrine, but then

> gradually he began to mix into his sermons doctrines that seemed to be inimical to Catholic dogma, and as he began to incite the commons to anger against the clergy, he attracted to himself some among the burghers who were eager for novelty.[14]

His superiors at St. Maurice's decided to protect their flock from Rothmann's increasingly radical views and so loaned him twenty gold florins for further study in Cologne. He neither made it there nor repaid the loan; instead, he headed straight to Wittenberg, home of Luther and Melanchthon.

The young priest returned to St. Maurice's in 1531 a confirmed Lutheran who, intoxicated by the pleasures of demagoguery, proved adept at attracting crowds to the small church that lay outside of the city walls. As recorded by von Kerssenbrock,

> Many people, especially those weighed down by debt, revered him like some godhead, hung from his every word, and were convinced that he was driven in his actions by the Spirit of God. Despite official orders to the contrary, they followed him in crowds from the city on account of their eagerness to hear him speak, their desire to do so being so great that they considered that there were no preachers but him and despised, condemned, and cursed the others along with the entire clergy.[15]

Von Kerssenbrock, a loyal Catholic, sniffed that Rothmann preached "not so much with solid arguments as with clumsy aspersions. The ignorant commoners, however, who cannot distinguish eloquence from bombast, thought that he had spoken excellently."[16]

Rothmann by this point had been removed as a priest at St. Maurice's, and soon enough he led a mob to the church that smashed idols, knocked over altars, crushed a silver chalice, and burned paintings of the Blessed Virgin. The authorities once more expelled him, and he repaired yet again to Wittenberg, where he impressed both Luther and Melanchthon, the latter of whom is said to have presciently remarked that "Rothmann would either be remarkably good or remarkably bad."[17]

Rothmann again returned to Münster in 1532, where he began to espouse frankly Anabaptist views. This was a double-edged sword. Adult baptism aroused not only the approval of his audiences, but also the approbation of the Church, which had by then shown scant compunction at burning Anabaptists at the stake or drowning them by tying rocks to their neck and tossing them into the water, "a little bit of a theological joke," in the words of Anabaptism scholar Christopher Mackay.[18]

At this point, the prince-bishop, von Wiede, still controlled the city and so forced the preacher to cease his blasphemies. He complied for a few weeks, but then threw caution to the wind and wrote to von Wiede, that "because my conscience is clear, I have no doubt that I can rely on God's mercy. He will protect me and rescue me from danger."[19]

In February 1532, Rothmann preached a sermon in the yard of one of the city's main churches, St. Lamberts, and so swayed the congregation that they spontaneously chose him as their pastor. More importantly, he had won enough support on the town council to prevent his expulsion. Münster's religious fervor was not limited to Anabaptism; churches all over the city were installing radical Lutheran preachers, all of them, except for Rothmann, from other cities.

Rothmann's success in converting the city to Anabaptism matched that of Hoffman and Matthys in the Low Countries. Shortly after Rothmann's St. Lamberts sermon, von Wiede resigned in frustration, and his immediate replacement died before he could be consecrated; in June Francis von Waldeck, the son of a count with little ecclesiastical background, ascended to prince-bishop. Late in the year, he blockaded the city, now fully under the control of the rebellious Anabaptists, who responded with a successful raid on von Waldeck's headquarters just outside the city walls. In February 1533, a compromise was reached: the parish churches could practice Lutheranism, while the cathedral would remain Catholic.[20]

Despite this compromise, time was running out for Münster's Catholics and Lutherans. Rothmann's pamphlets, underwritten by the wealthy Knipperdolling, had permeated the Low Countries. These flysheets labeled private property as a source of great evil: "God had made all things common, as today we can still enjoy air, fire, rain, and the sun in common, and whatever else some thieving man cannot grasp for himself." Rothmann portrayed Münster as a city of plenty that would welcome the faithful with open arms, and hundreds of the wretched from the Low Countries made the pilgrimage south to the new Anabaptist Jerusalem.

In early 1533, the city contained an uneasy mix of Catholics, conventional Lutherans, and Anabaptists, the last of whom had no intention of honoring the prince-bishop's compromise. At the same time, enough Anabaptists had flowed in from the Low Countries to trigger a special council election in March that resulted in a radical Lutheran majority, a substantial Anabaptist minority, and no Catholics.[21] The city council began its new reign by fining families who baptized babies in the cathedral.

Meanwhile in the Low Countries, Jan Matthys performed his first rebaptism on a man from Leiden named Jan Bockelson. Whereas Matthys, like Hoffman, was an impulsive, fiery preacher, Bockelson would fashion his theatrical skills and calculating nature into a formidable political force. Born into bitterness and disappointment as the bastard son of a town mayor and a serf woman, he was provided by his parents with rudimentary schooling and an apprenticeship in tailoring, at which he proved maladept. Nature, nonetheless, had endowed him with other attributes that he would shortly deploy in Münster: blond good looks, grace, cunning, oratorical prowess, and acting talent. In the words of millennialist scholar Norman Cohn, he used these gifts "to shape real life into a play, with himself as its hero and all Europe for an audience."[22]

In late 1533 Matthys sent several emissaries to Münster, who arrived the following January. These included Bockelson, who had himself visited the city the previous summer. Once there, they found that Rothmann and his followers had already rebaptized approximately one-fifth of the city's adults, and that as many as one-third of the population believed that the Apocalypse was imminent; Matthys himself came on February 9, 1534.[23] The arrivals of Matthys and Bockelson mark the merging of the two Anabaptist fuses: Rothmann's persuasive homegrown Münster Anabaptism, and the Low Country–derived hypnotic end-times delusions of Melchior Hoffman, then languishing in a Strasbourg prison cell. To both parties, the meaning of their arrival in Münster was crystal clear. In the words of scholar Ralf Klötzer,

That a prophet sent out his messengers to baptize was interpreted
as a sign that God was preparing the end of the world. Within this
context, wars, plague, and inflation, along with the Reformation in
the Empire, suddenly became portents of the last days.[24]

From this point, things moved rapidly. The Anabaptists sent envoys to
neighboring cities with the message that by Easter of 1534, God would
return to punish the wicked and that few would survive; safety and salvation could be had only in Münster, the New Jerusalem. The end of the
world was nigh.

On February 6, 1534, Rothmann performed an opéra bouffe for the
nuns of the Convent Across-the-River:

He gave a sermon in praise of marriage, and with the wondrous bat-
tering rams of his oration he broke open the barracks within which
their virginity was enclosed. He seemed to be urging the virgins to
propagate the human race, an act to which they were not particularly
averse. Next, to make them completely crazy instead of merely stupid, he convinced them that the tower of the convent along with its
entire structure and all those living in it would collapse at midnight
on the following day. . . . The oracle brought the nuns not so much
distress as joy. For their spirit, which was ablaze with lust, hated the
monastic life.[25]

The young ladies, who had nowhere else to go and perceiving Rothmann as
a man of God, decamped with their possessions to his house. Throughout
the city, citizens went sleepless to greet the End.

It did not come, and to save face, the preacher deployed a ripe biblical
chestnut, the story of Jonah, who had in error foretold the fall of Nineveh,
the Assyrian capital, which the Almighty then spared out of mercy. Two
mornings later Rothmann's Anabaptist colleagues, fearful that his forecasting incompetence had devalued their stock, comically attempted to
reinflate their credibility by rushing through the streets and declaiming
loudly with "horrifying shouts and insane bellows" for nonbelievers to
repent. That afternoon Bockelson and Knipperdolling joined the act, yelling
over and over, "Repentance! Repentance! Repentance! Repentance!" Their
remonstrations recruited others, who variously jumped up and down, rolled

their heads, and flopped in the mud. One Anabaptist galloped through the streets on horseback, announced the End, and told all who would listen of the tens of thousands of angels he had beheld.[26]

The madness so energized the Anabaptists that later the same day, five hundred of them seized the city market before the mainstream Lutherans finally pushed them back. The Lutheran comeback proved short-lived; the Anabaptists finally took complete control of the city council in the election of February 23. At month's end, armed Anabaptist enforcers gave the non-Anabaptists an ultimatum: rebaptism or expulsion. "Get out of here, you godless! God will punish you!"[27]

The Anabaptists destroyed church altars and spent days plundering the cathedral's gold and silver and burning its statues. They also received copper tokens bearing the letters "DWWF" (*das wort wird fleisch*—the word becomes flesh) that allowed them to pass the now heavily defended city gates. By the end of the month, the prince-bishop's troops had begun their siege of the city, and Bockelson informed the faithful that the scriptures demanded that when faced with end-times, the Lord granted Christians not the other cheek, but rather a heavily armed defense.

The first Catholics to depart were allowed to take their possessions, except for food, which was already in short supply; the last ones out went with just the clothes on their backs, usually minus their buttons and golden hooks, which were confiscated.[28] The Anabaptists, with the memory of the Lutheran counterattack against their coup still fresh in their minds, concentrated their ire on the menfolk. For their part, the Lutherans and Catholic men fully expected the prince-bishop to recapture the city, and so left behind their women to guard their houses and possessions. The resultant excess of women within the city's walls would soon produce dire consequences.[29]

Whereas in January the Anabaptists had merely volunteered all their physical possessions to the cause—since the world would end at Easter—in March the city council forbade private property, and Rothmann and Bockelson demanded that all silver, gold, and money be handed over at the city hall. In order to encourage the donations, Bockelson preached that there were three classes of believers: good Christians who totally divested themselves, those who held back some of their possessions and needed further prayer to a vengeful God, and those baptized only for convenience's sake who should expect nothing but fire at the End.

Matthys and Bockelson gathered all of the town's men in the cathedral square and shouted at them that the door to mercy had closed and that God was angry. Those who had been baptized were put to one side, and the rest, about three hundred men in all, were disarmed and forced to prostrate themselves and pray for mercy for an hour, expecting death at any moment. They were then led into the cathedral and forced to beseech God on their hands and knees for three more hours, at the end of which Bockelson, who had remained outside, theatrically threw open the doors and announced, "Dear brothers, I shall inform you for God's sake that you have mercy from God and are to remain with us and be holy folk." The next day, he repeated the process with the town's two thousand unbaptized women.[30]

As March ended, the city had undergone a religious cleansing; approximately two thousand Catholics and unbaptized Lutherans had been expelled, and a roughly equal number of Anabaptist immigrants had arrived from Holland and East Frisia, which left the population roughly unchanged at around nine thousand. Not only had the religious makeup of the town changed, but so had its psychological makeup as well. Non-suggestible Catholics had been replaced by far more suggestible Anabaptists, which aggravated the mass delusional behavior that had already become manifest. Further, the expulsion of the godless and in-migration of the faithful served only to strengthen the apocalyptic certitude of the new prophets—Rothmann, Matthys, and Bockelson—that the End was truly near.

Not only did the Anabaptists embrace the future; they would also exterminate the past, and so they ordered the destruction of all of the municipal records, especially debt ledgers. The zealots burned books, Luther's along with Aquinas's. In some homes and churches only the Bible remained. Eventually, Bockelson would also generically rename the city's gates and streets (St. Ludger's Gate, for example, becoming simply South Gate) and assign newborns' names according to alphabetical order.[31]

The new prophets began to brutally punish dissent; a blacksmith named Hubert Rüscher, who had lost his council seat in the February election and was unhappy, among other things, at the destruction of records, was brought before Bockelson, theatrically pardoned, then just as theatrically retrieved from his confinement, made to cry for mercy, and then stabbed in the back with a halberd. The vigorous and heavily muscled blacksmith survived the wound, so Bockelson then shot him in the back with a pistol; it took Rüscher eight days to die.[32]

Shortly before Easter, Matthys attended the wedding of some friends; Gresbeck recorded him prophesying his own death:

> He sat for an hour long, slapping his hands together, nodding his head up and down and sighing heavily, just as if he was about to die. . . . Eventually, he started to wake up again and said with a sigh, "Oh, dear Father, not as I will but as you will." He stood up, gave everyone his hand, and kissed them on the mouth. He said, "God's peace be with you all," and went on his way with his wife. (And at that time, the rebaptizers didn't have many wives yet.)[33]

In 1534, Easter fell on April 5, Jesus did not materialize, and the world did not end. On that day, Matthys and perhaps a dozen followers departed the city gates and rode toward the prince-bishop's *landsknechts*, who slaughtered them. Gresbeck reported that the besiegers cut Matthys's body into a hundred pieces and playfully struck each other with the gory fragments, affixed his head to a pike, and yelled back to the city that the inhabitants should retrieve their mayor.[34] The deluded Matthys may have been trying to entice Jesus to come, or, alternatively, to fulfill the passage in Revelation 11 suggesting that the deaths of Enoch (himself) and of Elijah (Hoffman, still rotting in a Strasbourg prison) would signal Jesus's return.

Bockelson's years of preaching around the countryside, which included a visit to Münster the previous summer, had honed his theatrical tradecraft. In nearby Schöppingen, he supposedly healed a sick girl by baptizing her, and by the time he arrived back in Münster in early 1534, a price was affixed to his head. He had likely been preparing for this precise moment. Until then he had kept a relatively low profile in Münster, but upon Matthys's death, he appeared high above the crowd in an upper-level window of a church clothed in a white robe and bathed in candlelight, with Knipperdolling to his right and Diewer, Matthys's beautiful and mysterious wife, whom history remembers by only her Christian name, to his left.

Bockelson shocked the crowd by telling them that Matthys deserved death for his vainglory and by taking so many along with him. He gestured to Knipperdolling and told the crowd that while living under his roof, he had a vision of Matthys's gory disembowelment and that the *landsknecht* who did the deed told Bockelson not to be afraid: Matthys would be judged by God, and he, Bockelson, must marry his widow, Diewer. As proof, Bockelson again pointed to Knipperdolling, who purported to also have witnessed the *landsknecht*'s speech and confirmed its truth. The crowd became excited at the divine vision, and not a few tore off their clothes and danced. No one needed to be told that Bockelson had inherited Matthys's mantle.[35]

He also inherited a problem from Matthys and Rothmann, for he had to explain to the faithful yet another no-show by Jesus. Christ, he divined, would now not return until the New Jerusalem had been purged of all impure elements.

Bockelson proved not only a brilliant demagogue, but also a competent military commander. He tightened the city's already formidable defensive cordon of twin walls, moats, and stone-roundel-guarded gates. Only nine thousand citizens faced a roughly equal number of largely mercenary *landsknechts*, and no dead weight was allowed: women not only assisted men at the gunpowder mill, but also fashioned flaxen wreaths dipped into boiling caldrons of pitch and quicklime to be dropped on the assaulting mercenaries from the city walls. At night, Bockelson's men slipped into their tents, cut throats, and left notes to the survivors that encouraged them to convert and join the Anabaptists.

On May 25, Bockelson's forces easily repulsed an assault by the prince-bishop's troops, many of whom defected into the city (though six of them soon had to be executed for drunken disorder).[36] The victory greatly inspired the Anabaptists; surely, God was on their side, and the defeat of the prince-bishop's troops solidified Anabaptist control of the city.

In July, Bockelson declared all previous marriages invalid and ordered all adults to remarry. Women now outnumbered men by almost three to one, a situation exacerbated by the left-behind Lutheran and Catholic women, and so the Anabaptists encouraged polygamy. At first, the more aggressive among the Anabaptist men engaged in a mad scramble through the city in search of young women and virgins on the theory that, in Gresbeck's words, "The more wives they had, the better Christians they were." Quickly, the leadership realized the resultant testosterone-fueled free-for-all had destabilized the city. They put a damper on the activity by requiring assent from primary wives, and also by freely granting divorce to all parties. Even so, first wives, understandably unhappy with their newly enlarged households, often mistreated the supernumeraries. In order to encourage compliance with the new regime, the leadership imprisoned the most recalcitrant wives, and decapitated not a few.[37]

The marriage law sparked an insurrection. About 120 men captured Bockelson and Knipperdolling, the latter of whom by now had been appointed executioner, a job he undertook with relish, before a counterattack freed them. Most of the rebels pled successfully for mercy, but Bockelson had 47 of them shot, beheaded, or, in a few cases, hacked to death. For good measure, he also had executed yet more women who had resisted forced marriage.

In August, another assault by the prince-bishop almost breached the inner wall but was ultimately beaten back. The attackers suffered horrific losses as the climbers looked up to find death in the form of boiling cauldrons and of wooden posts and trees that when dropped would strip several of them off their ladders at once. Deadly ambushes met those lucky enough to escape back through the breached outer wall. In the aftermath, the prince-bishop's army nearly dissolved.[38]

The victory buoyed Bockelson's spirits and grandiosity; he divined that he was the reincarnation of King David, and as such the planet's only legitimate ruler. He also wisely reasoned that such a startling claim had better come from someone else's mouth. Earlier that summer, a goldsmith with a limp from a nearby town named Jan Dusentschuer appeared in Münster. The new arrival claimed prophetic powers, and right on cue, after the defeat of the prince-bishop's second assault, he announced that the Lord had anointed Bockelson king.[39]

Now monarch, Bockelson declared Münster's old constitution inadequate to the new divine order, abolished the city council and the two mayoral positions, and replaced them with a royal court. The New Jerusalem was renamed the "People of God."

After the repulse of the prince-bishop's summer assault, the neighboring princes reinforced the blockade and appointed a new commander. Consequently, it became nearly impossible to sneak food and supplies into the city; the new king's subjects clad themselves in rags and slowly starved to death. This bothered Bockelson little. Quite the reverse: his sense of theater and costume took flight. As described by Gresbeck, Bockelson, made himself a velvet coat, and magnificent hose and doublet of magnificent silkwork, and magnificent golden cap, and a velvet bonnet with a crown, and a sword with a golden sheath and armor dagger with a golden sheath, and many golden chains, which he wore around his neck. . . . and on the chain he had the world hung, just like his coat of arms, with a golden round orb. This was blue speckled like his coat of arms.[40]

Bockelson's sense of pomp extended to outfitting his cavalrymen with flamboyant silk "made for half the body, so that one arm was without sleeve and the breast was without coat, so that it was impressive on horseback," and liveried up his household servants in red coats trimmed with gray and gold rings whose size announced their rank.[41]

In October, Dusentschuer extended Bockelson's dominion to the entire Earth and announced that the Lord would blow his trumpets three times to signal the town's journey to the Promised Land. Just before sunrise on October 31, 1534, the lame goldsmith climbed the tower of St. Lambert's Church and sounded a cow horn. He then descended and continued through the streets blasting his horn, while compatriots blew other wind instruments. Thousands of inhabitants trudged toward the cathedral square, the men bearing arms, and the women small children and their most precious possessions. More horns blew, and presently Bockelson arrived in full regalia mounted on a white stallion surrounded by a bodyguard of twenty and followed by Queen Diewer in a coach, her ladies in waiting, and fifteen more of his wives.

By now, Bockelson had elevated the art of the missing Apocalypse to high theater. He ordered a respected nobleman, Gerlach von Wullen, to lead a suicidal charge into the besieging forces. The king then had von Wullen announce that it was only a drill designed to test their wills, and that he was pleased to inform them that they had passed. Bockelson removed his scarlet robe and crown and put down his scepter, and he and his "Elders" served a feast to the hungry masses. In addition to their meal service, Bockelson and the Elders engaged the men in lighthearted banter about the number of their wives. Gresbeck wrote,

The brother that had no more than one wife sat shamefaced. Such a man was still an unbeliever, and he wasn't yet a real Christian. . . . They sat eating and drinking, and were of good cheer. Up at the cathedral square, it didn't look as if anyone was going to die. Each brother sat beside his wives, and in the evening he could go to bed with the one he hankered after.[42]

The burghers' appetites sated, Bockelson rose and tearfully announced in a broken voice that he had failed his people and would abdicate. No sooner had he finished than Dusentschuer relayed yet more news from the Almighty: a command to send forth himself and twenty-six others, listed in a document brandished in his hand, to four nearby towns to spread the Word, so as to speed the Apocalypse.

Moreover, Dusentschuer revealed that Bockelson should resume his kingly duties, prime among which was the punishment of Münster's ungodly. The goldsmith then placed the crown back on the king's head and handed him back his scarlet robe and scepter.

This dramatic production was perhaps Bockelson's finest; at a stroke he had heightened his authority and ridded himself of the potential rivals among the 27 messengers, along with their 134 wives. The king, along with his wives and his court, then had a sumptuous meal; before each course, his servants blew a fanfare. At the supper's conclusion, Bockelson sat silent for a while, then informed those present that he had received a revelation from God, and commanded that he be brought his sword and one of the captured *landsknechts*. He commanded the captive to sit down, and when he refused, threatened to cut him down the middle instead of merely beheading him, and so the prisoner complied. Having accomplished God's will, Bockelson concluded the meal.[43]

The messengers departed; all twenty-seven were caught and executed by the *landsknechts*, save one, Heinrich Graess, who was saved by his command of Latin, which attracted the attention of the prince-bishop, so allowing him the opportunity to turncoat.[44]

Graess returned to Münster with the story of his dramatic escape from the clutches of the ungodly, then left the city with priceless intelligence for the prince-bishop: food and arms were running low, and the city was split between the once loyal but now starving and demoralized populace and the Anabaptist elites, whose privilege allowed them to maintain their spirits and delusions.

Graess would also leave a damning letter to the town on his way out: "All the business that's now being conducted in Münster is a fraud, accordingly, it's my humble prayer that you will finally open your eyes—it's high time!—and see of your business that it's clearly contrary to God and His Holy Word."[45] Despite the disaster of the messengers, Bockelson comforted the believers that their deaths had been God's will and sent yet more messengers further afield to the Low Countries to recruit fresh Anabaptists to man the barricades. To prepare for the reinforcements' arrival, he ordered the manufacture of armored wagons with which to penetrate the blockade back into the city.

The second wave of messengers was likewise never heard from again, and the reinforcements failed to materialize. These continued misadventures, combined with the additional *landsknechts* sent to the prince-bishop by neighboring princes, smothered any chance of a military victory. Rothmann informed citizens that although they could not rely on the outside world to save them, God would do so. As food and resources grew scarce, Bockelson trimmed back his military forces and concentrated on theological efforts instead.

On New Year's Day of 1535, Bockelson issued a manifesto that ordained, among other things, that "only those governments that orient themselves by the word of God shall be preserved" and that "legal decisions are the prerogative of the king, his regents and judges." Also, "a government that refrains from unchristian coercion may not be interfered with, even if it has not yet accepted believers' baptism."[46]

Children as young as ten were executed for stealing food or on suspicion of treason. When it became apparent that a recently departed Danish nobleman named Turban Bill had been a spy, three women who had known of his activities were beheaded in the cathedral square. One of them was Knipperdolling's mistress, whom he had not added to his wives because she had been a prostitute. As she was led to the chopping block, she defiantly denounced Knipperdolling's treachery; enraged, Knipperdolling seized a sword and decapitated her.[47]

By Easter the relief force from the Low Countries hadn't materialized, and Bockelson declared that all along he had defined "victory" in a spiritual, and not a military, sense. Even stray cats and dogs had been eaten, and the starving citizens were allowed to depart.

Bockelson gave the emigrants a three- or four-day window in which to leave. They were made to change out of their own clothes into rags; those who were caught leaving Münster outside the approved time were hung. The unfortunate few who accepted this offer were slaughtered by the *landsknechts*, their heads displayed on stakes. As Gresbeck explained this Hobson's choice: "All the same, they defected from the city, such great hunger did they have in the city. For they much preferred to get themselves killed than to suffer in such great hunger."[48]

Several weeks later, Bockelson, in order to save food, allowed men to disown their lesser wives and their children so that they could leave, and Bockelson did the same with his wives and children. Observed Gresbeck, "Some rebaptizers would certainly have taken a piece of bread in exchange for a wife, if someone had offered it to them. There's poor holding of court when there's no bread."[49]

By this point, the *landsknechts* were beheading up to fifty male escapees daily, allowing women and children to huddle together in the no-man's land outside the walls, a hellish landscape a few hundred yards wide and four miles in circumference. The women and children languished there without sustenance or shelter for more than a month. The besiegers finally allowed the foreign women and children within to proceed home, and interned the locals until after the city fell.[50]

Around May 23, the carpenter Gresbeck and several others fled the city. As had most of the previous escapees, they were captured, but were lucky enough not to be killed; in Gresbeck's case, because of his youth, appealing nature, and the individual kindness of the *landsknechts* who caught him, he was granted the mercy of imprisonment.[51] His successful escape from Münster encouraged hundreds of others to flee the city, almost all of whom were slaughtered.

Gresbeck drew an earthen map for his captors on the floor of his cell that delineated how their troops could enter the city. On the night of June 22, Gresbeck and one of the former besiegers named "Little Hans of Long-street," who had previously defected to Münster and then escaped along with Gresbeck, swam a small floating footbridge into position across the moat, which thirty-five *landsknechts* quickly crossed, killed the sleeping sentries, and opened the gate with a key that Little Hans had created. At least three hundred more *landsknechts* followed over the short, tenuous causeway before the defenders finally closed the city gate. (The besiegers trusted Little Hans more than Gresbeck, perhaps because of Hans' original loyalties, and so he led the assault while Gresbeck stayed behind at the bridge.) Bockelson's troops nearly annihilated the invaders, now trapped within the city walls, but the invaders' crafty commander, Wilhelm Steding, stalled for time with sham negotiations that allowed the prince-bishop's main corps to stream into the city and mop up the remaining Anabaptists in brutal hand-to-hand fighting.[52]

The *landsknechts* slaughtered six hundred residents, and whatever guilt they may have felt disappeared when they found out that their individual booty shares amounted to 50 guilders for a year's brutal work (about $1,600 in today's money). Christian Kerckerinck, the Anabaptist moat captain, and possibly Queen Diewer were quickly executed, but Bockelson, Knipperdolling, and another lieutenant, Brend Krechtinck, were interrogated at leisure and condemned for various theological crimes, theft, and murder. A few days after the capture, the prince-bishop ruefully asked Bockelson, "Are you a king?" to which he insolently replied, "Are you a bishop?"[53] Among the revolt's leaders, only Rothmann possibly escaped, and in any case was never heard from again.

On January 22, 1536, two executioners began with Bockelson. Adhering to the procedure prescribed by the empire's new criminal code, they rendered him immobile with an iron collar attached to a pole and ripped off his flesh with glowing hot tongs. According to von Kerssenbrock, "When touched by the tongs, the muscles gave off visible flames, and thus made such a strong stench that it revolted the noses of the bystanders."[54]

On witnessing this, Knipperdolling tried to choke himself with his collar, upon which the executioners immobilized him firmly on his stake with a rope secured around his gaping mouth before returning to work on Bockelson, who silently withstood the torture. The other two did not stand up as well; the executioners tore at the throats of all three with the tongs and finally stabbed them in the heart. When done with them, the executioner stuffed their erect bodies into iron baskets, which were then hung from St. Lambert's tower for all to see.[55] Their bones remained there for fifty years, and the three cages can still be viewed from the street.*

---

* The church tower was later replaced; and in the 1880s the rusted cages themselves underwent extensive renovation, which was repeated following bomb damage in 1944.

The successors of the Münster Anabaptists learned from their experiences; the precept of adult baptism survives today mainly among the Amish and Mennonites, both quiet and peaceable sects.

A third large-scale medieval apocalyptic spasm played out amid the chaos that engulfed mid-seventeenth-century England. During the early 1600s, Parliament warred with the Stuart monarchs, who continued to claim the divine right of kings. Much of the discontent involved Charles I's support for High Anglicanism, which struck dissenters as near-Catholic.

The conflict, though, mainly revolved around fiscal issues. Unable to raise the necessary funds for his military adventures, Charles I attempted an end run around Parliament's power of the purse with a number of illegal strategies, most notably the right to raise "ship money." This ancient royal levy applied only during wartime, and only to coastal towns. His application of an extra-parliamentary tax in peacetime and extension of it to inland communities sparked a series of three separate conflicts known collectively as the English Civil War, which led to his beheading in 1649 and the brief establishment of Oliver Cromwell's commonwealth and protectorate. Cromwell's rule, and particularly his succession by his less capable and less politically engaged son Richard, proved disastrous enough to allow the monarchy's restoration under Charles II in 1660.

The turmoil spawned two major movements: the Levellers, who favored rule of law, democratic reform, and religious tolerance; and the Fifth Monarchists, a millennialist group whose eschatology espoused rule of the "saints," a self-identified cadre of the righteous, that was, like the Münster Anabaptists, anything but democratic, tolerant, or even modest. There would be no rest for the righteous after the Fifth Monarchists had brought England under their rule, a blessed act that would mandate the subsequent conquest of continental Europe. Although neither group survived intact, the Fifth Monarchists nearly gathered up the reins of government in the short-lived "Barebones Parliament" of 1653 (so named after one of its members, Praise-God Barebone), one of the dizzying succession of Cromwellian parliaments.[56]

As had been the case since Joachim, hard times yielded a bounty of number mysticism and apocalyptic arithmetic. An English diplomat, John Pell, wrote in 1655:

> Some that have heard that the end of Paganism is placed in the year
> 395, and that then there was not one heathen temple left standing in
> the Roman empire, will easily be induced to believe that the famous
> number, 1260, ought to be added to it; and then this year, 1655, must
> needs be pointed out for an apocalyptical epocha. Others pitch upon
> the year 1656, because, having summed up the lives of the patriarchs
> in the fifth chapter of Genesis, they find 1656 years from the creation
> to the flood, and thence infer, that the coming of Christ will be the
> next year, because it must be as in the days of Noah. Others will wait
> three or four years more, hoping that the 1260 years must be reckoned
> from the death of Theodosius, and the division of the Roman empire
> between his sons. Nor need we wonder, if we find some confident
> that eleven years hence we shall see the fatal change, because of the
> number 666 [that is, in the year 1666].[57]

A Fifth Monarchist named Arise Evans produced easily the silliest estimate.
One of the key elements of the group's eschatology was the current-day
identity of the book of Daniel's "little horn," which likely represented
Antiochus Epiphanes. Most Fifth Monarchists identified the current-day
little horn as King Charles I, which enraged Evans, a staunch supporter of
the late monarch and his archbishop, William Laud. To Evans, the latter's
name clearly dated the Apocalypse: the Roman numerals in VVILLIaM
LaVD added up to the year 1667.*

At the other end of the intellectual spectrum, Isaac Newton devoted
a large number of essays to the interpretation of apocalyptic scripture
(posthumously collected into a single volume, *Observations upon the
Prophecies of Daniel and the Apocalypse of St. John*), though he wisely
refrained from predicting the Second Coming's date.[58]

Perhaps the most influential computation was made by a preacher
named Henry Archer, who in 1642 published *The Personall Reign of Christ
Vpon Earth*, a fifty-eight page treatise that reinterpreted the shattered beast
of Daniel's dream as four monarchies: the Assyrian/Babylonian, Mede/
Persian, Greek, and Roman. The coming Fifth Monarchy would be that

---

* The lowercase *a* in the archbishop's name, which has no Roman numeral equivalent,
presumably carried a zero value. An obscure royal prerogative was the ability to cure
scrofula; after the Stuart restoration, Charles II rewarded Evans for his loyalty by touching
the latter's afflicted nose.

of Christ, from which the name Fifth Monarchy is derived. Archer's calculations placed His coming in either 1666 or 1700. Such a schema lay entirely within the realm of accepted Protestant theology; Luther himself considered both the Fourth Monarchy and the beast metaphors for the papacy.[59]

Many of the Fifth Monarchists were key participants in the English Civil War and in Cromwell's parliaments and protectorate. They saw themselves as passive observers of Christ's imminent return and judgment, and during the English civil wars, the most prominent of the group, Thomas Harrison, who rose to the rank of major general, demonstrated great courage and ability. He also served as a member of Parliament, where he advocated reform.

Most Fifth Monarchists, like Harrison, sought change by legal means, but a small minority, particularly a firebrand preacher named Christopher Feake, exhorted the public to a violent revolution that would usher in a millennialist theocracy of "the saints," an elite cadre of the pious, that is, themselves.[60]

Things started out well for the Fifth Monarchists, who had fought in and, as had Harrison, held high command in the New Model Army, which drove Cromwell's overthrow of the "Rump Parliament" of 1648. But over time, Cromwell proved either unwilling or unable to accept their political and theological demands, and their alliance frayed. The Fifth Monarchists reached the apex of their power in the evanescent Barebones Parliament in 1653. With its dissolution and the subsequent establishment of the dictatorial Protectorate, relations between Cromwell and the Fifth Monarchists worsened. Although Cromwell intermittently detained many of the Fifth Monarchists, including Harrison, he generally handled his old allies gingerly and executed none for their millennialist beliefs. For example, in 1654 Harrison, who may have been elected to the new Protectorate Parliament by as many as eight different constituencies, presented a petition that urged the restoration of "a state of perfect liberty." Cromwell spoke in opposition to it, detained Harrison, then released him after a few days with a mild warning.[61]

In the words of historian P. G. Rogers, Cromwell treated the Fifth Monarchists "like naughty, misguided children whom he disciplined against his will, and whom he did not wish to keep in confinement a day longer than was necessary."[62]

With the restoration of Charles II in April 1660, the Fifth Monarchist's luck finally ran out. The new king cast a jaundiced, vengeful eye on the group. Harrison, who had both guarded his imprisoned father, Charles I, and later played a prominent part in the judicial proceeding that condemned him to death, warranted special attention. Six months later the crown tried Harrison and his fellow regicides, some of whom were Fifth Monarchists. Most were convicted, and Harrison found himself first on the block, informed that he was to be

> drawn upon an hurdle to the place of execution; and there you shall
> be hanged by the neck, and being alive shall be cut down, your
> entrails to be taken out of your body, and, you living, the same to
> be burnt before your eyes, and your head to be cut off, your body
> divided into four quarters to be disposed of at the pleasure of the
> King's Majesty.[63]

Diarist Samuel Pepys, who had also attended Charles I's beheading, recorded on October 13,

> I went out to Charing Cross, to see Major Harrison hanged, drawn, and
> quartered; which was done there, he looking as cheerful as any man
> could in that condition. He was presently cut down, and his head and
> heart shown to the people, at which there were great shouts of joy.[64]

In the event, the King's pleasure saw Harrison's head and quarters displayed around the city. Two days later, Pepys attended the execution of another prominent Fifth Monarchist regicide, John Carew, who was "hanged and quartered at Charing Cross; but his quarters, by great favor, are not to be hanged up."[65] *

For several years a small Fifth Monarchist faction, led by a cooper named Thomas Venner, had labored under the delusion their popular

---

* In England before the seventeenth century, the most severe punishments featured live emasculation along with disembowelment, which may or may not have been applied to the regicides. Live evisceration was not formally abolished until 1814, though by the middle of the eighteenth century, executioners softened the procedure by hanging the condemned to death before eviscerating them. Quartering had by then fallen into disuse, but was not explicitly outlawed until 1870.

support was great enough that they could trigger the Second Coming through armed insurrection. Considered harebrained by more sober Fifth Monarchists like Harrison, Venner lived up to that reputation in April of 1657 when he plotted an uprising that was uncovered before it could be executed.

With typical tolerance, Oliver Cromwell had merely imprisoned Venner and his colleagues in the Tower of London; upon Cromwell's death, his son Richard released the inept plotters after less than two years' confinement. With the restoration of Charles II and the deaths of Harrison and the other Fifth Monarchists involved in the regicide, Venner's group, newly freed, grew desperate and decided to act. In December of 1660, one of Venner's drunken confederates bragged to a man named Hall that he was about to participate in a "glorious enterprise" (the aforementioned Second Coming). When Hall asked what it was, he replied, "We'll pull Charles out of his throne . . . for the Saints must reign." Hall promptly reported the conversation to the authorities and was then brought before the king himself, who ordered the arrest of the remaining known Fifth Monarchist discontents.

Venner and his band of about fifty confederates were not among the detained, which left them free to execute their plot on the night of January 6, 1661, a date chosen in the hope of finding the city's watchmen inebriated at the conclusion of the Twelfth Night revelry. They broke into St. Paul's cathedral and posted a guard outside, who promptly shot a passerby who, when asked about his loyalty, unluckily declared it to the king. Thus was the plot exposed, and Venner's woefully small force found themselves pursued through London's streets by a swelling group of "train-bands," as the city militias were called, later augmented by the king's troops. Over the next three days, Venner's men, now vastly outnumbered, fought an increasingly desperate and brutal series of house-to-house battles.

In a diary entry written on January 10, Samuel Pepys succinctly described the group as

> these Fanatics that have routed all the train-bands that they met with, put the King's life-guards to the run, killed about twenty men, broke through the City gates twice; and all this in the daytime, when all the city was in arms—are not in all above 31. Whereas we did believe them (because they were seen up and down in every place almost in

the City, and had been in Highgate two or three days, and in several other places) to be at least 500. A thing that was never heard of, that so few men should dare and do so much mischief. Their word was, "The King Jesus, and the heads upon the gates." Few of them would receive any quarter, but such as were taken by force and kept alive; expecting Jesus to come here and reign in the world presently.[66]

In the end, roughly half of Venner's followers were killed in the running battle, and most of the rest later hung, though the crown applied to only Venner and his chief lieutenant the full half-live disembowelment previously accorded Harrison and Carew.[67]

During the sixteenth and seventeenth centuries, northern Europeans sought escape from the travails of this world to the comforts of the wondrous one to come via compelling end-times narratives. In the case of the Swabian Peasants' War, Thomas Müntzer's apocalyptic theology was merely tacked onto what had initially been a largely secular populist uprising, with disastrous results, whereas the Anabaptist Madness and Fifth Monarchist revolts were end-times affairs from their starts to their equally disastrous finishes.

Beginning in the eighteenth century, entire nations would seek succor not from God, but rather from Mammon, as a succession of financial mass delusions swept through Europe. On their surfaces, the religious and financial events appear to represent different phenomena, but they were powered by the same social and psychological mechanisms: the irresistible power of narratives; the human proclivity to imagine patterns where there were none; the overweening hubris and overconfidence of both their leaders and followers; and, above all, the overwhelming proclivity of human beings to imitate the behavior of those around them, no matter how factually baseless or self-destructive.

3

BRIEFLY RICH

Throughout the length and breadth of the land, men's minds were engrossed by the same subject. Party politics were absorbed by it. Whig and Tory left off squabbling, and Jacobites ceased to plot. At every inn, on every road, throughout the country, the talk was the same. At Aberystwith, and Berwick-on-Tweed, at Bristol and St. David's, at Harwich and Portsmouth, at Chester and York, at Exeter and Truro—almost at the Land's End—the talk was only of South Sea Stock—nothing but South Sea Stock!

—William Harrison Ainsworth, 1868[1]

In the early eighteenth century, John Law, a brilliant Scottish financier, left behind a lurid trail of financial chaos hauntingly familiar to those savaged by the collapse of the 1990s internet bubble. Internet stocks merely damaged millions of investors; Law damaged France's faith in banks, a far more serious blow to a nation.

The young Scotsman hailed from a centuries-old lineage of distinguished Edinburgh goldsmiths that included his father, uncle, and three brothers. By the time of his birth in 1671, the very word "goldsmith" camouflaged that ancient profession's evolution into something quite different: banking.

Law's immediate ancestors lived on an island that bore no resemblance to the future majestic, free-trading Britannia. (And at the time, Scotland was, in any event, still independent from England.) As the seventeenth century dawned, the population of the future Great Britain was only a third that of France's—smaller than before the arrival of the Black Death in 1348–1349. The England of Law's era was weak, underdeveloped, and recently embroiled in a regicidal civil war, and its presence on the high seas involved piracy and smuggling as much as commerce. High-volume international trade had only just begun to slowly appear with the establishment of large trading organizations around 1600, the most famous of which was the East India Company.

When East India ships bearing gold and silver from the nascent spice trade sailed into London, their merchants met an immediate logistical problem: England had no banking system, and thus no reliable place to deposit their treasure. Goldsmiths, whose livelihoods depended on the safe storage of valuables, provided the most obvious alternative. In exchange for their valuables, the merchants received certificates. Critically, this paper could be exchanged for goods and services—in other words, it functioned as currency. Further, the goldsmiths tumbled onto the fact that they could create paper in excess of the amount of gold and silver (specie) they held.

This is to say, the goldsmiths could print money.

Only the most mendacious and shortsighted among them would manufacture and then spend their own certificates; rather, these pieces of paper were loaned out at high rates of interest. Since the prevailing rate for even the best borrowers was often well in excess of 10 percent per year (especially when England was at war), over a decade's span, lending a certificate was better than spending it, and it would remain so as long as the goldsmith remained solvent.

This daisy chain worked only so long as a large number of certificate holders didn't redeem them all at once. Say the goldsmith's safe contained £10,000 of specie, and he had issued £30,000 worth of certificates— one-third issued to the specie's owners and two-thirds to borrowers. If the holders of £10,001 of the certificates showed up demanding gold or silver—it did not matter whether they were borrowers or the original depositors—the goldsmith could be ruined. Worse, if the certificate holders even suspected this could happen, the growing line at the goldsmith's office would suffice to precipitate a run that would topple the entire house of cards. In this example, the ratio of certificates to specie was 3:1; the higher this ratio, the more probable a run. Even the most careful goldsmith/ bankers could come to grief; between 1674 and 1688 four documented "goldsmith runs" occurred, and between 1677 and the establishment of the Bank of England in 1694, the number of London goldsmith/bankers fell from forty-four to around a dozen.

As a practical matter, the goldsmith/bankers found a 2:1 ratio—£1 loaned to borrowers for every £1 of specie on deposit—reasonably safe. The importance of this system cannot be understated, for it heralded the birth of an elastic money supply that could be resized according to the hunger of borrowers for loans and the willingness of creditors to lend. When borrowers and lenders were euphoric, the money supply expanded, and when they were frightened, it contracted. The modern financial term for the amount of paper monetary expansion is "leverage": the ratio of total paper assets to hard assets.[2]

Bank-supplied leverage is the fuel that powers modern financial manias, and its birth in seventeenth-century Europe brought with it a roller coaster of bubbles and busts. Over the next four centuries, financial innovation has yielded a dizzying variety of investment vehicles; each, in its turn, was often simply leverage in a slightly different disguise, and would prove the tinder that would set alight successive waves of speculative excess.

The descendant of goldsmiths who had adopted English-style banking, John Law thus lived and breathed a system in which paper could function as money just as well as scarce specie. Even today, many resist the notion of paper money; at the turn of the eighteenth century, it struck the average person as ludicrous.

By 1694, the young Law, weary of filthy, poor, late-medieval Edinburgh, made his way to London, where he fashioned himself as Beau Law, a rakish man about town, especially at the gambling tables, and engaged in a duel with one Beau Wilson over their mutual interest in a young lady that resulted in Wilson's death. Tried, convicted to hang, then reprieved, then again sentenced to hang, Law escaped. The *London Gazette* in early 1695 read:

> Captain John Lawe, a Scotchman, lately a Prisoner in the King's-Bench for Murther, age 26, very tall black lean Man, well shaped, above Six foot high, large Pockholes in his Face, big high-Nosed, speaks broad and low, made his Escape from said Prison. Whoever secures him, so as he may be delivered at the said Prison, shall have £50 paid immediately by the Marshal of the King's-Bench.[3]

In the late seventeenth century, prisoners managed "escape" more easily than today, and Law's friends, with the likely connivance of King William III, probably arranged his flight.[4] The above physical description intentionally misled, since Law had an average-sized nose and fair complexion.

Initially, he traveled to France, where his mathematical ability astonished his contemporaries and served him well at the gambling tables. To have called Law a gambler, though, did not do his skills justice. Even today, quantitative ability and unblinking concentration serve well at the poker and blackjack tables (so long as the blackjack dealer does not shuffle between hands). Three hundred years ago, the less efficient casinos rewarded dispassionate calculation yet more richly. These opportunities attracted some of Europe's brightest mathematicians to games of chance, most famously Abraham de Moivre, whose *The Doctrine of Chances* forms much of the groundwork of modern statistics.[5] Wrote one acquaintance of Law's skills,

> You asked me for news of Mr. Law. He only sees other players with whom he plays from morning to night. He is always happy when gambling and each day proposes different games. He offered 10,000 sequins to any who could throw six sixes in a row, but each time that they fail to do so they give him a sequin.[6]

Since the odds of rolling six consecutive sixes are one in 46,656 (one in 6^6), Law's offer was a winning proposition. (From his perspective, the odds of losing or paying out before 10,000 series of six throws was 19 percent.) Further, whenever Law could, he served as "banker" at cards, which, depending on the rules of the particular game, usually conferred on him a small statistical advantage, since it allowed him to function as the casino, not as a customer.[7]

When Law left for France, he leveraged his casino winnings, estimated by economic historian Antoin Murphy to have totaled hundreds of thousands of pounds sterling, a massive fortune for the time.[8] He then decamped for Holland, where he observed firsthand the cutting-edge operations of both the Bank of Amsterdam and the city's new stock exchange. He also visited Genoa and Venice, where he familiarized himself with their centuries-old banking systems.

Because Frenchmen of that era did not trust their nation's governing institutions, the nation's banking system was nearly nonexistent. The spare livre went under the mattress or into a sock, not into a bank, thus depriving the economy of sorely needed capital.[9] Law marveled at the advanced financial systems in Italy and Holland, and endeavored to bring their benefits to France; in the decade or so of his continental peregrinations, he transformed himself from Law the professional gambler to Law the economist, a term that had yet to be invented.

Law intuitively understood how a stingy supply of money based on scarce gold and silver had strangled European economies, and how a generous one might stimulate them. Already familiar with the notion of privately issued paper money, his experience with Dutch banking hinted that paper money issued by a central national bank might solve the problem of an inadequate monetary base.

Law's intuition of how an ample supply of paper currency can prove an economic tonic can be understood via the famous story (at least among economists) of a babysitting cooperative in Washington, D.C., three centuries later. Such a cooperative involves the trading of childcare services. One of the most popular schemes involves the use of "scrip": paper chits, each worth one half hour of sitting; a couple desiring a three-hour movie outing would thus need six chits.

The success of such scrip/chit schemes depends greatly on the precise amount of chits in circulation. In the early 1970s, one such co-op in Washington, D.C., printed a stingy number of chits, and so parents horded them. Many were willing to babysit to earn chits, but fewer were willing to spend them, and so everyone spent fewer nights out than they would have liked.

This being Washington, D.C., many of the parents were lawyers, and, as lawyers are wont to do, they legislated a solution by mandating individual spending of the chits. In the economic sphere, legislative solutions often fail, as happened in this case, whereupon an economist couple convinced the co-op to print and hand out more. Flush with chits, parents spent them freely and so spent more nights out.[10]

In similar fashion, Law's goldsmith/banking background and experiences told him that Europe's economic stagnation was due to a shortage of specie, which could be remedied by, among other actions, printing paper money. Law was not the first to realize this; almost from the invention of elastic credit by the goldsmith/bankers in the early seventeenth century, some of them realized that monetary expansion with paper currency could be used to stimulate an economy. Three centuries before John Maynard Keynes famously labeled a gold-based monetary system a "barbarous relic," William Potter, a royal official, noted in 1650 that the limited amount of specie in circulation meant that,

though the *Store-house* of the *world* be never so full of *Commodity*,
yet seeing the *Tradesman* cannot afford to take it in faster than he
can find sale for what he hath already, it follows that if the people
through their extreme poverty are not able to take it off from the hands
of the *Tradesman*, the door in that respect is shut against *Trade*, and
by consequence against *Wealth*. . . . On the other side, let it be supposed that *money* (or that which goes for such) doth increase among
them; it follows that (they not hoarding it up, but laying it out in
commodity, as fast as they receive it) the more their hands are filled
with such money, by the increase thereof, so much more doth the sale
of *Commodity*, that is *Trading* increase; and this increase of *Trading*
doth increase *Riches*. . . . Therefore increase of *money*, or that which
goes for such, not hoarded up, is the *Key of Wealth*. (italics added)[11]

The banking systems in France and in his native Scotland were far more
primitive than the ones Law encountered in Holland and in Italy, and as
a result the French and Scottish economies functioned poorly. He was
particularly struck by the parlous state of the textile industry in the Rhône
Valley, and he formulated a plan for factories, nurseries, bakeries, and mills
financed by the issue of paper money. In late 1703, one of his contacts, the
French Ambassador in Turin, transmitted his proposal to the Marquis de
Chamillart, France's controller general, who politely rejected it.

Sometime around the new year, Law returned home to Scotland,
where things were in even greater flux. Earlier, in 1695, the Scottish Parliament had granted a monopoly on that nation's long-distance commerce to
the Company of Scotland Trading to Africa and the Indies, better known
as the Darien Company. Its plan was to establish a trading outpost on the
Isthmus of Panama at Darien in order to shorten the route from Europe
to Asia. The company sent two expeditions to the Isthmus, the first of
which failed because of poor planning and supply, while the second was
decimated by the Spanish.

When the outpost fell to the Spanish in 1699, the Bank of Scotland
had to suspend operations. The bank's difficulties profoundly affected
Law and so further refined his economic thinking, resulting in two tracts,
Essay on a Land Bank and *Money and Trade Considered*. The former
proposed the issuing of paper money backed by land; and the latter was

a detailed and incisive book that foreshadowed by seventy years many of the concepts in Adam Smith's *The Wealth of Nations*.

Law began to think deeply about the nature of money in a remarkably modern way. True money, he postulated, had seven essential features: stability of value, homogeneity (that is, it could be traded in constant units), ease of delivery, sameness from place to place, storability without loss of value, divisibility into smaller or larger quantities, and possessing a stamp or identification as to its value.[12]

Law thought that land met these criteria, and paper money yoked to it would be superior to a conventional currency anchored to silver. The notion of money denominated in units of land today seems odd, but in the early eighteenth century it made good sense. Beginning around 1550, silver flooded into Europe from the vast mines in Peru and Mexico, thus eroding its value. A certificate denoting a given piece of land, by contrast, could be valued according to the sum of its future grain, fruit, or animal production. In addition, silver has only a few circumscribed uses: as money, in jewelry and utensils, or in industrial employment. Land, by contrast, can simultaneously back paper money and be used in a wide range of agriculture.[13] As Law wrote, "Land is what produces everything, silver is only the product. Land does not increase or decrease in quantity, silver or any other product may. So land is more certain in its value than silver, or any other goods."[14]

Law gradually broadened his definition of money beyond land to include the shares in the era's great companies, particularly the English and Dutch East India companies and the Bank of England, whose profits, he thought, should likewise prove more stable than silver. This was a reasonable assumption; what Law did not foresee is that his system would itself introduce a fatal instability into those prices.

Foreshadowing Karl Marx, he postulated a three-stage progression of societal development. In the first stage, without money, barter served as the main form of exchange, under which large-scale manufacture was nearly impossible, since it requires significant up-front monetary outlay. In Law's words, "In this state of barter there was little trade, and few arts-men." (Law used the word "trade" in the modern sense of GDP: the total amount of goods and services consumed. In the modern era, the concept of barter in the pre-money era is recognized to be incorrect, since in aboriginal societies exchange is done by extending favors and accumulating markers, a state of affairs even more economically inefficient than barter.)[15]

In the second stage, the economy ran on metallic money, but far too little of it. While it is theoretically possible that if money is scarce, men would work for lower wages, manufacture is still stunted:

> It will be asked if countries are well governed why they do not process their wools and other raw materials themselves, since, where money is rare, labourers work at cheap rates? *The answer is that work cannot be made without money*; and that where there is little, it scarcely meets the other needs of the country, and one cannot employ the same coin in different places at the same time.[16]

In the third stage, when money and credit were plentiful, nations prosper. A case in point was England, which just a decade earlier had established the note-issuing Bank of England. The Bank periodically expanded and contracted the note supply; Law observed that "as the money in England has increased, the yearly value of [national income] has increased; and as the money has decreased, the yearly value has decreased."[17]

The heart of Law's theory, explained in a several-page passage in *Money and Trade Considered*, described, for the first time, an economic concept known as "the circular flow" model, which can be imagined as two concentric circles, with money flowing from one owner to another in clockwise fashion, and goods and services flowing in a counterclockwise fashion.

Law imagined an isolated island owned by a lord who rented out his land to one thousand farmers who grew crops and raised animals constituting 100 percent of the island's output. Manufactured items could not be produced locally, but rather were imported in exchange for the island's excess grain.

Furthermore, the island contained another three hundred unemployed paupers who subsisted on the charity of the lord and farmers. Law's solution to this sad state of affairs involved the lord printing up enough currency to establish factories that would employ as workers the three hundred paupers, whose wages would pay the farmers, now no longer idle, for food, and this would increase rents to the lord, with which he could continue to pay the workers.

Law summarized his example as any modern Keynesian would:

Trade [in modern terms, GDP] and money depend mutually on one
another: when trade decays, money lessens; and when money lessens,
trade decays. Power and wealth consists in numbers of people, and
magazines [warehouses] of home and foreign goods; these depend on
trade, and trade on money. So while trade and money may be affected
directly and consequentially; that which is hurtful to either, must be
so to both, power and wealth must be precarious.[18]

Law proposed a scheme for paper-note issuance by the Bank of Scotland,
which that nation's parliament voted down in 1705. Two years later, Scotland passed the Act of Union, which, by merging it with England, put
Law's neck at risk in Scotland, since he was still subject to imprisonment
and execution in London. Law requested a pardon from Queen Anne,
and when she turned him down, he fled back to the Continent, bouncing
around among Holland, Italy, and France for a decade before alighting in
Paris in 1715.[19]

During that time, he was once again turned down by Controller
General de Chamillart and saw another plan for a bank in Turin nixed by
the Duke of Savoy. Daringly, he next solicited the support of Louis XIV,
who by that point, in the summer of 1715, had reigned seventy-two years,
a record for European monarchs that stands to this day. (Queen Elizabeth
will have to live until age ninety-eight, in 2024, to exceed Louis's span.)
Louis was about to approve Law's proposal when he developed gangrene,
memorably telling the regent, the Duke of Orléans, "My nephew, I make
you regent of the kingdom. You are going to see one king in the tomb and
another in the cradle; always keep in mind the memory of the former and
the interests of the latter."[20] The attractive, charming, and wealthy Law
cultivated the regent, and eventually persuaded him to undertake a grand
financial experiment.

At the time of Louis's death in September 1715, France had been
bankrupted by the recent War of the Spanish Succession. Law had sought
to organize a large state bank, but beginning in 1716 the regent limited
him to the establishment of the Banque Générale Privée, a private firm,
as its name indicated, headquartered in the home of Law, a newly minted
French citizen.

At the time, only five states—Sweden, Genoa, Venice, Holland, and England—issued paper notes that did not function as everyday small-scale transactions, so Frenchmen regarded the new bank's notes suspiciously.[21] Law immediately mandated that they be convertible one-to-one into the gold and/or silver in circulation at the time of the bank's establishment. Since France, a chronically insolvent state, regularly debased its national coinage, this drove the new paper currency's value to a premium over that of the then circulating coins. To attract wealthy customers and increase confidence, he kept his reserve ratio low and offered several "loss leaders," including free foreign currency conversions and payment for the bank's notes at their face value, instead of at the much lower (highly discounted) price of ordinary government paper notes.[22]

Because they were guaranteed at par value, the desirability of Law's bank's notes and services could not help but attract attention. And just as Law predicted, the increased paper money supply perked up the kingdom's economy.

Law next targeted the Mississippi Company. Originally chartered in 1684, it later obtained monopolies on trade with French America through its mergers with other companies that held them, but it had been so unsuccessful at exploiting those monopolies that its manager, Antoine Crozat, turned his franchise back over to the crown in 1717. Law's reputation, now burnished by the success of the Banque Générale Privée, promised to save the nation's parlous finances by having the Mississippi Company buy up the crown's massive debt. In the process, Law multiplied his already staggering gambling wealth through speculation in the company's shares.

In order to enable the Company to do this, he had the crown expand its monopoly to trade with China, the East Indies, and the "South Seas"—all the oceans south of the equator—even though almost all of the relevant trade routes were under the control of England, Spain, and Portugal.[23] The inconvenient fact that the Company's "monopoly" on New World trade was worth little did not detract from the glamour of Law's new financial machinery.

The Company now held the crown's massive debt, mainly in the form of *billets d'état* by its citizens, which were then yielding 4 percent. Because of the kingdom's weakened financial state, the *billets* traded at a large discount to their face value; Law promised that his scheme would drive their price up to par, an offer the crown found irresistible. In December 1718, Law's successes allowed him to convert his Banque Générale Privée into a national bank, the Banque Royale, which completed the paper daisy chain: the new Banque would issue notes that would pay for shares in the Mississippi Company, which would buy up the *billets* and so mitigate the crown's war debts. Even more confusingly, Company shares could also be bought directly with *billets*; since the *billets* were debt, their disappearance in exchange for shares further improved the crown's finances.[24]

Law's power allowed him to indulge his war against silver currency, which he saw as the nation's economic ball and chain. Coins were out, and paper was in. The government had previously allowed tax payments to be made in his private bank's notes, and in early 1719, the Banque Royale established branches in the largest French cities, where silver transactions of more than six hundred livres had to be made in the bank's own notes or in gold; silver payment was forbidden. By late 1719, the Banque had bought up most of the *billets*, and the extinction of the nation's debt further buoyed the nation's animal spirits.

As the share price of the Mississippi Company rose, the bank printed more notes to meet the demand for the shares, further driving up their price, which then caused yet more note issuance. Soon, the first well-documented nationwide stock bubble was in process. The heedless monetary expansion was not entirely the work of Law, who understood the nature of an inflationary spiral, but also reflected the influence of the regent, who, buoyed by the scheme's success, did not comprehend this risk.

A modern company operates with what is known as "permanent capital," which is simply a fancy way of saying that if it needs a billion dollars for a given project, much of the money is raised from stock sales, and if the expense projections are accurate, the project will subsequently be completed.

Not so with Mississippi Company shares. Rather than being purchased outright for their full price, shares were sold by subscription—in the Company's case, for cash at a 10 percent premium. To acquire a share, purchasers had to pay only the 10 percent premium and the first of twenty monthly installments, or "calls," of 5 percent each—that is, a total of 15 percent of the share price. The call mechanism was an early form of financial leverage, and it served to magnify both gains and losses—if the price increased by 15 percent, the value of the investor's initial down payment doubled; and if the price fell by 15 percent, the investor was wiped out. The call structure can thus be thought of as the great-great-grandfather of the margin debt that underlay many subsequent financial crashes, most notably in 1929.[25]

To meet the demand for Company shares, Law's bank issued more of them; Charles Mackay described what happened next:

> At least three hundred thousand applications were made for the fifty thousand new shares, and Law's house in the Rue de Quincampoix was beset from morning to night by eager applicants. As it was impossible to satisfy them all, it was several weeks before a list of the fortunate new stockholders could be made out, during which time the public impatience rose to a pitch of frenzy. Dukes, marquises, counts, with their duchesses, marchionesses, and countesses, waited in the streets for hours every day before Mr. Law's door to know the result. At last, to avoid the jostling of the plebian crowd, which, to the number of thousands, filled the whole thoroughfare, they took apartments in the adjoining houses, that they might continually be near the temple whence the new Plutus was diffusing wealth.[26]

People talked of little else, and nearly every member of the aristocracy who was lucky enough to own stock was busy buying and selling it. Rents on Rue de Quincampoix rose fifteenfold.

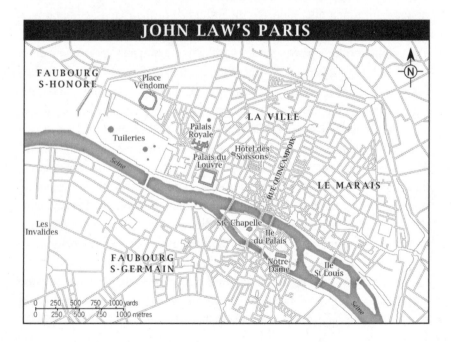

JOHN LAW'S PARIS

Law grew weary of the crowds and decamped for a residence in the more spacious Place Vendôme, but it too soon filled to capacity and attracted the ire of the chancellor, whose court lay on the square. Finally, Law moved to the Hôtel de Soissons, which had a garden large enough to accommodate the several hundred tents that sprang up; the lucky prince who owned the property rented them out for five hundred livres per month each.

Mackay recounted that "peers, whose dignity would have been outraged if the regent made them wait half an hour for an interview, were content to wait six hours for the chance of seeing Monsieur Law."[27] One lady cleverly exploited Law's famous gallantry by having her coachman overturn her vehicle in his presence. He predictably rose to her assistance; she soon confessed the ruse and so amused Law that he issued her shares. The prudish Mackay mentioned another episode that would make the reader "smile or blush according if he happens to be very modest or the reverse," but did not describe it, coyly leaving behind only a reference to a letter written by the Duchess of Orléans:

> Law is so run after that he has no rest day or night. A duchess kissed
> his hands before everyone, and if duchesses kiss his hands, what parts
> of him won't the other ladies salute?[28]

Other observers confirmed Mackay's lurid descriptions. In September 1719 a British embassy clerk reported to London that

> the rue de Quinquempoix, which is their Exchange Alley, is crowded
> from early in the morning to late at night with princes and princesses,
> dukes and peers and duchesses etc., in a word all that is great in
> France. They sell estates and pawn jewels to purchase Mississippi.

A week later, the same clerk wrote that "all the news of this town is of stock jobbing. The French heads seem turned to nothing else at present."[29] Paris became a boom town. During the bubble, its population swelled and the city suffered the inevitable side effects of ballooning prices for food, services, and real estate. In that heady milieu, the word "millionaire" first came into common usage to describe lucky shareholders.[30] Another embassy report read, "I was told yesterday that a shop had sold in less than three weeks lace and linen for 800,000 livres and this chiefly to people who never wore any lace before; the accounts of this kind everyday are so very extraordinary that will scarcely be believed in other countries."[31]

Bubbles typically end with a seemingly small disturbance, followed by a swift collapse. The tremor came in early 1720, when Prince de Conti, angered that he had not received a large enough allotment of the Company's stock, sabotaged it by sending to the Banque Royale three wagons to be filled with the gold and silver coin that supposedly backed the bank's new paper money. Law, who was by then the comptroller general of France— essentially, the prime minister—could not be seen refusing this disastrous request, so he did the next best thing: he complained to the regent, who forced Conti, an unpopular man, to back down. Perceptive investors sussed out the significance of the prince's demand and the regent's tacit refusal: The volume of the bank's outstanding notes grossly exceeded its reserves of gold and silver. A full-fledged run on the bank ensued.

Law now faced a dire choice. He could protect the currency by re-fusing to print more notes, which would damage share prices, or he could protect the share price by printing more notes to buy back shares at a floor price, which would worsen the already rampant inflation. The latter action would protect the aristocratic investors; the former would protect France.

Initially, Law chose to protect the currency, and thus the nation, or so he thought. In desperation, in late February 1720, he and the regent forbade trading in specie and limited personal possession to five hundred

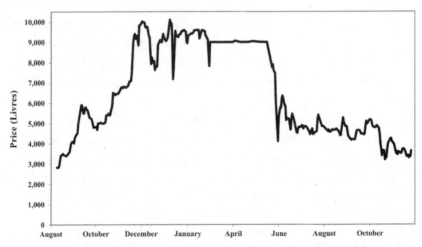

Figure 3-1.   Mississippi Company Share Price 1719–1720

livres in coin; the hoarding of silver plate and jewels was also forbidden, and informers and agents were recruited to enforce the odious new rules. The nation's social fabric began to unravel as servants ratted out masters and fathers betrayed sons.

So great was the social disruption that two weeks later Law switched gears to protect the share price, and thus the wealthy, by offering to pay nine thousand livres per share, which meant printing yet more bank notes. By then, the ensuing inflation brought about by the debasement of the livre was obvious, and in May he devalued the currency by 50 percent in two steps. Later in 1720, in an attempt to control inflation, he declared worthless large denomination bank notes, wiping out much of the nation's fortunes; economic historian Antoin Murphy estimates that the inflation-adjusted value of the entire system, consisting of Mississippi Company shares and banknotes, fell by approximately 87 percent. The final blow to Law's scheme of bank notes and Mississippi Company shares came that fall, when the plague ravaged Marseille and threatened Paris, further hobbling financial confidence.[32]

By this point, he had exhausted not only the Banque's capital, but his political capital as well. The regent, wishing to avoid further embarrass-ment, allowed him to depart Paris gracefully, first to the city's outskirts, and then abroad. Law, who by this point had received a royal pardon for the murder of Beau Wilson, spent his last years bouncing around England and the Continent and fending off creditors, the most famous of whom was Lord Londonderry, with whom he had placed a bet in September 1719 that the Mississippi Company would damage England's East India Company. The bet had Law effectively "short" the EIC's stock by promising to de-liver a large amount of shares to Londonderry at a later date. (A "short" is a wager on a share price fall.) Not only did the EIC's share price rocket during the South Sea Bubble, the Mississippi Company's London twin, but Law's scheme had greatly devalued the French currency relative to England's, making the bet yet more disastrous for him.[33]

Although Law had become a political liability to the Duke of Orlé-ans, the regent still valued his brilliance, and he might have been recalled to Paris had not the regent died in 1723. In the event, Law succumbed a poor man in his beloved Venice in 1729, his major asset by this point a substantial collection of art, and little else. All in all, he was lucky; future bubble protagonists often met grimmer ends.[34]

The Company did possess what eventually became the Louisiana Territory, but in the early eighteenth century it was underpopulated and malarial. In order to recruit settlers for the Company's New World operations, Law had produced fraudulent brochures describing it as an earthly paradise. When his advertising campaign failed, Law fell back on the conscription of thousands of white prisoners of both sexes and African slaves:

> Disorderly soldiers, black sheep of distinguished families, paupers, prostitutes, and any unsuspecting peasants straying into Paris were taken and transported by force to the Gulf Coast. Those who voluntarily came were offered free land, free provisions, and free transportation to the new territory.[35]

Louisiana's "capital," which alternated between modern-day Biloxi and Mobile, was little more than a deadly, fetid encampment of several hundred settlers, most of whom decamped for the new capital in New Orleans after the Company's collapse in 1721.[36]

For two centuries, history painted Law as a scoundrel. Typical was the advice of Daniel Defoe (writing under the nom de plume of Mr. Mist) to someone wishing to achieve great wealth:

> Mr. Mist says, if you are resolv'd upon it and nothing else will serve you but to do just so, what need you ask what you must do? The Case is plain, you must put on a Sword, Kill a Beau or two, get into Newgate, be condemned to be hanged, break Prison, IF YOU CAN,— remember that by the Way,—get over to some Strange country, turn Stock-Jobber, set up a Mississippi Stock, bubble a Nation, and you may soon be a great Man; if you have but great good luck, according to an old English Maxim:—
>
> > Dare once to be a Rogue upon record,
> > And you may quickly hope to be a Lord.[37]

Economic historians have been more kind. In Law's time, the idea of running an economy without gold- and silver-based money seemed revolutionary, even ludicrous. The overwhelming majority of today's economists believe that it is even more foolish to base the money supply on the amount of metal emanating from the ground or from people's jewelry boxes. Economic historian Barry Eichengreen, for example, an authority on the gold standard, observed that nations recovered from the Great Depression in the precise order they abandoned hard money.[38] In essence, we live in a Tinker Bell economy where, because everyone believes in the delusion of paper currency, it functions well. Much like the ancient mariners who met their ends voyaging out of the Mediterranean far beyond the Pillars of Hercules, Law's scheme—a mass delusion gone bad—came to grief through lack of experience, but also spotlit the way to the future.

The Mississippi Company bubble infected the entire Continent. During its fever, the stodgy Venetians dropped their ancient opposition to joint-stock companies; a few were enthusiastically floated, then disappeared as news of the subsequent disaster in Paris seeped south. The Dutch, not to be outdone by the French, also followed suit with forty-four stock flotations, thirty of which more or less immediately doubled in price. In the less developed parts of Europe, trading companies sprouted like wildflowers and disappeared just as rapidly; fully 40 percent of eighteenth century European stock issuance occurred in the year 1720.[39]

The French bubble resonated loudest in London in the person of Sir John Blunt, a man born at precisely the right time. He struck out on his own at age twenty-five in 1689, the year of the settlement that followed the Glorious Revolution of 1688, in which the Dutch stadtholder, William III, invaded England at the invitation of its Protestant forces and ascended the throne as King William III and ended the Stuart monarchy.

Before that date, England had no "national debt," only the financial obligations of the king and his family. When Charles II died in 1685, he, his brother, and his nephew owed about one million pounds sterling to London's bankers, to whom they repaid not a farthing of interest or principal.[40] Because of the ever-present threat of nonpayment of crown loans, bankers logically charged high rates, which stifled England's economy. The settlement that followed the Glorious Revolution, in which the crown surrendered the divine right of kings for a secure tax base, had the immediate effect of making government debt more attractive. This, in turn, lowered interest rates more generally; with high returns no longer available from relatively safe bonds, investors sought opportunity in riskier ventures. This, in turn, kick-started a boom in joint-stock companies over the next decade.

Blunt, the son of a dissenter-Baptist shoemaker, apprenticed as a scriv-ener, a writer of legal and financial documents, an occupation that imparted insider knowledge of real estate and financial activities. Blunt nurtured this entrée into a small commercial empire that included a linen business and a company that supplied London with water. He then obtained employment with the most aggressive of the new joint-stock companies, Sword Blade.

Initially, the company manufactured advanced French-style rapiers, but it soon expanded into land speculation and the trading of govern-ment debt. (Radical changes in a business model are a feature of bubble-associated chicanery; nearly three centuries later, Enron would morph from a dull power plant and pipeline company into a futures-trading juggernaut before blowing up.)

In 1710, Blunt's business acumen caught the eye of the chancellor of the exchequer, Robert Harley, who sought Blunt's assistance with the nation's massive debt, which, like France's, was the legacy of the War of the Spanish Succession. Blunt indeed had an idea or two. His solution to the debt featured a speculative frisson that would become his trademark: the government would issue conventional 6 percent bonds that contained lottery tickets sporting prizes ranging from £20 up to a mind-boggling £12,000. The offering's success led to an even more appealing scheme, "The Adventure of the Two Millions": a complex, layered lottery based on £100 tickets, with five successive drawings and a top prize increas-ing with successive escalating tiers of £1,000, £3,000, £4,000, £5,000, and, finally, £20,000; with each drawing, the possibility of a yet larger payoff kept the losers in the game.

The success of these ventures emboldened Harley, who founded the South Sea Company in 1711 with the express purpose of taking over all of England's considerable debt, with himself as governor and a board studded with Sword Blade hands, including Blunt.[41] In exchange for as-suming the government debt, the South Sea Company, like its older Pari-sian sister, the Mississippi Company, obtained a monopoly on trade with South America, despite the fact that Spain and Portugal controlled the continent and that nary one of the Company's board had experience with the Spanish-American trade. Partially in exchange for this "monopoly," the company assumed £10 million of government debt.

Ironically, although fear and envy of Law's French system triggered the English South Sea Bubble, which occurred nearly simultaneously with the one in Paris, the Mississippi Company's assumption of France's national debt in 1717 was in fact modeled on South Sea's previous assumption of England's. For eight years after the Company's 1711 chartering, the exchange of government debt for a "monopoly" on the New World trade was a relatively small-scale affair, but by 1720 the skyrocketing French Mississippi Company and the thousands mobbing Rue Quincampoix dazzled the English. Wrote Daniel Defoe from that Paris street in that year, as the French bubble blew the loudest:

> You, Mr. Mist in England, You are a Parcel of dull, phlegmatic Fellows in London; you are not half so bright as we are in Paris, where we drink Burgundy and Sparkling Champaign. We have run up a Piece of refined Air, a meer *Ignis fatuus* [wisp] here, from a hundred to two thousand, and are now making a Dividend of forty per cent.[42]

Fearing that the Bourbons had devised a financial perpetual-motion machine that would overpower their island kingdom, the South Sea Company and Parliament devised a similar scheme, in which the company assumed a much larger share of the nation's debts (around £31 million), mainly in the form of annuities. The holders of these debts, the annuitants, it was proposed, would voluntarily convert their government securities into the Company's shares.

The annuities, of course, were held mainly by English citizens to whom they yielded income. The annuity holders had to be made an attractive offer to part with them, and the easiest way to do so was to stimulate their limbic systems by convincing them that the price of the Company's stock was bound to rise.

The Company sold shares of varying complexity, typically, offering to purchase £100 of annuities from their owners for a single share of stock with a par value (at issuance) of £100. A high share price benefited the Company, since it enabled it to keep for itself a larger number of shares. If, for example, the share price rose to £200, the company only had to exchange half the number of the shares it would have at a price of £100, and could keep the other half; if the price rose to £1,000, as it did briefly, the company got to keep 90 percent of the shares held in its inventory. Further, as share prices rose, they became yet more desirable, a positive feedback loop that is the central feature of all bubbles.

Now, almost three centuries later, the nature of Blunt and Harley's command of psychology becomes more clear. They had stumbled across a powerful way to exploit a very old human phenomenon: our species' preference for "positively skewed outcomes"—ones with low-probability but enormous payoffs, even if the average of all payoffs is negative. No rational person, for example, spends $2.00 for a lottery ticket with a fifty-fifty chance of paying $3.00 or zero, since it produces a payoff of $1.50 (the average of zero and $3.00) for an average loss of 25 percent on the $2.00 ticket. Yet many people would buy a $2.00 ticket with a one-in-two-million chance of paying off $3 million, which carries the same average payout of $1.50 ($3,000,000/2,000,000) for the same average loss of 25 percent.[43]

In other words, Harley and Blunt had found a highway straight to the seat of human greed: the limbic system's powerful reward-anticipation circuitry. The instincts that profited the prehistoric hunter-gatherer proved irresistible and deadly on the balance sheet.

As we now know, the South Sea's monopoly was nearly worthless, but that did not prevent the company from floating the most fantastical rumors. Wrote Mackay:

> Treaties between England and Spain were spoken of, whereby the latter was to grant a free trade to all her colonies; and the rich produce of the mines of Potosi-la-Paz was to be brought to England until silver should become almost as plentiful as iron. . . . The company of merchants trading to the South Seas would be the richest the world ever saw, and every hundred pounds invested in it would produce hundreds per annum to the stockholder.[44]

To assure Parliament's assent to the scheme, the Company salted MPs with shares that appreciated after passage. The first share sales for cash took place on April 14, 1720, and the first conversions of annuities to shares took place two weeks later; the share price had already risen from £120 at the beginning of the year to around £300; by June, it had peaked above £1,000. The byzantine details of Blunt's structure raised the earlier Adventure of the Two Millions to a new level: the Company deployed successive subscriptions of different share classes designed specifically to capture the public imagination. Finally, as already mentioned, the higher the share price, the fewer the number of shares the Company had to provide the holders of the government debt/annuities, thus leaving yet more shares in the hands of Blunt and his colleagues.[45]

Four features distinguished the English bubble from the French one. First, while the French bubble revolved almost completely around the shares of one company, the English one was associated with share flotation in other ventures encouraged by the general euphoria of the time; Mackay listed no fewer than eighty-six of these so-called bubble companies, and subsequent historians have identified about twice that many. While most aimed at solid ends, such as the building of roads and houses and establishing trade in imported goods, other schemes were fantastical: "for trading in hair," "for a wheel of perpetual motion," "for drying malt by hot air," and "for the transmutation of quicksilver into a malleable fine metal." Contemporary sources listed numerous others. Many were likely apocryphal, such as an air pump to the brain, or "to drain the Red Sea with a view to recovering the treasure abandoned by the Egyptians after the crossing of the Jews," or, most famously of all, one "for carrying on an undertaking of great advantage; but nobody to know what it is."[46]

The second distinctive feature of the South Sea Bubble was the extreme degree of leverage in the English bubble companies. Similar to the 15 percent down payment required for Mississippi Company shares, South Sea Company shares could be purchased with a down payment of only 10 to 20 percent, with the rest due in subsequent calls. The leverage of the bubble companies was higher than that of South Sea—that is, their initial subscription prices were lower; in one case, one shilling for a share of stock supposedly worth £1,000 (0.005 percent of the stated purchase price). Accordingly, bubble companies were so poorly funded that they generally flamed out rapidly. Nonetheless, a few were capitalized and managed well enough that they survived, among which were two insurance firms: London Assurance and Royal Exchange.

Shareholders had a giddy ride up, and the effect on the more general public was seductive. Wrote Mackay, "The public mind was in a state of unwholesome fermentation. Men were no longer satisfied with the slow but sure profits of cautious industry. The hope of boundless wealth for the morrow made them heedless and extravagant for today."[47]

Early–eighteenth-century London could be imagined as two separate cities: to the west, the seat of government, Westminster, Parliament, St. James Palace, and Buckingham Palace, newly built for the Duke of

Buckingham; and to the east, its mercantile center, the "City." The latter's beating heart was the Royal Exchange, where the capital's merchant elite dealt in all manner of foreign and domestic commerce: wool, timber, grain, and a myriad of other goods.

The stock jobbers, despised by the mercantile hierarchy, were unwelcome in the Exchange's halls and thus banished to a warren of coffeehouses that clustered in a tiny street sandwiched in the acute angle formed by Lombard Street and Cornhill, dubbed "Exchange Alley."

Typically, the speculators lined up at the coffeehouses where the "financiers" hawked shares, usually acquired for the derisory initial

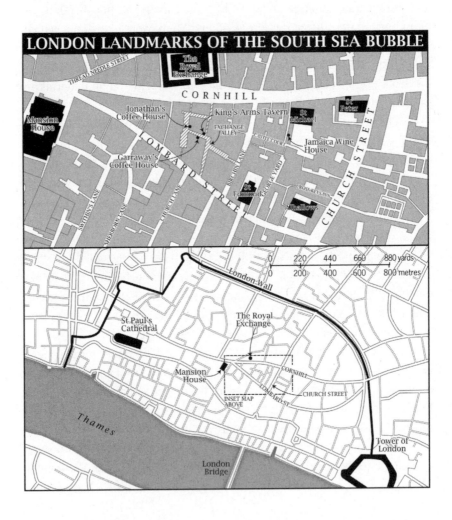

subscription. The new owners then hurried down to nearby 'Change Alley to flip their shares to even greater fools through the good offices of the stock jobbers. During the late spring and summer of 1720, the scene was as manic as in Rue Quincampoix: hackney cabs were in short supply, and even when procured, were likely to be gridlocked in the narrow streets. Caffeinated traders packed coffeehouses like Jonathan's, Garraway's, and Sam's, and pickpockets flourished; it was easier to find the king and his court in the alley than at the palace. The lawyer for a Dutch investor described the proceedings as "nothing so much as if all the Lunatics had escaped out of the madhouse at once."[48]

As in Paris, the speculation nourished a general price inflation. King George I threw the most lavish birthday party the nation had seen, and company directors demolished their mansions to make way for yet larger ones. Throughout most of modern financial history, property prices have ranged between five and twenty times annual rental values; in 1720, London property sold for forty-five times yearly rents, a ratio later approached during the real estate bubble of the early 2000s.[49] The South Sea enthusiasm also saw the birth of another characteristic feature of bubbles: securities speculations as a fashion statement. At the height of the action, London's social scene shifted east from St. James's Palace and Westminster to the City; there, a group of aristocratic ladies rented a shop just off 'Change Alley, where "at leisure times, while their agents are abroad, they game for china."[50] Nor was the excitement limited to the highborn:

> *Young Harlots too, from Drury-Lane,*
> *Approach the 'Change in Coaches,*
> *To fool away the gold they gain*
> *By their obscene debauches*[51]

Such an atmosphere was not conducive to rational decision-making. The speculation bubbled most intensely among the aristocracy. In June, near the peak, the worried chancellor of the exchequer, John Aislabie, advised King George to cash in his chips: £88,000 worth of Company stock. The famously rude monarch called his minister a coward, but Aislabie held his ground, and in the end George converted about 40 percent of his holdings into safe assets.[52]

    The third distinctive feature of the South Sea Bubble was the grow-
ing hubris of its perpetrators; while John Law retained his inherent de-
cency throughout the Mississippi episode, the same cannot be said of his
English counterparts. While it's easy to conceive of Blunt or Aislabie as
either credulous or mendacious, these two adjectives are only a starting
point. From their earliest histories, commercial societies equate riches
with intelligence and rectitude; people of great wealth appreciate hearing
of their superior brainpower and moral fiber. The wealth and adulation
that accompany financial successes inevitably instill an overweening pride
that corrodes self-awareness. Worse, great wealth not infrequently arises
more from dishonesty than from intelligence and enterprise, in which
case the adulation induces a malignancy of the soul, as indeed occurred
to Blunt, who by this point had evolved into the archetype of the modern
megalomaniacal CEO. An anonymous pamphlet, probably written just
after his downfall, describes how, shortly before the South Sea Company
imploded, he traveled to the newly fashionable resort of Tunbridge Wells:
"In what splendid equipage [Blunt] went to the Wells, what respect was
paid him there, with what haughtiness he behaved in that place, and how
he and his family, when they spoke of the Scheme, called it *our Scheme.*"[53]
The pamphleteer painted the classic picture:

> [Blunt] did never permit any body to make a motion in relation to
> [company transactions] but himself, during his first months reign;
> nor any minute, relating thereto, to be entered in the Court-Book, but
> what he dictated. He visibly affected a prophetic profile, delivering
> his words with an emphasis and extraordinary vehemence; and used
> to put himself into a commanding posture, rebuking those that durst
> in the least oppose any thing he said, and endeavouring to inculcate,
> as if what he spoke was by impulse, uttering these and such like ex-
> pressions: *Gentlemen, don't be dismayed: you must act with firmness,*
> *with resolution, with courage. I tell you, 'tis not a common matter you*
> *have before you. The greatest thing in the world is referred to you.*
> *All the money of Europe will center amongst you. All the nations of*
> *the earth will bring you tributes.*[54]

As pointed out by historian Edward Chancellor, bubbles, from South Sea
to the internet, often evoke megalomania from their principals:

> The plans of the great financier may act as a catalyst to a specula-
> tive mania, but the financier himself does not remain untouched by
> events. His ambition becomes limitless, a chasm opens up between
> the public appearance of success and universal adulation, on the one
> hand, and the private management of affairs which become increas-
> ingly confused and even fraudulent.[55]

Blunt engineered the manipulation of South Sea shares, including the
loaning out of money from subscriptions for further stock purchases. He
not only profited from the price increase before selling out most of his
shares near the top, but also secretly issued himself, friends, and many
MPs additional shares, some of which were fraudulent.

The end, as usually transpires, came from an unexpected direction.
In June 1720, with one eye on the bubble companies' drawing away of
capital from South Sea and the other on the collapse of the share price of
the Mississippi Company, Blunt had Parliament pass the Bubble Act just
as South Sea share prices were peaking. The act required parliamentary
approval for incorporation of new enterprises and restricted them to five
shareholders; Blunt also had the courts prosecute three of the existing
bubble companies for exceeding their charters.

As in Paris, Blunt's megalomania rippled outward. Mackay wrote that
one director, "in the full-blown pride of an ignorant rich man, had said that
he would feed his horse upon gold."[56] It was also reflected in the general
populace. "The overbearing insolence of ignorant men, who had arisen to
sudden wealth by successful gambling, made men of true gentility of mind
and manners blush that gold should have power to raise the unworthy in
the scale of society."[57] Blunt's actions against competing bubble companies
boomeranged, pricking not only the bubble companies, but also his own
South Sea; by late October, its share price had fallen to £210 from its peak
of £1,000, and by the end of 1721, it had sunk below £150.[58]

The fourth, and final, difference between the South Sea and the
Mississippi bubbles was their vision and scope. John Law was no ascetic,
but neither did he focus exclusively on his own self-interest; he genuinely
desired, through a revolutionary expansion of credit, to stimulate and
advance France's economy. Blunt's scheme, on the other hand, channeled credit narrowly through the Company into his own pocket; when the
credit expansion jumped the Company's boundaries into other ventures,

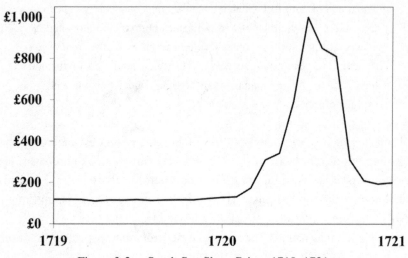

Figure 3-2.   South Sea Share Prices 1719–1721

his efforts to curtail it succeeded all too well and so destroyed not only his targets but South Sea as well. The narrowness of Blunt's scheme, from the national perspective, confined the relatively brief damage to the financial sector. This proved its saving grace, in distinction to the French catastrophic banking collapse, nationwide inflation, and subsequent long-lasting bank phobia.[59]

Also, unlike the Mississippi Company, South Sea was not a largely empty promise. Even in the early eighteenth century, a reasonable estimate of its intrinsic worth could be made. In the first place, it held the annuities tendered to it by the original annuitants, now company shareholders, and these assets had value amounting to, very roughly, £100 per share, approximately where it settled following the bubble's collapse.

Another distinguishing feature of South Sea was that it had inherited the monopoly on the slave trade in Spain's colonies (the *asiento*) granted to Queen Anne in 1707, which made up the lion's share of its supposed business volume, which by treaty with Spain virtually excluded New World products, limited to an "annual ship" containing five hundred tons of goods. The Company's New World trade was, however, nearly worthless, since its expertise lay in finance, and not international commerce; damningly, one of the directors was caught red-handed using sixty of the Company's five-hundred-ton annual allowance for his own benefit. By 1714, six years before the bubble collapsed, the Company's actual trade business was unprofitable, and the company withdrew from it; forty years later, it sold its *asiento* rights for a mere £100,000.[60] In the end, the value of the Company's New World ventures was beside the point; speculators cared not about the profits from the trade in slaves or sugar, but those from the buying and selling of shares whose prices seemed to grow to the sky.

Probably the most sophisticated contemporary calculations of share price were made by a barrister and MP named Archibald Hutcheson, who published a long series of reports on the Company's shares. Fortuitously, one was written in June 1720, just before the peak of the boom; it suggested a higher market value, £200, twice that calculated from the value of the company's annuity assets. At that point, the share price was £740; he predicted that "the present reigning madness should happen to cease." In the event, the madness went on a few more months; in July, at a prevailing price of £1,000 per share, Hutcheson reckoned that the total value of the company was nearly twice the value of all the land in England.[61] (This situation was echoed by the 1980s Tokyo real estate bubble, in which the hypothetical value of the Imperial Palace grounds exceeded that of all the land in California.)[62]

The next year, motivated not only by aggrieved constituents but also by its own swindled MPs, Parliament investigated the share price collapse and the massive wealth accumulated by Blunt, his colleagues, and government insiders. It settled on Chancellor Aislabie as scapegoat, forced his resignation, sent him to the Tower, and expelled six other MPs. The South Sea Company itself continued to function until 1853, not as a trading firm, but simply as a holder of government debt. The king, although the object of popular derision, avoided sanction.*

Some spoke of jailing or even hanging the company's directors, a fate they narrowly avoided after a brief imprisonment. Rather, Parliament confiscated their estates to compensate the scheme's victims; it allowed Blunt to keep £5,000 of his £187,000 in assets, and he retired in obscurity to

---

* George I was an accidental king; when his second cousin Queen Anne died in 1714, he was no better than fiftieth in the line of succession, and ascended to the throne only because the 1701 Act of Settlement forbade a Catholic monarch and so disqualified all those ahead of him. Upon his ascension to the throne, the prime minister became the nation's de facto leader.

Bath, founding a distinguished lineage of pious descendants that included a bishop and Queen Victoria's chaplain.[63]

The Bubble Act, passed at the height of the mania, which had not only put a brake on further speculative enterprises but also inadvertently helped sink South Sea, remained on the books for more than a century. Inevitably, memories of the frenzy and its collapse would fade and the market's animal spirits, buoyed by an exciting new technology and easy credit, and stoked by its promoters, the public, press, and politicians, would rise again, and so yield a wave of manias that would dwarf those of the early eighteenth century.

4

GEORGE HUDSON,
CAPITALIST HERO

In the early 1950s a Swarthmore College social psychologist named Solomon Asch performed a series of seminal experiments that make sense of the infectiousness of the medieval apocalyptic mass delusions and eighteenth-century financial manias.

Asch seated groups of about a half dozen male participants around an oblong table and told them that they were being tested for visual perception. All in the room were shown a card with a line of fixed length, say 3¾ inches. They were then shown a second card with three lines, one of which was the same 3¾-inch length, and the other two of slightly different lengths, say 3 and 4¼ inches. The participants were asked to pick the line that matched that on the first card. This task required some concentration but was easy enough that normal subjects made errors on each card pair about 1 percent of the time, and got all of a series of twelve card pairs correct 95 percent of the time.

Many, if not most, psychology experiments require fibbing to their subjects. This test wasn't about visual perception at all, and each group contained only one actual subject. The other participants were in fact Dr. Asch's assistants; the subject sat near the middle of the table, so as to minimize his average distance from the ringers.

The subject tested either last or next to last and was thus exposed to multiple responses from Asch's collaborators before answering. When the ringers answered correctly, the subjects performed similarly to those tested alone, getting all twelve card pairs correct 95 percent of the time. But when the ringers deliberately answered incorrectly, the actual subjects' performances plummeted. Only 25 percent of them scored all twelve pairings correctly, and incredibly, 5 percent answered all twelve incorrectly.[1]

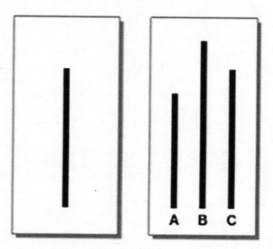

Card used in Asch Experiment.

Further, subjects performed consistently from trial to trial: Those who were highly influenced by the ringers' errors in the first six pairings were similarly influenced in the last six. That is to say, some of the subjects were reliably more suggestible than others.

Asch interviewed the subjects following the study, and their responses were revealing. The suggestible ones worried that their eyesight or mental processing were failing them; one commented, "I know the group can't be wrong."[2] Even the nonsuggestible ones were disturbed by their disagreement with the majority and sensed they were right, and few of these were completely sure.

Striking social science experiments often produce a fair amount of subsequent urban myth, and such was the case with Asch's results. In the decades following his research, its conclusions have been increasingly represented in the popular press, in textbooks, and even in the academic literature as suggesting that most people are strongly conformist.[3]

The data presented, however, a more nuanced picture. More than half of the subjects' responses in the presence of the confounding ringers were correct—that is, nonconformist. Further, the presence of even a single ringer who responded correctly significantly decreased the error rate of the subjects. A more accurate summary of the Asch experiment is that some people are more suggestible than others, and that many—25 percent of the subjects—are not at all suggestible. It is easy, though, to imagine that Asch would have identified those most susceptible to a financial bubble or to an apocalyptic creed.

Asch's results are especially striking, since few tasks are more emotionally neutral than estimating line length. So is yawning, a subject about which people tend not to have an emotionally driven opinion. Yet, as most of us know, and has been experimentally proven, yawning is infectious. Infectious yawning can be induced in normal, fully awake subjects not only by other people's yawns, but also by mere videos of yawning people, even those whose mouths have been obscured. Curiously, videos showing only the mouth fail to induce yawning.[4]

In emotionally laden situations, conformism rises. Charles Kindleberger's admonition about the detrimental effects of watching someone else get rich applies to Asch's findings about how some subjects were more suggestible than others; someone who successfully resists social pressure in the lab may not be able to resist an emotionally laden mass delusion.

Imitation is not just the sincerest form of flattery; it's also essential to our survival. Over the course of human evolution, our species has had to adapt to a wide variety of environments. That adaptation has taken two forms. The first is physical. To take an obvious case, Africans have darker skin than northern Europeans; darker skin protects the underlying tissues from damaging tropical sunlight, and, conversely, lighter skin allows for more efficient vitamin D production in less sunny northern latitudes.

The other adaptations are cultural and psychological. As pointed out by pioneering evolutionary psychologists Robert Boyd and Peter Richerson, the skill sets required for survival in the Amazon rainforest are very different from those required of people who live in the Arctic, who

> have to know how to make dozens of essential tools—kayaks, warm clothing, toggle harpoons, oil lamps, shelters built of skin and snow, goggles to prevent snow blindness, dog sleds and the tools to make these tools. . . . While we are rather clever animals, we cannot do this because we are not close to clever enough. A kayak is a highly complex object with many different attributes. Designing a good one means finding one of the extremely rare combinations of attributes that produces a useful boat.[5]

In other words, making a kayak from the locally available raw materials if you've never seen it done before is nearly impossible. The same is true of the very different skill set needed by an Amazon native. Humans needed less than ten thousand years to migrate from the Bering Strait to the Amazon, which means that we must have previously evolved the tendency to imitate accurately. In the words of Boyd and Richerson, being able to survive in such different surroundings means that humans have had to

> evolve (culturally) adaptations to local environments—kayaks in the Arctic and blowguns in the Amazon—an ability that was a masterful adaptation to the chaotic, rapidly changing world of the Pleistocene epoch. However, the same psychological mechanisms that create this benefit *necessarily* come with a built-in cost. To get the benefits of social learning, humans have to be credulous. . . . We get wondrous adaptations like kayaks and blowguns on the cheap. The trouble is that a greed for such easy adaptive traditions easily leads to perpetuating maladaptions that somehow arise.[6]

Over the past fifty thousand or so years, the human race has spread from its home in Africa to virtually every corner of the planet, from the arctic shores to the tropics to isolated islands in the middle of the vast Pacific Ocean. Our ability to adapt to such diverse environments during our species' late Pleistocene migration from the high Arctic to the Strait of Magellan rested on accurate imitation. Alas, many of our Stone Age adaptations have proved maladaptive in the modern world, the classic example being our ancient attraction to energy-rich fats and sugars, both scarce and life-giving in our evolutionary past but now dangerously available as cheap junk food. In the same way, our ancient proclivity to imitate is also now often maladaptive, carrying with it the modern propensity, in Mackay's famous words, to "extraordinary mass delusions and the madness of crowds."

The spread of mass delusions also feeds on another ancient psychological impulse, our propensity to suppress facts and data that contradict our every-day beliefs. In 1946, psychologist Fritz Heider posited the so-called "balanced state" paradigm to explain how people deal with the large amount of complex and often contradictory data presented to us in the course of daily life. Imagine that you know someone named Bob and that both you and he have an opinion about something that carries a modest amount of emotional freight, such as whether the Android phone or the iPhone is a superior mobile device.

If you admire Bob, and you both think the iPhone is better, then you're comfortable; you now occupy Heider's balanced state. Similarly, if you think the iPhone is better, but Bob loves his Android phone, and you think that he's an ignorant jerk, you're also in a balanced state, since your negative opinion of Bob allows you to dismiss his contrary opinion.[7] But if you admire Bob and disagree about phones, you're now in an uncomfortable "unbalanced state."

If you only modestly admire Bob, or if you really don't care that much about phones, you can easily ignore your discomfort. But if Bob is your dearest friend and you disagree strongly about something that carries more emotional weight, such as the Trump presidency, you're going to have to act to address the imbalance between your admiration of Bob and your political disagreement. Neuroscientists have recently found that such unbalanced states increase activity in the dorsomedial prefrontal cortex (dmPFC), brain areas in both hemispheres just above the top of the middle of your forehead. Further, this activity predicts a change in opinion, either about Bob or about Donald Trump. In other words, if you want your dmPFC to stop bugging you, you'll have to change your opinion about one or the other.[8] Conversely, when a subject learns that experts agree with his or her opinion, that is, has achieved a balanced state, another part of the brain, the ventral striatum, paired structures located deeply in both hemispheres, fires intensely.[9] This area receives its densest inputs from neurons responding to dopamine, our pleasure-providing neurotransmitter of choice.

In the original 1841 edition of *Extraordinary Popular Delusions*, Mackay wrote of the South Sea Bubble,

> Enterprise, like Icarus, had soared too high, and melted the wax of her wings; like Icarus, she had fallen into the sea, and learned, while floundering in its waves, that her proper element was the solid ground. She has never since attempted so high a flight.[10]

Yet within a few years of writing those words, the financial markets would prove Mackay wrong, for the Icarus of speculation soared again with a financial mania that would dwarf the 1719–1720 South Sea Bubble, this time surrounding the excitement and dislocation wrought by the first steam railways. Few writers captured the pre-steam human condition better than historian Stephen Ambrose:

> A critical fact in the world of 1801 was that nothing moved faster than the speed of a horse. No human being, no manufactured item, no bushel of wheat, no side of beef, no letter, no information, no idea, order or instruction of any kind moved faster. Nothing had ever moved any faster, and, as far as Jefferson's contemporaries were able to tell, nothing ever would.[11]

In 1851, English historian John Francis wrote the classic eyewitness account of the building of the nation's railway network. He described the state of premodern transport as follows:

> The machines which were employed to convey produce, rude and rough in their construction, were as heavy as they were clumsy. Even if the roads were tolerable, it was difficult to move [those machines], but if bad, they were either swallowed in bogs, or fell into dykes: sometimes, indeed, they sunk into the miry road so deep, that there was little chance of escape until the warm weather and the hot sun made their release easy. Markets were inaccessible for months together, and the fruits of the earth rotted in one place while a few miles off the supply fell far short of demand. . . . It was found cheaper to export abroad than to convey produce from the north to the south of England. It was easier to send merchandise from the capital to Portugal, than to convey it from Norwich to London.[12]

The idea of using steam power to perform physical work, previously the province of men, beasts, and water mills, goes back two millennia to the Ptolemaic Greeks, who supposedly used it to open and close the doors of a temple in Alexandria. An English inventor, Thomas Newcomen, produced the first working steam engine around 1712, which was so massive and inefficient that it could be used only to drain coal mines, where its fuel was plentiful. James Watt thus didn't invent the steam engine in 1776, as is commonly supposed, but accomplished something more subtle and effective: by adding an external condenser to the Newcomen design, he produced a device fuel-efficient enough to be used far from a coal mine. This innovation allowed Watt's partner, Matthew Boulton, to famously say, "I sell here, sir, what all the world desires to have—*Power.*"[13]

Over the next quarter century, Watt's bulky engines first drove boat paddles, then slimmed down enough for Richard Trevithick to mount one on a land carriage in 1801; by 1808, he was offering five-shilling rides near London's Euston Square. The early devices, made of soft iron, were so weak that one early engineer's wife, besides having to awaken at 4 A.M. to stoke the engine, also had to apply her strong shoulder to get it moving.[14]

At the turn of the nineteenth century, George Stephenson, the son of an illiterate Northumberland steam engine tender, acquired his father's trade, but unlike him also acquired reading, writing, and math skills in night school, and he applied his genius toward gradually improving the output of the early steam devices. In the immediate aftermath of the costly Napoleonic Wars, the high price of hay temporarily allowed steam to nudge out horse-drawn coal mine wagons, but not until 1818 did Stephenson convince mine owners at Darlington, near Newcastle, to build a marginal, but ultimately economically successful, steam rail line to the wharves at Stockton-on-Tees, twenty-five miles away, which opened in September 1825.[15]

The new rail technology transfixed the world: between 1825 and 1845, England experienced no fewer than three railway bubbles. The first followed on the heels of the Stockton and Darlington line. Stephenson's early engines were so unreliable that during their first years of operation the line's coal and passenger cars more often than not had to be pulled by horse. As the engines improved, as many as fifty-nine more rail lines were planned.[16]

The first projects met with no small opposition in Parliament, which, because of the Bubble Act, the now century-old relic of the South Sea episode, had to approve all incorporations. The canal and turnpike operators, who correctly perceived the damage rail transport would do their profits, were particularly active opponents. They and their minions told the public that engine smoke would kill the birds; that the weight of the engines would render them immobile; that their sparks would incinerate goods; that the elderly would be run over; that frightened horses would injure riders; that horses would become extinct and so bankrupt oat- and hay-growing farmers; that foxes would disappear; and that cows, disturbed by the noise, would cease to yield milk.[17]

In 1825, Parliament repealed the Bubble Act, but a generalized financial panic, combined with the primitive engine technology, put a damper on further projects. After a turbulent parliamentary passage in 1825–1826, Stephenson's Liverpool and Manchester Railway took four years to complete, formally opening on September 15, 1830. Thirty-five miles long, it was the engineering marvel of its age, requiring the construction of sixty-four bridges and the excavation of three million cubic yards of earth.

This remarkable new technology, which promised to transform everyday life, stoked the greed of those wishing to get in on its ground floor. The excitement peaked in 1836–1837. Wrote a journalist, "Our very language begins to be affected by [the railroads]. Men talk of 'getting up the steam,' of 'railway speed,' and reckon distances in hours and minutes."[18] One press report mentioned a merchant who traveled from Manchester to Liverpool, returned the same morning with 150 tons of cotton, sold it at great profit, and then repeated the feat. "It is not the promoters, but the opponents of railways, who are the madmen. If it is a mania, it is a mania which is like the air we breathe."[19] John Francis wrote, "The memory of those months which range from 1836 to 1837 will long be remembered by commercial men. Companies that engrossed the care and the capital of thousands, were projected."[20]

The allure of the hypnotic new technology was amplified, as is almost always the case with bubbles, by falling interest rates, which made investment capital more plentiful. A quarter century before, the borrowing needs necessitated by the Napoleonic Wars had raised interest rates; at their height in 1815 a wealthy Englishman could buy government bonds yielding nearly 6 percent in gold sovereigns. Over the following three decades rates fell to 3.25 percent.[21] When investors are unhappy with ultra-low interest rates offered on safe assets, they bid up the prices of risky assets with rosier potential income. Writing a generation after the English railway bubbles had burst, the great journalist (and an editor of *The*

Economist) Walter Bagehot wrote, "John Bull can stand many things, but he cannot stand two percent."[22] In other words, low interest rates are the fertile ground in which bubbles sprout.

The low interest rates, together with the success of the period's first mover, Stephenson's Liverpool and Manchester Railway, reignited railway speculation: "The press supported the mania; the government sanctioned it; the people paid for it. Railways were at once a fashion and a frenzy. England was mapped out for iron roads."[23]

Every bubble carries within it the seeds of its own destruction, in this case the excessive competition wrought by duplicate railway lines fed by cheap capital. The Liverpool and Manchester shareholders got the steak, while those who followed more often than not fed on more rancid fare. Noted the *Edinburgh Review* in 1836, "There is scarcely, in fact, a practicable line between two considerable places, however remote, that has not been occupied by a company. Frequently two, three, or four rival lines have started simultaneously." John Francis wrote that "in one parish of a metropolitan borough, sixteen schemes were afloat, and upward of one thousand two hundred houses scheduled to be taken down."[24]

These were merely the most credible of the schemes. In Durham, one entrepreneur began work on three parallel lines. The first was successful, and the other two, naturally enough, failed. Other promoters envisioned engines variously propelled by sails or rockets, the latter traveling at hundreds of miles per hour; elevated wooden rail lines; and another advertised, according to Francis, "to carry invalids to bed."[25]

Everywhere and always, freely available credit and credulous investors are catnip to the rogue promoter. One contemporary observer noted that, typically,

> A needy adventurer takes it into his head that a line of railway from the town A to the town B is a matter of great public utility, because out of it he may get great public benefit. He therefore procures an Ordnance map, Brooke's, or some other Gazetteer, and a Directory. On the first he sketches a line between the two towns, prettily curving here and there between the shaded hills for the purpose of giving it an air of truth, and this he calls a survey, though neither he nor any one for him had ever been over a single foot of the country. The Gazetteer,

Directory, and a pot of beer to a cad or coachman, supply him with
all the materials for his revenue, which fortunately never fails to be
less than 15, 20, or 30 per cent. per annum, and is frequently so great
that his modesty will not allow him to tell the whole.[26]

As supposedly said by Edmond de Rothschild, "There are three principal
ways to lose money: wine, women, and engineers. While the first two
are more pleasant, the third is by far the more certain."[27] As more lines
entered construction, the pool of available competent engineers and
laborers shrunk, leading to delays, massive cost overruns, and dubious
solutions to engineering difficulties, ending in the inevitable rash of
bankruptcies.

As already seen during the South Sea Bubble, English joint-stock
companies initially raised only a small percent of the needed capital.
Investors, who had initially put up only a fraction of the face value of
their shares, were liable for further calls of the capital needed for ongoing
railroad construction—a "leveraged" structure of dry tinder that inevitably
met its match.

The time of reaction was at hand. Money became scarce; the eyes of
the people were open to their folly; and shares of every description fell.
Then came that terrible revulsion, when ruin visits the social board,
and sorrow desolates the domestic hearth. Men who had lifted their
heads in the pride of presumed riches, mourned their recklessness,
and women wept that which they could not prevent.[28]

When the smoke from the 1830s bubble cleared, Parliament had sanctioned the building of 2,285 miles of track, less than a quarter of which
was actually open by 1838. The rest of the mileage, often unprofitable,
took several more years to complete; the ongoing construction required
substantial calls for capital from investors. Nonetheless, shares did recover
in price following the 1836–1837 plunge, and those who held on to their
railroad equities did not fare badly; share prices, which had been stable
before 1836, spiked upward by about 80 percent in that year, then just as
rapidly fell back to levels that were actually somewhat higher than pre-
bubble values.[29] By 1841, it was possible to travel the nearly three hundred

miles from London to Newcastle in seventeen hours: "What more can a reasonable man want?" crowed the *Railway Times*.[30]

By 1844, in fact, the average shareholder in the companies established during the previous decade was well pleased with their investment return. This paved the way for yet another, even more spectacular, bubble in the later 1840s, whose totemic figure was George Hudson. Born in 1800 the son of a small-landowning Yorkshire farmer, Hudson grew up on the reasonable assumption that he, too, would till the land, and thus received little formal education. When his father died at age nine, he was apprenticed to a linen draper in York, which proved a blessing in disguise. Hudson's energy, charm, and intelligence soon became apparent on the shop floor in a way that they would not have behind the plow, and he eventually married into his employer's family and took over the business. Fortune continued to smile on the young proprietor when, in 1827, he inherited £30,000 from a great uncle whose decline he had attended (and whose will had been suspiciously changed in Hudson's favor at the last moment).[31]

His newfound wealth allowed him entrée into politics and banking, which led, in 1833, to his nomination as treasurer of the York Railway Committee, charged with establishing a local line funded by a stock floatation. Hudson hired Sir John Rennie to survey the route, but the noted engineer disappointed the committee by recommending a horse-drawn system. Fortuitously, while visiting some property left to him by his great uncle, he met George Stephenson; subjected to the full glare of Hudson's charisma and vision, the now legendary engineer agreed to build the York and North Midland Railway, funded as a joint-stock company, whose first segment, just 14.5 miles long, opened in 1839.

Over the next decade, the "Railway King," as Hudson became known, created an empire of a dozen or so railway companies, including four of the nation's largest. He directed several corporate boards, here surveying a new line, there directing anger at the shareholder meeting of a failing one, and everywhere raising new capital. His life revolved around two centers of power: York, where he served several terms as a generous and well-loved mayor, and the nation's political center at Westminster.

Hudson could sell sand to a Bedouin. Able to turn even his most determined opponents, his signature victory was over William Ewart Gladstone. Perhaps the most formidable politician of the nineteenth century, Gladstone entered Parliament in 1832 at age twenty-two. Critically, in 1843 he became president of the Board of Trade, which functioned as the parliamentary gateway for railway legislation. He went on to serve four spells as chancellor of the exchequer and also four terms as prime minister between 1868 and 1894.

The two men could hardly have been more different: Hudson the boisterous, uneducated issue of Yorkshire peasant stock; Gladstone, the Eton- and Oxford-groomed heir of slaveholding wealth. They also differed on the most critical issues of the day; Hudson was an orthodox Tory opponent of repeal of the protectionist corn laws; Gladstone, while nominally a Tory, was a passionate free-trader.

Hudson would today be called a libertarian, opposed to any government interference with commerce, particularly with his cherished railways, while Gladstone early on saw the need for government regulation in an increasingly technologically advanced economy. Several decades before the cost-cutting predations of John D. Rockefeller, Gladstone also foresaw that the strongest railroads could drive their competitors out of business with aggressive fare reductions and thus leave the public at the mercy of the surviving railway monopoly—increasingly, it appeared to Gladstone, one run by Hudson.

In March 1844, testifying before the Board of Trade, Hudson deftly emphasized his points of agreement with Gladstone: it would well serve the public interest (to say nothing of his own) to limit the approval of further competing lines. The committee pushed back by closely questioning Hudson on precisely how he set his fares. What, the committee wanted to know, was wrong with Parliament periodically revising fares? Hudson was, as always, well prepared, answering that he would have no objection to allowing government-mandated fares in exchange for parliamentary limitation of charters for competing lines.

Somewhat placated by Hudson's answer, the committee proposed relatively mild railway legislation that mandated a "Parliamentary Class" fare of a penny per mile.[32] The bill allowed Parliament to revise the fares of companies that were so profitable that they could issue dividends in excess of 10 percent, and for the government to purchase any railway chartered after the bill's passage and after it had been operating for more than two decades.

This was too onerous for Hudson, who threw his legions into action and wrote a public letter to Gladstone, which, in the sweetest and most flattering tone, laid out his objections to the bill's provisions for fare reductions and option for government purchase. He arranged a deputation of railway owners to 10 Downing Street, and so impressed the prime minister, Robert Peel, that he made favorable comments about the railway companies on the floor of Commons.

Gladstone took the hint and met privately with Hudson, who turned his bluff Yorkshire charm up so high that the committee chair was later moved to observe, "It is a great mistake to look upon [Hudson] as a speculator. He was a man of great discrimination, possessing a great deal of courage and rich enterprise—a very bold, and not at all unwise, projector." Hudson so impressed Gladstone that he gutted the bill; of its original provisions, only the low fixed third-class fare remained.[33]

Hudson's close call with potential parliamentary oversight impressed upon him the need for more vigorous political involvement. While today a powerful industrialist might hire an army of lobbyists, the more relaxed ethical environment in nineteenth century Britain allowed for a more direct route: Hudson would simply buy himself a seat in Commons. In mid-1845, the opportunity arose. In exchange for taking over a failing local railway and wharf, the town fathers of sleepy coastal Sunderland nominated him as the Tory candidate for its seat, to which he was duly elected on August 14. The closest modern equivalent would be the chairman of Goldman Sachs simultaneously serving in the U.S. Senate.

That evening, a special train carried the news of his election from Sunderland to London, and the next day another train carried copies of the London morning papers' account of the event back to Sunderland, where, at a riotous victory celebration, Hudson flung the papers into the crowd, crowing, "See, see the march of intellect!"[34] Two months later, at a banquet in Sunderland, he again roused the locals by floating shares in his dock company: "I do not see why you should not have cotton from St. Petersburg, and the produce of China and other parts of the world come to the port of Sunderland, provided you offer the facilities . . . let us imagine we are going to be the Liverpool and Manchester of the world."[35]

He seemed barely to sleep; on the night May 2–3, 1846, for example, he worked in the House of Commons until 2:30 A.M., dozed briefly, then caught the early train to Derby, roughly halfway between

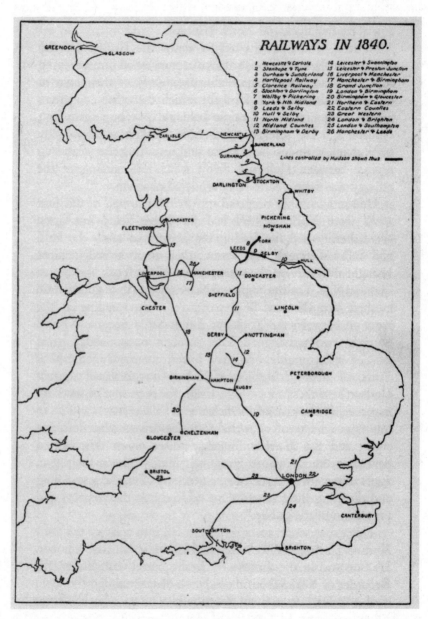

British Railway System in1840 (Hudson's lines in bold). Source: *The Railway King*, by Richard S. Lambert, London, George Allen & Unwin Ltd, © 1964, p. 57. Copyright ©1934 HarperCollins Publishers. All rights reserved.

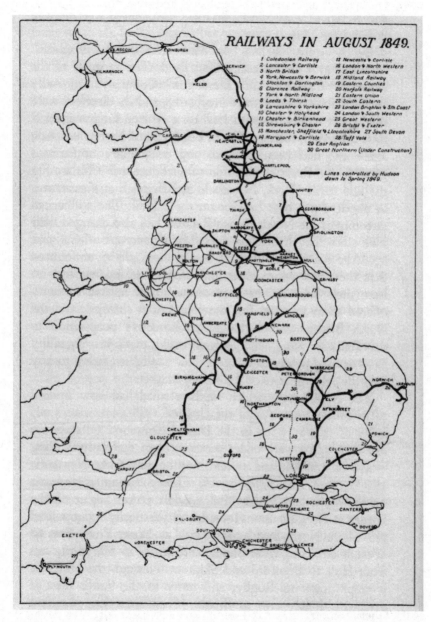

British Railway System in1849 (Hudson's lines in bold). Source: *The Railway King*, by Richard S. Lambert, London, George Allen & Unwin Ltd, © 1964, p. 238. Copyright ©1934 HarperCollins Publishers. All rights reserved.

London and York and the headquarters of the Midland Railway, one of his companies. There he explained to gobsmacked shareholders the essence of his twenty-six parliamentary bills that amalgamated rail and canal systems, built new ones, and extended others. This scheme required £3 million of investor capital; he freely admitted to the skeptical that many of the new lines would fail, but that in the aggregate they would forge an unassailable regional rail system. Already in possession of a raft of favorable proxies, he easily brushed aside scattered opposition from dissident shareholders to pass all twenty-six of his corporate proposals.[36] Wrote one contemporary observer,

> Nothing seemed to wear his mind; nothing appeared to weary his frame. He battled in parliamentary committees, day by day; he argued, pleaded, and gesticulated with an earnestness which rarely failed in its object. One day in town cajoling a committee—the next persuading an archbishop. In the morning adjusting some rival claim in an obscure office; in the afternoon astonishing the stock exchange with some daring *coup de main*.[37]

His powers of concentration and calculation mesmerized. Frequently, he was observed to throw back his head, cover his eyes, and accurately predict the dividend of an as-yet-unfinished line, or to intensely engage in two conversations simultaneously. Business associates found themselves cut off at the knees if their analyses were not to the point, but he forgave easily, and his generosity to both employees and strangers was legendary. Unfortunately, his facility with numbers and frenetic dealings had a downside: he relied excessively on verbal orders and did not keep books or records of his massive transactions, and simply assumed that his wishes would be carried out.[38]

England, which had not 2,000 miles of railroads in 1843, had more than 5,000 by the end of 1848; Hudson controlled some 1,450 of those iron miles and held a virtual monopoly over the nation's northeast.[39] Far more trackage was planned: Parliament approved 800 miles in 1844, 2,700 in 1845, and 4,500 in 1846. The modus operandi of Hudson, and of most of the other promoters, involved selling shares for a small down payment and completing the full purchase much later. The new shares usually advertised dividends approaching 10 percent per annum, despite the fact that construction, let alone operations and revenues, had not yet commenced;

most investors, attracted by the high yields, failed to notice that the absence of revenues implied that the earliest dividends would have to come out of new capital, which today would be labeled a Ponzi scheme, and that the later dividends were a fiction. Hudson fed the frenzy by leaking news of the parliamentary prospects of his own projects. As frosting on the cake, until the final stage of the bubble, Hudson's dense northeastern network blocked the flotations of competing lines.

In addition to promoters like Blunt and Hudson, the public, and politicians, a fourth *p* in the Theater of the Bubble emerged in the 1840s: the press. Broadly speaking, in that era, the fourth estate divided itself into two groups, the "old media," exemplified by *The Times* of London, and the "new media" of railway specialty reporting, such as the *Railway Times*; the former maintained a highly orthodox skepticism, while the latter fanned the flames of speculation. At the height of the bubble, the public could choose among at least twenty railway publications, upon which the railway company promoters lavished £12,000 to £14,000 per week in advertising revenues—funds that would have been more wisely spent on construction. Puff pieces about new proposals abounded; satirized one observer, "Its committee rejoiced in esquires and baronets. Its prospect of passing the House of Commons was certain. Its engineer was Stephenson [in this case, Robert Stephenson, George's son]; its potentate, Hudson; its banker, Glyn. The profits, it was modestly added, would not exceed fifteen percent."[40] Gushed one typical article, the railways were a new world wonder, encircling the globe:

> Not content with making Liverpool their lineage home . . . they are throwing a girdle around the globe itself. Far-off India woos them over its waters, and China listens to the voice of the charmer. The ruined hills and broken altars of old Greece will soon re-echo the whistle of the locomotive, or be converted to shrines sacred to commerce, by the power of those magnificent agencies by which rivers are spanned, territories traversed, commerce enfranchised, confederacies consolidated; by which the adamantine is made divisible, and man assumes a lordship over time and space.[41]

As late as 1843, the British economy was still recovering from the indigestion of 1836–1837, but in the fall of 1844, banks were loaning at 2.5 percent; even more ominously, they were happy to accept as collateral railway securities, widely considered "safe as houses." The subscription rolls saw entries that would make an early 2000s American mortgage broker blush: a half-pay military officer earning £54 per year down for a total of £41,500 on multiple lists; two charwoman's sons living in a garret, one down for £12,500 and the other for £25,000, almost all of which consisted of calls that they had no hope of meeting; millions more pounds sterling of calls came from shareholders with fictitious addresses.[42]

According to one anonymous observer, the English public,

> saw the whole world railway mad. The iron road was extolled at public meetings; it was the object of public worship; it was talked of on the exchange; legislated for in the senate; satirized on the stage. It penetrated every class; it permeated every household; and all yielded to the temptation. Men who went to church as devoutly as to their counting houses—men whose word had ever been as good as their bond—joined in the pursuit, and were carried away by the vortex.[43]

Observed the businessman and MP James Morrison,

> The subtle poison of avarice diffused itself through every class. It infected alike the courtly and exclusive occupant of the halls of the great and the homely inmate of the humble cottage. Duchesses were even known to soil their fingers with scrip, and old maids to inquire with trembling eagerness the price of stocks. Young ladies deserted the marriage list and the obituary for the share list, and startled their lovers with questions respecting the operations of bulls and bears. The man of fashion was seen more frequently at his broker's than at his club. The man of trade left his business to look after his shares; and in return, both his shares and his business left him.[44]

Parliament's Board of Trade established an annual deadline of November 30, by which date plans for new lines had to be filed. On the evening of the 1845 deadline, a frenzy engulfed the capital as promoters representing eight hundred schemes converged on the Board's Whitehall offices: special express trains that the lines allowed through sped toward London at speeds of eighty miles per hour. Railway companies blocked the trains carrying proposals from competing lines; one projector got around this hurdle by loading onto a train a fully decked-out hearse containing pro-posal documents.[45]

John Francis wrote that, as during the South Sea Bubble, 'Change Alley clogged with crowds and gridlock and was once again described as "almost impassable," and the surrounding neighborhoods were "like fairs." He continued,

> The cautious merchant and the keen manufacturer were equally unable to resist the speculation. It spread among them like a leprosy. It ruined alike the innocent and the guilty. It periled many a humble home; it agitated many a princely dwelling. Men hastened to be rich, and were ruined. They bought largely; they subscribed eagerly; they forsook their counting-houses for companies; if successful they continued in their course, and if the reverse, they too often added to the misery of the homes they had already desolated, by destroying themselves.[46]

Stephenson's offices on Great George Street in Westminster were more sought-after than the prime minister's on Downing Street; the price of iron doubled, and surveyors, particularly those working for the Ordnance Department, who often illegally entered private land without permission, could and did charge the earth. A parliamentary report yielded 157 MPs with share subscriptions in excess of £2,000; by the summer of 1845, "The neglect of all business has been unprecedented; for many months no tradesman has been found at his counter, or merchant at his office, east, west, south, or north. If you called upon business you were sure to be answered with 'Gone to the city.'" Even the Brontës got into the act: Emily and Anne owned York and North Midland shares, while the apparently better-grounded Charlotte was more skeptical.[47]

While many of Hudson's business practices, particularly his secrecy and high-handed approach to corporate governance, might have landed him in jail today, they were not yet illegal. Not for another eight decades would Charles Ponzi lend his name to operations that paid dividends out of fresh capital; in the early 1840s, such practices did not arouse legal scrutiny (though that would soon change). The end came not from fraud or deceit, but rather from simple overbuilding and regulatory reform.

Unlike the twin bubbles of the previous century, the collapse of the railway companies evolved in slow motion. By the late 1840s, Hudson's system, which stretched roughly from London almost to Edinburgh, found itself ever more hemmed in by competing lines to both the east and the west. In a desperate attempt to outflank the competition with further line extensions, he raised vast amounts of capital from individual investors; simultaneously, Parliament established a new regulatory regime in 1847 that finally did outlaw the Ponzi-like payment of dividends out of newly acquired capital.[48]

The Bank of England administered the coup de grâce in early 1847 when it raised the discount rate from 3.5 percent to 5 percent. This choked off the flow of capital needed to meet the calls required by share subscriptions. The failure of the potato crop in 1846 and the Continent-wide revolutionary disturbances of 1848 added to England's economic woes and forced Hudson and the other railway operators to cut dividends: panicked investors sold off, and by October 1848 share prices had fallen by 60 percent from their peak 1845 value.[49]

While the absolute share-price decline was not as great as those seen during the South Sea Bubble, or even during the great twentieth-century bear markets, the extreme degree of leverage inherent in the subscription purchase mechanism resulted in widespread devastation:

> Entire families were ruined. There was scarcely an important town in
> England but what beheld some wretched suicide. Daughters delicately

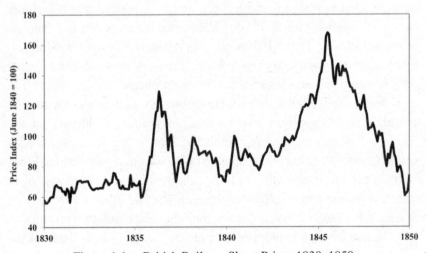

Figure 4-1.   British Railway Share Prices 1830–1850

nurtured went out to seek their bread. Sons were recalled from academies, households were separated: homes were desecrated by emissaries of the law. There was disruption of every social tie. . . . Men who had lived comfortably and independently found themselves suddenly responsible for sums they had no means of paying. In some cases they yielded their all, and began anew; in others they left the country for the Continent, laughed at their creditors, and defied pursuit. One gentleman was served with four hundred writs. A peer similarly pressed, when offered to be relieved of all liabilities for £15,000, betook himself to his yacht, and forgot in the beauties of the Mediterranean the difficulties that had surrounded him.[50]

By that point, minor indiscretions that might have been earlier forgiven of the great Hudson attracted greater scrutiny. Two rival members of the stock exchange, upon close examination of purchase and sales records, noticed that one of the Railway King's companies had bought shares of another that just happened to be owned by Hudson personally at higher-than-market prices; in other words, he had been caught red-handed bilking his own shareholders. Other, more serious infractions were soon uncovered that, while still not rising to the level of criminal liability, left him exposed to crippling civil judgments.

Hudson had one last ace up his sleeve: the gratitude of his Sunderland constituents kept him in Parliament for another decade, and as long as the House of Commons was in session, he was immune from arrest for debt. There followed an opéra bouffe sequence of sorties to and from the Continent. When Parliament was active, he could safely reside at home, where he desperately tried to salvage his holdings; upon adjournment, he decamped to Paris. When he went down to electoral defeat in 1859, the game was up; ignored by his friends and attended to only by his creditors, his last substantial holdings were confiscated. In the end, he subsisted on an annuity purchased by admirers.[51]

One day in 1863, Charles Dickens, returning to Britain on the Folkestone boat, encountered a friend, Charles Manby. Observed Dickens,

Taking leave of Manby was a shabby man of whom I had some remembrance, but whom I could not get into his place in my mind. Noticing when we stood out of the harbour that he was on the brink of the pier, waving his hat in a desolate matter, I said to Manby, "Surely I know that man." "I should think you did," said he; "Hudson!" He is living—just living—at Paris, and Manby had brought him on. He said to Manby at parting, "I shall not have a good dinner again, till you come back."[52]

Two of the three railway bubbles had ruined investors and endowed Britain with essential, if unprofitable, infrastructure. Between 1838 and 1848, its track mileage increased tenfold, and the 1848 railway map looks surprisingly like today's; almost another century passed before mileage doubled from that year.

The unfortunate railway investors had in fact provided England with an invaluable public good—its first high-volume, high-speed transport network. Before the early nineteenth century, the per capita GDP of England grew hardly at all; thereafter, it has grown by about 2 percent per year—approximately doubling once per generation—not only in England, but in other advanced Western nations as well. This transition was caused, in no small part, by the efficiencies of steam-driven land and sea transport.[53] Nor would this be the last time that ruined technology investors would provide their nation's economies with the infrastructure necessary for their growth.

Charles Mackay published the first edition of *Extraordinary Popular Delusions* in 1841, just before the railway mania reached its climax. More than anyone else in England, Mackay should have recognized the boom and bust as they played out. As a journalist and popular writer, he was perfectly placed to warn about it.

He did not, acknowledging the episode only in an oblique two-sentence footnote in the book's second edition, published in 1852.[54] As a young man in the 1830s, Mackay had written for and edited at two London papers, the *Sun* and the *Morning Chronicle*; in 1844, just before the railroad bubble burst, he assumed the editorship of the *Glasgow Argus*, a position he held for the three years of the boom and bust. A detailed analysis of the *Argus*'s articles, particularly the "leaders"—main articles, frequently reprinted from other papers—shows that Mackay was, in general, modestly enthusiastic about railway development. This was likely a reflection of the laissez-faire economic tenor of the time, which centered in that period around the repeal of the protectionist corn laws that benefited the landowning aristocracy and starved the urban poor by keeping grain prices high; the railways were thus a secondary concern of Mackay's circle.[55]

Under Mackay's editorship, the paper's leading articles did repeat the dire warnings about the bubble from *The Times*, but the *Argus* also reprinted favorable articles about the railway companies from other papers. It seems, though, that Mackay, whose name is today nearly synonymous with the word "mania," almost completely missed the massive one he lived through. In a leading piece published in October 1845, he forthrightly stated that the enthusiasm for railway shares had little in common with the South Sea Bubble, which "was founded upon no solid, but altogether an imaginary basis." The railway enthusiasm, he thought, had a foundation that was

> broad and secure. They are a necessity of the Age. They are a property
> real and tangible in themselves. . . . The quiet philosopher and the
> active man of business can perceive that there is not a more noble,
> or a more advantageous employment of British capital than in these
> projects.[56]

While no evidence exists that Mackay lost money in the railway mania, the blindness of the era's most astute observer of human financial irrationality testifies to the seductive power of financial bubbles. Even by the nineteenth century, this was old news: A century before, Isaac Newton showed how even extraordinary knowledge and intelligence failed to protect the investor from the bubble's siren song. Newton was no financial novice; by the time of the South Sea Bubble, he had been Master of the Mint for nearly a quarter century. He had earned a generous return in South Sea shares that he had bought in 1712, which he sold at a significant profit in early 1720, but later that year lost his head and bought them back at much higher prices. This lost him around £20,000 and caused him to supposedly remark that he could calculate the motions of the heavenly bodies, but not the madness of people.[57]

England's railway bubble reflected a technological ferment that promised to revolutionize the very fabric of everyday life. Nearly simultaneously and a continent away, a ferment of a very different sort yielded an extraordinary American end-times mania.

5

MILLER'S RUN

In the mid-1950s, a psychologist named Leon Festinger got lucky.

The son of a politically radical atheist Russian immigrant embroiderer, Festinger applied his considerable intellect over a long and distinguished academic career to the nascent field of social psychology, his luck arriving in the guise of a flying-saucer mania in the upper Midwest fortuitously close to where he taught. The affected group was led by a woman named Dorothy Martin, who claimed to have channeled spirits warning of massive earthquakes and floods; the twin cataclysms, they informed her, would consume North America on December 21, 1954.[1]

Social psychologists, aware of Solomon Asch's line-length experiments, had long known that social pressures tend to grind down differences of opinion among individuals to the point that both small groups and entire societies evolve distinct cultural, moral, and religious values. Further, they also knew that these values changes often occurred explosively, and that this rapid diffusion resembled that of contagious diseases.

Since the 1920s, epidemiologists have mathematically modeled disease spread, which depends mainly on two key parameters: the transmission rate, or infectiousness, of a pathogen, and its removal rate, either by cure or death. Social scientists found that they could understand the spread of ideas and beliefs in the same way. Festinger realized that Martin and her adherents provided him a laboratory in which he could observe this process in real time. More importantly, her group offered the rare opportunity to see just what happens after the inevitable failure of end-times prophecies.

The young researcher designed a study that no institutional review board would approve today, in which his assistants infiltrated Martin's circle "without either the knowledge or consent of the group members."[2] Festinger's project also ran afoul of the experimental and ethical injunction that field researchers should not interfere with their subjects' decision-making. Time and again, as Martin and her followers unknowingly drew out the opinions and advice of the planted observers, Festinger's infiltrators were forced to violate this noninterference mandate.

As an early Scientology devotee, Martin was no stranger to contact with the Beyond, having undergone the organization's "auditing" process, which enabled her to recall, among other things, her conception, birth, and earlier reincarnations. Her primary collaborator, Dr. Charles Laughead, had trod a more conventional path to his end-times beliefs. A physician at the student health service at Michigan State University, he performed foreign medical missionary work for a mainstream Protestant group; only when his wife began to suffer from incapacitating neuroses did his efforts to find help for her lead to inadvertent encounters with UFO enthusiasts, which led him to Ms. Martin.

About a year before the anticipated Apocalypse, Martin became a prophetess. She awoke with a tingling in her right arm: "I had the feeling that someone was trying to get my attention."[3] She picked up a pencil and soon found herself writing involuntarily in a strange hand. At first, unlike biblical prophets, she didn't relay messages from God, but from someone much closer to home: When she asked the commander of her willful limb for identification, he revealed himself as her departed father.

She quickly upped her channeling game; her tingling right arm and pencil began to relay messages from more exalted players: a creature called "Elder Brother" who advised her on her dead father's spiritual needs, followed by beings from the planets "Cerus" and "Clarion," with the most important entity being Sananda, who revealed himself as the contemporary physical embodiment of Jesus.

Sananda, a thoroughly modern messiah, was presently conducting advanced reconnaissance over the length and breadth of the U.S. and had already contacted others besides Ms. Martin. What Dwight Eisenhower would later call the country's military-industrial complex had angered Sananda and his associates, known as the Guardians; in retribution they would rend the continent asunder and inundate it with a massive flood near year's end. The Guardians instructed Martin to meet their flying saucers on the night of August 1, 1954. None appeared to her or the eleven followers she had brought along (none of whom were Festinger's plants); instead, they were met by an ordinary-appearing man to whom she offered fruit juice and a sandwich; he politely refused and walked away.

The saucers' nonappearance provided her group with its first jolt of disconfirmation, and seven members abandoned her immediately. Martin and the remaining four who kept the faith did not have to wait long: two days later, Sananda informed Martin that it was he who had turned down the refreshments and, satisfied with the moral character of her and her remaining colleagues, told her that they would be among the select few the saucers would rescue a few days before the apocalypse.[4]

Like almost all millennialists and apocalypticists, Martin was an earnest fool, not a knave. She devoted her time and fortune for the benefit of her followers, and her beliefs cost her dearly. When children in the Chicago suburb of Oak Park who heard from their parents of the imminent End developed nightmares, police brought charges of "inciting to riot" and placed her under psychiatric care, following which she fled her Chicago-area home. Laughead also lost his job over his involvement in the affair.[5]

The prospect of the spectacular disconfirmation of the disciples' belief system in late 1954, when both the rescuing saucers and the following apocalypse were nearly certain not to appear, was the main reason Festinger had put Martin and her colleagues under surveillance: to determine precisely how people behave when deeply held views are disconfirmed by events and data. The resulting work, *When Prophecy Fails*, became a classic among psychologists, sociologists, economists, and political scientists.* Festinger later coined the now familiar term "cognitive dissonance" to describe the emotionally unpleasant conflict between belief and fact or, slightly more subtly, between narrative and data. When compelling narrative and objective fact collide, the former often survives, an outcome that has cursed mankind since time immemorial.

Dorothy Martin's subsequent history typified how many people handle cognitive dissonance. Rather than modify her belief system in the light of contrary evidence, she and her group, which had initially been relatively secretive about their beliefs, doubled down and for the first time began to proselytize the coming of the saucers. After leaving the Chicago area, she spent the rest of her life dabbling in spirituality in alternative-lifestyle hotspots in South America, Northern California, and, finally,

---

* Festinger attempted to grant his involuntary subjects anonymity with pseudonyms; he referred to Dr. Charles Laughead as Dr. Thomas Armstrong, and Dorothy Martin as Marian Keech. Digital-age readers of *When Prophecy Fails* can easily pierce this veil.

Sedona, Arizona, where, nearly a half century after her 1954 brush with the Apocalypse, she died under the name Sister Thedra.[6]

While it's all too easy to dismiss Dorothy Martin as a caricature of New Age credulity, we are to one degree or another all the slaves of Festinger's demon. The "doubling down" demonstrated by Martin and her followers seems to be a near-constant of human behavior. When Münster's Anabaptists repeatedly saw Bockelson's end-times prophecies disconfirmed, their beliefs, at least for a while, grew stronger, as did their efforts to proselytize those in surrounding towns. The same would also happen with the wild end-times predictions of a substantial group of evangelical Protestants in the mid-nineteenth century.

This counterintuitive behavior makes a certain perverse sense. Disconfirmation of deeply held beliefs causes severe psychic pain; what better way of alleviating it than in the company of newly won believers? As put by Festinger, "If more and more people can be persuaded that the system of belief is correct, then clearly it must, after all, be correct."[7]

Beginning in 1620, the Puritans, who were closely associated with the Fifth Monarchists, sent the first colonists to Massachusetts. A decade later, the Bay Colony's new leader, John Winthrop, preached to his followers that they would found "a Citty upon a Hill" whose success and favor from God would be eagerly watched by the whole world.[8] The nation that evolved from the Bay Colony, with no state church and a hitherto unknown degree of religious and ideological liberty, provided fertile ground for the proliferation and growth of divinely inspired movements.

The early eighteenth and nineteenth centuries saw, respectively, the First and Second "Great Awakenings," religious revivals that swept the United States and England; both spawned a wide variety of unorthodox theologies that, like the Reformation before them, valued individual spiritualism and devalued organized religious hierarchies.

The craggy visage staring from a twenty-dollar Federal Reserve note represents a historical irony that directly contributed to the Second Great Awakening. Andrew Jackson despised the very idea of a central bank, and allowed the charter of the Second Bank of the United States to expire in 1837. His timing could not have been worse; almost simultaneously, the nation experienced a spectacular bubble, a complicated episode that featured massive sales of government land, real estate speculation, and a boom and bust in cotton prices. When the bubble burst that year, no national bank could act as lender of last resort to save the day. The resultant currency shortage plunged the nation into a painful depression that lasted for nearly a decade and caused approximately 25 percent unemployment. Detailed economic data from that era are unavailable, but Jackson's recklessness likely cost the nation as dearly as the Great Depression did a century later. Wrote the English novelist Frederick Marryat about his visit to New York after the Panic of 1837,

> Suspicion, fear, and misfortune have taken possession of the city. Had I not been aware of the cause, I should have imagined that the plague was raging, and I had the description of Defoe before me. Not a smile on one countenance among the crowd who pass and repass; hurried steps, care-worn faces, rapid exchanges of salutation, or hasty communication of anticipated ruin before the sun goes down. . . . Mechanics, thrown out of employment, are pacing up and down with the air of famished wolves. The violent shock has been communicated, like that of electricity, through the country to a distance of hundreds of miles. Canals, railroads, and all public works, have been discontinued, and the Irish emigrant leans against his shanty, with his spade idle in his hand, and starves, as his thoughts wander back to his own Emerald Isle.[9]

The Second Great Awakening, which was by then already well underway, accelerated among the wreckage strewn in the wake of the 1837 panic. Along the way the Awakening midwifed schisms that ranged from Mormonism to blatantly fraudulent spiritual movements like those of the Fox Sisters, whose supposed ability to communicate with the deceased hoodwinked no less than the great author and politician Horace Greeley.[10]

Most spectacularly, as many as a hundred thousand Americans came to believe that the world would end on October 22, 1844, a mass delusion spawned by the most unlikely of millennialist leaders: a modest, unassuming, and thoughtful man named William Miller.

Born in 1782, the first of sixteen children of desperately poor parents, Miller was brought up in a deeply religious Baptist farming family in the town of Low Hampton, in extreme eastern upstate New York. His mother taught him to read, but the family's poverty deprived him of a decent formal education. Like many farm children of the era, from ages nine to fourteen he attended school only during the three months between harvest and planting. At home, the boy, who loved books, had access only to his father's Bible, hymnal, and Psalter; generous neighbors loaned him copies of popular works like *Robinson Crusoe*. These literary interests displeased his father, who noticed that they distracted him from his farming chores, so young William would sneak down to the fireplace late at night to read by the dim light of burning pine knots.[11]

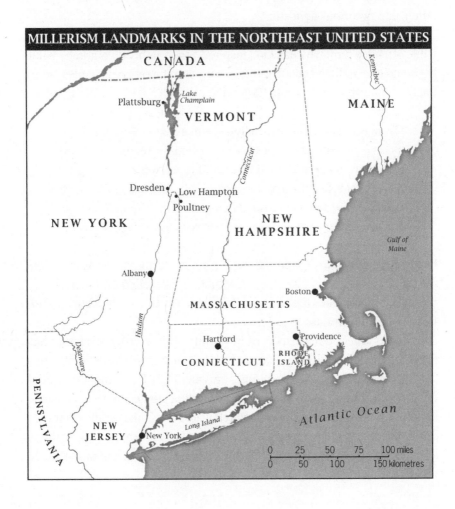

At age twenty-one he married and moved a few miles east across the Vermont state line to farm in his wife's home near Poultney. As fate would have it, the town was a hotbed of Deism, a philosophy that posited a detached supreme being, a "Divine Watchmaker" who observed his creation at a distance and viewed the Bible as a mere book that was anything but divinely inspired—nothing more than a useful guide to ancient history.

The town's extensive library collection reflected that liberality: Voltaire, Hume, and Paine, among many others, whose thinking Miller devoured in the process of becoming a Deist himself. In Poultney, Miller also came under the influence of its most famous townsman, Matthew Lyon, a congressman, Revolutionary War veteran, firebrand associate of Ethan Allen, and notorious agnostic.[12]

The more Enlightenment philosophy Miller consumed, the more the Bible offended him: why had God inspired a thoroughly incomprehensible book and then inflicted death, torture, exile, and starvation on hapless souls unable to interpret it properly? Mankind also fell short, in Miller's view:

> The more I read, the more dreadfully corrupt did the character of man appear. I could discern no bright spot in the history of the past. Those conquerors of the world, and heroes of history, were apparently but demons in human form. All the sorrow, suffering, and misery in the world, seemed to be increased in proportion to the power they obtained over their fellows. I began to feel very distrustful of all men.[13]

Poultney's iconoclasm well suited the young farmer; free at last from his family's stifling religious environment, he rebelled and mercilessly mimicked their pieties to their faces by impersonating his preacher grandfather's florid sermons.[14]

Miller did find one aspect of his family praiseworthy: his father had fought in the Revolutionary War, and so the son sought refuge from man's corruption in patriotism and military service. In 1810, as the prospect of conflict with Britain loomed, the Vermont militia granted him a lieutenant's commission; when the country declared war in 1812, the militia promoted him to captain, and the next year he transferred to the regular U.S. Army as a lieutenant. Even with the lower rank, the change of service was considered a promotion, and in any case, by early 1814 he had regained the rank of captain. In late summer, he found himself at Plattsburgh, on the shores of Lake Champlain, where an outnumbered and outgunned American force decisively defeated the British invaders in a swirling land-sea battle.

The military action overawed and horrified Miller, who wrote to his wife on September 11 that out of three hundred soldiers and sailors on one of the American vessels, only twenty-five survived. "Some of our officers, who have been on board, say the blood is knee deep." The next day he wrote to her again:

> My God! What a slaughter on all sides! . . . I cannot describe to you the general joy. At sundown, our forts fired a national salute, accompanied by a song called "Yankee Doodle. . . . " A naval and land engagement, within the compass of a mile or two, and fifteen or twenty thousand engaged at one and the same time, is superior to anything my eyes ever beheld before. How grand, how noble, and yet how awful![15]

The battle not only destroyed the British invasion force, but also Miller's Deism; how else to explain, beyond a God actively engaged on the U.S. side, the defeat of fifteen thousand crack British troops, battle hardened in the Napoleonic Wars, by a ragtag amalgamation of fifteen hundred American regulars and four thousand volunteers? "So surprising a result, against such odds, did seem to me like the work of a mightier power than man."[16]

Soon after the war, he returned to farm in Low Hampton, where, as a respected veteran and minor town official, he was expected to assume an increased role in his family's Baptist church.

His wartime experiences and the return to his childhood's conservative religious environment triggered a spiritual conflict, and given his love of reading, he applied literary analysis to the disjunction between his prior unbelief and his seemingly supernatural experiences in combat. Sometime around 1816, he began an arduous, word-by-word analysis of the Bible. If he came upon the word "beast," for example, in a context that suggested it symbolized a heathen empire, as in Daniel or in Revelation, he would compulsively search the rest of the Bible for the same word.

After several years of arduously scouring scripture, he found, he thought, the resolution between his prior unbelief and battle experiences.

Of Daniel's four kingdoms, only Rome, as represented by the Catholic Church, remained. He was particularly struck by Daniel 8:14: "And he said unto me, Unto two thousand and three hundred days; then shall the sanctuary be cleansed."

All was now clear to Miller: Chapter 7 of Ezra places the Persian Emperor Artaxerxes's command to return to Judah and build their house of worship in the seventh year of his reign, which the historians of the time estimated as 457 B.C. In that year, according to Miller's eschatology, the apocalyptic clock began ticking. Given the equivalency of the scriptural day and temporal year assumed by biblical scholars, the world would thus end 2,300 years later, in 1843.

Miller had inherited the long intellectual tradition of "number mysticism" that so enamored Joachim of Fiore, and which persists unabated into the present. The most spectacular modern example of this phenomenon is the late-nineteenth-century work of John Taylor and Charles Piazzi Smyth, who noted a number of mathematical coincidences in the structure of the pyramids, such as the fact that the ratio of twice the length of their base to their height was close to the value of π, that the ratio of the base length to that of its casing stone was 365, or that the distance from the earth to the sun was almost exactly a billion times the pyramid height. Smyth went on to write a bestseller, *Our Inheritance in the Great Pyramid*, which detailed these amazing discoveries.[17]

A century later, a Swiss man named Erich von Däniken deployed similar observations to prove that extraterrestrials had visited the earth in another bestseller, *Chariots of the Gods*.[18] And for nearly a millennium, theological cranks have deployed similar mathematical coincidences and biblical chronology to forecast the world's end. As recently as 2011, a Christian radio personality named Harold Camping predicted that the world would end that October 21. In 2012, he admitted his mistake and humbly acknowledged the exhortation of Matthew 24:36 "of that day and hour knoweth no man."[19]

The brilliant mathematical author, puzzle maker, and social commentator Martin Gardner wrote of the Smyth book, "*Our Inheritance* is a classic of its kind. Few books illustrate so beautifully the ease with which an intelligent man, passionately convinced of a theory, can manipulate his subject matter in such a way as to make it conform to precisely held opinions."[20] (Ironically, Gardner was raised in Seventh-day Adventism, the direct descendant of the theology Miller would help found.)[21] As he so often did, the late literary bad boy Christopher Hitchens coined a more pungent term for delusional biblical date-setting: an "odometer for idiots."[22]

Biblical number mysticism feeds off the "patternicity" phenomenon. The Bible, a vast compendium of numbers, narratives, and ofttimes poorly defined calendars, allows the studious millennialist to arrive at almost any future date as the End. In any case, Miller was hardly the first to employ biblical number mysticism to settle on 1843 as the apocalyptic date; in 1946 a Seventh-day Adventist minister named Leroy Edwin Froom published *The Prophetic Faith of our Fathers*, a four-volume history of end-times calculations, dozens of which centered on 1843. But none would deploy number mysticism to such devastating effect as William Miller.[23]

Number mysticism is inevitably amplified by another well-known psychological phenomenon, "confirmation bias," in which human beings, once they have settled on a hypothesis or belief system, pay attention only to data that support their beliefs and avoid data that contradict it.

The term is associated with a psychologist named Peter Wason. In a classic late-1950s experiment, he presented subjects with a sequence of three numbers such as 2–4–6, and asked them to derive the rule that produced the sequence, and then to test it with another sequence.[24]

The most obvious rule suggested by the above triplet is "successive even numbers," and so the test subject was most likely to respond with an answer sequence such as 8–10–12 and be told that it was consistent with the rule that actually generated the sequence. The subject might then come back with 24–26–28, and also be told that triplet was also consistent with the rule.

After several more successive "confirmations" of her "successive even numbers" rule, she might reasonably conclude that it was the correct one.

The problem is that all three sequences are consistent with multiple other rules as well, such as "numbers increasing in size" or "only positive increasing numbers." In other words, the subjects were only trying to confirm their own hypothesis, when in fact a more effective strategy is to test triplets that disproved the hypothesis, say, 5–7–9. If the examiner replied that this triplet was also consistent with the rule, then they would know that "successive even numbers" was incorrect, but that perhaps "numbers increasing in size" or "numbers increasing by two" still held true.

The majority of subjects most often tested only triplets that were consistent with their hypothesized rules, and not triplets inconsistent with their rules. By looking only for evidence that supported their hypotheses, they rarely arrived at the rules that generated Wason's number series.

As a scientist, Wason knew that the heart of the scientific method involved trying to *disprove* hypotheses, but as a psychologist he suspected that the natural human tendency was to *confirm* them.[25]

Psychologists soon expanded on Wason's work and performed a plethora of experiments that demonstrated our species' more general tendency toward seeking out and accepting confirmatory evidence, while ignoring or discounting contrary evidence. As the old saying goes, "a man convinced against his will is of the same opinion still."*[26]

In a classic late-1970s study, a group of Stanford University researchers surveyed 151 undergraduates about their views on controversial topics, such as capital punishment, and culled from that group 48 of them, 24 who strongly favored and 24 who strongly opposed it (proponents/opponents). They then presented the two groups with two different research findings, supposedly authentic but which were in reality fictional. One of the "studies" demonstrated that murder rates were lower in states with capital punishment, and the other, higher (pro-deterrence/anti-deterrence).

The proponents found the pro-deterrence study methodologically sounder than the anti-deterrence study, and were more convinced by the pro-deterrence study as well. Opponents, on the other hand, found the anti-deterrence study more sound and convincing. Most revealing of all, at the end of the experiment, after the participants had read and evaluated the two contradictory studies, each group hardened their proponent/ opponent views.[27]

William Miller, and later his followers, contracted a chronic case of confirmation bias. After he had calculated his chosen time, the year 1843, he focused on confirming evidence and so was able to convince himself of the accuracy of his prediction. Miller arrived at the startling conclusion

---

* This quote is often attributed to Benjamin Franklin, but a better documented source seems to be Mary Wollstonecraft, "Convince a man againft his will, He's of the fame opinion ftill," in *A Vindication of the Rights of Woman with Strictures on Moral and Political Subjects* (London: Printed for J. Johnson, 1796), 255.

of an 1843 Apocalypse. Christ would appear in the clouds and fire would consume the Earth. The righteous—those who believed—would ascend to heaven and immortality, while the wicked would be destroyed by God, who for good measure would eternally imprison their souls.[28]

For nearly a decade, Miller did not publicize this disturbing prophecy and discussed it only among his personal acquaintances.[29] His shyness and diffidence only enhanced his credibility, particularly among Methodist, Baptist, and Presbyterian clergy, who were impressed with an approach that was simultaneously scholarly and nondenominational; membership in any Protestant sect qualified one for salvation. Miller's friends, compelled by his eschatology, were perplexed at his reluctance to preach, which stemmed from his trepidation at becoming a laughing-stock, a fear that likely emanated from his social reticence and humble upbringing.[30]

In the summer of 1831, his Baptist sister and her husband invited him to speak in Dresden, Vermont, sixteen miles up Lake Champlain from Low Hampton. Although he had previously read sermons written by absent preachers, he had never given one of his own. By this point, he was close to fifty and not a well man. He had nearly died from spotted fever just before the Battle of Plattsburgh and had since suffered on and off from various skin infections.

History did not record his words on that particular occasion, but they were likely not much different from those of later written sermons: Christ would appear in the sky and resurrect dead saints, and the righteous would be "caught up to meet the Lord in the air where they will be married to him." Christ would then turn his attention to the sinners:

> Behold, the heavens grow black with clouds, the sun has veiled himself; the moon, pale and forsaken, hangs in the middle air; the hail descends, the seven trumpets utter loud their voices; the lightnings send their vivid gleams of sulphurous flames abroad; and the great city of the nation falls to rise no more forever and forever.[31]

His performance so mesmerized the Dresden Baptists that they held him over to the following Sunday, and over the next eight years he gave invited lectures throughout rural New England, New York, and Canada. When unable to fulfill a speaking request to distant congregations, he supplied them with written tracts, which led to a series of pamphlets and books, generating yet more speaking requests.

One contemporary eyewitness, who seems to have possessed an intuitive understanding of confirmation bias, simultaneously impressed and doubtful, described his pulpit presence:

> In person he was large and heavily built, his head broad and his brow high, with a soft and expressive eye, and all the inflections of his voice indicated the sincerest devotion. His imagination was quite fervid and having drawn his conclusion from a defective premise it became to him a real fact. In this state of mind he went about lecturing, using large charts illustrative of the visions of Daniel and John. Immense throngs came to hear him, a number of ministers and laymen of large mind embraced his views, and the greatest excitement prevailed over the eastern and northern parts of our country.[32]

Just as Miller's biblical number mysticism was centuries old, his vigorous preaching style also lacked originality. Beginning around 1825, a Presbyterian minister and Second Great Awakening principal named Charles Grandison Finney perfected the now familiar hellfire and brimstone evangelical delivery, soaked with audience participation. His sermons effected conversions by the score; one observer noted that after Finney had been through a town, it was "so deeply penetrated by religious feeling that it was impossible to organize a dancing party, and it was unprofitable to have a circus."[33] Miller himself viewed the new revivalist preaching style with disfavor, but there also seems little question that he had mastered the Finney technique, and that many of those who invited Miller to speak saw him as an effective practitioner of it.[34]

Like many early evangelicals, Finney was a staunch abolitionist and social activist. Early on, Miller shared these beliefs; Low Hampton was a stop on the underground railroad, and Miller is known to have sheltered at least one slave. But when in 1840 he attended a meeting of the Antislavery Society, he came away convinced that corruption so pervaded human society that it must look to divine intervention for help in solving its many ills, particularly slavery: "The year of Jubilee to the poor Slave is not near if man is the cause. But God can & will release the captive. And to him alone we must look for redress."[35]

Not only did Miller's florid oratory style hypnotize lay audiences, but his tolerance of other Protestant sects and steel-trap grasp of scripture beguiled churchmen. One skeptical church elder, in an effort to trip him up, recorded that he

> visited him in his room, with a formidable list of objections. To my surprise, scarcely any of them were new to him, and he could answer them as fast as I could present them. And then he presented objections and questions which confounded *me*, and the commentaries on which I had relied. I went home used up, convicted, humbled, and resolved to answer the question.[36]

Miller's popularity, which derived from his stem-winding sermons, came at a price: Congregations were moved far less by the Adventist theology that drove him than by his hellfire and brimstone delivery. Miller's raison d'être revolved around saving souls from the fire, whereas those who invited him wanted to fill pews. Still, by the late 1830s he had attracted a cadre of supporters who spread the message. For example, in 1838, the editor of Boston's *Daily Times* published a series of Miller's sermons, and at nearly the same time a minister named Josiah Litch wrote an approving pamphlet called *The Midnight Cry!*, which circulated widely around New England. A Boston pastor named Charles Fitch, one of William Lloyd Garrison's abolitionist lieutenants, reread Litch's tract several times in succession; Litch, Fitch, and several other Miller acolytes would, over the next several years, support Miller's movement and, eventually, encourage his most disastrous apocalyptic forecast.[37]

At first, this support did not greatly hearten Miller; by 1839, hobbled by age and ill health, and discouraged that he had convinced few of the advent of the end-times four years hence, he considered himself a failure. Speaking invitations continued to arrive, but he knew that his scattered rural preaching would save only a few souls from the coming Apocalypse.[38]

Though his followers thought him a prophet, technically, he wasn't one, for he steadfastly denied any communication with the Almighty. Rather, he claimed an ability to divine the future from scripture. However he thought of himself, he clearly underestimated how his persuasive Adventism had stirred clergymen in the Northeast. In 1838, for example, he had refused a speaking request from one Joshua Himes, a Boston minister and, like Fitch, a lieutenant of Garrison's.

Where Miller was humble and rough around the edges, Himes was urbane, polished, and well connected in Boston progressive circles. The First Christian Church proved too conservative for Himes, so he founded his own house of worship named, naturally enough, the Second Christian Church, which grew so rapidly under his leadership that it had to build a five-hundred-seat chapel on Boston's Chardon Street. The forceful, outgoing, and charismatic Himes was in no way put off by Miller's diffidence. Sometime in the autumn of 1839, he convinced Miller to preach to his congregation, a performance that so impressed Himes that he devoted his considerable energy, organizational skills, and mastery of the era's print media to Miller's cause, and so effectively took it over.

Himes sent Miller not just to sleepy rural congregations, but also to packed churches in New York City and Albany. He republished Miller's pamphlets and books and established a successful newspaper, *The Signs of the Times*, initially a biweekly, soon enough a weekly. Himes also had extensive contacts with others swayed by Miller's eschatology. These acolytes published their own Millerite newspapers, most notably Nathaniel Southard, who eventually edited the most famous Adventist publication of all, *The Midnight Cry!* (which confusingly had the same name as Litch's pamphlet).

Himes intuitively grasped the synergy between the publications and the preaching, from the smallest meetings to the largest lectures. Pamphlets, newspapers, and books that featured the compelling Adventist end-times narrative begat the call for preaching, and the preaching begat greater sales of the publications. Believers spread the word by leaving bundles of pamphlets on seagoing ships and canal barges for disbursement in ports and by hanging posters in train carriages.[39]

Beginning in 1840, Himes organized the first of several general conferences that brought together and coordinated Miller's Adventist campaign. This involved not only conventional church venues but also massive "camp meetings."

Himes did not invent the camp meeting; the first were organized soon after the birth of the new nation, and by 1840 they were an established institution. Part revivalist congregation and part social club, they initially attracted otherwise isolated farmers in the frontier territories of South Carolina, Tennessee, and Kentucky with sorely needed social intercourse. Typically, their Baptist and Methodist organizers cleared a plot of forest and fashioned the felled trees into crude benches and pulpits, which functioned as itinerant churches. (Episcopalians and Congregationalists, on the other hand, turned their noses up at the camps, and at evangelism in general.)

Miller's followers held the first two camp meetings in late June, 1842: one in East Kingston, New Hampshire, and the other in Hatley, Quebec. The New Hampshire meeting was a stunning success: As many as ten thousand Baptists and Methodists came, as did a sprinkling of Deists and "infidels," presumably attracted by the nondenominational good fellowship. Himes proved himself a master of logistics: The ideal site for these gatherings had to be easily reached by rail and required, according to one historian, "an abundance of pure cold water, tall hemlock trees with their cool shade, and secluded groves for prayer and devotion."[40] Medium-sized and large cities sponsored their own tent accommodations, and the railroads established temporary stations, slashed fares for the faithful, and let preachers ride for free. At the conclusion, each "tent master" provided a tally of souls saved from the eternal fire.

So successful was the East Kingston meeting that Himes and his colleagues decided to purchase a "Great Tent," 55 feet high and 120 feet in diameter, with a seating capacity of four thousand and room for perhaps a few thousand more in the aisles. In the event of inclement weather, it could accommodate services indoors and came equipped with stoves to allow for cold weather meetings; the tent attracted thousands in Rochester, New York, and to as far west as Ohio. Over the ensuing two years, Himes and his colleagues organized 125 camp meetings attended by approximately half a million people.[41]

At the conclusion of each camp meeting, ministers arranged a farewell prayer or song, the favorite being "Never Part Again":

> *We are marching through Immanuel's ground*
> *We shall soon hear the trumpet sound,*

And soon we shall with Jesus reign,
And never, never part again.

What? Never part again?
No, never part again.
For soon we shall with Jesus reign,
And never, never part again.[42]

The minister then led the congregation out of the tent in a single-file spiral, which doubled back on itself so each could shake the hand of everyone else. Since the end-time was imminent, believers expected their next meeting in the "heavenly camp."[43]

Miller himself paid a high personal price for his success. Not a well man to begin with, he estimated that in 1841 alone he gave 627 rousing ninety-minute lectures.[44] Throughout this period, Miller's skin condition and exhaustion, coupled with the enthusiasm of his acolytes, loosened his influence over the movement he had founded. On more than one occasion, ill health forced him to return home early to Low Hampton.[45]

Unless carefully managed, emotionally laden mass events can get out of hand, as happened at subsequent camp meetings. While Himes was busy spreading Miller's message, he had placed his second-in-command, Charles Starkweather, in charge of the Chardon Street chapel, where he proved adept at whipping the congregation into frenzies. Fearing his influence, Himes eventually fired Starkweather but could not prevent his presence at camp meetings, where his sermonizing convinced believers that he hosted the Holy Ghost and had "gifts" that included the ability to stop steam engines or walk on water. At one meeting, another attendee claimed to read a believer's character and heart, and then recruited followers to gang up on his skeptics to recant on pain of eternal damnation. When they resisted, he talked in tongues and thrashed about, and when observers attempted to intervene, they too were condemned to Hell.[46]

More importantly, Miller and Himes began to lose control of the increasingly powerful Adventist media. Believers began to publish their own newspapers, with titles like *Voice of Truth and Glad Tidings of the Kingdom at Hand*, *Advent Chronicle and Tent Reporter*, *Jubilee Trumpet*, and *Western Midnight Cry*, the last founded by George Storrs, a Methodist minister who had been jailed in New Hampshire for his abolitionist activities. Storrs would, with disastrous results, pursue the Adventist cause with equal zeal.

On New Year's Eve, December 31, 1842, Adventists around the country gathered to welcome in 1843, the final year of Creation, at Chardon Street. Himes and Starkweather, the latter of whom had not yet been fired, preached to the packed chapel. The increasingly infirm Miller sent out a letter to believers:

> This year, according to our faith, is the last year that Satan will reign in our earth. Jesus Christ will come, and bruise his head. The kingdoms of the earth will be dashed to pieces . . . And he whose right it is to reign will take the kingdom and possess it forever and ever.[47]

By February, Miller had recovered enough from his illnesses to travel to Philadelphia, where the massive Chinese Museum Hall was rented for his sermons. So palpable was the excitement, and so unruly was the crowd waiting outside, that the city authorities canceled the first lecture on February 9 for fear of civic mayhem. The next day, Miller preached to great effect without incident, and shortly thereafter in Trenton at the mayor's invitation. On his way home, Miller sickened and remained confined to Low Hampton until the fall. Himes and several associates divided the country into theaters of operation and preached in churches and rented halls and distributed literature as far west as Wisconsin and Missouri and as far south as the Carolinas.

In Boston, at the movement's urban epicenter on Chardon Street, those wanting to hear Himes overwhelmed the chapel's seating, and so a larger site on Howard Street with a capacity of three thousand was planned. City ordinance required that a building of that size be enclosed on four sides by brick, and since The End was near, the Howard Street lot was ideal, being already walled on three sides and necessitating only the construction of a twelve-foot wall on the fourth side.

At this point, the movement, which had long engendered skepticism and derision within the wider public, encountered outright hostility. Newspapers piled warning and scorn upon a belief system viewed as not only dangerous but foolhardy in the extreme: if the world's end was imminent, the large tabernacles under construction not only in Boston, but in Cincinnati and Cleveland, served no purpose. Despite the increasing public opposition, the faithful dedicated the Howard Street tabernacle on May 4, 1843.

As within most closed belief systems, Millerites deployed confirmation bias to buttress their theology; as always, the Bible proved a treasure trove of supporting data:

> Knowing this first, that there shall come in the last days scoffers, walking after their own lusts, And saying, Where is the promise of his coming? For since the fathers fell asleep, all things continue as they were from the beginning of the creation. (2 Peter 3:3–4)

To buck up the troops discouraged by the increasing public scorn, *The Midnight Cry!* carried "The Liars Column" and "Scoffers Corner" as regular features.[48]

Miller had always been noncommittal about the End's precise date. His calculation had added the twenty-three hundred years from Daniel 8:14 to Artaxerxes's supposed order in 457 B.C. that the Jews return home and rebuild the Temple. This simple arithmetic scheduled Jesus's return for 1843. As the year marched uneventfully on, Miller began to fudge: Since biblical events ran according to the Jewish rabbinical calendar, which began in March or April, there was still plenty of time; the Jewish "1843" did not end, according to this computational adjustment, until March 21, 1844.[49]

In early 1844, Miller returned to the fray and preached to huge audiences in Boston and New York City. As the fateful date approached, he joined Josiah Litch and Himes for a grand finale in Washington, D.C. That "Caesar's Household," as Miller dubbed the capital, seemed more consumed with that year's presidential election than with the coming Apocalypse annoyed him no end:

> Our rulers and political men are not yet ready to give up their power, but they are much engaged in their political squabbles for the next Presidency, as if their little "brief authority," were to last forever. But with the help of God's Word, the Holy Spirit, and the history of past ages, I will show them that an important revolution will take place before long, which will supercede the necessity of choosing a president.[50]

By March 3, Miller had delivered nineteen sermons in the capital, then several more on his way back home to Low Hampton, where he arrived, exhausted, to await the End on March 21.

The day came and went uneventfully; Miller wrote hopeful letters to Himes via private post and messages to the faithful via the Adventist newspapers: His calculations were never exact, so what if they were off by a week or a month or two? The Lord was still coming; Himes, for his part, warned readers, "It is not safe, therefore, for us to defer in our minds the event for an hour, but to live in constant expectation, and readiness to meet our Judge. With such views, we can make no certain arrangements for the future."[51]

There was still plenty of wiggle room. For example, an unsigned article the previous year in one of Himes's newspapers, *The Signs of the Times*, pointed out the computational error in Miller's calculation: Since there is no year zero in the Christian calendar, only 2,999 years separated 457 B.C. and A.D. 1843, not 3,000. Thus, the End should occur in the "Jewish year" of 1844, not 1843.

This article further took issue with Miller's use of the rabbinical Jewish calendar. After the Romans scattered the Jews into the diaspora, the Judean barley harvest, upon which the date of Yom Kippur was based, could no longer be observed, and so almost all Jews adopted the rabbinical calendar, a precise mathematical dating system that relied on a nineteen-year cycle. That newer calendar, though, did not come into use until the fourth century A.D.; far better, the writer thought, to observe the "Kairate" calendar system used in biblical times that started the year with the appearance of the new moon nearest the Judean barley harvest. By this method, the Apocalypse would occur on April 29, 1844.[52]

That date passed uneventfully as well. Public derision mounted, and a Millerite was apt to hear from his neighbor some variant of "What—not gone up yet? We thought you'd gone up! Wife didn't leave you behind to burn, did she?"[53]

The Bible was once again mined for plausible explanations for the nonevent. One of the most obscure Old Testament books, Habakkuk, contains this passage (2:3): "For the vision is yet for an appointed time, but at the end it shall speak, and not lie: though it tarry, wait for it; because it will surely come, it will not tarry." The word "tarry" helpfully popped up elsewhere in the Bible, most importantly in Matthew 25, a parable in which ten virgins await the "bridegroom," who represents Jesus. Verses 5 and 6 explain, "While the bridegroom tarried, they all slumbered and slept. And at midnight there was a cry made, Behold, the bridegroom cometh; go ye out to meet him" (hence the name of Litch's pamphlet and the best known Adventist newspaper, *The Midnight Cry!*). This rationalization reassured the disappointed faithful: Christ's work was largely done, he was just tarrying.

The Millerites followed the same playbook used by Dorothy Martin's adherents when the flying saucers first failed to appear. Some followers left, but those who remained doubled down and began, for the first time, to proselytize. The camp meetings continued, but the doubt sown after the Spring Disappointment, as it became known, while reducing membership, simultaneously provided an opening for more zealous elements. The fanatical Starkweather took many of his adherents with him after Himes ejected him from the Chardon Street congregation. Another fanatic, Calvin French, taught that not only could believers avoid hellfire, but they could also achieve perfection, a state that condoned and blessed anything they did. Such sanctioned activities conveniently included carnal knowledge of "spiritual wives" outside the bounds of marriage, a privilege often enjoyed by end-times leaders in all eras, which Starkweather also enthusiastically claimed.

The volatile mix of disappointment and fanaticism exploded in a camp meeting held in Exeter, New Hampshire, in August 1844. In the midst of a dull party-line speech by Joseph Bates, one of Miller's lieutenants, a woman interrupted: One Samuel Snow, a previously unknown figure, had urgent news.

Snow told the crowd that he had performed an exhaustive survey of both the Old and New Testaments and had made an amazing discovery: there was a one-for-one concordance between four Judean sacred days and four Christian ones. Three of the Christian ones had already been celebrated that year, but the fourth, which corresponded to Yom Kippur, the Jewish Day of Atonement, had not. That observance, the holiest one in the Jewish religion, occurred on the tenth day of the seventh month of the Jewish calendar, Tishri.

Snow disagreed with that date, which in 1844 put Yom Kippur on September 23. He felt it more accurate to use the ancient Kairate calendar, which ran a month later than the rabbinical one; accordingly, the End would come on October 22. (Even with such "precision," there was still a bit of uncertainty. Because in that era the appearance of the new moon in Jerusalem was thousands of miles away and thus unobservable from the New World, at least a few disciples thought that the actual date might fall as late as October 24.)[54]

Snow's message electrified the camp and bowled over even the inter-rupted Bates, who wrote:

> It worked like leaven throughout the whole camp. And when that meeting closed, the granite hills of New Hampshire were ringing with the mighty cry, "Behold the bridegroom cometh; go ye out to meet him." As the loaded wagons, stages, and railroad cars, rolled away through the different States, cities and villages of New England, the cry was still resounding, "Behold the bridegroom cometh!" Christ, our blessed Lord, is coming on the tenth day of the seventh month! Get ready! Get Ready![55]

The "bridegroom" reference again pointed to Matthew 25. Imitating Himes, Snow founded a new newspaper entitled *The True Midnight Cry*. Snow's calculation wasn't original; Miller himself had earlier toyed with the "tenth day of the seventh month" formulation. During the summer of 1844, the beleaguered Millerites, fevered with cognitive dissonance and confirma-tion bias, seized upon Snow's formulation, which was soon seconded by the fiery George Storrs.

Both Snow and Storrs were hardy individualists: Snow began as a self-described "infidel" who had written for the *Boston Investigator*, an avowedly atheist newspaper; like many nonbelievers of the period, he converted to Adventism upon reading Miller's works. Storrs, on the other hand, had started out as a Methodist, and on one occasion had been ar-rested and dragged on his knees from a church to prevent the abolitionist sermon he had been invited there to give.

One by one, like the more susceptible of Solomon Asch's line-test subjects, the senior Adventist hierarchy signed on to the "tenth day of the seventh month," October 22 in the then current calendar. In late September, Nathan Southard, the editor of *The Midnight Cry!*, put the movement's flagship publication on record in favor of the October 22 date. Himes, ever the pragmatic organizer, detected his troops' change of heart and reminded Miller of his previous flirtation with the tenth day/seventh month concept;

both committed themselves to the October 22 date on October 6. The End was now just a fortnight away.[56]

Wrote Miller in *The Midnight Cry!*,

> I see a glory in the seventh month which I never saw before. Although the Lord had shown me the typical bearing of the seventh month, one year and a half ago, yet I did not realize the force of the types [concordance of holy days between New and Old Testaments]. Now, blessed be the name of the Lord, I see a beauty, a harmony, and an agreement in the Scriptures, for which I have long prayed, but did not see until to-day.—Thank the Lord, O my soul. Let Brother Snow, Brother Storrs and others be blessed for their instrumentality in opening my eyes. I am almost home. Glory! Glory!! Glory!!![57]

The faithful, by and large, accepted Snow's math; the most skeptical of the old guard, Josiah Litch, fell into apocalyptic lockstep on October 12:

> My difficulties have all vanished, and I now rejoice in the glorious light which shines forth from the word of God from the types of the Old Testament. . . . I feel myself humbled under his mighty hand, and now lift up my head in joyful expectation of seeing the King of kings within ten days.[58]

The Howard Street tabernacle filled to overflowing, and *The Midnight Cry!*'s and *Advent Herald*'s state-of-the-art steam-powered presses ran round the clock in a frenzied effort to save as many souls as possible from hellfire before Jesus shuttered the window of salvation.

By now, the faithful had become acutely aware that the rest of the world considered them mad, and so faced a fearful choice: either continue their ordinary activities and business and be labeled hypocrites, or cease them altogether and be damned as fanatics. The leadership, ever conscious of the movement's public image, counseled the former course: Believers were to live their normal lives until the End.

The last edition of *The Midnight Cry!* before the foretold End was published on October 19 and contained heartfelt expressions of faith. Perhaps the most impressive came from one William Nicholass, who had just looked in on his fellow Adventist neighbor, one Mrs. Baxter:

This is the *twenty-ninth day* since she has eaten anything, and yet she is in apparently good health, looking well, and the neighbors say that her strength has lately been increased. She says that she is not sick, but in good health. Yesterday as well as this morning, she was out of doors.[59]

Miller, a modest man, estimated that 50,000 believed in the 1844 Advent, while others put the number at a million out of the total U.S. population of twenty million; the respected American Antiquarian Society pegged the movement at between 150,000 and 200,000 adherents.[60] On October 22, most of them met the anticipated End with calm certitude, gathered quietly with their families in their homes and churches, and said goodbye to those they knew would not avoid hellfire. Himes traveled from Boston to Low Hampton to be with Miller to greet the Savior.

Miller and Himes had exhorted their followers to go about their ordinary activities based on the biblical injunction "Occupy till I come" (Luke 19:13). Despite this advice, many did not sow crops in the spring of 1844, or if they did, failed to harvest them as an expression of faith. Others closed their businesses, sounded public alarms, and absented their children from school. Some took things yet further and gave away the contents of their shops and bakeries and, in more than a few cases, most of their money and worldly possessions.[61] Adventist papers reported camp meetings at which scores confessed their sins and bank notes littered pulpits as the faithful attempted unsuccessfully to give their money away. Believers forgave thousands of dollars of debts owed them, the New York legislature excused one member so that he could prepare for the end of the world, and in Rochester a woman confessed to a murder she had committed years before in England and asked to be returned there for trial.[62] According to one comprehensive nineteenth-century history of Philadelphia,

> The Millerite Church was on Julianna Street, between Wood and Callowhill, and there his followers met, night and day, and watched the stars and sun, and prayed and warned the unrepentant that the "day of judgment was at hand." Many of them began to sell their lands and their houses at prices which were merely nominal. Others gave away their personal effects, shut up their business, or vacated their

houses. On a store on Fifth Street, above Chestnut, was a placard, which read thus: "This shop is closed in honor of the King of kings, who will appear about the 20th of October. Get ready friends, to crown Him Lord of all!"[63]

Mainstream Millerites, who approached October 22 calmly, viewed with alarm the fanaticism engendered in some by their end-times theology:

> Deluded ones withdrew entirely and set up for themselves holding meetings, as the time drew near in a private dwelling in the neighbor-hood night and day, and all night long, neglecting almost wholly their temporal affairs, and in some, leaving their little children to take care of themselves, or to be cared for by others less infatuated than their natural guardians.[64]

The effects on believers understate the overall societal effect of the scheduled Advent, since for every confirmed Millerite there were surely several unbelievers who, as October 22 approached, wondered if, whenever the wind picked up or the sky darkened, they shouldn't have hedged their bets. In Ithaca, New York, a man awakened by shouts of "fire!" investigated and found an Adventist meeting hall to be the source of the conflagration and expressed relief that "the Temple of the Millerites was in flames, instead of the world."[65]

Well after the fact, in the early 1920s, a privately tutored Yankee blueblood named Clara Endicott Sears took an interest in Millerism and solicited firsthand accounts of the episode via newspaper advertisements. She collected about 160 of them in a book entitled *Days of Delusion*, which greatly influenced the modern impression of the Millerite madness, although historians have concluded that many, if not most, of the tales, filtered over eight decades via parents, grandparents, aunts, and uncles, were probably either embellished or patently untrue.

Still, several themes ran consistently through the accounts she received: Many Millerites waited on hilltops, and lesser numbers in graveyards. Many of Sears's anecdotes do carry the ring of truth: One of her elderly correspondents, who had been a small girl in 1844, remembered asking the assistance of a neighbor girl, the daughter of Millerite parents, for help with cooking. Her parents told her that she was preparing her soul for the ascension, to which the little visitor responded, "Can she come over the week after if this doesn't happen?" She later recalled, "Young as I was, I never forgot the horrified look that came over her face, or the tears that filled her large blue eyes."

Another Sears anecdote has an ardent Millerite declaiming the End to Unitarian minister Theodore Parker and poet Ralph Waldo Emerson, to whom Parker replied, "It does not concern *me*, because I live in Boston," and Emerson said, "The end of the world does not affect me; I can get along without it."[66]

The best-remembered stories from Sears describe the Millerites waiting in white "ascension robes" or breaking necks and limbs by launching themselves out of trees, on one occasion with homemade wings. While plausible, such reports were most likely the result of anti-Adventist propaganda.

Critics also charged that Millerism packed the asylums with lunatics, but this was also likely mythical: religious thought frequently tinges schizophrenia, a common disorder, and New England asylum records mentioned Millerism in only a few cases.[67] Moreover, the relatives of a Millerite who had given away all his worldly goods might understandably attempt to get him committed. When a believer named J. D. Poor sold his possessions in order to pay for a trip from Boston to the West in 1843 to proselytize and distribute literature, he was lured to the house of one of his brothers, who attempted to pack him off to an asylum, but he was rescued by his Adventist traveling companion.[68]

The October Disappointment, with its hard target of October 22, knocked the wind out of the faithful more forcefully than the one in the spring, with its squishy arrival date. Their collective despair was overpowering. According to Miller, "It seemed as though all of the demons from the bottomless pit were let loose upon us."[69] One movement elder, Louis Boutelle, observed,

> The 22nd of October passed, making unspeakably sad the faithful
> and longing ones; but causing the unbelieving and wicked to rejoice.
> All was still. No *Advent Herald*; no meetings as formerly. Every one
> felt lonely, with hardly a desire to speak to any one. Still in the cold
> world! No deliverance—the Lord not come! No words can express the
> feelings of disappointment of a true Adventist then. Only those who

experienced it can enter into the subject as it was. It was a humiliating thing, and we all felt it alike. All were silent, save to inquire, "Where are we?" and "What next?"[70]

Piled atop the salvation's failure was widespread scorn. Given that many of the Adventists were followers of the abolitionist William Lloyd Garrison, his description of them as suffering from "a deplorable fantasy of the brain, now plainly demonstrated to be such" must have particularly stung. (Garrison had his own ax to grind, since he saw the Millerites as draining personnel and resources away from his own movement.)[71]

Believers suffered indignities great and small, from the taunts of small boys, "Have you not gone up yet?" to serious accusations of fraud against Himes, whose apparently prosperous periodicals presented an inviting target; one Boston newspaper advised him to avoid appearing on the street.

Of these charges Himes was innocent. He offered fourfold repayment for any evidence of demonstrable fraud (none was produced); found witnesses who recanted falsely quoted statements as to his malfeasance; and had his banks testify as to his modest holdings.[72] Himes then vigorously organized financial relief for those who had neglected their personal and financial affairs for the Second Coming. In the immediate aftermath of the Great Disappointment, violent mobs ransacked and burned down tabernacles and broke into meetings and brandished firearms. Miller himself would suffer the ultimate indignity when, on January 29, 1845, the Low Hampton Baptist Church disfellowshipped him.

As with Dorothy Martin's adherents, Adventists responded to the massive cognitive dissonance in widely varying ways. Snow followed the same path as Ms. Martin and her most loyal followers by doubling down and holding fast to the imminence of the End. Snow's mentor, George Storrs, did the opposite and disavowed his prior belief in an imminent Apocalypse.

Others fudged in one of two ways. The first, and eventually the most important, were the "spiritualizers," led by a Millerite from upstate New York named Hiram Edson, who asserted that Christ *had* acted on October 22, but in bookkeeping mode, rather than in apocalyptic mode. Instead of returning to Earth, he had entered the "Holy of Holies" to laboriously divide humanity into the naughty and the nice. Eventually, he would finish his list, and only then return to the world to wreak final judgment.

The second cognitive dissonance coping strategy for October 22's disappointment was that of the "door shutters," who postulated that Jesus had not returned, but had on that date shut the door of Rapture on those who had not seen the light, and would save only the Elect—that is, themselves. And, as often with Elects, their perfection endowed them with various sexual privileges, from "promiscuous feet washing" to "holy kissing" to the ultimate carnal reward of spiritual wifery.[73]

Miller, as he often did, took a nuanced, poorly defined course, hemming, hawing, and finally laying blame on the inaccuracy of the available historical data; the End would certainly come soon, but because of the uncertainty of the calculation, it might be as long as several years away.

By this point an exhausted, sick, and broken man, he lingered for five years before dying, and the energetic and brilliantly competent Joshua Himes attempted to bind the movement together. His previous commitment to October 22 was more pragmatic than theological, and he quickly backpedaled from it. He disavowed any further date setting and tried to suppress the spiritualizers and door shutters, the latter of whom he despised. This outraged door shutters like Snow, who condemned both Miller and Himes to hell for their apostasy.[74]

Himes could not help but fail; Millerite congregations withered, newspaper subscriptions fell off drastically, and the movement splintered beyond repair. Snow's orthodox faction quickly disappeared; the mainstream one, represented by Himes and Miller, admitted their forecasting error but continued to believe in an imminent Second Coming. Himes, for his part, drifted away from the movement and eventually returned to his childhood Episcopalianism.

Like the sixteenth-century Anabaptists, a small faction of the spiritualizers survived and evolved into a peaceable modern sect, in their case, today's Seventh-day Adventists, a mild-mannered modern mainstream group that is socially conservative, encourages vegetarianism, and observes strict Sabbath prohibitions. While preaching the imminence of the Second Coming, the sect understandably abstains from settling on a precise date.[75]

But the embers of delusional Adventist apocalypticism never completely burned out. A century and a half after the Great Disappointment, a tiny breakaway sect of Seventh-day Adventists, David Koresh's Branch Davidians, would trigger one of the most tragic episodes in American religious history.

Date setting, as Leon Festinger described, produces an inherently unstable dynamic. The more precise the prediction, the more compelling it becomes. With the first few no-shows, the resultant cognitive dissonance encourages believers to proclaim their faith and proselytize with increasing vigor and precision, which attracts yet more adherents. Finally, there comes a prediction so bold and precise that its failure becomes blindingly obvious and shakes out most followers, leaving only a small die-hard remnant. Festinger's findings explain the Millerite episode in a way that describes true belief of all stripes, not just religious, but also political and cultural:

> Although there is a limit beyond which belief will not withstand disconfirmation, it is clear that the introduction of contrary evidence can serve to increase the conviction and enthusiasm of the believer.[76]

Never again would a mainstream Christian sect make the date-setting mistake. As put by religious historian Ernest Sandeen,

> The Millerite movement appears to have virtually destroyed premillennialism in America for a generation. . . . But in concentrating on the year 1843, Miller had also introduced an element that would destroy the movement. . . . Miller's success before 1844 is matched only by the difficulties he created for anyone brave enough to attempt to preach a millenarian message after 1844. It took a long time for Americans to forget William Miller.[77]

Yet the urge to transmute the Bible's ambiguity into exact prophecy remains irresistible to some. In the twentieth century, Miller's theological heirs learned to be coy about the *when* of the end-times, but they would prove embarrassingly overeager about its *how*; just as Miller and his followers could not resist divining an exact date from the Bible, his modern followers found irresistible the extrapolation of the day's newspaper headlines into seemingly plausible end-times narrative arcs that inevitably failed to play out. As with Dorothy Martin's flying saucers, each disconfirmation generated yet more proselytization and increasingly outlandish narratives.

Alarmingly, these narratives would exert great influence among those in control of the world's doomsday machinery.

6

WINSTON CHURCHILL'S
EXCELLENT ADVENTURE IN
MONETARY POLICY

All people are most credulous when they are most happy; and when much money has just been made, when some people are really making it, when most people think they are making it, there is a happy opportunity for ingenious mendacity. Almost everything will be believed for a little while.

—Walter Bagehot[1]

In the early autumn of 1929, Winston Churchill conducted a leisurely private railcar tour of Canada. He arrived in New York on October 24, 1929, Black Thursday, the first calamitous stock market drop of many that fall, where he observed, "Under my window, a gentleman cast himself down fifteen stories and was dashed to pieces, causing a wild commotion and the arrival of the fire brigade." The next day, a total stranger invited Churchill into the visitor's gallery of the New York Stock Exchange, where he noted the following:

> I expected to see pandemonium; but the spectacle that met my eyes was one of surprising calm and orderliness. [The brokers] are precluded by the strongest rules from running or raising their voices unduly. So there they were, walking to and fro like a slow-motion picture of a disturbed ant heap, offering each other enormous blocks of securities at a third of their old prices and half their present value, and for many minutes together finding no one strong enough to pick up the sure fortunes they were compelled to offer.[2]

He sailed for home shortly thereafter, oblivious to the connection between his financial ineptitude four years before and the momentous events that had just unfolded before his eyes. The crash, though, did catch Churchill's eye in one regard. It devastated his speculative investment portfolio and plunged him into debt. His personal misfortune carried a silver lining for posterity: In order to repay his creditors, he fell back on his most reliable meal ticket, his pen. Over the ensuing decade he produced some of his finest books as well as many articles and even a screenplay.

To call Churchill's political career before 1929 "checkered" would be an understatement. As first lord of the Admiralty during the First World War, he had vigorously supported the disastrous Gallipoli invasion, which resulted in thousands of casualties and his demotion. A decade later Prime Minister Stanley Baldwin, unaware of Churchill's financial incompetence, appointed him chancellor of the exchequer, the British equivalent of Treasury secretary. (Churchill described his interactions with his exchequer mavens thusly: "If they were soldiers or generals, I would understand what they were talking about. As it is they all talk Persian.")[3]

One name, Hyman Minsky, comes up most often when economists discuss financial bubbles. Minsky cut a curious figure in the economics profession from the 1950s to the 1980s—a long-haired iconoclast who believed that capitalism was fundamentally unstable: a modern, more grounded version of Karl Marx. Better than any other twentieth-century observer, he understood and described the pathophysiology of bubbles and busts which, he thought, required two necessary conditions: the easing of credit wrought by falling interest rates and the advent of exciting new technologies.

First, interest rates. Before the First World War, pound sterling notes were freely convertible into gold sovereign coins at £4.86 per ounce, and note holders had confidence that there was plenty of bullion on hand to meet any demand for it. Because the pound seemed solid, relatively few took advantage of this convertibility; of what use, after all, was a hunk of yellow metal? But England had run the printing presses to pay for its war effort, and the ballooning number of notes eroded this faith with a downward spiral in which the holders of paper currency became ever more likely to exchange it for gold.

Since following the war not nearly enough gold existed in Britain to cover paper currency, England had to suspend convertibility, lest the holders of the devalued notes drain away the nation's bullion reserves. In 1925, Churchill disastrously resumed convertibility by returning the pound to the gold standard at the old £4.86 rate. The now overvalued pound made British goods more expensive and thereby decreased exports; in addition, the artificially high exchange rate also made foreign goods cheaper, thereby encouraging imports; by 1926, England saw its gold reserves fall by an alarming £80 million, 10 percent of its total amount.[4]

Ever since the birth of the United States, high American and British government officials have developed close personal friendships, and at this juncture one such relationship proved particularly unlucky: that between the world's two most important central bankers, Federal Reserve Chairman Benjamin Strong and Bank of England Governor Montagu Norman.

The surest way to boost the value of the pound and to staunch the gold outflow was to lower American interest rates, which made sterling-denominated assets relatively more attractive. Strong did so in 1927 and thus bailed Norman out of his difficulties, but only temporarily. Lower interest rates in the United States, already in the midst of a vigorous economic boom, set alight a speculative fever that broke just as Churchill, nearing the end of his North American tour, alighted in New York.

By 1929, the developed world had grown used to periodic financial upheavals. Casual observers and historians alike often refer to these booms and busts as illnesses, and the medical model indeed provides a window into both the patient and the disease, whether for persons or societal events.

Physicians understand illness through three fundamental lenses: pathophysiology, the underlying biochemistry and physiology of the disease process; anatomy, the parts of the body affected; and the symptoms and signs, what the patient feels and what the doctor sees at the bedside.

We can understand bubbles and crashes in the same way. For example, their pathophysiology involves the vagaries of human psychology and the unstable supply of credit from a modern banking system. Their anatomy consists of the "four *ps*": promoters, public, politicians, and press. Finally, their signs and symptoms include the contagious societal infatuation with nearly effortless wealth, the hubris of the promoters, and their veneration by the public.[5]

Recall that Hyman Minsky theorized that the blowing of a bubble required not only the sort of credit easing produced by Benjamin Strong's 1927 lowering of interest rates, but also an exciting new advance in technology. Such a technological advance could be in the sciences or in engineering, such as the railroad in the nineteenth century; or in finance, such as the joint-stock company in the seventeenth and eighteenth centuries.[6] Investors, excited about new technologies or financial products, begin to pour money into them, be they stocks, real estate, or some other instrument. Since these assets can also be used as collateral for loans, rising prices mean that speculators can borrow yet more to pour into these assets, thus raising prices even further and enabling them to borrow even more—a self-reinforcing "virtuous cycle," but only on the way up. It's thus no accident that manias, panics, and crashes became a permanent and recurring part of Western life around 1600 precisely because both "displacement" and elastic paper-based credit first appeared around that time.

Today, technological displacement can take many forms. The dizzying pace of scientific advance seems a permanent feature of modern life: a mere twenty years ago, people would have blinked in disbelief at being told that worldwide personal video communication would become ubiquitous and nearly free. As recently as the 1940s, common bacterial diseases such as cholera, typhoid, bacterial pneumonia, and meningitis routinely struck down people in their prime, with no respect for wealth or social class. In developed nations, these scourges became vanishingly rare events after the advent of antibiotics such as penicillin.

By contrast, before 1600, the lack of progress was not just accepted, but assumed. Until the advent of the printing press, many a technological advance was lost simply because the manual reproduction of its documentation was so laborious and expensive that not enough copies survived down the generations. Furthermore, the rarity of literacy meant that artisans often failed to record their techniques, which consequently disappeared with them. The Romans, for example, invented concrete, but its use effectively died with the Empire; not until 1756 did John Smeaton rediscover the secret of Portland cement.

Gutenberg's invention of mass-produced moveable type around 1450 removed this particular roadblock to technological advance, but others remained; per-capita GDP hardly grew at all before 1600 in the West, and not until much later in the East.

In 1620, philosopher Francis Bacon published his *Novum Organum Scientiarium* ("new instrument of science"; in English, *The New Organon*). Before Bacon, "natural philosophers," as scientists were then called, developed their models via the Aristotelian, "deductive" method that proceeded from axioms—unquestioned principles that formed the basis of all further reasoning. In this system, observable facts were almost an afterthought.

The New Organon was itself a form of displacement, and its genius was twofold. First, it recognized that the old Aristotelian system of deductive reasoning stifled human progress; and second, it proposed a viable alternative: an "inductive" process that meticulously gathered empirical data, which could then be matched against theory—the essence of the modern scientific method. Within a few generations, Bacon's intellectual children—Hooke, Boyle, and Newton, to name but a few—established the Royal Society for the Promotion of Natural Knowledge (now known simply as the Royal Society). This spawned similar groups throughout Europe, and with them followed a prodigious acceleration of scientific discovery.[7]

The seventeenth century midwifed not only the scientific method, but also a second societal revolution: the appearance of elastic currency. Most Americans labor under the misconception that money consists of green pieces of paper decreed by the government to be "legal tender for all debts, public and private," or, in years past, stamped round disks of gold and silver. But in the ancient world, almost anything could be money: a fixed measure of wheat, oil, or, as time passed, silver. Only in the middle of the seventh century B.C. did the Lydians in Asia Minor stamp out the first coins made of electrum, a mixture of gold and silver.

Today, we live in a very different world. In the United States, only one-tenth of money consists of circulating notes and coins; keystroke entries in government and bank computers create the rest of it. For example, a bank doesn't issue a mortgage in the form of a gym bag filled with green linen with pictures of Alexander Hamilton, Ben Franklin, and assorted dead presidents; rather, it sends a packet of electrons to the title company. And those checks and electrons are most certainly not backed by a corresponding amount of notes and coins, let alone gold, silver, or cattle.

This credit system is today known as "fractional reserve banking" and has become ever more elastic in the centuries following its creation by seventeenth-century goldsmiths. If early banks issued certificates much above a reserve ratio of 2:1, they risked a run by depositors demanding their money back. With the development of banking consortiums and government-run central banks, this ratio grew to around 10:1 for commercial banks, and much higher, on occasion, for investment banks. How high the reserve ratio climbs depends upon how much consumers and investors want to borrow, how willing banks are to lend, and, with increasing frequency, how much leverage government regulators will allow.[8] A rubber band provides an apt metaphor for the stretching of the reserve ratio: enshrined in the 1913 legislation that established the Federal Reserve Bank is the mandate to "Furnish an Elastic Currency."[9]

The housing market of the early 2000s provides a perfect example of Hyman Minsky's paradigm. Before 2000, the housing market was reasonably sedate, stable, and dull. Banks extended mortgages to only the safest borrowers: those with superb credit histories, steady incomes, and little other debt, and who needed to borrow much less than the market value of their homes. Consequently, they almost always paid off these mortgages on schedule, default rates were low, and the banks made a modest profit.

Bank managers began to notice, however, that competing institutions with looser loan requirements serviced more borrowers and thus made more money; eventually, nearly everyone followed suit. Around the same time, another phenomenon gained steam: Banks began to sell their mortgages to Wall Street firms that assembled them into increasingly dodgy packages such as collateralized debt obligations (CDOs). This so-called securitization of the loans transferred the risk of homeowner mortgage default from the originating banks, which were in a good position to know the initial borrowers, to gullible institutions and governments around the world, who did not know them from Adam.

This corrosion of lending standards spread throughout the banking system, and defaults began to creep up. At first, the value of the underlying collateral, in this case, the homes, rose, and the banks and holders of the mortgage securities sustained few net losses, since defaulting properties could be seized and resold at a profit. Beginning around 2007, the increasing forced sales of homes depressed their prices, and the banks and securities holders started to lose money; eventually some went bankrupt and/or got federal bailouts. In the end, everyone tightened lending standards. This shutoff in lending from banks further decreased house prices and forced homeowners to walk away from their mortgages.

This sequence played out not just in the United States but globally. For the first five years of the housing bubble, roughly 2002–2007, the major mortgage qualification seemed to be possession of a pulse; after the collapse, banks counted a loan applicant's gold fillings. Similarly, consumers, investors, and prospective homeowners became much more interested in paying down debt than in acquiring it, so the supply of credit, and with it the money supply, fell.

Minsky, who died in 1996, had taught that this cycle is the inevitable result of an elastic currency in which banks, both the government central one (the Federal Reserve) and private ones, can expand and contract the supply of money. Further, he understood that this monetary expansion and contraction occurs in just about all areas of the market economy, not just in housing, but in corporate management and in the stock and bond markets as well.

Minsky's famous "instability hypothesis" states that in a safe and stable financial environment, money inevitably migrates away from safe borrowers and toward increasingly risky ones. Eventually, things get out of hand, resulting in a blowup of the sort described above, which makes lenders and investors more prudent, and the cycle begins anew, a process that seems to play out, very roughly, once per decade. In short, stability begets instability, and instability begets stability, with lenders periodically cycling the economic system through fear and greed.[10] Of course, without intermittently greedy borrowers, greedy lenders would lack customers.

Minsky must have intuitively understood that two more conditions, in addition to "displacement" and credit easing, had to be met, though he didn't explicitly spell them out: amnesia for the previous boom and bust, and the abandonment of customary and prudent objective methods of valuing investments.

Amnesia is implicit in the instability hypothesis. In the aftermath of a financial crisis, with the memory of painful losses still fresh, bankers and investors shy away from risk; the former will make only the safest of loans, while the latter are loath to purchase stock shares. As markets slowly recover and the unpleasant memories fade, participants become more open to risk and the instability cycle begins anew.

The abandonment of hardheaded financial calculations in favor of compelling narratives is the last factor that precipitates financial manias. When human beings are confronted with difficult or impossible analytical tasks, such as valuing a company that has never produced a profit, let alone a dividend, they default back to simpler methods of analysis; psychologists apply the term "heuristics" to such mental shortcuts.

Over the past several decades, psychologists have expanded our understanding of how humans apply heuristics when confronted with challenging or impossible problems; this work is directly applicable to finance, and particularly to understanding manias. In the 1940s, a Hungarian-born psychologist named George Katona began to study the intersection of economics and the human mind at the University of Michigan, where he pioneered psychological measurements relating to the economy. Among other accomplishments, he developed the now widely used Index of Consumer Sentiment, and the university became a hotbed of psychological research.

Another area pioneered at the University of Michigan was research into decision-making, which caught the attention of a particularly brilliant Israeli researcher named Amos Tversky.[11] (His acquaintances liked to joke about the Tversky Intelligence Test: "The faster you realized that Tversky was smarter than you were, the smarter you were.")[12] The Michigan researchers had assumed, as do many economists even today, that humans were skilled intuitive statisticians; that just as we effortlessly acquire the rules of grammar and syntax, so do we also for statistics and probability.

Initially, this seemed reasonable to Tversky, but when he debated the question with a fellow academician at the Hebrew University of Jerusalem, Daniel Kahneman, he found himself persuaded otherwise. Around 1970, the two embarked on a remarkable series of experiments that revolutionized the way both economists and psychologists regard decision-making. It turned out, not only human beings in general had lousy statistical intuition, but so did even their fellow psychologists, who should have mastered it.[13] In a classic study, they presented subjects with the following vignette:

Steve is very shy and withdrawn, invariably helpful, but with little
interest in people, or in the world of reality. A meek and tidy soul, he
has a need for order and structure, and a passion for detail.

Kahneman and Tversky then asked subjects if Steve was most likely a
farmer, salesman, airline pilot, librarian, or physician. Most people chose
librarian, since the above description best fits the librarian stereotype.
Nevertheless, farmers outnumber librarians by a factor of twenty, and
since there are plenty of shy farmers, Steve is more likely to be one of
them than he is to be a librarian.[14]

The two proceeded to uncover a wide range of systematic analytic
errors made by even the smartest people: the blindness to baseline frequencies (not recognizing, for example, that there are far more farmers than
librarians), not realizing that large samples are more reliable than small
ones, underestimating how easily humans perceive nonexistent patterns
in random data, and not grasping that particularly good or bad task performance usually reverts toward normal on successive attempts, to name
but a few.* The two came away from their work deeply disappointed with
the sad state of human rationality:

What is perhaps surprising is the failure of people to infer from
lifelong experience such fundamental statistical rules as regression toward the mean, or the effect of sample size on sampling
variability. Although everyone is exposed, in the normal course of
life, to numerous examples from which these rules could have been
induced, very few people discover the principles of sampling and
regression on their own.[15]

Their exercises revealed that humans are by nature cognitively lazy. Rather
than stop to rigorously analyze which of the five listed professions Shy

---

* A classic example of the phenomenon of "reversion to the mean" is provided by Daniel
Kahneman's experience with Israeli flight instructors who mistakenly believed that praise/
scolding for good/bad performance was effective, when in fact relative performance was
mostly due to chance. Thus, the instructor's yelling had nothing to do with the "improvement" in the pilot's prior performance, which was merely randomly poor and had subsequently "reverted to the mean." See Daniel Kahneman, *Thinking Fast and Slow*, 175.

Steve was most likely to practice, it's far easier to default back to the following shortcut: Steve fits the stereotype of a librarian—end of story.[16]

The relevance of Kahneman and Tversky's findings to financial bubbles is obvious. Rather than attempt the nearly impossible estimation of the value of a stock with high projected future earnings—the South Sea Company in 1720, RCA in 1928, Pets.com in 1999, or Tesla today—investors default back to this simple heuristic: "South Sea/RCA/Pets.com/Tesla is a great company that's going to change the world, and it's worth paying almost any price for it."

Kahneman, Tversky, and other researchers also found that one of the most powerful heuristics is the human susceptibility to salience, our overemphasis of dramatic events. As an extreme example, a defining U.S. event of the past half century, the 9/11 attacks, killed nearly three thousand individuals. Even the death of a single individual in a terrorist attack will make headlines, yet individual deaths as a result of ordinary gun violence, opioids, or car accidents pass largely unnoticed in the media, despite the fact that more than thirty thousand lives are lost in each of these three categories annually in the United States.[17] An American is far less likely to die from a terrorist attack than from a lightning strike, yet the United States devotes far more resources to antiterrorism efforts than to preventing the hundred thousand or so total deaths from guns, cars, and narcotics. (In a similar vein, any tourist who contemplates a visit to Israel is likely to be asked by a friend or family member if she isn't worried about terrorism, despite the fact that since 2005 the average Israeli is roughly twenty times more likely to die in a road accident.)[18]

Kahneman and Tversky refer to the above salience fallacies as the "availability heuristic." Salience has another dimension, which is temporal; you're more likely to buy insurance for an earthquake or flood immediately following one. Naturally enough, they refer to this as the "recency heuristic."

Humans, in short, are prisoners of salience, and this applies to financial manias in several different ways. The dramatic novelty of a new technology, such as the ability to fly around the planet at hundreds of miles per hour or to instantaneously bring entertainment or current world events into the home, is salient in the extreme—until the novelty wears off.

The recency heuristic also distorts investors' perception of long-term reality: If stock prices have been rising for the past several years, they will come to believe that equity levels will continue to do so forever; as prices climb, shares become more attractive, which drives prices up even more. This becomes a self-perpetuating "virtuous cycle" that can drive stocks into the stratosphere. The reverse, of course, happens during long bear markets.

Like most economists, Minsky didn't bother much with psychology, but he clearly understood the all-too-human preference for narratives over quantitative reasoning. We all like a good story; in the grip of a bubble, when faced with an unpleasant or difficult calculation, a compelling narrative provides easy escape from the eye-crossing effort of rigorous analysis. It's not too much of an oversimplification to consider the narratives as the pathogen that spreads the bubble disease throughout a society.

Understanding how bubbles pop requires extending the elastic money metaphor only a bit. Imagine a rubber band an inch in diameter and several hundred feet long. Around the rubber band cluster hundreds of observers, most of whom are just milling about. Several dozen of them, though, are engaged in stretching it out. Further imagine that the rubber band's increasing length imparts wealth to the pullers; as it gets longer, it attracts more idle crowd members. Their more naïve members believe that the rubber band will be stretched out forever, but a large number know that sooner or later it will contract violently. The latter group is programmed to let go at the first sign of contraction and is confident that they will know when to do so; that is, they are primed to release it.

Eventually, a few let go, which increases the strain on those remaining. Then, those primed to let go do so in a rush, and soon enough, the band snaps back not just to its natural length, but curls into a tight coil. Eventually, a few smart observers find it easy to lengthen the crumpled coil out again, and the cycle begins anew.

By the 1920s, all four of Hyman Minsky's conditions were well established.

After the First World War, five technological advances rocked peoples' lives. The internal combustion engine, invented in the late nineteenth century, came first, and facilitated two more: the Wright brothers' invention of heavier-than-air flight and the spread of the motorcar, which freed people to travel long distances at will. By 1925, more than one-third of American families owned an automobile.[19]

The fourth was radio. In 1895, Guglielmo Marconi transmitted a Morse code letter *s* over a few kilometers of Italian countryside, but for the succeeding two decades the expensive new technology was reserved for the private transmission of sensitive and valuable information, and even in the United States, radio was reserved primarily for one domain: maritime communication, since the telegraph proved far more reliable and less expensive over land, as well as between continents via undersea cables.

In 1915, a Marconi employee named David Sarnoff wrote the famous "Radio Music Box Memo," which proposed opening the medium up to the public "to bring music into the house by wireless." It took some doing for Sarnoff to get Marconi to throw open to the public his profitable private medium, but in 1919, Marconi and General Electric incorporated Radio Corporation of America (RCA), and by 1920, the first two radio stations, KDKA in Pittsburgh and WWJ in Detroit, began operations. For the first time in history, concerts, sporting events, and breaking news could be broadcast live; without question, radio ranked with the invention and spread of the telegraph and the internet in the way that it transformed everyday life.

Bringing the news, George Burns and Gracie Allen, or the 1921 heavyweight championship fight between Jack Dempsey and Georges Carpentier into the nation's living rooms astounded even more than the arrival of the world wide web in the early 1990s. RCA became the darling of investors, and by the late 1920s, when someone uttered the word "radio," he or she was almost as likely to be referring to the stock's nickname as to the medium or the hardware.

The fifth transformative technology involved the rapid expansion of the electrical utility companies that increasingly lit the nation's homes and powered its factories. Although J. P. Morgan and his colleagues had incorporated General Electric more than a generation before, GE and its competitors needed decades to fully electrify the nation.

All five of these "displacements"—the internal combustion engine, airplane, automobile, radio, and widely available electrical power—stimulated the Roaring Twenties economy, as did Henry Ford's mass-production techniques and the influence of Frederick Winslow Taylor, a mechanical engineer who, beginning in the late nineteenth century, led the "efficiency movement" that turned the stopwatch into a driver of worker productivity and corporate earnings. Between 1922 and 1927, the output of American workers increased by 3.5 percent per year, which delighted company shareholders; the response of company employees was less enthusiastic.[20] Such was his influence that "Taylorism" entered the English vocabulary; ironically, Lenin and Stalin were fans, whereas in the United States, the term was not always a compliment, particularly within the rapidly growing union movement.

The second Minsky criterion during the 1920s was the easing of credit in the United States. Minsky knew that displacements could be financial as well as technological, and the 1920s produced a bumper crop of "advances" in leverage: brokers' loans, investment trusts, and holding companies. All of these provided new and powerful sources of funds that could be borrowed and then deployed to flood the stock market, and which appeared to an increasing number of Americans as nothing so much as a wealth-spewing fountain. As put by economist John Kenneth Galbraith, "The world of finance hails the invention of the wheel over and over again, often in a slightly more unstable form."[21]

Before the twentieth century, the primary form of stock market leverage was the low initial subscription amount for shares, followed by mandatory calls for further capital. Greed-fevered participants assumed they could meet those calls by selling their partially owned but appreciating shares; a lucky few did, most did not, and many were ruined.

The speculators of the 1920s, by contrast, had fully purchased their shares, but with borrowed money, sometimes as much as 90 percent of the shares' value. Consider, for example, the investor who had paid for shares of stock worth $1,000 with $100 of his own money on top of a $900 "brokers' loan." If the shares increased in value by 10 percent, they were now worth $1,100, leaving him with $200 after paying back the loan, thus doubling his original $100 investment. Alas, if the value of the investment fell by 10 percent to $900, the creditor demanded more funds to protect his $900 loan with a "margin call" to the plunger, and if the funds were not forthcoming, the loan's terms allowed the creditor to sell out the position in order to protect his $900 loan. Brokers' loans did not come cheap; as stock prices rose, so did the demand for the loans, which by 1929 had raised their rates to as high as 15 percent annual interest which served to gradually tighten the screws on those who purchased shares with them.

While all but the most optimistic plungers at least dimly perceived the risks of equity speculation, the brokers' loans themselves seemed perfectly safe to the banks, which could access funds from the Federal Reserve at 5 percent and loan out to speculators at double or triple that rate, a simple and spectacularly profitable operation. The primary function of financial capitalism is to efficiently funnel money from those with an excess of it to those who need it. Bubbles distort that flow and so corrode a nation's economy; the 1920s provided a spectacular example of this distortion when not a few large corporations diverted the capital needed to maintain and grow their businesses to the margin-loan market.[22]

The high brokers' loan rates focus a bright light on just how hard it is, even today, for the Federal Reserve to safely puncture an established bubble. In 1929, the Fed could theoretically have staunched the flow of brokers' loans, but since banks and corporations benefited from double-digit loan rates, the Federal Reserve would have had to raise interest rates almost this high, which would have been economically disastrous. Nor would raising the brokers' loan rates themselves, if such a thing could be mandated by the government, have had much effect on the enthusiastic speculators, whose net worth, at least on paper, was giddily increasing at a much higher clip as yesterday's price rise drove tomorrow's in a self-sustaining cycle. The Fed found itself in the position of a skateboard rider barreling out of control down a hill, for whom there are only two options: intentionally crashing into a tree or continuing forward in a deep crouch and crashing later at higher speed. It chose the latter course. (The initial crash in October 1929 did in fact dampen the demand for brokers' loans, whose rate fell to 7 percent.)

During the 1920s, the financial mania also infected the by-then well-established institution of investment trusts. During the late eighteenth century, a Dutch merchant named Abraham van Ketwich created what may have been the first mutual fund, a publicly available collection of shares in businesses from all over Europe and in New World Plantations: Eendragt Maakt Magt (Unity Creates Strength).[23] Over the following century the investment trust concept spread throughout Europe, particularly to Scotland, and in 1893, to the United States with the formation of the Personal Property Trust in Boston. These conservatively run funds generally traded as stocks that could be bought and sold on demand. A few of those created during the 1920s have survived to the present day: General American Investors, Tri-Continental, Adams Express, and Central Securities.

The story of another trust, the Goldman Sachs Trading Corporation, did not end as happily. The brokerage firm that created the Trading Corporation, Goldman, Sachs & Co., did not get into the investment trust business until late in the game when it sponsored the Trading Corporation in December 1928. The Trading Corporation's first steps were timid; it owned all of its stocks and bonds outright—that is, without leverage; further, the parent brokerage firm, Goldman, Sachs & Co., retained ownership of 90 percent of the Trading Corporation's shares, selling only 10 percent of them to the public. In today's terms, the Trading Corporation could be thought of as a simple mutual fund set up by Vanguard or Fidelity, which then owned almost all of the shares.

That conservatism soon fell by the wayside. A few months later, the Trading Corporation was merged with another Goldman creation, the Financial and Industrial Securities Corporation, and so bubbly was the market that, a few days after the February 1929 merger, the newly configured Goldman Sachs Trading Corporation was priced at twice the value of the securities it held; in effect, selling dollar bills to the public for two dollars.

Most companies would have been happy with such a showing, but Goldman then had the Trading Corporation buy up its own shares, which boosted its value yet further. At this point, Goldman, Sachs & Co. began unloading the shares it held in the Trading Corporation to the general public at hugely inflated prices. Next, in rapid succession, the Trading Corporation itself sponsored a new trust, the Shenandoah Corporation, which, piling absurdity upon absurdity, sponsored yet a third trust layer, the Blue Ridge Corporation. As put by Galbraith:

> The virtue of the trust was that it brought about an almost complete divorce of the volume of corporate securities outstanding from the volume of corporate assets in existence. The former could be twice, thrice, or any multiple of the latter.[24]

Within the remarkable Goldman Sachs edifice Shenandoah and Blue Ridge each issued both common and "convertible preference" shares, the latter being essentially the same as a bond, with an obligation to pay 6 percent in interest to its owners. The two trusts had, in effect, written themselves brokers' loans with their convertible preference shares, magnifying the price changes of the common shares according to the "multiple" described by Galbraith.

By ordinary standards, the leverage was not that great: only about one-third of Shenandoah's shares and slightly less than half of Blue Ridge's were the bond-like convertible preference shares. But the multiplication of these two leverages, and of the ownership structure, of which Trading Corporation sat on top, destabilized things disastrously. Shenandoah controlled Blue Ridge, and so got paid only after Blue Ridge's convertible preference owners got their 6 percent interest payments, and the Trading Corporation got paid only after Shenandoah's convertible preference holders got their interest payments, and so the price changes multiplied as they wound their way up the pyramid to the Trading Corporation, which by this point had also taken on its own debt. Shenandoah, for example, paid exactly one paltry dividend to its common shareholders before suspending payment in December 1929 for good.

Goldman had designed its fleet of trusts for calm winds and glassy seas, and as long as prices rose, the sailing was smooth. But almost immediately after the three trusts were formed, the skies turned foul, and the funds sank in reverse order of their creation: Blue Ridge first, then Shenandoah, then finally the Trading Corporation.

The effects of the leveraged structure were devastating. By year-end 1929, for example, the Dow Jones Industrial average had recovered somewhat from the October crash, and had suffered a decline of "only" 35 percent from its September peak. The three trusts, by contrast, fell by around 75 percent. By the low point of the market in mid-1932, the Dow had fallen 89 percent, the trusts by 99 percent. The total losses borne by the public in the three Goldman Sachs trusts alone totaled approximately $300 million. During just August and September of 1929, American corporations issued more than a billion dollars' worth of similar investment trusts, a staggering amount for the era, most of which was lost by 1932.[25] The Great Depression was by this point fully established and would grind on until the Second World War, which functioned as a massive public works project that brought the economy back to life.[26]

* * *

By 1929, the third factor, amnesia for the last bubble, was also solidly established. The preceding generation did see two market declines. The first, the Panic of 1907, was a rather curious affair. Its triggering event was indeed a failed stock speculation, but on a very small scale, a disastrously unsuccessful attempt by two brothers, copper mining magnates named Otto and Augustus Heinze, to execute an arcane maneuver known as a short squeeze of the shares of their company, United Copper.*

Augustus also owned a small Montana bank, the State Savings Bank of Butte, which went under with the failed short squeeze. Andrew Jackson's euthanasia of the Second Bank of the United States in 1837 had left the nation without a "lender of last resort" to supply sorely needed capital when private lending dried up. Banks lend to each other, and the failure of one can spread domino-like; absent a central bank to ride to the rescue, a mild recession can turn into a full-fledged panic and depression. This is precisely what occurred during the financial crisis of the late 1830s, one of the worst in United States history.

In 1907, the failure of Heinze's bank took out ever larger banks and eventually depressed stock prices by about 40 percent, and the panic stopped only when J. P. Morgan "drew a line," above which were banks that were, in his estimation, solvent and thus worthy of support, and below which were banks that were allowed to fail. By historical coincidence, Morgan was born in 1837, the year of the death of the nation's last central bank, and he died in 1913, with the passage of the Federal Reserve Act, which reestablished it. For much of that seventy-six-year lifetime, he effectively was the country's central banker, and on one occasion in 1893, when an economic depression drained the U.S. Treasury's gold reserve, he orchestrated its rescue.

The second market decline before 1929 occurred at the end of the First World War. The conflict had buoyed U.S. stock prices, but this speculation soon gave way to despair as farm prices fell; during the year following the market peak in the summer of 1919, stocks gradually fell

---

* A short seller borrows shares from an existing owner, then sells them to a third person with the expectation that the short seller can later buy them back to repay their lender at a lower price. A short squeeze attempts to profit from the knowledge that the shares will eventually need to be repurchased by the short seller; the squeezer buys up enough of them to inflate their price and so force the short seller to close out his trade at great profit to the squeezer, and great loss to the short seller.

by about one-third, though part of that was ameliorated by the generous dividends that stocks yielded in that period.[27] As market declines went, this was relatively mild.

Before the First World War, only wealthy Americans owned stock shares, so neither the Panic of 1907 nor the market decline of 1919 made much of a lasting impression on the general public. By 1929 a new investing public, attracted by the wonders of the internal combustion engine, aircraft, automobile, radio, and electrical power, thus had no memory of prior bubbles.

The fourth bubble prerequisite was the abandonment of conservative, traditional methods of stock valuation. The United States funded the First World War partly through the issue of billions of dollars of Liberty Bonds, yielding between 3.5 and 4.5 percent, and in the process introduced the average American into the securities markets. Liberty Bonds served as the public's investment "training wheels," and provided a safe and modest rate of return.

Government bonds can be thought of as a baseline, or what financial economists call the "risk-free rate" for safe assets. For centuries, investors bought stocks solely for their dividends, and since they were risky, in order to attract buyers, the dividend yield of stocks had to be higher than those provided by safe government securities. George Hudson, for example, had to promise the buyers of his railways shares dividends far higher than the 3 to 4 percent yields of British government bonds. Like their British counterparts, rational American investors did not require, nor did they expect, to benefit from share price increases, but they did desire to collect a dull but steady dividend flow higher than that offered by safe bonds; before the First World War, U.S. stock yields averaged around 5 percent.[28] By the 1920s, it was generally accepted that stocks should sell for approximately ten times their annual profits, so as to easily cover that payout.

Today, investors, wisely or not, take long-run rises in company profits and share price for granted and so tolerate much lower dividend payouts, but before the twentieth century, sustained share price increases were a rarity, seen only with the most successful companies. Even in the most favorable cases, the price increases were tiny. For example, the two most successful early English joint-stock companies were the Bank of England and the East India Company, and even this cherry-picked pair saw share price appreciation averaging only 0.7 and 0.6 percent per year, respectively, between 1709 and 1823.[29]

How, then, could even the most accomplished investors value RCA, which by the time of the 1929 crash had not yet produced any dividends, and, in the event, would not do so until 1937?[30] By the late 1920s, while investors obviously thought that the company had stellar prospects, they did not have the tools to estimate an appropriate price to pay for the company's expected future profits. Not for another decade would financial economists like Irving Fisher, John Burr Williams, and Benjamin Graham work out the complex mathematics of calculating the intrinsic value of a stock or bond, particularly one with highly speculative future prospects. Even today, this technique, the so-called discounted dividend model, which estimates the value of all future dividends and "discounts" them back to the present, challenges the average investor, and in any case, is of such limited accuracy that even professionals more often than not run afoul of it.[31]

In the bubbling technological environment of the 1920s with the development of radio, automobiles, and airplanes, it was easy for the public to believe that the old rules of security valuation didn't apply anymore. As supposedly put by a great twentieth-century investor, John Templeton, "The four most expensive words in the English language are 'This time it's different.'"*

Writing about that time, Benjamin Graham observed:

> If a public-utility stock was selling at 35 times its *maximum* recorded earnings, instead of the 10 times its *average* earnings, which was the preboom standard, the conclusion to be drawn was not that the stock was now too high but merely that the standard of value had been raised. . . . Hence, all upper limits disappeared, not upon the price at which a stock *could* sell, but even upon the price at which it

---

* This sentence is one of the most repeated in finance, contributing the title, for example, to a classic in international economics, Carmen M. Reinhart and Kenneth S. Rogoff, *This Time Is Different* (Princeton NJ: Princeton University Press, 2009). It is mainly attributed to Templeton, but sometimes to David Dodd, Benjamin Graham's coauthor. I am unable to find a definitive source for this quote.

would *deserve* to sell. . . . An alluring corollary of this principle was
that making money in the stock market was now the easiest thing in
the world.[32]

By 1929, the full panoply of Kahneman and Tversky heuristics, especially the salience of the era's new technologies, the recency of ballooning security prices, and the availability of credit-fueled prosperity, had
overwhelmed the rational analysis of security prices.

The economist Max Winkler put it most simply. Alluding to the
newly described discounted dividend model, Winkler archly observed in
the crash's aftermath that the 1920s stock market discounted not only the
future but the hereafter as well.[33]

7

SUNSHINE CHARLIE
MISSES THE POINT

Just as with the Mississippi Company, South Sea Company, and railway bubbles, the anatomy of the 1929 crash involved the "four *ps*": the promoters, the public, the press, and the politicians.

In the early twentieth century, Samuel Insull inherited the mantle of John Law and George Hudson by creating an industrial goliath; in his case, one that powered the nation's great factories and illuminated the homes of millions.

Born in 1859 to a ne'er-do-well London lay preacher and a temperance hotel keeper, Insull toiled through his teenage years as a clerk and stenographer. As did many ambitious young men in that era, he idolized Thomas Edison, and after losing his job in a London auctioneer's office, he was thrilled to come across a help-wanted ad for one of Edison's British phone companies, where he secured employment.

His superiors quickly recognized that he had arrived with office skills that extended well beyond shorthand transcription and bookkeeping. A few years later, when offered employment at the company's head office in the United States, he replied, "I'll go if I can be secretary to Edison himself." He grew sideburns so as to look older than his tender twenty-one years, and in early 1881 crossed the Atlantic to work at the great man's side, where he stayed for eleven years and gradually rose through the company's ranks.

Increasingly, Insull's fortunes were bound up not only with Edison's, but with those of J. P. Morgan, who was a supporter of the great inventor. By that point, Morgan was reaching the apex of his influence and technological acumen, and as an early electricity enthusiast, he had outfitted his home at 219 Madison Avenue with Edison's first incandescent bulbs. In the absence of an electrical grid, this was no small feat, a deficiency he later remedied by bankrolling Manhattan's first large-scale generating plant and transmission lines.

Unfortunately for Edison General Electric, because its low-voltage DC system was ill-suited to long-distance transmission, it began to lose market share to the AC high-voltage grid constructed by Thomson-Houston, a competing company founded in 1882 by electrical engineers Elihu Thomson and Edwin Houston. The beginning of the end for Edison General Electric came in 1883 with the issuance of an English patent for a transformer that "stepped down" the high-voltage current in long-distance AC transmission wires for residential use. It was quickly licensed by American George Westinghouse, who deployed it in Thomson-Houston's system.

Morgan, in a master stroke of investment banking, staved off Edison General Electric's demise by merging it in 1892 with Thomson-Houston to form General Electric. Edison himself never accepted the superiority of AC transmission; he sold his GE shares in a fit of pique, and when reminded later how much they would have been worth, remarked, "Well, it's all gone, but we had a hell of a good time spending it."[1]

Insull proved to be a genius at running electrical utilities, and in the decade before the merger, he had gradually swallowed up Edison's rivals to achieve monopoly status in the Chicago area.[2] Insull wound up running the company's Chicago organization, which had been cut adrift by the 1892 merger, and so left him at loose ends. The next year he struck out on his own by taking over Edison's now orphaned operations in Chicago, where he proceeded to adroitly acquire, manage, and combine smaller utility companies into larger organizations. By 1905 he had expanded his operations well beyond Chicago into the Midwest; he operated his companies competently and, for the era, in the public interest. The industry's growing scale allowed him to gradually reduce rates and introduce low off-peak pricing. Insull welcomed statutory regulation of the increasingly essential electrical service, and on one occasion he even suggested that if his companies could not properly service their customers, then the government should do so.[3]

Had he limited his horizons to merely powering industries and lighting cities, he would still be well remembered. Sadly, his scrupulous regard for his companies' electrical customers did not extend to his companies' shareholders. Typical of Insull's early financial machinations was his 1912 floatation of the Middle West Utilities Company, whose primary purpose was not to produce electricity, but rather to raise capital for his other operations. At the heart of his complex financial machinations was his personal purchase from Middle West Utilities of all of its preferred and common shares for $3.6 million. Then, he turned around and sold all of the preferred shares, but only one-sixth of the common shares, to the public for the same $3.6 million, effectively acquiring for himself five-sixths of the company for nothing.

Like Hudson, Insull was public spirited and worked like a Trojan. Also like Hudson, he gave generously to civic projects and the arts, including Chicago's Civic Opera House, known to locals as "Insull's Throne." He built a 4,445-acre estate in Libertyville, north of Chicago, where inhabitants "built homes on Insull real estate, sent to an Insull school children born in an Insull hospital, used Insull lights, cooked with Insull gas, traveled on an Insull road, saved in an Insull bank, and played golf on an Insull golf course."[4] The town represented in microcosm his vast empire, which at its height constituted scores of companies that employed seventy-two thousand workers in power plants that served ten million customers. He sat on or chaired the boards of sixty-five companies and was president of eleven.[5]

As early as 1898, Insull had intuited that oversight by state agencies was preferable to competition from city-run utilities, and by the First World War, largely as a result of Insull's personal leadership of the industry, the utilities companies were solidly under the thumb of government regulation.[6] This limited their profits, but Insull, like Hudson before him, grasped that the biggest money lay not with providing goods and services, but in financing them.

The complexity of Insull's holding companies outran the ability of most observers, and perhaps even of Insull himself, to understand. He stacked hundreds of companies into layers, with the bottom layers sometimes owning pieces of those at the top of the structure. Historian and journalist Frederick Lewis Allen described one small corner of Insull's Rube Goldberg apparatus as follows:

> The little Androscoggin Electric Company in Maine was controlled
> by the Androscoggin Corporation, which was controlled by the Cen-
> tral Maine Power Company, which was controlled by the New Eng-
> land Public Service Company, which was controlled by the National

Electric Power Company, which was controlled by Middle West
Utilities.[7]

The common shares of Middle West Utilities, which conferred ownership
and control, were by that point held by Insull's personal vehicle, Insull
Utility Investments, Inc.—seven layers in all. The leverage described above
was thus multiplied many times, not just the skimming of cream, but, in
Allen's words, of "superrich cream" and "super-superrich cream" that came
from stacking multiple organizational levels.[8] By 1928, Insull's byzantine
agglomeration was hardly the exception, but rather the rule. In that year,
of the 573 entities listed on the New York Stock Exchange, 92 were purely
holding companies, 395 were both holding and operating companies, and
only 86 were pure operating companies.[9]

Selling the shares of these stacked companies to the public at inflated prices required the illusion of profitability. Insull did so with an
arsenal of financial legerdemain worthy of Blunt and Hudson, most
notoriously by having his companies buy assets from each other at escalating prices and then booking each operation as a profit. It was as if
a husband sold to his wife for $1,500 the Chevrolet he had previously
bought for $1,000, and the wife sold him her Ford in the same fashion,
each claiming a $500 gain.

As with Blunt and Hudson before him, and as with the internet moguls
after him, both the public and press worshipped Insull. His august image
graced the cover of *Time* twice in the 1920s, and to be glimpsed with him
in front of the Continental Bank was said to be worth a million dollars.[10]

Insull salesmen propelled the final act in this leveraged farce. In early
1929, this specially trained corps began selling to the public, for the first
time, shares in his top-level company, Insull Utility Investments, initially
at prices that were ten times what he had paid for its assets, and later at
more than thirty times as the popular enthusiasm surrounding it grew.
These were structures, like the Goldman Sachs trusts, designed for boom
times. Any bump in the economy that impaired the ability of his electrical companies to pay off the interest and dividends on their bonds and
preferred stock (which had first claim on their revenues) would savage the
dividends and prices of their common shares. The net worth of the common
share holders, who often owned them on margin, would also suffer. This
process accelerated with each step up Insull's holding company pyramid.

This is precisely what happened to him and most of his six hundred thousand shareholders after 1929. Like Hudson, he sincerely believed in his scheme to the end and borrowed millions in a vain attempt to keep aloft company share prices in his many-layered contraption as it collapsed in slow motion during the long, grinding 1929–1932 bear market. In April 1932, just three short months before the stock market itself finally bottomed, his bankers summoned him to a New York office and informed him that they would not support him further. "Does this mean receivership?" he asked. "Yes, Mr. Insull, I'm afraid it does."[11] The damage to the investing public was immense; one accounting estimated that by 1946, when the prolonged legal wrangling surrounding the bankruptcy of Middle West Securities was finally completed, it amounted to $638 million.[12] By that year, the stock market had largely recovered; the losses sustained immediately after the 1932 collapse, near the market's nadir, must have run into the billions.

Insull's final act was no less convoluted than the layers of his holding companies and echoed Hudson's downfall. Indicted for mail fraud connected to sales of utility company stock a few months after his bankruptcy, he fled to France, and when the government tried to bring him back for trial, he decamped for Greece, which had not yet inked a pending extradition treaty with the United States. Authorities in Athens ignored that nicety and packed him off home via Turkey anyway.[13] Back in the United States, he appeared again on the cover of *Time*, this time with his hat shielding his face. Stripped of most of his wealth, he could still mount a high-powered legal defense that eventually beat the multiple counts against him. He returned to France an embittered and frail seventy-eight-year-old shadow of his former self. On July 16, 1938, he descended into a Paris Metro station, extended his hand to the ticket taker, and dropped dead with a few francs in his pocket. His wife had repeatedly warned him to avoid the subway because of his bad heart.[14]

Insull's holding companies were only a relatively small piece of a much larger debt pie. The major effect of the late-1920s mania, as with the Mississippi, South Sea, and railway episodes, was to infect the population and business community with an extreme optimism, which led them to borrow excessively against the future.[15] Between 1922 and 1929, the nation's total debt increased by 68 percent, but its total assets increased by only 20 percent, and its income by only 29 percent.[16] Debt can grow faster than the rest of the economy for only so long before they implode. This is particularly true of private debt; individuals and corporations, unlike governments, cannot tax or print money, and since individuals and corporations were the main engines of debt in the 1920s, their obligations proved especially explosive when the music finally stopped.

Another major promoter of the 1920s bubble was the stock pool, which typically consisted of an ad-hoc group of brokers and financiers who manipulated the share price of a particular company by buying and selling shares to each other in a carefully choreographed sequence. The procedure was designed to catch the attention of small investors who, clustered in front of the tickers and chalk boards in brokerage galleries, concluded that a stock had been "taken in hand," and jumped in themselves, driving the price up yet further.

The key player in such a pool was the stock exchange floor "specialist" in the target company's shares: the broker who bought and sold them on the exchange floor for the public, and who kept a precious "order book" of customer buy and sell orders that predicted future share direction. When the order book's list of public buy orders grew fat enough, the participants would sell their shares to investors aroused by the steep price rise and reap millions in profits.

The most notorious pools of all centered on Radio, as RCA was known, and its participants read like a who's who of American politics and business: John J. Raskob, the treasurer of DuPont and General Motors; U.S. Steel chief Charles Schwab; Walter Chrysler; Percy Rockefeller; and Joseph Tumulty, a former aide to Woodrow Wilson. To the modern reader attuned to insider trading, an act that was not illegal in the 1920s, another name sticks out: Mrs. David Sarnoff, the wife of Radio's president and founder.

The greatest stock pool impresario of all time, though, was Joseph P. Kennedy, Sr. Popular mythology associates the Kennedy family fortune with bootlegging. No credible evidence supports this, and in any case the illicit manufacture of spirits would hardly have been a rational career choice for a Harvard economics graduate, a pedigree far better suited to Wall Street, where his legendary pool operations amassed a fortune that he later expanded into, among other venues, Hollywood and real estate.

Just as George Hudson's Ponzi-like financing of his railroads—initially paying dividends to existing shareholders out of capital from new ones—was acceptable and legal in the 1840s, so too was the pools' behavior in the 1920s, and such blatant manipulation of stock prices would not be prohibited until the passage of the Securities Acts of 1933 and 1934.

The third and fourth anatomical components of financial manias, the politicians and press, were both neatly encapsulated in John J. Raskob. When his father, a middling cigar manufacturer, died in 1898, he had the same good fortune as Insull when he became the personal secretary to a titan of industry, Pierre S. du Pont, eventually rising to treasurer of the giant chemical firm. When du Pont rescued troubled General Motors in 1920, Raskob took over the automaker's finances as well. As the 1920s wore on, Raskob became a stock enthusiast and participated in some of the most successful stock pools.[17] In 1928, the Democratic Party appointed him the chairman of its national committee.

Raskob is best remembered, though, for an infamous interview, entitled "Everybody Ought to Be Rich," given in *Ladies' Home Journal*, which by that point had more than two million subscribers. It was published in the August 1929 issue, the most infamous passage from which explains the thrust of the title:

> Suppose a man marries at the age of twenty-three and begins a regular savings of fifteen dollars a month—and almost anyone who is employed can do that if he tries. If he invests in good common stocks and allows the dividends and rights to accumulate, he will at the end of twenty years have at least eighty thousand dollars and an income from investments of around four hundred dollars a month. He will be rich. And because anyone can do that, I am firm in my belief that anyone not only can be rich but ought to be rich.[18]

A classic bubble-era media paean to effortless wealth, this quote neatly illustrates the heuristic shortcuts taken by even the chief financial officer of two great corporations. Today only modest competence with a spreadsheet or financial calculator is needed to determine that turning savings of fifteen dollars each month over twenty years into $80,000 requires earning an average annual return of 25 percent. In 1929, that estimation was more difficult, and while it's possible that Raskob got out his pencil, paper, and compound interest tables, the fact that he didn't mention the implied long-term investment return (ludicrously high even for 1929) makes it more likely that he simply pulled his numbers out of thin air.

The role during bubbles and crashes of politicians like Raskob is twofold. First, like everyone else, they become intoxicated by the pursuit of effortless wealth, as did King George I and the Duke of Orléans in 1719–1720, and much of Parliament during the railway bubble. In recent decades, modern political probity and legislation have tamped down such graft, at least in the developed West, leaving political leaders with a more priestly function, the unceasing incantation that the economy is fundamentally sound. On the way up, no mention of speculative excess is hinted at, and on the way down, a nation's leaders steadily avoid any hint of fear or panic.

And so it was in the 1920s. In his 1928 acceptance speech at the Republican convention, Herbert Hoover solemnly intoned, "We in America today are nearer to the final triumph over poverty than ever before in the history of our land. The poorhouse is vanishing from among us."[19] After the crash, both Hoover and his Treasury secretary, Andrew Mellon, repeatedly reassured the public that the economy was "fundamentally sound." Hoover also pioneered what would become the standard response of modern leaders around the world when faced with an economic crisis: what John Kenneth Galbraith labeled the "no-business meeting," in which the nation's political, financial, and industrial leaders are called to the White House "not because there is business to be done, but because it is necessary to create the impression that business is being done."[20]

Is it possible to spot a bubble in real time?

One of the great advances in modern finance was the formulation of the Efficient Market Hypothesis (EMH) by the University of Chicago's Eugene Fama, who in the 1960s realized that financial markets rapidly incorporated new information—that is, surprises—into prices. Since, by definition, it's impossible to predict surprises, it's also impossible to predict future price direction.

And, as the EMH posits that the current market price accurately reflects existing information, manias by definition should not occur. As Fama pungently remarked: "The word 'bubble' drives me nuts, frankly."[21]

The antipathy of EMH enthusiasts toward the existence of bubbles is understandable; the heart of modern finance formulates and tests mathematical models of market behavior. While it's easy to toss off Isaac Newton's supposed lament that he could calculate the motions of the heavenly bodies but not the madness of men, it illuminates a deeper truth: Newton was one of the greatest mathematical modelers the world has ever seen, and if he couldn't describe a bubble in mathematical terms, then perhaps no one ever could.

Robert Shiller of Yale University, who shared the 2013 Nobel Prize in Economics with Fama, suggests that bubbles occur when price rises become self-sustaining, in his words, "if the contagion of the fad occurs through price."[22] While true of all bubbles, this phenomenon alone does a poor job of identifying them, since investors everywhere and always chase assets with recent high returns. Large-scale bubbles, however, like the ones in 1719–1720, the 1840s, and 1920s are rare, and the mere existence of everyday self-sustaining price rises yields a high false-positive rate.

Supreme Court Justice Potter Stewart confronted the same problem in the case of *Jacobellis v. Ohio*, which involved a different arena, and his approach offers another way of considering bubbles:

> Under the First and Fourteenth Amendments, criminal laws in this area are constitutionally limited to hard-core pornography. I shall not today attempt further to define the kinds of material I understand to be embraced within that shorthand description, and perhaps I could never succeed in intelligibly doing so. *But I know it when I see it.* (italics added)[23]

Just as Newton could not model the madness of men, and just as Professor Fama pushes back against the very word "bubble," Justice Stewart's famous construct conveys that although he couldn't linguistically model hard-core pornography, he knew what it looked like. *Jacobellis v. Ohio* applies equally well to finance: Even if we can't model bubbles, we surely by now know what they look like qualitatively.

The financial manias covered thus far—the Mississippi Company, South Sea, English railway, and 1920s stock market—all exhibited four highly characteristic features. First, financial speculation becomes the primary topic of everyday conversation and social interaction, from the throngs in Rue Quincampoix and Exchange Alley to those in American brokerage galleries in the 1920s. Frederick Lewis Allen recalled that during the 1920s,

> stories of fortunes made overnight were on everybody's lips. One financial commentator reported that his doctor found patients talking about the market to the exclusion of everything else and that his barber was punctuating with the hot towel more than one account of the prospects of Montgomery Ward. Wives were asking their husbands why they were so slow, why they weren't getting in on all this, only to hear that their husbands had bought a hundred shares of American Linseed that very morning.[24]

The second characteristic bubble feature is that a significant number of ordinarily competent and sane people abandon secure, well-paying professions for full-time financial speculation. Absent the financial excitement of their times, for example, both Blunt and Hudson would have remained modestly successful linen dealers. Allen described an actress who outfitted her Park Avenue residence as a small brokerage operation and "surrounded herself with charts, graphs, and financial reports, playing the market by telephone on an increasing scale and with increasing abandon," while an artist "who had once been eloquent about only Gauguin laid aside his brushes to proclaim the merits of National Bellas Hess [a now-defunct mail-order house]."[25]

The third, and most constant, feature of any bubble is the vehemence that believers hurl at skeptics. If anyone had the pedigree and sense of history to express doubt and warn the public about the looming disaster during the late 1920s, it was Paul M. Warburg. Born in 1868 into a German-Jewish family with banking roots in medieval Venice, he rose meteorically through the European financial apparatus before becoming a naturalized U.S. citizen in 1911; in 1914 he was sworn in as an inaugural member of the Federal Reserve Board.

Warburg had seen this movie before he emigrated from Europe, and he knew how it ended. In March 1929, while serving as the head of the International Acceptance Bank, he noted the complete detachment of stock prices from any rational valuation measures and pointed out with alarm the burgeoning amount of loans that caused an "orgy of unrestrained speculation," which would not only eventually savage the speculators but "would also bring about a general depression involving the entire country."[26]

This stunningly accurate prognostication was met with a wall of public condemnation. The mildest label applied was "obsolete"; angrier observers accused Warburg of "sandbagging American prosperity," foreshadowing nearly word for word the invective hurled at internet bubble skeptics two generations later.[27]

The same fate met the famous investment adviser Roger Babson when, on September 5, 1929, speaking at a well-attended business conference at Babson College, which he had founded a decade before, he said that "sooner or later a crash is coming, and it may be terrific." Like Warburg, he predicted a significant depression. That day, the market fell sharply, the so-called Babson Break. If Warburg was easy to attack with nativism and dog-whistle anti-Semitism, Babson presented an even fatter target because he had proved himself a bit of a crackpot and had authored, among other works, a manifesto entitled *Gravity—Our Enemy Number One*, and established the Gravity Research Institute, whose major purpose was the invention of a protective shield against this deadly force.

In normal times, Babson's prognostications would have been met with, at worst, good-humored skepticism. But these were not normal times. Newspapers sarcastically referred to him as "The Sage of Wellesley" and pointed out the inaccuracies of his previous prognostications. One investment house warned its clients, "We would not be stampeded into selling stocks because of a gratuitous forecast of a bad break in the market by a well-known statistician."[28]

Minsky's amnesia requirement usually reveals a generational divide during bubbles; only participants old enough to recall the last boom and bust are likely to be skeptical. Their younger and more enthusiastic colleagues will deride them as old fogies, out of touch with the new realities of the economy and the financial markets. Bubbles are, in short, the province of young people with short memories.

Whatever the mechanism, such vehemence is perfectly understandable as a manifestation of Fritz Heider's theory of balanced and unbalanced states. Mirroring the expectations of end-times adherents, few beliefs are more agreeable than the promise of effortless and unbounded wealth, and its acolytes do not easily part with so comforting a notion. For the faithful, the path of least resistance runs through a balanced state of disagree/dislike, labeling skeptics dim bulbs who "don't get it."

The fourth, and final, symptom of a bubble is the appearance of extreme predictions, such as the South Sea forecasts of Spain miraculously ceding its New World trade monopoly to England, investments of £100 yielding hundreds in annual dividends, the railway's impending "lordship over time and space," or Raskob's implicit projection of 25 percent annual market returns.

In 1929, the prediction to end all predictions, though, came from Yale's Irving Fisher. Perhaps the greatest financial economist of his time, Fisher is today revered for developing much of the underpinning of modern mathematical finance. Alas, he is even better remembered for a remark made on October 15, 1929, to the Purchasing Agents Association in Manhattan, nine days before Black Thursday: "Stocks have reached what looks like a permanently high plateau."[29]

No history of the 1929 crash is complete without the tale of "Sunshine Charlie" Mitchell. Insull and Hudson had at least endowed posterity with vital infrastructure, a bequest that mitigated their sins. Nothing, on the other hand, redeemed Charlie Mitchell, the great financial promoter—and predator—of the era.

Like Insull, Mitchell came from humble origins and became an assistant to a corporate titan, in his case Oakleigh Thorne, president of New York City–based Trust Company of America in 1907, just in time for the great panic of that year. Thorne led the large firm through the bank run at the storm's epicenter, and throughout the crisis, Mitchell, his thirty-year-old aide, put in punishing hours and often slept on his boss's office floor in lieu of returning home. Between 1911 and 1916 he ran his own brokerage firm, then was hired by the National City Bank (the predecessor of today's Citibank, hereafter "the Bank") to run its tiny stock-and-bond sales arm, the National City Company (hereafter, "the Company").

The commercial banker performs three near-sacred functions central to any capitalist society: the safeguarding of other people's money; the provision of working capital to businesses, without which the economy cannot function; and the creation of money. By contrast, the investment banker sells stocks and bonds to the public, a much riskier and morally more ambiguous activity.

Banking regulators had long understood this distinction, and in fact, prohibited commercial banks from owning investment banks. But that did not mean that a commercial bank could not control an investment bank without actually owning it, which is how Mitchell and the Bank's lawyers managed to structure its relationship with the Company.[30] Charlie Mitchell, in short, was a pirate disguised as an officer of the queen who sailed under the flag of the Bank. For substantial fees, the Company became an investment bank, whose main function was to generate capital for corporations by selling their newly issued stock shares and bonds to the public. Unfortunately, many of the stocks and bonds sold by the Company were dodgy, and it compounded the malfeasance by selling these securities to the Bank's unsuspecting customers. Later, the Company and Bank would underwrite even dodgier bonds issued by foreign governments.

When Mitchell took over the Company in 1916, it occupied one room and housed just four employees in the Bank's headquarters. Promoters need not only the public, their customers, but also the press, which during boom times provides an army of credulous recruits. The 1920s prototypical media shill was a magazine writer named Bruce Barton, the son of a preacher who once described Jesus as an "A-1 salesman." In 1923, he wrote a puff piece on Mitchell entitled "Is There Anything Here that Other Men Couldn't Do?" In an interview, Mitchell recounted for Barton how, when one of his young salesmen encountered a slump, he would take him to the top floor of the Bankers' Club to survey the multitudes below. "Look down there. There are six million people with incomes that aggregate in the thousands of millions of dollars. They are just waiting for someone to come and tell them what to do with their savings. Take a good look, eat a good lunch, and then go down there and tell them."[31]

Mitchell's charisma, drive, glowing press, and the mania of the 1920s stock market swelled the Company's operations; by 1929, it employed fourteen hundred sales and support personnel scattered among fifty-eight branch offices, all connected to its New York headquarters by eleven thousand miles of private wires (hence the modern pejorative for a full-service brokerage firm, "wirehouse"). Mitchell emitted a nearly constant stream of exhortation to his charges: "We do want to be absolutely sure that, with the exception of the cubs, we have no one in our sales force but producers."

The Company met this aspiration and more, issuing in excess of $1.5 billion annually during the 1920s in the stocks and bonds it had underwritten, more than any other investment bank.[32]

The Bank heavily marketed the Company's investment banking "expertise" to its trusting customers. In place of traditional low-yielding but safe passbook accounts, they were advised to buy bonds with alluring fat coupons and stocks with even more alluring nosebleed-inducing price increases.

Mitchell probably didn't invent the brokerage sales contest, but he refined it to a high art, offering prizes as large as $25,000 to the winning "producer" (an unlovely term still unselfconsciously used in the financial industry). So successful was Mitchell's apparatus that it ran out of bonds to sell. Normally, companies and foreign governments court investment banks to issue their bonds, but the Company reversed this dynamic by actively encouraging companies to issue more of them. Even more egregiously, Mitchell's salesmen fanned out to shaky Balkan and South American nations to offer cheap capital to their needy governments.

Despite the salesmen's reports of ineptitude and mendacity among foreign governments such as Peru and the Brazilian state of Minas Gerais, and of the near-certainty of their default, Mitchell and the Company kept selling these foreign bonds to the Bank's trusting customers.

In 1921, he ascended from the presidency of the Company to that of the Bank itself, removing the last major roadblock to his sales steamroller. Literary critic Edmund Wilson best captured Mitchell's spirit, describing how he sent out his salesmen "knocking at the doors of rural houses like men with vacuum cleaners or Fuller brushes." During the early- and mid-1920s, the Company mainly sold bonds; as the decade wore on and the bull market gained momentum, it shifted its focus from bond sales to stock sales, not only risky issues such as the indebted Anaconda Copper Company but even the Bank's own stock, which would have been illegal but for the fig leaf of the legal separation of the Company and the Bank.[33]

In 1958, Wilson described how Mitchell

> sold the American public, over the course of ten years, over fifteen billion dollars' worth of securities. He sold them the stock of motor-car companies that were presently to dissolve into water; he sold them the bonds of South American republics on the verge of insolvency; he sold them on the stock of his own bank, which dropped in the course

of three weeks, after October, 1929, from $572 to $220, and which was recently worth $20.[34]

Mitchell had made his customers ground zero for the crash, the popular image of which centers on the dramatic "black days" of October. Black Thursday, the 24th, saw a consortium led by the J. P. Morgan organization stage a dramatic rescue that broke the panic by midday. But by Black Monday and Black Tuesday, the 28th and 29th, the titans who had saved the day on the 24th—Mitchell, Thomas Lamont of Morgan, and Albert Wiggin of Chase National—had run out of both nerve and capital. On those two successive days, the market fell by 13.5 percent and 11.7 percent, respectively.[35]

By the close of business on October 29, the market had fallen by 39.6 percent from its September peak: bone-rattling, to be sure, but not as bad as the price falls seen in 1973–1974, 2000–2002, and 2007–2009. Further, by mid-April 1930, stocks had recouped more than two-fifths of that loss.*

During the 1907 crash, only a few percent of Americans owned equities, and even by 1929 that figure had risen to only about 10 percent, and so the initial 1929 fall had relatively little direct economic effect on the general population.[36] But over the next several years, the rot spread to the beating heart of business activity, the banking system, and the economy entered a tailspin. By mid-1932, stock prices had plummeted by nearly 90 percent from their 1929 peak level. On December 11, 1931, still six months from the market's ultimate bottom in mid-1932, a small investor named Benjamin Roth wrote of the impoverishment of investors in his diary,

> A very conservative young married man with a large family to support tells me that during the past 10 years he succeeded in paying off the mortgage on his house. A few weeks ago, he placed a new mortgage on it for $5000 and invested the proceeds in good stocks for long-term investment. I think in two or three years he will show a handsome profit. It is generally believed that good stocks and bonds can now be bought at very attractive prices. *The difficulty is that nobody has the cash to buy.* (italics added)[37]

---

* On October 19, 1987, the Dow Jones Industrial Average fell by 22.6 percent, which marked "only" a 36.1 percent price fall from its previous high eight weeks prior.

Figure 7-1.   Dow Jones Industrial Average 1925–1935

A cashless public is an angry public and, as in 1720 and 1848, it wanted scalps. The financial humorist Fred Schwed put it most succinctly: "The burnt customer certainly prefers to believe that he has been robbed rather than that he has been a fool on the advice of fools."[38] By 1929, the Bank had 230,000 customers; it's not known exactly how many of those established brokerage accounts at the Company, but the number ran at least well into the tens of thousands, and likely more.[39] Unlike other brokers' customers, who had willingly come in the front door to purchase securities, Mitchell's had sought a safe place for their money in a commercial bank and instead stumbled into a bordello.

The fates afflicted Charlie Mitchell with a most unlikely avenging angel: a plainspoken Italian-American attorney named Ferdinand Pecora, whose education had been cut short when his father, a shoe factory worker, sustained a disabling industrial injury. Pecora dropped out of college as a teenager in the late 1890s to support his parents and siblings, and somehow managed to cram in a law degree. Subsequently, his career included a long stint as an assistant district attorney in New York City, where he successfully prosecuted a number of financial cases.

The crash and subsequent bear market prompted an investigation of the securities industry by the U.S. Senate's Committee on Banking and

Currency. It began its hearings in 1932 and questioned Mitchell, among many others. So ineffectual was the interrogation by the first two counsels that the committee fired them.

Pecora's brilliance in cross examination had caught the eye of Bainbridge Colby, a distinguished attorney who had served as secretary of state under Woodrow Wilson, who recommended the young assistant DA to Peter Norbeck, the outgoing Republican chair of the Committee, who by this point was desperately looking for a replacement for his previous hires.[40]

Pecora began work as chief counsel on January 24, 1933; he had to hit the ground running and started out well behind the curve. During his first crack at the participants in the Insull trusts, just three weeks after he was hired, he landed nary a punch, so when the tall, imposing, tanned, and supremely self-confident Mitchell strode into the committee room on February 21, 1933, the new chief counsel seemed hopelessly overmatched.

But Pecora soon found his prosecutorial legs, so dominating the hearings and thoroughly destroying its targets that history remembers the proceedings as the "Pecora Commission." Great wealth, as we've seen, confers upon its recipients great adulation. This, in turn, corrodes self-awareness, a fatal flaw when criminal behavior is involved. Further, criminal enterprises typically anesthetize participants to their organizations' moral failings, who come to view their activities as normal, even laudable.

The same thing often happens with skullduggery at financial companies, where employees learn to rationalize their behavior as in their clients' best interests. This phenomenon applies in spades to charismatic and successful corporate leaders; as the old saw goes, the fish rots from the head down. Pecora, a connoisseur of criminal behavior, quickly recognized that Mitchell, typical of such corporate thoroughbreds, saw nothing legally or ethically amiss with National City's modus operandi, and that the most effective way to indict him would simply be to have him explain how he directed his salesmen. Over eight days of testimony, Pecora completely dismantled the haughty Mitchell by leading him methodically, in polite, understated fashion, through the moral swamp that was the National City sales apparatus.

How much did Mitchell have to pay his salesmen to induce them to sell their clients stocks and bonds? Not much, answered Mitchell, only about $25,000 per year—at a time when the average American worker earned $800 per year. How did National City pay its executives? According to the profits from selling securities, and not according to how those securities performed for the customers. How much did this system award Mitchell? Over one million dollars per year, an unheard of salary even for the highest executives in that era.

To make matters worse, Mitchell sold National City stock to his wife at a loss, then immediately bought it right back from her, and thus paid no income tax in 1929; engaged in a classic stock pool manipulation of the Bank's shares; and made extravagant forgivable "loans" to high executives while simultaneously sandbagging his ordinary employees with mandatory purchases of Bank stock, journaled against their future paychecks at well above the market price. When his rank and file finally paid off their overpriced purchases, he fired them.[41]

As the shocking salaries and loans, tax shenanigans, and employee abuse filled the headlines, it slowly dawned on the initially confident Mitchell that he was in deep trouble. Pecora, though, aimed higher: He wanted to expose the twisted incentives that pushed securities salesmen in general, not just National City's, to sell customers high volumes of risky securities with borrowed money, a prescription for bankrupting thousands of hardworking Americans. He began this task on the fourth day of the hearings and demonstrated how the Company, with full access to the list of ordinary Bank depositors, "ruthlessly," as worded in a sales directive, sold them stocks and bonds.[42]

On the sixth day of the hearings, February 28, Pecora again shifted gears and focused on the damage done to individual investors. Prior to the hearings, the committee had received hundreds of letters from National City's ruined customers. Their common thread involved prudent, thrifty people who had managed to acquire a comfortable cushion of government bonds, and whom National City salesmen then methodically reduced to penury through repeated leveraged purchases of risky stocks and bonds.

Pecora picked one of the most sympathetic and engaging of them, one Edgar D. Brown from Pottsville, Pennsylvania, to testify. Brown had recently sold a theater chain and desired to move to California for health reasons, and he decided that he needed the financial advice and logistical support from a national financial institution. He came across this advertisement in a national magazine:

Are you thinking of a lengthy trip? If you are, it will pay you to get in touch with our institution, because you will be leaving the advice of your local banker and we will be able to keep you closely guided as regards to your investment.[43]

Critically, the advertisement had been placed by National City Bank, but Brown was contacted by Fred Rummel of National City Company to help him invest his nest egg of $100,000, most in cash coming due from the sales of his theaters. One quarter of this sum was already in bonds, mainly U.S. government securities. Brown made only one request: He wanted to avoid stocks.

Rummel purchased a wide variety of domestic and foreign bonds for Brown, with his permission, well in excess of his $100,000 nest egg, which required that he take out loans from various banks, including National City, totaling $180,000 more. When his bond portfolio plummeted, even before the crash, Brown complained.

BROWN: And [Rummel] said, "Well, that is your fault for insisting upon bonds. Why don't you let me sell you some stock?" Well, the stock market had been continually moving up. So then I took hook, line and sinker and said, "Very well. Buy stock."

PECORA: Did you tell him what stocks to buy?

BROWN: Never.

PECORA: Did he buy stocks then for your account?

BROWN: Might I answer that facetiously—Did he buy stocks?

To which the committee's clerk dutifully recorded, "Great and prolonged laughter."[44]

Brown then produced for the committee a record of stock purchases so voluminous that Pecora did not burden the clerk with their entry. Brown recounted how he traveled to the National City headquarters to complain that Rummel had so aggressively traded his account that despite the rising stock market, his portfolio's value had declined. He was told that the Company would look into the matter and that he would hear back.

Brown did hear back from Mr. Rummel, who recommended the purchase of more stocks, including National City Bank; by October 4, 1929, the value of his portfolio had declined yet further. Brown marched into National City's Los Angeles office and demanded the sale of all his positions, and recounted what happened next: "I was placed in the category of the man who seeks to put his own mother out of his house. I was surrounded at once by all of the salesmen in the place, and made to know that that was a very, very foolish thing to do."

The Company finally did sell Brown's stocks on October 29, Black Tuesday, when he had run out of margin, leaving him with nothing. Further, it had done so in the most mendacious way possible, purchasing Brown's securities themselves at prices well below the going market price.

Brown, who two years prior had been worth $100,000, about $1.5 million in today's money, was now a pauper. Amazingly, what Brown wanted most at this point was an additional loan of $25,000 so that he might speculate further in Anaconda stock. The Bank, of course, refused, on the grounds that Brown was unemployed and broke.[45]

Before 1929, successful businessmen attained near-cult status as the ultimate arbiters of what was good for the nation; for a time after 1933, the Pecora Commission made Wall Street public enemy number one. It also introduced the word "bankster" into the American vocabulary, two generations before it was resuscitated with a vengeance by the 2007–2009 global financial crisis.

The hearings wound down on March 2, just two days before the inauguration of Franklin Roosevelt, and amid massive bank failures that modern economic historians have attributed in no small part to FDR's campaign rhetoric, particularly pertaining to his threat to devalue the dollar relative to gold, which he eventually carried out.[46] The public thirsted for revenge, and within two months of the hearings, Mitchell found himself on trial for fraud. As with Blunt and Hudson, Mitchell had probably not done anything that violated the lax fraud and securities laws of that time, and he was acquitted on all charges, although he did later have to settle with the government for back taxes. Over the next two decades, he even regained some semblance of wealth and respectability; his last residence on Fifth Avenue now serves as the French consulate.

Just as happened after the South Sea debacle two centuries prior, the law belatedly changed. Within fifteen months of the hearings, Roosevelt would sign a panoply of securities legislation inspired by the Pecora Commission, including the Glass-Steagall Act, which rigorously separated investment banking and commercial banking; the Securities Acts of 1933 and 1934, which regulate, respectively, the issuance and trading of securities; and the Investment Company Act of 1940, which governs financial advisors and investment trusts, the progenitors of today's mutual funds.

In one of finance's greatest ironies, the first commissioner of the Securities and Exchange Commission, established by the 1934 act and charged with enforcing its provisions, was none other than pool operator par excellence Joseph P. Kennedy, Sr. When the incongruity of Kennedy's appointment was pointed out to FDR, he quipped, "It takes a thief to catch a thief."[47]

A contemporary perspective on the crash was offered by Fred Schwed, who, with his characteristic fey humor, explained it thusly:

> In 1929 there was a luxurious club car which ran each week-day morning into the Pennsylvania Station. When the train stopped, the assorted millionaires who had been playing bridge, reading the paper, and comparing their fortunes, filed out of the front end of the car. Near the door there was placed a silver bowl with a quantity of nickels in it. Those who needed a nickel in change for the subway ride downtown took one. They were not expected to put anything back in exchange; this was not money—it was one of those minor conveniences like a quill toothpick for which nothing is charged. It was only five cents.
>
> There have been many explanations of the sudden debacle of October, 1929. The explanation I prefer is that the eye of Jehovah, a wrathful god, happened to chance in October on that bowl. In sudden understandable annoyance, Jehovah kicked over the financial structure of the United States, and thus saw to it that the bowl of free nickels disappeared forever.[48]

A quote apocryphally attributed to Albert Einstein posits compound interest as the most powerful force in the universe. It is not. Amnesia is. Just two short years after the Pecora hearings, Frederick Lewis Allen presciently observed that

> St. George attacks the dragon and is furiously applauded; but there comes a time when St. George is dead, when the audience has dispersed, and when St. George's successor finds the dragon a very persuasive fellow and begins to wonder why such a to-do was ever made

over dragon-slaying, whether times haven't changed, and whether there is any need for subjecting the dragon to anything more than the mildest restraint.[49]

As the Pecora Commission faded into memory, Saint George fell not merely off his guard, but lay bleeding by the roadside, unable to protect a public with little recollection of Raskob, Insull, and Mitchell from their erstwhile late-twentieth-century successors.

8

APOCALYPSE COW

Speak unto the children of Israel, that they bring thee a red heifer without spot,
wherein is no blemish, and upon which never came yoke.

—Numbers 19:2

During the twentieth century, a once obscure branch of Protestant theology exploded onto the American religious and political scene to become an influential social movement not only in the United States, but around the globe. It's no exaggeration to label this theology a religious mass mania— one that has already yielded several small tragedies, and also carries the seeds of Armageddon. A minor incident in Israeli animal husbandry reveals its end-times potency.

In the mid-1990s, Jubi Gilad, a dairyman at the Orthodox Kfar Ha-sidim agricultural school in northern Israel's Jezreel Valley, was having a hard time impregnating one of his Holsteins. He imported some bull semen from Switzerland, and in August 1996, the black-and-white cow gave birth to Melody, a startlingly red female. To a small minority of the world's Jews and Christians, the calf's color could only mean one thing: The world was about to end. Melody, in short, was the Apocalypse Cow.[1]

Like a crimson strand of wool, the bovine cataclysm's lineage winds through nearly three thousand years of millennialist history. The ancient Israelites believed that anyone who came into contact with a corpse, or who had been under the same roof as one, was impure, and so that person could not enter Jerusalem's Holy Temple. In those days, this meant all but the very young. This impurity could only be removed, as alluded to in the above epigraph from the Book of Numbers, by a ritual in which priests sacrificed a heifer (a young cow that had never given birth) with pure red hair, which had never been yoked and was blemish-free. She was then burned on a pyre along with red wool, a cedar branch, and a hyssop sprig. Priests performed the rite on the Mount of Olives, which overlooked the Temple. There, they mixed the heifer's ashes with pure water drawn from the Shiloach Spring. If, and only if, the ash water was sprinkled on the impure believer on both the third and the seventh days after proximity with the dead was the impurity removed.[2]

The destruction of the Second Temple by the Romans in A.D. 70 rendered this complex procedure impossible. A millennium later, the great Jewish intellectual of the medieval world, Maimonides, tried to make sense of the now meaningless purification ritual.

Born in Islamic Spain around 1135, Maimonides excelled academically, practiced medicine, and eventually led the Jewish community of Cairo during the turbulence of the Crusader invasions. His most lasting accomplishment was the Mishneh Torah, a compendium of ethics and Jewish law. But the rationale for ritual purification flummoxed even this great scholar, who classified it as a *chok* (mystery): "not matters determined by a person's understanding."[3] He was more forthcoming, though, about the procedure's history:

> The first [sacred red heifer] was brought by Moses our teacher. The second was brought by Ezra. Seven others were offered until the destruction of the Second Temple. And the tenth will be brought by the king Mashiach [messiah]; may he speedily be revealed. Amen, so may it be God's will.[4]

To certain Jews and Christians, the meaning of Melody was thus startlingly clear: She was the tenth red heifer, which foretold the Messiah's coming. A tiny minority believed that the birth of a perfect red heifer predicted, in approximately the following order, the imminent Rapture of believers to the safety of heaven; a fearsome Tribulation featuring a titanic battle with the Antichrist, global chaos and hellfire; the return of Jesus and a millennium of his rule; God's final judgment; and finally the end of time.

Melody's saga resonates because it goes to the heart of the most prominent, and dangerous, mass delusion running like a red thread through human history, the end-times narrative. Well into the modern period, end-times stories like it have produced a bumper crop of tragedies ranging from the disastrous Anabaptist Madness to more numerous relatively small-scale ones, such as the Solar Temple episode.

Over the last half century, a new and highly characteristic form of the end-times narrative now espoused by most evangelical Protestants, "dispensationalism," has given rise to a belief system that pervades America and cleaves its society into two camps with very different worldviews. Most alarming of all, a story similar to Melody's could at some future date become a cataclysmic self-fulfilling prophesy, just not in the way that Jewish, Christian, and also Muslim believers imagine.

Soon after Melody's birth, a fundamentalist rabbi named Yisrael Ariel found out about her. After he pronounced the heifer sacrificially fit, the story broke into the mainstream media and then went global as reporters from the major American and European television networks broadcast amusing stories about the Cow at the End of the Universe.

Israelis found themselves less entertained; one local journalist referred to Melody as a "four-legged bomb . . . equal in its ability to set the entire region on fire to the power of non-conventional weapons in the hands of the Iranian Ayatollahs."[5] Fortunately, Melody's minders had noted white hairs on her udder soon after birth, and when more white hairs appeared on her tail at the age of one year, the rabbis declared her unfit. (She would have had to make it to pristine full-fledged heiferdom at age three to qualify for ritual sacrifice.)

The similarity between Melody's Jewish backstory and the Christian end-times theology of Müntzer's rebellion, the Anabaptist Madness, Fifth Monarchism, and Millerism is obvious. In theological terms, three of these four Christian episodes were "premillennial"—Jesus's return was to occur *before* the millennium, which had yet to happen. (The fourth, Fifth Monarchism, had both pre- and postmillennialist believers.) The triggering of the millennium by Christ's second coming is necessarily a dramatic, and usually violent, event.

Contrariwise, Saint Augustine's earlier and more conventional end-times theology, which informs modern Catholicism and most mainstream Protestant sects, downplays the entire concept of the millennium: Jesus doesn't dramatically return to rule for a thousand years. This more conventional "amillennialist" scheme is accordingly a far more placid process and, because of the psychological precept that "bad is stronger than good," a less compelling one.

The last half of the nineteenth century would see the evolution of an even more dramatic, violent, and compelling version of the end-times narrative, a creed that has increasingly influenced the lives of ordinary Americans: The world is hopelessly corrupt and cannot be saved or reformed by the efforts of mere men. Only divine intervention, in the form of the Rapture, Tribulation, Armageddon, and the final judgment, will suffice.

This end-times sequence does not conform to accepted Catholic or conventional Protestant doctrine. Over a century ago most mainstream Christian denominations on both sides of the Atlantic discarded the notion of the Bible's literal truth. In the process, they alienated a significant portion of their flocks; even today, Gallup and Pew polls find that about a quarter of Americans still believe that the Bible is the actual word of God. A similar percentage believe that Jesus will return to Earth in their lifetime, and 61 percent of Americans think that Satan exists, percentages that were almost certainly higher in the early twentieth century.[6] These American believers were unwilling to let go of the comfort of literal biblical truth and to embrace modern scientific knowledge and the moral ambiguity of mainstream churches that granted legitimacy to Judaism, Catholicism, or, God forbid, atheism.

The result was dispensationalism, which restores the comfort of literal biblical truth along with a large dollop of old-fashioned Manichean thinking, the clean black-and-white separation of the world between good and evil, with believers placed squarely and comfortably in the former camp.*

This belief system has become so embedded in our political system that at least one U.S. president, Ronald Reagan, subscribed to it, as do a large swath of politicians at all levels, such as Mike Pence, Dick Armey, Michelle Bachmann, and Mike Huckabee, to name but a few. Indeed, its tenets pervade nearly every aspect of national discourse, particularly social issues such as abortion and gay rights, and foreign policy issues, most especially pertaining to the conflict-ridden Middle East.

*   *   *

---

* Named after Manichaeism, a syncretic Christian/pagan religion promulgated by a third-century A.D. Persian named Mani, who conceived the universe as a struggle between good and evil.

At roughly the same time that William Miller's eschatology took hold in mid-nineteenth-century America, an Irish Anglican named John Nelson Darby lit a slow-burning theological fuse that would not yield its ultimate explosion for another century.

Unlike the humble and unassuming Miller, Darby was both intellectually imposing and socially endowed. Born in 1800 to a wealthy merchant family, he acquired his middle name by way of an uncle knighted for serving with Horatio Nelson at the Battle of the Nile. He earned gold medals in literature, Latin, and Greek at Dublin's Trinity College and gained admission to the Irish bar. Finding the law unsatisfying, in 1826 he was ordained in the Irish branch of the Anglican Church. His abandonment of the bar so disappointed his father that he was disinherited.

The intellectually restless Darby soon enough grew disenchanted with rigid and hierarchical Anglicanism; just one year after his ordination, he attended a conference on biblical prophecy and concluded, like Luther, that the authentic church could be any group of true believers in Christ ordained by God to carry humanity from the crucifixion of Jesus to his Second Coming.

The key to Darby's belief system was a series of five "dispensations," or periods of history, in which God tested humanity, hence the formal name that theologians assign it: "dispensational premillennialism." Darby's God evidently graded on a very strict curve, and mankind accordingly flunked all four dispensations leading up to the modern time. Brilliant as Darby was, he, like the author/authors of Revelation, wrote dense, indigestible prose, and it was left to others to clarify the precise nature of his dispensations/historical periods. Darby's later followers expanded the number of dispensations to the seven standard ones used today:[7]

1. Innocence, from the creation to the expulsion of Adam and Eve from Eden;
2. Conscience, from the expulsion from Eden to Noah;
3. Government, from Noah to Abraham;
4. Promise, from Abraham to Moses;
5. Law, from Moses to Jesus;
6. Grace, the current period of Darby's true church, from the crucifixion to the Second Coming;
7. Millennium, the final reign of Christ.

The Bible fairly bursts with contradictory passages, and the genius of Darby's dispensational system was that it cleared away much of the chaos by pigeonholing its contents into separate dispensations so as to lessen that internal conflict. From the arcane and inbred perspective of biblical interpretation, many theologians considered this rearrangement of scripture a masterstroke that organized it into a more coherent whole.

All organized religions have, in addition to their theology, or belief system, an "ecclesiology"—an organizational structure. In Darby's case, the ecclesiology was so-called gospel assemblies, small groups organized around a charismatic leader who ordained that group's gospel truth. Darby intentionally did not name these congregations, but they informally came to be called the Church of God, or, more simply, the Brethren, the most famous of which was Darby's Plymouth Brethren.

In stark contrast to emotionally wrought modern American fundamentalist church services, the Brethren's meetings were intensely intellectual affairs whose methodology closely resembled Miller's, in which a single word in the Bible, such as "creation," was traced through its contents. Given the ambiguous richness of the Bible and the powerful intellects involved, the movement soon became caustically fractious. All Brethren, though, agreed on the movement's basic tenets, which centered on the division of the world into Jews, Christians, and everyone else: the Gentiles. They further agreed on the centrality of Paul's First Epistle to the Thessalonians, whose two key verses are

> *For the Lord himself shall descend from heaven with a shout, with the voice of the archangel, and with the trump of God: and the dead in Christ shall rise first.*

> *Then we which are alive and remain shall be caught up together with them in the clouds, to meet the Lord in the air: and so shall we ever be with the Lord.*[8]

To those who accept the literal truth of the Bible, the meaning of these two verses is clear. At the End, Jesus descends partway down to Earth and gathers up all true Christians into the clouds, halfway to heaven, first the resurrected dead, then the living: the Rapture.

Darby's Plymouth Brethren then skipped ahead to Revelation's phantasmagorical narrative: in approximate order, a seven-year Tribulation of unspeakable horrors, Christ's victory over Satan and his army, followed by a thousand years of peace capped with another brief battle with Satan, and the final judgment of both the living and the dead. Those who remain on earth during the Tribulation are also eligible, by dint of their repentance amid the chaos, for redemption. (The fictional exploits of this group would be lucratively mined more than a century later in fundamentalist novels such as Tim LaHaye and Jerry Jenkins's *Left Behind* series.)[9]

While at Trinity College, Darby had come under the influence of the popular Regius Professor of Divinity, Richard Graves, whose tutoring of classics and theology inspired generations of students. According to Graves, the Jews would return to the Holy Land and accept Jesus, and with the passion of recent converts guide the rest of humanity to the Savior. The homecoming and conversion of the Jews would hasten the end-times, and so true Christians had the duty to help the Jews return. Graves, as have millennialists before and since, sought confirmation of his biblical prophecies in current events, in this case the weakening of Turkish rule over Palestine and the rise of British naval power.[10] This "alliance" of Jews and Christians became known as "Christian Zionism," and would, in tandem with Jewish Zionism, grow ever stronger over the next century and a half.

Just as with the Anabaptist Madness and Fifth Monarchist revolt, by the late twentieth century millennialism became a potentially destructive self-fulfilling prophecy for two reasons: First, as with Graves, Darby, and the Brethren, the millennialist narrative centers on the Holy Land, the modern world's powder keg; and second, in the past several decades, dispensationalists have begun to influence American foreign policy and exert a control over military weapons that could, at a stroke, incinerate a large portion of humanity without one iota of assistance from Jesus or the biblical beasts of Daniel and Revelation.

Among the world's developed nations, dispensationalism has gained its most enthusiastic following in the United States; it now exerts far less influence in its birthplace in the British Isles, or, for that matter, in all other developed nations.

The early- to mid-nineteenth century saw one of the great inflection points in Western scientific development. Charles Darwin's *On the Origin of Species* would shortly be published (1859), and over the course of the nineteenth century, scientists gradually realized that the Earth was a good deal older than the biblical 6,000 years. In 1779, the Comte de Buffon modeled the cooling of the Earth with heated spheres and estimated the planet's age at 75,000 years, and in 1862 the physicist William Thomson— later Lord Kelvin—put it between 20 million and 400 million years. With subsequent advances in laboratory technique, these estimates gradually increased, by the mid-twentieth century, to the current consensus of 4.6 billion years; the wider universe is thought to be three times as old. These inconvenient facts disturbed many Christians. The Brethren, for example, rejected Darwin, and they struggled to incorporate the concept of geological time into their interpretation of the Book of Genesis.[11]

Before these nineteenth-century discoveries, leading politicians and scientists often dabbled in eschatology. Most notably, Isaac Newton published an entire body of work, later assembled into a posthumous volume, which expounded on the meaning of Daniel and Revelation.[12]

Joseph Priestley's mid-eighteenth-century training, like almost all higher education in that era, was theological; he began his career as a minister but soon became interested in the natural sciences, in which he accomplished groundbreaking early work on the nature of electricity, gases, and, most famously, the codiscovery of oxygen. Like Newton, Priestley also extensively engaged in biblical prophecy, which included speculation on the return of the Jews to Palestine:

> The present dispersed state of the Jews is the subject of a whole series
> of prophecy, beginning with Moses. And if this remarkable people
> should be restored to their own country, and become a flourishing
> nation in it, which is likewise foretold, few persons, I think, will doubt
> of the reality of a prophetic spirit.[13]

Priestley, who died in 1804, was one of the last high-profile natural philosophers who combined prophecy with the sciences; after Darwin and the blossoming of geology, any mainstream scientist who cited the Bible as a foundation for their beliefs about the physical or biological sciences would incur the ridicule of peers. Likewise, this new scientific knowledge demolished the notion of literal biblical truth for many Christian believers and clergy.

German theologians were the first to backpedal from biblical infallibility and treat the Bible's narratives as allegorical rather than factual, a school of thought that came to be known as "higher criticism." Over the course of the nineteenth century, this movement spread to England, where the hierarchical and highly educated Anglican clergy gradually adopted it; by the end of the century, the literalist Brethren found themselves marginalized in their home country. Moreover, the natural centrifugal forces fed by intense dispensationalist intellects like Darby, when applied to ambiguous scriptural texts, splintered the British Brethren movement into dozens of obscure, powerless sects that became, in some cases, objects of derision.[14]

Dispensationalism found more fertile soil in the theological free-for-all of American Christianity. Not only did the United States lack an English-style hierarchical state church, but the American temperament was also radically different. The 1800s were truly the British Century, a profoundly optimistic period during which faith in technological progress was near absolute and Britannia ruled the waves, a mindset inconsistent with dispensationalism's dim assessment of humanity. Although the United States also initially considered itself the New Jerusalem, a beacon for all mankind, the Civil War shattered that faith, and the badly bruised nation proved far more receptive to the pessimistic Darby and the Brethren, who toured North America for a decade and a half after the war. Darby himself spent months at a time visiting major American cities, where he and his colleagues spread the dispensationalist creed.

The most important of dispensationalism's American recruits were Dwight Moody, C. I. Scofield, and Arno Gaebelein. Moody, a fiery evangelical preacher who had previously come into contact with the Brethren while touring England, had also met Darby during one of the Irishman's American sojourns. Initially the lowborn Moody and the aristocratic and intellectual Darby did not get along, but over time Moody's steadfastness won Darby over.[15] Further, Moody possessed the common touch that Darby lacked; he packed churches, stadiums, and gardens with thousands of worshippers on both sides of the Atlantic. In 1886, four years after Darby's death, he founded the Chicago Evangelization Society, which upon his death was renamed the Moody Bible Institute. Over the following decades, it would train dozens of leading American dispensationalists.

More than fifty American evangelical colleges followed on the heels of Moody's, whose primary goals were to promote prophecy based on biblical literal truth and to combat the rise of scientifically centered "higher criticism" among the mainstream Protestant sects. In 1924, an Oberlin graduate named Lewis Sperry Chafer founded the most famous of these, the Evangelical Theological College. Twelve years later he renamed it the Dallas Theological Seminary (DTS).*[16] The DTS is the most important educational institution that most secular Americans have never heard of. It has trained much of the top level of the dispensationalist movement's leaders, "Dallas men" as they are known in evangelical circles, and has heavily influenced most of the rest.

The second key early American dispensationalist, C. I. Scofield, was a Confederate war veteran who practiced law after the conflict and served variously as a Kansas legislator and U.S. attorney before undergoing a sudden evangelical conversion in 1879. Shortly thereafter, he came under the spell of a dispensationalist leader named James Brookes, the organizer of the Niagara Bible Conferences, held annually between 1876 and 1897 at Niagara-on-the-Lake in Ontario. Scofield also came into contact with Moody and the third key early American dispensationalist, Arno Gaebelein.

The Niagara conferences highlighted yet another reason why dispensationalism flourished more strongly in America than England. The hands-off attitude of the U.S. Constitution toward religion encouraged the growth of a wide variety of Protestant sects, and Brookes welcomed all of them to Niagara-on-the-Lake. This avoided the fractious infighting that characterized the British movement, an ecumenism evident today in the wide range of American churches that embrace the dispensationalist end-times narrative.

Gaebelein was an even more singular intellectual figure than Darby. After emigrating to the United States from Germany in 1879 at age eighteen, he learned Latin, Greek, and especially Yiddish in his quest to convert New York's Jews, going so far as to establish a Yiddish-language newspaper. He also founded an English-language paper that played to American

---

* Among Protestants, the word "evangelical" involves three basic tenets: salvation through the acceptance of Jesus, the inerrancy of the Bible, and the duty to proselytize. Not all evangelicals are dispensationalists, but all dispensationalists are evangelicals. A more formal definition of "evangelism," the "Bebbington Quadrilateral," involves four tenets: the requirement to change lives, the integration of the gospel into everyday action, belief in the Bible's inerrancy, and an emphasis on Jesus's sacrifice to humanity on the cross.

fundamentalists, including Chafer and Scofield, the latter of whom was so impressed with Gaebelein's brilliance that the two began work on an annotated version of the King James Bible, the Scofield Reference Bible. Initially published in 1909, its annotations served as the inspiration behind Chafer's founding of what became the DTS.

It is difficult to overestimate the importance of the Scofield Reference Bible; religious historians recognize it as the single most influential dispensationalist publication, which to this day informs modern Christian fundamentalism. The 1909 edition sold three million copies, which was more than matched by a heavily revised 1967 edition whose estimated sales run well in excess of ten million copies; over the past century, the two versions have guided large numbers of Americans through the dispensationalist system.[17]

The nexus of Gaebelein, Scofield, Moody, and Brooke's Niagara Conferences marks the point at which dispensationalist doctrine began its entanglement with geopolitics. In 1878, Brooke created a fourteen-point creed, officially adopted by the 1890 Niagara Bible Conference. The last of the fourteen points stated,

> We believe that the world will not be converted during the present dispensation but is fast ripening for judgment, while there will be a fearful apostasy in the professing Christian body; and hence that the Lord Jesus will come in person to introduce the millennial age, when Israel shall be restored to their own land . . . and that this personal and premillennial advent is the blessed hope set before us in the Gospel for which we should be constantly looking.[18]

Heretofore, Darby and his immediate followers had maintained a strict hands-off stance toward the restoration of the Jews. Christians, they thought, should at most be interested observers of the processes leading up to the Rapture and millennium, but they should limit their actions to saving souls from the awful Tribulation that separated these two events; under no circumstances would they attempt to trigger the sequence by encouraging or aiding the return of the Jews to Palestine. This passive approach would change as four more dispensationalists, Robert Anderson, William Blackstone, Arthur Balfour, and Orde Wingate, emerged onto the historical stage as Christian Zionists; all aimed their formidable rhetorical and political power at the Jewish return to the Holy Land. Wingate in particular would violate Darby's policy of noninterference in the most violent way possible: through force of arms as a British army officer.

Like Darby, Anderson hailed from aristocratic Irish stock and studied law at Dublin's Trinity College, which launched him into a distinguished career at the British Home Office. He eventually headed Scotland Yard, where he supervised the Jack the Ripper investigation. Unusually for that era, he had one foot each in two very different groups, the dispensationalist camp and the ruling aristocracy, and was thus uniquely placed to influence British foreign policy toward Palestine, then under Turkish rule. Even though the Brethren were social and theological outcasts in Britain, Anderson greatly admired Darby and personally knew Scofield and Moody. In addition, during his decades at the Home Office, he rubbed elbows with, among others, a succession of prime ministers, including Gladstone, Asquith, Salisbury, and, fatefully, Balfour.[19]

Anderson was smitten with an obscure book published in 1863 by a Plymouth Brethren member named Benjamin Wills Newton, entitled *Prospects of the Ten Kingdoms Considered*. Newton focused on the ten toes of the beast from Daniel; since contemporary Christians interpreted the clay feet as the Roman Empire, its ten toes represented, he thought, its ten nationalities, or kingdoms. Newton imagined that the second sign of the end-times, along with the centuries-old prophecy of the return of the Jews to Palestine, would be when those ten ancient kingdoms reassembled themselves into a new Roman Empire:

> The final subdivision into the Ten Kingdoms, denoted by the ten *toes*, is an event which will almost immediately precede the end, and will probably be contemporaneous with the national establishment of unbelieving Israel in their own land.[20]

To Newton, the establishment of modern nation-states around Europe in the wake of the Napoleonic Wars and the 1815 Congress of Vienna constituted this new Roman Empire, events that surely presaged the imminent End because

> the establishment of governments that are virtually or actually democratic-monarchies in England, Belgium, France, Algeria,

> Portugal, Spain, Italy, Austria, and Greece, and the favour with
> which the principles of the western European nations are regarded
> at Constantinople, Egypt, and Tunis, indicate the approach of the
> period, when clay, mingled with iron, will fitly represent the char-
> acter of governmental power throughout the Roman Empire.[21]

The concept of a resurgent ten-member Roman Empire led by the Antichrist
is a superb example of confirmation bias. So popular did this prophecy
become among dispensationalists that almost any biblical passage containing the number ten was seen to predict the reassembly of ancient Rome.
Darby, for example, was equally impressed with the ten-horned beast
from Revelation:

> As much excitement has been caused by the question, as to whether
> Louis Napoleon is the Antichrist or not, I add that I have not the
> slightest doubt that he is the great agent of the Latin or ten-horned
> beast at present, and that his operations distinctly mark the approach
> of the final scenes. Blessed be God![22]

In 1881, Anderson, inspired by Newton, published *The Coming Prince*, a
bold and provocative work of prophecy that endures to the present day. (Typical of the fractiousness of dispensationalists in all eras, Newton had by this
point become an independent Baptist and fierce critic of dispensationalism.)[23]
Anderson's social status allowed him the autonomy to develop a prophetic
system that formed the basis for the lurid late-twentieth-century predictions
of Jerry Falwell and Hal Lindsey, and the even more lurid and phenomenally
lucrative novels of Tim LaHaye and Jerry Jenkins.

Anderson's late-nineteenth-century interpretation of dispensationalism, which derives directly from Daniel 9:24–27, is essential to understanding the roots of today's American Protestant fundamentalism. These
four chapters of the Book of Daniel describe a biblical period of "seventy
weeks" between the Jews' return from the Babylonian exile and the coming of the Messiah. Confusingly, these verses subdivide this length of
time into three periods of, respectively, seven weeks, sixty-two weeks,
and one final week that is further subdivided into two half-weeks. (The
title of Anderson's book refers to "the prince that shall come" of Daniel
9:26—the Antichrist who leads the ten-nation confederation.)

This recalls the Millerites' fascination with the preceding chapter from Daniel, the eighth, which mentions the 2,300 biblical days—that is, years—between the Jews' return from Babylon and the end-times, which calculated out to A.D. 1843 or 1844.[24] Anderson instead decided to focus on the seventy "weeks" that is—490 days/years—of Daniel's ninth chapter as the time span between the return from Babylon and the Second Coming. The 1,810-year discrepancy between Anderson's and the Millerites' estimates for the interval between the end of the Babylonian captivity of the Jews and the Second Coming puts into sharp perspective the slipperiness inherent in biblical prophecy, in this case how the Bible's interpreters deal with the cognitive dissonance of a nearly two millennia difference between these two conclusions about the length of this time span.

To deal with the 1,810 years missing from Anderson's estimate, a gargantuan fudge was needed—a suspension of both disbelief and of theological time. Anderson, channeling Darby, stopped the apocalyptic ticktock with the Crucifixion at the end of week sixty-nine, at which point the Messiah was "cut off," and started it up again with the appearance of the Antichrist. The restarting of time at the apocalyptic seventieth week

> would be signalised by the advent of another Prince [the Antichrist], who would make a seven years' covenant (or treaty) with the Jews; and in the middle of the week (i.e., after three years and a half), he would violate that treaty and suppress their Temple worship and the ordinances of their religion. All this is so plain that any intelligent child could understand it. (parentheses original)[25]

Anderson had little doubt that this sequence was already in its early stages, and that it would involve

> the outcome of some great European crisis in the future, this confederation of nations shall be developed, and thus the stage will be prepared on which shall appear the awful Being, the great leader of men in the eventful days which are to close the era of Gentile supremacy.[26]

The dispensationalists had already identified two occurrences that would mark the end of this hiatus and the resumption of time and God's renewed attention to the Jews, and so bring about the end-times: the return of the

Jews to the Holy Land and the reassembly of the Roman Empire into the Antichrist-led European ten-nation confederation. While Darby left behind dozens of volumes, his unreadable prose confined his readership to a small core of literate and determined true believers. On the other hand, not only did Anderson's prose go down like fine claret, but his accurate prediction of the return of the Jews to Palestine in *The Coming Prince* electrified his later twentieth-century readers.

The book's prophetic bona fides were enhanced by the fact that he published it in 1881, more than a decade before Theodor Herzl jump-started the modern Zionist movement with the publication of *Der Judenstaat* and the calling of the First World Zionist Congress, and a third of a century before General Edmund Allenby seized Jerusalem from the Ottoman Turks. Before those events, the prospect of a renewed Jewish state in Palestine seemed remote, even to Anderson, who wrote,

> The prophecies of a restored Israel seem to many as incredible as predictions of the present triumphs of electricity and steam would have appeared to our ancestors a century ago.[27]

Even today, Anderson's prediction of the restoration of the Jewish nation in Palestine astounds. The same, alas, cannot be said of his prophecy of a renewed Roman Empire, which has embarrassed Christian fundamentalist prophecy ever since. For example, a century and a half after Richard Graves identified the post-1815 rise of European constitutional monarchies as the new Roman Empire, dispensationalists would do the same for the European Union, which has thus far failed to produce the Antichrist or form a strategic alliance with Israel, let alone invade it.*

The Great Disappointment of Millerism cured fundamentalist Christians of date-setting. But starting with Darby, dispensationalists have been magnetically drawn toward divining biblical prophecy from current events, especially the labeling of groups of nations as the New Rome and given

---

* With one fleeting exception: In 1956, Great Britain and France cooperated with Israel during the 1956 Sinai-Suez invasion, which President Dwight Eisenhower scuttled by, among other actions, threatening to sell British government bonds.

individuals as the Antichrist. The problem is that while a similarity between biblical and current events may seem plausible and alarming in the
moment, the passage of a few decades always reveals such prophecies and
their prophets as foolish.

As if all this weren't complicated enough, Darby's fertile dispensationalist imagination had added yet one more major player to the final
battle between the restored Jewish nation and the new Roman Empire: the
King of the North, repeatedly mentioned as an invader of Israel in Daniel,
whom he identified as modern Russia. (Darby's scheme also featured a
poorly identified "King of the East" and "King of the South," the latter
likely Egypt.)[28]

For someone of Darby's intellectual horsepower, finding biblical text
supportive of a coming Russian invasion of the Holy Land was child's
play. Genesis 10:2 lists two of Japheth's six sons as Meshech and Tubal; in
Darby's fevered imagination, this could only mean that they represented,
respectively, Moscow and Tobolsk, the latter of which is well east of the
Ural Mountains.[29]

In the mid- and late-nineteenth century, an apparently vigorous Imperial Russia threatened the feeble Ottoman Turks, and Darby asserted
that Russia would steal from Turkey the lands of Gog and then invade the
restored Jewish state. In the mid- and late-twentieth century, Darby's followers would embellish this prophecy with the idea that the Jews would
ally themselves with the Antichrist-led New Roman Empire in response
to this Russian threat, an alliance that the Antichrist would end three and
a half years later by betraying the Jews.[30]

However complex, bizarre, and nonsensical this nineteenth-century theological speculation seems today, the story of its evolution over nearly two
centuries is essential to the understanding of recent American domestic
politics and foreign policy. The next step on the long and winding road
from Darby, Anderson, Moody, Scofield, and Gaebelein to Melody the cow
and the recent rampant growth of dispensationalist beliefs in the United
States belongs to the crucial figure of an American businessman named
William Blackstone.

Blackstone can be thought of as the American Robert Anderson,
a well-connected dispensationalist enthusiast for the Jewish return to

Palestine. Although Blackstone came from humble origins, he inherited a large estate from his father-in-law and grew even wealthier through his insurance business, thrift, judicious investments, and book sales.* And like Anderson, he had contacts at the highest levels of government.

Born in 1841 in upstate New York, Blackstone had undergone religious conversion at age eleven, and subsequently he became Moody's close associate. In 1886, he published *Jesus Is Coming*, which trumpeted the centrality of the restoration to Palestine of the Jews and their conversion to Christianity; the book eventually sold more than a million copies and was translated into forty-three languages.[31] He became so convinced of the dispensationalist end-times narrative that sometime around 1888 he hid thousands of copies of his book, along with other works of prophecy in Hebrew, Yiddish, and Aramaic, around Petra, in current-day southern Jordan, so that "someday the terrified survivors of the Antichrist's bloodbath will welcome the opportunity to read God's work."[32]†

Blackstone engaged in the usual combination of number mysticism (for example, seven years times 360 [*sic*] days in the year equals 2,520, which when added to the Babylonian conquest in 606 B.C. [*sic*] yielded a Second Coming in the year 1914) and historical coincidence (the First World War beginning in that year), but, as his hiding of books around Petra indicated, he was not averse to giving a personal shove to the advent of the end-times.

Theodor Herzl organized the Zionist Congress in Basel three years after the publication of *Jesus Is Coming*, and in the ensuing decades Blackstone collaborated warily with the Zionists through his Chicago Hebrew Mission. Blackstone went so far as to convene a joint conference of Christian premillennialists and Zionists shortly after his return from his book-burying sojourn in Jordan. Buoyed by the agreement between the conference's Jewish and Christian participants, he drafted a letter to President Benjamin Harrison known to history as the "Blackstone Memorial," which skipped lightly over Ezekiel and Isaiah, then focused on the suffering of Russia's Jews under the pogroms. The obvious solution to the Jews' tribulations: "Why not give Palestine back to them again?"

---

* His family lore asserted that he was the descendant of the legendary English jurist Sir William Blackstone, though documentation for this connection is lacking.
† Petra's exotic, majestic ruins have enchanted visitors for centuries, most recently as the setting for *Indiana Jones and the Last Crusade*.

With naïve optimism, the Memorial suggested that the Ottomans would freely give up this valuable real estate in exchange for the assumption of their considerable debt by Western nations. More impressive were the Memorial's 413 signatories, who included the chief justice of the Supreme Court, the House speaker, the House Foreign Relations Committee chairman, numerous other congressional members, leading theologians, journalists, and captains of industry such as John D. Rockefeller and J. P. Morgan.

President Harrison promised Blackstone that he would look into the matter and forwarded the letter to Secretary of State William Blaine, who made inquiries with the U.S. embassy in Constantinople. As U.S. diplomats were wont to do in that era, they ignored Jewish issues, and the Memorial then disappeared from public view; after Blackstone resubmitted it to Theodore Roosevelt in 1903, it vanished again.

In 1916, Louis Brandeis, whom Woodrow Wilson had just appointed as the first Jewish justice on the Supreme Court, came across the document. By that point, it was so obscure that when Brandeis made inquiries at the State Department, its officials denied any knowledge of it. In the words of historian Paul Charles Merkley,

> [The State Department's professed ignorance of the Memorial] seems extremely unlikely. Probably, they were simply resisting giving support to the embarrassing notion that the President of the United States—or worse still, the State Department!—was in the habit of giving the time of day to end-times pamphleteers.[33]

Over the coming decades the State Department gave ample evidence of an institutional anti-Semitism that before and during the Holocaust hindered the flight of refugees from Germany and occupied Europe and cost an untold number of lives, but the above quote identifies an additional reason for the State Department's willful dismissal of a petition signed by the country's ruling elites, namely,

> the contempt of the well-educated for the unsophisticated, especially the theologically unsophisticated. In the Episcopalian, Congregational, Unitarian, and occasionally Presbyterian circles in which the policy-making elite were reared, nothing was so vigorously despised . . . as

the end-times pamphleteer. So long as the only constant champions of "Jewish Destiny" were Fundamentalist pamphleteers, there was no need to give Zionism the time of day. Simple, old-fashioned, country-club anti-Semitism is as nothing in this equation, compared to the fear and loathing of Fundamentalism among properly educated Protestants.[34]

The State Department's neglect of the Memorial both amazed and alarmed Brandeis. He struck up a warm correspondence with Blackstone, and in 1917 the two of them resubmitted a revised Memorial to President Wilson, a devout Protestant. But by this point, the military and diplomatic situation in the Middle East had overtaken the duo's efforts.

By the end of his life, Blackstone had become a wealthy man, and he sent Brandeis (who was also well-to-do) large sums, much of it donated by oilman Milton Stewart, with which to support his Zionist work. Shortly before Blackstone's death in 1935 at age ninety-four, he told Brandeis that he had squirreled away funds, just as he had his books in Petra, so that "if the Rapture does come [after I die] and you are not among those who participate in it," that the funds would be used to support his fellow un-raptured Jews who had subsequently converted to Christ so that they might proselytize the rest of heathen humanity. (He further counseled Brandeis, one of the nation's greatest jurists, that "there are apparently no human laws which provide for any such event as this.")[35]

The event that overtook Brandeis's Jewish Zionism and Blackstone's dispensationalist Christian Zionism came in the person of Arthur Balfour. From an early age, Balfour had inherited his parents' piety and was obsessed with the Old Testament. Otherwise, he was the archetypical languid, detached British aristocrat who, according to his biographer, belonged to "an easily recognizable type, represented both in England and France by a number of statesmen who owe their fame less to any specific performance than to the impression created by their intellectual brilliance."[36]

Balfour's father was a member of Parliament, and both his parents, particularly his mother, were evangelical Protestants. Balfour was also strongly influenced by a Brethren member named William Kelly, who, like Darby, was a fellow Trinity graduate. More importantly, Kelly edited Darby's mammoth *Collected Writings*, and like Anderson was well connected in Conservative Party circles.

Balfour's uncle, Lord Salisbury, was thrice prime minister, and almost as a matter of course Balfour succeeded him in 1902. As is often the case, the intellectual brilliance and rapier debating skills that power the rise to high office in England did not equate with administrative competence, and Balfour resigned after three years, largely over trade issues.[37]

At nearly the same time as his resignation, he met with one of Herzl's aides, the young Zionist Chaim Weizmann, a chemistry professor who had recently moved to England and eventually became Israel's first president; the young chemist's vision of a Jewish homeland is reported to have moved the religious Balfour "to tears."[38]

Over the ensuing decade, Balfour's relationship with the Zionists deepened, and on November 2, 1917, now foreign secretary, he wrote a letter to Lord Rothschild, arguably the foremost member of Britain's Jewish community, the text of which was publicly released a week later:

> His Majesty's government view with favour the establishment in Palestine of a national home for the Jewish people, and will use their best endeavours to facilitate the achievement of this object, it being clearly understood that nothing shall be done which may prejudice the civil and religious rights of existing non-Jewish communities in Palestine, or the rights and political status enjoyed by Jews in any other country.[39]

This momentous letter, the Balfour Declaration, electrified Zionists around the world and played no small part in Israel's birth three decades later in the wake of the Holocaust. But while Balfour's religiosity clearly drove the Declaration and subsequent British foreign policy, it's doubtful that his contacts with dispensationalists such as Kelly directly affected his policy toward Palestine. From this point forward, the Holy Land's fortunes would be driven not by theologians content to observe history from the sidelines, but rather by those who wished to shape it themselves.

9

GOD'S SWORD

The Jews did return to the Holy Land, first as a trickle as the nineteenth century ended, then in increasing numbers as Zionism gained influence in the wake of Eastern Europe's pogroms, and finally as a flood immediately after the Holocaust.

In the decades following the 1948 birth of Israel, only a small number of its citizens subscribed to the Jewish version of the end-times narrative, which, like the dispensationalist version, also featured the return of the Jews and rebuilding of the Temple. Because of the extraordinarily sensitive nature of the Temple Mount, this tiny group caused, and continues to cause, no end of civil strife that threatens at any moment to explode into a regional, or even a global, conflict.

Christian Zionists, imbued with a dispensationalist fervor that mushroomed during the second half of the twentieth century, proved, and continue to prove, just as dangerous, both inside and outside the Holy Land.

John Nelson Darby and his immediate followers were content to observe events play out from the sidelines, but in the 1930s dispensationalist theology finally collided with realpolitik in the person of a remarkable British army officer named Orde Wingate—"Lawrence of the Jews," as described by the famous British military historian Basil Liddell Hart.[1]

In 1920, the League of Nations granted Britain custodial rule over the Holy Land—the British Mandate for Palestine—where Wingate served between 1936 and 1939.* There, his dispensationalist beliefs combined with his military skill and British resources to move the millennium along; unfortunately, he did so by grossly violating the Mandate's supposed equal treatment of Arabs and Jews.

---

* Granted in 1920, the Mandate did not formally take effect until 1923.

Wingate's maternal grandfather was a Scottish captain in the British army who resigned his commission to found a local chapter of the Brethren, and both of his parents were also members. Young Wingate grew up listening to his father's dispensationalist church sermons, and his mother was even more doctrinaire. In 1921, he joined the army, and in 1936, he was fatefully deployed to Palestine, where the Old Testament became his field manual. The great Israeli general Moshe Dayan describes their first meeting:

> Wingate was a slender man of medium height, with a strong, pale face. He walked in with a heavy revolver at his side, carrying a small Bible in his hand. His manner was pleasing and sincere, his look intense and piercing. When he spoke, he looked you straight in the eye as someone who seeks to imbue you with his own faith and strength. I recall that he arrived just before the sunset, and the fading light lent an air of mystery and drama in his coming.[2]

His arrival in Palestine coincided with a violent series of Arab attacks on both Jewish settlements and British Mandate troops, charged with keeping the Arabs and Jews from each other's throats. Wingate's single-minded sympathy for the Jews soon disturbed the fragile diplomacy required for this task and annoyed his commanders, who tended to be pro-Arab.

Wingate thought the Jews too passive in the defense of their settlements against Arab raids and urged them to go on the offensive. He had a career-long fondness for commando-style raids behind enemy lines; although initially assigned as an intelligence officer, he soon formed the Special Night Squadrons (SNS), a unit of around two hundred men, three-quarters of whom were Jewish, commanded by British officers. The unique unit was tasked with protecting the strategically important oil pipeline that ran from Iraq to the Mediterranean. In the summer of 1938, the SNS conducted a series of largely successful raids against Arab forces.

As hinted at by Dayan, to call Wingate eccentric would be an understatement. He was given to addressing his troops stark naked or wearing only a shower cap, and occasionally scrubbed himself as he spoke. He also consumed large amounts of raw onions and repeatedly exposed himself and his troops to contaminated food and water in the belief that this increased disease resistance.

Wingate's family's dispensationalist theology drove his actions in Palestine; he once told his mother-in-law that "The Jews should have their homeland in Palestine and that, in this way, the prophecies of the Bible would be fulfilled."[3] Wingate was also not averse to combining his biblical aspirations with more earthly ones, as he viewed a militarily strong Jewish people as a bulwark of the British Empire.

His pro-Zionist bias soon earned him the enmity of both the Arabs, who put a price on his head, and of his superiors, who found his hit-and-run tactics and "dressing up Jews as British soldiers" unsporting. Eventually, the brass confined him to desk work in Jerusalem and then in May 1939 reassigned him to antiaircraft duty in Britain.[4] He remained there only a short time before the Second World War began, upon which he was sent to Sudan and then Ethiopia to lead the "Gideon force," a guerrilla unit that harassed the region's Italian occupiers. The outbreak of the Pacific war saw him transferred to Burma, where he organized his most famous behind-the-lines unit, the Chindits (also known as "Wingate's Raiders"), whose British army commandos harassed Japanese forces in the effort that protected the subcontinent from invasion. On March 24, 1944, he died in a plane crash in India.[5]

Wingate had not only disturbed the neutrality of the British Mandate, but at least as important, he had egregiously breached the dispensationalist injunction against actively working to bring about the end-times through his SNS operations, whose tactical brilliance awed his Jewish subordinates. He mentored almost the entire cohort of Israeli high commanders in the coming 1948 War of Independence and in the 1967 Six-Day War, including Moshe Dayan, Yigal Allon, Yigael Yadin, and Yitzhak Rabin. He also helped bring about what is today known in Middle East politics as "facts on the ground"—conquered territory and established settlements.[6] In Dayan's words, "Wingate was my great teacher. His teaching became part of me and was absorbed into my blood."[7] One does not have to travel far in Israel to see streets and public places named after him, as is a training center for the country's national sports teams.

He had planned to resign his British army commission at war's end and return to Palestine; David Ben-Gurion, the nation's founder, thought him the "natural choice" to command the Israeli forces.[8] His counterfactual survival is surely one of the great what-ifs of Middle East history: Would a Wingate-led Israeli army have held on to Jerusalem's Old City during the War of Independence? Would his charismatic leadership have led to a more complete victory in that war and possession of the West Bank in 1948, or would his notoriously erratic personal behavior have proven fatal for the nascent Jewish state?

Wingate's ghost haunts the Middle East down to the present. In September 2000, Ariel Sharon, acting in his capacity as leader of the opposition Likud Party and surrounded by nearly a thousand armed riot police, single-handedly sparked the deadly Second Intifada and derailed the Oslo Accords with a visit to the Temple Mount. Wingate was Sharon's boyhood hero; further, he had trained and commanded a young soldier named Avraham Yoffee, who in turn became Sharon's mentor.

Sharon's fateful visit to the Temple Mount brings into focus its status as the world's most contentious piece of real estate, a 35-acre tract in Jerusalem's labyrinthine 220-acre Old City, which itself is intimately bound up in the end-times narratives, and thus the religious manias, of Christianity, Judaism, and Islam. It is thus arguably the place where the Third World War is most likely to begin, with Jewish, Christian, and Muslim millennialists as the dramatis personae.

Roughly speaking, the Old City can be envisioned as a square with the Temple Mount at its southeastern corner. As one circles the Old City's perimeter in a clockwise direction from the Mount, one passes successively through the Jewish, Armenian, Christian, and Muslim quarters before arriving back at the Mount, which is where Christian and Jewish religious extremists, each with their own apocalyptic scripts, want to build the Third Temple.

No one is certain precisely where the First Temple, built by Solomon and destroyed by the Babylonians, was located, but the Mount's Dome of the Rock shrine is the most commonly mentioned site. (And even before the Jews occupied Canaan, it was likely a place of worship of the Jebusites, whom Solomon's father, David, had conquered.) The Second Temple was constructed after the return from the Babylonian exile in the late sixth century B.C., restored and expanded under the Maccabees, and massively enlarged into the current Temple Mount site by Herod before being destroyed by the Romans in A.D. 70.

The Arabs conquered Jerusalem in A.D. 637 and completed the Dome of the Rock in A.D. 692. The Mount's second major structure, the al-Aqsa Mosque, started as a simple shack and was reconstructed several times after earthquakes before taking its final form around 1035. The holiness of the Mount to Muslims derives from a dream of the Prophet's in 621 in which he visited it, as well as heaven, in a single night on Buraq, his winged steed. (Upon his "return" to Mecca the next day, Muhammad offered the account of his supposed journey to the city's skeptical inhabitants.)

Jewish religious scholars divide into three different groups over the current status of the Temple Mount. The first, and largest, group considers it permissible for Jews to visit the Temple Mount but not to pray there. A second, smaller group considers even a visit forbidden, since not only is the sacrificial red heifer missing, but so is knowledge of the precise location of the Ark of the Covenant (the Holy of Holies). According to this second

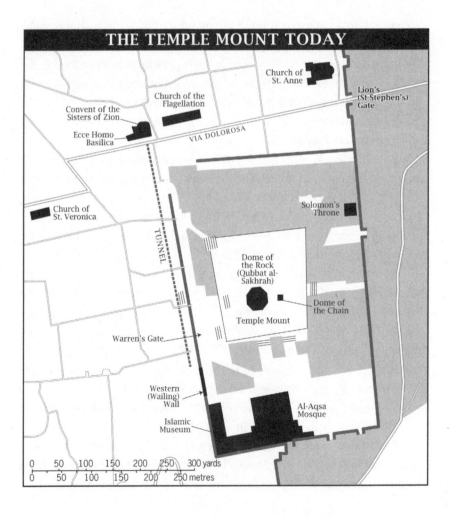

THE TEMPLE MOUNT TODAY

Church of St. Anne

Church of the Flagellation

Lion's (St Stephen's) Gate

Convent of the Sisters of Zion

Ecce Homo Basilica

VIA DOLOROSA

Church of St. Veronica

Solomon's Throne

TUNNEL

Dome of the Rock (Qubbat al-Sakhrah)

Dome of the Chain

Temple Mount

Warren's Gate

Western (Wailing) Wall

Al-Aqsa Mosque

Islamic Museum

0 50 100 150 200 250 300 yards
0 50 100 150 200 250 metres

group, visitors are thus impure and might accidentally contaminate the Ark, wherever it actually happens to be located within the Mount. Finally, a tiny minority on the far-right fringe wants to build the Third Temple. Right now.[9]

Theological considerations aside, the overwhelming majority of Jews don't want to rebuild the Temple for one good, practical reason: It would necessitate razing the Dome of the Rock and possibly the al-Aqsa Mosque, and no great geopolitical acumen is required to realize that the willful Jewish demolition of these structures would trigger a cataclysmic regional, and possibly a worldwide, conflict.

The Brethren and early dispensationalists had relatively little to say on this contentious subject, and for good reason: As they often do, the Old and New Testaments offer conflicting advice regarding the future temple, or, more precisely, on the necessity to perform sacrifices there. On the one hand, Ezekiel 40–48 describes a future temple, and the sacrifices to be performed within; and on the other hand, Hebrews 10:1–18 argues that the Messiah's sacrifices sufficed, and that animal sacrifices, and hence the rebuilding of the Temple, are unnecessary.[10]

The long and tangled history of Jerusalem suffuses the explosive modern status of the city. In A.D. 70 the Romans destroyed the Temple and expelled much of the rebellious Jewish population, and most of the remainder in A.D. 135 after a second revolt led by Simon bar Kokhba. The city was then occupied, sequentially, by the Romans, Byzantines, Sasanian Persians, and the Muslim Umayyad, Abbasid, and Fatimid Caliphates. In 1099, the crusaders ejected the Fatimids and slaughtered the city's Jewish and Muslim inhabitants; the crusaders then temporarily lost the city to Saladin in 1187, and decades of seesaw control between Christian and Muslim forces ensued. In the last half of the thirteenth century, the Muslim Mamluks and Mongols dueled for control of the city, but after about 1300 the Mamluks won out and so ushered in over six centuries of uninterrupted Muslim rule. The Ottomans took over from the Mamluks in 1516 and retained control until December 1917, when British forces under General Edmund Allenby entered the Holy City.

Around 1929, six years after the Mandate's establishment, Jews and Arabs began slaughtering each other in incidents ranging from attacks on single individuals to large-scale riots and terrorist operations, and the carnage continued throughout the 1930s as the Arabs reacted violently to the large numbers of newly arrived Jewish immigrants fleeing Nazi persecution and in the aftermath of the Holocaust. The United Nations offered a partition plan for the territory in 1947, but when the Jews declared the establishment of the state of Israel at midnight on May 14, 1948, full-scale war broke out between the new nation and its Arab neighbors.

The partition plan, which divided Palestine roughly in half, also envisioned an internationally administered greater Jerusalem, a "corpus separatum" of about a hundred square miles, which would include the Old City, the more modern precincts to the west, and the surrounding territory.

The Palestinians and adjacent Arab countries rejected the partition and would settle for nothing less than the complete destruction of the new Jewish state. Both Arabs and Jews attacked Jerusalem at the moment of independence on May 14, 1948, from multiple directions.

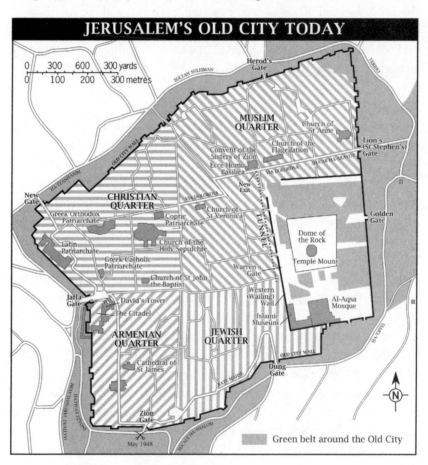

JERUSALEM'S OLD CITY TODAY

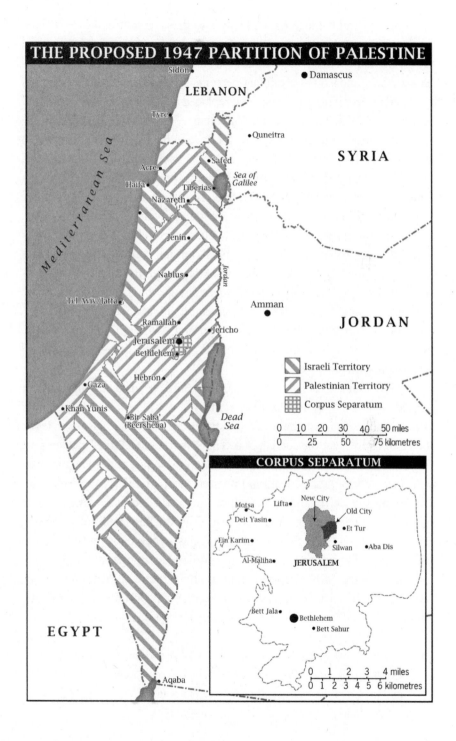

THE PROPOSED 1947 PARTITION OF PALESTINE

In a critical battle at the Old City's southern entrance, the Zion Gate, Jewish forces under the command of a twenty-two-year-old officer named David Elazar penetrated the entrance long enough to extract the Jewish Quarter's civilians and wounded military personnel. The attack exhausted Elazar's unit, and the less well trained one that replaced it was forced to withdraw and left the Old City in the hands of the Jordanians.[11] Until that point, Jews had resided there more or less continuously for three millennia. Even under Muslim rule, Jews had access to the Temple Mount and, critically, its Western Wall, the holiest site in Judaism. The Jordanian forces proceeded to level the Jewish Quarter. Despite the loss of the Old City, the new nation survived, contrary to the expectations of the international community and also of many Jews.

The initial reaction of American Christians to Israel's founding was tepid at best. American Catholics, for example, followed the Vatican's lead in denying any Jewish claim to the Holy Land. In 1943, the Vatican's secretary of state declared that it did not recognize the Balfour Declaration, and on the same day that Israel announced its independence in 1948, the Vatican's newspaper, *L'Osservatore*, claimed, "Modern Israel is not the heir to biblical Israel. The Holy Land and its sacred sites belong only to Christianity: the true Israel."[12]

Mainstream Protestants were hardly more enthusiastic; they largely agreed with the Vatican that Christians, not Jews, represented the new Israel. Further, Episcopalians and Presbyterians had other reasons to favor the Arab cause over the Jewish one. They worried that American support for the new Jewish state would hamper their missionary activity in the Arab world as well as their educational institutions, particularly the American Universities in Beirut and Cairo, which had by that point become hotbeds of Arab nationalism. Last and not least, Episcopalians and Presbyterians packed the executive suites of oil companies with increasingly lucrative and strategically important potential Middle Eastern operations.[13]

During the early twentieth century, the American Protestant establishment publication *Christian Century* emitted a constant stream of anti-Zionist editorial opinion. For example, in 1929 it questioned:

The Jew is respected and honored in all the regions where he has exhibited his powers in the fields of industry, commerce, politics, art and literature. Does he really desire to emigrate to a small, poverty stricken and unresourceful land like Palestine?[14]

Most egregiously, when Hitler took power in 1933, most mainstream Protestants looked the other way. As Nazi racial legislation gave way to outright genocide, *Christian Century* repeatedly counseled against a rush to judgment; more data were needed, its editors thought. A decade later, the publication urged Jews to bring Jesus back into their synagogues after his two-millennia absence and thus demonstrate their fealty to the United States, "a simple gesture [of which] would be the unconstrained observance of Jesus' birthday."[15]

In 1942, the first stories about deportations, concentration camps, and mass killings began to appear in American newspapers, and when the American Zionist rabbi Stephen Wise began to publicize their full extent, *Christian Century* questioned whether his charges served "any good purpose." The publication was particularly outraged by Wise's assertion, later proved tragically true, that Jewish corpses were occasionally being processed into soap.[16]

Not all mainstream Protestants proved so oblivious to the truth, most notably the great American theologian Reinhold Niebuhr. As with many of his political analyses, his early observations on a Jewish state have endured well and speak volumes to the current Middle East situation. As a liberal Protestant, Niebuhr rejected the Bible's literal truth and took a more realistic and pragmatic approach to the Zionist question. Writing early in the Second World War, he observed that the Jews deserved nationhood, not to bring about the millennium, but for more down-to-earth reasons. First, "every race finally has the right to a homeland where it will not be 'different,' where it will neither be patronized by the 'good' people nor subjected to calumny by bad people." Second, it was painfully apparent that no one nation could absorb all of the refugees from Nazi oppression, and that Palestine would serve as a necessary safety valve for the overflow.[17]

Critically, unlike Wingate and the Christian Zionists, Niebuhr recognized that it was folly to ignore the Arab population:

> [The American and British eventual victors of the Second World War] will be in a position to see to it that Palestine is set aside for the Jews, that the present restrictions on immigration are abrogated, and that the Arabs are otherwise compensated. Zionist leaders are unrealistic in insisting that their demands entail no "injustice" to the Arab population since Jewish immigration has brought new strength to Palestine. It is absurd to expect any people to regard the restriction

of their sovereignty over a traditional possession as "just," no matter
how many benefits accrue from that abridgement.[18]

Like most dispensationalists, the brilliant Yiddish-speaking Arno Gaebelein
differentiated between Orthodox Jews, whom he revered, and more secular
Jews, whom he regarded with suspicion. A virulent anti-Communist, he
fell for the most notorious of all anti-Semitic frauds, the *Protocols of the
Elders of Zion*, which bruited a vast Jewish conspiracy to control the global
economy, take over national governments, and kill Christians (and which
has recently been resurrected by the current global crop of extreme-right
nationalists).

At the same time, Gaebelein proved spectacularly prescient about
the Holocaust at a time when most mainstream Protestants and Catholics
had averted their gazes. As early as 1932, he condemned Hitler's rabid
anti-Semitism and predicted that "he evidently is headed for the end and
the same fate as Haman in the Book of Esther." By 1942, he was one of the
earliest to relay reports of mass murder in occupied Europe and of Hitler's
desire to exterminate the Jewish people; by the next year he correctly ap-
proximated that by that point the Germans had killed two million of them.[19]

The fault line between fundamentalist and mainstream Protestantism at
Israel's birth played out at the highest levels in 1948 in the persons of Harry
Truman, a Baptist who had read the entire Bible twice by age twelve, and his
secretary of state, George C. Marshall, an Episcopalian.[20] Two days before
the end of the British Mandate, Truman met with Marshall, Under Secretary
Robert Lovett, and a young Clark Clifford, the White House counsel.

Truman had already promised Chaim Weizmann, by now the president of the Zionist Organization, U.S. recognition of Israel, and asked
Clifford to present the case for doing so to Marshall and Lovett. Before
Truman even got started, Marshall interrupted the president: "I don't even
know why Clifford is here. He is a domestic adviser and this is a policy
matter," to which Truman responded, "Well, General, he's here because I
asked him to be here," to which Lovett, who had been a Skull and Bones
member at Yale and whose father had been chairman of the Union Pacific
Railroad, added that recognizing Israel was "obviously designed to win the
Jewish vote." Truman and Marshall went at each other for a while longer
before Marshall finally declared, "If you follow Clifford's advice, and if
I were to vote in the election, I would vote against you."[21]

Eventually, Marshall backed down and promised to keep secret his opposition to the recognition of Israel. Truman had been born to devout Baptist parents, regularly attended Sunday school, and rebaptized himself as an adult; no matter where he was, he almost always attended Sunday services. In his personal papers, he recorded, "I'm a Baptist because I think that sect gives the common man the shortest and most direct approach to God."[22]

Shortly after he left the White House, he visited the Jewish Theological Seminary, where a friend introduced him as "the man who helped create the state of Israel." Truman responded by referring to the Persian king who had released the Jews from Babylonian captivity, "What do you mean 'helped to create'? I am Cyrus. I am Cyrus."[23]

The 1949 armistice agreements left the Old City and the West Bank in Jordanian hands; at its narrowest point, Israel's "waist," the distance between Jordanian troops and the sea, spanned just nine miles. Jerusalem's newer western half remained under Israeli control, but the Jordanians held Latrun, just a stone's throw from the critical road that ran through the neck of territory that connected the New City with the rest of Israel. During the Independence War, Latrun had been the site of a ferocious battle that ended in defeat for the Israelis, following which they built a new road a few miles to the south that rendered the link only slightly less vulnerable.

In contrast to their mainstream Christian cousins, American dispensationalists reacted ecstatically to Israel's establishment. Typical of these was Schuyler English, who had attended Phillips Academy and Princeton and spoke Hebrew and Aramaic, headed the Philadelphia School of the Bible, and later spent more than a decade working on the 1967 edition of the Scofield Reference Bible. In 1949, he declared that "the Messianic age is about to begin." Further, he detected an "imminent alliance" between Israel and Britain as the start of the dispensationalist compact between the Jews and the restored Roman Empire. That the British might not be eager to ally with Zionists who had heretofore been blowing up their soldiers seemed to have escaped him. Other dispensationalists went further and concluded that God had intentionally shortened the life of Franklin Roosevelt, who had developed close relations with the Arabs, in order to make the pro-Israel Harry Truman president.[24]

While the establishment of Israel certainly stirred the souls of bookish dispensationalists, it resonated little beyond their rarified circle, of whom Schuyler English was typical. Further, although the founding of Israel had returned the Jews to the Holy Land, they didn't control the Temple Mount, and in fact for the first time in millennia no longer even had access to it. They thus were in no position to fulfill an essential dispensationalist requirement: the resumption of worship and sacrifices in a rebuilt Third Temple.

Nineteen years later, that would change. In May 1967, as Arab mobs filled the streets and demanded Israel's destruction, Egyptian president Gamal Abdel Nasser blockaded Israel's access to the Red Sea and expelled United Nations peacekeepers from the Sinai Peninsula. (The Israelis had conquered the Sinai during their brief 1956 military alliance with the French and British. The peninsula was returned to Egypt under a subsequent agreement, according to which both of Nasser's actions constituted acts of war.) Critically, Nasser also sent two commando battalions to Latrun, a dagger aimed directly at Israeli west Jerusalem; at the end of May, he publicly announced that he would destroy the Jewish state.

Nasser calculated that this provocation would yield an Israeli attack, which would end in the tiny country's liquidation by superior Arab forces. He was half right. The six days from June 5 to June 10 saw the Israeli armed forces destroy the Egyptian air force on the ground and occupy the Sinai, West Bank, Golan Heights, and the Old City and Temple Mount.

Initially, the Israelis had not planned to take the Old City. The nation felt itself on the brink of annihilation, and the existential threat from Egypt demanded their full attention and resources. The nation's leadership thus desperately sought to keep the Jordanians, who could cut Israel in two at its vulnerable "waist," out of the war. To the extent that the Israelis had any strategic interest in the Jerusalem area, it centered on the Mount Scopus enclave, with its small garrison and abandoned university and hospital, which were completely surrounded by Jordanian territory.

The Israelis relayed a message to Jordan's King Hussein that if he avoided hostilities, they would not attack his forces on either side of the Jordan River. He replied that his answer would be "airborne," and it soon came via fighter aircraft and artillery strikes. Hussein's aircraft proved ineffective, but when the Jordanians shelled Jerusalem and the nation's international airport outside Tel Aviv, the Israelis had little choice but to respond. Even at that point, Moshe Dayan, who had become defense minister just three weeks before in response to the crisis, wanted to proceed carefully, but the cabinet's hawks, particularly Menachem Begin, demanded that the army take Jerusalem; for the first two days of the war, Dayan's restraint won out.[25]

It is hard to imagine anyone better equipped than Moshe Dayan to deal with the evolving dynamic in the Old City. The one-eyed defense minister grew up on a farm in everyday contact with Arabs, spoke Arabic, developed boyhood friendships with them, and admired their parents' quiet dignity. During the War of Independence, the young lieutenant colonel had commanded Jewish forces in the Jerusalem area. In the midst of the delicate and prolonged armistice talks that eventually ended the 1948 conflict, he had dealt extensively, and increasingly warmly, with his Jordanian counterpart Abdullah el-Tell, whom Dayan trusted enough to travel with, dressed in Arab garb, to Amman, where he negotiated with King Abdullah, Hussein's father; years later Dayan returned the favor when el-Tell requested that the *Palestine Post* (predecessor of the *Jerusalem Post*) pen scathing criticisms of him and so enhance his credibility in Amman.[26]

With the Egyptian and Jordanian threats neutralized and a cease-fire imminent, the Israeli cabinet finally authorized the taking of the Old City; the local commander, Uzi Narkiss, who had fought in the unsuccessful 1948 battle for the Old City, ordered Mordechai Gur, a paratroop officer, to execute the final assault.

Gur, whose reservist unit had initially been scheduled to deploy into the Sinai, proceeded to fight a series of bloody battles with Jordanian forces to secure the Old City's northern and eastern outskirts, an approach that had the added advantage of establishing a corridor to Mt. Scopus. Israeli aircraft scattered a westbound relief column urgently requested by the Old City's Jordanian garrison, which allowed Gur's paratroopers relatively easy final entry through its gates on June 7. Dayan, mindful of world opinion, authorized no air cover over the Old City, kept artillery rounds away from the Temple Mount, and directed sparse small-arms fire only at snipers in the al-Aqsa minaret.[27] That was fortunate: The Jordanians had stored a massive amount of munitions adjacent to the Mount, which close fighting would likely have ignited, with catastrophic geopolitical results.*

Gur, upon occupying the world's most sacred site, radioed to Narkiss perhaps the most famous sentence in the modern Hebrew language, *"Har HaBayit BeYadeinu!"* ("The Temple Mount is in our hands!") Two officers followed Gur to the Mount: Narkiss and the ecstatic Shlomo Goren, the

---

* Of historical note, the ruined state of Athens' Parthenon is largely due to the detonation of an Ottoman munitions dump during the Venetian siege of 1687.

army's chief rabbi since independence, who ascended the Mount shouting biblical verses and repeatedly blowing his ram's horn trumpet (*shofar*).

Goren belonged to the small Jewish minority who wanted to rebuild the Third Temple. He took Narkiss aside to talk. Only decades later, just before he died, did Narkiss give this account of the exchange to the newspaper *Haaretz*:

> GOREN: Uzi, now is the moment to put 100 kilograms of dynamite into
>   the Mosque of Omar [the Dome of the Rock] and that will be it.
> NARKISS: Rabbi, stop.
> GOREN: Uzi, you enter the pages of history for such an act. You don't
>   grasp the very important implications for such an action. This is
>   an opportunity which it's possible to exploit now at this moment.
>   Tomorrow, it won't be possible to do anything.
> NARKISS: Rabbi, if you don't stop, I will take you from here to prison.[28]

Goren left in silence. As soon as he heard the news of the Old City's capture, Dayan headed for Jerusalem to deal with the Temple Mount situation, then as now the fuse attached to the time bomb of Middle East politics. As Dayan described in his memoirs,

> For many years, the Arabs had barred Jews from their most sacred site,
> the Western Wall of the Temple compound in Jerusalem, and from the
> Cave of the Patriarchs in Hebron. Now that we were in control, it was
> up to us to grant what we had demanded of others and to allow members
> of all faiths absolute freedom to visit and worship in their holy places.[29]

Immediately after he arrived on the Mount, Dayan ordered the Israeli flag removed from the Dome of the Rock. The next day he consulted with a Hebrew University professor of Islamic history on how best to approach the clerical officials who ran the site, the Waqf. Shortly thereafter, he and his staff found themselves ascending the Temple Mount toward the al-Aqsa Mosque for a fateful meeting:

> As we continued [upward] to reach the mosque compound, it was
> as though we . . . had entered a place of sullen silence. The Arab
> officials who received us outside the mosque solemnly greeted us,
> their expression reflecting deep mourning over our victory and fear
> of what I might do.[30]

Dayan ordered his soldiers to leave their shoes and weapons at the door, and after hearing the initial orientation from the Waqf, asked them to speak of the future. They greeted this request with silence, and so he and his staff sat on the floor cross-legged, in Arab style, and made small talk. Eventually, the officials opened up: Their immediate concern was the cutoff in water and electricity attendant to the battle. Dayan promised them both back within forty-eight hours.

At that point he told the Waqf why he had come: his soldiers would depart the Mount, which he would leave in their hands. Dayan asked that they resume services, and told them that the Israelis would not censor the traditional Friday sermon, as had the Jordanians. His forces would secure the Mount from without, and the Western Wall, the holiest site in Judaism, which bulldozers had just cleared of adjacent Arab dwellings, would remain in Israeli hands.

Dayan later recorded, "My hosts were not overjoyed with my final remarks, but they recognized that they would not be able to change my decision."[31] A prodigious womanizer and archeological thief, Dayan was no angel. Observed journalist Gershom Gorenberg, "If God does stick his finger in history, He has a sense of humor in His choice of saints."[32] Dayan had come up with this arrangement on his own, with little input from the cabinet; as is usually true of prudent and enduring compromises, neither side was happy with it.

Nonetheless, the hastily brokered state of affairs has yielded an incessant series of incidents, each of which has carried the potential for catastrophe. Almost from the start, Rabbi Goren proved troublesome. He started by bringing small groups of followers up to the Mount to pray. Initially, the Waqf did not object, but on the ninth of the month of Av, when Jews commemorate the destruction of both temples, he pushed the envelope yet further. On that day, which fell on August 15, 1967, the nettlesome rabbi brought to the Mount fifty people and a portable Ark, blew his ram's horn, and prayed.

The city's Muslims grew agitated, and the Waqf locked the main entrance to the Mount and began to charge Jews an entrance fee; Goren responded by promising to bring a thousand followers the following Sabbath. By this point the Israeli cabinet had tired of Goren's antics and decided that while Jews could visit the Mount, they could not pray upon it, and almost simultaneously, the Chief Rabbinate, Israel's supreme religious council, forbade Jews to visit it at all. Although not all Jews recognized the Rabbinate's authority, a large portion of the Orthodox did, and since they tended to be the most ideologically extreme, this prohibition kept the lid on Mount-related tension—at least for a while.[33]

The small minority of Jews who wanted to evict the Muslims from the Mount, dynamite the Dome and the Mosque, and rebuild the Third Temple were outraged and labeled Dayan a traitor and worse. Although history has thus far vindicated Dayan, the last has not yet been heard from temple-building zealots or from the Waqf.

Almost from the start, Dayan's compromise largely nullified Gur's famous exclamation; on a day-to-day basis, the Temple Mount is in fact in the hands of the Muslim community, and that control has only solidified over the half century since the 1967 war, and the political volatility surrounding God's little thirty-five acres has only increased along with it.

The next major incident at the Mount involved a schizophrenic Australian Christian named Denis Michael Rohan, who, suffused with psychosis-derived religious fervor, entered the al-Aqsa Mosque on August 21, 1967, poured kerosene onto the stairs to the pulpit, and tossed in a match. The fire destroyed much of the interior and weakened supporting pillars.

Rohan was a disciple of Herbert Armstrong, the American founder of the fundamentalist Radio Church of God, one of the first preachers to exploit the new medium in the early 1930s. Armstrong wasn't a dispensationalist, but rather believed that Britons and Americans were descendants of the Ten Lost Tribes of Judaism. Nonetheless, the garden-variety dispensationalist belief that the Second Coming of Jesus required renewed worship and sacrifices at a rebuilt Temple motivated the actively hallucinating Rohan, who simply took the next logical step: since the Mosque was the site of the First Temple, it had to be destroyed to make way for the new Temple's rebuilding (despite the fact that most authorities place the site of the First Temple at the Dome of the Rock, not at the adjacent Mosque).

When Israeli police finally caught up with Rohan two days later at his east Jerusalem guesthouse, he cheerfully confessed that since God wanted him to build the Temple, he had to first destroy the Mosque. In the end, Rohan was tried, convicted, confined to psychiatric detention, and finally in 1974 deported to Australia, where he remained hospitalized for two decades until his death.

Despite Rohan's lack of a Jewish connection, the Arab world erupted; both Nasser and Saudi King Faisal declared a sacred war against Israel. In this particular instance, the Israelis were lucky, since both Nasser and Faisal had locked up the radical Islamists most likely to take up the call.[34]

The al-Aqsa Mosque fire illustrated the two most explosive characteristics of Temple Mount politics. First, it is everywhere and always suffused with paranoia; despite Rohan's manifest insanity and lack of Zionist connections, many in the Arab world still accused the Jews of setting the fire and Israeli firemen of pouring gasoline on it. Contrariwise, one Israeli cabinet minister accused Muslims of setting the fire as a provocation. Second, if the Temple Mount tinderbox ever sets the world alight, it will likely be with the flame of religious delusion, whether that of the Zionist extremist, radical Islamist, dispensationalist Christian, or merely an everyday schizophrenic. Their madness will offer little solace for the ensuing Armageddon.

It is probably not too much of an overgeneralization to apply this principle to all of the world's great faiths. Mainstream Judaism, Christianity, and Islam are all religions of peace until they fall into the hands of the deluded true believer or the overtly insane; as regards the latter, schizophrenia's cardinal symptom, auditory hallucination, often speaks in the voice of God.[35]

Christians hardly possess a monopoly on end-times delusions, and the Jews had a half-millennium head start in that department. Islam, starting almost with the Prophet himself, has also sprouted its own varieties, which have recently mushroomed in both the bookstore and on the battlefield.

Desperation is the fertile soil in which end-times narratives grow, and in the sixth century B.C., having just been exiled into servitude along the shores of the Euphrates, the ancient Jews were certainly in need of a break. The books of Ezekiel and Daniel bruited the destruction of the Jews' oppressors, but theologians generally mark the first explicit mention of the Jewish Messiah with the Book of Isaiah. Similar to Daniel, Isaiah was written centuries after he supposedly lived in the eighth century B.C., probably by a series of authors writing both during the Babylonian exile and after the return to Judah. Its chapters prophesized the appearance of a savior who would end time and institute a universal Kingdom of God in Jerusalem.

Messianism runs as a constant theme throughout Jewish history, sometimes as a thin red ribbon, other times as an unfurling crimson cloth that smothers reason. It could become a nationwide movement, as during the Roman period when the Zealots plotted the A.D. 70 rebellion in which a Zealot splinter group, the Sicarii, assassinated Jews who refused to rebel; some of its members later committed mass suicide at Masada, high above the Dead Sea. Or it could be the work of talented but deluded, and occasionally psychotic, individuals such as Sabbatai Zevi, a bipolar Sephardic rabbi who declared himself the Messiah in 1648 during a manic break, became the religious leader of the large Jewish community of Smyrna in Asia Minor, then skittered around the eastern Mediterranean gathering converts and congregations. The mid-seventeenth century saw pogroms that decimated the Continent's Jewish population, and Sabbatai Zevi's messianic promises of salvation attracted a vast following that ended when he was imprisoned by the Ottomans and chose conversion to Islam over death.[36]

In the aftermath of the Holocaust, the fractious Israeli independence movement featured its own version of the drama between the ancient Judean Zealots, who generally didn't murder their fellow Jews, and the Sicarii, who did. During the pre-Independence conflicts, two terrorist groups, the Irgun and Lehi, would, respectively, reenact these two roles. Each participated in murderous attacks on both Arabs and British officials, most famously the 1944 assassination in Cairo of Lord Moyne, a British deputy minister of state, and the 1946 bombing of Jerusalem's King David Hotel, which killed ninety-one people.

When the Second World War erupted, the Irgun called a temporary halt to its attacks on the British, which angered its more radical members, who coalesced under the leadership of Avraham Stern to form Lehi (better known in the English-speaking world as the Stern Gang). Like the Irgun, Lehi targeted Arabs and British nationals and was responsible for not only Moyne's assassination, but in 1948, that of Count Folke Bernadotte, the U.N. representative, whom they feared was about to push through an unfavorable armistice settlement with the Arabs. (During the war, Bernadotte had secured the release of tens of thousands from German concentration camps, among whom were about sixteen hundred Jews.)

In addition to the temporary Second World War cease-fire with the British, two issues separated the Irgun and Lehi. As with the Zealots and their splinter Sicarii faction, the Irgun generally did not kill their fellow Jews, whereas the Lehi did. Both the ancient Sicarii and modern-day Lehi murdered Jewish collaborators, and occasionally those with whom they merely had ideological differences. More importantly, like the Sicarii, the Lehi were enthusiastic messianists, whereas the Irgun were more secular.

Lehi's manifesto, the "National Revival Principles," listed eighteen points, which included the infamous promise to the Jews from Exodus of the land "from the River of Egypt to the great Euphrates River," and also the building of the Third Temple.[37] The last leaders of the Irgun and Lehi, before being absorbed into the Israeli armed forces and intelligence services, were, respectively, Menachem Begin and Yitzhak Shamir. Both later became Israeli prime ministers.

Messianic groups garner relatively little support in Israel, where the populace is well informed, and there are few ruder things than phoning someone during the evening news; their body politic thus well understands the suicidal potential of rebuilding the Temple. While the nation is still the target of frequent terrorist attacks and of the more recent looming Iranian presence, the raw fuel for messianism, an existential threat on the scale of the Babylonians, Seleucids, Romans, Nazis, or Nasser's Egypt, is no longer present; Israel, after all, has signed peace treaties with Egypt and Jordan, and the remaining traditional threat, Syria, is in disarray.

Even so, the 1967 conquest of the Old City did energize a small corner of Israeli millennialists, especially the Gush Emunim (Bloc of the Faithful), who took Exodus's territorial maximalism as gospel: The Lord had deeded Gaza, the West Bank, the Golan Heights, and even the desolate Sinai to the Jews in perpetuity. Almost immediately after the 1967 war, the Gush began building settlements in the West Bank, and in 1974, they clashed with the new prime minister, Yitzhak Rabin, over building projects there; eventually, the settlers wore the prime minister down and outfoxed him with an end run through Rabin's rival, defense minister Shimon Peres, who was more sympathetic to the settlements. Three years later, Menachem Begin became the Israeli leader, and he opened the floodgates to West Bank expansion. (Gush was less successful in preventing implementation of the 1978 Camp David Accord, which returned the Sinai to Egypt.)

Other Jewish messianists focused on rebuilding the Temple. One such Temple enthusiast is Yisrael Ariel, the rabbi intrigued by Melody the cow. As a young man in 1967, Ariel had served in the paratroop brigade that captured the Western Wall. For him and a tiny group of ultra-Orthodox Jews, the Messiah (the first, and as yet unarrived, one) cannot come until the Temple is up and running, and in 1988, he helped found the Temple

Institute, which is dedicated not just to rebuilding the Third Temple, but also to recreating it down to the finest detail, including the flaxen robes, musical instruments, and rituals of ancient Jewish worship.

Such attention to detail is simply a matter of time, artistry, and money, of which Ariel and his colleagues have plenty. More difficult to accomplish is supplying the priests who will perform the ritual sacrifice required for the Messiah's return. This represents a theological catch-22, since sacrifices generally can be performed only by a priest purified with red-heifer ash, which itself requires slaughtering the rare bovine.

Yosef Elboim, a rabbi associated with another messianic group, the Movement for the Establishment of the Temple, sought to surmount this difficulty through the creation of priests who have never been under the same roof with a dead person. Willing expectant mothers descended from the ancient priestly caste, the *cohanim*, would give birth in a special compound, raised off the ground so as to avoid another priestly taboo, mistakenly stepping on an unmarked grave. The Movement would allow parental visits, but the boys could never venture outside the compound; a specially raised courtyard would be provided for play. They would receive priestly training, including sacrificial technique, and at some future date after their bar mitzvahs they would slaughter genetically engineered red heifers.[38]

In 1975, a small group of Jewish messianists entered the Temple Mount and prayed just inside one of the gates forbidden to them, as had Goren and his followers eight years previously.* A joint Arab-Israeli police unit removed the praying nationalists, but an Israeli court ruled in favor of their actions and provoked riots in which several Arabs were killed and dozens injured. Arab nations protested at the U.N., and the Waqf ruled that the entire Mount, including the Western Wall, was a mosque. An Israeli higher court finally nullified the decision to allow Jewish Temple Mount prayer, but subsequently three Likud prime ministers, Menachem Begin, Ariel Sharon, and Benjamin Netanyahu, have vowed to reverse it. None has yet delivered on that incendiary promise.

---

* The Mount has eighteen gates; six are sealed, and one is physically open but prohibited for public use. Muslims can use the remaining eleven, but non-Muslims can enter by only one, the Mughrabi Gate at the southwest corner, next to the Western Wall.

In 1982, two separate Jewish extremist groups attempted to plant explosives on the Mount; in the first, the Kach movement, a floridly racist anti-Arab group led by Rabbi Meir Kahane, tried to set off a bomb near the wall of the Dome of the Rock, while the second, a shadowy group called the Lifta Gang, attempted to blow up both the Dome and the al-Aqsa Mosque.* In response to the attempts, the Harvard University Center for International Affairs performed a geopolitical simulation predicated on a successful destruction of the Dome and concluded that it would start a third world war.

Yet more seriously, another group, the Jewish Underground, which had by the early 1980s killed five Arab students in Hebron and had attempted assassinations of West Bank mayors and bombings of mosques and Arab buses, made the most serious attempt of all. In 1984, they performed extensive reconnaissance of the Dome and acquired sophisticated explosives before calling off their plans. As later put by one member of an extremist group, thirty people planning such an operation could be called an underground; three hundred, a movement; and three thousand, a revolution.[39] The next year an Israeli court sentenced twenty-seven Underground members for the attempt on the Mount and their other terrorist attacks to prison terms ranging from a few years to life. By 1990, though, pressure from Israeli right-wing groups saw all of them freed.[40]

Almost until his death in 1994, Rabbi Goren continued to cause trouble. On his infamous first visit to the Mount, he began to measure and survey it. A few years before his demise, he published those measurements along with a scriptural commentary that declared that a large southern strip of the Mount lay outside the Temple's sacred confines, and so was suitable for building a synagogue. The article ignored the fact that the site is currently occupied by the al-Aqsa Mosque.

Archaeology under the Mount incites the same Arab anger as prayer on its surface. Despite overwhelming historical and archaeological evidence, Muslims generally deny the existence of both the First and Second Temples and consider any excavation of the layers under the Mount's surface as a Jewish attempt to justify building a third one.

Over the centuries, human settlements accumulate successive layers

---

* Eight years later, Kahane was assassinated in Brooklyn by El Sayyid Nosair, an American citizen who had been born in Egypt and trained in Pakistan by an organization founded by Osama bin Laden.

of sediment, so the deeper an archaeologist digs, the further back she travels in time. Vivid demonstrations of this are occasionally visible in cities with ancient histories such as Rome and Jerusalem, where excavations dating to the time of Christ are seen one or two dozen feet below the modern streets.

In Jerusalem, this means that an archaeologist first encounters artifacts from the Ottoman period, followed by those of successively earlier Muslim kingdoms, then Roman, Greek, Jewish, and, if very lucky, the Canaanite rulers. After the 1967 conquest, for the first time Jewish researchers, led by Hebrew University archaeologist Benjamin Mazar, gained access to the area surrounding the Mount.

Mazar's most significant discovery was from the period of the late Second Temple of Herod, which uncovered a large public area with extensive housing, broad streets, and a sophisticated water system adjacent to the Mount, as well as monumental steps leading up to it, as close to dispositive proof of the Second Temple as an archaeologist might find.

The Waqf complained to UNESCO that the excavations undermined the stability of the Mount, and the U.N. organization appointed a series of independent investigators who found no evidence of structural compromise and praised the archaeological results, though one participant did criticize the fact that the excavations had been performed without the permission of the Arab landowners.[41]

Far more serious problems resulted from the Western Wall Tunnel, which runs underground along the entire western edge of the Mount. Begun in 1969 by the Israelis, its excavation destroyed multiple structures from the Mamluk period and greatly upset the Waqf; the digging resulted in denouncements in the U.N. General Assembly and subsequent U.N. sanctions. In protest against the U.N. sanctions, the United States and some of its allies stopped their contributions to UNESCO, which nearly bankrupted it.

The nineteenth-century English archaeologist Charles Warren had extensively excavated on and under the Mount, and one of his many discoveries was an ancient gate under the Western Wall that opened into a tunnel under the Mount, and thence to a staircase to its surface near the Dome of the Rock. Warren later wrote *The Land of Promise*, a pamphlet that suggested that a European consortium, "similar to the old East India Company," colonize Palestine with Jews.[42]

In 1981, workers in the Western Wall Tunnel under the direction of Rabbi Yehuda Getz re-encountered "Warren's Gate" and the eastbound tunnel beyond, which Getz believed led to the Holy of Holies and perhaps even to the lost Ark of the Covenant. His team began to excavate eastward under the Mount itself toward the Dome, apparently with the cooperation of the Israeli Religious Affairs Ministry. Several weeks after Getz's discovery, Waqf guards heard noise coming from the excavation below and descended through the cisterns, where they battled with the Jewish archaeologists.[43]

True to form, Goren proclaimed the new tunnel even holier than the Western Wall. Arabs, on the other hand, saw a naked attempt to gain control of the Mount, and the Israelis, faced with intense Arab hostility, sealed off the tunnel with a thick concrete wall, placing it off limits, possibly forever, to further investigation.

Shortly after the Western Wall Tunnel's completion in the mid-1980s, the Israelis opened it to tourists. Because of the passageway's narrowness, visitors had to double back to exit from its southern entrance near the Wailing Wall; the resulting congestion seriously limited traffic. To remedy this problem, the Israelis built an exit at its northern terminus, which again inflamed the Arab populace, who saw the new portal as an attempt to undermine and collapse the Mount; angry crowds gathered, and work was temporarily halted.

At midnight on September 23, 1996, the Israelis cracked open the street over the northern portal and quickly placed an iron door there. Two days later riots broke out all over the Palestinian territories that featured a pitched battle between the Israeli army and the Palestinian National Security Force, newly created under the Oslo Accords; dozens were killed on both sides, and hundreds were injured.[44] The situation became fraught enough for President Clinton to call an international summit, which proved inconclusive. Subsequently, the unrest died down and the exit remained open; today, tourists who exit the tunnel are surprised to find themselves greeted by Israeli guards who escort them back to the Wailing Wall.

Israel's 1967 conquest of the Old City and West Bank would change not only the political complexion of the Middle East and of Arab-Israeli relations, but it would also increasingly impinge upon politics, religion, and culture in both the United States and Israel. It would do so in ways that the direct combatants in that year's events could hardly have predicted. Most alarmingly, its American dispensationalist protagonists would be driven by a belief system so delusional and divorced from real-world facts as to make John Nelson Darby blush.

10

ENTREPRENEURS OF
THE APOCALYPSE

To get a ground-level sense of America's current cultural polarization, watch *Left Behind*, a B-movie starring Nicolas Cage as airline pilot Rayford Steele. On a flight from New York to London, Steele's plane suffers the inexplicable disappearance of dozens of passengers and a collision with an apparently pilotless airliner and is then improbably guided by Steele's daughter to a fiery emergency landing on a stretch of abandoned highway.

The film, which chaotically shifts between scenes of mayhem in Steele's aircraft and on the ground, neatly separates its viewers into two groups: those who find the plot line bizarre and kick themselves for watching it, and those who consider it an entertaining version of a story as familiar as *Ocean's Eleven* or *Casablanca*.

Nowhere is the nation's cultural divide more noticeable than that cleaved by dispensationalism: To one side lie those to whom it supplies the very real prospect of salvation from a fearsome Tribulation and eternal damnation; and to the other side it seems a belief system that, to the extent they're aware of it at all, echoes the incoherent jumble of *Left Behind*.

President George W. Bush's address to the nation announcing military action in Afghanistan on October 7, 2001 nicely illustrated this divide. To the secular ear, it struck a tolerant, anodyne tone almost devoid of religious content, and mentioned Islam only in terms of American open-armed acceptance of and good wishes toward its nearly two billion adherents.

Evangelical listeners, on the other hand, heard a rather different message in phrases such as "lonely path" (Isaiah), "killers of innocents" (Matthew), and "there can be no peace" (Jeremiah, Ezekiel, Chronicles, Isaiah) that suggested the wrath of a Judeo-Christian God. Religious scholar Bruce Lincoln observed that such phrases were "plainly audible to portions of his audience who are attentive to such phrasing, but likely to go unheard by those without the requisite textual knowledge."[1] Bush's speech was a loud and piercing dog whistle; as put by *Christianity Today* after Lincoln published those words, "Sadly, we'll no longer be able to secretly nod and wink to each other as Bush talks."[2] (Bush himself is noticeably silent regarding dispensationalist beliefs; officially a Methodist, most observers classify him as mainline Protestant.)[3]

The prevalence of the dispensationalist delusion in the United States also separates this country from the rest of the developed world, and carries with it the potential for catastrophe.

While Jewish messianists constitute only a tiny percentage of Israelis, the vast majority are justifiably horrified at the prospect of a Third Temple, since they well understand the catastrophic consequences of the requisite destruction of a Muslim holy shrine. The same cannot be said for American evangelicals. Thanks to Darby and his heirs, many more Christians than Jews share the messianist dream of resuming sacrifices in a rebuilt Temple.

The theological justification for doing so is tenuous. Dispensationalists, for unclear reasons, generally fall back on the annoyingly redundant and vague 2 Thessalonians 2:4:

> Who opposeth and exalteth himself above all that is called God, or that is worshipped; so that he as God sitteth in the temple of God, shewing himself that he is God.

The *Moody Monthly*, the house organ of the Moody Bible Institute, devoted much of the issues following the 1967 war to the prophetic meaning of the capture of the Old City and newly regained access to the Temple Mount. In a sterling example of confirmation bias, one of the participants in a roundtable-style article reported in the magazine summarized the conflict's significance as follows:

> The Bible is almost an encyclopedia of Middle Eastern events, and certainly in this hour the Middle East is the focus of attention. And to me these events confirm the literal interpretation of Old Testament and New Testament prophecies.[4]

In those same pages, Dallas Theological Seminary (DTS) president John Walvoord discussed the renewal of Temple animal sacrifices, noting that "many therefore predict the early reactivation of a temple by the victorious state of Israel," and that "surely this is the finger of God indicating The End of the Age."[5]

Walvoord was not a household name, as neither were Anderson, Scofield, Gaebelein, and English, who despite their publishing successes led modest, quiet lives. Walvoord's article, fatefully, was followed on the next page by one penned by Hal Lindsey, then an even more obscure DTS graduate who had been Walvoord's protégé between 1958 and 1962.[6]

Within a few short introductory paragraphs, Lindsey served up a burbling cauldron of current-day secular apocalypses: the Vietnam War, domestic race riots, nuclear obliteration of the planet within minutes of the first intercontinental ballistic missile launches, the rising power of Communist China, and the starvation of billions from global overpopulation.

Equally disastrous, according to Lindsey, was liberal Protestantism's denial of literal biblical truth and its bruiting of God's death. In his fevered imagination, the geopolitical stars were perfectly aligned with Daniel and Revelation: the resurgent Roman Empire/European Union; the "king of the north," Russia; the "king of the south," Egypt; and finally, the "king of the east," China. According to Lindsey, Revelation 9:13–21 foretold that it would field a vast oriental horde (in Lindsey's unfortunate phrasing, a "yellow peril"): "A recent television documentary, filmed inside of Red China, stated that at this present hour there are 200 million Chinese under arms. An interesting coincidence?"[7]

The cited passages from Revelation do not in fact mention the king of the east; its 9:16 cites two hundred thousand horsemen of obscure provenance, not two hundred million. At its height in the 1970s, the People's Liberation Army boasted about four million men. Despite this factual looseness, all was clear to Lindsey, according to whom the overwhelming litany of global horrors of that era consisted of

> pieces of a great jig-saw puzzle which after much vagueness finally fit into place. We are living at a time when the pieces in a divine puzzle are suddenly fitting where they belong. The most important development, of course, is the re-establishment of Israel in its own

land after almost two thousand years of global dispersion, coupled
with the events since then in the Middle East.[8]

Lindsey's 1967 essay in *Moody Monthly* hinted at the slow, dangerous dispensationalist segue from passive observation of the end-times sequence to
active involvement powered by the wholesale confabulation of ludicrous
geopolitical assertions. Lindsey fondly quoted "an Israeli historian" who,
when asked with the rebuilding of the Temple what would become of the
Dome of the Rock, answered coyly, "Who knows? Perhaps there will be an
earthquake."[9] An Israeli who happened upon this sentence would likely have
laughed out loud: the "Israeli historian" in question was one Israel Eldad,
the right-wing Lehi ideologue who had penned the organization's "National
Revival Principles," which proclaimed the Jewish right to all land between
the Nile and Euphrates and the immediate construction of the Third Temple.

While well known in dispensationalist circles, *Moody Monthly* had
little readership among the broad American public, but Lindsey's riveting
staccato of doomsday scenarios foretold a prose talent that would shortly
carry the dispensational message to tens of millions of Americans over the
next half century. In the process, he would achieve wealth and worldwide
celebrity and transform the American religious landscape. Even more
incredibly, his patented brand of geopolitical fantasy would infect the
American body politic.

Born in Houston in 1929, Lindsey had a traditional Southern fundamentalist upbringing, which did not seem to immediately stick; baptized
three times, he found religion irrelevant and depressing, "so I just kissed it
off."[10] He drifted through a business education at the University of Texas,
deployment in the Coast Guard, a stint as a Mississippi tugboat captain,
and an unsuccessful marriage, all of which left him pessimistic about the
world. On the brink of suicide, he picked up a Gideon's Bible and read
that if he received God's truth, he would receive spiritual rebirth.

Intrigued but still not convinced, he taught himself to read Greek and
immersed himself in the Bible, which initially he thought full of historical
errors. By and by he met a young preacher named Jack Blackwell who
introduced him to biblical prophecy: "A fire was kindled within me that
has never gone out."[11]

His newfound faith led him to the DTS, where he earned a master's
in theology and remarried. Upon graduation the newlyweds began work

as campus missionaries and spread the dispensationalist narrative during the turbulent 1960s at schools like U.C. Berkeley and San Francisco State. Preaching to skeptical left-wing campus audiences sharpened his rhetorical skills into a theological scalpel; one observer noted how he attracted auditoriums filled with young men of draft age to whom Armageddon was not an abstraction, and whom the handsome, charismatic, and lucid Lindsey would mesmerize with rapid-fire renditions of current events supplemented with blackboard-drawn maps.[12]

He and his wife eventually tired of barnstorming college towns and settled down in Los Angeles, where they concentrated their efforts at UCLA. The success of his *Moody Monthly* piece encouraged him to write a book. Under the mentorship of the well-established religious writer Carole Carlson, who had worked with Billy Graham, he began work:

> As I wrote, I'd imagine that I was sitting across from a young person—a cynical, irreligious person—and I'd try to convince him that the Bible prophecies were true. If you can make a young person understand, then others will understand too. A young person isn't hesitant to call you on something, and it forces you to come to grips with people who aren't in the religious "club."[13]

The result, *The Late Great Planet Earth*, was like nothing ever seen in evangelical literature: Echoing the style of his 1967 *Moody Monthly* piece, it blended breezy current geopolitics, gee-whiz technological futurism, and current popular culture, all deftly laid over a gossamer-thin framework of dispensationalism. Bookstores, instead of burying it on the musty religion shelves, placed it in the red-hot New Age section next to works on the I Ching, transcendental meditation, and reflexology.

Lindsey and Carlson had mastered the art of literary transportation, and their output captivated readers. Within a year, the book had sold ten million copies, and to date, at least thirty-five million. It found its way into the hands of President Ronald Reagan and several of his cabinet secretaries and was followed by similar volumes that also sold in the millions.

It's nearly impossible to overestimate the book's influence. In the words of the late Paul Boyer, one of America's most well respected theological observers,

The significance of Hal Lindsey, I think, is he represents another one of those moments of breakthrough, when interest in Bible prophecy spills out beyond just the ranks of the true believers and becomes a broader cultural phenomenon. And people who had never paid much attention to prophecy at all hear about this book. They pick up the paperback. They see the way Lindsey weaves together current events and finds Biblical passages that seem to foretell those events, and they say, "Wow, this is amazing. There must really be something to this." . . . [Lindsey] seems to have had considerable influence not just on the part of the public as a whole, but at some of the highest levels of government.[14]

First published in 1970, the book synthesizes the works of Darby, Anderson, Scofield, and Gaebelein into a breezy, free-flowing narrative exposition, but where Lindsey excels is at the selling of biblical inerrancy. Time and again, he breathlessly relates the predictions of Jesus and the prophets that have come true with uncanny accuracy decades, and even centuries, later.

Confirmation bias does not merely involve actively seeking favorable evidence, no matter how vague, but it also casts a willfully blind eye over contrary data, in this case the large number of biblical prophecies that failed to materialize. To name but a few: the prediction that Egypt would become a permanent wasteland and that the Nile would evaporate (Ezekiel 29:8–15 and 30:12); that the Egyptians would adopt the Canaanite language (Isaiah 19:18); and, most famously of all, that a Jewish kingdom would stretch east several hundred miles from the Nile to the Euphrates (Exodus 23:25–31).

Lindsey's influence reached from the humblest believers to commanding heights of American politics. Ronald Reagan's devout mother, Nellie, imparted to her young son a deep religious devotion; while most Americans of a certain age know of his graduation from Eureka College, few are aware of its religious affiliation with the Disciples of Christ, the Reagan family's church. Although a mainstream Protestant denomination, the sect is deeply imbued with both social and economic conservatism.

By young adulthood, Reagan had bought into evangelical Protestantism. Early in his political career, he enthusiastically proclaimed his devotion to Christ, and during his governorship of California, he became a devotee of *The Late Great Planet Earth*.[15] He also met regularly with the biggest dispensationalist and evangelical names of his day, including Jerry Falwell, Jim Bakker, Pat Robertson, and Billy Graham. All of them recall having animated end-times discussions with the up-and-coming politician. One witness to an eschatological conversation between Graham and Reagan marveled about how the governor "held his own."[16]

Nor did Reagan confine his eschatological conversations to evangelists. In 1971, the California governor told James Mills, the Democratic president pro tempore of the state senate, "For the first time ever, everything is in place for the Battle of Armageddon and the second coming of Christ." As he continued, his voice rose,

> It can't be long now. Ezekiel says that fire and brimstone will be rained upon the enemies of God's people. That must mean that they'll be destroyed by nuclear weapons. They exist now, and they never did in the past.[17]

Reagan even cornered Jews on the topic. In 1981, the newly elected president discussed end-times eschatology with Thomas Dine of the American-Israel Public Affairs Committee: "I turn back to your ancient prophets in the Old Testament and the signs foretelling Armageddon, and I find myself wondering if, if [*sic*] we're the generation that's going to see that come about." Shortly thereafter he repeated the sentiment to Alabama's Senator Howell Heflin and added, "Russia is going to get involved in it."[18]

Reagan was especially taken with the Russian role in Lindsey's dispensationalist narrative; not coincidentally, his most famous speech was given in 1983 to the National Association of Evangelicals, in which he referred to the Soviet Union as "an Evil Empire" and that "we are enjoined by scripture and the Lord Jesus to oppose this evil." Those flourishes out of the way, he went on,

> A [nuclear] freeze would reward the Soviet Union for its enormous and unparalleled military buildup. Yet let us pray for the salvation for all of those who live in that totalitarian darkness. Pray that they will discover the joy of knowing God. But until they do, let us be aware that while they preach the supremacy of the state, declare its omnipotence

The Scottish songwriter, poet, and journalist Charles Mackay is best known as the author of *Memoirs of Extraordinary Popular Delusions and the Madness of Crowds*. First published in 1841, it is still in print. *Wikimedia Commons*.

The illegitimate son of a small town mayor, Jan Bockelson had charisma and theatrical skills that propelled him into the leadership of the catastrophic 1534–1535 Münster end-times rebellion. *Courtesy of Stadtmuseum Münster.*

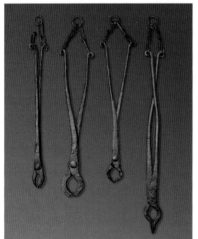

The tongs used to torture Bockelson and his lieutenants, and the cages in which their bodies were hung from a church tower. The cages are still visible today. *Courtesy of Stadtmuseum Münster.*

Nature endowed John Law with a steel-trap grasp of mathematics that enabled him to transform France's banking structure and ignite the world's first widespread stock bubble. Reviled in his time, he is now recognized as one of the forefathers of today's paper-currency–based financial system. *© The Trustees of the British Museum.*

This 1720 Dutch cartoon depicts John Law as Don Quixote. *Courtesy of Baker Library, Harvard University.*

The Mississippi Bubble in Paris triggered a similar mania in London, the South Sea Bubble, whose central character, John Blunt, became the prototype of today's arrogant and fraudulent CEO. *Private Collection/ Bridgeman Images.*

"The South Sea Bubble, a Scene in 'Change Alley in 1720,'" painting by Edward Matthew Ward, 1847. Digital photograph: *Photo © Tate Gallery, London.*

George Hudson, the indefatigable railroad magnate of the 1840s, simultaneously ruined thousands of investors and endowed England with the world's first high-speed transport network. *Wikimedia Commons*.

Psychologist Peter Wason's 1950s experiments established today's widely quoted concept of confirmation bias. *Courtesy of Armorer and Sarah Wason.*

The early agnosticism of William Miller gave way to intense religious belief and fixation on the imminence of the end-times. *Courtesy of the Adventist Digital Library.*

The wealth, social connections, and organizational skills of Joshua V. Himes propelled Miller's theology into a powerful mass movement. *Courtesy of the Adventist Digital Library.*

Between 1842 and 1844, the end-times followers of William Miller organized 125 "camp meetings" attended by up to several thousand believers. The railroad companies often built special stations to receive attendees; preachers rode for free. *Courtesy of the Adventist Digital Library.*

The front page of *The Midnight Cry!* from October 19, 1844, three days before the world was to end. *Courtesy of the Adventist Digital Library.*

In the 1960s and 1970s, the iconoclastic economist Hyman Minsky described the instability inherent in a modern economic system built on financial leverage. *Courtesy of Beringer-Dratch/Levy Economics Institute of Bard College.*

During the 1920s, "Sunshine" Charlie Mitchell sold the unsuspecting customers of National City Bank, the predecessor of today's Citicorp, billions of dollars of dodgy stocks and bonds. *Wikimedia Commons.*

A seasoned prosecuting attorney, Ferdinand Pecora questioned Charlie Mitchell so deftly that he incriminated himself, such that his tenure as chief counsel of the U.S. Senate's Committee on Banking and Currency became known as the "Pecora Commission." *Wikimedia Commons.*

The British commando Orde Wingate deeply imbibed his family's dispensationalist end-times theology and mentored many in the Israeli army's high command, including Moshe Dayan. *Wikimedia Commons.*

In 1948, Moshe Dayan, the Israeli Jerusalem front commander, dressed himself in Arab garb and traveled by car with his opposite number, Abdullah el-Tell, pictured in the above photograph, to Amman for talks with the Jordanian king. *Wikimedia Commons.*

From left to right, the local Israeli commander, Uzi Narkiss, Defense Minister Moshe Dayan, and Chief of Staff Yitzhak Rabin stride into the Old City on June 7, 1967, in this iconic photo. *The National Photo Collection of Israel.*

Immediately following the June 1967 conquest of the Old City, the fanatical chief rabbi of the Israeli Army, Shlomo Goren, blew a ceremonial ram's horn (shofar) at the Western Wall. Later, he unsuccessfully tried to convince Uzi Narkiss to blow up the Dome of the Rock. *Wikimedia Commons.*

A Seventh-day Adventist salesman with a third-grade education, Victor Houteff convinced himself that he alone had arrived at the proper interpretation of the Book of Revelation's end-time sequence. *Wikimedia Commons.*

The sect eventually wound up under the leadership of Lois Roden, the widow of one of Houteff's lieutenants. *Wikimedia Commons.*

The son of an unmarried fourteen-year old girl, Vernon Howell endured a chaotic childhood. After Lois Roden's death, he changed his name to David Koresh (after, respectively, the Jewish King David and Persian King Cyrus), and led the sect towards its apocalypse in Waco, Texas, on April 19, 1993. *Wikimedia Commons.*

Fire erupts at the Mount Carmel Branch Davidian complex on April 19, 1993, killing 76. Timothy McVeigh witnessed the conflagration in person, and in revenge perpetrated the Oklahoma City bombing on its second anniversary, killing 168 innocents. *Wikimedia Commons.*

Ronald Reagan was an enthusiastic believer in apocalyptic dispensationalist theology, which he could knowledgeably discuss with its best-known leaders, such as Jerry Falwell, founder of the Moral Majority. *White House/ Ronald Reagan Presidential Library via Wikimedia Commons.*

During the tech bubble of the 1990s, this barber shop became the improbable center of stock speculation on Cape Cod, as proprietor Bill Flynn dispensed investing advice while clipping hair. *Courtesy of the Wall Street Journal.*

Between 1984 and 1993 a small-town ladies' investment club in Beardstown, Illinois, reported mistakenly calculated returns that seemed to show them beating the market averages, launching its middle-aged members into media stardom. *The LIFE Images Collection, Getty Images.*

One of Islam's holiest sites, the Temple Mount's Dome of the Rock is thought by some Jews to be the site of Solomon's First Temple. *Jane A. Gigler.*

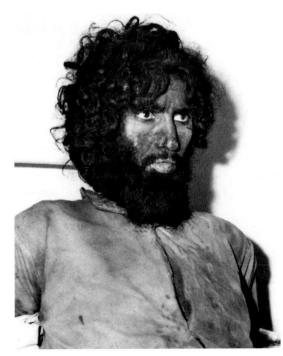

Former Saudi national guard corporal Juhayman al-Uteybi, expecting the end-times and the return of the Prophet, launched a suicidal attack on Mecca's Grand Mosque, Islam's holiest site. This picture was taken shortly before he and several dozen comrades were executed. *Wikimedia Commons.*

The Palestinian Muhammad al-Maqdisi (right), deeply influenced by Juhayman al-Uteybi's life and writings, in his turn inspired a large number of Islamic extremists, most notably the bloodthirsty Abu Musab al-Zarqawi, killed by a U.S. air strike in 2006. Al-Maqdisi renounced his end-times beliefs and today lives peaceably in Jordan. *Getty Images News.*

Yemeni-American Anwar al-Awlaki's apocalypse-laden internet content inspired numerous terrorist attacks in the United States, most notably "underwear bomber" Umar Farouk Abdulmutallab and the Fort Hood shooter Army psychiatrist Nidal Malik Hasan. His videos continued to inspire deadly attacks even after his death in a 2011 drone strike. *Wikimedia Commons.*

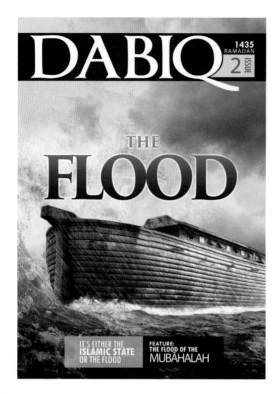

The cover of Issue 2 of *Dabiq*, the highly influential Islamic State publication named after the site of a famous battle in 1516 fought against the Christian Byzantine Empire. This issue was published just after the declaration of the caliphate on June 29, 2014. *Dabiq, Issue 2, Ramadan 1435 AH (June–July 2014).*

From the same issue of *Dabiq*, a celebration of the demolition of the Ahmad Al-Rifa'i shrine in southern Iraq named after the founder of the Sufi order, a sect considered heretical by IS. *Dabiq, Issue 2, Ramadan 1435 AH (June–July 2014).*

over individual man, and predict its eventual domination of all peoples on the earth, they are the focus of evil in the modern world.[19]

One wonders what the Soviet leaders made of Reagan's infatuation with the glories of a millennium whose antechamber featured nuclear holocaust. Their intelligence reports would also have informed them of the end-times beliefs of his long-serving defense secretary and fellow Hal Lindsey enthusiast, Caspar Weinberger. After his Jewish parents had left the faith, Weinberger became a deeply religious Episcopalian, impressed by the Bible's last book: "I have read the Book of Revelation, and, yes, I believe the world is going to end—by an act of God, I hope—but every day I think time is running out."[20] (Besides Reagan and Weinberger, Interior Secretary James Watt and Attorney General Edwin Meese were also Lindsey acolytes.)[21]

Reagan's dispensationalist influence ran in both directions. Not only did evangelical leaders bolster Reagan's end-times beliefs, but the president in turn supplied ammunition to his evangelical allies. In 1983, he had the National Security Council prepare a greatly simplified nuclear arms briefing for Falwell, who in his turn condensed the information yet further for Moral Majority–sponsored newspaper ads: "We cannot afford to be number two on defense! But sadly enough, that's where we are today. Number two. And fading!"*[22]

Happily for the planet, after 1983 both Reagan's eschatology and his hawkishness faded. The former actor was not the best informed of commanders in chief; according to one of his biographers, Lou Cannon,

> When Bill Clark became Reagan's second national security adviser at the beginning of 1982, he found that the president knew next to nothing about what was going on in many corners of the globe. . . . Clark knew that the president responded to visual aids and reasoned that he would be most receptive of all to films. So he took Reagan to the movies. [23]

* All evangelicals, however, were not defense hawks; in 1987, Billy Graham, who had counseled presidents since Eisenhower, labeled the arms race as "madness" and advocated not only SALT II, but "Salt 10."

The president was particularly affected by an ABC made-for-television movie, *The Day After*, about the vaporization of Lawrence, Kansas, during a nuclear exchange. Afterward, he recorded in his diary,

> It's very effective and left me greatly depressed. So far they haven't sold any of [the show's advertising], and I can see why. . . . My own reaction: we have to do all we can do to have a deterrent and to see that there is never a nuclear war.[24]

Reagan's diary failed to mention the reason for the absence of advertising: Jerry Falwell, who felt the program a propaganda effort by anti-nuclear activists, had threatened a boycott against its potential sponsors. A subsequent Reagan diary entry that detailed a meeting with Joint Chiefs Chairman General John William Vessey, Jr. described nuclear war planning as "a most sobering experience."[25]

It soon became apparent that both Reagan's television viewing and military briefings had underestimated the outcome of a thermonuclear exchange. By that point weapons experts knew that the firestorms generated by thermonuclear bombs would claim more victims than the initial blast and subsequent radioactive fallout; within a few months of *The Day After*, a landmark article in *Science* suggested that the stratospheric soot from those firestorms would linger for years and cause dramatic falls in global temperatures that would likely kill more people than even the blasts, firestorms, and radioactive fallout from the initial exchange.[26]

Reagan's apocalyptic beliefs became an issue during his 1984 reelection campaign against Walter Mondale. When journalists Georgie Anne Geyer and Marvin Kalb pressed him on the issue during the October 21 presidential debate, he soft-pedaled his previous end-times beliefs by suggesting that "a number of theologians" believed in Armageddon, but that he did not think that any nation could prevail in a nuclear war. (Nancy Reagan was said to have groaned "Oh, no" at Kalb's question.)[27]

By his second term, the prospect of nuclear war so horrified Reagan that diplomat Jack Matlock, Jr., the president's adviser on Soviet affairs, doubted that he would retaliate against a nuclear attack: "I think deep down he doubted that, even if the United States was struck, that he could bring himself to strike another country with [nuclear weapons]. He could never hint, but I sort of sensed [that]."[28] His Manichean anti-Soviet stance had evaporated, going so far as to propose to Mikhail Gorbachev a total ban on nuclear weapons at the 1986 Reykjavík Summit. Even though the two leaders failed to achieve this breakthrough, U.S.-Soviet tensions deescalated, and a year later they signed the far-reaching Intermediate-Range Nuclear Forces Treaty.

While both theologians and publishing industry observers have marveled at Lindsey's phenomenal success, they have paid less attention to his incessant stream of factual inaccuracies.[29] In one remarkable passage, he describes a large Japanese invasion force that steamed westward through the Indian Ocean in 1942 toward North Africa: "Nothing could have stopped them." Luckily, Admiral Yamamoto decides at the last minute to turn the fleet around and instead invade the U.S. West Coast. The American Navy intercepts his task force in the Coral Sea, where it decisively defeats the Japanese and turns the tide of the war.[30]

In the real Second World War, the Japanese didn't attempt to invade Northern Africa or even plan an invasion of the West Coast. The Battle of the Coral Sea was a relatively minor and inconclusive naval action that, if awarded on points, would have gone to the Japanese, not to mention the fact that a Japanese armada sailing from the Indian Ocean to the U.S. West Coast would not have come within two thousand miles of that body of water. In another passage, Lindsey describes Hitler seizing power in a "Putsch." Since he capitalized the word, he was referring to Hitler's 1923 opéra bouffe beer hall fiasco; in fact Hitler's National Socialists would not gain power for almost an additional decade via a legitimate parliamentary election victory. Further illustrating Lindsey's often hallucinatory grasp of everyday facts, the book predicts that Israel's geothermal resources will endow her with great wealth:

> I was talking to a prominent Los Angles engineer . . . and we discussed the need for a cheap source of energy. . . . He said that he is certain that there is enough steam trapped under the numerous faults in the earth around Israel to provide power to run turbines to produce electricity very economically. He called this new process geo-thermal energy. In the near future Israel will discover a way to produce cheap energy to develop this gold mine of riches.[31]

The vague reference to "a prominent Los Angeles engineer" is typical of the gauzy sourcing of many of Lindsey's assertions. (Other Lindsey favorites: "a television documentary," "scientists tell us," "a graph in a news magazine," "a major television station," or, simply, "it was reported to me.") Geothermal power is hardly a new technology; mankind has been heating homes and buildings with terrestrial steam for centuries, and geothermal electrical generation was invented around 1904. Finally, Israel doesn't have much in the way of geothermal vents, and its geothermal industry nicely demonstrates the real source of the modern state's wealth: its intellectual capital, and not its natural resources, which Lindsey mistakenly and repeatedly cites. An Israeli company, Ormat Technologies, is indeed one of the world's largest producers of geothermal equipment, but the country doesn't harbor enough geothermal potential to support any of the company's plants.[32]

More seriously, from the viewpoint of biblical interpretation, Lindsey repeatedly cites the Book of Daniel's supposed prophecy of around 550 B.C. about the successful Macabbean revolt against the Seleucid Empire four centuries hence as one example of a myriad of the Bible's unerring prophetic accuracies. As described in Chapter 1, biblical scholars in fact place Daniel's composition shortly after that event, probably fictitiously set during the earlier period of exile so as to enhance its prophetic bona fides.[33] As did Darby, Lindsey identifies the biblical Meshech's location as Moscow, despite the fact that modern historians date the city's founding in A.D. 1174, long after the Bible was written.[34]

Given Lindsey's lack of analytical and factual rigor, it's not surprising that his prophecies have not worn well. Early on in the book, he stresses the imminence of The End, triggered by the 1948 establishment of Israel. He quotes Jesus's statement in Matthew 24:34: "Truly I say to you, *this generation* will not pass away until all these things [the return of the Jews to Israel] take place." He interprets the passage as literally as possible:

> What generation? Obviously, in context, the generation that would see the signs—chief among them the rebirth of Israel. A generation in the Bible is something like forty years. If this is a correct deduction, then within forty years or so of 1948, all these things could take place. Many scholars who have studied Bible prophecy all their lives believe that this is so.[35]

Darby and his immediate followers, with the memory of Miller's Great Disappointment fresh in their memories, would never have made such a precise prediction. More than a century later, with that donnybrook far from the dispensationalist consciousness, Lindsey spun a combination of current events and biblical interpretation that predicted The End no later than 1988.

In the book, Lindsey also prophesizes the rise of a single worldwide religion synthesized from a mashup of mainstream Protestant and Catholic ecumenism and New Age "astrology, spiritualism, and even drugs."[36] At the beginning of the planet's seventieth "week" (in the dispensationalist calendar, seven years), Israel allies itself with the charismatic and mighty dictator of the all-powerful European Alliance, the Antichrist, and the Jews resume sacrifices at the rebuilt Third Temple. Because of its supposed abundant natural resources, Israel becomes one of most powerful and prosperous nations on the Earth, but at the three-and-a-half-year mark, the European dictator/Antichrist betrays the Israelis and begins slaughtering Christians. At this point, the Russians, along with Arab allies angered by the desecration of the Temple Mount, invade Israel via both an amphibious assault through the Bosporus Strait and the Mediterranean Sea and an overland expedition through the Caucasus and Turkey, a narrative Lindsey helpfully embellishes with detailed invasion route maps.

The Russians then double-cross their Arab allies and invade Egypt. The European dictator/Antichrist, alarmed by this turn of events, calls on the "Red Chinese" for help, who march the aforementioned two-hundred-million-strong horde clear across Asia to attack Israel. (Lindsey divines this attack from an "Indian report" that told of twelve thousand Chinese troops building a road across Tibet through Pakistan to facilitate the massive troop movement.) The Russian army, distracted in Egypt, returns to Israel, where it is destroyed (it's not clear whether by God or the Europeans). There ensues a great final battle at Megiddo (the biblical Armageddon, in present-day Israel) between the Europeans and the Chinese. This momentous clash of armies echoes around the world in a cataclysm of global destruction; Jesus then returns to end time. There is, happily, one bright spot in the carnage. A third of Jewry converts to Christianity and so save themselves. Alas, the remaining two-thirds burn.[37]

Lindsey's engaging prose style and the apocalyptic social and geopolitical atmosphere of the late 1960s opened a rich literary bank-teller's
window. *The Late Great Planet Earth* sold so well that the Mutual Insurance Company of New York began to offer policies that would pay off the
left-behind beneficiaries of raptured policy owners.[38]

Others soon clamored aboard the Tribulation gravy train. One of the first
was Lindsey's old teacher and president of the DTS, John F. Walvoord.
By the time of Lindsey's publication, he had headed the school for almost
two decades, but he had published relatively little in the mass-market
realm. Inspired by Lindsey's success, Walvoord cranked out a flood of
popular books, the most prominent of which was *Armageddon, Oil, and
the Middle East Crisis.* First published in 1980, it underwent a reworking
necessitated by the 1991 First Gulf War, eventually sold more than two
million copies, and is still in print.[39]

The book retraced the same modern dispensationalist narrative of
The Late Great Planet Earth: the return of the Jews to Israel, rise of the
Antichrist-led new Roman Empire, successive invasions by the Russians
and Chinese, followed by the Rapture, Armageddon, the return of Jesus,
and the final judgment. As did Lindsey, Walvoord enthusiastically wove
a thick red thread of current events into his narrative. In the four years
between the publication of the two books, the Arab oil embargo, triggered
by the 1973 Yom Kippur War, raised the specter of a vast transfer of the
world's wealth and power to the OPEC cartel, particularly the Arab nations
and Iran. As dispensationalist writers are wont to do, Walvoord seized upon
a dramatic current event, in this case the oil embargo, as the detonator for
an imminent end-times story.

Walvoord clearly saw through his dispensationalist-tinted glasses
that the United States, damaged beyond repair by the shift in the global
economic balance of power, would slink off the world stage and be
replaced by an all-powerful Muslim confederation led by an alliance of
Sunni Saudi Arabia and Shiite Iran, never mind that the two sects have
been slaughtering each other for the past fourteen centuries. The Antichrist would head the Europeans, who would be even more threatened
by the oil embargo than the United States, and the Muslim and European
confederations would broker an encompassing Middle East peace plan,

which would be enthusiastically embraced by another harmonious pair, the Israelis and Arabs.

At the usual three-and-a-half-year point, the Antichrist would cynically abrogate the pact and trigger the whole dispensationalist scenario: invasion by the Russians and two hundred million "Red Chinese," Armageddon, the Second Coming, and ultimate end-times. As did Lindsey, Walvoord predicted the rise of a "world church," which would be a tool of Satan, and yet an even more improbable amalgamation of ecumenical Christians, astrologers, other New Agers, and even Muslims.

With his academic orientation, Walvoord commanded historical fact more securely than Lindsey. For example, he clearly understood, as Lindsey did not, that the small Valley of Armageddon would not accommodate two hundred million Chinese fighters, and so he expanded its battlefield out by hundreds of miles.[40] His better grasp of history and geography, though, didn't improve his forecasting accuracy or limit his fantasies.

As with Dorothy Martin and her flying saucers, when the future disconfirmed the predictions of Lindsey and Walvoord, they doubled down and altered their narratives. Lindsey exploited the phenomenal success of *The Late Great Planet Earth* with several more volumes like it.[41] *The 1980's: Countdown to Armageddon*, first published in 1980, served up the usual menu of world-ending catastrophes: widespread revolution, war, and famine. In one typical example of Lindsey melodrama, an unnamed Israeli source, "one of that country's most brilliant and aggressive generals," tells him that during one of the direst moments in the Yom Kippur War, Moshe Dayan advised Prime Minister Golda Meir, "The Third Temple is falling. Arm the doomsday weapon."[42] While the Israelis did briefly consider the use of nuclear weapons during both the 1967 and 1973 wars, and Dayan probably did utter the first sentence in the above quote, the B-movie second sentence was reported nowhere else, least of all in his memoirs.

Such errors pop up in *The 1980's: Countdown to Armageddon* with even greater frequency than in *The Late Great Planet Earth*. At one point, Lindsey informs readers that "the number of earthquakes per decade has roughly doubled in each of the 10-year periods since 1950."[43] Were this true, temblors would now be about one hundred times more frequent than in 1950. Not unexpectedly, authoritative studies of worldwide earthquake frequency show no increase over the past century.[44]

Like the proverbial stopped clock that is accurate twice a day, Lindsey hits the odd bull's-eye, as when *The 1980's: Countdown to Armageddon* highlighted Egyptian leader Anwar Sadat's risk of assassination.[45] (And even so, Middle East national leadership has always been a high-risk proposition.) The ensuing years otherwise monotonously disconfirmed Lindsey's lurid predictions; the melody of increasing global cataclysms remained the same, only the lyrics required alteration. The near-total disappearance of godless communism personified by the Soviet Union's 1991 collapse forced Lindsey to find new bogeymen. *Planet Earth—2000 A.D.* duly identified new world-ending threats: the aforesaid pan-Islamic confederation of Shiites and Sunnis and terrifying natural cataclysms, especially the apparently unstoppable AIDS epidemic. ("No One Is Safe Any More" reads one chapter subheading.) Even the *Star Trek* television show exercised Lindsey, who fulminated against the fondness of Captain James T. Kirk, commander of the *Starship Enterprise*, for both secular philosophical concepts and Eastern religious notions such as reincarnation.[46]

Today, a pan-Muslim confederation currently seems as likely as Elvis's reappearance; since 9/11, twice as many American lives have been lost to right-wing terrorists than to Islamic terrorists, and an order of magnitude fewer than from lightning strikes and choking deaths.[47] Treatment and prevention advances have made HIV infection largely preventable and curable. (Death and infection rates for the disease peaked, depending on the source, at about the same time as the book's 1996 publication, and have been in slow decline ever since.)[48] As this is being written, the nonagenarian Lindsey continues to preach doom and dispensationalism in internet videos and on obscure cable channels.[49]

Although there is little question as to where Lindsey's political sympathies lay, he usually avoided direct advocacy; perhaps he chose to focus more on the next world than on this one. Whatever the reason, it fell to others to inject their dispensational beliefs into everyday politics, and few had more success in this endeavor than the dispensationalist preacher Jerry Falwell.

Falwell's family traced its Virginia roots back to 1669. His father was a successful, irreligious businessman who, among many other ventures, operated a bus company whose vehicles featured battery-powered movie projectors, and who drank himself to death at age fifty-five. Falwell, instead, took after his devout mother, who began every Sunday by blaring Charles Fuller's *Old-Fashioned Radio Hour* throughout the house.

In his early twenties, the newly ordained minister, who saw in his parents the battle between good and evil in miniature, took a page from Fuller's radio script with his own *Old-Time Gospel Hour*, which attracted a wide following after its 1956 debut. Although he personally opposed civil rights legislation, he hewed to that era's evangelical dictum to save souls but stay away from politics.[50]

That changed on January 22, 1973, with the Supreme Court's announcement of the *Roe v. Wade* decision:

> I will never forget the morning of January 23, 1973. . . . I couldn't believe that seven justices on that Court could be so callous about the dignity of human life. Were they misinformed? Had they been misled? Were they plunging the nation into a time of darkness and shame without even knowing what they were doing? . . . I knew something more had to be done, and I felt a growing conviction that I would have to take my stand among the people who were doing it.[51]

Several years later, one of Falwell's political allies, Paul Weyrich, said to him, "Jerry, there is in America a moral majority that agrees about the basic issues. But they aren't organized." The Moral Majority, which Falwell and Weyrich helped found, burst onto the national scene with their opposition to abortion and gay rights, determination to "clean up" television and the movies, and fervent support for the state of Israel.

The Moral Majority deserves significant credit for the election of Ronald Reagan and dozens of Republican congressional candidates in the 1980 election, and Falwell himself gave the opening benediction at the 1984 Republican Convention, in which he praised Reagan as "our greatest president since Lincoln."[52]

Within a decade, the movement fizzled and finally disbanded. For starters, Reagan's presidency did not seem to improve the nation's morals, film and television only got smuttier, and fellow evangelists Jimmy Swaggart and Jim Bakker disgraced evangelism with their sordid sex and financial scandals. Several years after the movement's disbandment, the Senate's acquittal of Bill Clinton moved Weyrich to write to his supporters that maybe there was no "moral majority" after all.[53]

Probably the most lasting, and potentially dangerous, legacy of the political movement spawned by Falwell and his dispensationalist colleagues has been America's ever more fervent support for Israel. While much has been made of the powerful pro-Israel lobbying machine exemplified by the American Israel Public Affairs Committee (AIPAC), its influence on American Middle Eastern policy is easily surpassed by that of Christian evangelicals. As succinctly put by UCLA political scientist Steven Spiegel in *Congressional Quarterly* (*CQ*) in 2002, "If you just focus on the power of Jewish members [of Congress] and Jewish groups in forming U.S. policy on Israel, you're missing the boat."[54]

The same *CQ* piece contained two salient quotes from fundamentalist Christian U.S. House members. The first was from a newly elected representative from Indiana named Mike Pence:

> My support for Israel stems largely from my personal faith. In the Bible, God promises Abraham, "Those who bless you I will bless, and those who curse you I will curse." So in some way, I don't fully understand [U.S. Policy]. I believe our own security is tied to our willingness to stand with the people of Israel.[55]

Representative James Inhofe was more concise. Asked why Israel had the right to occupy Gaza and the West Bank, he answered simply, "God said so."[56] The piece ended with Falwell, who remarked,

> There are about 200,000 evangelical pastors in America, and we're asking them all through e-mail, faxes, letters, telephone, to go into their pulpits and use their influence in support of Israel and the prime minister.[57]

No one, though, exemplifies the shift of fundamentalist influence onto the potentially cataclysmic arena of geopolitics as does Pat Robertson, whom diplomat and journalist Michael Lind labeled "the single most important purveyor of crackpot conspiracy theories in the history of American politics."[58]

Robertson grew up the child of conservative Southern privilege, the son of Absalom Willis Robertson, whose two-decade-long U.S. Senate career ended when Lyndon Johnson, angered by Robertson's snubbing of Lady Bird during a Virginia visit pursuant to the passage of the 1965 Civil Rights Act, recruited and successfully ran an opponent against him in the 1966 senate primary.

After graduating near the top of his Yale Law School class, the young Robertson failed the New York Bar examination and so undertook a business career. Disillusioned by the high life in Manhattan, he found Jesus, returned to Virginia, borrowed $37,000, and in 1960 started what became the Christian Broadcasting Network. The media venture succeeded beyond his wildest expectations and grew into, at its height, the third largest U.S. cable consortium.[59]

Robertson has led a protean career that has ranged from comical faith healing performances to control of a worldwide media and business empire with annual revenues of $150 million per year that endowed him with a net worth in the hundreds of millions of dollars.[60] He adheres to the basic dispensationalist Christian Zionist narrative, but with two important exceptions: He does not believe in the Rapture, and he practices "charismatic evangelism," a fancy way of saying that he possesses the ability to heal, to speak in tongues, and to talk to, or at least hear from, God.

In the mid-1980s, he decided to seek the 1988 Republican presidential nomination. The party's national establishment initially dismissed him as a fringe candidate, but soon the GOP found that his television ministry could turn out thousands of volunteers for "Brother Pat" and fund salaried staffs in twenty states. In 1987, he stunned political observers when he took control of that year's Michigan Republican Party convention, besting the two front-runners, Vice President George H. W. Bush and the glamorous, libertarian ex–football star Jack Kemp. Later that year, he would turn in impressive performances at caucuses and delegate meetings in Iowa, South Carolina, and Florida, and he would go on to win primaries in Hawaii, Alaska, Washington, and Nevada.

Ultimately, Robertson's campaign foundered on the shoals of three jagged political reefs. As a charismatic who did not completely subscribe to the dispensationalist timeline, he failed to unify the fundamentalist right. Although he did gain the endorsement of Falwell and Jimmy Swaggart, Jim Bakker's support was lukewarm, and another staunchly dispensationalist author, Tim LaHaye, pointedly snubbed him in favor of Jack Kemp.[61]

While his fellow evangelicals did not completely close ranks behind Robertson, the reaction of the secular body politic was withering. Reported Christopher Hitchens on a 1986 Robertson rally,

> There is something frightening about stupidity; more especially, about stupidity in the mass, organized form. . . . The man who drew the job of introducing Robertson to the throng was Harald Brede-sen . . . [who] is a self-defined "evangelical-charismatic," with alleged Pentecostal powers to speak in tongues.[62]

Furthermore, the partial evangelical support he did manage to get from Swaggart and Bakker backfired when their respective sex and financial scandals broke. Swaggart's played out at the worst possible time, right before the 1988 Super Tuesday primaries. (Two years prior, Swaggart himself had set a slow-burning fuse to his ministry when he called out a fellow minister for adultery, who then staked out Swaggart's favorite Baton Rouge no-tell motel with a telephoto lens.)

Robertson formally suspended his campaign two months after Super Tuesday, but his presidential run, at least in the short term, only enhanced his influence at the state and local levels. He took credit for Senator Jesse Helms's come-from-behind 1990 reelection; in the 1993 election for Arkansas lieutenant governor, he helped to launch the career of evangelical politician Mike Huckabee, a particularly sweet victory for Robertson, who despised Bill Clinton, who had backed Huckabee's opponent, Nate Coulter.[63]

One of the most salient aspects of Robertson's outsized life has been his involvement in Middle Eastern politics. By the time his television network, and especially its popular *700 Club* news show, burst into American living rooms in the 1960s, the American evangelical presence in Middle Eastern affairs had already been well established. Energized by the 1977 Israeli parliamentary election's elevation of Menachem Begin to prime minister, evangelicals subsequently founded the International Christian Embassy Jerusalem (ICEJ) in 1980, to which successive Likud governments pandered. In 1982, for example, Begin, an assiduous biblical scholar, accepted an invitation to speak at a pro-Israel rally at an evangelical church in Dallas, which was canceled at the last minute because of his wife's death.

The ICEJ went so far as to criticize the 1978 Israel-Egypt Peace Treaty's return of the Sinai Peninsula to Egypt as a violation of the biblical promise that all the land of Canaan belonged to the Jews; it also vigorously supported Israel's lethal 1982 incursion into southern Lebanon.[64]

Every year, between Christmas and New Year's, Robertson retreats into the Bible for additional study and prayer:

> During these periods, I have earnestly asked the Lord for any insight or direction He wishes to give me for the year ahead. At some times, His word to me has been remarkably precise and subsequent fulfillment amazing. At other times, either my spiritual perception was lacking or else subsequent prayer or actions by others caused a different result than what I anticipated.[65]

If there is a cataclysmic war in the Middle East, it will likely result from God telling different people different things, and in this regard, Robertson was, and remains, especially dangerous, as he has misheard God with some frequency, as when He told him that the world would end in 1982, that a tsunami would hit the Pacific Northwest in 2006, that worldwide mass terrorist killings would occur in 2007, and that Mitt Romney would win the 2012 presidential election.[66] (He also hears strange things from less exalted places as well: In 1984, on the *700 Club,* he quoted mysterious sources who reported that American troops had just invaded Lebanon. When mainstream sources contradicted the story, Robertson responded darkly that obviously the State Department or CIA were hushing things up; in 1988, he imagined that the Soviets had stationed squadrons of SS-5 and SS-24 missiles in Cuba.)[67]

At the height of his influence in the 1980s and 1990s, his sway in Israel equaled that in the United States; he still has close ties with Israeli Temple activists, particularly Gershon Salomon, leader of the Temple Mount Faithful, which advocates for the expulsions of Muslims and their shrines from the Mount and for rebuilding the Third Temple. Robertson has met with six of the last eight Israeli prime ministers, and he is especially close with hard-liner Benjamin Netanyahu.[68]

The geopolitical dangers inherent in Robertson's brand of theologically driven foreign policy extend well beyond the Middle East. For example, he was overjoyed when José Efraín Ríos Montt, a fellow charismatic Christian, became president of Guatemala after a military coup. Even after it became apparent Ríos Montt had embarked on a murderous campaign of ethnic cleansing against the country's indigenous populations that had killed thousands and displaced hundreds of thousands, Robertson averted his eyes: "I know Ríos Montt and he has not allowed his army to kill, rape, and torture over 4,000 men, women, and children. . . . There are those who would like to see [Montt's regime] replaced by communists. I prefer a Christian."[69]

The conventional explanation for the unique, widespread influence of dispensationalism in the United States is that it is more religious than other nations. In 2012, when the National Opinion Research Center (NORC) queried citizens around the world about their religious beliefs, fully 81 percent of Americans agreed with the strong and categorical statement "I believe in God now and I always have," versus only 37 percent in Great Britain, 25 percent in Japan, and 29 percent in France.[70]

In the past few decades, religiosity does seem to be waning even in the United States, although less dramatically than in the rest of the world; in 1967, for example, 98 percent of Americans answered yes to the simpler and less categorical Gallup survey question "Do you believe in God?"; by 2017 that number had fallen to 87 percent.[71]

The same is also true of Protestant evangelical fervor; between 2004 and 2018, a Pew survey of the number of self-identified evangelicals, most of whom are dispensationalists, declined from 23 to 15 percent. But while their numbers have decreased, their influence has actually increased

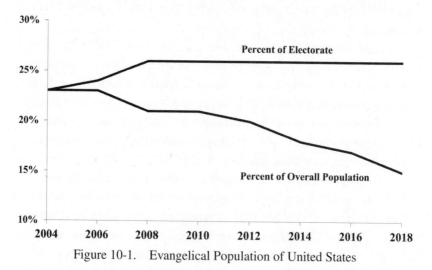

Figure 10-1.   Evangelical Population of United States

from 23 to 26 percent of voters, the inescapable conclusion being that evangelicals have more than maintained their political power in the face of declining numbers with increased electoral participation.

Although the world's developed nations have shown drops in religious belief and participation, this is not true for developing nations. Sociologists have long known that as societies become wealthier and better educated, they become less religious—the so-called secularization hypothesis. Because poorer developing nations have higher birth rates than wealthy developed ones, the percentage of the world population with strong religious beliefs is increasing, not decreasing.[72]

There are many reasons why societies grow less religious as they become more wealthy, including increasing existential security and the assumption by the state of social welfare functions formerly borne by religious organizations, but for our purposes the most important driver of the developed world's increasing secularization is the expansion of scientific knowledge, which displaces the need for religious explanations of natural phenomena.[73]

Mankind is blessed with an insatiable curiosity about the natural world, and particularly its most frightening phenomena, such as violent storms, floods, droughts, plagues, and earthquakes, as well as its most mysterious ones, particularly the origin of life on Earth. Today, the well-educated person has scant need for a theological explanation of any of these questions. Certainly, there are, and will likely forever be, gaps in our knowledge of the physical world, but as science continues to narrow these gaps, religion lags ever further behind science in explaining the natural world.

Although the more highly educated are less religious, the effect does not at first blush appear that powerful: according to a different 2014 survey by the Pew Forum, 66 percent of Americans with no college education believed in God with absolute certainty; this percentage fell only modestly to 55 percent among college graduates.[74]

Scientific education, though, makes a much bigger difference; among those at the pinnacle of that summit, belief in God has shrunk to derisory levels. Between 1914 and 1916, psychologist James Leuba surveyed five hundred American scientists; his results provide a fascinating snapshot of religious belief among the nation's leading biologists, chemists, and physicists at a time when belief in God in the general population was near universal.

Leuba divided the scientists according to his assessment of their status and accomplishment as "lesser" or "greater," and he also looked separately at biological and physical scientists:

	Physical Scientists	Biological Scientists
Lesser	50%	39%
Greater	35%	17%

Figure 10-2.   Belief in God among American Scientists 1914–1916

These data present a striking picture: Belief in God was lowest among the most accomplished scientists, especially elite biologists, whose need for a divine explanation for the origins and diversity of life was presumably less than for the chemists and physicists. And in any case, the average of all scientists' belief in God was certainly far lower than in the general population of that era.

In 1998, two American historians repeated this study among members of the prestigious National Academy of Sciences, a group that corresponds to Leuba's "greater" scientists. Eight decades after the Leuba study, belief in God ran to only 5.5 percent among biologists, 7.5 percent among physical scientists, and, most interesting, 14.3 percent among mathematicians, likely because their grasp of evolution and molecular biology is less secure than that of biologists.[75] A 2013 study among a group of similarly eminent British scientists, the fellows of the Royal Society, showed nearly identical results, including the same differentiation between biological and physical scientists: 76 percent of the biologists strongly felt that God did not exist and only 3 percent strongly felt that He did; versus 51 and 7 percent, respectively, of the physical scientists.[76]

Is it thus possible that many Americans tolerate the factual looseness of the likes of Lindsey and Robertson, and the tenets of dispensationalism in general, because they are less well informed than the citizens of the rest of the developed world?

The susceptibility of Americans to the dispensationalist narrative, along with the high degree of their religiosity compared with that of other developed nations, is a complex phenomenon. Obviously, other factors besides a lack of factual knowledge contribute to a person's devoutness, prime among which are their social and familial milieu; sociologists have long noted that belief systems are especially well transmitted via strong social ties to other believers.[77] But after social factors are considered, it's also likely that the larger a person's fund of general knowledge, the less likely they are to accept a dispensationalist narrative studded with the bald factual inaccuracies of a Hal Lindsey or a Pat Robertson.

The United States consistently ranks near the bottom of developed nations for the OECD's PISA international educational evaluations, and when compared with the citizens of other developed nations, Americans know depressingly little about both their own country and the rest of the world. The latest PISA cycle, completed in 2015, showed American students ranked fortieth, well behind the likes of Slovenia, Poland, Vietnam, Russia, Portugal, and Italy, let alone top scorers like Singapore, Hong Kong, Japan, and South Korea.[78]

A study from 1994 throws this problem into sharp relief: fully 37 percent of Americans got all of five representative basic facts about the world wrong, versus only 3 percent of Germans. (Of Spaniards, 32 percent got all five wrong; of Mexicans, 28 percent; of Canadians, 27 percent; of French, 23 percent; of British, 22 percent; and of Italians, 18 percent.) Italians and Germans who didn't attend college outscored Americans who did.*[79]

Individual performance correlated negatively with exposure to television news. As put by the study's authors, "American television is noteworthy for the cognitive busyness of its jump cuts, advertisements, and staccato style, and cognitive busyness makes it harder for some people to absorb information." The authors dryly noted that American researchers are "generally reluctant to ask too many factual questions for fear of embarrassing the respondents, who might terminate the interview or become too flustered to answer other questions." This may explain why the Germans did so well, since they were far more likely to be regular newspaper readers than those in the other six nations studied.[80]

Another study in 2009 that extensively examined Americans, Britons, Danes, and Finns also showed that Americans knew little about domestic as well as international current events, and even international popular culture.

---

* The five questions asked in the 1990s: for the president of Russia (Yeltsin) and the country threatening to withdraw from the nuclear nonproliferation treaty (North Korea), to identify Butrous Butrous Ghali (U.N. General-Secretary), who was attacking Muslims in Bosnia (the Serbs), and the party that had signed the Oslo Accords with the Israelis (Palestinians).

In the most glaring instance, only 37 percent of Americans knew that the Kyoto Accords pertained to climate change, as opposed to 60 percent of Britons, 81 percent of Danes, and 84 percent of Finns. Only in one area, domestic popular culture, did Americans score nearly as well as the Britons, Danes, and Finns, and even then, slightly worse than the average.[81]

This study's authors also ascribed this difference to international variances in media structure: In the United States, the media's mission centers more on entertainment than education, whereas Scandinavian governments vigorously support high-quality news and informational programming. The U.K., which possesses both a prestigious and well-endowed public news outlet, the BBC, and a prosperous private media sector, occupies a position midway between the United States and Scandinavian nations.

This study's other striking finding was that the knowledge gap between Americans of high and low educational status was much larger than in the other three nations studied: A poorly educated Briton, Dane, or Finn knows far more about the world around them than a poorly educated American.[82] It's hard to escape the conclusion that the poorly educated in the United States, relative to those in other countries, are uniquely

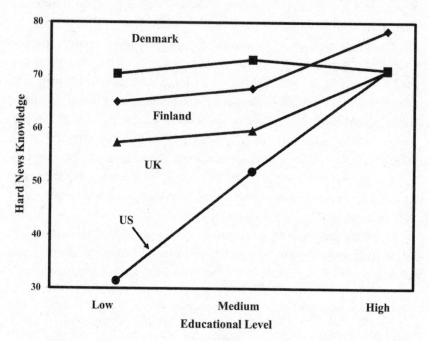

Figure 10-3.   Hard News Knowledge versus Educational Level

susceptible to dispensationalist narratives that even the most educationally disadvantaged in the rest of the developed world resist because of their better grasp of everyday facts.

Journalist Gershom Gorenberg makes a related point. In the late 1990s, dispensationalists became increasingly obsessed with the Y2K computer bug; many thought that it might trigger the Apocalypse as the calendar clicked over to 2000; true to form, Hal Lindsey published a how-to on surviving the year 2000 end-times titled *Facing Millennial Midnight*.[83] Observed Gorenberg:

> Future historians, I suspect, will study the buildup [to January 1, 2000] to the very boring day when computers didn't crash as part of America's cultural, not technological, history. The point is not the glitch, but how strident the rhetoric was in a country saturated with millennial beliefs, relative to less religious societies elsewhere in the West.[84]

The deeply moralistic dispensationalist end-times narrative imposes a societal cost. Ever since the historian Richard Hofstadter wrote *The Paranoid Style in American Politics*, the nation's marked tendency toward conspiracy theories has been well recognized. Recent research by a pair of political scientists, J. Eric Oliver and Thomas Wood, demonstrated that two closely related factors most powerfully predict susceptibility to conspiracy theories. The first is a belief in the end-times narratives. The second is the tendency to view human existence as a Manichean struggle between good and evil that typifies evangelical, and particularly dispensationalist, theology: the belief that we and those like us epitomize goodness and light, and that those who disagree with us are in league with the devil. Oliver and Wood noted that while those on the right tended to espouse dispensationalist narratives about Satan and God, those on the left favored ones about unseen secular forces, such as 9/11 conspiracy theories.[85]

Man is not only the ape that can mindlessly imitate and favor stories over facts and data, but, darkest of all, he is also the ape that can morally condemn others, at times a Manichean beast that constructs ludicrously convoluted theologies tailored to flatter himself and demonize others. Manichean thinking permeates both the far right and far left of the political spectrum, and it's not unusual for true believers at one end of it to flip to the opposite side—"serial true belief." Adolph Hitler remarked that whereas he could never convert a trade unionist or Social Democrat to Nazism, he could always convert a communist: "I have . . . given orders that former communists are to be admitted to the party at once."[86] More recently, many prominent neoconservatives such as Irving Kristol, Nathan Glazer, Albert Wohlstetter, and Sidney Hook began as Marxists.

Evolutionary psychologists have hypothesized that the Manichean mindset likely evolved from the need for tribal cohesiveness in early hunter-gatherer societies. The tribe benefits if its members behave altruistically toward one another and, more critically, if it treats other tribes with homicidal ruthlessness. Psychologists call this in-group/out-group dichotomy "groupishness," a behavior that is facilitated by the notion that one's own tribe embodies a variety of virtues and is favored by the deities, and that other tribes embody evil and are in league with malign forces (or, in monotheistic societies, the devil).[87]

A classic high school psychology demonstration involves dividing pupils into high- and low-status groups according to their shirt or hair color; the former soon enough develop derogatory opinions of the latter.[88] In 1954, sociologist Muzafer Sherif and his colleagues demonstrated the phenomenon in a more elegant fashion: the famous (at least among sociologists) "Robbers Cave" experiment.

This complex study assembled twenty-two boys, nearly all eleven years old, at a Boy Scout Camp at the isolated, wooded Robbers Cave State Park in Oklahoma. Sherif screened out candidates with psychological problems, and all those chosen also came from two-parent Caucasian Protestant families. The average IQ of this highly selected group was well above average (112); critically, none of the boys knew each other before they assembled on the park campground.

The experiment proceeded through three phases. In the first, Sherif matched the twenty-two into pairs that closely matched their skills in various areas, such as sports, cooking, and music. To make each group equally endowed with this panoply of skills, he randomly split each pair and created two groups of eleven each.

During the first week each group participated separately in the usual range of summer camp activities—swimming, hiking, and sports—but also in problem-solving exercises that required extensive discussion, strategizing, and cooperation, such as cooking, tent-pitching, and rope-bridge building. Each group was unaware of the presence of the other, and toward the end of this bonding period, the groups chose names for themselves: Rattlers and Eagles. Sherif then produced shirts and flags with those motifs.

In the second phase, the Rattlers and Eagles were thrown together in a several-day-long multievent competition (the "color war" familiar to many summer camp veterans). Unlike the typical color war, the winning team received awards: medals, a trophy, and fancy pocketknives, all of which were prominently displayed at mealtime. The losing team got nothing.

Almost immediately, the two groups began hurling taunts at each other; early on the Eagles burned the Rattler's flag and then tore up its replacement, followed by a violent retaliatory nighttime raid. Only when the Rattlers threatened to respond with a rock attack did the experimenters intervene. Both groups marked their territories with "Keep Off" signs, and raids became a nearly nightly event.

The Rattlers and Eagles almost immediately evolved classic out-group derogation, referring to each other as "stinkers," "braggers," and "sissies," and objected to eating meals in the same mess hall.[89] Even after the competition ended in an Eagle victory, the two groups kept to themselves and pointedly avoided mixing. When the two groups were brought together at meals, the Eagles usually gave way to the Rattlers, remarking "ladies first." Sherif extensively measured the boys' opinions of each other, and found, not surprisingly, that they rated their in-group companions much more highly than the out-group members.

In the third phase, which began soon after the tournament's end, Sherif explored ways of decreasing the in-group/out-group behavior generated in the second phase. When the two groups were brought together for meals or passive entertainment, such as a movie, the antagonism remained. He then had the two groups work together on critical tasks, such as restoring the camp's water supply, which had been intentionally cut off at the end of the day, as the campers grew thirsty when their canteens ran dry. After a series of such tasks, the groupishness lessened significantly, though it did not completely disappear. For example, at the end of phase 2, only 6 percent of the Rattlers' friend choices were Eagle members; by the end of phase 3, that increased to 36 percent.[90]

Given that such random and meaningless distinctions seen in classroom shirt color demonstrations and in the Robbers Cave Experiment produced dramatic demonization of out-groups, it's not surprising that a Manichean mindset came to permeate the dispensationalist landscape, whose theology differs greatly from that of other mainstream religions.

While the first few generations of dispensationalists eschewed political involvement, by the time of the Balfour Declaration this stricture had largely fallen away, and by the 1970s, Lindsey, Falwell, and many of their dispensational literary brethren labeled all those to the left of them as evil and, wherever plausible, as the Antichrist; they further transformed Jesus into a paragon of Manichean, hawkish right-wing political and social conservatism.

Soon after the 1991 breakup of the Soviet Union, Lindsey divined that Russia and Germany had concluded a secret agreement that carved up Europe between them. Always on the lookout for satanic cultural icons, *Planet Earth—2000 A.D.* settled on undersea explorer Jacques Cousteau, beneath whose warm, fuzzy marine environmentalism supposedly lay a hard core of "one-world socialism." (Such dispensational fearmongering is nothing new; during the early twentieth century, fundamentalist Christians saw the universal language Esperanto as a tool of satanic globalism.)[91]

Planet Earth—2000 A.D. also inveighed against even the most non-controversial elements of the nation's social safety net and environmental protections. Apparently unaware of the fate of the passenger pigeon, Dodo bird, and the world's fish stocks, Lindsey flatly stated that "resources in private hands are always the best protected." He listed the thinning of the earth's ozone layer as one of the many cataclysmic disasters heralding the end-times. While he admitted that manmade chlorofluorocarbons (CFCs) contributed to its depletion, he implied that the Montreal Protocol that limited worldwide CFC production was an unnecessary government intrusion on our individual freedoms. Further, volcanic activity, not CFCs, was the major culprit: "What's so scary is that there isn't anything we can do to repair a damaged ozone layer."[92]

Volcanic eruptions do reduce ozone levels, but only temporarily. They've been blasting away for hundreds of millions of years without permanently thinning this protective layer, which is a more modern phenomenon; the most recent data demonstrate that the Montreal Protocol is indeed slowly repairing the damage.[93]

Over the years, Lindsey has increasingly trumpeted his wide-ranging influence. In his book *The 1980's: Countdown to Armageddon,* written just at the beginning of the decade, he makes the unsubstantiated claim that he had been invited by an Israeli pilot to lecture on prophecy to the

U.S. Air War College, where he was met by an "enthusiastic ovation." He writes that a year later he was invited back and "was amazed to find hundreds of people jamming the room. Outside, others were trying to crowd in. All of these people wanted to hear what the prophets had to say about our destiny. When I finished, the response was overwhelming."[94] Later, he lectured to "an elite group charged with awesome responsibility" whose membership he was not at liberty to reveal. Once again, this high-level audience was "visibly moved" by his prophecies. "A few days before our meeting, their computer had predicted the same events and outcomes that had been forecast by Daniel. Needless to say, they were more surprised by Daniel's words than I was by theirs."[95]

Closer to home, over the past several decades evangelicals have increasingly permeated the ranks of the American military. While the overall percentage of personnel who identify themselves as evangelical or Pentecostal seems to be about the same as in the general population—about 22 percent—its actual influence is much greater than that number suggests, particularly in the chaplaincy and in the Air Force high command.[96]

Beginning in the 1950s, the evangelicals' reliably anticommunist rhetoric endeared them to the military hierarchy. This military-evangelical bond further strengthened in the 1960s and 1970s, when evangelical support for the Vietnam War contrasted starkly with the mainstream Protestant churches' opposition to it. As put by historian Anne C. Loveland, "Formerly regarded with skepticism, if not suspicion, evangelicals gained respect and influence within the armed forces as a result of the support they demonstrated for military service, the war, and the men who fought it."[97]

Evangelicals came to see military chaplaincy less as ministering to the spiritual needs of young men and women exposed to the horrors of warfare and more as an opportunity to help them find Jesus. An article in the magazine of the National Evangelical Association noted that one half of enlisted men had no significant religious background, and most of the rest were mainline Protestants, Catholics, or Jews: "This is the ripe harvest field in which our chaplains are working."[98]

In order to avoid the constitutional prohibition against a state religion, the military relies on "endorsing agents" from religious denominations for their chaplaincy candidates. Before 1987, the military assigned chaplains according to denomination; if 5 percent of enlistees were Episcopalian, then so would be 5 percent of chaplains. In that year a regulatory adjustment not only lumped all Protestants together into a single category, but it also allowed evangelical and Pentecostal endorsing agencies to nominate chaplains. By 2009, approximately 80 percent of active-duty chaplains were evangelical or Pentecostal.[99]

In addition, for the past several decades the heart of American military culture has lain below the Mason-Dixon Line. As it became less acceptable for white Southern officers and enlisted men to emphasize their racial supremacy, evangelism took the place of skin color as a way of asserting superiority.[100]

All four armed service branches have suffered proselytization scandals, ground zero for this phenomenon being the Air Force Academy, located in politically and religiously conservative Colorado Springs. The Academy had already been rocked by a sexual assault scandal in the early 2000s; a few years later a different sort of abuse became apparent as evangelical instructors turned a blind eye to overt anti-Semitism, exhorted athletes that they were playing for "Team Jesus," and officially mandated viewings of Mel Gibson's inflammatory *The Passion of the Christ*, a violent, moralistic movie that received lavish praise from evangelical Christians and criticism from secular viewers for its implicit anti-Semitism.[101]

While comforting to know that during the 1980s an American president backed away from an apocalyptic belief system, its dangers remain in place at lower levels of command; what if, for example, a high-level American, Russian, Israeli, or Pakistani military officer suffers, like the Temple Mount arsonist Denis Michael Rohan, a psychotic break and wields, instead of a bottle of kerosene, a nuclear weapon?

11

DISPENSATIONALIST
CATASTROPHES:
POTENTIAL AND REAL

In 1964, nuclear-war planner Daniel Ellsberg, who would later become famous for his unauthorized release of the Pentagon Papers, went with his boss at the RAND think tank, Harry Rowen, to see the movie *Dr. Strangelove*, "for professional reasons." Stanley Kubrick's iconic film tells the story of a Soviet "doomsday machine" (several thermonuclear bombs in a buried "Cobalt-Thorium G" container triggered to explode with the first enemy atomic bomb), and a mad U.S. Air Force base commander, Brigadier General Jack D. Ripper, who launches his strategic bombers toward Russia. All but one of Ripper's aircraft are successfully recalled; the movie ends with that plane's pilot, memorably played by Slim Pickens, riding a hydrogen bomb down, bronco style, from his aircraft's bomb bay.

Simultaneously, Dr. Strangelove himself, played by Peter Sellers, explains to the American president and Soviet ambassador his plan for post-apocalyptic survival in deep mineshafts as films of nuclear explosions mushroom to the tune of "We'll Meet Again." Ellsberg wrote, "We came out into the afternoon sunlight, dazed by the light and the film, both agreeing that what we had just seen was, essentially, a documentary." Ellsberg and Rowen were particularly impressed with how accurately the film had portrayed the then top-secret nuclear command procedures; in fact, the movie had been based on a novel, *Red Alert*, written by a Royal Air Force officer named Peter George, who later served as one of the film's screenwriters.

By that point, Ellsberg had already learned how dangerously decentralized was U.S. nuclear authority; several years before he had toured

U.S. military bases. His research made obvious that a nuclear war might mean the extinction of the human race, and he was mortified to discover that general officers, and in one case a mere major, could on their own authority launch a nuclear strike.[1]

Ellsberg and Rowen had not been the first nuclear planners to be impressed with the accuracy of *Dr. Strangelove* and *Red Alert*; five years before the movie was produced, a colleague of theirs, John Rubel, sent a copy of the novel to each member of the Pentagon's Scientific Advisory Committee for Ballistic Missiles.

Even without the risk of a religiously inspired, psychotic commander, the world's nuclear weapons command system is alarmingly unstable and accident-prone. Almost from the dawn of the nuclear age, the world's atomic arsenals, its real-life doomsday machines, have brought the world to the brink of incineration several times. Eric Schlosser's masterful book *Command and Control* documents dozens of hair-raising nuclear accidents ranging from the loss of thermonuclear weapon-bearing planes and missiles to false warnings of massive enemy attacks.

In 1961, a wing-tank fuel leak on a B-52 bearing a pair of four-megaton thermonuclear bombs resulted in a weight imbalance that sent the plane into an uncontrollable spin. The pilot dumped both of the presumably unarmed weapons; the parachute on one bomb failed to open, and the device plunged seventy feet into the wet ground near Faro, North Carolina. Its explosive trigger and "primary" plutonium core were recovered, but the uranium "secondary," the source of the weapon's high yield, was never found. The parachute on the other weapon did open, and when it struck the ground its nose sensor sent a firing signal that cascaded through several safety mechanisms. All but one failed.

Had that second weapon detonated, it would have effected a "groundburst," which produces vastly more radioactive fallout than the "airburst" of the Hiroshima and Nagasaki weapons, which had less than 1 percent of the yield of the B-52's bombs. Had the explosion occurred with southerly winds, the deadly fallout would have blanketed most of the Northeast and rendered much of North Carolina uninhabitable.[2]

Even more alarming, during the 1962 Cuban Missile Crisis, an overeager American destroyer skipper, unaware that Soviet vessels were armed with nuclear-tipped torpedoes, dropped dummy depth charges on the Russian submarine *B-59*. Both the submarine's commander and commissar wanted to fire one of its atomic weapons at the destroyer, but luckily, the overall flotilla commander, Vasili Arkhipov, was on board and refused to agree. When the episode became public decades later, Arkhipov became widely known as "the man who saved the world."[3] In general, the Soviet leadership kept their arsenal on a much shorter leash than the United States did. According to Princeton University's Bruce Blair, a leading authority on nuclear control today, "The architecture of [the Russian] system of control and safeguards is much more impressive than that of the United States."[4]

A good thing, that: When Ronald Reagan became president in 1981, he filled his national security apparatus with defense hawks who consciously and enthusiastically rattled the Soviets with nearly continuous provocations. As often as several times a week, SAC would send bombers over the North Pole, or shorter-range fighter-bombers would threaten Warsaw Pact airspace or the Soviet Asian borders. Recalled William Schneider, Jr., the undersecretary of state for military assistance, "They didn't know what it all meant. A squadron would fly straight at Soviet airspace and their radars would light up and units would go on alert. Then at the last minute the squadron would peel off and return home."[5]

On other occasions, radar systems have produced false warnings of massive missile attacks. At 2:30 A.M. on June 3, 1980, amid cold war tensions over the Russian invasion of Afghanistan and the U.S. boycott of the Moscow Olympics, Bill Odom, a military aide to national security adviser Zbigniew Brzezinski, woke him with a report of 220 incoming missiles. Brzezinski had Odom confirm that SAC alert crews were sprinting to their B-52s and firing up their engines, and to call him back; he decided not to wake up his wife so that she would be vaporized, unaware, while asleep. When Odom called a few minutes later, he told Brzezinski that there were now 2,200 incoming missiles. With just minutes to activate the nation's arsenal, he was about to phone President Carter when Odom called a third time to report that other systems had failed to confirm the attack. The world, it turned out, had come within a minute of incineration because someone had mistakenly inserted a training tape into a command computer system.[6]

As the size of the nation's nuclear arsenal grew, so did the risk of an accidental catastrophe. Civilian leaders faced an uphill battle against military commanders more interested in making sure the weapons would launch than in preventing accidental launches; ensuring the former simultaneously makes the latter more likely. For example, the introduction of permissive action links (PALs), with their eight-digit code and limited-try feature, theoretically prevented an unauthorized launch. Alas, in order to ensure that bungling the code didn't prevent such a launch, the SAC high command set all the codes to the easy to remember eight-digit "00000000," thus effectively eliminating this safeguard.[7]*

Furthermore, as with automobile antilock brakes, the introduction of safety features to a system often makes it paradoxically less safe by increasing user confidence. As Charles Perrow, the leading theoretician of "normal accidents" in complex systems has noted, such seemingly beneficial changes "often merely allow those in charge to run the system faster, or in worse weather, or with bigger explosives."[8]

The most fateful decision any commander or leader may ever face will have to be made within minutes on the basis of incomplete data. With luck, it will not be colored by the belief that the Elect, to which they belong, will be raptured before the bombs strike. The psychotic General Ripper of *Dr. Strangelove* deployed his bombers toward the Soviet Union out of concern over the fluoridation of the water supply, delivering one of moviedom's most famous monologues: "I can no longer sit back and allow Communist infiltration, Communist indoctrination, Communist subversion, and the international Communist conspiracy to sap and impurify [*sic*] all of our precious bodily fluids." Fluoridation today remains a bugaboo of the dispensationalist right, particularly Jim Bakker, whose website repeats the ludicrous claim that "more people have died in the United States from fluoridation than all the military deaths of [*sic*] entire country."[9]

Beyond the obvious danger of a psychotic or religiously fanatical military commander, the dispensationalist narrative carries a subtler and perhaps more serious risk of Armageddon. Dispensationalists like Lindsey and Falwell have argued vigorously against any and all efforts at arms control and in favor of bloated arsenals that, by sheer force of numbers, increase the probability of accidental annihilation.

This came across most strongly in Lindsey's book *The 1980's: Countdown to Armageddon*. In his view, the SALT Treaty did not reduce the risk of a nuclear holocaust; rather, it destroyed the military superiority of America, placed it in mortal danger, and would allow the evil Soviets

---

* In addition, the PAL at underground sites locked only the missile, not the warhead.

to "sweep through Europe." The U.S. government was little more than a puppet of the great bugaboo of conspiracy theorists, the Trilateral Commission (a high-profile nongovernmental organization that prominently featured the Rockefeller family and Zbigniew Brzezinski). Worse, the nation had foolishly abandoned stalwart allies such as Chiang Kai-shek, the shah of Iran, and the apartheid South African government.[10] Lindsey conjured up the following scene:

> The Soviet Premier may soon telephone the American President. The Premier will say: "We can destroy your missile silos. We can intercept and destroy all incoming submarine launched missiles with our laser beams. We can destroy your obsolete bombers with our MIG-25 fighters and SS-5 ground-to-air missiles. So, Mr. President, will you surrender? Or shall we destroy your country? You have 20 seconds to decide.[11]

Lindsey had also pounded the same hawkish drum in *Planet Earth—2000 A.D.*, which identified the now long-forgotten Gorbachev Foundation in San Francisco's Presidio, "one of America's most hallowed military posts," as evidence of the demolition of American influence by a satanic new world order. UFOs weren't alien spacecraft, but rather Satan's demons.[12]

Moreover, "normalizing" Armageddon risks making it a self-fulfilling prophecy. As put by Paul Boyer, an authoritative observer of end-times theology,

> My own sense is that the connection between grassroots prophecy belief and nuclear-weapons policy, while real, was subterranean and indirect. Few post-1945 prophecy believers consciously sought to bring on Armageddon as quickly as possible. Rather, convinced that the Bible foretells The End and secure in the knowledge that believers will be spared, they tended toward passive acquiescence in the nuclear-arms race and Cold War confrontation.[13]

In the early 1980s, novelist Grace Mojtabai traveled to Amarillo, Texas, to investigate the relationship between that deeply religious town and the nearby Pantex plant, which today assembles and maintains the entire American nuclear arsenal. Her magazine piece eventually turned into a full-length book, *Blessed Assurance*. Mojtabai, who is Jewish, wound up living in Amarillo.

She found that dispensational beliefs so thoroughly permeated the city that even the publisher of its newspaper, a well-educated liberal Democrat, subscribed to its tenets. After the plant's mission became widely known in the 1980s, Amarilloans instantly understood that the entire area was a prime target and would be wiped from the face of the earth in the first moments of a nuclear exchange. The town's largest denomination, the First Baptist Church, does not itself subscribe to dispensationalist doctrine; nonetheless, its members accepted that risk with equanimity and even took some comfort in the fact that their instant vaporization would be preferable to the more agonizing demise of many of their countrymen.

The Reverend Royce Elms, the leader of the town's smaller Jubilee Tabernacle, had a different take. As recounted by Mojtabai, he told his parishioners that they need not fear a nuclear exchange at all, since they would be raptured before everyone else was immolated:

> You know, they're spending a fortune on the space program. A fortune! If they'd just shut it all down, see, and wait for the sound of the trumpet, that, my friend, is going to be one space program! I never even put my name in to be an astronaut on this little rinky-dink thing they got going now. But I've got my name, by the grace and help of God, in that other astronaut program. . . . When them rockets take off . . . we're going to leave a trail of Holy Ghost fire!

"Goodbye! Goodbye!" the reverend shouted, to Amarillo, and to Houston, Dallas, and Los Angeles as the bombs vaporized them. One of Elms's parishioners, while comforted by the belief that she would escape nuclear Armageddon on the same rocket ship, agonized that she might leave her children and grandchildren behind.[14] (The title of Mojtabai's book refers to the "blessed assurance" that believers would be spared the horrors of a nuclear tribulation.)

Like Boyer, Mojtabai only briefly considered the possibility that religiously crazed Pantex workers might help the millennium along by getting their hands on a nuclear weapon. Rather, as did Boyer, she worried that ordinary citizens, like the Amarilloans she had grown to know so well, had adopted a Manichean dispensationalist worldview and anesthetized themselves to the risk of nuclear warfare.

If the world is divided between absolute good and absolute evil, between followers of the Lord and Satan, accommodation or negotiation with the enemy becomes unthinkable. In a world of absolute polarization, peace is humanly impossible, and war is inevitable.[15]

In his 1982 presidential address to the American Academy of Religion, theologian Gordon Kaufman further pinned down dispensationalism's threat to humankind. He pointed out that for the first time in history, the human race has the potential to extinguish the entire species, and that dispensationalism's apocalyptic worldview is thus "an ultimate evasion of our responsibility as human beings; it is demonically to invoke the divine will as a justification for that very evasion." Kaufman further described the Rapture as "cutting the nerve of human responsibility."[16] To wit, the belief that our ability to save ourselves from extinction is, to even a small extent, in God's hands diminishes our will to prevent it and thus increases the risk that it will happen.

While the dangers inherent in the intersection of nuclear weapons and dispensationalism have thus far thankfully remained theoretical, the apocalyptic beliefs of one of Miller's spiritual heirs would propel him and scores of his innocent followers toward a tragic end. Since the dawn of recorded history, Freud's narcissism of small differences has yielded a steady stream of religious mutations, and Seventh-day Adventism would produce a poisonous twig on Protestantism's luxuriant tree.

In the 1920s, an Adventist named Victor Houteff began to preach his own unique interpretation of scripture. A salesman with a third-grade education, Houteff was drawn to Revelation's lurid narratives. In particular, he focused, as had so many before him, on the 144,000 believers of the book's seventh chapter, 12,000 from each of the twelve Hebrew tribes, "sealed [branded] the servants of our God in their foreheads."

The Seventh-day Adventists considered themselves the 144,000; the problem, Houteff imagined, was that as the sect had grown well beyond that number, it had lost its zeal and devotion. As is typical of dispensationalists, he inveighed against Seventh-day brethren who indulged in modernity's sinful cultural activities: "beach parties and moving picture shows."[17] He compiled, as heretics are wont to do, a list of "abominations" of the Church; as he saw it, his mission was to winnow the Seventh-day Adventist's ranks down to 144,000 members of requisite purity.

Houteff hadn't meant to start his own sect, but rather to reform the parent church. However, as the charismatic salesman began to attract adherents, his more conventional brethren grew alarmed and "disfellowshipped" him in 1934 (as Low Hampton Baptists had done to Miller in 1845).

Initially, his sect was known as the Shepherd's Rod, the title of Houteff's manifesto, or simply "the Rod." Reflecting their belief in the centrality of the ancient Holy Land, the Kingdom of David, they changed their name to the Davidian Seventh-day Adventists—Davidians for short. As their membership grew, in 1935, the Davidians established a national headquarters at the Mount Carmel Center, a compound in Waco, Texas. Although the Center itself held only thirty-seven followers, Houteff expected the end-times within a year, by which point he would lead the full complement of 144,000 to Palestine.

Since he hungered for a devout and pure Adventism, he and his successors aimed their proselytization only at their fellow Seventh-day Adventists, and not at the general population, who were beyond redemption.[18] Although Houteff had attracted thousands of followers by the time he died in 1955, the sect's move to Palestine, by then mostly under Israeli rule, never occurred. The Davidians by that point had outgrown the original Waco compound and moved nine miles east to Elk, Texas, their "new" Mount Carmel.

The Bible is history's most analyzed and discussed book, read over the centuries by billions. Millions of its readers, by the laws of probability, must have been of extremely high intelligence, and hundreds of thousands have had extensive academic training in biblical interpretation. Yet Houteff, whose education ended in elementary school, decided that he alone had found a meaning hidden to all previous Bible readers, and anointed himself the "angel ascending from the east" who would lead 144,000 faithful to the Holy Land in the end-times. Starting with Houteff, the Davidians produced a succession of similarly egomaniacal leaders who would, with an assist from tone-deaf federal law enforcement agencies, lead the sect toward catastrophe.

On November 5, 1955, shortly after Houteff's death, his widow, Florence, announced that she had further decoded the end-times sequence of Revelation. On April 22, 1959, exactly 1,260 days hence, Jesus would come.[19] Her prophecy attracted nine hundred followers to Mount Carmel to greet the end-times, where the expectant faithful replayed a smaller version of Miller's Great Disappointment. And like the disappointed of 1844, the sect subsequently splintered into competing groups, the largest led by a Houteff acolyte named Ben Roden, who took over Mount Carmel.[20]

Roden had inherited the Houteffs' egomania and announced that God had revealed him to be the "Branch," a term used in Zechariah and John to describe the Lord's servants, who would lead the group toward the Second Coming, hence the group's new name: the Branch Davidians. He would exhort believers with "Get off the dead Rod, and move onto a living Branch."[21]

When Roden died in 1978, a power struggle ensued between his wife, Lois, to whom the Lord had revealed that she was the Holy Spirit, and their unstable son, George. Eventually, Lois won out with the help of a young man named Vernon Howell. Up to that point Howell had led a chaotic life as the son of an unmarried fourteen-year-old girl. As a boy, he had bounced around among different households and suffered from dyslexia and loneliness before he finally dropped out of ninth grade.

Only three things held the interest of the awkward but good-looking young man: his guitar, his Bible, and sex. In 1981, he impregnated a fifteen-year-old girl and then announced to his Seventh-day brethren that God intended him to marry a different young lady, the pastor's daughter. He also had a habit of "witnessing" almost continuously and once interrupted a service to mount the pulpit and preach, activities that soon got him disfellowshipped. In 1983, he settled at Mount Carmel, where he had previously done carpentry.[22]

There, attracted by Lois Roden's leadership position and semi-divine status, Howell found a home. Raised in the Seventh-day Adventist Church, he read the Bible compulsively; she, in her turn, was taken with his steel-trap grasp of scripture and good looks. Howell soon shared with the now sixty-seven-year-old widow leadership of the Davidians, and her bed as well.

Within the Davidians, a woman who claimed divine power did not raise as many eyebrows as it might have in mainstream Protestant sects; one of Seventh-day Adventism's founders, Ellen G. White, was considered a prophetess, whose writings Howell revered. The Bible guided nearly every

aspect of his life; he copulated with Roden, he said, in the hopes of fulfill-
ing biblical prophecy of Isaiah 8:3: "And I went unto the prophetess; and
she conceived, and bare a son." He would later half-joke that had he "gotten a seventy-year-old woman pregnant then he must be God after all."[23]

Recall theologian R. H. Charles's description of Revelation as "the
most difficult book of the entire Bible" and his admonition that "not only
is it the cursory reader that is bewildered but also the serious student."[24]
Until around 1983, Howell might have agreed with that assessment. But
in that year, the twenty-four-year-old high school dropout decided that he,
like Houteff and unlike the billions who had read the Bible since the advent
of mass literacy a few centuries ago, could unlock the seven seals and so
uncover the true meaning of Revelation, which itself, thought Howell,
held the key to the rest of the Bible.

In January 1984, Howell married the fourteen-year-old daughter of
a fellow Branch Davidian and thus estranged Lois; later that year George
Roden, now back in his mother's good graces, managed to eject Howell
and his supporters from the compound at gunpoint and rename it Roden-
ville. Howell and a few followers settled a hundred miles to the east into
a hovel in Palestine, Texas, and with time on his hands and desirous of
better scenery, he visited Israel.

While there, he seems to have contracted Jerusalem Syndrome, a
well-described disorder in which visitors to Israel, overly stimulated by
direct contact with the holy places and shrines they have read and heard
about all their lives, become overwhelmed with religious fervor and often
imagine themselves as biblical characters.[25] One victim, a schizophrenic
bodybuilding tourist, convinced himself that the Western Wall was located
in the wrong place and tried to move one of its huge stones: the "Sampson
Syndrome." Denis Michael Rohan, the al-Aqsa arsonist, likely had a variant of the condition as well.

The Kfar Shaul Psychiatric Hospital, just a few miles from the Temple
Mount, specializes in the disorder. Between 1980 and 1993, psychiatrists
there treated 470 sufferers, the overwhelming majority of whom, like the
Sampson Syndrome sufferer and Rohan, had preexisting psychopathology. Forty-two patients, however, or 9 percent of the study sample, had no
previous psychiatric history. While the 91 percent with previous psychiatric
episodes were widely distributed among Jews and mainstream Christian
sects, forty of the forty-two of those lacking previous psychopathology

were evangelical Protestants, a fact that would tragically play out in Waco less than a decade later.[26]

Vernon Howell returned from Israel visibly changed. While there, God had told him that he was His servant; subsequently his preaching waxed dynamic, and he became more adept at connecting and mixing together scriptural passages. God's voice now instantly provided the Bible's true meaning to him whenever he read its passages. Prior to the trip he had taught that he expected to receive, by and by, the "full message" from God, but that it hadn't come yet. On his return, likely in the grip of Jerusalem Syndrome, his message from God had finally arrived.[27]

Prophecy had been an intrinsic part of Seventh-day Adventism at its birth in the late 1840s, as it was also in the Davidians under Houteff and the Rodens, and as it would be under Howell. Davidians strove to be more or less continuously "in the message"—that is, in reception of a stream of prophecy from the Almighty. They considered the modern Seventh-day Adventist Church, which had in their view given up on prophecy, as apostate.

Howell was particularly taken by the description of the three prophecy-bearing angels described in Revelation 14:6–9 and, for whatever reason, thought that there must actually be seven prophecies. The first two would be William Miller's seminal messages—of the end-times and that Babylon had fallen. The third would be Ellen White's message of the seventh-day Sabbath; the fourth, Victor Houteff's prophecy; the fifth, Ben Roden's; and the sixth, Lois Roden's. Howell was now, God had informed him, the bearer of the seventh message, the last angel before the end-times, which was imminent.

After Howell's 1987 return from Israel, a strange scene ensued when George Roden, who still controlled Mount Carmel, dug up the grave of a follower named Anna Hughes, who had been buried a quarter century previously at age eighty-five. Roden challenged Howell to a competition to resurrect her dead body; in response, Howell and seven followers raided the Mount Carmel compound to take photographs of Anna's body with which to accuse George of corpse abuse. The resultant forty-five-minute gun battle produced no deaths or serious injuries, and in 1988, Howell and his seven accomplices were tried for attempted murder. The jury acquitted the accomplices but hung on Howell's verdict, and the prosecution elected not to pursue him further.

This legal outcome unhinged Roden, who emitted multiple bizarre profanity- and threat-filled court filings against Howell, which landed him in jail for contempt. His incarceration allowed Howell to pay the compound's back taxes and move back into it. After his release in 1989, Roden axe-murdered his roommate, whom he suspected had been sent by Howell to kill him. He was committed to a mental facility, from which he escaped on multiple occasions; shortly after doing so in 1995, he was found dead from a heart attack on the hospital grounds.

Over the next few years, Howell refined his apocalyptic roadmap with passages from the usual places: Ezekiel, Daniel, Matthew, and Revelation. As the end-times, whose date he had not yet precisely determined, approached, he would lead his followers to Israel, where the Davidians would convert the Jews, triggering a U.S.-led United Nations force from the north, the presumably now Christian Israelis with whom the Davidians would stand and die. There's no recorded evidence that Howell had read Hal Lindsey, but given the pervasiveness of his books during that period, it's hard to imagine that he extracted his far-fetched narrative from scripture by himself. Later he would shift the locus of Armageddon from Israel to the Mount Carmel compound.

Howell's Jerusalem syndrome–fueled scriptural brilliance dazzled listeners, and during evangelizing tours both in the United States and abroad he recruited to Mount Carmel about a hundred followers. While he collected converts in Australia and the United Kingdom, he had no success among more skeptical and biblically jaded Israelis.

It was an eclectic, multiracial group that included two dozen British converts. In 1990, he filed court papers in California to legally change his name to David Koresh after, respectively, the biblical kingdom he fancied himself leading and the Hebrew name of Cyrus. As had John Bockelson almost half a millennium before, he satisfied his growing sexual appetite with a convenient combination of polygamy for himself and celibacy for the other men. He "married" five additional females ranging in age from twelve to twenty, and to avoid prosecution for bigamy, arranged their sham marriages to male followers. While touring Australia, he so impressed a couple of his divinity that they allowed him to have sex with both the wife and their nineteen-year-old daughter so that they could have "children for the Lord."[28]

In preparation for the end-times, he demanded that the compound's married members purify themselves through sexual abstention and "nullified" the marriages of all of New Carmel's couples including, presumably, the "husbands" of his five auxiliary wives. Sex with Koresh, on the other hand, became a sacrament, and he bedded many of the "ex-wives" with the full approval of their "ex-husbands."

He made followers comfortable with this setup by prophesying that the children he fathered, of which there were at least a dozen, would enjoy favored status in Jerusalem's New Kingdom. Explained one of "the ex-husbands": "You don't understand at all. We as Branch Davidians aren't *interested* in sex. Sex is so *assaultive*, so aggressive. David has shouldered that burden *for* us." For his part, Koresh considered procreation with his followers a grim sacred duty. On occasion, though, he did confess his lust to partners and would sheepishly admit that God had made him do it.

This felicitous carnal arrangement, he explained, arose from a specific imperative in Revelation 4:4, which describes twenty-four elders wearing crowns of gold who exclaim that God "hast made us unto our God kings and priests: and we shall reign on the earth" (5:10). Koresh had made a revolutionary advance in scriptural interpretation: The words "made us" implied that Revelation had foretold that he was destined to father said twenty-four elders, who would rule in the millennium. The women chosen to bear the twenty-four were thus sacred vessels, which mandated Koresh's control over every aspect of their lives, including their diets. Needless to say, no reputable biblical scholar interprets Revelation's fourth chapter in so agreeable a fashion.[29]

Koresh's magnetism lay in his "Bible teachings," sessions that could last hours during which he would accurately recall and lucidly interpret scripture. Even though he had dropped out of the ninth grade, the brilliance of his biblical interpretation mesmerized even the most well educated of his flock, which included a Harvard Law School alumnus and several others with graduate-level theology training.

Koresh thought that the seven seals of Revelation 5:1 held the key to both the exact events of the end-times and the Branch Davidians' path to salvation: "And I saw in the right hand of him that sat on the throne a book written within and on the backside, sealed with seven seals."

Koresh titled the "book" mentioned in the above passage the "Mind of God," his heretofore secret plan for mankind entrusted to "the Lamb." Koresh, who by this time had self-identified with the Lamb, deduced from other parts of the New and Old Testaments clues to opening each of the seven seals and consequently had the unique ability to reveal the mind of God to his followers.[30] (The Davidians viewed "Christ" as a dynamic manifestation sent by God on a mission that could take multiple forms; sometimes as Jesus, sometimes as the Lamb, and sometimes, according to Koresh, as himself.)[31]

As early as 1987, the Davidians had attracted the attention of Rick Ross, a controversial high-profile "cult buster" who over the decades had "deprogrammed" hundreds of individuals and testified in multiple court cases. At the behest of concerned relatives, Ross deprogrammed two Koresh followers in New York, and he subsequently received calls for help from other families. Ross listed six criteria for designating an organization a "dangerous cult": an absolute and unaccountable authority figure, conformation to the leader's wishes, filtering of outside information, "us against them" mentality, denigration of those outside the group, and biblical or philosophical justification for the leader's financial and sexual gratification.[32] While Koresh didn't filter outside information, he did meet the other five criteria.

Beginning in the late 1980s, Koresh and several of his followers accumulated large arsenals and also raised money dealing weapons at gun shows, which do not require background checks. By 1991, an Australian follower named Marc Breault had grown disaffected with Koresh's accumulation of weapons, theological grandiosity, and sexual exploitation of young girls. His concerns attracted widespread media attention, first in Australia and then in custody proceedings that ordered the removal of a child from Mount Carmel. Both Breault and Ross relayed their concerns to the Bureau of Alcohol, Tobacco, and Firearms (BATF), which planned a raid on the compound for late February 1993, by which time the group had acquired at least three hundred weapons, including sixty M16s, sixty AK-47s, and thirty AR-15 assault rifles.[33]

The gun-loving Koresh had said before the raid, "Nobody is going to come to my home, with my babies around, shaking guns around, without a gun back in their face." In Texas, state law allows citizens to fire at law officers who exert "improper force."[34]

Ross also contacted the *Waco Tribune-Herald*, which on February 27, 1993, published the first in a sensationalistic "Sinful Messiah" series, which the wider national media soon picked up. The articles alleged that Koresh physically abused children, had sex with underage girls, and claimed a divine right to other men's wives, of whom he had enjoyed at least a dozen.[35]

Texas child-welfare authorities had in fact investigated the compound in the previous year and found happy, well-cared-for children with little evidence of abuse beyond occasional spoon-on-buttocks spanking, considered well within the bounds of acceptable Texas parenting. On the other hand, the *Tribune-Herald*'s allegations of Koresh's sexual conduct were largely true.[36]

At 9:45 A.M. the next day, February 28, the BATF executed a search warrant, based not on any of the lurid allegations in the "Sinful Messiah" series, but rather on possession of firearms. At the time, it was legal to own and operate automatic weapons in Texas, so long as they were properly registered with federal authorities; the alleged illegality involved the failure to do so.*

The BATF's ineptitude was epitomized when it tipped off a television reporter, who then asked directions to the compound from a letter carrier, who turned out to be Koresh's brother-in-law. The BATF knew through an informant in the compound that they had thereby lost the element of surprise, with armed conflict therefore all but certain. Despite this, the BATF proceeded with the raid. The forewarned Koresh first ordered a prayer service, then placed armed men around the entrances. Exactly who fired first has never been determined, but Koresh told followers as he headed for an entrance that he was going out to talk to the agents. According to the subsequent Treasury Department investigation, Koresh opened the door and asked the agents "What's going on?" To which they replied, "Freeze!" Koresh slammed the door, and gunfire erupted through it from the inside and from the windows. Another agent observing from outside the compound reported seeing Koresh shot twice, which means that he must have opened the door and may not have been the one to fire first, not the act of someone executing an ambush, as the BATF later alleged.[37]

A running gun battle swirled throughout the compound that saw four agents and six Davidians killed, two of whom were Koresh's sixteen-month-old child and the infant of another member; dozens more were

---

* Current federal and state laws surrounding the ownership, operation, and registration of machine guns are complex. See, for example, https://thefederalist.com/2017/10/02/actual-federal-laws-regulating-machine-guns-u-s/.

injured. The BATF had prepared the raid so poorly that the Davidians outgunned and outsupplied them; when the BATF ran low on ammunition, they withdrew.[38]

Most chroniclers agree that the Davidians, had they desired, could have killed many more of the BATF agents. A later government investigation specifically noted that the Davidian response to the raid typified the sort of "defensive violence" that characterizes "groups that wish to withdraw from the dominant culture."[39] Indeed, the most striking communication that day was the frantic phone call of Wayne Martin, the Harvard Law–trained follower, to the Waco sheriff's office: "Tell them there are women and children in here and to call it off!"—hardly suggestive of someone bent on apocalyptic violence.[40] Even more damning is the fact that the BATF, which had a long history of aggressive door-busting assaults for minor weapons violations, knew that Koresh took regular solitary jogs around the neighborhood, during which they could have easily served a warrant or arrested him.[41]

Following the fiasco, the FBI relieved the BATF. Over the next fifty-one days, the FBI negotiated with Koresh, who had been shot in the wrist on February 28. From the start, the FBI portrayed the siege as a hostage-rescue situation, but after the BATF raid twenty children, accompanied by several adults, left the compound, and there was ample subsequent testimony that none of the remaining Davidians wanted or needed rescue, save from the federal government, which, in classic dispensationalist fashion, they referred to as "Babylon."

The siege riveted the country; almost immediately after the BATF raid, Koresh communicated directly with the public via a local radio station and CNN, on which he spun lengthy quotes from the King James Bible that, although familiar to his adherents and Christian theologians, sounded like Swahili to the secular audience. On one occasion he told a befuddled radio interviewer, "We are now in the fifth seal."

Among those who heard that interview was theologian James Tabor, who before 1993 had not known of Koresh. On the evening of February 28, along with millions of other Americans, he tuned into CNN as it interrupted its regular broadcasting to cover the aftermath of the BATF raid. As the young Davidian leader rambled on, Tabor's mind snapped to attention with the mention of the seven seals. Not only was he intimately familiar with this central feature of the Book of Revelation, but he also knew that

"Koresh" was the Hebrew word for Cyrus; a fast consultation with Isaiah 45 revealed that Cyrus had been anointed by God as a Messiah, the Hebrew term for which, *Mashiach*, translates into Greek as *Christos*—Christ. Koresh called himself "the Lamb," an Adventist manifestation of Christ—to Tabor a dead giveaway for the Book of Revelation.

As the siege evolved, it became clear to Tabor that the FBI had no knowledge of the apocalyptic narrative world inhabited by Koresh. Tabor called another theologian, Phillip Arnold, who contacted the FBI agents, who admitted that Koresh's biblical soliloquies had them flummoxed.

A few agents had even begun to inhale the apocalyptic books of their hotel room's Gideon's Bibles, a task that overwhelms even expert theologians. As put by Tabor, the mental image of the agents frantically paging through their Bibles was "almost comical, but at the same time frightening." Tabor and Arnold immediately grasped that the Davidians saw themselves as navigating the world of the seven seals; they also knew that the fifth seal, the one Koresh considered the Davidians living currently in, was the most violent and dangerous of the seven.

If the siege was going to end peacefully, Tabor and Arnold thought, it would be accomplished by engaging Koresh on his home ground of Revelation. The government gave Tabor and Arnold access to a jailed Davidian named Livingstone Fagan, whom Koresh had sent out of Mount Carmel as its public face. Fagan confirmed their analysis: The Davidians were living through the tumultuous fifth seal, but God had told them to wait. The two theologians appeared on a radio talk show on April 1 that discussed Revelation's eschatology at length and hinted at a peaceful outcome. They knew that Koresh regularly listened to the show, and just to be sure, they had his attorneys send him a recording of it.

On April 14, whether influenced by the radio show or not, God finally spoke again to David Koresh. All was now clear to him; on that day, he wrote a letter to his attorneys in which he announced that he was in the process of composing an epistle that would inform the world about the "decoded messages of the Seven Seals." As soon as he finished it, he would release a copy. Then, "I will come out and then you can do your thing with this beast." Arnold and Tabor were elated; perhaps the looming catastrophe could be averted after all. It would be the last communication the world would hear from Koresh.[42]

Tabor and Arnold weren't the only theologians who understood Koresh's devoutness and hoped for a peaceful outcome; many in the wider evangelical community did so as well. Early in the siege, officials of the National Council of Churches and Baptist Joint Committee wrote a letter to President Clinton that opened with the heartfelt plea: "*Please demilitarize the confrontation in Waco, Texas.*" (italics original) It observed that "threats of vengeance and the mustering of troops and tanks are but proof to the 'faithful' that the powers of the world are arrayed against them" and presciently observed that "it would be even more tragic if the government has invested so much money and credibility in this no-win situation that it cannot be satisfied with less than a total eradication of the offending sect."[43]

And yet, after more than seven weeks of standoff, the hard-line faction among the FBI besiegers won the day with Attorney General Janet Reno, who gave the go-ahead for a direct assault.

While Tabor and Arnold may or may not have moved Koresh in the right direction, the hardliners within the FBI considered Koresh a dissembling con man who cynically used "Bible babble" as a delaying tactic; to the theologically untrained agents on the receiving end of hours of biblical harangues from Koresh, it certainly sounded that way.[44] The FBI ridiculed the April 14 letter, particularly the pretentiousness of a "book" written by a ninth-grade dropout and considered it yet one more dilatory tactic. They also ignored Koresh's lawyers, who told them that they were in the process of working out a surrender agreement.[45] Instead of approaching Koresh on the one subject that mattered to him, prophecy, the FBI upped the ante and cut off the electricity, destroyed the followers' parked cars, and blasted music and shone searchlights at the compound.

The siege ended in an FBI assault on April 19. Starting around 6 A.M. on that day, agents repeatedly rammed the building with armored vehicles and deployed CS tear gas (a chemical agent similar to that used by the Grand Mosque besiegers). Shortly after noon, fire broke out; it spread quickly, engulfed the compound, and collapsed its roof. Seventy-six Davidians, two of whom were pregnant, perished in the blaze, and only nine escaped. The majority of the dead were found trapped in the basement to which they had fled from the conflagration. At least twenty members had been shot, including Koresh, apparently to escape burning to death.

While multiple subsequent government investigations concluded that the Davidians had set the fires prior to the FBI raid, the surviving Davidians vigorously denied any talk of suicide, which the Davidians considered a sin. They also related that when the FBI cut off the electricity, they resorted to oil lamps, which the armored vehicles knocked over. Further, on April 19, the wind was blowing at up to thirty miles per hour and would have quickly spread the fire from room to room through the open windows and holes cut by the FBI vehicles. Nor was the FBI's credibility enhanced when they had the site bulldozed two weeks after the fire.[46]

One of the survivors carried out with her a data disk bearing the unfinished manuscript Koresh had mentioned in the April 14 letter, which the FBI had thought a ruse. His letter covered thirteen typewritten pages and contained an introduction and discussion of the first seal; the missive would likely have taken a few more weeks to finish.[47]

In the words of James Tabor,

> Koresh was a master at his own form of biblical exegesis. His message was systematic, consistent, and internally logical when understood within the theological perspective of the Branch Davidians. However, to one untutored in the details of the prophetic portions of the Bible, this message, delivered in typical nonstop style, with lengthy quotations from the King James Version, would appear nonsensical.[48]

We can never know if Koresh would, as promised in the April 14 letter, have peacefully surrendered, but it's also obvious that the FBI never attempted to seriously engage with the theological issues that consumed him. Six months after the disaster, the Department of Justice directed a massive report to the deputy attorney general, the redacted version of which ran to 489 pages. The short shrift given to theological expertise is obvious even in the table of contents, which lists just four pages of consultations with religious scholars, and which conveyed almost no useful information beyond their identities. These four pages were followed by twenty-eight pages of analysis from psychological consultants, nearly all of whom considered Koresh a con man. One of them, Pete Smerick, a behavioral specialist and instructor at the FBI Academy, actively recommended against even allowing theologians to participate.[49]

As the siege progressed, the overwhelming popular impression of David Koresh, similar to that of the FBI, was of a self-interested con man. The truth was likely more subtle. Like George Hudson, Samuel Insull, William Miller, and almost all propagators of mass delusions, Koresh sincerely believed his own narrative, a self-deception that magnified his ability to disastrously mislead his followers.

Over the past half millennium, the human predisposition to imitate and to seek compelling stories has settled on the most hypnotic narrative of all, the end-times delusion. The resulting theologies usually bind their adherents into peaceful, and often prosperous, communities. From time to time, however, this narrative jumps the guardrails of normal behavior to yield—as with Müntzer's Peasants' War, Bockelson's Anabaptist Madness, Venner's Fifth Monarchism, and Koresh's Branch Davidians—catastrophe.

And as with William Miller and his followers a century and a half prior, Koresh's bizarre theology, sexual aggrandizement, and statutory rape virtually guaranteed his demonization by the press and public—a demonization that led, in turn, to the tragic final law enforcement over-reaction. Had the initial BATF response been more deft, and had the FBI been more conversant with the nuances of end-times narratives, the Waco standoff would likely not have ended tragically.

A significant minority of the public did, correctly as it turned out, blame the federal government, and the Branch Davidian tragedy did not end on April 19 at Waco. The carnage played out on live TV, but the inferno's most important witness saw it from close up—a young Army veteran named Timothy McVeigh, already incensed by the government siege at Ruby Ridge the year before. Similar to the Waco siege, it involved a weapons charge against Randy Weaver, an evangelical U.S. Special Forces veteran; the standoff resulted in the deaths of Weaver's son Sammy and wife, Vicki, the latter of whom held strong end-times beliefs. McVeigh had traveled to Waco during the standoff to hand out gun-rights pamphlets. As the flames rose, he vowed to avenge the deaths of innocent men, women, and children. On the second anniversary of the FBI raid, he and his accomplice, Terry Nichols, carried out a truck bomb attack on the Alfred P. Murrah Federal Building in Oklahoma City that killed yet another 168 innocents. McVeigh had selected their target because it contained both FBI and BATF offices and, in addition, a large number of other federal employees.[50]

12

RAPTURE FICTION

By the dawn of the new millennium, the Branch Davidian disaster and Lindsey's off-base predictions had again driven home the perils of overly precise prophecy and date-setting, and dispensationalists increasingly turned toward a genre immune to disconfirmation: end-times fiction.

As early as the turn of the twentieth century, Christian writers began to produce novels about the Rapture of the righteous, the rise of the Antichrist, Tribulation, Armageddon, and final judgment. In 1905, an Ohio physician named Joseph Burroughs published one of the earliest known Rapture novels, *Titan, Son of Saturn.* The title's Titan refers to the now easily recognized Antichrist character, "a young Greek, who is to unite the radical Socialists and lead them in a world-wide effort to destroy the Christian Church." Burroughs's preface states that the novel was not the mere product of his imagination, but that it threw "a searchlight out over the consecutive distant events that are surely coming to the Church."[1]

While the Rapture scenes and description of the rise of Titan/Antichrist engaged readers, the characters spouted entire chapters of stupefying biblical exposition. *Titan* sold well enough to require ten printings and sold more than ten thousand copies over the decade following initial publication—respectable, to be sure, but hardly a bestseller.[2]

Nonetheless, the book exuded what would become the hallmarks of Rapture fiction, and of American evangelicalism in general: xenophobia, Islamophobia, and both ideological and moral panic. The nation-hero of Burroughs's novel, England, stands alone against the Antichrist-led ten-nation confederation. The United States, sadly, cannot come to the mother country's aid because of "the twenty-five million European-born citizens in the States." American "Saxons" rush to help England but are overwhelmed by the dark confederation, now aided by Muslims screaming, "Allah! Allah! Allah!" The European/Muslim force invades the United

States and dissolves the culture of "the Saxon people" in an evil cauldron of foreign-derived socialism.[3]

Over the ensuing decades Rapture novelists improved their art by adding compelling narratives that fed off current events.[4] By the 1980s, the foremost practitioner of dispensationalist fiction was Frank Peretti, a skilled literary craftsman whose most famous book, *This Present Darkness*, sold more than two million copies.

By the time of its initial publication, with the threat of godless communism in rapid decline, dispensationalists needed a new enemy. They were forced to settle for a decidedly down-market world-ending scourge: New Age movements, particularly any that gave off even the faintest whiff of Satanism.

Set in the idyllic fictional college town of Ashton, *This Present Darkness* pits its two heroes, the devout minister Hank Busche and hard-bitten newspaperman Marshall Hogan, against an obscenely wealthy city slicker, Alexander Kaseph, who for inexplicable reasons plots a takeover of the small burg.

Kasepth's allies include a battalion of winged, red-eyed, scaly-skinned, sulfur-breathing demons who suck the will out of ordinary mortals, but are fortunately uniquely vulnerable to the devout, especially Busche. These creatures, though, cannot match the satanic potential of Juleen Langstrat, a feminist professor at the local college who attempts to despoil the religious faith of Hogan's daughter with courses such as "Introduction to God and Goddess Consciousness." Kaseph conspires to frame Busche and Hogan, who find themselves in the same cell, compare notes, and join forces to defeat Kaseph and his minions, both inhuman and human.[5]

Peretti's sense of moral panic was nothing new. Hal Lindsey's books, for example, conducted a cultural jihad that deemed the writings of Darwin, Kant, Marx, and Freud "thought bombs" that doomed modern society. A year before he wrote *The Late Great Planet Earth*, Lindsey published *Satan Is Alive and Well on Planet Earth*, which contains an interview with a Los Angeles "police commander" who described a "Kiss-In" on a Santa Monica beach that reminded him of "the rites of African Savages":

> There were about four hundred people, so tightly packed together that they were just one big mass swaying to the throb of drums and weird music. . . . Some of them began to peel off their clothes. Some began

to indulge in open sex, oblivious to any around them. We noticed that most of them wore charms around their necks. They believe in the spirit world and will readily tell you that the Devil is very real to them.[6]

Historically, end-times movements have flourished in the worst of times: the slavery and dislocation of the Babylonian exile, the slaughter and wholesale physical destruction of the two Jewish revolts against Rome, and the horrors of the medieval European religious wars and pogroms. End-times believers who live in prosperous, secure, and peaceful modern nations are forced to settle their outrage on less tangible societal plagues: astrology, the cognitive dissonance of evolutionary and geological science, ecumenism, sex, drugs, rock and roll, and an ever-present Satan.

Such end-times fear-mongering is far from harmless. During the 1970s and 1980s, the dispensationalist aversion to New Age spiritualism and astrology morphed into a classic "moral panic"—itself a form of mass delusion—over nonexistent outbreaks of satanic child sexual abuse and mass murders. A profusion of self-proclaimed Satanism experts, including prominent law enforcement officials, gained national prominence and spoke of tens of thousands of child ritual murder victims. Supposedly, Satanists abducted young women and forced them to become "breeders" to supply infant victims; newborns were plucked from hospitals before their birth certificates had been filled out so that "they were never missed."[7]

One such "expert" was Ted Gunderson, a former FBI official who had worked on the suicide of Marilyn Monroe and the assassination of John Kennedy, and who had headed the Bureau's Los Angeles, Memphis, and Dallas offices. Gunderson postulated that four thousand American children were ritually murdered each year:

> I have been told it is a common occurrence for these groups to kidnap their victims (usually infants and young children) from hospitals, or-phanages, shopping centers and off the streets. I have been informed that Satanists have been successful in their attempts to influence the Boy Scouts and, in recent years, have concentrated their efforts in recruiting Little League baseball players by infiltrating the coaching staffs and establishing pre-schools throughout the US. . . . A Boise, ID police officer believes that fifty thousand to sixty thousand Americans disappear each year and are victims of human sacrifices of satanic

cults. Most of the victims are cremated, thus there is no body and no evidence. I know of an occult supply store in Los Angeles, California that sells portable crematory equipment. . . . I have alerted the Federal Bureau of Investigation (FBI), the U.S. Department of Justice, and members of Congress of these facts, and suggested that these matters be investigated by the Federal Government. *My requests have been ignored.* (italics original)[8]

In 1988, the nationally syndicated *The Geraldo Rivera Show* ran an episode entitled *Devil Worship: Exposing Satan's Underground* on the supposed mass murders; "investigations" into the phenomenon even appeared in mainstream media programs such as *20/20* and NPR's *Morning Edition.*[9]

The most infamous episode of the era played out with the 1985 Mc-Martin trial, precipitated when a psychotic young mother, in an incident eerily reminiscent of Denis Michael Rohan's schizophrenia, reported to the police that her toddler had been sodomized at his preschool. Her story was wildly implausible: children lured into airplanes and tunnels, where horses were slaughtered and teachers dressed as witches flew through the air and conducted rituals in which their young charges were sexually abused and exploited to make child pornography.

"Experts" on satanic abuse and social workers converged on the school, run by an extraordinarily unlucky woman named Peggy McMartin Buckey, and they soon extracted descriptions of the abuse from children far too young to accurately convey what had allegedly happened. The trial of Buckey and six other nursery school workers for the abuse took seven years, cost $15 million, and ruined the defendants' lives: in an egregious miscarriage of justice, Buckey spent two years in prison, and her son, five years, while awaiting trial. Ultimately, investigators found no tunnels or child pornography, none of the children's parents reported seeing dead horses, and the one black robe entered into evidence turned out to be Ms. Buckey's graduation gown.[10]

Their trial involved just one of roughly a dozen large-scale Satanism/childcare moral panics, complete with fraudulent prosecutions, that swept the nation during the 1980s, many of which actually resulted in draconian sentences. When the ensuing appeals and investigations trials made obvious the bogus nature of the cases and highlighted the hallucinatory character of the moral panic, evangelical paranoia moved on to other pastures and prosecutions dried up. Warned *New York Times* journalist Margaret Talbot, "Ambivalence is a difficult state of mind to sustain; the temptation to replace it with a more Manichean vision is always close at hand," especially when the Antichrist and end-times loom on the immediate horizon.[11]

This Present Darkness and Peretti's stream of sequels proved merely the opening act of a far larger publishing phenomenon: Tim LaHaye and Jerry Jenkins's previously mentioned *Left Behind* series. Born in 1926, LaHaye enrolled in Bob Jones University in Greenville, South Carolina, whose atmosphere accorded with his religious beliefs. The school's provenance ran deeply through the fundamentalist backlash against the mainstream Protestant church's acceptance of modern science, particularly evolution. LaHaye's ideology had its roots in a 1924 Bible conference during which William Jennings Bryan supposedly leaned over to Bob Jones, an evangelist preacher, and said, "If schools and colleges do not quit teaching evolution as a fact, we are going to become a nation of atheists."[12] The next year, Bryan, a former secretary of state, two-time presidential candidate, and famous orator, went on to prosecute the infamous Scopes Monkey Trial case. His concern about the evils of secular influences in the nation's institutions of higher learning rang clear in the ears of Jones, who in 1927 founded his university.

In the early 1950s, with his Bob Jones diploma fresh in his hands, LaHaye bounced around the country ministering to various congregations before settling in California, where he crusaded for Jesus and family values, his zeal perhaps related to the loss of his father at age nine. Along with his wife, he branched out into television with *The LaHayes on Family Life* show, which transformed him into a battle-hardened culture warrior who inveighed against homosexuality, secularism, and feminism. Over the years, he produced a series of both fiction and nonfiction books that explicitly warned of the dangers of the National Organization for Women, the United Nations, and the American Civil Liberties Union.[13]

Sometime in the mid-1980s, while flying to a prophecy symposium, LaHaye noticed his aircraft's captain flirting with the head flight attendant. The captain wore a wedding ring, and she did not. Mused LaHaye: Wouldn't it be interesting if the Rapture occurred and the pilot recognized that the hundred people that suddenly were gone from his aircraft meant that his Christian wife and son would be missing when he got home?[14]

Disappearing passengers and crews had in fact figured in at least two Rapture narratives that predated LaHaye's: Salem Kirban's novel *666* and an essay by William T. James, "When Millions Vanish."[15] Originality aside, history's most successful venture into religious multimedia, the *Left Behind* phenomenon, had been born.

LaHaye initially envisioned a "Rapture Trilogy," but he knew he lacked the requisite fictional narrative skill, so his literary agent connected him with a broadly experienced author, ghostwriter, and dispensationalist named Jerry Jenkins, who over his long career wrote 190 books. The personable LaHaye was about the age of Jenkins's beloved mother, and the two connected immediately. While LaHaye supplied the series' theological framework, Jenkins wrote the books' texts.[16] The pair published their first title, *Left Behind: A Novel of the Earth's Last Days*, in 1995.

Jenkins's previous literary output had ranged from children's fiction to sports writing, and his mastery of the art of the taut potboiler shines through on every page of the series, as illustrated by the book's opening:

> Rayford Steele's mind was on a woman he had never touched. With his fully loaded 747 on autopilot above the Atlantic en route to a 6 A.M. landing at Heathrow, Rayford had pushed from his mind thoughts of family. Over spring break he would spend time with his wife and twelve-year-old son. Their daughter would be home from college too. But for now, with his first officer fighting sleep, Rayford imagined Hattie Durham's smile and looked forward to their next meeting. Hattie was Rayford's senior flight attendant. He hadn't seen her in more than an hour.[17]

Heretofore faithful to his fanatically religious wife, Irene, who expected the Rapture at any moment, Steele screws up his courage, leaves the controls in his copilot's sleepy hands, and wanders back to the galley for a tryst with Hattie. To his disappointment, he finds her hysterical: between sobs, she tells him that dozens of passengers are missing, their seats empty save for their clothes. One by one, awakening passengers scream as they notice only the apparel of their now departed companions. Hattie begs for an explanation from Steele, who feigns ignorance, but "the terrifying truth was that he knew all too well. Irene had been right. He, and most of his passengers, had been left behind."[18]

Around the world chaos reigns as pilotless planes rain down from the skies like pheasants at a shoot and driverless vehicles careen off highway shoulders; millions have disappeared and millions more are dead. The world epicenter of unbelief, New York City, is rendered immobile because of the devoutness of subway drivers and the crashes resulting from their abrupt disappearance. Europe closes to air traffic, and so Steele brings his plane back to the one functioning major American airport in Chicago (as opposed to the improbable highway landing in the movie version).

TV news cameras capture the capricious bizarreness of the Rapture: the belly of a woman in labor, for example, suddenly deflates as her baby ascends directly to heaven, and the clothes of her nurse collapse to the floor as she joins the infant on its way up. Upon his return home, Steele finds his wife and young son gone, while Chloe, his agnostic college student daughter, remains. Almost the entirety of Irene's church's congregation, of course, has departed; its minister thoughtfully leaves an "I told you so" DVD for those remaining, so well produced and convincing that it effects Rayford Steele's immediate rebirth.

By wondrous coincidence, a passenger on Steele's plane, a brilliant journalist named Buck Williams, investigates the events. About a year before, he had gone to Israel to interview a biologist who had discovered a chemical fertilizer that turned sand into rich cropland, and who also possessed another mysterious and fantastically valuable scientific secret that made that nation the wealthiest place on earth. During Williams's visit to Israel, the Russians attempted a massive nuclear strike on the country, but miraculously all of their missiles and planes exploded in midair.

The third major player in the novel is the Antichrist, in the person of a Romanian named Nicolae Carpathia, possessed of fluency in nine languages, impossibly attractive looks, a powerful intellect, and irresistible charm. Williams had interviewed him while he was still a minor local politician, but his mercurial rise soon saw him as head of the United Nations, whose Security Council he reorganized into the familiar dispensationalist ten-nation confederation. Now the world's most powerful human, he institutes a global currency system and economic union, brings about universal disarmament, inks a seven-year peace agreement with Israel, and moves the now all-powerful U.N. to the site of ancient Babylon.

Normally the slowest-moving of bodies, the world organization agrees within hours to all these requests from Carpathia, who then announces a unified world religion.

Buck discovers Carpathia's true identity and joins forces with Chloe. In contrast to the almost uniformly Raptured congregation at Chloe's mother's church, all of Chloe's left-wing Stanford University chums must stick around for the Tribulation; Chloe and Buck are born again, marry, and ally with her father to organize the Tribulation Force, which employs technological magic to combat Carpathia.[19]

Internationalist conspiracies sprout up everywhere. Decades before, an all-powerful biotech financier named Jonathan Stonagal had Carpathia's mother artificially inseminated to produce a hypnotic surrogate, Nicolae, who would advance Stonagal's nefarious ambitions. The military pointedly ignores UFO reports from professional pilots. Stonagal rearranges world leadership and effects high-level "suicides" on an almost daily basis before finally being assassinated by Carpathia himself, who brainwashes all of the crime's witnesses, save one, the God-protected Buck Williams, into believing that Stonagal killed himself.

LaHaye's Manichean culture-warrior-hood suffuses the book: those who oppose abortion and vote Republican get raptured, while merely wearing sensible shoes or reading New Age books condemns their owners to burn.

Buck Williams's page-turning exploits chop the otherwise indigestible lump of dispensationalist eschatology into easily swallowed bites. The book maintains a highly transporting narrative flow by alternating passages that describe Williams's relentless pursuit of Carpathia's true identity with sections laying out the now born-again Steele's exploration of the dispensationalist end-times scheme.

Over the twelve years following *Left Behind*'s 1995 publication, LaHaye and Jenkins wrote fifteen more sequels and prequels that together spanned the entire dispensationalist sequence, from the evil Carpathia's genetically engineered birth to the (final) Kingdom Come.

The first volumes sold a few hundred thousand copies each, but by the fourth installment, word of mouth drove the series to the top of *The New York Times* bestseller list.[20] The eighth installment's initial print run totaled 2.5 million copies. In 2001, sales of the tenth book, which rocketed after the 9/11 attacks, displaced John Grisham's *A Painted House* as the best-selling novel for the whole year, the first time that Grisham had not held that title since 1995, all the more remarkable since bestseller lists generally did not track religious bookstore purchases, which accounted for a third of the series' sales. About one in ten Americans had read one of the books, and fully a quarter of Americans were aware of them.[21]

The series' total sales topped 65 million copies. In 2002, LaHaye and Jenkins made the cover of *Time* (and of *Newsweek* in 2004); both authors then spun off their own series, with LaHaye jumping that year from the religiously oriented Tyndale House Publishers to the mainstream Random House organization to earn a $45 million advance for another series.[22]

Such outsized success drew critical scrutiny of dispensationalism. Wrote Nicholas Kristof in *The New York Times*,

> The "Left Behind" series, the best-selling novels for adults in the U.S., enthusiastically depict Jesus returning to slaughter everyone who is not a born-again Christian. The world's Hindus, Muslims, Jews, and agnostics, along with many Catholics and Unitarians, are heaved into everlasting fire. . . . Gosh, what an uplifting scene!

Kristof then turned his attention to Lindsey's spotty prophetic track record and concluded, "Being wrong has rarely been so lucrative."[23] Another secular critic sniffed that Jenkins's style amalgamated "Jerry Falwell and Tom Clancy."[24] Other observers made note of rapture fiction's general lack of empathy for the hundreds of millions of humans immolated in their novels with an almost obscene relish.

Jerry Jenkins meanwhile projected the image of an easygoing, non-ideological yeoman scribbler. In a wide-ranging interview with *Newsweek*, he observed,

> Pedestrian writing, thin characters—I can handle the criticism. I write to pedestrians. And I am a pedestrian. I write the best I can. I know I'm never going to be revered as some classic writer. I don't claim to be C. S. Lewis. The literary-type writers, I admire them. I wish I was smart enough to write a book that's hard to read, you know?[25]

Jenkins's mention of C. S. Lewis was no random literary allusion; according to theologian Mark Ward, "The bylaws of Christian publishing require at least one chapter in each Christian book begin with a C. S. Lewis quote." Nor did Jenkins romanticize his readers, noting that he once came across a shopper at Sam's Club carrying out one of his books along with a fifth of whiskey and concluded that either way, she was gong to sleep well that night.[26]

By contrast, in the same *Newsweek* article LaHaye expressed both hard-edged theological certainty and burning resentment toward the nation's cultural and religious elites: "Those millions that I'm trying to reach take the Bible literally. It's the theologians that get all fouled up on some of these smug ideas that you've got to find some theological reason behind it. It bugs me that intellectuals look down their noses at we ordinary people."[27]

LaHaye's "ordinary people" live predominantly in the South and Midwest, which accounted for 71 percent of the series' readers, as opposed to only 6 percent in the Northeast.[28] The LaHaye heartland is the stronghold of the antiabortion, antigay social conservatism that served to energize American dispensationalists, and evangelicals in general; both Jerry Falwell and Pat Robertson hailed from Virginia, Hal Lindsey from Texas, Jimmy Swaggart from Louisiana, and Jim Bakker from Missouri.

An increasing number of dispensationalist parishioners, many enthusiasts of Lindsey, LaHaye, and Jenkins, throng Israel, particularly Jerusalem, to indulge their millennialist beliefs; of the country's 3.6 million visitors in 2017, it's estimated that one in eight was an evangelical. Many religiously oriented travelers book dispensationalist-centered tours, the highlight of which is a visit to Jerusalem's Temple Institute's visitor center, which shows off the vessels and instruments constructed for the rebuilt Temple. Most of these visitors, in the words of academic Yossi Mekelberg, are "completely oblivious to the Palestinian side of the story. It's about religion; with friends like that, who needs enemies?"[29]

Central to the building of the Third Temple is the arrival of a red heifer devoid of discoloration, blemish, or yoke. The appearance of white udder hairs disqualified Melody as the apocalypse cow, but her birth inspired a more serious dispensationalist visitor to Israel named Clyde Lott, a Mississippi cattleman who in 1989, came across the relevant passage in Numbers 19 and wondered how he might breed such a fully qualified sacrificial animal. It would not be all that difficult, he decided, since although such heifers are rare in Europe and Asia, the American Red Angus comes close to filling the bill.

The next year he visited the international trade office of the Mississippi Department of Agriculture and Commerce, which sent this memo to a State Department trade attaché:

> Clyde Lott is prepared to offer Red Angus suitable for Old Testament Biblical sacrifices, will have no blemish or off color hair, genetically red will produce red eye, nose pigmentation will be dark, heifers a year old will weigh approximately 700 pounds. These cattle will adapt quickly to Middle East climate, also excellent beef quality [*sic*].[30]

Eventually, the memo found its way to the rabbis at the Temple Institute, whose director, Chaim Richman, noted with pleasure that the biblical Lot, of Sodom fame, had also bred cattle.[31] Over the ensuing years, Lott and Richman visited each other in Israel, and the sensation surrounding Melody's 1996 birth encouraged them to plan big: a December 1997 shipment of five hundred pregnant cows to, of all places, the powder keg occupied West Bank. The scheme, which likely would have produced an entire herd of genuine apocalypse cows, got snarled in red tape and financial difficulties and never got off the ground. Lamented Lott,

> Something deep in my heart says God wants me to be a blessing to Israel. But it's complicated. We're just not ready to send any red heifers over there. If there's a sovereign God with his hand in the affairs of men, it'll happen, and it'll be a pivotal event.[32]

In the dispensationalist scheme, a thin red line separates "pivotal" and "cataclysmic." Melody, Lott, and Richman encapsulate a kind of bizarre theological theater in which the different players act on the same stage and read scripts that are nearly identical. The actors happily support each others' performances until its denouement, when their fates radically diverge. In the Jewish script, the Messiah comes for the first time and establishes forever the Jews and their Temple in Jerusalem, whereas the Christian script adds several additional scenes in which a vengeful God consigns one-third of the Jews to renounce their old faith and proselytize a new one, and roasts the other two-thirds.

Needless to say this play involves industrial quantities of cynical mutual exploitation. Israeli extremists, unable to garner majority electoral support for their biblical right to all of Judah and Samaria and the rebuilding of the Temple, happily accept financial and political help from evangelical Christians, who in their turn believe that the play's end liquidates their new Jewish allies through either conversion or incineration. In the words of journalist Gershom Gorenberg,

> And perhaps it wouldn't matter, except that well-intentioned people warming themselves with the idea that Jews building the Temple will lead to the world's final salvation sometime lend their hands to extremists who act, not in the realm of myth, but in a real country where real conflicts claim real lives.[33]

13

CAPITALISM'S PHILANTHROPISTS

During the same decade that Clyde Lott and Chaim Richman indulged their respective, and potentially cataclysmic, Christian and Jewish end-times delusions, American investors lost their collective wits in an orgy of financial speculation.

One evening in early 2000, after a long day's work at *Money* magazine's midtown Manhattan office, journalist Jason Zweig caught a taxi home. As the driver pulled into traffic, the vehicle was obstructed by four young men in expensive suits, one of whom rat-a-tatted the driver's window to demand a ride to a destination just a few blocks away. When informed by the cabbie he already had a fare, the gentleman thrust a $100 bill in the driver's face and said, "Throw him out and we'll give you a hundred bucks."

The cabbie shut the window, and, as recorded by Mr. Zweig, "We sped away from the scene like two maidens escaping the tent of Attila the Hun." What flabbergasted Zweig, an experienced New Yorker, was not so much that the whiz kids offered a Ben Franklin for his ejection, but that the four could have gotten to their destination faster on foot.[1]

Like Blunt, Hudson, and Insull, these brash young men had drunk of the hubris of sudden wealth, and probably also from more mundane spirits. They were rich, and, according to the logic of our materialistic society, thus smart and important, never mind that their lucre more likely flowed from dumb luck, sharp practices, or both.

The financial mania that so intoxicated Zweig's assailants lasted, roughly speaking, from the mid-1990s until mid-2000, and then collapsed in slow motion over the ensuing two and a half years, a deflation nearly identical in length to that following 1929's Black Thursday. The devastation was widespread: in the aggregate, 100 million investors lost $5 trillion, roughly a third of their stock market wealth. The most aggressive of them, still many millions of Americans, having been deluded into believing that they had found the financial fountain of youth in dot-com stocks and mutual funds, had, like Edgar Brown in 1929, lost most of their life savings in the deluge.[2]

As with previous manias, the bubble's underlying pathophysiology of Hyman Minsky's four necessary conditions applies: technological and financial displacement, credit loosening, amnesia, and the abandonment of time-honored valuation principles.

To paraphrase the bubble's mantra, the era's great displacement, the internet, really did change everything.[3] It came into existence in 1969, when the Defense Department's Advanced Projects Research Agency linked together its first four "nodes" at UCLA, UC Santa Barbara, the University of Utah, and the Stanford Research Institute. The new "information superhighway" titillated investors, but its initial slowness and difficulty of use, combined with the expense and clumsiness of the first personal computers, meant that for its first twenty years it impinged little on everyday life. The first commonly used networks, such as AOL and Compuserve, were initially not even connected to the wider internet, and even later, when they were, functioned as walled gardens that did not allow direct navigation to web pages outside their domain.

That would change in 1990, when Tim Berners-Lee, a computer scientist working at CERN, the European high-energy physics center that straddles the Swiss-French border, invented the first primitive browser, which he prophetically named WorldWideWeb. At the time, he merely sought to connect the facility's myriad different computers; almost by accident, he wired up the planet and created a sensation that roiled the financial markets and transformed the very way we live.[4]

Berners-Lee's first browser required too much technical expertise for general purposes, but other programmers soon improved on its user-friendliness. In 1993, the National Center for Supercomputing Applications (NCSA) at the University of Illinois released Mosaic, a relatively easy to install and deploy Microsoft Windows–based application. Marc Andreessen, a University of Illinois student, headed the NCSA team; after he graduated, he moved to California, where he joined forces with a computer science Ph.D. named Jim Clark.

A decade earlier, Clark had founded Silicon Graphics, which made high-end computers. In tech argot, these devices were "workstations," custom-made devices designed for a specific task that usually ran their own proprietary operating systems and software. In the 1980s, the manufacturers of workstations made billions, but for most companies, this profitability proved a golden trap, since increasingly capable personal computers would shortly displace them, an eventuality that the visionary Clark foresaw. Frustrated at his inability to convince the firm's management of this, he left Silicon Graphics, angry not only that the company he had founded had veered off course, but also that his share was worth only $20 million—in his words, "relatively little to show for a dozen years of creativity, leadership, risk, and hard work in an industry that has produced vast personal wealth."[5] He vowed that next time he'd have more control and be better rewarded.

In 1994, Clark and Andreessen incorporated the Mosaic Communications Corporation. The University of Illinois, miffed at their use of the Mosaic moniker, asked them to find a new company name; they settled on Netscape Communications. Like Mosaic, the company made the browser freely available, and it spread like wildfire. By mid-1995, millions of users thrilled to the meteor shower and the *N*-monogrammed planet in the upper-right corner of the screen that announced that they were *online* and able to access web pages from anywhere on the globe.

Easy credit, the second of Minsky's pathophysiolgical factors, provides the raw fuel for bubbles. In a modern fractional reserve system, a nation's central bank—in the United States, the Federal Reserve—plays the money supply's guard dog. The Fed's job is to keep the economy humming with an adequate money supply, but also, in the immortal words of former chairman William McChesney Martin, to "take away the punch bowl just when the party gets going."[6]

Under most circumstances, the Federal Reserve Board cares about two things: the overall state of the economy, as measured by GDP growth and the unemployment rate, and keeping inflation under control. Stock prices are of lesser concern, and often wind up an "innocent bystander" to these twin concerns.

By the middle of the twentieth century, the Fed's primary tool was the federal funds rate, the interest rate at which member banks lend to each other overnight—effectively, the short-term rate on government securities. When the interest rate on these safe securities is high, they attract investors.

This draws money away from risky assets such as stocks and lowers their prices; contrariwise, when the Fed lowers rates, investors seeking a higher return purchase stocks, and thus raise prices.*

The early 1990s saw a moderately severe recession that precipitated two major events. First, it cost George H. W. Bush a second term; as put by the de facto campaign slogan of the victor, Bill Clinton, "It's the economy, stupid." Second, the recession triggered a dramatic loosening of credit by the Federal Reserve, which nourished the stock market bubble.

Under the chairmanship of Alan Greenspan, the Fed attacked the early 1990s recession by buying Treasury bills, which lowered the federal funds rate from 8.3 percent in January 1990 to around 3.0 percent in late 1992, where it remained for two full years. This fueled the initial phase of the stock market boom, and investors began to speak of the "Greenspan Put," the impression that the chairman actively sought to keep stock prices aloft.†

By all rights, the Fed should have taken away the punch bowl around 1997, by which time the economy was clipping along nicely, with inflation falling to about 3 percent. It looked like Greenspan was about to do just that, but a sequence of events intervened that was eerily similar to the 1920s, when Chairman Strong inadvertently touched off a U.S. stock market frenzy by lowering rates to protect the English pound.

In 1997 and 1998, global events conspired to keep the punch bowl full. A series of currency and debt crises swept through world financial markets, beginning with the collapse of the Thai currency, the baht, and spread in domino-like fashion to Malaysia, Indonesia, and Hong Kong. Initially, the evolving contagion did not greatly alarm Greenspan, since those Asian economies were relatively small, but when late in 1997, the same sequence played out in Korea, a wealthier nation that hosted tens of thousands of American troops, he was forced to respond. The Fed and Treasury strong-armed America's banks to keep lending to Korea as cheaply as possible—that is, at the lowest possible interest rate, not only in Korea but in other Asian nations as well. Lower interest rates abroad

---

* The federal funds rate is in reality just a target. The actual overnight rate is negotiated between the lending and borrowing banks; the Fed influences it by either buying Treasury bills on the open market, which tends to lower rates, or by selling them, which tends to raise them.

† A "put" is an option to sell a security at a given floor price, thus insuring against a large loss.

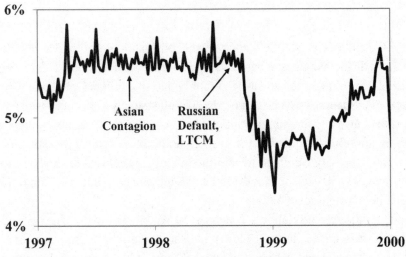

Figure 13-1.   Federal Funds Rate 1997–2000

depressed these foreign currencies, which appreciated the dollar. In early 1997, the Fed had, in response to the booming economy, already begun to raise interest rates, but in order to prevent this dollar appreciation, held them steady; as in the 1920s, the persistent relatively low rates fed the by-then well-established stock market mania.

The international financial dominoes continued to fall; in late 1998, a similar shrinkage of the Russian economy precipitated a default on its debt and deflation of the ruble. This time, the contagion spread directly to the United States, where a large and prestigious hedge fund, Long Term Capital Management (LTCM), which had bet heavily on Russian debt, went under. The evaporation of the fund's massive holdings threatened the rest of the financial system and hammered stock prices around the world.

By that point, the markets considered Greenspan the virtual author of the 1990s economic boom, and he had acquired near mythical status as "the maestro," as Bob Woodward would later title his best-selling book about the chairman, who saw his outsized reputation threatened by the potentially catastrophic fallout of LTCM's collapse. Not only did Greenspan engineer the fund's bailout by private banks, but he also eased credit by aggressively lowering the federal funds rate, and kept it low for a full year. This, in turn, sent stock prices into the stratosphere.[7]

*   *   *

By the end of the twentieth century, the third pathophysiological bubble factor, financial amnesia, had developed over several decades. The 1929–1932 bear market had so savaged family and institutional wealth and so seared the national psyche that for decades after stocks were not considered prudent investments; for example, as late as 1945, the first date for which there are reliable statistics, the average dollar of individual investments, which is heavily weighted toward the savings of the wealthy, hovered at around only 30 cents in stocks, and it was the rare corporate pension fund that held a significant amount.

Although only about 10 percent of Americans owned stocks and got directly burned in the 1929–1932 bear market, the subsequent Great Depression affected everyone.[8] Almost all Americans of a certain age carry with them a burden of family Depression baggage (in this author's case, his mother's habit of carefully wrapping and saving even a single leftover restaurant asparagus). For millions of Americans, still-vivid memories of the brutal 1929–1932 period diminished the appeal of stocks for a generation or more.

A stock bubble of sorts did occur in the late 1950s to early 1960s that revolved around the invention of the semiconductor transistor a few decades previously by a Bell Labs team led by physicist William Shockley, sparking an explosion of increasingly miniaturized and capable electronic devices. By 1959, affixing "-tronics" to a company's name served to stimulate public interest and juice the stock price in the same way that adding "dot-com" to a company would do so a generation later. One staid manufacturer of phonographs and vinyl records, American Musical Guild, went public with a sevenfold price pop simply by changing its name to Space-Tone. Some other meaningful corporate names from the era were Astron, Vulcatron, several ending in "-sonics," and, most impressive of all, Powertron Ultrasonics. Investment banks learned to favor insiders with large share allotments and simultaneously limit the amount available for purchase by the wider public, and thereby fed the public enthusiasm, which collapsed in 1962, as almost all previous bubbles had, when the frenzy ran out of eager buyers.[9]

The tronics mania involved only a small corner of the equity market, and since relatively few Americans owned stocks in that era, it left little lasting impression on the public memory.[10] By the 1990s, the average U.S.

citizen was two generations removed from the last society-wide securities bubble. When one finally arrived, only three tiny groups had the tools to recognize it: nonagenarian investors with intact memories; economic historians; and those who had read, absorbed, and retained the lessons of the first three chapters of *Extraordinary Popular Delusions*.

The 1990s tech mania prominently featured the fourth pathophysiological bubble factor, the abandonment of traditional valuation criteria for stocks. Even the highest-flying stock darlings of the late 1920s produced a solid stream of profits, and all but a few "high tech" companies (most notably, RCA and Remington Rand) sported healthy dividends as well.[11] By contrast, in the 1990s, only a handful of the new tech companies produced enough revenue to pay for their lavish spending on personnel and equipment. As to dividends, tech investors thought them a quaint echo from a remote horsewhip-and-buggy era; what few turned up lay more than a decade away. Microsoft, which issued its first shares to the public in 1986, did not declare its initial dividend until 2003; as of this writing, the two biggest winners of the dot-com sweepstakes, Amazon and Google, have yet to do so. As the 1990s progressed, investors somehow convinced themselves that earnings and dividends didn't matter at all; the true value of a company's stock lay in fuzzier metrics, measured in millions of eyeballs or billions of clicks.

As supposedly put by a great twentieth-century investor, John Templeton, "The four most expensive words in the English language are 'This time it's different.'" During the 1990s, the emerging digital world really did look different, and many of the era's wildest-sounding promises came true: near universal broadband coverage, ubiquitous and nearly free voice and video telephony, and an efficient online shopping environment that would swallow many traditional brick-and-mortar outlets whole.

Regrettably, the average investor in these technologies didn't profit. Of the hundreds of companies that went public during the late 1990s, just a small handful survived. Only one of them, Amazon, became a dominant economic force, and even it has yet to show the earnings an investor might expect from its commanding position in the retail industry.[12]

Just as during the English railroad and 1920s bubbles, the 1990s tech boom, while mauling investors, left society with valuable infrastructure. Bubble companies are best understood as a three-level pyramid structured

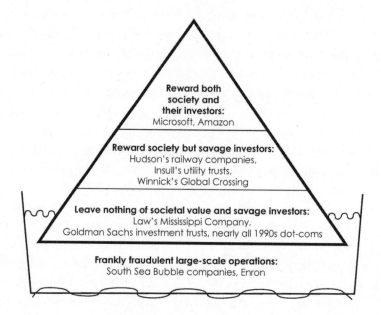

according to the relationship between the profitability and societal benefit of those companies, as depicted above.

At the apex of the pyramid sit companies that not only benefited society but also made their investors wealthy, like the East India Company or the Bank of England, and, at least as of this writing, Amazon and Google. The second and perhaps most important level consists of companies that benefit society but lose their investors money, such as George Hudson's railway empire and Samuel Insull's utilities trusts.

Global Crossing Ltd. was the tech bubble era's poster child for this seemingly counterintuitive outcome. Between 1998 and 2002, during the blowing and collapse of the dot-com mania, telecommunications firms strung most of today's current half-million miles of global submarine fiber-optic cable. One man, Gary Winnick, was responsible for nearly a third of that frenzied effort.

Winnick, a former bond salesman and protégé of junk-bond king and convicted felon Michael Milken, possessed in spades the same talent as his business ancestors, Blunt, Hudson, and Insull: a genius for raising billions in stock and bond offerings from credulous investors.

Unfortunately, Winnick possessed none of Hudson's and Insull's business acumen; before he founded Global Crossing in 1997, his knowledge of telecommunications did not extend greatly beyond, as one journalist put it, "an ability to make a cold call," a deficiency compounded by his never having run a large enterprise.[13] Whether the company's failure was due to incompetence, malfeasance, or merely bad luck is still a matter of dispute. While Winnick tended to absent himself from the company's day-to-day affairs, he, along with other top executives, did have the presence of mind to sell hundreds of millions of dollars of stock just before the firm went belly-up. Civil and regulatory actions stripped him of most of that ill-gotten gain, but in the end prosecutors declined to indict.

Winnick's culpability is beside the point. However badly Global Crossing battered its investors' fortunes, the company contributed in no small part to the making of today's interconnected world. At the height of the market frenzy surrounding it and other internet-era stocks, the company was valued in excess of $40 billion, $6 billion of which Winnick owned. ("Getting Rich at the Speed of Light," gushed the 1999 *Forbes* cover.)[14]

His scheme was neither fraudulent nor lacking in vision, as his appraisal of the importance of global bandwidth proved correct. Rather, as have many business visionaries throughout commercial history, he underestimated the two things that everywhere and always diminish profits. First, as sure as death and taxes, profits attract competition, increase supply, and depress prices and subsequent profits. Winnick's 1997 completion of two high-capacity transatlantic links, for example, was followed within six years by ten more competing cables. Second, technological improvement also increases the supply of the goods produced, further depressing prices. In the case of sub-marine cables, over the subsequent decades, improvements in "dry plant," the optical transmitters and receivers at either end of the cables, have resulted in a seven- to tenfold increase in the carrying capacity of the originally laid strands. Global data traffic is now roughly a thousand times greater than it was in 2002, despite the fact that companies laid no new transatlantic cables between 2003 and 2014; on average, less than a quarter of the world's sub-marine cable capacity is currently "lit" with signal.[15]

As is almost always the case during bubbles, the enthusiasm of Global Crossing's investors led them to pay far too much for their piece of the action. On January 28, 2002, the company filed for bankruptcy, following which two Asian firms scooped up a controlling interest in Winnick's net-work for $250 million, literally a penny on the dollar. While the company eventually emerged from its reorganization and still operates a large slice of the internet's backbone, the original shareholders were left with nothing beyond a few crumbs from resulting legal settlements.

The carnage was widespread: Besides individual investors, pension and mutual fund pools lost billions. Commenting on Mr. Winnick's well-timed stock sales, Linda Lorch, an elementary school teacher who lost $120,000 in the stock, said, "I don't know how the management of this company did so well while small shareholders did so poorly."[16] Many of Global Crossing's employees owned the company's shares in their 401(k) plans and fared even worse than Lorch, losing their savings as well as their jobs.[17]

Global Crossing's executives weren't the only ones who profited from well-timed sales of its stock. In March 1999, former president George H. W. Bush gave a speech to its executives; in lieu of his $80,000 speaking fee, he took company shares that he sold several months later for approximately $4.5 million, which the *Wall Street Journal* speculated may have gone to pay for upkeep at the family's Kennebunkport retreat.[18]

While Global Crossing crippled the financial futures of unfortunates like Lorch and the company's employees, it benefited the rest of the world by blessing it with a surfeit of bandwidth. The same cannot be said for the third level down the pyramid, the hundreds of dot-coms that disappeared without a trace, not only trampling their investors but also leaving behind nothing of societal or economic value. Perhaps the most spectacular story in the futile dot-com pursuit of eyeballs and mindshare was the Webvan episode, a fiasco on a scale unimaginable before 1995.

Louis Borders, who had founded the eponymous bookstore chain, was hardly a wild-eyed twentysomething techie with an outlandish idea. In 1997, five years after he had retired from bookselling to found an investment firm, a package containing some rare spices he had ordered online, a novelty at the time, arrived on his doorstep. A lightbulb fired off: could he convince Americans to order their groceries that way?

Borders dreamed big. In order to deliver perishable goods to millions of consumers, he needed to build out a novel, massive logistical system. His first facility in Oakland was twenty times the size of a standard supermarket, housed four and a half miles of conveyor belts, and carried a vast variety of food, including more than seven hundred kinds of meat and fish.[19] He then engaged Bechtel, the nation's largest construction concern, to erect a national network of twenty-six similar complexes at a total cost of more than $1 billion—impressive for a firm that didn't exist the year before.

Borders, who had studied mathematics at MIT, projected that each facility would assemble eight thousand twenty-five-item orders daily and each bring in a third of a billion dollars in annual revenue; human "pickers," strategically placed among a ballet of food-bearing rotating carousels, would put together customers' purchases and then feed them down the miles of conveyor belts to idling refrigerated trucks for delivery to homes within an hour of order. Because of its scale, Webvan's operations were projected to spend less than 1 percent of revenues on its physical plant, versus 6 percent for soon-to-be-obsolete conventional supermarkets. Borders mused that after conquering retail food, he would move on to videos, consumer electronics, and dry cleaning.[20]

Webvan attracted A-list financial backing from the likes of Goldman Sachs, Oracle, Hewlett-Packard, and Knight Ridder, as well as a tsunami of popular enthusiasm. To stoke the frenzy, the initial stock offering sold off only a small percentage of the company; when applied to all of Webvan's shares, this implied a market valuation of $8.4 billion, half that of Safeway's, not bad for what at that point amounted to an operation centered on the twenty-six eventually constructed oversized supermarkets.[21]

Two problems doomed the venture. First, Webvan was hardly the first internet food seller; it had several competitors, among which was a larger and more established company, HomeGrocer.com, backed by, among others, Amazon's Jeff Bezos. Second, the model didn't work; the untested technology proved balky, and even had it functioned smoothly, consumers didn't yet trust someone else to pick out perishable produce and deliver it on time. Both Webvan and HomeGrocer.com posted month after month of losses.[22]

HomeGrocer.com was better managed, but Webvan generated more enthusiasm and thus began with more cash, which meant that HomeGrocer.com ran dry first. In the dot-com opéra bouffe style of the late 1990s, the less competent but better-funded Webvan absorbed HomeGrocer.com, which only served to accelerate the newly merged company's cash consumption; in July 2001, it declared bankruptcy, vaporizing billions in wealth and leaving 3,500 employees out of work.[23]

* * *

The three-level bubble pyramid of the 1990s sat on a slimy pool of malfeasance and deceit, as occurred at Enron, one of the biggest corporate frauds in United States history, costing investors upwards of $70 billion. The episode speaks volumes about the get-rich-quick atmosphere of the era. Unlike the likable, philanthropic, and visionary Winnick, Enron's management consciously conjured up the mass of criminal behavior that regularly accompanies financial bubbles, and its dramatis personae came straight out of central casting's villain folder: the sanctimonious and socially ambitious Kenneth Lay; the hyperkinetic Jeffrey Skilling; and the dark, larcenous Andrew Fastow.

Unlike Global Crossing and the dot-coms, Enron began life in one of the economy's most unglamorous commodities: natural gas, which, until the mid-twentieth century, was most often burned off as waste. The company's principals, in contrast, shone with dazzling brilliance, and in the memorable and pithy words of journalists Peter Elkind and Bethany McLean, were "the smartest guys in the room."[24]

Born in 1942 into grinding poverty in rural Arkansas, Kenneth Lee Lay did not live in a house with an indoor toilet until he was eleven. From that point forward, though, fortune repeatedly smiled upon him, as when his father moved to Columbia, Missouri, the home of the state's public university. All three Lay children attended at little cost, and there Kenneth encountered great good fortune in the person of an economist named Pinkney Walker.

After graduation, Lay began work at Humble Oil, Exxon's predecessor, earning a night-school economics doctorate along the way. Next, he enlisted in the Navy, where in 1969, Walker's connections landed him a procurement job at the Pentagon. Shortly thereafter, President Nixon appointed Walker to the Federal Power Commission, and he took his young protégé with him. The commissioner's young aide so impressed Nixon that he tapped him for undersecretary of energy at the Interior Department.

Public utilities run through public rights of way, and ever since their birth in the late nineteenth century, the states and federal governments had heavily regulated the industry. But by the early 1970s, deregulation was in the air, and Lay found himself in the middle of the action. His Washington connections found him positions in Texas and Florida energy companies, eventually winding up in 1984 as CEO of Houston Natural Gas, where he engineered a merger with Omaha's venerable pipeline company, InterNorth. Lay hired a consulting firm to name the merged entity, which came up with Enteron; embarrassingly, *The Wall Street Journal* noted that the new moniker was a synonym for the gastrointestinal tract. It was shortened to Enron.[25]

Lay envisioned vast profits from deregulation. Tragically, he possessed qualities that would in due time turn the name Enron into a synonym for corporate malfeasance: a love of luxury and prestige, a weakness that prevented him from reining in the accomplished and arrogant young men he hired to execute his vision; and a moral blindness that equated his own self-interest with that of both his company and of society at large. He compounded this unfortunate combination of traits by gradually absenting himself from the company's day-to-day operations, as he spent ever more time hobnobbing in Washington, D.C., and Manhattan, and ever less time at the company's Houston headquarters. Despite Lay's stratospheric compensation (over $100 million in 2001, including stock options and "loans"), his social and material ambitions drove him deep into debt, more than $100 million worth when Enron failed.[26]

Corporate jets provide a useful window into corporate behavior. While their purchase does not by itself indicate poor management, let alone malfeasance, excessive use, and particularly personal use, does.[27] Enron owned six, which Lay's wife and children viewed as their private property, the "family taxi," as the fleet became known within the company. Among the ultrarich, the size, range, and speed of an aircraft mark the owner's place in the pecking order, and at the turn of the last century, private aviation's ne plus ultra was the three-engine Falcon 900. Enron had two, over which the Lay family held priority. On one occasion in 1999, for example, when daughter Robin wanted to return from France, the company sent an empty Falcon over to pick her up. In 2001, as the company was beginning to implode, Lay enthusiastically buttonholed Jeffrey Skilling, by then about to become CEO, for his opinion regarding the choice of upholstery for yet one more newly ordered aircraft.[28]

The Lay family taxi informed the consumption choices of other executives, many of whom owned fleets of luxury cars, multiple luxury vacation homes, and Manhattan apartments. One exception to the Enron culture of excess stood out: a sober and competent executive named Richard Kinder, who was in line to be Enron's CEO. Lay forced him out over personal issues, and when Kinder went through the door in 1996, the last brake on Enron's downhill slide departed with him. (Kinder then helped found another energy company, Kinder-Morgan. It owned no private jets, and when Kinder, a billionaire, needed one, he rented it out of his own pocket.)[29]

Lay's corporate vision went well beyond the everyday world of domestic pipelines; he wanted to extend the company's ambit in both space and scope, with ambitious overseas infrastructure projects and forays into the enticing new world of energy futures trading and, once established there, to create from scratch a futures market in internet bandwidth. Once Enron had conquered these, it would move into massive industries such as steel and paper, as well as services such as freight hauling.[30] In order to do so, the company needed to borrow vast amounts of money, which in turn required demonstrating the ability to earn profits early on; since the firm's new ventures were in fact sustaining significant losses, the appearance of profits would have to suffice.

Enter Jeffrey Skilling. Raised in the suburbs of both New Jersey and Chicago, in the early 1970s, he attended Southern Methodist University, where he studied electrical engineering. He soon found that money thrilled him in a way that circuitry did not. In one class he came across a Ph.D. thesis that described how to "securitize" futures contracts into marketable financial products, in the same way that mortgages would later be disastrously bundled together and sold to credulous investors. Skilling saw a way to extract money from mathematical abstraction, in which he had excelled at SMU, and soon thereafter, at Harvard Business School, where he graduated with top honors in 1979.

The logical next step for top-flight business school graduates was McKinsey & Company, before its recent scandals the planet's most prestigious consulting firm, where cool abstract reasoning was valued above all other skills. He made director at its Houston office within a decade, often consulting for Enron, and in 1990, it lured him away from McKinsey.

Enron, like most other companies, reported the income from gas sales as it arrived. To practitioners in the world of high-level consulting like Skilling, several things stood out about this seemingly antiquated notion of making profits from the sales of a mere commodity. He envisioned, for example, that the long-term contracts between the pipeline companies and their customers could be bought and sold in the financial markets like any other security. Even more critically, reporting income as it arrived offended

Skilling's rarified intellect. If the customer signed a contract to purchase gas over the next decade, he thought that it could be reported up front.

This technique, known as "mark-to-market" accounting, stood just on the edge of legality, so before deploying it, he asked for the SEC's blessing. Incredibly, in 1992, the commission gave it. At Enron headquarters, the accounting change effected the pouring of champagne, for Skilling had just acquired the nearest thing to a license to print money: sign long-term contracts, book all the revenue at once and thus immediately report spectacular earnings, borrow capital based on those fictitious earnings to build out natural gas capacity, on the strength of which yet more contracts could be signed, more future earnings booked immediately, and more money borrowed for yet more expansion.[31] It was as if Lockheed Martin, which expects to sell twenty-five hundred F-35 fighters to the U.S. armed forces for a total of more than a trillion dollars during the next decade, booked that revenue immediately upon signing the deal, then went out to borrow money on the strength of those projected earnings to begin the manufacture of automobiles, then booked the projected income from those future sales to build out a nationwide hospital chain.

Enron had already borrowed massively to expand the company beyond pedestrian gas delivery. Among other ventures, over the next decade the company built an enormous gas-fired power plant at Dabhol, south of Mumbai; established Azurix, a conglomeration of water companies around the globe as far-flung as Romania, Peru, and Morocco; and set up trading platforms for natural gas, for electricity, and, most seductively of all for credulous tech investors, for internet capacity (the last of which meant doing business with Winnick's Global Crossing).

Like Winnick, Enron's crew excelled at accounting legerdemain and dazzled inattentive stock analysts and small investors, and just like Winnick, few at Enron knew how to run a real-world business. Almost all of their operations lost boatloads of money, most spectacularly the Dabhol power plant, whose output cost so much that the local electricity board refused to pay for it, following which the plant sat mothballed for five years. Enron's international adventure in water companies, run by a charismatic and glamorous executive named Rebecca Mark, who had little prior experience with water utilities, imploded even more rapidly. Most incredibly of all, Enron contracted to deliver electrical power to twenty-eight thousand sites around the world, what the cerebral types at the Houston headquarters derisively called "butt-crack businesses," and because they had little experience with electrical utilities, they then had to hire the technical and administrative expertise to do so. Skilling, who envisioned a high-tech globe-circling broadband trading platform, tellingly had to have his secretary print out his emails and turn on his computer terminal for him.[32]

Rather than come clean to their shareholders about the company's losses and debt load, Skilling ordered twenty-eight-year-old new hire Andrew Fastow to conceal them. In order to borrow, companies need to demonstrate not only an ability to earn profits, but also that they are not already burdened with preexisting debt. Skilling had previously "solved" the earnings problem with his aggressive mark-to-market booking of future earnings; Fastow would surmount the borrowing problem by hiding the company's massive existing debt.

Fastow had acquired expertise in securitization of loans at his previous employer, the Continental Bank. Securitization involves the assembly of packages of loans and other debt that could next be marketed to buyers and traders. These highly complex and shadowy structures, so-called special purpose entities (SPEs), assumed the burgeoning debt and so theoretically took it off Enron's accounts; analysts, institutional investors, small investors, and even Enron's own board no longer saw them on its balance sheet and this deception made it appear as if the company was not heavily indebted.

Fastow constructed more than thirty-five hundred of these SPEs, featuring names like Marlin, Rawhide, Braveheart, Raptor, JEDI, Chewco (named after Chewbacca, a furry Star War's character), and LJM1, LJM2, and LJM3 (named after Fastow's wife and children, Lea, Jeffrey, and Matthew). Many of them were specifically designed to transfer money to the personal accounts of Fastow and other executives from shareholders, lenders, and even its own lower-level employees.[33]

Each of Skilling's and Fastow's accounting shenanigans kicked the cans of Enron's debt down the road, and all those cans accumulated into a massive garbage heap that eventually could no longer be hidden. What's remarkable is why shareholders and analysts took so long to recognize what should have become plainly visible far sooner.

The man who finally did so was James Chanos, who runs a hedge fund that specializes in so-called short sales. In the normal course of events, share buyers hope that they can buy low, then sell high, and thereby profit.

Counterintuitively, a trader can do the opposite: sell first at a high price, then reap a profit by purchasing the shares back later at a lower price. In order to do so, he must first borrow the shares from someone else; the share lender receives a fee for lending the shares, while the share borrower alone reaps the return—and the risk—of the short sale operation.*

Mr. Chanos was not the first analyst to realize that Enron's financial reports didn't make sense; rather, his edge lay in better handling the cognitive dissonance between the socially acceptable, happy narrative of Enron's genius and the contrary financial data, and in acting on it by shorting the stock.[34] The loans made to Enron depended on its credit rating, which in turn depended upon Fastow's ability to hide Enron's debt with the SPEs. Those loans also hinged on the value of Enron's stock, which was offered as collateral for their loans; when word of the shenanigans finally seeped out, the stock price fell, the banks called in the loans, and the house of cards came tumbling down. On October 16, 2001, Enron finally came clean about its losses; Ken Lay remained optimistic about the company's prospects right up to the moment it declared bankruptcy six weeks later. When he and his lieutenants went to New York to file the Chapter 11 papers, they flew there on an Enron jet and stayed at the Four Seasons.[35]

As with Charlie Mitchell's National City Bank, the collapse pummeled Enron's rank and file, who had been encouraged to lard their 401(k) plans with Enron stock; in 2005, for example, twenty thousand former Enron employees received a class-action award of $85 million, pennies on the dollar of their actual losses, which were estimated to be in the billions. (The money was recovered from insurance and banking firms, not from defunct Enron.)[36]

Adding insult to injury, employees were unable to sell the shares held in their retirement plans for a month, ostensibly because of ongoing changes made to the accounts, during the steepest stock price decline. On the other hand, Enron's top brass could unload their shares en masse ahead of the collapse, Skilling doing so to the tune of $71 million. When Dynergy, another utility company, offered to rescue Enron, the latter's executives demanded bonuses and payouts totaling more than $100 million, most for Lay, which Dynergy refused.[37]

---

* In order to protect the lender of the shares, the short seller must provide her with cash collateral of greater than the value of the share loan.

Unlike in the cases of Blunt, Hudson, and Mitchell, justice was served: Multiple executives, including Skilling and Fastow, did jail time (eleven and six years, respectively), and Lay died of a heart attack just before his sentencing.

The Enron episode, along with other similar scandals of that era, such as Dennis Kozlowski's Tyco International and Bernard Ebbers's WorldCom, were merely one end of a continuum of accounting manipulation that emanated from an obscure regulatory tweak.

In 1993, in a well-meaning effort to rein in excessive executive compensation, the IRS limited corporate tax deductibility for direct executive salaries to $1 million; this shifted executive payment toward stock options, which become more valuable as the stock price increases. Theoretically, payment in options aligns the incentives of both the executives and the shareholders, but in a classic example of the law of unintended consequences, options payment also incentivizes executives to fudge quarterly earnings numbers to show consistent, reliable earnings increases.

All other things equal, at a given average level of earnings, a small quarter-to-quarter variation in them makes the shares more valuable. Since real-world corporate fortunes fluctuate a lot, this questionable "management" of earnings reports proved too tempting for many CEOs, who made "adjustments" in accounting technique.

General Electric epitomized this legal but sleazy practice, rearranging the inevitable occasional losses seen in a normally operating far-flung empire from quarter to quarter to generate the appearance of smooth, dependable earnings growth.[38] The engineer of that prestidigitation, Jack Welch, had done nothing out of the ordinary, let alone fraudulent. Quite the contrary; the financial and popular press hailed him as the second coming of Thomas Edison.

Still, the point cannot be overemphasized: The stock bubbles that emanated from previous revolutionary technologies—the railroad in the nineteenth century and radio and automobiles in the early twentieth century—provided the free-flowing capital that powered economies and advanced societal well-being.

The same was true of the 1990s internet bubble. Even after taking into consideration the nonproductive companies at the bottom of the pyramid like Webvan and the frankly fraudulent companies in the muck under it like Enron, incalculable online intellectual, entertainment, shopping, and banking benefits flowed from investments, most of them money-losers, made in those technologies during that heady period. It's not too much of a stretch, then, to label bubble investors as capitalism's unwitting philanthropists, who unconsciously and tragically sacrifice their wealth in the service of the greater public good.

By the late twentieth century, large investment banks, the folks who manufactured the stocks and bonds of new and existing companies, had become the prime bubble promoters. Financier Jay Gould pioneered this industry during the Civil War by selling the government bonds necessary to finance the Union army. In the wake of the 1929 crash, the Pecora Commission blew the lid off Charlie Mitchell's seamy investment banking practices at National City and brought about the Glass-Steagall Act of 1933, which separated commercial and investment banking by forbidding Main Street banks from issuing stocks and bonds and investment banks from taking deposits from and loaning to ordinary citizens.

Over the succeeding decades, lobbying by investment banks brought about a gradual weakening of Glass-Steagall's enforcement. This eventually culminated, under the direction of free-market ideologue Republican lawmakers such as Phil Gramm and with the acquiescence of the triangulating Democratic president Bill Clinton, in the act's repeal at the bubble's height in 1999.

During the tech bubble, the investment banks revved up their issuance of stock shares in the new companies, and the public, ecstatically connected by the Netscape browser to the internet for the first time at speeds ten thousand times slower than today's broadband connections, needed no convincing to buy them. Netscape founders Marc Andreessen and Jim Clark, aware that giant Microsoft was developing its own browser, moved quickly to cash in with an initial public offering (IPO).

The Glass-Steagall Act had forced the Morgan company, which had kept its nose clean during the 1920s, to split off from the investment banking half and become Morgan Stanley, Inc. In the 1990s, Morgan Stanley, now the nation's largest issuer of new stock shares, would float Netscape's IPO, the most spectacular of the dot-com bubble.

Morgan Stanley, heretofore the great bastion of establishment wealth and privilege, had changed; one of its executives, Frank Quattrone, who hailed from Italian immigrant roots and still spoke with a strong accent, had already taken public Cisco, a major producer of the internet's backbone hardware. With Netscape's initial offering on August 9, 1995, he proved himself the worthy successor to Sunshine Charlie Mitchell (and like Mitchell, Quattrone narrowly avoided serving jail time in a series of trials that included a conviction—later reversed on appeal—on obstruction and witness tampering charges).

A major question vexed Quattrone, Clark, Andreesen, and Jim Barksdale, who had just been hired as Netscape's CEO: How much should investors pay for the company's shares? Properly pricing an IPO is a fine art. Ideally, in order to sustain enthusiasm, a stock should experience a significant "pop" up from the offering price on its first day of trading; if that offering price is too high, it may discourage retail investors by falling on the first trading day; if set too low, the company and its founders get shortchanged. The four decided on $28 per share, which valued the company at about a billion dollars. When the market opened that morning, the four held their collective breath.

Demand for the stock was so heavy that at the 9:30 A.M. opening bell in New York, Morgan Stanley's traders couldn't arrive at a sensible price; one brokerage firm quickly added a new phone prompt: "Press one if you're calling about Netscape." Unaware of the frenzy, a bewildered Clark looked at his monitor at 9 A.M. Pacific time, two and a half hours into the east coast trading day, and saw the stock flatlined at $28. He called a broker at Morgan Stanley, who told him there was a "trade imbalance." Not fully comprehending what that meant, Clark wondered if the IPO had bombed.

"Trade imbalance" did not even begin to describe the deafening scene at Morgan Stanley's New York IPO desk. At its heart sat approximately two hundred workstations, each manned by a trader desperately trying to answer several simultaneously ringing extensions, each of which, in turn, conveyed a demand for Netscape shares.

Shortly after Clark's initial call, the broker rang back to inform Clark that it had opened at $71, which meant that his net worth had abruptly shot past a half billion dollars, and that the company had raised much more than that. As put by one of the chapter titles in Clark's memoir, "One Billion Is the Best Revenge."[39]

The Grateful Dead's Jerry Garcia died later that day of a massive heart attack. His last words supposedly were, "Netscape opened at *what*?"[40]

14

HUCKSTERS OF THE DIGITAL AGE

We don't get up every morning thinking business is bad.
—Roger Ailes[1]

The reason many chose to ignore the obvious signs of a bubble, and particularly the Enron accounting garbage pile, can be summed up in two words: "investment banker." Over the past few decades, that job description has become shorthand for "someone who makes an obscene amount of money." When an investment bank floats an IPO, it earns a commission of 5 to 7 percent of the proceeds. Netscape yielded fees of $130 million, and Webvan, $375 million; later IPOs would earn the banks billions. Individual employees garnered a large slice of this pie. When Frank Quattrone moved from Morgan Stanley to Credit Suisse in 1998, his next year's personal share of this bonanza rose to approximately $100 million.[2]

One of the more bizarre features of the dot-com era was the rise to celebrity status of the once lowly stock analyst, who before the 1990s toiled away in modestly well-compensated anonymity in the bowels of investment companies. The dot-com bubble propelled a handful of them to a visibility usually reserved for superstar athletes and movie actors, as an eager public followed their every pronouncement about the prospects of this or that dot-com. The two most famous were Morgan Stanley's Mary Meeker and Merrill Lynch's Henry Blodget. The problem was that the same companies that cranked out the stocks and bonds also employed the folks who "analyzed" the stocks and bonds.

The financial industry is the eight-hundred-pound gorilla of the U.S. economy, representing nearly one-fifth of both GDP and the value of stock market shares. Because investment banking represents the biggest source of this bounty, analysts who didn't play along with a steady stream of "buy" recommendations could be pressured, as John Olson, who covered Enron for Merrill Lynch, learned.

Enron executives obsessively followed the company's stock price, especially Fastow, whose schemes depended on it, and their major investment banking interest lay in the bond offerings that fueled their breakneck global expansion. These offerings generated enormous fees for the investment banks, a fact about which Enron never ceased to remind its banks. One analyst reported being told by the company, "We do over $100 million of investment-banking business a year. You get some if you have a strong buy [recommendation to clients]."[3]

Unhappily for Olson, he didn't follow that playbook. Unlike James Chanos, who suspected fraud, Olson wasn't overly negative about Enron, reporting that he simply didn't understand its accounting and noting in one media interview, "They're not very forthcoming about how they make their money. . . . I don't know an analyst worth his salt who can seriously analyze Enron."[4] Enron chairman Lay despised Olson and wrote a note to his boss at Merrill Lynch, Donald Sanders: "Don, John Olson has been wrong about Enron for over ten years and is still wrong, but he is consistant [sic]." (When Sanders showed Olson the note, he observed that he might be old and worthless, but at least he knew how to spell "consistent.")[5] Eventually, a pair of Merrill Lynch investment bankers complained to the company's president, Herbert Allison, who apologized to Lay. Merrill Lynch let Olson go and kept its seat on the Enron gravy train.[6]

During the 1990s, different versions of the Merrill/Enron/Olson drama were played out by thousands of actors on hundreds of stages, and while every script was different, the plotline remained constant, as stock analysts abandoned their craft and became cheerleaders for their investment banking colleagues. One researcher compiled more than fifteen thousand stock reports from just one year, 1997; fewer than 0.5 percent recommended selling shares.[7]

Along with the promoters, the investing public forms the second anatomic locus of financial manias. In the years preceding the internet bubble, more and more Americans had become their own investment managers, and while increasing incomes and wealth largely drove this phenomenon, something else was happening as well: They had to.

In the decades following the 1929 crash, the U.S. economy and social structure had undergone profound changes, prime among which was the gradual lengthening of life expectances, and with it, the extension of retirement. When Otto von Bismarck established the concept of old-age pensions in Germany in 1889, the median life expectancy of European adults was forty-five, decades below the seventy-year qualifying age, and in any case, families generally took care of their elderly members. By the end of the twentieth century, Americans contemplated retirements lasting more than three decades, and increasing geographical mobility often made direct family care impossible. All these factors increased the onus on individuals to fund their ever-more expensive golden years.

The luckiest American workers spent their careers at large companies that provided so-called defined benefit plans that supplied a pension until the employees, and usually their spouses, died (assuming the company did not fire them just before they qualified for a pension, an all-too-common practice). Studebaker, an automobile manufacturer, was one such benevolent employer, but when it closed its last U.S. plant in 1963, it set in motion a series of congressional investigations that eventually gave rise to the Employee Retirement Income Security Act (ERISA) in 1974, which governs pension operations to this day. One of the act's more obscure sections established Individual Retirement Accounts (IRAs), which allowed workers for the first time to accumulate savings free of income tax until withdrawal in retirement; in 1981, the government loosened initial restrictions on their use, making them more attractive to employers and available to more workers.

At roughly the same time, a pension benefits consultant named Ted Benna was growing increasingly dissatisfied with his work, which primarily involved answering the following question for employers: "How can I get the biggest tax break, and give the least to my employees, legally?"[8] This troubled the devout and generous Benna, who sought a way to get companies to do right by their workers.

Benna noticed that the Revenue Act of 1978 had added an obscure subsection to the IRS Code, § 401(k), which allowed employers to directly defer their employees' salaries into retirement savings. Benna imagined the number of workers doing so would increase if employers could induce them by offering to match their contributions. Benna had connections at the IRS, which approved the scheme. His invention mushroomed; today, the trillions of dollars in 401(k) assets roughly match those in IRAs.[9]

These individual accounts consequently allowed companies to abandon their commitment to traditional defined-benefit pension plans; along with the loosening of intergenerational bonds brought about by increased geographical mobility, workers and small businessmen suddenly became their own pension managers, a job that requires a combination of quantitative skills, historical knowledge, and emotional discipline that few finance professionals, let alone lay people, possess.

The inability of ordinary investors to competently invest is evident, for example, in data on the performance of mutual funds that are now by far the most common retirement vehicles; they are essentially the only choices available in defined-contribution retirement schemes such as company 401(k) plans. Were investors competent, their "internal rate of return" (IRR, which accounts for all fund shares bought and sold) on these vehicles should exactly equal the underlying return of the fund. Sadly, researchers have found that, on average, employees time their fund purchases and sales so poorly that the IRR they earn on them is almost always lower than the return of the funds themselves.[10] In other words, more often than not, small investors buy high and sell low, robbing themselves of the full market return available from a given fund.

CNBC epitomized the third anatomic location of bubble anatomy, the press, during the dot-com era. Its predecessor in television business and investment information, the Financial News Network, began operations at the wrong time, in 1981, toward the tail end of a long, brutal bear market that marked a nadir in public interest in investing; a decade later, it went bankrupt. In 1989, NBC, eager to improve its anemic ratings and sensing renewed public interest in investing, founded the Commercial News and Business Channel.

NBC's timing could hardly have been better, for the markets had begun to turn around, and tens of millions of people, as much out of necessity as out of interest, began to follow stocks. Initially, its programming was soporific: anchors faced the cameras from behind card tables and presented shows on dinner preparation and managing children's tantrums.[11] In 1991, its fortunes improved a little, as the bankrupt remains of FNN fell into its hands, along with much of its talent, and it shortened the channel's name to its acronym, CNBC.

In 1993, the media gods smiled even more broadly on the fledgling network with the arrival of Roger Ailes, then at the apex of his legendary grasp and deployment of television's raw emotive power. Born with hemophilia and saddled with a father fond of corporal punishment—a particularly unfortunate combination—his frequent bleeding episodes resulted in long periods of confinement at home, where his real classroom became 1950s television, which he spent endless hours analyzing. Unsurprisingly, he majored in media studies, and after college graduation cut his teeth on production work at local east coast television stations.[12] Ailes then hired on with the nationally syndicated *Mike Douglas Show* as a prop boy; within three years he became its producer. Shortly after that promotion, in 1968, he encountered Richard Nixon, then pursuing his second presidential bid, in the show's studio. Nixon expressed distaste that "a man has to use gimmicks [like television] to get elected," to which Ailes replied, "Television is not a gimmick." Shortly after that encounter, Nixon aide Leonard Garment hired him.[13] Thus did Ailes begin a quarter-century career in media consulting for Republican presidents, making Nixon more likable in 1968 and in 1988 helping George H. W. Bush defeat Michael Dukakis.

Upon becoming president of CNBC, Ailes kept what had worked from the old FNN format, particularly the ubiquitous stock ticker "crawl" running at the bottom of the screen, which would become the metaphorical background soundtrack of the financial bubble's soap opera. Otherwise, he overhauled every aspect of the look and feel of the network, and later applied the same techniques to his new charges that had worked so well with national politicians and business giants. Instead of simply announcing a new segment with theme music, he added voiceovers with tight head shots of the anchors. Recipes and child temper tantrums were out; Geraldo Rivera and the engaging political commentator Mary Matalin were in. Ailes personally instructed camera operators on how to properly frame corporate executives to make them appear more alive, prodded writers to come up with more compelling "don't touch that dial" patter, and sent anchors to breathlessly report the price action from the stock exchange floor. The more flamboyant the guest, the better. As put by the *New Yorker*'s John Cassidy,

Their ideal studio guest was a former beauty queen who covered technology stocks, spoke in short declarative sentences, and dated Donald Trump. Since there weren't many of these women available, the producers generally had to settle for balding, middle-aged men who revered Alan Greenspan and tried their best to speak English.[14]

Ailes taught his anchors and production staff to treat finance as a spectator sport; after one particularly brutal week in the market, one of his advertising clips caustically compared the new network to its archrival: "The Dow plummets in heavy trading. But first, today's weather. CNN tells you if your shirt will get wet; CNBC tells you if you've still got one." He also married sex and finance by promoting a new recruit from CNN, Maria Bartiromo, into an anchor position; with her Sophia Loren looks, dense Brooklyn accent, and blatant sex appeal, she quickly became known as "the Money Honey."[15]

In 1996, CNBC forced Ailes out for the bullying behavior that would haunt his later career, but by then his media makeover had proven hugely profitable. By the mid-1990s, CNBC had opened sister networks in Europe and Asia, and the sun never set on the constant drama, real or manufactured, of the world's capital markets.

Ailes intuitively understood that his audiences preferred the cotton candy of entertainment to the spinach of information and analysis; and best of all was a confection that spun unlimited wealth. Under Ailes, CNBC mastered that genre and perpetrated a feat of modern cultural alchemy by transmuting the tedious world of mainstream finance into wildly successful entertainment. The new venue's attention centered on the internet, which small investors could use to instantaneously act on what they had just viewed on CNBC through online brokerages such as E-Trade and Datek, the latter favored by day traders.

Investigative reporting went out the window; it cost gobs of money, and worse, it offended the all-important investment banks, whose parent companies purchased the lion's share of the advertising. Better to fill broadcast time slots with interviews of corporate executives who talked enthusiastically about their companies, and "market strategists" who spoke authoritatively about where stocks were headed. Best of all, the executives and strategists appeared for free and arrived in hired cars from across the Hudson to CNBC's studios in Fort Lee, New Jersey.

CNBC's offerings lacked any critical examination of the uniformly optimistic pronouncements of both its corporate executive and most brokerage analyst guests. In 2000 and 2001, CNBC anchor Mark Haines interviewed, respectively, Ken Lay and Jeffrey Skilling. Haines had graduated from the University of Pennsylvania's law school and fancied himself a sharp inquisitor, but when faced with the perpetrators of one of history's greatest corporate frauds, he exuded only a wide stream of praise and puff questions.[16]

When major corporations like IBM, Sears, and AT&T laid off tens of thousands of employees, CNBC cheered the company's buoyed bottom line, oblivious to the human cost of mass firings. When corporations committed apparent felonies, CNBC simply looked the other way, at least as long as the resulting scandal stayed off newspapers' front pages, as when the network brushed off reports in May 2012 that J. P. Morgan had hid $2 billion of trading losses from its shareholders.[17]

Nor did the network do much good for viewers' bottom lines. Two representative academic studies looked closely at the value of acting on the show's guest list and recommendations; their conclusions were not

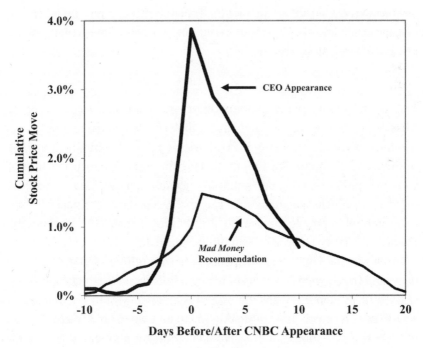

Figure 14-1.   CNBC and Stock Prices

encouraging. The first examined the reaction of stock price to the appearance of corporate CEOs on CNBC, and the second researched the performance of the stock picks of one of the network's most popular current programs, *Mad Money*, hosted by the frenetic, boisterous James Cramer. The results of both studies, shown in figure 14-1, are nearly identical: A price bump, relative to the rest of the stock market, peaked on the day of, or day after, the show, then fell. As alarming as the postshow price fall was, the rise beforehand suggested that participants with foreknowledge of the show's schedule of guests played CNBC's viewers like two-dollar banjos. Despite his clownish appearance, Cramer was no dummy, and well understood this dynamic. On at least one occasion he had sold stock in a company touted on Bartiromo's show, then bought it back a few days later after its price drifted back down.[18]

Even more telling were those CEOs who elected not to participate in the circus. Jeff Bezos, the chairman and founder of the period's most successful IPO, Amazon, enjoyed intellectual back-and-forth with informed journalists and often granted interviews to even minor publications. He saw little point, though, in appearing on CNBC, which he knew would focus on the short-term outlook for the company's stock price, and which he considered a worthless distraction. If he took care of his customers, he felt, the company would prosper in the long run, no matter how the stock price wandered along the way.[19]

The fourth locus of bubble anatomy centers on political leaders. During the Mississippi, South Sea, and railway bubbles, leaders at the highest levels had thrust their hands deeply into the cookie jar, including the monarchs of France and Britain. Starting in the late nineteenth century, because of increased public scrutiny and antigraft legislation, politicians figured less often as prominent speculators: During the 1920s, direct political involvement in bubble propagation reached little higher than John Raskob, the Democratic Party National Committee chairman.

During the 1990s, the prospect of tens of millions of 401(k) participants and IRA owners, each his or her own little capitalist, enthralled conservatives; influenced by the theories of Ayn Rand, Milton Friedman, and Friedrich von Hayek, they gloried in the new "ownership society." While the 1990s tech bubble did not involve significant political acts of commission—that is, outright graft and corruption—political acts of omission took center stage, namely inattention to the regulatory safeguards that were put in place during the 1930s in the wake of the Pecora Commission; by the 1980s the Glass-Steagall Act's strict separation of commercial and investment banking operations had been rendered toothless from inattention long before its final repeal in 1999.

CNBC's coverage and tone gloried in the ideological underpinnings of the great bull market. In what amounted to the opening prayer of its "Kudlow Report" segment, its host Lawrence Kudlow would intone, "Remember, folks, free market capitalism is the best path to prosperity!"[20] Conservative journalist James Glassman, perhaps more than anyone else, cemented the connection between the tech bubble and free-market ideology. Best known as the author of multiple investing books, he was, and remains, a favorite on conservative venues, especially *The Wall Street Journal*. In the 1990s he rhapsodized about how the market's meteoric rise was a mere prelude to what was to follow from free-market capitalism's cornucopia. So when stocks began to crumble in April 2000, he blamed Uncle Sam for stifling those markets. Reacting to a ruling favorable to the government's antitrust suit against Microsoft, he observed:

> No one ever knows for sure why a stock falls on a given day, but my interpretation of Nasdaq's sharp decline is that investors, jarred by the Microsoft decision, have suddenly woken up to these threats of government intervention. If they haven't woken up, they had better. And so should [Vice President and presidential candidate] Al Gore. The Clinton administration likes to take credit for a stock market that has quadrupled in the past decade. It can't avoid the blame for Nasdaq's collapse.[21]

George Gilder, a former speechwriter for Richard Nixon and Nelson Rockefeller, to whom the connection between the great 1990s bull market and the superiority of unfettered free markets was an article of faith, provided the most extreme example of 1990s tech enthusiasm. In a remarkable editorial in *The Wall Street Journal* published on the portentous date of January 1, 2000, Gilder posited that the internet didn't merely change everything, but transformed the very "space-time grid of the global economy." He deployed grandiose metaphors that invoked the vastness of the empty reaches inside the atom, the "manipulation of the inner structure of matter," and even slipped quantum mechanics and "centrifical [*sic*] force" past the *Journal*'s editors, concluding that only through the bounteous application of faith, love, and religious commitment would mankind triumph in the brave new digital age.[22] High above at the Pearly Gates, the editors of the *Railway Times* applauded.

How did Gilder, Kudlow, and Glassman, all of whom possessed formidable intellectual horsepower burnished with Ivy League educations, get things so spectacularly wrong in the late 1990s? Starting in the twentieth century, psychologists began to realize that people use their analytical ability not to *analyze*, but rather to *rationalize*—that is, to conform observed facts to their preconceived biases. (Economists have long observed that "if you torture the data long enough, it will eventually confess.") Understanding the two main reasons why humans do so lies at the heart of both individual and mass delusions.

The first reason for the proclivity all of us—the smart, the dumb, and the average—have for such irrationality is that true rationality is extraordinarily hard work, and few possess the ability to do it. Further, the facility for rationality correlates imperfectly with IQ. In the early 2000s, an academic named Shane Frederick, who had acquired a doctoral degree in the relatively new discipline of decision sciences, invented a famous paradigm that demonstrates just how difficult pure analytical rigor is.

Not long after earning his doctorate, Frederick wrote a classic paper describing a simple questionnaire. Known among psychologists as the cognitive resource test (CRT), it measured the quotient of rational ability—call it RQ—as opposed to IQ. It consisted of only three puzzlers, the most famous of which (at least in economic circles) is this one: Suppose that a baseball and a baseball bat together cost $1.10, and that the bat costs a dollar more than the baseball. How much does the ball cost? Most people, even highly intelligent ones, will quickly answer $0.10. But this cannot be, since it means that the bat costs $1.10, and so makes the total price $1.20. Rather, the ball must cost $0.05, which makes the bat $1.05, and the total cost of both the desired $1.10.*

---

* The other two questions in Frederick's battery: (1) If it takes 5 machines 5 minutes to make 5 widgets, how long would it take 100 machines to make 100 widgets? Answer = 5 minutes. (2) In a lake, there is a patch of lily pads. Every day, the patch doubles in size. If it takes 48 days for the patch to cover the entire lake, how long would it take for the patch to cover half of the lake? Answer = 47 days. Over the past decade, the baseball/bat question has become so well known in economics and finance that it's now hard to stump anyone in these fields with it.

If you found the baseball/bat question and the two others in the footnote easy, you might find another puzzler, half a century old, a little more challenging. Wason's Four Card test involves cards with a letter on one side and a number on the other. Start with this rule: "If a card has a vowel on its letter side, it has an even number on its number side." Four cards are showing: K, A, 8, and 5. Which two cards do you turn over to prove or disprove the rule?

The overwhelming majority of subjects will intuitively answer A and 8, but the correct answer is A and 5. With typical academic understatement, Wason, who pioneered the concept of confirmation bias, wrote, "The task proved to be peculiarly difficult." To answer correctly, one first has to realize that the rule, when carefully considered, allows that cards with even numbers can have both vowels and consonants on the other side, so it does no good to turn over the 8 card. To disprove the conjecture, one must turn over the 5; if it has a vowel, then the conjecture is false, as will also be true in the easier case of turning over the A and finding an odd number.[23]

Rational thought takes considerable effort, and almost all human beings are mentally lazy or "cognitive misers," in psych-speak, and they intuitively seek analytical shortcuts like the heuristics described by Kahneman and Tversky. The intense cognitive effort demanded by rigorous rationality is not at all pleasant, and most people avoid it. As put by one academic, we "engage the brain only when all else fails—and usually not even then."[24]

IQ and RQ thus measure different things. While IQ measures the ability to handle abstract verbal and quantitative mechanics, particularly algorithms, RQ focuses instead on what comes *before* those algorithms are applied: Before analyzing the facts, does the subject carefully lay out the problem's logic and consider alternative analytical approaches? And after arriving at an answer, does she consider that her conclusions may be wrong, estimate that probability, and calculate the consequences of such an error? A high IQ, it turns out, provides little protection against these pitfalls. In the droll assessment of Keith Stanovich, the inventor of an expanded RQ-measuring battery, the Comprehensive Assessment of Rational Thinking (CART), "Rationality and intelligence often dissociate."[25]

The second main reason for our propensity to act irrationally is that we more often than not apply our intellects to rationalization, and not to rationality. What we rationalize, generally speaking, are our moral and emotional frameworks, as evidenced by the division of our cognitive processes into a fast-moving System 1, seated in our deeply placed limbic systems—our "reptilian brains"—and a plodding System 2 that analyzes the rationality-demanding tasks of the CRT and CART.

For most of humanity's history, our two-system apparatus served us well. In the words of psychologist R. B. Zajonc, "It was a wise designer who provided separately for each of these processes instead of presenting us with a multiple-purpose appliance that, like the rotisserie-broiler-oven-toaster, performs none of its functions well."[26]

In the postindustrial world, whose planning horizon, particularly for financial affairs, stretches decades into the future, the decisions we face look less and less like the second-to-second System 1 functioning that decided the survival of our ancestors on the African savannahs and more and more like the mind-twisting System 2 questions in the CRT and CART, a problem compounded by the fact that, more often than not, we use our System 2 to rationalize the conclusions already reached by our emotionally driven System 1. In other words, the vaunted human System 2 functions mainly as, in the words of Daniel Kahneman, System 1's "press secretary."[27]

Because of this greater need for cognitive effort, even the best and brightest prove inadequate to the forecasting and decision-making societal tasks facing us. By the 1970s, Kahneman, Tversky, and others sensed that human beings were terrible at forecasting, but not until more recently have researchers begun to measure just how terrible we are.

Beginning in the late 1980s, psychologist Philip Tetlock began to quantify the predictive abilities of supposed authorities in their fields by examining the performance of twenty-eight thousand predictions made by 284 experts in politics, economics, and domestic and strategic studies. First and foremost, he found that experts forecast poorly—so poorly that they lagged simple statistical rules that fed off the frequencies of past events: the "base rate."

For example, if the average investing "expert" is asked about the likelihood of a market crash in the coming year, defined as a fall in price by more than, say, 20 percent, he will likely spin a narrative about how Fed policy, industrial output, debt levels, and so forth affect that possibility. What Tetlock discovered was that it was best to ignore this sort of narrative reasoning and simply look at the historical frequency of such price falls. For example, monthly stock market price falls of more than 20 percent have occurred in 3 percent of the years since 1926, and this simple data point proves more accurate in forecasting the likelihood of a crash than narrative-based "expert" analysis.

Tetlock also found that certain experts did especially badly. His research broadly separated them into two categories, as described in a famous essay by social and political theorist Isaiah Berlin entitled "The Hedgehog and the Fox."[28] In Tetlock's taxonomy, the hedgehog is an ideologue who interprets everything he sees according to an overarching unitary theory of the world, whereas the fox entertains many competing explanations. Foxes tolerate ambiguity better than hedgehogs and feel less compelled to come to firm conclusions. Hedgehogs possess greater confidence in their predictions and make more extreme ones; critically, they change their opinions less frequently than do foxes when presented with contrary data, a behavior that corrodes forecasting accuracy.

Analysis-killing hedgehoggery infects the political right and left equally: For example, radical environmentalists to this day defend Paul Ehrlich's famously off-base 1970s predictions of imminent global starvation and natural resource shortages, and libertarians do the same for influential economist Martin Feldstein's high-profile warning that Bill Clinton's budgets and social policies would wreck the economy.

Ever since our prehistoric ancestors began consulting shamans, people have sought certainty in an uncertain world by consulting experts. Tetlock tested the forecasting ability of three broad groups: undergraduates, recognized authorities in the area of a given forecasting question, and "dilettantes" who were knowledgeable in one field but were forecasting outside it. Not surprisingly, the undergraduates performed the worst. More remarkably, the experts performed no better than the dilettantes; further, when Tetlock then broke down these results between foxes and hedgehogs, specialty expertise in the area in question seemed to benefit the forecasts of the foxes but worsened those of the hedgehogs.

In other words, a foxy environmental scientist will likely better forecast a military outcome than a hedgehoggy military specialist, and vice versa. The reason for this seems to be that while the experts and dilettantes both tended to overestimate the probabilities of extreme outcomes, the experts did so more of the time, and paid the price in forecasting accuracy attendant to extreme predictions. The dilettantes, it would seem, behaved more like foxes, at least outside their field of expertise. The sweet spot of knowledge would thus appear to be, in Tetlock's words, "in the vicinity of savvy readers of high-quality news sources such as the *Economist*, the *Wall Street Journal*, and the *New York Times*, the publications that dilettantes most frequently reported as useful sources of information on topics outside their specialties."[29]

This somewhat startling statement stems from Tetlock's finding that experts generally use their knowledge to rationalize how the data conform to their preexisting worldview. Since hedgehogs hold on to their preexisting views more tightly, they rationalize their errors more reliably. For example, Tetlock found that "loquacity," the ability to enumerate a large number of arguments in support of a prediction, was a marker for poor forecasting. Tetlock suggests a simple rule of thumb for identifying an expert's animal mascot: hedgehogs use the word "moreover" more than "however," whereas foxes do the opposite.[30]

Most of us suffer from strong bias toward self-affirmation, the desire to think well of ourselves, and thus misremember our forecasts as more accurate than they actually were; conversely, we erroneously remember our opponents' forecasts as less accurate. Hedgehogs, though, have an especially marked tendency to do this, and Tetlock enumerated the most notable excuses they deploy: "A bolt out of the blue derailed my prediction," "I was almost right," "I wasn't wrong, I was just early," and finally, when all else fails, "I haven't been proven right yet." He succinctly summarized this tendency: "It is hard to ask someone why they got it wrong when they think they got it right."[31]

Finally, Tetlock identified a particularly potent forecasting kiss of death: media fame. For its part, the media seeks out "boomsters and doomsters"; that is hedgehogs fond of extreme predictions, who appeal to viewers more favorably than do equivocating foxes. Further, media attention produces overconfidence, which itself corrodes forecasting accuracy. The result is a media-forecasting death spiral that seeks extreme, and hence poor, forecasters, whose media exposure then worsens their predictions. Tetlock observed, "The three principals—authoritative-sounding experts, the ratings-conscious media, and the attentive public—may thus be locked in a symbiotic triangle."[32] In retrospect, Kudlow, Gilder, and Glassman, the tech bubble's ideological cheerleaders, had hit the Tetlock trifecta: media-darling hedgehogs fond of extreme predictions.

The dot-com era exhibited all of the classic signs and symptoms of a financial bubble: the dominance of stock investing in everyday conversation, the abandonment of secure jobs for full-time speculation, the scorn and ridicule heaped on skeptics by true believers, and the prevalence of extreme predictions.

Never before had extreme market ebullience and the subsequent disaster been so closely observed and recorded in real time on TV screens and, increasingly, on the internet itself. The ebullience infected venues in the tech industry's pampered nerve centers in Silicon Valley, on Wall Street, and in CNBC's studios in Fort Lee, but the market fever that gripped everyday conversation was most acutely felt on Main Street, in social gatherings and investment clubs.

A poignant ground-level narrative of this obsession played out in that bastion of working-class male solidarity, a barber shop, on Massachusetts's Cape Cod. In normal times, the talk in such places runs mainly to sports and politics, and if the establishment is graced with a television set, it is tuned to a baseball, football, or basketball game. But the turn of the last century was no normal time, and Bill's Barber Shop in Dennis, Massachusetts, owned and operated by Bill Flynn, was no ordinary haircutting establishment.

By 2000, Flynn had been cutting hair for a third of a century and was no stranger to the stock market. His great-grandfather, also a barber, had offered him superb advice: save 10 percent of his earnings and put it into equities. Bill's execution of that wisdom proved less than stellar, for he was driven by the human phenomenon exploited so well by South Sea's John Blunt, the preference for lottery-like outcomes. In the mid-1980s, Cabbage Patch Dolls were all the rage, and large numbers of children and adults "invested" in them, never mind the fact that they could be manufactured at will. At the height of the frenzy, Flynn bought shares on margin—that is, with borrowed money—in Coleco, Inc., the company that made them.

The company's 1988 bankruptcy decimated his original savings, but he stoically soldiered on and continued to put his spare earnings into the market. Over the course of a decade, he socked away $100,000 into the most glamorous high-tech names he could find: AOL, Yahoo!, and Amazon, among others. By 2000, his nest egg had grown to $600,000. Bill had told himself that he would retire when his portfolio hit two commas; given how well he was doing, he figured, he would be there shortly.[33]

If manias resemble epidemics, "the internet changes everything and it's going to make us all rich" narrative was the virus, and Bill Flynn was Cape Cod's Patient Zero. By 2000, the patter around the barber chair had switched from the Red Sox, Celtics, and Patriots to EMC and Abgenix, Bill's two favorite stocks. The TV was tuned to CNBC.

The toxic combination of round-the-clock financial entertainment and instantaneous online trading played out tragically in Bill's shop. He spun compelling narratives and cajoled his small-business-owner customers into purchasing the shares of his chosen companies.[34] When *Wall Street Journal* reporter Susan Pulliam first visited the shop in the winter of 2000, just as the market was peaking, the talk was all tech stocks, all the time. Bill suggested Abgenix, a biotech firm, to one customer. Others in the shop variously volunteered that they had purchased Coyote Technologies, had owned Network Appliance, or, if less adventurous, were merely considering a mutual fund offered by Janus, an investment company that specialized in tech-oriented portfolios.

Bill's favorite was a data storage firm, EMC: "I'd say I've put 100 people into EMC." None of them seemed to care that Bill had settled on the company not through rigorous security analysis, but rather via a tip from another barber. By mid-2000, stocks had encountered several severe downdrafts, but Bill and his customers were confident of their staying power. As put by one, a painter/wallpaperer, "Even if we do go down 30 percent, we'll come right back." Weaker souls drew ridicule. Flynn pointed out a customer in the parking lot: "See that guy? He had $5,000 set aside two years ago, and I told him to buy EMC. Would've been worth $18,000 right now if he'd have listened."[35]

When Ms. Pulliam returned to the shop three months later, tech stocks had just recovered from severe declines, but were still about 40 percent below their peaks. Said Bill, "I'm not just buying any biotechnology or high-tech stock," but he was still sticking with his old standby, EMC. He had also just bought more Abgenix, whose share price had strongly rebounded, and his portfolio value had reached a new high.[36]

In February 2001, the beloved EMC shares he had purchased on margin fell to the point that his broker had to liquidate the position. The stock, which had peaked at $145 shortly after Ms. Pulliam's first visit, eventually fell to under $4 in late 2002. Bill's shop, once the town's social hive, fell silent and emptied out. Observed one customer, "Everyone knows Bill has lost a lot of money. You don't want to talk about it so much."[37]

Not all of Bill's customers got shorn; one, for instance, cashed out of his EMC stock to purchase a new home. But the damage, in general, had been done; the 2000–2002 bear market so demoralized Bill that he did not start buying stocks again until 2007, when, on the advice of a stock broker, he purchased shares in Eastman Kodak. It went bankrupt five years later; in 2013, at age seventy-three, he was still cutting hair. Even after the crash, EMC executives, who had grown understandably fond of Mr. Flynn, stopped by for haircuts during their summer vacations.[38]

Bill and his customers, for the most part, got fleeced in time-honored fashion, by trading shares in individual companies, frequently on margin. But during the 1990s, increasing numbers of Americans got their stock exposure from another route: mutual funds, the direct descendants of the investment trusts of the 1920s, which provided not only easy diversification of risk through ownership of a large number of companies, but also stock

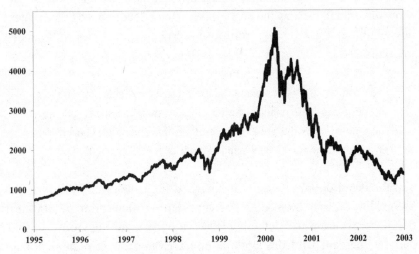

Figure 14-2.   NASDAQ Composite Index 1995–2003

selection by supposedly skilled managers. Between 1990 and 2000, the assets of U.S. stock mutual funds increased by almost twentyfold, from roughly $200 billion to $3.5 trillion—that is from about 7 percent to about 23 percent of the value of the total stock market in those two decades.[39]

Just like the Cape Cod barber shop denizens, mutual fund investors increasingly gravitated toward the highest fliers. The Jacob Internet Fund, one of the most popular, shot up by 196 percent in 1998, and the Van Wagoner Emerging Growth Fund gained a jaw-dropping 291 percent in 1999. Janus Capital ran an entire series of tech-heavy domestic and international funds, many of which also posted triple-digit returns that halcyon year.

The sizzling performance of these offerings attracted more assets, particularly in the burgeoning 401(k) accounts, whose sponsors thoughtfully supplied participants with fund performance statistics so that they might select the offerings with the highest recent returns.

Several strands of interwoven logic drove the tech fund mania. Most obviously, the best-performing funds attracted the largest flow of assets, which further drove up the prices of these stocks and, temporarily, the funds' performance. The mutual fund companies, paid in proportion to the assets they manage, responded by churning out new tech funds. Finally, investors' increasingly short time horizons drove the fund managers to trade more frenetically. In 1997, a remarkable PBS *Frontline* program filmed Garrett Van Wagoner, manager of his eponymous Emerging Growth Fund, emitting a near-continuous stream of trades into his phone.[40] The show illustrated just how the press played along. It contained this ebullient description of Van Wagoner from Joseph Nocera, a well-known financial journalist:

> The competition is fierce and the top mutual fund managers are like modern-day alchemists, creating magical market gains. And right now no one has the golden touch more than this man, Garrett Van Wagoner, who runs a one-man shop out of San Francisco.[41]

Ten thousand dollars invested in his fund on January 1, 1997, grew to $45,000 by March 2000 (a 350 percent return), then fell to $3,300 near the market bottom in September 2002 (a 67 percent fall from $10,000, and a 93 percent fall from top to bottom). Even these grim numbers understate the damage. The *Frontline* segment notwithstanding, relatively few investors knew about the fund in 1997, while it was taking off. Over the course of just the calendar year 1999 alone, the fund size grew from $189 million to $1.5 billion. Therefore, many more investors took the sickening 93 percent ride down than enjoyed the heady 350 percent way up. In the end, Nocera was right: Van Wagoner was indeed an alchemist, albeit one who transmuted gold into lead; in 2008 he finally stepped down as the manager of his eponymous portfolio, which had the worst ten-year performance of any actively managed mutual fund—a 66 percent loss of value, versus 72 percent gain for the overall stock market.[42]

A remarkable strand ran through the railway, 1920s, and internet bubbles: the part played by the central technologies that underlay them. Hudson depended on the newfound swiftness of rail travel to hopscotch among his offices, construction sites, shareholder meetings, and Parliament. During the 1920s bubble, speculators, even on ocean liners, eagerly perused ticker tapes fed by incoming radio signals and traded via outbound signals from shipboard trading desks. Internet chat rooms and online trading magnified the frenzy in the stocks of internet companies, which were themselves traded over the internet.

The second signature bubble symptom—the abandonment of comfortable and respectable professions for full-time speculation—also manifested itself during the internet bubble. More often than not, during the 1990s, this meant day-trading, as millions of individuals, overwhelmingly male, took time off work or even quit their employment entirely to sit in front of computer monitors and execute dozens, and sometimes hundreds, of trades per day.

Day-trading involves the rapid-fire purchase and sale of stocks and aims at numerous small profits. In an ideal day-trading world, a typical transaction might involve purchasing one thousand shares of a stock at 31½ and selling it the same day, sometimes within a few minutes, for 31⅝, resulting in a gross profit of $125. In reality, most day traders' gross returns average close to zero and each trade gets nicked by commissions that, over hundreds and thousands of transactions, will more often than not ruin even moderately successful/lucky participants.

For sheer addictiveness, nothing matched online trading, which kept participants glued to their terminals. As one observer put it,

I do not know if many of you readers have played video poker in Las
Vegas (or anywhere). I have, and it is addicting. It is addicting despite
the fact that you lose over any reasonable length period (i.e., sit more
than an hour or two and [nine out of ten] times you are walking away
poorer). Now, imagine video poker where the odds were in your
favor. That is, all the little bells and buttons and buzzers were still
there providing the instant feedback and fun, but instead of losing
you got richer. If Vegas was like this, you would have to pry people
out of their seats with the jaws of life. People would bring bedpans
so they did not have to give up their seats. This form of video poker
would laugh at crack cocaine as the ultimate addiction. In my view,
this is precisely what on-line trading has become.[43]

Before 1997, only large institutions engaged in this sort of rapid-fire trading, since small investors could not obtain the necessary favorable and
accurate pricing from the stock exchanges; that year "level 2 quotes," which
display pending limit orders on their computer screens, became available
to retail investors, who joined in the fun and games.

Unlike the crowd at Bill's, most day traders are tech savvy, quantita-
tively gifted, and highly educated. The problem is that whenever someone
buys a stock, someone else is selling it, and vice versa. In other words,
security trading is akin to playing tennis with an invisible partner; what
most day traders fail to realize is that almost all of the folks on the other
side of the net are the investment world's Williams sisters: savvy institutional participants to whom the company is far more than a mere symbol
or computer algorithms that can steamroll human traders.

By the late 1990s, about a hundred companies established "training
programs" that skipped lightly over these long odds. For several thousand
dollars, "trainees" typically got three days of orientation and "boot camp"
followed by a week of "paper trading." The "trainers" dispensed optimism
in tank-car quantities: Anyone could succeed if they just followed the rules.
As put by one trainer, "It's just like golf. If you're careful about how you
place your feet, how you lift the club, and follow through, you'll stand a
better chance of hitting the ball straight rather than hooking it. The same
principle applies to day trading."[44]

By the late 1990s, approximately five million Americans were trading
online, although the number doing so full-time was estimated to be much

lower.[45] As long as the markets rose, the day traders stood half a chance, but just like the plungers in the 1920s and during the railway bubble, when the seas got choppy, most got wiped out.

The Beardstown ladies could not have been more different from the customers at Bill's Barber Shop or the frenetic day traders at their desks, but the women's trajectory was even more spectacular and just as emblematic of a gold rush atmosphere that convinced people lacking any visible expertise in finance of their bright prospects in that field.

In any other era, no one would have paid attention to a traditional investment club consisting of middle-aged and elderly homemakers in the Illinois burg of Beardstown who followed the relatively conservative playbook that had governed this small corner of American civil society for decades: gather for cookies and coffee, research established companies with reliable earnings, and hold them for the long term.

The ladies weren't even dealing with serious money: Membership required $100 up front and $25 monthly after that. The trouble started when they began sending in their returns to the national organization, the National Association of Investors Corporation, which earned them an "All-Star Investment Club" award for six straight years. For the decade between 1984 and 1993, they reported an astonishing 23.4 percent annualized return, more than 4 percent better than the stock market.

The story of how these matrons beat Wall Street played compellingly to the 1990s narrative of casually investing one's way to easy street. The club's members shed their identities as small-town housewives and became full-time financial gurus. They jetted around the world, often spoke to audiences larger than the population of their hometown (pop. 5,766) that sometimes had waited in the rain for tickets, earned fat consulting fees from investment companies, and sold eight hundred thousand copies of *The Beardstown Ladies' Common-Sense Investment Guide*, a compendium of their "secrets." Remarked one, "I got off an airplane in Houston and the limousine driver was apologizing because he had to bring an extra-large car. I always used to see limos go by and say, 'I wonder who's in there.' Well, now it was me in there."[46]

There was just one problem with the ladies' sudden celebrity: the 23.4 percent figure included their monthly membership dues. If one starts out with $100, earns nothing on it but adds another $25 of one's own money along the way, one hasn't made a 25 percent return. Sometime around 1998, more than two years after the book came out, the publisher noticed the mistake and inserted a disclaimer that stated, "this return may be different from the return that might be calculated for a mutual fund or a bank."

During a bull market, journalistic skill atrophies; not until the 1998 edition hit the shelves did Shane Tritsch, a reporter for *Chicago* magazine, hardly a frontline venue for investment reporting, notice and report the disclaimer. The ladies were at first indignant, and an executive at Hyperion, their publisher, called Mr. Tritsch "malicious" and fixated on smearing "the most honest group you ever want to meet."[47]

Honest mistake or not, the ladies hadn't earned 23.4 percent for the ten years in question: 9 percent was closer to the truth. Ultimately, Hyperion withdrew the book and had to settle a lawsuit by agreeing to exchange it for any other one it published, and the ladies vanished back into obscurity.

When all was said and done, the women hadn't done badly: for the full fifteen-year period between 1983 and 1997, auditors found that their account had earned a properly calculated 15.3 percent per year, only 2 percent worse than they would have done in an index fund, but respectable nonetheless, and certainly leagues better than the folks at Bill's and the day-trading firms. Nonetheless, only during the 1990s could a math error turn a group of ordinary women earning mediocre stock market returns into cultural icons.

Like the Beardstown ladies, the armies of day traders, and the customers at Bill's Barber Shop, by the late 1990s millions thought themselves stock market geniuses. The mood was best captured by the literate and insightful Barton Biggs of Morgan Stanley:

> The sociological signs are very bad. . . . Everybody's son wants to work for Morgan Stanley. Worthless brothers-in-law are starting hedge funds. I know a guy who is fifty and he's never done anything. He's starting a hedge fund. He's sending out brochures to people. I've got one here somewhere.[48]

*   *   *

The bubble's third symptom, vehemence, verging on raw anger, directed at doubters, became manifest by the mid-1990s. Decades before Roger Ailes made CNBC into a media powerhouse, as many as thirty million viewers tuned in Friday nights to *Wall $treet Week with Louis Rukeyser*, a panel show broadcast nationwide on PBS and hosted by the urbane and witty Rukeyser, himself the son of an esteemed financial journalist.

Rukeyser rigidly choreographed the show's production, and its most coveted slots were on the rotating panel of stock brokers, analysts, and newsletter writers who bantered with him at the show's start and later questioned the week's featured guest. Almost as sought after was membership in his off-screen panel of "elves" who purported to predict future market direction. Rukeyser knew two things: first, that bullishness benefited his show, as well as his brand, which included two newsletters and the Louis Rukeyser Investment Cruise at Sea; and second, that a regular slot on the panels was priceless advertising for the brokers and analysts lucky enough to get one. Accordingly, he kept his panelists on a short leash, especially in the heady days of the tech bubble.

During the late 1990s, Gail Dudack, who was an analyst at UBS Warburg and a regular on both Rukeyser panels, began to get queasy. She had read Charles Kindleberger and recognized his bubble criteria, especially "displacement" and easy credit, in the then current market conditions. She warned her clients, one of whom accused her of being unpatriotic, just as her firm's founder, Paul Warburg, had been libeled seven decades before. She thus knew how doubters got treated during bubbles: "You'll be scorned, you'll be terrorized, and when the bubble begins to collapse, the public will be very angry. It will need a scapegoat." In November 1999, five months before the bubble burst, Rukeyser fired her from the show in the most humiliating way possible, on a night when she was not appearing, by drawing a dunce cap atop her image. He replaced her with an engaging Dartmouth ex-basketball player, Alan Bond, who four years later would be the recipient of a twelve-year sentence for stealing from pensioners.[49]

The internet bubble was hardest on "value investors" who owned stock in well-established brick-and-mortar and smokestack companies that sold at reasonable prices and lagged during the mania. Julian Robertson, a well-regarded value-oriented hedge fund manager, was forced to close down his firm, Tiger Management, which until the mid-1990s had compiled an enviable record. Remarked Mr. Robertson, "This approach isn't working and I don't understand why. I'm sixty-seven years old, who needs this?" Mr. Robertson announced the firm's closing on March 30, 2000; although he could not know it at the time, the tech-heavy NASDAQ had peaked three weeks earlier at 5,060, a level it would not see for another decade and a half.[50]

The final identifying bubble characteristic is the presence of extreme predictions. In normal times, pundits predict market rises or falls in a given year rarely exceeding 20 percent. Forecasts outside these narrow bounds risk branding their maker as a lunatic, and most range in the single digits up or down. Not so during bubbles. James Glassman, along with his economist coauthor Kevin Hassett, wrote a book in 1999 that predicted that the Dow Jones Industrial Average would more than triple from its prevailing level of approximately 11,000 to 36,000 within a few short years. Not to be outdone, others had no choice but to raise that estimate as high as 100,000.[51]

The way in which Glassman and Hassett arrived at a stock market price of more than three times its then current level illustrates the lengths gone to rationalize stratospheric bubble prices. They did this by manipulating the so-called discount rate applied to both stocks and bonds. Loosely speaking, the discount rate is the return demanded by investors before they will bear the risk of owning securities; the higher the risk, the greater the return demanded (the discount rate) for owning them. For example, in mid-2019, ultrasafe long-term Treasury bonds yielded 2.5 percent, whereas the return demanded for owning much riskier stocks was roughly triple that, currently around 7.5 percent, and about 10 percent before about 1990.

The price of a long-dated asset, such as a thirty-year Treasury bond or a stock, is approximately inversely related to the discount rate: Halve the discount rate (say from 6 percent to 3 percent), and the price doubles. (Since a stock has no expiration date, it is, at least theortically, even "longer-dated" than a thirty-year Treasury.) Conversely, when the economy or global geopolitical status deteriorates, investors require a much higher return—that is, discount rate—for owning stocks, and so their prices plunge.

Glassman and Hassett's *Dow 36,000* declared that investors had evolved into a new type of *homo economicus* who knew that stocks weren't so risky in the long term since they always recovered from price declines. This new human subspecies had thus decided to apply a 3 percent Treasury-like discount rate to stocks rather than the approximately historical 10 percent discount rate; this theoretically revalued their price upward by a factor of more than three (10 percent/3 percent).[52]

Glassman and Hassett had forgotten Templeton's famous warning about the costliness of "This time it's different." Nearly simultaneously with the 2000 publication of *Dow 36,000*, the internet bubble foundered on the sudden return of risk, marking the denouement of the greatest financial mania of all time. Within the span of less than two years, U.S. stocks lost $6 trillion of market value, as if seven months of the nation's entire economic output had disappeared. Whereas in 1929, only 10 percent of the households owned stocks, by 2000 the expansion of personal brokerage and mutual fund accounts, IRAs, and employment-based 401(k) plans saw stock ownership swell to 60 percent of households. Tens of millions who thought themselves financially secure found out otherwise, and millions more who considered their nest eggs adequate for retirement were forced to postpone it.

In a story as old as the financial markets, in 2000–2002 investors reacquainted themselves with the indescribable misery of sudden financial loss. In the words of humorist Fred Schwed,

> There are certain things that cannot be adequately explained to a virgin either by words or pictures. Nor can any description I might offer here even approximate what it feels like to lose a real chunk of money that you used to own.[53]

15

MAHDIS AND CALIPHS

The internet bubble rang down the curtain on the twentieth century's theater of popular manias. As the twenty-first opened, the now familiar end-times narrative of the world's youngest Abrahamic religion would astound the world with its ability to attract adherents from around the world, and with its violence.

On November 16, 2014, rebels of the Islamic State (IS) beheaded an American named Peter Kassig, along with eighteen Syrian captives. The ex–U.S. Army Ranger had been doing humanitarian work. The perpetrators' video did not show the atrocity itself; rather, Kassig's severed head lay at the feet of "Jihadi John," believed to be a U.K. citizen named Mohammed Emwazi, who intoned in a British accent, "Here we are, burying the first American crusader in Dabiq, eagerly awaiting for the remainder of your armies to arrive."[1]

Over the preceding year, IS's slick and effective social media campaign had drawn thousands of fighters and other volunteers, even from the prosperous and peaceful West, to one of the world's worst places. The town mentioned by Jihadi John, Dabiq, and the IS magazine of the same name go a long way toward understanding the remarkable success of their recruitment efforts.*

The magazine was named after the town in northwestern Syria where the Ottoman Turks defeated the Egyptian Mamluks in 1516, a victory that gave the Turks control over the Levant and, symbolically for modern jihadis, marked the rebirth of a caliphate—a state led by a successor of Muhammad with dominion over all Muslims—that would last four

---

* On June 29, 2014, when Abu Bakr al-Baghdadi declared the caliphate, its name was shortened to the Islamic State (IS, Daesh). Before that date, it was most commonly referred to as ISI (Islamic State of Iraq), ISIL (Islamic State of Iraq and the Levant), or ISIS (Islamic State of Iraq and al Sham (Syria).

centuries. The town's association with the Ottoman caliphate places it, despite its unimposing appearance and strategic unimportance, front and center in the Islamic end-times narrative.

The apocalyptic traditions of Judaism, Christianity, and Islam resemble one another, which is not surprising in light of their common origins. During the early medieval period, both the Byzantines and Muslims divined their battle plans against each other from the same verses of Daniel.[2] Because of its military history, Dabiq became an Islamic Armageddon, a place where the forces of the Antichrist, in Islam most commonly called the Dajjal, would battle the armies of the righteous.

There are differences. Christian eschatology springs mainly from a small number of well-circumscribed scriptural locations, especially Ezekiel, Daniel, and Revelation, whereas Islamic eschatology has more diffuse, and so less well defined, wellsprings: the hadith, the recorded sayings of the Prophet (in Arabic, "news" or "reports"). In contrast to Christian eschatology, the Muslim "book," the Koran, contains almost no prophecy and, like Saint Augustine and subsequent Catholic theological tradition, specifically warns against calculating the date of the end-times.

But as it does for Christians, date-setting irresistibly tempts Muslims, and their end-times narratives spring like desert wildflowers from the hadith.[3] Because of their great number, Islamic eschatology is even messier than the Christian variety. The Sunni tradition, for example, relates roughly ten thousand separate hadith, and different observers report each of them in often widely varying ways. One medieval scholar alone listed more than thirty thousand versions. For centuries following the Prophet's death in 632, scholars have graded and cataloged his sayings according to their authenticity, from "authentic" down to "fabricated."

The Prophet complicated matters by leaving no testament. His first four successors, or caliphs—Abu Bakr, Omar, Othman, and Ali—saw the rapid expansion of Muslim territory well beyond the confines of western Arabia to the frontiers of Byzantium and Persia. Over the following centuries, the Arab empires warred with these two great neighboring infidel powers. In addition, the assassination of the fourth caliph, Ali, the Prophet's cousin and son-in-law, and the subsequent death of Ali's youngest son, Husayn, and his followers at Karbala in modern Iraq, set off a bloody sectarian split that has raged ever since. On one side of this great Islamic conflict lay the followers of Husayn, the Shiites, who limit the Prophet's succession to his bloodline. The victors at Karbala, who evolved into the Sunnis, do not share this restriction of leadership.

Political scientist Samuel Huntington's highly controversial *The Clash of Civilizations and the Remaking of the World Order* tabulated the large number of armed conflicts among Muslim countries, as well as their conflicts with their non-Muslim neighbors, and concluded that "Islam's borders *are* bloody, and so are its innards."[4] Critics accused him of "orientalism" and pointed out that Islam's modern wars arose from Western domination. While Western colonialism certainly plays a prominent role in the troubles of the modern Middle East, Huntington's infamous quote applies just as well to the medieval Islamic world, which, as the possessor of one of the world's most intellectually advanced, wealthy, and powerful civilizations, was little troubled by the backward and impotent early post-Rome West.

And therein lies the appeal of apocalyptic Islam. American and European Christians live in relatively prosperous, safe, and geopolitically stable societies; furthermore, their religions are culturally dominant. Western Christian apocalypticists are thus forced to pick among a dog's breakfast of moral panics for signs of The Hour (end-times): pervasive sexuality, socialism, and Satanism (or at least astrology).

Islam, by contrast, has been in relative political and economic decline ever since Vasco da Gama first rounded the Cape of Good Hope in 1497 and began to dismantle the immensely prosperous Muslim-dominated Indian Ocean trade emporium. For the devout Muslim, then, signs of The Hour loom all too obvious and painful, with a long litany of humiliation and defeat that demands apocalyptic justice: in the twentieth century alone, the secret 1916 Sykes-Picot Agreement that carved up the Muslim heartland between the French and British; the 1948 establishment of Israel; its 1967 seizure of the West Bank and Old City of Jerusalem with its sacred Temple Mount; the 1979 peace treaty between Israel and Egypt; and the 1990 First Gulf War, which made embarrassingly visible the Western military presence in, among other Middle East locations, Saudi Arabia, the custodian of the religion's holiest shrines. Far more than Christians and Jews, Muslims have reasons to yearn for an Apocalypse that overturns the existing world order. It is impossible to miss the bitterness and anger felt by Muslim apocalypticists and their audiences. Wrote one,

Thus the Jewish slap on the faces of Christians continues, who apparently enjoy and allow this sort of humiliation. . . . The Crusader West continues like a whore who is screwed sadistically, and does not derive any pleasure from the act until after she is struck and humiliated, even by her pimps—who are the Jews in Christian Europe—and it will not be long before they are under the rubble as a result of the Jewish conspiracy.[5]

As do all seekers of the end-times, Muslim apocalypticists pine for Hesiod's age of "golden men," in their case, the *salaf*: the first three generations of Muslims, the Prophet's companions and their offspring, the religion's founding fathers. It's not surprising, then, that today's Muslim apocalypticist scholars and leaders plumb the hadith for the inspiration that will return Islam to its rightful place as the world's dominant theology. A large number of hadith speak of the battles with the Byzantines, especially at Constantinople, that occurred during the few centuries after the Prophet's death, when these sayings were first recorded. This explains IS's obsession with a small dusty town in northern Syria, Dabiq, which is mentioned in one of the most famous and highly respected of the apocalyptic hadith: "The Last Hour will not come until the Byzantines attack Amaq or Dabiq."[6]

The hadith scholar's main task is establishing the provenance of their oral sources that stretch centuries back to the Prophet's lifetime, a treacherous game of generational whispering down the lane. Two Persian scholars, Abu al-Husayn Muslim and Isma'il al-Bukhari, working two hundred years after Muhammad's death, produced the most highly respected compilations. Bukhari reportedly dreamed of himself swatting away flies swarming around Muhammad, and decided to devote his life to the banishment of inauthentic hadith. Only 1 percent of them survived his exacting criteria.[7] The hadith of Muslim and Bukhari occupy the highest tier, and the authority of any Islamic cleric, political leader, military leader, or commentator rests in no small part on his command of hadith, especially those compiled by these two scholars.

Needless to say, even the most "authentic" of hadith wind through several generations of oral transmission, and, in the words of Arabist William McCants,

End-times prophecies were an especially inviting target for fabricators. In the internecine wars that tore apart the early Muslim community, each side sought to justify its politics by predicting its inevitable victory and the other side's preordained defeat. What better way to do this than to put the prophecy into the mouth of the Prophet. . . . Throughout the centuries, new politics would give the residue new meaning, a phenomenon familiar to readers of the Christian Book of Revelation.[8]

Many of Islam's end-times narratives evolved out of those unhappy with the victors at Karbala, the Umayya clan, who established the first great Muslim dynasty and ruled it from Damascus. The central character who would rescue the devout from their increasingly corrupt and despotic masters in Damascus was the Muslim messiah, the Mahdi: "the Rightly Guided One."

The Umayyads's Arab and Persian opponents spread prophecies of soldiers flying black flags from Khorasan (roughly, modern eastern Iran and Afghanistan), who would sweep in from that direction to defeat the Umayyads: "If you see the black banners coming from Khorasan, go to them immediately even if you must crawl over ice because indeed among them is the caliph, al-Mahdi."[9] In 750, rebels flying the black flag overthrew the Umayyads. The rebels' leader was a descendant of the Prophet's uncle named Abbas, hence the name of the Baghdad-centered empire he founded, the Abbasid Dynasty, which would last half a millennium.

Hadith passages, like the ones quoted by the victorious Abbasid rebels, tend to be fragmentary and brief, usually of sentence or paragraph length, and rarely more than a page or two. As put by David Cook, the foremost American scholar of Muslim apocalyptic literature,

Because the Muslim traditions have no apparent context, except that provided artificially by the lengthy traditions (which are essentially attempts by scholars to place the material into usable chronological order), it is hardly surprising to find that there has been considerable disagreement as to the order in which events are to take place before the end of the world.[10]

In other words, the large number and brevity of hadith make possible an infinite number of end-times narratives; pour into this batter the day's headlines and add a large dollop of confirmation bias, and the clever

Islamic scholar has an even easier time serving up the desired apocalyptic narrative than his Christian dispensationalist cousin.

Nonetheless, hadith-derived Muslim apocalypses do have certain features in common with Christian eschatology: The world will, at some point, end. Jesus, who is a prophet, not the son of God, returns to Earth, most often via the east minaret of the Damascus Umayyad Mosque, borne by two white angels. He does battle with the Dajjal, who is almost always a Jew, and often the Jewish messiah. Unlike the beguiling Christian Antichrist, the Dajjal has a displeasing personality and cuts a hideous physical figure, with a large hooked nose, one deformed, bulging eye, and hands of different sizes—a nonpareil demonstration of the role of anatomic symmetry in the perception of beauty.[11]

Anti-Semitism is such an established part of Muslim apocalypticism that it accepts even the most fraudulent racist canards. The late Saudi king Faisal routinely harangued foreign dignitaries about the communist-Jewish world conspiracy, and at the end of meetings he would turn to his protocol chief and ask, "Have they got the book?" meaning *The Protocols of the Elders of Zion*. On one occasion, the American ambassador pointed out to him that *Protocols*, a screed postulating a global conspiracy by Jews for world rule, had been forged by the czar's secret police. Nonsense, answered Faisal; the kingdom had printed it up in multiple languages to widen its circulation. The king was and still is not alone in his anti-Semitism; for virtually all Muslim apocalypticists, *The Protocols of the Elders of Zion* is Exhibit A of Jewish treachery.[12]

Muslim apocalypticists, also like Christian dispensationalists, search current events for signs of The Hour that herald the End. These are of two types. The first are known as "lesser signs," and would warm the hearts of Lindsey and LaHaye: sexual laxity, including bestiality and both male and female homosexuality, and, most prophetic of all, public intercourse. Even song and dance, wealth, and men's silk clothing also come in for approbation, as do automobiles, since they allow women to drive. Other lesser signs include earthquakes, floods, droughts, and financial misbehavior, particularly the charging of interest and the employment of men by women (the last of which ignores the fact that the young Prophet was hired by the widowed trader, Khadija, who eventually became his wife and first follower).

One particularly well-known hadith states that the "Last Hour" will be characterized when "two figures come to blows," even though the two preach the same thing; when thirty false messiahs appear; when all religious knowledge vanishes; when murder becomes frequent; when everyone is so wealthy that none will accept alms; and when tombs are so magnificent that the living wish themselves inside them.

Muslim apocalypticists also look for "Greater Signs": more specific predicted events. During the early Muslim period, the yet-to-be accomplished Muslim conquest of Christian Constantinople stood at the top of the list. Successive Muslim rulers deployed the hadith to justify multiple unsuccessful attempts to conquer the city; when the Ottomans finally succeeded in 1453 and the End did not follow, theologians alternatively prophesized great battles would take place at other locations, most recently, Dabiq.

As with Christian Zionists, another Greater Sign is the return of the Jews to the Holy Land. And if the Christian version is, from the Jewish perspective, grim—convert and proselytize or be destroyed—the Muslim version is even more brutal: Allah will return the Jews to Palestine as, in the words of one apocalypticist, "a declaration of the proximity of God's vengeance upon them by gathering them into [Palestine]": the apocalyptic Muslim version of the Final Solution.[13]

Other Greater Signs include the appearance of the Dajjal (who is in one hadith dispatched by Jesus's lethal halitosis) and the sun rising in the west. Gog and Magog make appearances in the hadith, as does a character unique to Islam known as the Sufyani, a powerful Sunni tyrant who rampages through Syria. As a Sunni, he is reviled by Shiites, a sentiment not always shared by Sunnis; the Umayyad opponents of the Abbasid caliphate in Baghdad, for example, lionized him.[14]

The Sufyani's ultimate goal is the murder of the central character of The End, the Mahdi, but he is most commonly stopped short when the earth swallows him. In most tellings, not until Jesus has dispatched the Dajjal does the Mahdi lead the armies of Islam to victory and establish just rule over the world. Shiites believe that the twelfth, or "hidden" imam, Muhammad al-Mahdi, who disappeared in the tenth century, will, as suggested by his name, reappear at The End.[15]

In 1978, Anwar Sadat and Menachem Begin signed the Camp David Accords, which led directly to the 1979 Egypt-Israeli Peace Treaty, which

Islamists considered an abomination. In particular, in 1987, an obscure Egyptian journalist named Sayyid Ayyub wrote a book entitled *Al-Masih ad-Dajjal* (*The Antichrist*), which had a simple message: The entire history of the human race was poisoned by the perfidy of the Jews, who would be defeated by the forces of Islam in an apocalyptic battle.

Prior to the 1980s, Muslim apocalyptic literature was a sleepy genre, heavy on the Mahdi and the millennium, and light on Gog and Magog, and on Jesus doing single combat with the Dajjal. The publication of *The Antichrist* was Muslim apocalyptic literature's Hal Lindsey moment. Similar to the shift in Christian apocalyptic literature that occurred with *The Late Great Planet Earth*, Ayyub's book invigorated the genre by emphasizing a lurid, bloody final victory over the Jews and deemphasizing the goodness and light that presumably follows.[16]

According to Ayyub, the Dajjal's first Jewish agent on earth was Saint Paul, followed by Constantine, then the Freemasons, American Jews, and Atatürk, followed by the United States, NATO, and, finally, Israel. Ayyub wrote that "earthquakes, volcanic eruptions, and droughts will precede the appearance of the Antichrist, [and] the temperature will rise perceptibly." There follows a final great battle whose hallucinatory details give Revelation and Lindsey a run for their money. In The End, Israel is destroyed, and the capital of world-dominant Islam is relocated from Damascus to Jerusalem. Along the way Ayyub condemns the pope for once visiting a synagogue and denies the Holocaust.

As with Christian dispensationalist fiction, the Temple Mount plays a leading role. Taking his cue from Denis Michael Rohan and Rabbi Goren, Ayyub wrote, "The dwelling place of [the Dajjal] will be in the Temple in Jerusalem. For this reason they sometimes try to burn al-Aqsa, and try to conduct archaeological excavations, and even try to buy the ground through the Masons of America."[17] The similarities among the end-times narratives of the three Abrahamic religions are so striking that Israeli journalist Gershom Gorenberg observed,

> The theater of the End is triangular, and in the eyes of apocalyptic believers on all three sides, the great drama has begun. The sound system is hope and fear; each time an actor speaks, his words reverberate wildly. Three scripts are being performed. The cast of Jewish messianists has starring roles in the Christian play; Jews and Christians

alike have parts in the Muslim drama. What one sees as a flourish of rhetoric can be the other's cue for a battle scene.[18]

The Antichrist sold wildly in the Arab world, and as did Lindsey, Ayyub followed his success with a stream of similar titles and spawned a host of imitators, some of whom made nearly everyone a Jew, including Martin Luther; one of Ayyub's imitators, Fahad Salim, generously allowed that Saddam Hussein wasn't Jewish, but that a close associate had a Jewish father and thus tainted his regime. One of the most prominent of Ayyub's emulators was another Egyptian journalist, Muhammad Isa Dawud, who wrote for the Saudi press and who once published an apparently serious interview with a *jinn* (genie).

Dawud evidently considered Ayyub's work too sober and tolerant toward the Jews, and in 1991, he published *Beware: The Antichrist Has Invaded the World from the Bermuda Triangle*, which is the location both for an eight-century midway point of the Dajjal's sojourn to North America and a base for the flying saucers of an avenging Islamic air force.[19]

Popular apocalyptic literature pervades souks in Cairo, Riyadh, Beirut, Baghdad, and East Jerusalem and fills bookstore shelves from Morocco to Indonesia. More importantly, with the advent of social media, these books have become freely available and more influential, effectively providing the background music to twenty-first-century jihadism.[20] Islamic scholar Jean-Pierre Filiu describes the genre's increasingly anti-Semitic and anti-Western tone:

> There is nothing harmless about this intensifying delirium, for it is saturated with a profound sense of resentment and vindictiveness. . . . The messianics of the third millennium distill their venomous bile with the self-assurance of those for whom the future—and the end—of the world is obvious. America, unalterably hostile to Islam and fundamentally Machiavellian, is damned and fated to die a dreadful death; Islam is truth, irresistible power, and everlasting victory.[21]

For centuries, then, Muslims pinned their hopes for delivery from humiliation and oppression on the savior figure of the Mahdi. This narrative has paid at least as much attention to round date numbers as have Christian millennialist narratives, and Mahdist eruptions have tended to punctuate the dawn of new Muslim centuries.

The Muslim calendar begins with the Prophet's flight from Mecca to Medina in 622, the *hijra*, and the fourteenth century A.H. (anno hegirae) began on November 12, 1882.* In the late thirteenth century A.H., which corresponded to the late 1870s A.D., a Sudanese Sufi cleric named Muhammad Ahmad became angered by the heresies of the Egyptian rulers of Sudan, who gave nominal tribute to the Ottoman Turks, but in fact were more beholden to the British. Ahmad thought the November 12, 1882, date a portent of The End, and in preparation he declared himself Mahdi in 1881 in order to give himself enough time to establish his rule in Khartoum to ring in the new century.[22]

His revolt initially succeeded, and his regime would likely have survived had not British general Charles "Chinese" Gordon been killed during Ahmad's later siege of Khartoum. While Gordon had become a popular hero back home, he had annoyed the British crown and high command by exceeding his brief, the evacuation of Egyptian troops and administration, and instead attempting to defend the entire city.

The popular outrage in England over Gordon's death forced the deployment of a costly expedition under Field Marshall Horatio Herbert Kitchener in 1898 to recover Khartoum. In the meantime Ahmad had died of typhus; Kitchener defeated Ahmad's successor, Abdullah al-Taashi, at the Battle of Omdurman, in which British troops with advanced weaponry slaughtered twelve thousand Muslim soldiers while sustaining only light losses themselves.[23] (Also present at the battle was a young lieutenant named Winston Churchill; the one-sidedness of this and other late-nineteenth-century colonial battles inspired poet Hilaire Belloc to rhyme, "Whatever happens we have got / The Maxim gun, and they have not.")[24]

Khartoum, the location of the uprising marking the dawn of the fourteenth century A.H., is a peripheral site in Muslim geography. The

---

* The Islamic year runs on a lunar cycle for 354 or 355 days, so converting from A.D. to A.H. (anno hegirae) is not a simple matter of subtraction; with each passing century, the gap between A.D. and A.H. decreases by about two years. (This is a little counterintuitive; in the year of the *hijra*, the A.D./A.H. gap was obviously 622 − 1, or 621 years. The year of this book's publication in 2021 corresponds, depending on the exact month, to around A.H. 1442; the A.D./A.H. gap has thus shrunk to 2021 − 1442 = 579 years.)

tumultuous events that unfolded at the beginning of the fifteenth century A.H. would take place at Islam's very epicenter, Mecca's Grand Mosque. The shrine's roots stretch back to well before Islam's birth in 610, when the archangel Gabriel was said to dictate the first verses of the Koran on Mount Hira just outside his home city of Mecca to the trembling Prophet, by then a successful merchant.

Mecca's wealth derived from the Kaaba, a granite building supposedly built by Abraham, and the probably meteoric Black Stone embedded in it. Long before Muhammad, pilgrims made the hajj to circumambulate the Kaaba and Black Stone, which were likely shrines to al-Llah, the principal god of the polytheistic pre-Islamic Arabs.

A trader of humble origins who prospered under the tutelage of his future wife Khadija, Muhammad was also a Qurayshi, the tribe that ruled Mecca, though hailing from one of its minor branches. His religious fervor, and particularly his efforts to cleanse the Kaaba of idolatrous totems to the city's 360 pagan gods, threatened Mecca's hajj trade and so angered the Qurayshi elite, who forced him to flee to Yathrib (Medina) in 622—the hegira, as his journey became known. When he finally returned to Mecca at the head of victorious Islamic forces in 630, he denied nonbelievers entry into both cities, a ban that stands to this day.*

The tension between the rich and luxury-loving merchant elites and the devout and ascetic faithful has intermittently roiled the peninsula ever since. In the early 1700s, a jurist by the name of Muhammad Ibn Abd al-Wahhab began to preach a radical brand of Islam that revolved around two principles: the return to the Prophet's original teachings and a resolute opposition to the luxury and wealth enjoyed by the aristocracies in Baghdad, Damascus, Istanbul, and Cairo. Dancing, jewelry, and even tobacco were *haram* (forbidden); so was Shiism, whose adherents were offered the choice between conversion and death.

Ibn Abd al-Wahhab allied himself with a fearsome warrior by the name of Muhammad bin Saud, and the synergy of the jurist's theological chops and bin Saud's military prowess swept Wahhabi Islam centrifugally out from its birthplace in the sun-baked emptiness of Arabia's deep interior desert to command almost the entire peninsula and beyond.

---

* The ban now applies to all of metropolitan Mecca, but only the immediate vicinity of the Prophet's Mosque in Medina.

As Ottoman power crumbled in the nineteenth century, one of Muhammad bin Saud's descendants, Abdulaziz, known in the West as Ibn Saud, seized the Ottoman fort at Riyadh in 1902 and established a dynasty that retains power to this day. The new regime's shock troops, the ultradevout Ikhwan, literally, "brothers," hailed from Bedouins in whose blood ran centuries of desert raiding and warfare. In 1924, Ikhwan troops besieging Mecca slaughtered four hundred residents of the neighboring town of Taif, sliced open the bellies of expectant mothers, and so frightened the Meccans into surrendering without a fight.

Unfortunately for the Ikhwan, the First World War altered the Middle East's political landscape. Abdulaziz now needed to assuage the British Christians, the recent war's victors who now loomed on his northern border. Additionally, the legitimacy of his guardianship of Islam's holy shrines rested on the approval of the broader Muslim world that included not only the apostate Shiites but also Sufis and less adherent Sunnis. Accordingly, Abdulaziz began to back away from the monarchy's Wahhabi Ikhwan allies.

Abdulaziz strained his relations with the Wahhabis by enthusiastically embracing modernity's bounties, especially the automobile and telephone. He clamped down on the Wahhabis, who were intent on liquidating the eastern Arabian Shiites. Angered by the king's heresies, the Ikhwan, the most conservative among the Wahhabis, revolted; in 1927, they launched an attack on Kuwait, and in due course experienced humiliation at the hands of another of modernity's handmaidens, British military aircraft. Two years later Abdulaziz, who by that point had had enough of the Ikhwan, drove north from Riyadh in cars mounted with machine guns toward a deep interior oasis at Sbala, where he offered the Ikhwan an honorable surrender. The refusal of the horse- and camel-borne Ikhwan was answered with their slaughter.[25]

The Ikhwan flame had been smothered, but not extinguished, and among the survivors of the Sbala massacre was an Ikhwan named Mohammed bin Seif al-Uteybi; years after the battle, in 1936, he sired a son with a face seemingly fixed in a permanent scowl. Since Saudis are fond of rough-and-ready names, the baby was called Juhayman: "angry face," an appellation he would later more than live up to.[26]

Just two years after Juhayman's birth, American oilmen drilled the first gushers at Dhahran and visited upon the heretofore impoverished and devout nation a grand economic experiment of nature that endowed

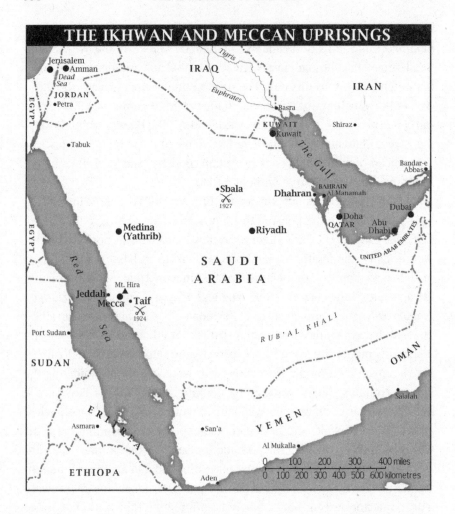

THE IKHWAN AND MECCAN UPRISINGS

Abdulaziz's heirs and hangers-on with unimaginable wealth. Six of Abdulaziz's sons, born of different wives, one half-brother after another, have ruled the kingdom since his death in 1953.

The second of the half-sibling kings, Faisal, further angered the Wahhabi faithful when he abolished slavery in 1962, instituted education for girls in 1963, and introduced television into the kingdom in 1965. Ten years later, he was assassinated by a member of the royal family whose relative had been killed in the rioting incited by the kingdom's adoption of television.

While the sons of the new Saudi elites joined the army and air force, the more devout Ikhwan were shunted into the less prestigious National

Guard. When Juhayman came of age, he served there for eighteen years before mustering out in 1973 as a mere corporal. While his undistinguished National Guard service did not advance his social or material status, its intense religious orientation drove him to more transcendent matters, especially Islamic eschatology.

After retiring from the Guard, he settled in Medina and joined a Wahhabist organization, the al-Jama'a al-Salafiyya al-Muhtasiba: the Salafi Group That Commands Right and Forbids Wrong (JSM). The organization was particularly influenced by Abdulaziz bin Baz, a brilliant, charismatic, and ambitious Islamic scholar, blind since age eight, who opposed the kingdom's headlong rush into modernity.

The royal family's fondness for the fleshpots of the French and Spanish Mediterranean particularly inflamed bin Baz; closer to home, he inveighed against tobacco, barber shops, and hand-clapping at public events.[27] With bin Baz and other Islamists as their spiritual guides, the JSM built a theology straight out of Freud's narcissism of small differences: Adherents broke the Ramadan fast not with the sunset, but with the disappearance of all light. (It was permissible, though, to hasten the meal by closing the room curtains.) Sandals could be worn at prayer, a deviation that annoyed other Muslims, and their mosques did not contain the traditional "niche" that faced Mecca (*mihrab*). The JSM established chapters in most of Saudi Arabia's major cities, many with their own dedicated buildings, and quickly developed an international reputation and attracted adherents from around the Muslim world, particularly from Egypt and Pakistan. To the chagrin of the JSM, the Saudi monarchy gradually co-opted bin Baz, whose evolving realpolitik drove a wedge between him and the Ikhwan; while the blind cleric had chastised the royals' modernizing and libertine proclivities, he nonetheless did not challenge the legitimacy of the regime. Eventually, the government appointed bin Baz to head the prestigious and influential Council of Senior Scholars, in which capacity he appeared every week with the king on the same medium, television, that had gotten the king's half-brother assassinated, and served as the Saudi Grand Mufti from 1993 until his 1999 death.

The JSM's theological quirks and, more importantly, its hostility to the royal family, soured its once-warm relationship with bin Baz, who by this point had departed for the monarchy's capital in Riyadh. In the summer of 1977, it fell to bin Baz's lieutenants in Medina to call a meeting with the JSM on a rooftop and demand that they renounce their heresies. The majority of JSM members, who were in their twenties, refused and reorganized themselves under the leadership of the older, charismatic Juhayman, and took the name of their Wahhabist forefathers, the Ikhwan.[28]

Sometime in December 1977, perhaps a few months after the rooftop meeting, the regime arrested two dozen of the followers of Juhayman, who escaped and appealed to bin Baz for help. The blind cleric interviewed the detainees and had the government release them.[29]

Juhayman elected to remain at large. For millennia, his ancestors had evaded their Byzantine, Ottoman, Persian, and Abyssinian overlords by vanishing into the desert on the one domesticated animal able to survive in that hostile, nearly waterless environment: the camel. For two years after his 1977 flight, Juhayman fell back on this Bedouin heritage and successfully avoided arrest in the peninsula's empty interior. In the process he became a legend, generally traveling with three to five followers and arranging clandestine meetings with others; more frequently, he attended these conclaves in spirit only. On one occasion, he was warned off visiting his mother when informed at the last moment that the police were watching her home; on another he suffered a prolonged painful toothache before finding a dentist who would not report him to the authorities.[30]

Unhappy with bin Baz's compromises, Juhayman dissociated himself from him. During his peregrinations, Juhayman buried himself in the hadith, particularly those involving the Mahdi and the end-times. He drew inspiration from perhaps the most famous apocalyptic saying of the Prophet,

> The Last Hour will not come until the Byzantines attack Amaq or Dabiq. A Muslim army consisting of some of the best men on earth at this time will be sent from Medina to thwart them. . . . Then the battle will be joined. A third part of the [Muslim] army will admit defeat; Allah will never forgive them. A third will die; they will be excellent martyrs in the eyes of Allah. And a third will conquer: they will never have been tested and they will [go on] to conquer Constantinople.[31]

Dabiq and Amaq are, respectively, a town in Syria and a valley in Turkey; IS named its magazine after the former, and named its news agency after the latter. In Juhayman's eschatology, Mecca and Medina took their places.

All Juhayman needed to trigger the end-times was a Mahdi, who happily turned out to be one of his Saudi followers, an otherworldly fair-skinned poet with light brown eyes named Mohammed Abdullah al-Qahtani. After he joined forces with Juhayman, the poet's sister dreamed that her brother received the *baya* (oath of allegiance) by the Kaaba, in the courtyard of the Grand Mosque. Within the standard Islamic end-times narrative, the dream made sense: Qahtani was a light-skinned Qurayshi, as was the Prophet, as had to be the Mahdi. As a bonus he also had a birth-mark on his left cheek, as did, according to one widely quoted hadith, the Mahdi as well. Others in this group, including Juhayman himself, soon had the same dream.

Dreams have a special meaning in Islam, especially when experi-enced collectively, since Allah transmitted many of his revelations to the Prophet through them. (As put by one of Juhayman's followers, "The fact that we dream proves that we are more religious.")[32] Qahtani grew close to Juhayman, who went so far as to divorce his wife and marry Qahtani's dreaming sister.[33]

As Hal Lindsey would say, the pieces of the great jigsaw puzzle finally fit into place. Not only did Juhayman now have his Mahdi, his reading of the hadith also confirmed the precise spot where the Mahdi would re-ceive the *baya*, adjacent to the graves of Hagar and Ishmael (respectively, Abraham's first wife and son) just outside the Kaaba, exactly as dreamed by Qahtani's sister. Juhayman's research also revealed the date: a Sunni tradition predicts that a scholar known as the "renewer of the century" would appear on the first day of each *hijri* century: 1400 A.H. was to begin on November 20, 1979. Juhayman and his followers would thus have to seize the Grand Mosque in order that the Mahdi receive the *baya* at the prescribed spot next to the Kaaba, and on that exact date.

During his desert exile, Juhayman recorded audio cassettes and composed "letters of Juhayman," in which he laid out his theology and eschatology. (He had only a fourth-grade education; although not illiter-ate, his writing skills were poor, so the "letters" were likely dictated.)[34] No Saudi publisher would touch them, but eventually a left-wing Kuwaiti house printed up two separate compendiums, known as "the seven letters" and "the four letters," which were widely circulated around the peninsula.

By recommending the release of Juhayman's accomplices, bin Baz had committed a grave error; on the first day of 1400 A.H., Juhayman spectacularly reemerged into the public eye along with around three hundred of his followers at the Grand Mosque.* Over the previous days, they had smuggled in weapons and provisions in the traditional shroud-covered litters used to bear the dead for final blessing. The occupation itself was nearly bloodless, initially killing only two unarmed policemen and an assistant imam. Juhayman grabbed the microphone from the imam while his men fired celebratory rifle shots and shouted, "Behold the Mahdi! Behold the right-guided one!"[35]

Juhayman then deployed snipers to the upper floors and minarets and left it to Qahtani's older brother Sayyid, who spoke fluent classical Arabic, to announce the presence of the Mahdi to the crowd. So impressive was Sayyid's performance, and particularly the offerings of the *baya* to Qahtani, that some of the hostages joined in with the occupiers and convinced at least one of the Mosque's security guard commanders that the pale young poet was indeed the Mahdi.

Juhayman released many foreigners, particularly those who spoke no Arabic. But the nearly bloodless initial takeover would turn deadly as the rebels barred the tens of thousands of Saudi and other Arab pilgrim hostages from leaving the Grand Mosque, and instructed them to take up arms or assist the occupiers. Government troops and policemen who approached within a half kilometer of the shrine quickly found themselves under fire.

Two factors paralyzed the initial government response to the takeover: Even though the heavily armed rebels shot at any uniform they saw, the army was reluctant to return fire because the Prophet had banned weapons from Mecca. Also, a large number of the hostages, and the government forces themselves, worried that Qahtani just might be the Mahdi.

Only one governing body could resolve this standoff, namely, the *ulema*, or high religious council, led by bin Baz. Angered by the royal family's impiousness, loose morals, and profligacy, the august body drove a stiff bargain: Not until the fifth day of the occupation did it declare Qahtani an impostor and bless a counterattack. In exchange, the Saudi king, Khalid, would clamp down on public morals, most especially on alcohol

---

* Sticklers will note that just as with the Western Gregorian calendar, the new century did not in actuality begin until 1401 A.H.

and women appearing on television—precisely the same agenda at the core of Juhayman's appeal.

Theological clearance in hand, the horrific assault began. Although the government quickly took out the minaret snipers with antitank missiles, the rebels firing from the main building remained in place, and infantry could not enter the Mosque itself without being cut to pieces at close range. The heavily Ikhwan-influenced National Guard made matters worse by refusing to fire on their tribal and theological brethren, in some cases supplying them with weapons.

Regular army units replaced the National Guard, but they had even less training in urban guerrilla warfare. Not until the Army trundled armored personal carriers inside the Mosque was any progress made. In addition to the losses on both sides, hundreds, and perhaps thousands, of pilgrim hostages perished in the crossfire. Told too many times he was the Mahdi, Qahtani considered himself invulnerable and somehow survived exposure to direct fire. His immortality thus confirmed, he took to hurling back the army's grenades until his luck finally ran out and one blew him almost to bits. The rebels slowly retreated to the Mosque's basement, which the armored vehicles entered but in whose narrow passages they became immobilized.

The assault was stalemated. Although exact figures were never published, a week into the assault government casualties represented a significant portion of the nation's thirty thousand army and twenty thousand National Guard personnel. King Khalid needed to call in foreign help. The Jordanians, the only Arab country both on friendly terms with the Saudis and with a credible commando force, offered assistance.

From the Saudi perspective, the Jordanian offer was a nonstarter. In the 1924–1925 campaign that included the brutal 1924 attack on Taif, Ikhwan forces, still allied at that point with Abdulaziz, Khalid's father, had ejected the Hashemite great-grandfather of the current Jordanian monarch, Hussein, from his Hejaz kingdom, which contained Mecca and Medina; to accept assistance from the despised Hashemites would have entailed an unacceptable loss of face.[36]

The kingdom was thus forced to countenance the unthinkable: aid from Christian forces at Islam's holiest site. This would be the hadith's infidel "army from the north"; it eventually arrived, but in diminutive and fleeting form. Khalid, who considered President Jimmy Carter and the

CIA impotent after the ongoing Tehran embassy hostage fiasco, settled on the French intelligence service for assistance. Because of the extreme sensitivity of allowing nonbelievers, let alone Christian troops, into Mecca, the French sent just three elite operatives, along with a large amount of advanced weaponry, which included several hundred pounds of an advanced irritant anesthetic gas.

Essential to the ongoing attack's planning were the building plans for the Mosque's extensive renovation and expansion in the 1960s, drawn by the man who had undertaken the vast project, a construction magnate named Muhammad bin Laden. His son Salem, who had taken over the firm's leadership after the 1967 death of his father, hurried to the Mosque with the plans, and he and his employees drilled holes in the Mosque floor through which to toss the French gas canisters down onto the rebels in the basement. The tactic proved only temporarily effective, which forced the Saudis to mount an almost unimaginably brutal French-designed coordinated final direct assault on the rebels' basement redoubt.[37]

When the siege ended on December 4, fourteen days later, thousands of combatants and hostages lay dead. At least a hundred rebels were taken captive, among whom was a dejected Juhayman. Doctors examined the prisoners; shoulder pain or bruises, which suggested the active firing of weapons, marked 69 prisoners for public beheading, with Juhayman first on the list. The Saudis executed others secretly, and the rest received long jail sentences. No one took seriously the official death toll of just 270 rebels, troops, and hostages.[38]

Although Juhayman's strategy was largely driven by his apocalyptic delusions, subsequent interviews with the surviving participants made clear that many did not believe his end-times theology, but rather paid it lip service out of their respect for him; others participated because the operation furthered their political goals. In any case, even those who swallowed Juhayman's apocalyptic scenario were discouraged when Qahtani, the supposedly invulnerable Mahdi, fell to a grenade on the siege's third day.[39] But the fact remains: Absent end-times belief, the Grand Mosque siege would not have occurred.

The Saudis had smothered the Ikhwan fire of 1979, just as they had done with the Ikhwan Revolt of 1927–1930. But in both cases, that fire continued to smolder, and in the coming decades the winds of global conflict would carry the embers of the Grand Mosque siege well beyond the kingdom's borders. This time, new technology would enable Juhayman's heirs to fan the flames much hotter and brighter than in 1979.

Those embers began to burn brighter even before the Mosque had been cleared of blood and debris. Three weeks after Saudi forces had taken care of the last of Juhayman's rebels, Soviet forces invaded Afghanistan. This was no coincidence; the Soviets sensed weakness in both the American response to Iran's 1979 Tehran embassy siezure and also in the Saudi monarchy, which had just suffered not only the Grand Mosque siege, but also an unrelated Shiite rebellion in the eastern peninsula.

The Soviet invasion of Afghanistan proved a catastrophic mistake; the country became a magnet for the new breed of jihadis, many of whom were supporters and sympathizers of Juhayman, who had gained legendary status in the Afghan mujahideen camps. Smarting from its hands-off policies in the Middle East, the United States aggressively supported the fighters who flooded into Afghanistan from around the Muslim world. One combatant was the son of the man who had renovated and expanded the Grand Mosque, and whose brother's blueprints proved invaluable in its retaking: the young Osama bin Laden.

In the wake of the Mosque seizure, a Palestinian living in Kuwait named Isam al-Barqawi, who at some point changed his name to Muhammad al-Maqdisi, discovered Juhayman's letters and found his way to that nation's JSM branch, which provided refuge to the sect's fugitive members. Maqdisi then went to Medina for religious study and in the following years traveled around Saudi Arabia and Jordan prior to arriving in Peshawar, Pakistan, the main portal into Soviet-occupied Afghanistan. At each stop, he sought out Juhayman's followers. Maqdisi was so taken with Juhayman's legend that he mimicked his hero's physical appearance by growing long hair and a tangled beard and claiming a nonexistent blood relationship with the Ikhwan hero.[40]

Eventually, Maqdisi settled down in Jordan, where he rotated in and out of jails between 1995 and 2014. More than any other Muslim thinker, he laid the ideological foundation for today's jihadism. A recent study of jihadi scholars found that Maqdisi, who had spent his adult life immersed in the Koran and hadith, was the radical Islamist most cited in Muslim apocalyptic literature.[41]

During his first Jordanian jail stint in 1995–1999, Maqdisi mentored a Jordanian petty criminal named Abu Musab al-Zarqawi. Both were released in 1999, at which point they separated in both space and theology. The teacher remained in Jordan, and while he at times criticized extreme colleagues, he was certain of one thing: Devout Muslims were duty-bound to travel to Syria to participate in the coming end-times struggle against the Dajjal, and if not to Syria, then to Yemen. The student, Zarqawi, decamped for Afghanistan and developed an intolerant and murderous ideology that endures to this day despite his death.

Zarqawi had an uncanny knack for arriving at places just before U.S.-led military actions, first Afghanistan, and then upon his escape from there, Iraq, where he almost single-handedly wrote the violent jihadi playbook of suicide attacks, kidnapping, and beheading of Westerners, along with skillful internet-based recruitment.

In 2004, Zarqawi participated in both battles for Falluja and declared his allegiance to Osama bin Laden. By this point, Maqdisi had rejected Juhayman's apocalypticism, but Zarqawi did not, and with the swift defeat of Saddam Hussein's forces, Zarqawi's propaganda took on an increasingly end-times tenor. Early on, he learned that apocalyptic propaganda attracted recruits, a lesson that the Islamic State would later absorb, which set in motion a vicious cycle: The worse things went for him on the battlefield, the more apocalyptic his tone became, attracting yet more recruits, which yielded yet more battlefield casualties.

Zarqawi never took his eye off his primary goal, the overthrow of the Jordanian monarchy, which in 1994 had inked a peace treaty with the Israelis. Describing the Jordanians as "slaves of the Zionists," he often applied the prophetic term "the corrupt ruler" to its king, Abdullah II. Zarqawi also despised Shiites and their Iranian power center, and he often referred to ancient prophecies that denigrated Shiism, especially those relating to the initial Arab defeat of the Persian Sasanian Empire at al-Qadisiyah in A.D. 636, as well as other prophecies that associated later Persian Islam with the hated Mongols. To Zarqawi, it was clear that Shiites, not the Jews, were the Dajjal, as were the U.S. invaders; not only was murdering them a theological necessity, but as a bonus such acts would ignite a sectarian war that would hasten the end-times.

By exploiting the rich apocalyptic literature associated with the early Muslim struggles against the Byzantines, Zarqawi referred to U.S. forces using the ancient shorthand for both the Byzantines and western Rome, *rum*. (Al-Qaeda, by contrast, applied the equally damning label of "crusader" to U.S.-led forces.) Whenever he could, he likened the battles of the Prophet to his own. He was especially fond of the well-known hadith of Thawban, in which the Prophet tells his followers that "the nations are about to flock against you from every horizon, just as hungry people flock to a kettle." He viewed Iraq's 2005 democratic constitution a catastrophe, and to console himself quoted from a Bukhari-approved hadith that even when the righteous are defeated, "in this way the messengers are tested then they win in the end." [42]

Zarqawi's indiscriminate suicide bombings, beheadings, and disregard for innocent lives eventually alienated even members of his organization, who likely betrayed the location of his "spiritual adviser," Sheikh Abd al-Rahman, which then enabled bomb-laden U.S. F-16s to find Zarqawi on June 7, 2006.[43]

Zarqawi had also spoken of reestablishing the caliphate, the last pale iteration of which had been abolished by Turkey in 1924, a goal he ultimately rejected, since a legitimate caliphate required conquered territory and the support of its population. The caliphate would have to wait; both he and bin Laden had proclaimed a less exalted entity, an "emirate," in, respectively, Iraq and Afghanistan.

The difference between an emirate and a caliphate is critical; an emirate rules over limited territory, whereas the caliphate rules over all Muslims, and it also implies the onset of the end-times. While Zarqawi thought the Apocalypse was drawing near, he did not think it had arrived yet. Nonetheless, the issue of the precise arrival of the end-times and caliphate would split apart bin Laden's "Al-Qaeda Central" operation in Afghanistan from Zarqawi's in Iraq. Just before Zarqawi succumbed in the 2006 air attack, he commanded his followers to declare the Islamic State of Iraq (ISI). His organization did so four months later, on October 15, 2006, an action that gobsmacked al-Qaeda, which deemed it foolish to announce the new state without territorial control.

The split between al-Qaeda and the ISI in some way resembled that between mainstream and evangelical Protestants. Just as urbane and well-educated Episcopalians and Presbyterians looked down disdainfully on the end-times speculation of their dispensationalist co-religionists as gibberish spouted by the unwashed, so, too, did the privileged bin Laden disdain the uninformed apocalypticism of Zarqawi as that of a barely literate small-time thug. His terrorism notwithstanding, bin Laden was an aristocrat. His father, Mohammed bin Laden, was a patriarch peculiar to that part of the world. Originally from Yemen, he began his adult life as a porter in Mecca's port city of Jeddah, and eventually became the general contractor for the Saudi royal family; today, the Saudi Binladen Group is one of the world's largest contracting firms. He married no fewer than twenty-two women and fathered fifty-four children, the seventeenth of whom was Osama, whose mother gave birth to him at age fifteen.

Mohammed divorced her soon after Osama's birth and married her off to a company executive, who became Osama's stepfather, and although the boy was no longer under Mohammed's roof, the two maintained loose ties; more importantly, the young man enjoyed his father's largess. This included an elite education at multiple private institutions, most importantly at Jeddah's prestigious Al-Thagr School, at that time a hotbed of both Arab nationalist and Islamist ideology, the latter of which the young Osama adopted. In 1967, his father died in a plane crash when Osama was only ten; later, after graduating from King Abdulaziz University in 1979, he joined the family construction business. When the Soviets invaded Afghanistan that same year, it became fashionable for young Saudis to journey there to do humanitarian work or fight with the mujahideen. Initially sent there by the company, Osama segued from the business of construction to the business of jihad.[44]

To the high-born and engineering-minded bin Laden, jihad was a methodical, hardheaded affair, not a messianic one. To cite just one example, he would later warn his apocalyptic-minded followers in Somalia, al-Shabab, that climate change threatened Islam in its arid homelands as much as did foreign troops, and would recommend that they plant heat-resistant trees. Wisecracked Arabist William McCants, "If you didn't know he ran the world's most notorious terrorist organization, you'd think bin Laden was an officer working for the United States Agency for International Development."[45]

Bin Laden had another reason to distrust Zarqawi's apocalypticism. His 1979 graduation year saw the Grand Mosque seizure, which his brother Salem, with his knowledge of its renovation, had participated in retaking.[46] The bin Ladens thus saw firsthand just what happens when a poorly thought-out end-times–soaked strategy collides with real-world geopolitical power, particularly when the former possesses neither political nor military control of its geographical base.

Al-Qaeda's first order of business would be to strike at the "far enemy," the United States, and drive its troops out of Saudi Arabia and the Middle East. The 9/11 attacks accomplished exactly the opposite. Bin Laden's strategy for the "near enemy" in the Middle East was the overthrow of its corrupt leaderships, and doing so required a "hearts and minds" approach that eschewed the suicide bombings, beheadings, and the mass extermination of Shiites perpetrated by his more zealous followers in Iraq.

The concept of near and far enemies had been coined by an Egyptian Islamist named Mohammed Abd al-Salam Faraj, who applied the former term to his own government, and the latter term to Israel. This terminology was picked up by Ayman al-Zawahiri, an Egyptian surgeon who became bin Laden's lieutenant. In 1982, the Egyptians executed Faraj for his role in the Sadat assassination, while the prickly and uncharismatic Zawahiri inherited al-Qaeda's leadership after bin Laden's elimination in 2011, and shared his disdain for apocalypticism.

ISI stopped short of establishing the caliphate, but in 2006, its nominal ruling body, the Mujahideen Shura Council, named an almost completely unknown figure, Abu Umar al-Baghdadi, as "commander of the faithful." Baghdadi claimed descent from the Prophet and was thus technically qualified as caliph, but his putative prophetic bloodline was likely bogus. His real name was Hamid al-Zawi, a former policeman, electronics repairman, and imam of no great learning or repute. In reality, an Egyptian disciple of Zarqawi, Abu Ayyub al-Masri, was running ISI's operations.

Earlier in that same year, ISI had chosen as its symbol the black flag, which carried the seal of the prophet and the inscription "No god but God, Muhammad is the Messenger of God." Given the apocalyptic hadith prophecy that spoke of "the black banners coming from Khorasan" (i.e., Afghanistan), the end-times augury of ISI's flag could hardly have been more clear.[47]

ISI had struck a rich vein in a Muslim world riven by strife and poverty. Survey data show that even more of the world's Muslims expect the end-times than do Christians. One Pew Center study found that 51 percent of the Middle East's Muslims believe in the Mahdi's imminent return, a figure that was likely higher in the cauldron of post-invasion Iraq.[48] (As with other sociologic data on religiosity, the poorer the nation, the more fervent the belief; the figure was 60 percent among South Asian Muslims, but only 18 percent among Balkan Muslims.)[49] Intentionally or not, ISI had adopted an apocalyptic narrative far more compelling than the stale salafist theology of bin Laden, and particularly that of his uncharismatic successor, Zawahiri.

If anyone believed in the imminence of the Mahdi's arrival, it was ISI's de facto leader, Masri. To expedite the process, he had his troops build pulpits for the Mahdi's transit through the three great mosques in Medina, Jerusalem, and Damascus. Masri also needed to conquer and hold territory to speed the Mahdi's arrival. To doubters, he offered this simple reply: "The Mahdi will come any day."[50]

Masri's zeal and granite religious certitude justified a string of atrocities even worse than Zarqawi's. ISI slaughtered not only Shiites, but also any Sunni who withheld allegiance; used as human shields women and sick children; and blew up homes and hospitals. It widely enforced *hudud*: the stoning of adulterers, amputation for theft, and flogging for alcohol consumption. On one occasion ISI beheaded an eight-year-old girl.

As reports of escalating ISI butchery reached al-Qaeda in Afghanistan, bin Laden and Zawahiri tried to regain control of their Iraqi franchise, but received back only dilatory responses, when they got them at all.[51] American officials observed Masri's gross strategic and tactical errors with wonder and reduced the price on his head from $5 million to $100,000; some analysts speculated that he was an actor playing a theatrical role. Masri's wife offered perhaps the most succinct description of her husband's pigheaded, inept brutality: "Where is the Islamic State of Iraq you're talking about? We're living in the desert!" On April 18, 2010, a joint raid by Iraqi and American forces cornered both Masri and Baghdadi near Tikrit, Saddam Hussein's hometown. Faced with surrender, they blew themselves up.[52]

For all its failures, ISI had rediscovered a truth well known to Lindsey, LaHaye, and Jenkins: Apocalypse sells, and the bloodier, the better. In the twenty-first century, ISI could advertise the Apocalypse to the whole world via websites and social media. Its most common media product was the simple press release:

A brave, daring brother, one of the heroes of the Islamic State of Iraq, a member of the Martyrdom-Seekers-Brigade . . . plunged his explosives-laden car into a command post of the American crusader army at the Jerusalem intersection in the Al-Mafriq district of Diyala Governorate. Our heroic brother cried out, "Allahu Akbar," and detonated the car . . . killing more than 11 soldiers of the Idolatrous Guard and destroying two Bradley armored fighting vehicles.[53]

The internet made possible not only a wide range of written material, but even more compelling videos. ISI sympathizers in both the Middle East and the West thrilled to clips depicting attacks on "crusader" troops, often from multiple camera angles; the caption of one video of the destruction of an American truck with an improvised explosive device read, "Their last moments." Longer videos featured "greatest hits" attack compilations, martyr profiles, plan-to-execution documentaries, and motivational montages. Nor were American and Iraqi troops the only targets; films featuring the execution of Shiite prisoners proved especially popular.[54]

As early as 2008, the Yemeni bin Laden franchise, al-Qaeda in the Arabian Peninsula (AQAP), had already advanced the art of Islamic apocalyptic propaganda with a pair of magazines, *The Echo of Battles* and *Inspire*. The latter was an English-language periodical run by a Pakistani raised in North Carolina, Samir Khan, who had a knack for catchy article titles, such as "Make a Bomb in the Kitchen of Your Mom"; around 2010, he began to write apocalypse-laden pieces for *Inspire*.

Khan was the disciple of a charismatic and influential imam, an American-raised U.S. citizen of Yemeni extraction named Anwar al-Awlaki, who intoned in one of his articles:

Mu'jam al-Kabir and others by way of Ibn Abbas [report that] the Prophet said: "An army of twelve-thousand will come out of Aden-Abyan [Yemen]. They will give victory to Allah and His messenger. They are the best between myself and them!"

About that hadith the honorable Shaykh Sulayman ibn Nasir al-Ulwan—may Allah hasten his release—said that the hadith's chain is good and its narrators are acceptable.[55]

Rather than rely on his own analysis of the first paragraph of the above passage, Awlaki cited a higher authority in the second, in this case a prestigious, and imprisoned, Saudi Islamist theologian named Sulayman ibn

Nasir al-Ulwan, who vouched for the integrity of the hadith's transmission chain back to the Prophet.[56]

Awlaki's apocalypse-laden articles, lectures, and videos inspired a number of terror attacks. Some of them were effected by disciples he had been in personal contact with, and may even have directed, such as "underwear bomber" Umar Farouk Abdulmutallab; while others were inspired to act from afar, such as Fort Hood shooter Nidal Malik Hasan, a U.S. Army psychiatrist with whom he had exchanged emails; and the Times Square bomber, Faisal Shahzad, who described himself as merely Awlaki's "fan and follower."[57]

In the end, AQAP went down the same senselessly violent road as ISI; this drew the disapproval of the parent organization in Afghanistan, whose command had devolved to Zawahiri after bin Laden's death in 2011. AQAP failed to provide adequate services to people in the small territory it controlled and succumbed to superior foreign forces. On September 30, 2011, a controversial U.S. drone strike in Yemen killed Khan and Awlaki—both U.S. citizens. Tragically, another drone strike killed Awlaki's sixteen-year-old son Abdulrahman, supposedly by accident; and on January 29, 2017, a disastrous commando raid resulted in the death of a Navy SEAL and Awlaki's eight-year-old daughter.[58]

By 2010, ISI seemed to be on the ropes, but this would change when the United States withdrew its fighting troops from Iraq during the beginning of the Obama administration, leaving behind a much smaller cadre of trainers and advisers. The United States threw its support behind Iraqi prime minister Nouri al-Maliki, a highly partisan Shiite politician whose repressive tactics drove even moderate Sunnis into the arms of ISI.

A month after the April 2010 deaths of Masri and Abu Umar al-Baghdadi, an opportunist and minor Islamic scholar named Abu Bakr al-Baghdadi assumed leadership.* Little is known for sure about him, since his immediate family members, said to be of descent from the Prophet,

---

* The similarity in names is trivial: "al-Baghdadi" simply indicates that someone is from Baghdad (which also conveys the historical prestige of the former Abassid capital). Abu Bakr and Umar are common Arabic appellations, since those were the first and second caliphs after Muhammad; Abu Bakr al-Baghdadi is thus the Iraqi equivalent of "David from New York."

have disappeared. He seems to have been a bookish young man whose poor eyesight kept him out of Saddam's army and who early on earned the nickname "the Believer." He immersed himself in the Koran and hadith and may or may not have earned a Ph.D. from Baghdad's Saddam University for Islamic Studies, which the dictator established to co-opt the religious establishment.

Aside from Islamic scripture, the "new Baghdadi" had two other passions: soccer, at which he excelled, and the enforcement of public morality. He was said to have a fiery temper that could be ignited either by a missed goal attempt or the sight of mixed couples dancing at a wedding.

Soon after the 2003 American invasion, Baghdadi organized an obscure resistance group and was captured in Falluja in February 2004. He was popular among his fellow inmates at Camp Bucca, which held twenty-four thousand detainees and was called by one observer a "virtual terrorist university" where jihadis compared notes, networked, and wrote each other's contact information in the elastic bands of their boxer shorts. Almost immediately after release, they would undress, cut out the critical data from their underwear, and use it to regroup and organize.

Baghdadi charmed his American captors into an early release, likely after just several months, upon which he almost immediately connected with Zarqawi's outfit. As a religious scholar, he was a valuable commodity who could provide theological cover for ISI's brutal campaign of stoning adulterers, amputating the limbs of thieves, and massacring Shiites and other apostates. In 2007, he took a break from these labors and traveled to Baghdad to defend his doctoral dissertation.

The April 2010 loss of Masri and Abu Umar opened up the leadership positions to Camp Bucca alumni, and Baghdadi, with his charisma, scholarly reputation, internment camp connections, and supposed Qurayshi descent, topped the list.[59]

Over the next several years, the dwindling American presence in Iraq allowed Baghdadi to expand his influence throughout the country, and then into Syria. In April 2013, he asserted leadership over al-Qaeda's franchise in Syria, much to its surprise as well as that of al-Qaeda Central, now under the control of Zawahiri, who kicked ISI out of its organization. With the Syrian civil conflict in full swing, President Bashar al-Assad effectively sided with ISI by selectively bombing its rivals and leaving ISI nearly untouched.

By mid-June, ISI had conquered Mosul, Iraq's third-largest city, and Baghdadi now found himself in charge of a fiefdom that had obliterated the frontier between Syria and Iraq, drawn in 1916 by the hated Anglo-French Sykes-Picot Agreement.[60] The turnaround in ISI's fortunes stunned the Western alliance; only six months before, President Obama had told journalist David Remnick that "if a jayvee team puts on Lakers uniforms, that doesn't make them Kobe Bryant." Although Obama was talking specifically about al-Qaeda's ability to strike U.S. territory, his timing could not have been worse.[61]

As with Hal Lindsey and Juhayman's Grand Mosque siege, "the great jigsaw puzzle" had fallen nearly into place for ISI: with the world in moral and political disarray and a borderless kingdom under the rule of one of the prophet's descendants, the caliphate was surely at hand. All that was needed was a theological foundation for the caliph's anointment.

That task fell to a jihadi scholar by the name of Turki al-Binali, a Bahraini theologian formidable enough to be considered Maqdisi's heir apparent. Like his teacher, he had moved in and out of prison, and as ISI was gathering steam in Syria in early 2014, he arrived there to witness the birth of the caliphate: "Is it reasonable that we would return, having arrived in the Sham [Syria] of epic battles and warfare? . . . A land wherein the rule is Islam is my home; there is my dwelling and there do I belong."[62]

To the chagrin of his mentor Maqdisi, who certainly didn't believe that the caliphate was at hand, Binali would shortly pen an essay entitled "Extend Your Hands to Give Baya to Baghdadi."[63]

On June 29, 2014, the first day of Ramadan, Baghdadi declared the reestablishment of the caliphate, with himself as Caliph Ibrahim. Five days later, the caliph, who had never before appeared before a public gathering, mounted the pulpit of the Great Mosque of al-Nuri in newly conquered Mosul bedecked in a black turban and robe, humbly accepted leadership, then demanded obedience from the world's Muslims. In addition to the classical clerical garb, he also sported a flashy, expensive watch of the sort favored by high-level jihadis that, among other features, announced the five daily prayers.[64]

Henceforth, ISI's leadership decided that it was now to be known simply as the Islamic State (IS). Several weeks later, IS propagandists would publish the first issue of *Dabiq*, headlined "The Return of Khilafah":

the rebirth of the caliphate. Initially posted only on the "dark web," *Dabiq* published fifteen issues between 2014 and 2016 that are now freely available on the open internet.[65]

By late 2015, approximately thirty thousand foreign fighters, hailing from at least eighty-six nations, had traveled to join IS, about one-sixth of them from Western nations.[66] The contrast with bin Laden's lengthy, turgid Arabic language communiqués could hardly have been more striking; IS aimed its snappy English-, French-, and German-language editions of *Dabiq*'s maiden issue squarely at potential Western recruits, especially those lacking a deep understanding of Islamic eschatology.

Prophetic allusions to the coming Armageddon with the West filled its pages, starting with its version of the most famous apocalyptic hadith, in their printing, "The Hour will not be established until the Romans land at Amaq or Dabiq," and proceeded through the prophesized return of Jesus, before whom the enemy "will melt as salt melts with water." For those who still didn't grasp the prophetic meaning, the authors supplied an abbreviated version:

> According to the hadith, the area [around Dabiq] will play a historical role in the battles leading up to the conquests of Constantinople, then Rome. Presently, Dabiq is under the control of the crusader-backed sahwat [Sunni puppets], close to the warfront between them and the *Khilafah* [caliphate].[67]

Shortly, IS would fulfill that prophecy by taking the symbolic but strategically inconsequential town of Dabiq. The Islamic State's forces, swollen with fighters from around the globe, would, according to its narrative, re-create the caliphate and restore Islam to its proper place in the world: "Soon, by Allah's permission, a day will come when the Muslim will walk everywhere as a master, having honor, being revered, with his head raised high and his dignity preserved."[68]

Save for the identity of the heroes and villains, the magazine's Manichean worldview was nearly identical to Lindsey and LaHaye's:

> Indeed the world today has been divided into two camps and two trenches, with no third camp present: The camp of Islam and faith, and the camp of kufr (disbelief) and hypocrisy—the camp of the

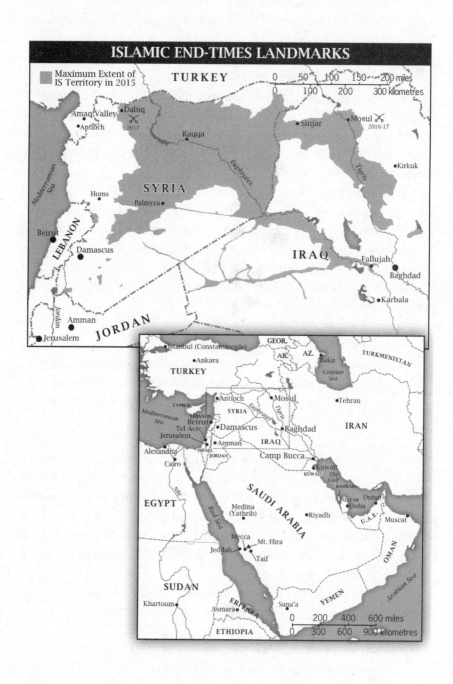

Muslims and the mujahidin everywhere, and the camp of the Jews, the crusaders, their allies, and with them the rest of the nations and religions of kufr, all being led by America and Russia, and being mobilized by the Jews.[69]

This prophecy was followed by gory images of atrocities against Sunnis and the execution of their Shiite perpetrators, the former to generate sympathy among supporters, the latter to generate fear among opponents. Glowing descriptions ensued of Caliph Ibrahim and, bizarrely, a photo of a distinguished-looking U.S. National Security Council official, Douglas Ollivant, behind a Cato Institute podium accompanied by text of his description of IS's fearsome capabilities.[70] The magazine then laid out IS's five-step roadmap to victory, which led from hegira (emigration to IS territory) to *Khilafah*.

Strangely, the Mahdi, who had figured so prominently in the Grand Mosque siege, went largely unmentioned. Exactly why is uncertain; perhaps his appearance demands a date and is thus prone to a Great Disappointment; perhaps the Mahdi's disastrous role in the 1979 siege devalued his stock. Instead, the IS narrative, rather, focused to a great extent on the victory of the prophet Jesus over the Dajjal.[71]

The Westerners who made the hegira to IS territory generally didn't speak Arabic and had no military training, and so were of little use, with one exception: those with media experience. One of IS's productions, a thirteen-minute video, featured multiple jihadis from Europe and Australia who extolled the caliphate: "We understand no borders—we have participated in battles in Sham [Syria] and we will go to Iraq in a few days and fight there and come back. We will even go to Jordan and Lebanon with no problems." Another video showed an IS fighter bragging of attacking Israel and lamenting deformed babies born to "our sisters in Falluja," while another delivered the punch line: leave your "fat jobs" in the West: "Ask yourself what prevents you and what keeps you behind. It's your wealth."[72]

Jihadi media specialists used music, the royal road to the limbic system, as adroitly as did Leni Riefenstahl in *Triumph of the Will* or as in the slickest American campaign ad. Since devout Muslims eschew musical instruments, the Islamist tunes featured hypnotic a cappella songs, *anashid* (singular, *nashid*) that declaimed the praises of the coming caliphate and exhorted the faithful to martyrdom.

Anashid have figured prominently during multiple Islamist terror attacks. For example, after the Tsarnaev brothers perpetrated the deadly 2013 Boston Marathon bombing, when they failed to connect their iPhones to the stereo of their carjacked vehicle to listen to militant *anashid*, they took the risk of driving back to their own abandoned car to retrieve the CD that contained them. Anwar al-Awlaki was especially impressed with the magnetism of jihadi music: "A good *nashid* can spread so widely it can reach to an audience that you could not reach through a lecture or a book."[73]

The prospect of taking part in a grand adventure built on a fourteen-century-old apocalyptic narrative proved irresistible to many young people alienated by their aimless and seemingly meaningless lives in the West, and was manifest in a high percentage of recent converts among European jihadi recruits.[74] As one Syrian Sunni rebel told a Reuters correspondent, "If you think all these mujahideen came from across the world to fight Assad, you're mistaken. They are all here as promised by the Prophet. This is the war he promised—it is the Grand Battle."*[75]

As psychologists Timothy Brock and Melanie Green pointed out, the more powerful the narrative, the more it corrodes critical thinking. To the alienated recruits fed up with a Western-dominated world, IS's narrative was powerful enough to supply theological cover for a chamber of horrors that included ethnically based mass murder, rape, and slavery.

Following the spectacular IS conquests in August 2014 in northern Iraq, members of the large Yazidi sect of Islam in Sinjar Province found themselves under IS rule. The fourth issue of *Dabiq*, published on October 11, 2014, did not just rationalize the persecution of the sect, but glorified it as a means of encouraging adherents to participate in racially driven mass slavery, rape, and murder.

The Yazidis believe that Allah entrusted the world to seven angels, prime among them being the Malik Tous, whom they especially revere. Such heresy, explained *Dabiq*, rendered the Yazidis "mushrikin"— polytheists/pagans: "Their creed is so deviant from the truth that even cross-worshipping Christians for ages consider them devil-worshippers and Satanists." And when it came to mushrikin, the Koran, said *Dabiq*, was clear:

---

* In Arabic, "Grand Battle" also translates as "slaughter."

And when the sacred months have passed, then kill the mushrikin wherever you find them, and capture them, and besiege them, and sit in wait for them at every place of ambush. But if they repent, establish prayer, and give zakah [tax paid by Muslims], let them [go] on their way. Indeed, Allah is Forgiving and Merciful.

Unlike Christians and Jews, "people of the book" who could skate by with payment of a *jizyah* (tax paid by non-Muslims) IS viewed the Yazidis as pagans. IS theologians debated whether Yazidis had always been pagans, or had first been Muslims who later became apostate. This distinction was critical, since apostate women had to be offered the same choice as their men—conversion or death—whereas women of an originally pagan race could be enslaved.

Dabiq informed readers that IS had decided the Yazidis had always been pagans, which condemned their women to slavery. But Allah is merciful, and did not allow their sex slaves to be separated from their children. Better yet, according to one hadith, when "the slave girl gives birth to her master," it is a sign of The Hour, though there seemed to be confusion as how to interpret this ambiguous phrase. Maybe it meant that the child of the master becomes the master, or that the increase in slaves by itself is a sign of The Hour, or that in the End men turn away from marriage and make do with concubines alone. In any case, taking the women of nonbelievers, according to *Dabiq*, "is a firmly established aspect of the Sharia that if one were to deny or mock, he would be denying or mocking the verses of the Koran and the narrations of the Prophet, and thereby apostatizing from Islam."[76]

As a consequence, IS offered Yazidi men conversion; IS fighters slit the throats or blew out the brains of those who refused, often in front of their families. Four-fifths of the women and children were divided among the fighters, and the remaining fifth went to the organization, with the women captives often enduring repeated gang rape. Many Yazidis did manage to escape only to die of starvation. As of 2017, the United Nations estimated that IS had killed three thousand Yazidis and abducted seven thousand.[77]

Beginning in mid-2014, IS directed and inspired attacks around the world, most spectacularly the November 13, 2015, slaughter at the Bataclan concert hall and other Paris locations that killed 130 and injured 530; and the July 14, 2016, National Day truck attack in Nice that killed 84 and injured 458. It's estimated that by August 2019, IS-directed and IS-inspired attacks outside Syria and Iraq had taken more than 3,800 lives.[78]

The mid-2014 ascension of Baghdadi to Caliph Ibrahim more or less marked the apogee of IS, which then controlled a population of approximately eight million and vast stores of arms and income from oil fields and refineries. Its shocking victories in Iraq and Syria and worldwide terrorism capability drew a Western military response, and the combination of IS's extreme brutality and the replacement of Iraqi prime minister Maliki with the more conciliatory Hiader al-Abadi loosened IS's hold on Sunnis. Beginning in October 2016, an increasingly effective Iraqi military, aided by U.S.-led air strikes and Kurdish forces, slowly regained territory in the Mosul region, capped by the cataclysmic recapture of the eastern section of the city in late January 2017. In excess of ten thousand civilians and about one thousand coalition forces may have died in the assault; as many as sixteen thousand of IS's fighters were killed in this single action, by which point it was a shadow of its former self; on October 26, 2019, a U.S. Special Forces raid in northwestern Syria cornered al-Baghdadi, who detonated an explosive vest that killed him and two of his children.[79]

Over the course of the entire conflict with ISI/IS, Iraqi- and U.S.-led foreign forces may have killed as many as sixty thousand IS fighters. The reversal of IS's fortunes on the battlefield corroded its ability to plan and inspire terrorist attacks in the West, although it is still capable of mounting devastating operations in the Middle East and Asia. *Dabiq* ceased publication in 2016, and by early 2018, the flow of propaganda had fallen by about two-thirds.

As predicted by many observers of Islamic apocalypticism, the cessation of further conquest was preordained by mid-2014; IS already controlled the Sunni heartlands of Iraq and Syria, and it was hardly going to make further conquests into Turkey, Kurdish-held territory, and Shiite areas. Absent any ongoing conquests, the caliphate lost its legitimacy and recruiting power.[80]

In addition, IS's initial victories produced a strategic backlash from Iraqi Shiite militias, particularly from forces led by the influential imam Muqtada al-Sadr. In late 2014, a plea from the usually peaceable Grand Ayatollah Ali al-Sistani, Iraq's highest Shiite cleric, for fighters to "defend the country, its people, the honor of its citizens and its sacred places" produced a torrent of enthusiastic recruits. These Shiite militia forces were heavily supported by Iranian money, men, and matériel of the elite Quds Force, led by its legendary commander, Qassem Soleimani (who was killed in 2020 by a U.S. drone strike). In the brutal follow-up revenge operations, they murdered thousands of otherwise innocent Sunnis.[81]

With no further territory to acquire and a rapidly reversing military situation, the prospect of accelerating the Apocalypse, along with its financial reward and infidel sex slaves, shrank; and by mid-2016, those training camps that had not been bombed into rubble closed for lack of recruits. On October 17, 2017, IS's "capital" at Raqqa, Syria, fell to a force of Syrian rebels backed by U.S. Special Forces, and in late March 2019, coalition forces conquered the last IS-held territory.[82]

While the Islamic State remains a potent actor in the Middle East and its disciples in the West are still capable of mounting lone-wolf attacks, the apocalyptic narrative leading to a triumphant, ever-expanding caliphate has evaporated, and IS no longer attracts thousands of starry-eyed young adherents from developed nations.

Nonetheless, wherever there is society-wide humiliation and disappointment, apocalypticism can and will flourish. This is certainly true in much of the Muslim world today, especially where it has suffered defeat, real or imagined, at the hands of the West.

Furthermore, as the late-twentieth-century rise of Christian apocalypticism demonstrates, end-times narratives can flourish even in successful, prosperous societies, and all three Abrahamic faiths have proven fertile ground for them. The human hunger for compelling narratives, of which the end-times is the most seductive, almost invariably exacerbates another unfortunate human tendency, our proclivity to in-group/out-group behavior. A significant minority of people will always find irresistible the notion that they are members of an elect few who will usher in a virtuous new order that condemns nonbelievers to burn, a delusion that has driven religious mass manias for centuries, from John Bockelson and his followers in Münster to William Miller's and Jerry Falwell's in the United States, to the tens of thousands attracted to the inferno of the Islamic State.

Epilogue

We are survival machines—robot vehicles blindly programmed to preserve the selfish molecules known as genes.

—Richard Dawkins[1]

Were Charles Mackay able to journey through time to the present day, the stories of the 1844 Great Disappointment, of the stock bubbles of the 1920s and 1990s, and of the rise of the recent end-times delusions of all three Abrahamic religions would not surprise him in the least. He would, at the same time, be riveted by Darwin's exposition of human evolution, described a generation after the 1841 publication of *Extraordinary Popular Delusions*, and wonder how it applied to the episodes he wrote about. And he would be just as fascinated, for the same reason, by twentieth-century psychology and social psychology research.

First and foremost, Mackay would have been fascinated to learn that we are the slaves of the hardwired instincts of our Stone Age ancestors, who depended on mutual cooperation, communication, and, above all, mimicry, to survive in an environment of scarce food, poisonous berries, venomous snakes, and faster-footed and bigger-toothed predators.

We are only about three hundred generations removed from the end of the Stone Age and are still driven by these ancient survival instincts. Not only have those three hundred generations not been long enough to evolve more analytical cognition, but it's doubtful whether such improved mental abilities would even confer a survival advantage to the individuals that possessed them in a relatively more humane industrial or postindustrial world. In other words, we're likely doomed to limp along with our Stone Age minds on a space-age planet.

Indeed, much of our behavior has far more ancient roots; we share many genes that are hundreds of millions of years old, such as those that regulate appetite, with earthworms.[2] Our evolutionary fondness for energy-laden sweet and fatty foods, which likely originated in our vertebrate ancestors eons before our species evolved, has become profoundly maladaptive in a modern world saturated with cheap sugar and lipids.

From the perspective of *Extraordinary Popular Delusions*, mimicry is probably the most important of our hardwired evolutionary characteristics. Besides our advanced cognitive and language ability, the human capacity to rapidly learn through imitation new skill sets—kayaks in the arctic, bison-hunting on the Great Plains, and blowguns in the Amazon Basin—has allowed us to thrive in most places on the planet. Sadly, our proclivity toward mimicry applies equally to maladaptive, and ofttimes abhorrent, behavior.

Probably the most famous experimental demonstrations of this unfortunate phenomenon were Stanley Milgram's "obedience" and Philip Zimbardo's "Stanford Prison" studies. In Milgram's study, subjects (the "teachers") were frequently persuaded by the "experimenters" to deliver "lethal" shocks to "learners" for incorrect answers.[3] Similarly, the Stanford Prison Experiment divided the subjects between "prisoners" and "guards." Within a few days, both groups mimicked and internalized their roles to the point that violence broke out between the two groups.[4]

While both of these studies have attracted serious criticism, the contagion of moral and intellectual rot is hardly a theoretical or experimental issue, for the real world abounds with far better examples of how aberrant behavior spreads among apparently normal, well-adjusted people.[5] The Enron scandal of the 1990s, for example, demonstrated just how contagious both irrationality and moral corruption could be. None of the protagonists—Kenneth Lay, Jeffrey Skilling, and Andrew Fastow—considered themselves unethical or immoral; after all, everyone around them told them they were fine, highly intelligent people who were revolutionizing the American economy. And, similar to the subjects exposed by psychologist Solomon Asch to the erroneous line measurements of tablemates, Enron's personnel accepted the nearly unanimous but incorrect judgments of their colleagues and of journalists.

Perhaps the most spectacular examples of aberrant moral contagion manifested themselves in totalitarian societies such as the Cambodia of Pol Pot, the China of the Cultural Revolution and, of course, the Germany of Hitler. When historian Laurence Rees interviewed Nazi death camp guards and administrative personnel near the end of their lives, he found them more open about their work than they had been decades before. He was stunned to find that, rather than evil robots who blindly followed orders, these Germans, almost to a man and woman, were normal-appearing, intelligent individuals who considered themselves ethical participants in a worthy enterprise, namely, ridding the world of Jewish vermin. Like junior executives at an elite firm, they competed and innovated to complete their horrific tasks with maximum efficiency.[6]

Still, there were limits to the Germans' peer-driven inhumanity, particularly when it came to machine-gunning thousands of Jews at a time, which produced psychological distress even among hardened SS troops. Consequently, the most "efficient" death camps at Sobibór, Belżec, Treblinka, and Birkenau (Auschwitz) relied on the labors of non-German prisoners for the dirtiest work, and required only relatively small numbers of German personnel—approximately twenty at Belżec, for example, at which six hundred thousand were murdered.*

It is hard to avoid the dark conclusion that if enough of our peers deem genocide desirable, many, if not most, of us are capable of it. Those who still think that German exceptionalism was a major factor in the Holocaust should consider the behavior of English officials on the German-occupied channel islands of Jersey and Guernsey, who willingly cooperated in sending their Jewish residents to the camps. In the words of one former Nazi official, "The trouble with the world today is that people who have never been tested go around making judgments about people who have."[7] Or, more succinctly, one should never underestimate the human tendency toward mimicry, and especially of how the everyday beneficial mass delusions that help businesses and whole societies function smoothly can rapidly mutate into fraudulent or genocidal mass delusions.

Mackay would also agree with the observation that we are the apes who tell stories—he was a master narrator himself. When our remote ancestors needed to communicate with each other to survive, they did not do so with syllogisms, numerical data, or mathematical formulae. The

---

* The Nazis discovered early on that separating parents and children created disturbances that slowed down the process. Rees, perhaps the only researcher to have interviewed camp guards from all three of the Second World War's totalitarian powers—Germany, Japan, and the Soviet Union—noted that, by contrast with German camp personnel, Soviet and Japanese guards were largely driven by fear, and not ideological commitment.

primary mode of that communication was, and still is, narration: "You go right, I'll go left, and we'll spear the mastodon from both sides." Humans are narrative animals, and no matter how misleading the narrative, if it is compelling enough it will nearly always trump the facts, at least until those facts cause great pain or, as in the case of the Islamic State forces in the Middle East and the Münster Anabaptists, the facts decimate the believers themselves.

Further, we listen to stories not only because we enjoy them for their own sake, but also because we want to know their ending, and no story compels and transports more than that of the world's ultimate fate. The more a narrative transports someone, the more it corrodes their analytical skills; a skillfully crafted end-times narrative can convince men to give away all their worldly goods or to happily send their wives and daughters to the storyteller's bed.

Mackay would concur that we mold the facts to fit our preexisting opinions, and not the other way around. Everywhere and always, we fall prey to confirmation bias and cling to those facts most consistent with our beliefs and intentionally ignore those that disconfirm them.

In technical terms, were we truly rational, we would formulate our opinions about the world according to "Bayesian inference," a method of analysis invented by Thomas Bayes, an eighteenth-century English philosopher who invented a mathematical rule for altering our forecasts in the face of new data. If one thinks that there is a 50 percent chance that a politician one dislikes is guilty of criminal behavior, and then a new and powerful piece of exculpatory evidence appears, according to Bayesian inference, one's estimate of the probability of his or her guilt should now fall below 50 percent.

But that's not how people behave; when we hold strong opinions on a topic, we intentionally avoid exposing ourselves to contrary data, and when disconfirming information can no longer be ignored, it can trigger the proselytization of delusional beliefs, as happened with Dorothy Martin's flying saucer sect. Human beings, far from being rational Bayesians, are indeed often "anti-Bayesians," a fact that serves to spread delusional beliefs.

Mackay undoubtedly understood that a compelling narrative can act as a contagious pathogen that rapidly spreads through a given population in the same exponential fashion, as when a COVID-19 virus super-spreader

infects a large number of contacts. Moreover, as Asch's experiments illustrated, if an incorrect belief becomes prevalent enough, it acquires a
critical mass.

As ever more of those around us share the same delusion, the more
likely we are to believe in it, and so the more likely those around us will
do so as well, a vicious cycle for which we lack an analytical emergency
brake. In the presence of delusional contagion for which no effective de-
fenses exist, runaway manias gain ever more momentum until they finally
smash into the brick wall of reality.

Finally, Mackay described time and again the human tendency to
view life in Manichean terms—a stark black-and-white struggle between
good and evil—and had Darwin's *On the Origin of Species* been published
a generation earlier, he would have understood this as yet one more piece
of our Stone Age evolutionary baggage. He would further have realized
that the near universal human tendency toward overconfidence both enables
our survival and also leads us to assume that we sit on the right side of
the moral fence: Both this book and Mackay's fairly burst with religious
multitudes who believed that those not sharing their worldview were hell-
bound, and in extreme cases, deserved to die.

The Islamic State is only the latest float in this parade of the Manichean delusion; for a while, the Islamist group commanded the most compelling and agreeable narrative available to those suffering from poverty,
war, and oppression: that the afflicted were engaged in a black-and-white
struggle as the forces of righteousness, and that Allah would sooner or later
deliver them final and everlasting victory over oppressors who embodied
the essence of evil. This Islamic apocalyptic twenty-first-century narrative
is thus little different from John Bockelson's sixteenth-century narrative,
or from Hal Lindsey's twentieth-century one. (Although Lindsey's post-
communist opponents—socialists, Satanists, and astrologers—are weak
tea indeed compared with the Habsburg Empire or the might of the Israeli
and Western militaries.)

The descriptions of delusional financial manias in this book and in
Mackay's differ only in quality from their end-times ones. In both cases, the
narratives are highly agreeable: in the latter case, the promise of membership in an elect that will be spared life's tribulations through miraculous
spiritual means, and in the former case, by miraculous financial means.

And in both cases, confirmation bias and human mimicry play starring roles as well.

The main difference is that financial delusions largely lack the Manichean element that is front and center in religious ones. But even this lack isn't total. Recall that one of the cardinal diagnostic features of a bubble is a vehement response to skepticism. As I write these words, the excitement surrounding cryptocurrencies, of which bitcoin is the exemplar, seem to exhibit all of the signs and symptoms of earlier financial manias. Perhaps the most famous endorsement of bitcoin came from antivirus entrepreneur John McAfee, who opined that if bitcoin's price did not reach $500,000 within three years, "I'll eat my dick on national television," the implication being that anyone who doubted bitcoin's value was, if not evil, at least an idiot.[8] (Having reached a price of $20,000 in late 2017, by mid-2020 it was trading at $11,800.)

Just as Mackay would have been fascinated with modern psychological and evolutionary insights into mass delusional behavior in general, he would also have learned a great deal from recent research by economists such as Hyman Minsky and Charles Kindleberger specific to financial manias, work that clearly demonstrates that these episodes revolve around the explosive combination of exciting new technologies, the loosening of credit, amnesia, and the abandonment of time-tested financial analysis. And once again, cryptocurrencies such as bitcoin are instructive; while it seems likely that few will grow wealthy from direct investment in these instruments, the so-called blockchain technology underlying them may well benefit society at large by revolutionizing both banking and government finance.

Mackay, while a consummate storyteller, was hobbled by his era's lack of scientific knowledge about human behavior, genetics, and natural selection, and his marvelous descriptions of mass delusions, while enormously instructive, took him only so far. But Mackay must surely have suspected that mankind is condemned to step repeatedly on the same financial and religious rakes even if he did not know, as we now do, the reasons why.

ACKNOWLEDGMENTS

This volume combines elements of neuropsychology, social psychology, evolutionary psychology, financial economics and history, macroeconomics, the eschatology of all three Abrahamic religions, and wide swaths of historical analysis, from the ancient to the modern periods. Not many are conversant with more than a few of these subjects, let alone all of them. I am therefore indebted to a wide range of individual experts in these areas:

Michael Barkun, on the relationship between millennialism and violence; David Blitzer and Kimberly Boyle, for access to Dow Jones returns data; Scott Burns and Laura Jacobus, for archival newspaper material; the late John C. Bogle, Burton Malkiel, and Richard Sylla, for perspectives on the 1960s technology investing craze; D. Campbell-Meiklejohn, on the fMRI data on bias disconfirmation; Edward Chancellor, for perspectives on equity bubbles; Henry Clements, for help with translation of Arabic sources; Chris Dennistoun, for bringing Richard Davenport, a predecessor of Mackay, to my attention; Jacob J. Goldstein, for help with NPR archives; Henrique Gomes, for access to and help with the marvelous Adventist Digital Library; Gershom Gorenberg, on the history of Melody the cow; Joel Greenblatt, for comments on his extension of the Galton experiment; Thomas Hegghammer, on the eschatology of the Meccan siege; Ron Inglehart, for quantitative data on religiosity; Philip Jenkins on the 1980s Satanism moral panic; Philip Johnson-Laird and Barry Popik, on the origins of the modern concept of confirmation bias; Toby C. Jones, on the eastern Saudi Shiite rebellion; Brendan Karch, on Hitler's power of suasion; Ofir and Haim Kedar, on Zionist history; Daniel Levitin, on the role of music in delusional propagation; Peter Logan, on Mackay's literary history; Mike Piper, on the history of retirement plans; Susan Pulliam and Penny Wang, on the ground-level history of the 1990s internet bubble; Peter Richerson, on the group evolution controversy; Jean-Paul Rodrigue, on the explosive growth of internet traffic; Terry Ann Rogers, for general editorial comments; Greg Schramm, on internet history; Robert Shiller, on the relevance of the epidemic equations to finance; Matthew Avery Sutton, on modern dispensationalism; Robert Trivers, on the finer points of evolutionary psychology; Brett Whalen, on the connection between the Jaochites and Munster Anabaptists; Barrie Wigmore, on Franklin Roosevelt's preinauguration stance on the gold standard; and Jason Zweig, for comments on early financial bubbles and artistic advise.

I am especially grateful to David Cook and Jean-Pierre Filiu for detailed help with Islamic apocalyptic thought and literature. Crawford Gribben generously guided me through the intricacies of the historical origins of dispensationalism. Richard Gerrig described in detail the ability of compelling narratives to corrode analytical ability. Ronald Numbers and Andrew Odlyzko availed me of their encyclopedic knowledge of, respectively, Millerism and early financial bubbles.

Finally, Christopher Mackay (no relationship to Charles Mackay), more than generously availed me of his singular knowledge of the Anabaptist Madness.

All of the above prevented me from more grossly exposing the lacunae in my knowledge of these areas.

George Gibson shepherded the book from the initial drafts through production, and along the way not only transformed a jumble of indecipherable and disconnected chapters into a coherent whole, but also imparted to me some sorely needed editorial discipline and large blocks of wisdom accumulated over his decades in publishing.

Emily Burns for help with image permissions, Gretchen Mergenthaler for the jacket, Julia Berner-Tobin for precision, John Mark Boling for publicity, Martin Lubikowski for the maps, and Lewis O'Brien for permissions advice and support.

And, as always, Jane Gigler, my wife and first reader, provided invaluable editorial and substantive input from the earliest stages.

I would be lost without her.

ILLUSTRATION CREDITS

Figure 1-1, page 34, drawing by Mason Wiest.

Figure 3-1, page 84, Mississippi Company Share Price, 1719–1720. Source Data: Antoin E. Murphy, *John Law* (Oxford: Clarendon Press, 1997), 208.

Figure 3-2, page 96, South Sea Share Prices, 1719–1721. Source Data: Larry Neal, *The Rise of Financial Capitalism* (Cambridge: Cambridge University Press, 1990), 233–234.

Figure 4-1, page 118, British Railway Share Prices 1830–1850. Source Data: Arthur D. Gayer, W.W. Rostow, and Anna Jacobsen Schwartz, *The Growth and Fluctuation of the British Economy 1790*–1850 (Oxford, UK: Clarendon Press, 1953), I:375.

Figure 7-1, page 187, Dow Jones Industrial Average 1925–1935. Source Data: http://stooq.com/q/?s=^dji, accessed November 6, 2019.

Figure 10-1, page 258, Evangelical Population of the United States. Source Data: Pew Foundation from https://www.theatlas.com/charts/JMn6Nk_nM, accessed March 11, 2020.

Figure 10-2, page 260, Belief in God among American Scientists 1914–1916. Source Data: James H. Leuba, *The Belief in God and Immortality* (Chicago: The Open Court Publishing Company, 1921), 255.

Figure 10-3, page 262, Hard News Knowledge versus Educational Level. Source Data: Source: James Curran et al., "Media System, Public Knowledge and Democracy: A Comparative Study," *European Journal of Communications* Vol. 4, No. 1 (2009): 19 (Table 5).

Figure 13-1, page 305, Federal Funds Rate 1997–2000. Source Data: Federal Reserve Board, https://fred.stlouisfed.org/series/FEDFUNDS, accessed February 20, 2019.

Figure 14-1, page 327, CNBC and Stock Prices. Source Data, J. Felix Meshcke, "CEO Appearances on CNBC," working paper; and Ekaterina V. Karniouchina et al., "Impact of Mad Money Stock Recommendations: Merging Financial and Marketing Perspectives," *Journal of Marketing* Vol. 73 (November 2009): 252 (Table 1).

Figure 14-2, page 337, NASDAQ Composite Index 1995–2003. Source Data: https://finance.yahoo.com/quote/%5EIXIC/history?p=%5EIXIC, accessed March 19, 2020.

BIBLIOGRAPHY

20/20, "The Devil Worshippers," see https://www.youtube.com/watch?v=vG_w
-uElGbM, https://www.youtube.com/watch?v=gG0ncaf-jhI, and https://www
.youtube.com/watch?v=HwSP3j7RJlU.

Ahamed, Liaquat, *Lords of Finance* (New York: Penguin, 2009).

Ainsworth, William Harrison, *The South Sea Bubble* (Leipzig: Bernhard Tauchnitz, 1868).

Akenson, Donald Harman, *Discovering the End of Time* (Montreal: McGill-Queen's University Press, 2016).

Allen, Frederick Lewis, *The Lords of Creation* (Chicago: Quadrangle Paperbacks, 1966).

Allen, Frederick Lewis, *Only Yesterday* (New York: Perennial Classics, 2000).

Al-Awlaki, Anwar, full text of "Anwar Nasser Aulaqi" from FBI files, https://archive.org/stream/AnwarNasserAulaqi/Anwar%20Nasser%20Aulaqi%2010_djvu.txt.

Ambrose, Stephen E., *Undaunted Courage* (New York: Simon and Shuster, 1996).

Anderson, Robert, *The Coming Prince* (London: Hodder and Stoughton, 1881).

Anderson, Robert, *Unfulfilled Prophecy and "The Hope of the Church"* (London: Pickering & Inglis, 1923).

Anglim, Simon, *Orde Wingate and the British Army, 1922–1944* (London: Routledge, 2010).

Anonymous, *Advent Herald*, Vol. 8, No. 3 (August 21, 1844): 20.

Anonymous, "Apocalypse Cow," *The New York Times*, March 30, 1997.

Anonymous, *Bend Bulletin* (Oregon), July 16, 1938, 1, 5.

Anonymous, "Bible Prophecy and the Mid-East Crisis," *Moody Monthly* Vol. 68, No. 1 (July/August 1967): 22–24.

Anonymous, "The Book of Tribulations and Portents of the Last Hour," https://sunnah.com/muslim/54/44, accessed September 6, 2019.

Anonymous, "Christian evangelicals from the US flock to Holy Land in Israeli tourism boom," *Independent*, April 6, 2018.

Anonymous, "Doctor Claims World Will Upheave, Not End," *Pittsburgh Post-Gazette*, December 17, 1954.

Anonymous, "Fisher Sees Stocks Permanently High," *The New York Times*, October 16, 1929, 8.

Anonymous, "Former Ruler of Utilities Dies in France," *Berkeley Daily Gazette*, July 16, 1938.

Anonymous, "Hearings before a Subcommittee of the Committee on Banking and Currency of the United States Senate, Seventy-Second Congress on S. Res. 84 and S. Res. 239," 2170, http://www.senate.gov/artandhistory/history/common/investigations/pdf/Pecora_EBrown_testimony.pdf.

Anonymous, "History and Timothy McVeigh," *The New York Times*, June 11, 2011.

Anonymous, "Insull Drops Dead in a Paris Station," *The Montreal Gazette* Vol. 167, No. 170 (July 18, 1938): 9.

Anonymous, "Jacobellis v. Ohio," https://www.law.cornell.edu/supremecourt/text/378/184#ZC1-378_US_184fn2/2.

Anonymous, *The Midnight Cry!* Vol. 7, No. 17 (October 19, 1844): 132 (courtesy of Adventist Digital Library).

Anonymous, "The Partisan Brain," *The Economist* (December 7, 2018).

Anonymous, "Recent Views of the Palestine Conflict," *Journal of Palestine Studies* Vol. 10, No. 3 (Spring 1981): 175.

Anonymous, "Reveal Stock Pool Clears 5 Million in Week," *Chicago Tribune* Vol. 91, No. 121 (May 20, 1932): 1.

Anonymous, "The Revival of Slavery before the Hour," *Dabiq* Vol. 4 (September 2014): 17.

Anonymous, "The Secret History of the South Sea Scheme," in *A Collection of Several Pieces of Mr. John Toland* (London: J. Peele, 1726).

Anonymous, *The Signs of the Times* Vol. 6, No. 16 (June 23, 1843): 123 (courtesy of Adventist Digital Library).

Anonymous, *The Signs of the Times* Vol. 6, No. 17 (December 13, 1843): 144.

Anonymous, *The South Sea Bubble* (London: Thomas Boys, 1825).

Anonymous, "William Martin," *The Economist*, August 6, 1998.

Applebome, Peter, "Jerry Falwell, Moral Majority Founder, Dies at 73," *The New York Times*, May 16, 2007, A1.

Archer, Henry, *The Personall Reign of Christ Vpon Earth*, Early English Books Online, http://eebo.chadwyck.com.

Arcuri, Luciano, and Gün Semin, "Language Use in Intergroup Contexts: The Linguistic Intergroup Bias," *Journal of Personality and Social Psychology* Vol. 57, No. 6 (1989): 981–993.

Armitage, Thomas, *A History of Baptists* (New York: Bryan, Taylor & Co.), 1887.

Arnold, Phillip "The Davidian Dilemma—To Obey God or Man?," in James R. Lewis, Ed., *From the Ashes* (Lanham, MD: Rowman & Littlefield Publishers, Inc., 1994).

Arthur, Anthony, *The Tailor-King* (New York: Thomas Dunne Books, 1999).

Asch, Solomon E., "Studies of Independence and Conformity: A Minority of One Against a Unanimous Majority," *Psychological Monographs* Vol. 70, No. 9 (1956): 1–70. See also Asch, *Social Psychology* (New York: Prentice-Hall, 1952), 450–501.

Asness, Clifford, "Bubble Logic: Or, How to Learn to Stop Worrying and Love the Bull," working paper, https://ssrn.com/abstract=240371.

Aspray, William, et al., *Food in the Internet Age* (New York: Springer Science & Business Media, 2013).

Associated Press, "Davidian Compound Had Huge Weapon Cache, Ranger Says," *Los Angeles Times*, July 7, 2000.

Auerbach, Jerold S., *Hebron Jews* (Plymouth, UK: Rowman & Littlefield Publishers, Inc., 2009).

Axtman, Chris, "How Enron awards do, or don't, trickle down," *Christian Science Monitor*, June 20, 2005.

Bacon, Francis, *The New Organon* (New York: The Bobbs-Merrill Company, Inc., 1960).

Bagehot, Walter, *Lombard Street* (New York: Scribner, Armstrong & Co., 1873).

Balen, Malcolm, *The Secret History of the South Sea Bubble* (New York: HarperCollins, 2003).

Balmer, Randall, *Encyclopedia of Evangelism* (Waco, TX: Baylor University Press, 2004).

Banerjee, Neela, "Religion and Its Role Are in Dispute at the Service Academies," *The New York Times*, June 25, 2008.

Bar-El, Yair, et al., "Jerusalem syndrome," *British Journal of Psychiatry* 176 (2000): 86–90.

Barrett, Richard, "Foreign Fighters in Syria," The Soufan Group, June 2014.

Barrionuevo, Alexi, "Did Ken Lay Demonstrate Credibility?" *The New York Times*, May 3, 2006.

Barton, Bruce, "Is There Anything Here that Other Men Couldn't Do?" *American Magazine* 95 (February 1923): 128.

Bates, Joseph, *The Biography of Elder Joseph Bates* (Battle Creek, MI: The Steam Press, 1868).

Baumeister, Roy F., et al., "Bad Is Stronger Than Good," *Review of General Psychology* Vol. 5, No. 4 (2001): 323–370.

BBC News, "Dabiq: Why is Syrian town so important for IS?" October 4, 2016, http://www.bbc.com/news/world-middle-east-30083303.

Bebbington, David W., *Evangelicalism in Modern Britain* (London: Routledge, 1989).

Beck, Julie, "Vaccine Skepticism and 'Big Government,'" *The Atlantic*, September 17, 2015.

Bell, Eric Temple, *The Magic of Numbers* (New York: Dover Publications, Inc., 1991).

Belloc, Hilaire, *The Modern Traveler* (London: Edward Arnold, 1898).

Benaziz, Amar, and Nick Thompson, "Is ISIS leader Abu Bakr Baghdadi's bling timepiece a Rolex or an 'Islamic watch'?" CNN, July 10, 2014, http://www.cnn.com/2014/07/10/world/meast/iraq-baghdadi-watch/index.html.

Bergman, Ronen, *Rise and Kill First* (New York: Random House, 2018).

Berle, Adolph A. Jr., and Gardiner C. Means, *The Modern Corporation and Private Property* (New York: The Macmillan Company, 1948).

Berlin, Isaiah, *The Proper Study of Mankind* (New York: Farrar, Straus and Giroux, 1998).

Berners-Lee, Tim, *Weaving the Web* (San Francisco: HarperSanFrancisco, 1999).

Berns, Gregory S., et al., "Predictability Modulates Human Brain Response to Reward," *The Journal of Neuroscience* Vol. 21, No. 8 (April 15, 2001): 2793–2798.

Bernstein, William J., "The Market Villain: It's Not Your Uncle," *The Wall Street Journal*, April 19, 2000.

Bernstein, William J., *The Birth of Plenty* (New York: McGraw-Hill Inc., 2004).

Bernstein, William J., *The Four Pillars of Investing* (New York: McGraw-Hill, Inc., 2002).

Bernstein, William J., *The Intelligent Asset Allocator* (New York: McGraw-Hill, Inc., 2000).

Bernstein, William J., *Masters of the Word* (New York: Grove/Atlantic, 2013).

Bersaglieri, Todd, et al., "Genetic Signatures of Strong Recent Positive Selection at the Lactase Gene," *American Journal of Human Genetics* Vol. 74, No. 6 (April 2004): 1111–1120.

Bigler, Rebecca S., et al., "When Groups Are Not Created Equal: Effects of Group Status on the Formation of Intergroup Attitudes in Children," *Child Development* Vol. 72, No. 4 (July/August 2001): 1151–1162.

Blackstone, William E., *Jesus Is Coming* (Chicago: The Moody Bible Institute, 1916).

Blair, Bruce, *Frontline* interview, https://www.pbs.org/wgbh/pages/frontline/shows/russia/interviews/blair.html.

Blair, Bruce, *The Logic of Accidental Nuclear War* (Washington, DC: The Brookings Institution, 1993).

Blau, Benjamin M., et al., "Gambling Preferences, Options Markets, and Volatility," *Journal of Quantitative and Financial Analysis* Vol. 51, No. 2 (April 2016): 515–540.

Blickle, Peter, *The Revolution of 1525*, trans. Thomas A. Brady, Jr. and H.C. Erik Midelfort (Baltimore: The Johns Hopkins University Press, 1981).

Bliss, Sylvester, *Memoirs of William Miller* (Boston: Joshua V. Himes, 1853).

Block, Brian P., and John Hostettler, *Hanging in the Balance* (Sherfield Gables, UK: Waterside Press, 1997).

Blum, Ben, "The Lifespan of a Lie," https://medium.com/s/trustissues/the-lifespan-of-a-lie-d869212b1f62.

Boutelle, Louis, *Sketch of the Life and Religious Experience of Eld. Louis Boutelle* (Boston: Advent Christian Publication Society, 1891).

Boyd, Robert, and Peter J. Richerson, "Culture and the evolution of human cooperation," *Philosophical Transactions of the Royal Society* Vol. 364, No. 1533 (November 12, 2009): 3281–3288.

Boyer, Paul, "America's Doom Industry," https://www.pbs.org/wgbh/pages/frontline/shows/apocalypse/explanation/doomindustry.html.

Boyer, Paul, *When Time Shall Be No More* (Cambridge: The Harvard/Belknap Press, 1992).

Bradford, R.W., "Who Started the Fires? Mass Murder, American Style," and "Fanning the Flames of Suspicion: The Case Against Mass Suicide at Waco," in *Armageddon in Waco* (Chicago: University of Chicago Press, 1995).

Breiter, Hans C., and Bruce R. Rosen, "Functional Magnetic Resonance Imaging of the Brain Reward Circuitry in the Human," *Annals of the New York Academy of Sciences* Vol. 877, No. 1 (February 6, 2006): 523–547.

Bromley, Edward D., and Edward G. Silver, "The Davidian Tradition," in Stuart A. Wright, *Armageddon at Waco* (Chicago: University of Chicago Press, 1995).

Brown, Ira V., "The Millerites and the Boston Press," *The New England Quarterly* Vol. 16, No. 4 (December 1943): 599.

Bryan-Low, Cassel, and Suzanne McGee, "Enron Short Seller Detected Red Flags in Regulatory Filings," *The Wall Street Journal*, November 5, 2001.

Bryce, Robert, "Flying High," *Boston Globe Magazine*, September 29, 2002.

Bunzel, Cole, *From Paper State to Caliphate: The Ideology of the Islamic State* (Washington, DC: Center for Middle East Policy at Brookings, 2015).

Bunzel, Cole, "The Caliphate's Scholar-in-Arms," http://www.jihadica.com/the-caliphate%E2%80%99s-scholar-in-arms/, accessed June 10, 2018.

Burke, Jason, "Rise and fall of Isis: its dream of a caliphate is over, so what now?" *The Guardian*, October 21, 2018, https://www.theguardian.com/world/2017/oct/21/isis-caliphate-islamic-state-raqqa-iraq-islamist.

Burr, William, and Thomas S. Blanton, "The Submarines of October," National Security Archive (October 31, 2002), https://www.webcitation.org/67Zh0rqhC?url=http://www.gwu.edu/%7Ensarchiv/NSAEBB/NSAEBB75/.

Burroughs, Joseph Birkbeck, *Titan, Son of Saturn* (Oberlin, OH: The Emeth Publishers, 1905).

Burton, Jonathan, "From Fame, Fortune to Flamed-Out Star," *The Wall Street Journal*, March 10, 2010.

Butler, Jonathan M., and Ronald L. Numbers, Introduction, in Ronald L. Numbers and Jonathan M. Butler, Eds., *The Disappointed* (Bloomington and Indianapolis: Indiana University Press, 1987).

Callimachi, Rukmimi, and Eric Schmitt, "ISIS Names New Leader and Confirms al-Baghdadi's Death," *The New York Times*, October 31, 2019.

Campbell-Meiklejohn, Daniel K., et al., "How the Opinion of Others Affects Our Valuation of Objects," *Current Biology* Vol. 20, No. 13 (July 13, 2010): 1165–1170.

Cannon, Lou, *President Reagan: The Role of a Lifetime* (New York: Simon & Schuster, 1991).

Capp, B. S., *The Fifth Monarchy Men* (London: Faber and Faber, 1972).

Carhart, Mark M., "On Persistence in Mutual Fund Performance," *Journal of Finance* Vol. 52, No. 1 (March 1997): 57–82.

Carswell, John, *The South Sea Bubble* (Gloucestershire, UK: Sutton Publishing, Ltd., 2001).

Cassidy, John, *dot-con* (New York: Penguin Press, 2002).

Cetorelli, Valeria, "Mortality and kidnapping estimates for the Yazidi population in the area of Mount Sinjar, Iraq, in August 2014: A retrospective household survey," *PLOS Medicine* May 9, 2017, https://doi.org/10.1371/journal.pmed.1002297.

Chancellor, Edward, *Devil Take the Hindmost* (New York: Plume, 2000).

Charles, R.H., *Lectures on the Apocalypse* (London: Humphrey Milford, Oxford University Press, 1922).

Cheng, Jonathan, "A Barber Misses Market's New Buzz," *The Wall Street Journal*, March 8, 2013.

Chibi, Allan, *The Wheat and the Tares* (Eugene, OR: Pickwick Publications, 2015).

Christiansen, Paul, *Orchestrating Public Opinion* (Amsterdam: Amsterdam University Press, 2018).

Chulov, Martin, "ISIS: the inside story," *The Guardian*, December 11, 2014,

Church, Philip A.F., "Dispensational Christian Zionism: A Strange but Acceptable Aberration of Deviant Heresy?," *Westminster Theological Journal* Vol. 71 (2009): 375–398.

Clapham, J. H., *An Economic History of Modern Britain: The Early Railway Age 1820–1850* (Cambridge, UK: Cambridge University Press, 1939).

Clark, Jim, *Netscape Time* (New York: St. Martin's Press, 1999).

Cohen, Yoel, "The Political Role of the Israeli Chief Rabbinate in the Temple Mount Question," *Jewish Political Studies Review* Vol. 11, No. 1 (Spring 1999): 101–105.

Cohn, Norman, *Cosmos, Chaos, and the World to Come* (New Haven, CT: Yale University Press, 1995).

Cohn, Norman, *The Pursuit of the Millennium* (New York: Oxford University Press, 1970).

Coleman, Calmetta Y., "Beardstown Ladies Add Disclaimer That Makes Returns Look 'Hooey,'" *The Wall Street Journal*, February 27, 1998.

Coll, Steve, *The Bin Ladens* (New York: The Penguin Press, 2008).

Collins, John J., *The Apocalyptic Imagination* (Grand Rapids, MI: William B. Erdmans Publishing Company, 1988).

Condorelli, Stefano, "The 1719 stock euphoria: a pan-European perspective," working paper, 2016, https://mpra.ub.uni-muenchen.de/68652/, accessed April 27, 2016.

Cook, David, "Abu Musa'b al-Suri and Abu Musa'b al-Zarqawi: The Apocalyptic Theorist and the Apocalyptic Practitioner," private working paper, cited with permission from the author.

Cook, David, "Fighting to Create a Just State: Apocalypticism in Radical Muslim Discourse," in David Cook, Ed., *Contemporary Muslim Apocalyptic Literature* (Syracuse, NY: Syracuse University Press, 2008).

Cook, David, *Studies in Muslim Apocalyptic* (Princeton, NJ: The Darwin Press, Inc., 2002).

Cook, John, and Marni Leff, "Webvan is gone, but HomeGrocer.com may return," *Seattle Post-Intelligencer*, July 9, 2001.

Cornwall, Marie, "The Determinants of Religious Behavior: A Theoretical Model and Empirical Test," *Social Forces* Vol. 66, No. 2 (December 1989): 572–592.

Cosmides, Leda, and John Tooby, "Cognitive Adaptations for Social Exchange," in Jerome H. Barkow et al., *The Adapted Mind* (New York: Oxford University Press, 1992), 180–206.

Court, John M., *Myth and History in the Book of Revelation* (Atlanta, GA: John Knox Press, 1979).

Cowie, Ian, "Oriental risks and rewards for optimistic occidentals," *The Daily Telegraph*, August 7, 2004.

Cross, Whitney R., *The Burned-over District* (New York: Harper Torchbooks, 1950).

Crowquill, Alfred, "Railway Mania," *The Illustrated London News*, November 1, 1845.

Crowther, Samuel, "Everybody Ought to Be Rich: An Interview with John J. Raskob," *Ladies' Home Journal*, August 19, 1929, reprinted in David M.P. Freund, *The Modern American Metropolis* (New York: Wiley-Blackwell, 2015), 157–159.

Cuevas, John, *Cat Island* (Jefferson, NC: McFarland & Company, Inc., 2011).

Cumming-Bruce, Nick, "ISIS Committed Genocide Against Yazidis in Syria and Iraq, U.N. Panel Says," *The New York Times*, June 16, 2018.

Cuomo, Joe, "Joe Cuomo and the Prophecy of Armageddon," 1984 WBAI-FM audiocassette recording.

Curran, James, et al., "Media System, Public Knowledge and Democracy: A Comparative Study," *European Journal of Communications* Vol. 14, No. 1 (2009): 5–26.

Dabiq, "The Return of the Khilafah," https://jihadology.net/2016/07/31/new-issue-of-the-islamic-states-magazine-dabiq-15/.

Dale, Richard, *The First Crash* (Princeton: Princeton University Press, 2014).

Davenport, Richard Alfred, *Sketches of Imposture, Deception, and Credulity* (London: Thomas Tegg and Son, 1837).

Dawkins, Richard, *The Selfish Gene* (New York: Oxford University Press, 2009).

Dayan, Moshe, *Story of My Life* (New York: William Morrow and Company, Inc., 1976).

De Baviére, *Letters of Madame Charlotte Elizabeth de Baviére, Duchess of Orleans*, ii274, https://archive.org/stream/lettersofmadamec02orluoft/lettersofmadamec02orluoft_djvu.txt.

Dejevsky, Mary, "Totally Bananas," *The Independent*, November 9, 1999.

De Long, J. Bradford, and Andrei Schleifer, "The Stock Market Bubble of 1929: Evidence from Closed-end Mutual Funds," *The Journal of Economic History* Vol. 51, No. 3 (September 1991): 675–700.

Department of the Treasury, "Report of the Department of the Treasury on the Bureau of Tobacco, Alcohol, and Firearms investigation of Vernon Wayne Howell, also known as David Koresh," September 1993, 95–100, available at https://archive.org/stream/reportofdepartme00unit/reportofdepartme00unit_djvu.txt.

Dick, Everett N., "Advent Camp Meetings of the 1840s," *Adventist Heritage* Vol. 4, No. 2 (Winter 1977): 5.

Dick, Everett N., *William Miller and the Advent Crisis 1831–1844* (Berrien Springs MI: Andrews University Press, 1994).

Dickinson, Emily (Mabel Loomis Todd and T.W. Higginson, Eds.), *The Poems of Emily Dickinson* (Raleigh, NC: Hayes Barton Press, 2007).

Di Giovanni, Janine, "The Militias of Baghdad," *Newsweek*, November 26, 2014.

Di Giovanni, Janine, "Who Is ISIS Leader Abu Bakr Baghdadi?," *Newsweek*, December 8, 2014.

Dimock, Michael, and Samuel L. Popkin, "Political Knowledge in Comparative Perspective," in Shanto Iyengar and Richard Reeves, Eds., *Do the Media Govern?* (Thousand Oaks, CA: Sage Publications, 1997).

Doan, Ruth Alden, *The Miller Heresy, Millerism, and American Culture* (Philadelphia: Temple University Press, 1987).

Dougherty, Philip H., "Advertising; Who Bought Time on 'The Day After,'" *The New York Times*, November 22, 1983.

Easton, Thomas, and Scott Wooley, "The $20 Billion Crumb," *Forbes* April 19, 1999.

Edwards, I.E.S, Ed., *The Cambridge Ancient History*, 3rd Ed. (Cambridge, UK: University Press, 1975).

Eichengreen, Barry, *Golden Fetters* (Oxford: Oxford University Press, 1995).

Eisenstein, Elizabeth, *The Printing Press as an Agent of Change* (Cambridge, UK: Cambridge University Press, 1979).

Eliade, Mircea, *Cosmos and History*, trans. Willard R. Trask (New York: Harper Torchbooks, 1959).

Elkind, Peter, et al., "The Trouble With Frank Quattrone was the top investment banker in Silicon Valley. Now his firm is exhibit A in a probe of shady IPO deals," *Fortune*, September 3, 2001.

Ellison, Christopher G., and John P. Bartkowski, "Babies Were Being Beaten," in Stuart A. Wright, *Armageddon in Waco* (Chicago: University of Chicago Press, 1995).

Ellsberg, Daniel, *The Doomsday Machine* (New York: Bloomsbury, 2017).

Emshwiller, John R., and Rebecca Smith, "Murky Waters: A Primer On the Enron Partnerships," *The Wall Street Journal*, January 21, 2001.

England, Mark, "9-1-1 records panic, horror," *Waco Tribune-Herald*, June 10, 1993.

England, Mark, and Darlene McCormick, "The Sinful Messiah: Part One," *Waco Tribune-Herald*, February 27, 1993.

Ennis, Thomas W., "E. Schuyler English, Biblical Scholar, 81," *The New York Times*, March 18, 1981.

Evensen, Bruce, "Robertson's Credibility Problem," *Chicago Tribune*, February 23, 1988.

Evans, Clark, Ed., *The Internal Debts of the United States* (New York: The Macmillan Company, 1933).

Federal Bureau of Investigation, "The Megiddo Project," October 20, 1999, 28–29, available at http://www.cesnur.org/testi/FBI_004.htm.

Festinger, Leon, et al., *When Prophecy Fails* (New York: Harper Torchbooks, 1956).

Filiu, Jean-Pierre, *Apocalypse in Islam*, trans. M.B. Devoise (Berkeley: University of California Press, 2011).

Filkins, Dexter, et al., "How Surveillance and Betrayal Led to a Hunt's End," *The New York Times*, June 9, 2006.

Fisher, Irving, *The Theory of Interest* (New York: The Macmillan Company, 1930).

Fishman, Hertzel, *American Protestantism and a Jewish State* (Detroit: Wayne State University Press, 1973).

Fitzgerald, F. Scott, "The Crack-Up," *Esquire* (February 1936), http://www.pbs.org/wnet/americanmasters/f-scott-fitzgerald-essay-the-crack-up/1028/, accessed March 5, 2016.

Forbes, Bruce David, "How Popular are the Left Behind Books . . . and Why?," in Jeanne Halgren Kilde and Bruce David Forbes, Eds., *Rapture, Revelation, and the End Times* (New York: Palgrave Macmillan, 2004).

Forster, John, *The Life of Charles Dickens* (London: Clapman and Hall, 1890).

Foster, Kevin R., and Hanna Kokko, "The Evolution of Superstitions and Superstition-like Behaviour," *Proceedings of the Biological Sciences* Vol. 276, No. 1654 (January 7, 2009): 31–37.

Francis, John, *A History of the English Railway* (London: Longman, Brown, Green, & Longmans, 1851).

Frederick, Shane, "Cognitive Reflection and Decision Making," *Journal of Economic Perspectives* Vol. 19, No. 4 (Fall 2005): 25–42.

Friend, Ronald, et al., "A puzzling misinterpretation of the Asch 'conformity' study," *European Journal of Social Psychology* Vol. 20 (1990): 29–44.

Friesen, Abraham, *Thomas Muentzer, a Destroyer of the Godless* (Berkeley: University of California Press, 1990).

Froom, Leroy Edwin, *The Prophetic Faith of Our Fathers* (Washington, DC: Review and Herald, 1946).

Fryckholm, Amy Johnson, *Rapture Culture* (Oxford: Oxford University Press, 2004).

Galbraith, John Kenneth, *The Great Crash 1929* (Boston: Houghton Mifflin Company, 1988).

Galbraith, John Kenneth, *A Short History of Financial Euphoria* (Knoxville, TN: Whittle Direct Books, 1990).

Galton, Francis, "The Ballot-Box," *Nature* Vol. 75, No. 1952 (March 28, 1907): 509.

Galton, Francis, "Vox Populi" *Nature* Vol. 75, No. 1949 (March 7, 1907): 450–451.

Galton, Francis, Letters to the Editor, *Nature* Vol. 75, No. 1952 (March 28, 1907): 509–510.

Gardner, Dan, and Philip Tetlock, "What's Wrong with Expert Predictions," https://www.cato-unbound.org/2011/07/11/dan-gardner-philip-tetlock/overcoming-our-aversion-acknowledging-our-ignorance.

Gardner, Martin, *Fads and Fallacies in the Name of Science* (New York: Dover Publications, 1957).

Garrison, William Lloyd, *The Letters of William Lloyd Garrison*, ed. Walter M. Merrill (Cambridge: Belknap Press of Harvard University Press, 1973).

Gates, David, "The Pop Prophets," *Newsweek*, May 24, 2004, 48.

Gates, Robert M., *From the Shadows* (New York: Simon & Schuster Paperbacks, 1996).

Gelertner, David, "A Religion of Special Effects," *The New York Times*, March 30, 1997.

Gerolymatos, André, *Castles Made of Sand* (New York: Thomas Dunne Press, 2010).

Gerrig, Richard J., *Experiencing Narrative Worlds* (New Haven, CT: Yale University Press, 1993).

Gibbs, Nancy, "Apocalypse Now," *Time* Vol. 160, No. 1, (July 1, 2002): 47.

Gilbert, Martin, *Winston S. Churchill* (Boston: Houghton Mifflin Company, 1977).

Gilder, George, "The Faith of a Futurist," *The Wall Street Journal*, January 1, 2000.

Gilovich, Thomas, "Biased Evaluation and Persistence in Gambling," *Journal of Personality and Social Psychology* Vol. 44, No. 6 (June 1983): 1110–1126.

Gladwell, Malcolm, *David and Goliath* (New York: Little, Brown and Company, 2013).

Glassman, James K., "Is Government Strangling the New Economy?," *The Wall Street Journal*, April 6, 2000.

Glassman, James K., and Kevin A. Hassett, *Dow 36,000* (New York: Times Business, 1999).

Goldgar, Ann, *Tulipmania* (Chicago: University of Chicago Press, 2007).

Gonen, Rivka, *Contested Holiness* (Jersey City: KTAV Publishing House, 2003).

Gongloff, Mark, "Where Are They Now: The Beardstown Ladies," *The Wall Street Journal*, May 1, 2006.

Goodstein, Laurie, "Air Force Chaplain Tells of Academy Proselytizing," *The New York Times*, May 12, 2005.

Gordon, Keith, "The End of (the Other Side of) the World: Apocalyptic Belief in the Australian Political Structure," *Intersections* Vol. 10, No. 1 (2009): 609–645.

Gorenberg, Gershom, *The End of Days* (New York: The Free Press, 2000).

Graeber, David, *Debt* (New York: Melville House, 2012).

Graham, Benjamin, and David Dodd, *Security Analysis* (New York: Whittlesey House, 1934).

Graham, John R., and Campbell R. Harvey, "Grading the Performance of Market Timing Newsletters," *Financial Analysts Journal* Vol. 53, No. 6 (November/December 1997): 54–66.

Graham, Stephen R., "Hal Lindsey," in Charles H. Lippy, Ed., *Twentieth-Century Shapers of American Popular Religion* (New York: Greenwood Press, 1989).

Graves, Richard Hastings, *The Whole Works of Richard Graves, D.D.* (Dublin: William Curry, Jun. and Company, 1840).

Green, Melanie C., and Timothy C. Brock, "The Role of Transportation in the Persuasiveness of Public Narratives," *Journal of Personality and Social Psychology* Vol. 79, No. 5 (2000): 701–721.

Greenblatt, Joel, and Barry Ritholtz, *Masters in Business*, April 20, 2018, https://assets.bwbx.io/av/users/iqjWHBFdfxIU/vcNFFMk_gBGg/v2.mp3.

Gribben, Crawford, *Evangelical Millennialism in the Trans-Atlantic World, 1500–2000* (New York: Palgrave Macmillan, 2011).

Gribben, Crawford, *Writing the Rapture* (Oxford: Oxford University Press, 2009).

Gullapalli, Diya, "Van Wagoner to Step Down As Manager of Growth Fund," *The Wall Street Journal*, August 4, 2008.

Haag, Matthew, "Robert Jeffress, Pastor Who Said Jews Are Going to Hell, Led Prayer at Jerusalem Embassy," *The New York Times*, May 14, 2018.

Halberstam, David, *The Best and the Brightest* (New York: Random House, 1972).

Hall, Carla, et al., "The Night of 'The Day After,'" *The Washington Post*, November 21, 1983.

Hamilton, W.D., "The Genetical Evolution of Social Behaviour I," *Journal of Theoretical Biology* Vol. 7, No. 1 (July 1964): 1–16; and Part II, 17–52.

Haney, C., et al., "Interpersonal Dynamics in a Simulated Prison," *International Journal of Criminology and Penology* Vol. 1 (1973): 69–97.

Harding, Susan Friend, *The Book of Falwell* (Princeton, NJ: Princeton University Press, 2000).

Harrell, David Edwin, Jr., *Pat Robertson* (Grand Rapids, MI: William B. Eerdmans Publishing Company, 2010).

Harrison, Paul, "Rational Equity Valuation at the Time of the South Sea Bubble," *History of Political Economy* Vol. 33, No. 2 (Summer 2001): 269–281.

Hashimi, Sohail H., Ed., *Just Wars, Holy Wars, and Jihads* (Oxford: Oxford University Press, 2012).

Heider, Fritz, "Attitudes and Cognitive Organization," *The Journal of Psychology* Vol. 21 (1946): 107–112.

Herapath, John, *The Railway Magazine* (London: Wyld and Son, 1836).

Herbers, John, "Religious Leaders Tell of Worry on Armageddon View Ascribed to Reagan," *The New York Times*, October 21, 1984, 32.

Heresco, Aaron, *Shaping the Market: CNBC and the Discourses of Financialization* (Ph.D. thesis, Pennsylvania State University, 2014).

Herodotus, *The Histories* (Baltimore: Penguin Books, 1954).

Herzog, Chaim, *The Arab-Israeli Wars* (New York: Random House, 1982).

Hesiod, *Works and Days*, http://www.theoi.com/Text/HesiodWorksDays.html.

Hetzel, Robert L., *The Monetary Policy of the Federal Reserve* (New York: Cambridge University Press, 2008).

Heukelom, Floris, "Measurement and Decision Making at the University of Michigan in the 1950s and 1960s," Nijmegen Center for Economics, Institute for Management Research, Radboud University, Nijmegen, 2009, http://www.ru.nl/publish/pages/516298/nice_09102.pdf.

Himes, Joshua V., *The Midnight Cry!* Vol. 6, No. 13 (April 11, 1844), 305 (courtesy of Adventist Digital Library).

Himes, Joshua V., Ed., *Miller's Works*, http://centrowhite.org.br/files/ebooks/apl/all/Miller/Miller%27s%20Works.%20Volume%201.%20Views%20of%20the%20Prophecies%20and%20Prophetic%20Chronology.pdf.

Himes, Joshua V., *Views of the Prophecies and Prophetic Chronologies, Selected from Manuscripts of William Miller* (Boston: Josuhua V. Himes, 1842).

Himmelstein, Linda, "Can You Sell Groceries Like Books?," Bloomberg News, July 25, 1999, http://www.bloomberg.com/news/articles/1999-07-25/can-you-sell-groceries-like-books.

Hitchens, Christopher, *God Is Not Great* (New York: Hachette Group, 2007).

Homer, Sidney, and Richard Sylla, *A History of Interest Rates*, 4th Ed. (Hoboken, NJ: John Wiley & Sons, 2005).

"H.R.K.," *Life in the Future*, unpublished manuscript, courtesy of Crawford Gribben.

Huertas, Thomas F., and Joan L. Silverman, "Charles E. Mitchell: Scapegoat of the Crash?," *The Business History Review* Vol. 60, No. 1 (Spring 1986): 81–103.

Hull, David L., *Science and Selection* (Cambridge, UK: Cambridge University Press, 2001).

Hullinger, Jerry M., "The Problem of Animal Sacrifices in Ezekiel 40–48," *Bibliotheca Sacra* Vol. 152 (July–September 1995): 279–289.

Huntington, Samuel P., *The Clash of Civilizations and the Remaking of the World Order* (New York: Simon & Shuster, 1996).

Hyde, Montgomery, *John Law* (London: W. H. Allen, 1969).

Ilmanen, Antti, "Do Financial Markets Reward Buying or Selling Insurance and Lottery Tickets?," *Financial Analysts Journal* Vol. 68, No. 5 (September/October 2012): 26–36

Ipsos Global Advisor, "Mayan Prophecy: The End of the World?," https://www.ipsos .com/sites/default/files/news_and_polls/2012-05/5610-ppt.pdf.

Izuma, Keise, and Ralph Adolphs, "Social Manipulation of Preference in the Human Brain," *Neuron* Vol. 78 (May 8, 2013): 563–573.

Jenkins, Philip, *Moral Panic* (New Haven, CT: Yale University Press, 1998).

Jenkins, Philip, and Daniel Maier-Katkin, "Satanism: Myth and reality in a contemporary moral panic," *Crime, Law and Social Change* Vol. 17 (1992): 53–75.

Jensen, Michael C., "The Performance of Mutual Funds in the Period 1945–64," *Journal of Finance* Vol. 23, No. 2 (May 1968): 389–416.

Johnson, H. Clark, *Gold, France, and the Great Depression, 1919-1932* (New Haven, CT: Yale University Press, 1997).

Johnson, Paul, *The Birth of the Modern* (New York: HarperCollins, 1991).

Johnson, Paul, *A History of the Jews* (New York: HarperPerennial, 1987).

Jones, Julie Scott, *Being the Chosen: Exploring a Christian Fundamentalist Worldview* (London: Routledge, 2010).

Jürgen-Goertz, Hans, *Thomas Müntzer*, trans. Jocelyn Jaquiery (Edinburgh: T&T Clark, 1993).

Kadlec, Charles W., *Dow 100,000* (Upper Saddle River, NJ: Prentice Hall Press, 1999).

Kahneman, Daniel, *Thinking, Fast and Slow* (New York: Farrar, Straus and Giroux, 2013).

Kahneman, Daniel, and Amos Tversky, "Intuitive Prediction: Biases and Corrective Procedures," *Advances in Decision Technology* (Defense Advanced Research Projects Agency, 1977).

Kahneman, Daniel, and Amos Tversky, "On the Psychology of Prediction," *Psychological Review* Vol. 80, No. 4 (July 1973): 237–251.

Kahneman, Daniel, and Amos Tversky, "On the study of statistical intuitions," *Cognition* Vol. 11 (1982): 123–141.

Kahneman, Daniel, and Amos Tversky, "Subjective Probability: A Judgment of Representativeness," *Cognitive Psychology* Vol. 3 (1972): 430–454.

Kaminker, Mendy, "Meet the Red Heifer," http://www.chabad.org/parshah/article_cdo/ aid/2620682/jewish/Meet-the-Red-Heifer.htm.

Karlgaard, Richard, "The Ghost of Netscape," *The Wall Street Journal*, August 9, 2005, A10.

Karniouchina, Ekaterina V., et al., "Impact of *Mad Money* Stock Recommendations: Merging Financial and Marketing Perspectives," *Journal of Marketing* Vol. 73 (November 2009): 244–266.

Karouny, Miriam, "Apocalyptic prophecies drive both sides to Syrian battle for end of time," Reuters, April 1, 2014, https://www.reuters.com/article/us-syria-crisis -prophecy-insight/apocalyptic-prophecies-drive-both-sides-to-syrian-battle -for-end-of-time-idUSBREA3013420140401.

Kaufman, Gordon D., "Nuclear Eschatology and the Study of Religion," *Journal of the American Academy of Religion* Vol. 51, No. 1 (March 1983): 3–14.

Kechichian, Joseph A., "Islamic Revivalism and Change in Saudi Arabia: Juhaymān Al'Utaybī's 'Letters' to the Saudi People," *The Muslim World* Vol. 80, No. 1 (January 1990): 9–15.

Kellner, Mark A., "John F. Walvoord, 92, longtime Dallas President, dies," *Christianity Today* Vol. 47, No. 2 (February 2003): 27.

Kelly, Dean M., "The Implosion of Mt. Carmel and Its Aftermath," in Stuart A. Wright, Ed., *Armageddon in Waco*, 360–361.

Kelly, William, Ed., *The Collected Writings of John Nelson Darby* (London: G. Morrish, 1867–1900).

Kennedy, Susan Estabrook, *The Banking Crisis of 1933* (Lexington KY: The University Press of Kentucky, 1973).

Kestenbaum, David, "What's a Bubble?," http://www.npr.org/sections/money/ 2013/11/15/245251539/whats-a-bubble.

Kestenberg-Gladstein, Ruth, "The 'Third Reich': A fifteenth-century polemic against Joachim, and its background," *Journal of the Warburg and Courtauld Institutes* Vol. 18, No. 3–4 (July–December 1955): 245–295.

Keynes, John Maynard, *A Tract on Monetary Reform* (London: Macmillan and Co., Limited, 1924).

Kimmage, David, and Kathleen Ridolfo, *Iraqi Insurgent Media* (Washington, DC: Radio Free Europe/Radio Liberty, 2007).

Kindleberger, Charles P., *Manias, Panics, and Crashes* (New York: John Wiley & Sons, 2000).

King, Wayne, "Robertson, Displaying Mail, Says He Will Join '88 Race," *The New York Times*, September 16, 1987, D30.

Kirban, Salem, *666* (Wheaton, IL: Tyndale House Publishers, 1970).

Kirkland, Frazar, *Cyclopedia of Commercial and Business Anecdotes* (New York: D. Appleton and Company, 1868).

Kirkpatrick, David D., "A best-selling formula in religious thrillers," *The New York Times*, February 11, 2002, C2.

Kirsch, Jonathan, "Hal Lindsey," *Publishers Weekly*, March 14, 1977, 30–32.

Klötzer, Ralf, "The Melchoirites and Münster," in John D. Roth and James M. Stayer, Eds., *A Companion to Anabaptism and Spiritualism, 1521–1700* (Leiden: Brill, 2007).

Knight, George R., *Millennial Fever* (Boise, ID: Pacific Press Publishing Association, 1993).

Kohut, Andrew, et al., *Eight Nation, People & The Press Survey* (Washington, DC: Times Mirror Center for People & The Press, 1994).

Koresh, David, uncompleted manuscript, https://digital.library.txstate.edu/bitstream/handle/10877/1839/375.pdf?sequence=1&isAllowed=y.

Kristof, Nicholas D., "Apocalypse (Almost) Now," *The New York Times*, November 24, 2004), A23.

Krugman, Paul, "Baby Sitting the Economy," http://www.pkarchive.org/theory/baby.html.

Kurtz, Howard, *The Fortune Tellers* (New York: The Free Press, 2000).

Kyle, Richard, *Apocalyptic Fever* (Eugene, OR: Cascade Books, 2012), https://www.youtube.com/watch?v=W0hWAxJ3_Js.

Lacey, Robert, *Inside the Kingdom* (New York: Viking Press, 2009).

LaHaye, Tim, and Jerry B. Jenkins, *Left Behind* (Wheaton, IL: Tyndale House Publishers, 1995).

LaHaye, Tim, Jerry B. Jenkins, and Sandi L. Swanson, *The Authorized Left Behind Handbook* (Wheaton, IL: Tyndale House Publishers, 2005).

Lahoud, Nelly, and Jonathan Pieslak, "Music of the Islamic State," *Survival* Vol. 61, No. 1 (2018): 153–168.

Lambert, Richard S., *The Railway King* (London: George Allen & Unwin Ltd., 1964).

Landman, Isaac, Ed., *The Universal Jewish Encyclopedia* (New York: Universal Jewish Encyclopedia, Inc., 1940).

Larsen, Stephen, *The Fundamentalist Mind* (Wheaton IL: Quest Books, 2014).

Larson, Edward J., and Larry Witham, "Leading scientists still reject God," *Nature* Vol. 344, No. 6691 (July 23, 1998): 313.

Laurent, Lionel, "What Bitcoin Is Really Worth May No Longer Be Such a Mystery," https://www.bloomberg.com/news/features/2018-04-19/what-bitcoin-is-really-worth-may-no-longer-be-such-a-mystery.

Law, John, *Essay on a Land Bank*, ed. Antoin E. Murphy (Dublin: Aeon Publishing, 1994).

Law, John, *Money and Trade Considered* (London: R. & A. Foulis, 1750).

LeDoux, J.E., "The lateral amygdaloid nucleus: sensory interface of the amygdala in fear conditioning," *The Journal of Neuroscience* Vol. 10, No. 4 (April 1990): 1062–1069.

Lee, William, *Daniel Defoe: His Life, and Recently Discovered Writings* (London: John Camden Hotten, Piccadilly, 1869).

Lettow, Paul, *Ronald Reagan and His Quest to Abolish Nuclear Weapons* (New York: Random House, 2005).

Leuba, James H., *The Belief in God and Immortality* (Chicago: The Open Court Publishing Company, 1921).

Lewis, Clayton H., and John R. Anderson, "Interference with Real World Knowledge," *Cognitive Psychology* Vol. 8 (1976): 311–335.

Lewis, James, R., *From the Ashes* (Lanham, MD: Rowman & Littlefield Publishers, Inc., 1994).

Lilliston, Lawrence, "Who Committed Child Abuse at Waco," in James R. Lewis, Ed., *From the Ashes* (Lanham, MD: Rowman & Littlefield Publishers, Inc., 1994).

Lincoln, Bruce, *Holy Terrors*, 2nd Ed. (Chicago: University of Chicago Press, 2006).

Lind, Michael, *Up from Conservatism* (New York: Free Press Paperbacks, 1999).

Lindsey, Hal, *Planet Earth—2000 A.D.* (Palos Verdes, CA: Western Front, Ltd., 1996).

Lindsey, Hal, *The 1980's: Countdown to Armageddon* (New York: Bantam Books, 1981).

Lindsey, Hal, "The Pieces Fall Together," *Moody Monthly* Vol. 68, No. 2 (October 1967): 26–28.

Lindsey, Hal, and C.C. Carlson, *The Late Great Planet Earth* (Grand Rapids MI: Zondervan Publishing House, 1977).

Lindsey, Hal, and C. C. Carlson, *Satan Is Alive and Well on Planet Earth* (Grand Rapids MI: Zondervan Publishing House, 1972).

Lindsey, Hal, and Cliff Ford, *Facing Millennial Midnight* (Beverly Hills, CA: Western Front, Ltd., 1998).

Lipin, Steven, et al., "Deals & Deal Makers: Bids & Offers," *The Wall Street Journal*, December 10, 1999.

Lippman, Thomas, *Inside the Mirage* (Boulder, CO: Westview Press, 2004).

Lister, Tim, et al., "ISIS goes global: 143 attacks in 29 countries have killed 2,043," CNN, February 12, 2018, https://www.cnn.com/2015/12/17/world/mapping-isis-attacks-around-the-world/index.html.

Litch, Josiah, letter to Nathaniel Southard, *The Midnight Cry!* Vol. 7, No. 16 (October 12): 125 (courtesy of Adventist Digital Library).

Lloyd, John, and John Mitchinson, *If Ignorance Is Bliss, Why Aren't There More Happy People?* (New York: Crown Publishing, 2008).

Lloyd, Marion, "Soviets Close to Using A-Bomb in 1962 Crisis, Forum is Told," *The Boston Globe*, October 13, 2002.

Logan, Peter Melville, "The Popularity of Popular Delusions: Charles Mackay and Victorian Popular Culture," *Cultural Critique* Vol. 54 (Spring 2003): 213–241.

Lord, Charles G., et al., "Biased Assimilation and Attitude Polarization: The Effects of Prior Theories on Subsequently Considered Evidence," *Journal of Personality and Social Psychology* Vol. 37, No. 11 (June 1, 1979): 2098–2109.

Loveland, Anne C., *American Evangelicals and the U.S. Military 1942–1993* (Baton Rouge, LA: Lousiana State University Press, 1996).

Lowenstein, Roger, *Origins of the Crash* (New York: The Penguin Press, 2004).

Mackay, Charles, *Memoirs of Extraordinary Popular Delusions* (London: Richard Bentley, 1841).

Mackay, Charles, *Memoirs of Extraordinary Popular Delusions and the Madness of Crowds* (London: Office of the National Illustrated Library, 1852).

Mackay, Christopher, *False Prophets and Preachers* (Kirksville, MO: Truman State University Press, 2016).

Mackey, Robert, "The Case for ISIS, Made in a British Accent," *The New York Times*, June 20, 2014.

Macleod, Hugh, "YouTube Islamist: how Anwar al-Awlaki became al-Qaida's link to local terror," *The Guardian*, May 7, 2010.

MacPherson, Myra, "The Pulpit and the Power," *The Washington Post*, October 18, 1985, Friday Style D1.

Madden, Mike, "Mike Huckabee Hearts Israel," https://www.salon.com/2008/01/18/huckabee2_4/.

Mahar, Maggie, *Bull!* (New York: HarperBusiness, 2003).

Malkiel, Burton G., *A Random Walk down Wall Street* (New York: W. W. Norton & Company, Inc., 1999).

Mallaby, Sebastian, *The Man Who Knew* (New York: Penguin Press, 2016).

Mangalindan, Mylene, "Webvan Shuts Down Operations, Will Seek Chapter 11 Protection," *The Wall Street Journal*, July 10, 2001.

Mann, Walter, *The Follies and Frauds of Spiritualism* (London: Watts & Co., 1919).

Marryat, Frederick, *A Diary in America* (New York: D. Appleton & Co., 1839).

Mashala, Nur, *Imperial Israel* (London: Pluto Press, 2000).

Mazetti, Mark, et al., "Two-Year Manhunt Led to Killing of Awlaki in Yemen," *The New York Times*, September 30, 2011.

McCants, William, "The Believer," *Brookings Essay*, September 1, 2015, http://csweb.brookings.edu/content/research/essays/2015/thebeliever.html.

McCants, William, *The ISIS Apocalypse* (New York: St Martin's Press, 2015).

McCollister, John, *So Help Me God* (Louisville: Winchester/John Knox Press, 1991).

McGinn, Bernard, *Apocalyptic Spirituality* (New York: Paulist Press, 1977).

McGinnis, Joe, *The Selling of the President, 1968* (New York: Trident Press, 1969).

McGonigle, Steve, "Former FBI superstar falls onto hard times," *Dallas Morning News*, January 2, 1983.

McLean, Bethany, and Peter Eklind, *The Smartest Guys in the Room* (New York: Penguin Group, 2003).

McQueen, Allison, *Political Realism in Apocalyptic Times* (Cambridge, UK: Cambridge University Press, 2018).

Mearsheimer, John, and Stephen M. Walt, *The Israel Lobby and U.S. Foreign Policy* (New York: Farrar, Straus and Giroux, 2007).

Melton, J. Gordon, *Encyclopedia of American Religions* (Detroit: Gale Press, 1999).

Merkley, Paul Charles, *American Presidents, Religion, and Israel* (Westport, CT: Praeger, 2004).

Merkley, Paul Charles, *Christian Attitudes Towards the State of Israel* (Montreal: McGill-Queen's University Press, 2001).

Merkley, Paul Charles, *The Politics of Christian Zionism 1891–1948* (London: Frank Cass, 1998).

Meshcke, J. Felix, "CEO Appearances on CNBC," working paper, http://citeseerx.ist.psu.edu/viewdoc/download?doi=10.1.1.203.566&rep=rep1&type=pdf.

Michel, Lou, and Dan Herbeck, *American Terrorist* (New York: ReganBooks, 2001).

Mieczkowski, Yanek, *The Routledge Historical Atlas of Presidential Elections* (New York: Routledge, 2001).

Milgram, Stanley, "Behavioral Study of Obedience," *Journal of Abnormal and Social Psychology* Vol. 67, No. 4 (1963): 371–378.

Milgram, Stanley "Some Conditions of Obedience and Disobedience to Authority," *Human Relations* Vol. 18, No. 1 (February 1965): 57–76.

Miller, William, "A New Year's Address," *The Signs of the Times* Vol. 4, No. 19 (January 25, 1843): 150 (courtesy of Adventist Digital Library).

Miller, William, letter, *The Advent Herald* Vol. 7, No. 5 (March 6, 1844): 39.

Miller, William, letter to Joshua Himes, *The Midnight Cry!* Vol. 7, No. 16 (October 12, 1844): 121 (courtesy of Adventist Digital Library).

Minksy, Hyman, "The financial-instability hypothesis: capitalist processes and the behavior of the economy," in Charles P. Kindleberger and Jean-Pierre Laffargue, Eds., *Financial crises* (Cambridge, UK: Cambridge University Press, 1982), 13–39.

Mojtabai, A.G., *Blessed Assurance* (Syracuse, NY: Syracuse University Press, 1997).

Moore-Anderson, Arthur Posonby, *Sir Robert Anderson and Lady Agnes Anderson*, http://www.casebook.org/ripper_media/rps.apmoore.html.

Morningstar Inc, "Mind the Gap 2018," https://www.morningstar.com/lp/mind-the-gap?cid=CON_RES0022.

Mortimer, Edward, *Faith and Power* (New York: Vintage Books, 1982).

Mortimer, Ian, "Why do we say 'hanged, drawn, and quartered?," http://www.ianmortimer.com/essays/drawing.pdf.

Moser, Whet, "Apocalypse Oak Park: Dorothy Martin, the Chicagoan Who Predicted the End of the World and Inspired the Theory of Cognitive Dissonance," *Chicago Magazine*, May 20, 2011.

Mounce, Robert H., *The Book of Revelation* (Cambridge, UK: William B. Eerdmans Publishing Company, 1984).

Mulligan, Thomas S., and Nancy Rivera Brooks, "Enron Paid Senior Execs Millions," *Los Angeles Times*, June 28, 2002.

Müntzer, Thomas, *The Collected Works of Thomas Müntzer*, trans. Peter Mathesen (Edinburgh: T&T Clark, 1988).

Murphy, Antoin E., *John Law* (Oxford: Clarendon Press, 1997).

Neal, Larry, *I Am Not the Master of Events* (New Haven, CT: Yale University Press, 2012).

Neal, Larry, *The Rise of Financial Capitalism* (Cambridge, UK: Cambridge University Press, 1990).

Newton, B.W., *Prospects of the Ten Kingdoms Considered* (London: Houlston & Wright, 1863).

Newton, Isaac, *Observations upon the Prophecies of Daniel and the Apocalypse of St. John* (London: J. Darby and P. Browne, 1733).

Nichol, Francis D., *The Midnight Cry!* (Takoma Park, Washington DC: Review and Herald Publishing Association), 337–426.

Nicholas, William, *The Midnight Cry!* Vol. 7, No. 17 (October 19): 133 (courtesy of Adventist Digital Library).

Nickerson, Raymond S., "Confirmation Bias: A Ubiquitous Phenomenon in Many Guises," *Review of General Psychology* Vol. 2, No. 2 (1998): 175–220.

Niebuhr, Gustav, "Victims in Mass Deaths Linked to Magical Sects," *The New York Times*, October 6, 1994.

Niebuhr, Reinhold, *Love and Justice* (Louisville, KY: Westminster John Knox Press, 1992).

Nietzsche, Frederich, *Beyond Good and Evil* (Cambridge, UK: Cambridge University Press, 2001).

Norris, Pippa, and Ronald Inglehart, *Sacred and Secular* (Cambridge, UK: Cambridge University Press, 2004).

Noyes, Alexander Dana, *The Market Place* (Boston: Little, Brown and Company, 1938).

NPR Weekend Edition Saturday, March 12, 1988, courtesy of Jacob J. Goldstein.

Numbers, Ronald L., and Jonathan M. Butler, Eds., *The Disappointed* (Bloomington and Indianapolis: Indiana University Press, 1987).

O'Brien, Timothy L., "A New Legal Chapter for a 90's Flameout," *The New York Times*, August 15, 2004.

O'Doherty, John P., et al., "Neural Responses during Anticipation of Primary Taste Reward," *Neuron* Vol. 33, No. 5 (February 28, 2002): 815–826.

Odlyzko, Andrew, "Charles Mackay's own extraordinary popular delusions and the Railway Mania," http://www.dtc.umn.edu/~odlyzko/doc/mania04.pdf.

Odlyzko, Andrew, "Newton's financial misadventures during the South Sea Bubble," working paper November 7, 2017.

Odlyzko, Andrew, "This Time Is Different: An Example of a Giant, Wildly Speculative, and Successful Investment Manias," *The B.E. Journal of Economic Analysis & Policy* Vol. 10, No. 1 (2010), 1–26.

Oliver, J. Eric, and Thomas J. Wood, "Conspiracy Theories and the Paranoid Style(s) of Mass Opinion," *American Journal of Political Science* Vol. 58, No. 4 (October 2014): 952–966.

Oliver, Moorman, Jr., "Killed by Semantics: Or Was It a Keystone Kop Kaleidoscope Kaper?" in James R. Lewis, Ed., *From the Ashes* (Lanham, MD: Rowman & Littlefield Publishers, Inc., 1994), 75–77.

Olmstead, A.T., "The Text of Sargon's Annals," *The American Journal of Semitic Languages* Vol. 47, No. 4 (July 1931): 263.

Olsham, Jeremy, "The inventor of the 401(k) says he created a 'monster,'" http://www.marketwatch.com/story/the-inventor-of-the-401k-says-he-created-a-monster-2016-05-16.

Olson, Ted, "Bush's Code Cracked," *Christianity Today*, September 1, 2004, https://www.christianitytoday.com/ct/2004/septemberweb-only/9-20-42.0.html.

Oppel, Richard A., Jr., "Merrill Replaced Research Analyst Who Upset Enron," *The New York Times*, July 30, 2002.

Oreskes, Michael, "Robertson Comes Under Fire for Asserting That Cuba Holds Soviet Missiles," *The New York Times*, February 16, 1988, 28.

Ortega, Tony, "Hush, Hush, Sweet Charlatans," *Phoenix New Times*, November 30, 1995.

Orwell, George, *Animal Farm*, https://archive.org/details/AnimalFarm-English -GeorgeOrwell.

Osgood, Charles E., and Percy H. Tannenbaum, "The Principle of Congruity and the Prediction of Attitude Change," *Psychological Review* Vol. 62, No. 1 (1955): 42–55.

Palast, Gregory, "I don't have to be nice to the spirit of the Antichrist," *The Guardian*, May 23, 1999, available at https://www.theguardian.com/business/1999/ may/23/columnists.observerbusiness1.

Paul, Helen, *The South Sea Bubble* (Abingdon, UK: Routledge, 2011).

Pepys, Samuel, *The Diary of Samuel Pepys* (London: Macmillan and Co., Ltd, 1905).

Peretti, Frank, *This Present Darkness* (Wheaton, IL: Crossway, 2003).

Perino, Michael, *The Hellhound of Wall Street* (New York: The Penguin Press, 2010).

Perrow, Charles, *Normal Accidents* (Princeton, NJ: Princeton University Press).

Peterson, Alan H., *The American Focus on Satanic Crime, Volume I* (Milburn, NJ: The American Focus Publishing Company, 1988).

Pew Foundation, *Spirit and Power: A 10 Country Survey of Pentecostals* (Washington, DC: The Pew Forum on Religion & Public Life, 2006).

Pew Research Center, "In America, Does More Education Equal Less Religion?," April 26, 2017, http://www.pewforum.org/2017/04/26/in-america-does-more -education-equal-less-religion/.

Pew Research Center, "Jesus Christ's Return to Earth," July 14, 2010, https://www .pewresearch.org/fact-tank/2010/07/14/jesus-christs-return-to-earth/, accessed August 29, 2019.

Pew Research Center, "The World's Muslims: Unity and Diversity," http://assets .pewresearch.org/wp-content/uploads/sites/11/2012/08/the-worlds-muslims -full-report.pdf.

Pierard, Richard V., "Religion and the 1984 Election Campaign," *Review of Religious Research* Vol. 27, No. 2 (December 1985): 98–114.

Pomper, Miles A., "Church, Not State, Guides Some Lawmakers on Middle East," *Congressional Quarterly* Vol. 58 (March 23, 2002): 829–831.

Potter, William *The Key of Wealth* (London: "Printed by R.A.," 1650).

Priestly, Joseph, *Letters to a Philosophical Unbeliever, Part I, Second Ed.* (Birmingham: Pearson and Rollason, 1787), 192.

Provine, Robert R., "Yawning," *American Scientist* Vol. 93, No. 6 (November/ December 2005): 532–539.

Pulliam, Susan, "At Bill's Barber Shop, 'In Like Flynn' Is A Cut Above the Rest— Owner's Tech-Stock Chit-Chat Enriches Cape Cod Locals; The Maytag Dealer Is Wary," *The Wall Street Journal*, March 13, 2000, A1.

Pulliam, Susan, "Hair Today, Gone Tomorrow: Tech Ills Shave Barber," *The Wall Street Journal*, March 7, 2001, C1.

Pulliam, Susan, and Ruth Simon, "Nasdaq Believers Keep the Faith To Recoup Losses in Rebound," *The Wall Street Journal*, June 21, 2000, C1.

Quittner, Joshua, and Michelle Slatalla, *Speeding the Net* (New York: Atlantic Monthly Press, 1998).

Rabinovich, Abraham, "The Man Who Torched al-Aqsa Mosque," *Jerusalem Post*, September 4, 2014.

Rasmussen, Sune Engel, "U.S.-Led Coalition Captures Last ISIS Bastion in Syria, Ending Caliphate," *The Wall Street Journal*, March 23, 2019.

Rauschning, Hermann, *Hitler Speaks* (London: Eyer & Spottiswoode, 1939).

Raymond, E.T., *A Life of Arthur James Balfour* (Boston: Little, Brown, and Company, 1920).

Reagan, Ronald, *An American Life* (New York: Simon and Schuster, 1990).

Rees, Laurence, *Auschwitz: A New History* (New York: Public Affairs, 2005).

Reese, Alexander, *The Approaching Advent of Christ*, https://theologue.wordpress.com/2014/10/23/updated-the-approaching-advent-of-christ-by-alexander-reese/.

Reeves, Marjorie, *Joachim of Fiore & the Prophetic Future* (Stroud, UK: Sutton Publishing, 1999).

Remnick, David, "Going the Distance: On and off the road with Barack Obama," *The New Yorker*, January 27, 2014.

Reinhold, Robert, "Author of 'At Home with the Bomb' Settles in City Where Bomb Is Made," *The New York Times*, September 15, 1986, A12.

Reuters, "Ex-Money Manager Gets 12 Years in Scheme," *Los Angeles Times*, February 12, 2003.

Riding, Alan, "Chalets Burn—2 Others Dead in Canada: 48 in Sect Are Killed in Grisly Rituals," *New York Times*, October 6, 1994.

Riding, Alan, "Swiss Examine Conflicting Signs in Cult Deaths," *The New York Times*, October 7, 1994.

Riedel, Bruce, *Kings and Presidents* (Washington, DC: Brookings Institution Press, 2018).

Roberts, Andrew, *Churchill: Walking with Destiny* (New York: Viking Press, 2018).

Robinson, Jennifer, *Deeper Than Reason* (Oxford: Clarendon Press, 2005).

Rogers, P.G., *The Fifth Monarchy Men* (London: Oxford University Press, 1966).

Romero, Simon, "In Another Big Bankruptcy, a Fiber Optic Venture Fails," *The New York Times*, January 29, 2002.

Rostow, W.W., and Anna Jacobsen Schwartz, *The Growth and Fluctuation of the British Economy 1790–1850* (Oxford: Clarendon Press, 1953).

Roth, Benjamin, *The Great Depression: A Diary* (New York: Public Affairs, 2009).

Rouwenhorst, K. Geert, "The Origins of Mutual Funds," in *The Origins of Value*, William N. Goetzmann and K. Geert Rouwenhorst, Eds. (Oxford: Oxford University Press, 2005).

Rowe, David L., *God's Strange Work* (Grand Rapids, MI: William B. Eerdmans Publishing Company, 2008).

Rowe, David L., *Thunder and Trumpets* (Chico, CA: Scholars Press, 1985).

Rozin, Paul, et al., "Operation of the Laws of Sympathetic Magic in Disgust and Other Domains," *Journal of Personality and Social Psychology* Vol. 50, No. 4 (1986): 703–711.

Rushay, Samuel W., Jr., "Harry Truman's History Lessons," *Prologue Magazine* Vol. 41, No. 1 (Spring 2009), https://www.archives.gov/publications/prologue/2009/spring/truman-history.html.

Sahagun, Louis, "The End of the world is near to their hearts," *Seattle Times*, June 27, 2006.

Saint Augustine, *The City Against the Pagans*, http://www.loebclassics.com/view/augustine-city_god_pagans/1957/pb_LCL416.79.xml.

Sandeen, Ernest, *The Roots of Fundamentalism* (Grand Rapids, MI: Baker Book House, 1970).

Sanders, Ralph, "Orde Wingate: Famed Teacher of the Israeli Military," *Israel: Yishuv History* (Midstream—Summer 2010): 12–14.

Savage, Charlie, "Court Releases Large Parts of Memo Approving Killing of American in Yemen," *The New York Times*, June 23, 2014.

Schacter, Stanley, "Leon Festinger," *Biographical Memoirs* Vol. 94 (1994): 98–111.

Scharf, J. Thomas, and Thompson Westcott, *History of Philadelphia* (Philadelphia: L. H. Everts & Co., 1884).

Schlosser, Eric, *Command and Control* (New York: Penguin Press, 2013).

Schmemann, Serge, "50 Are Killed as Clashes Widen from West Bank to Gaza Strip," *The New York Times*, September 17, 1996.

Schmitt, Eric, "U.S. Commando Killed in Yemen in Trump's First Counterterrorism Operation," *The New York Times*, January 29, 2017.

Schneer, Jonathan, *The Balfour Declaration* (London: Bloomsbury, 2010).

Scholem, Gershom, *Sabbatai Sevi* (Princeton, NJ: Princeton University Press, 1973).

Schorr, Daniel, "Reagan Recants: His Path from Armageddon to Détente," *Los Angeles Times*, January 3, 1988.

Schultz, Ellen, "Enron Employees' Massive Losses Suddenly Highlight 'Lockdowns,'" *The Wall Street Journal*, January 16, 2002.

Schultz, Wolfram, et al., "A Neural Substrate of Prediction and Reward," *Science* Vol. 275, No. 5307 (March 14, 1997): 1593–1599.

Schwartz, John, "Enron's Collapse: The Analyst; Man Who Doubted Enron Enjoys New Recognition," *The New York Times*, January 21, 2002.

Schwed, Fred, *Where Are the Customers' Yachts?* (Hoboken, NJ: John Wiley & Sons Inc., 2006).

Schweizer, Peter, *Victory* (New York: Atlantic Monthly Press, 1994).

Scofield, C.I., *The Holy Bible* (New York: Oxford University Press, American Branch, 1909).

Scofield, C.I., *The New Scofield Reference Bible* (New York: Oxford University Press, 1967).

Sears, Clara Endicott, *Days of Delusion* (Boston: Houghton Mifflin Company, 1924).

Segev, Tom, *One Palestine, Complete*, trans. Hiam Watzman (New York: Holt Paperbacks, 1999).

Segev, Zohar, "Struggle for Cooperation and Integration: American Zionists and Arab Oil, 1940s," *Middle Eastern Studies* Vol. 42, No. 5 (September 2006): 819–830.

Sharlet, Jeff, "Jesus Killed Mohammed: The Crusade for a Christian Military," *Harpers* (May 2009), 31–43.

Shearer, Peter M., and Philip B. Stark, "Global risk of big earthquakes has not recently increased," *Proceedings of the National Academy of Sciences of the United States* Vol. 109, No. 3 (January 2012): 717–721.

Sherman, Gabriel, *The Loudest Voice in the Room* (New York: Random House, 2014).

Shermer, Michael, "Patternicity," *Scientific American* Vol. 209, No. 6 (December 2008): 48–49.

Shragai, Nadav, "Raiders of the Lost Ark," *Haaretz*, April 25, 2003.

Siddle, Ronald, et al., "Religious delusions in patients admitted to hospital with schizophrenia," *Social Psychiatry and Psychiatric Epidemiology* Vol. 37, No. 3 (2002): 130–138.

Simpkinson, C.H., *Thomas Harrison, Regicide and Major-General* (London: J.M. Dent & Co., 1905).

Shapiro, T. Rees, "Harold Camping, radio evangelist who predicted 2011 doomsday, dies at 92," *The Washington Post*, December 18, 2013.

Sherif, Muzfir, et al., *Intergroup Conflict and Cooperation: The Robbers Cave Experiment* (Norman, OK: Institute of Group Relations, 1961).

Shiller, Robert, *Market Volatility* (Cambridge: MIT Press, 1992).

Simonson, Tatum S., et al., "Genetic Evidence for High-Altitude Adaptation in Tibet," *Science* Vol. 329, No. 5987 (July 2, 2010): 72–75.

Smith, Rebecca, "New SEC Filing Aids Case Against Enron," *The Wall Street Journal*, May 15, 2003.

Smith, Tom W., *Beliefs about God Across Time and Countries*, NORC/University of Chicago working paper (2012).

Snow, Mike, "Day-Trade Believers Teach High-Risk Investing," *The Washington Post*, July 6, 1998.

Snow, S.S., *The True Midnight Cry* Vol. 1, No. 1 (August 22, 1844): 3–4 (courtesy of Adventist Digital Library).

Solomon, Susan, et al., "Emergence of healing in the Antarctic ozone layer," *Science* Vol. 253, No. 6296 (July 16, 2016): 269–274.

Sontag, Sherry, and Christopher Drew, *Blind Man's Bluff* (New York: HarperPaperbacks, 1999).

Soufan Group, "Foreign Fighters: An Updated Assessment of the Flow of Foreign Fighters into Syria and Iraq," December 2015.

Stanovich, Keith E., "The Comprehensive Assessment of Rational Thinking," *Educational Psychologist* Vol. 51, No. 1 (February 2016): 30–34.

Stanovich, Keith E., and Richard F. West, "Individual differences in reasoning: Implications for the rationality debate?," *Behavioral and Brain Sciences* Vol. 23 (2000): 645–726.

Stanovich, Keith E., et al., *The Rationality Quotient* (Cambridge: MIT Press, 2016).

Stirrat, Michael, and R. Elisabeth Cornwell, "Eminent Scientists Reject the Supernatural: A Survey of Fellows of the Royal Society," *Evolution Education and Outreach* Vol. 6, No. 33 (December 2013): 1–5.

Stross, Randall E., *eBoys* (New York: Crown Business, 2000).

Sutton, Matthew Avery, *American Apocalypse* (Cambridge: Belknap Press, 2014).

Surowiecki, James, *The Wisdom of Crowds* (New York: Anchor, 2005).

Sweeney, Joan, and Richard James Sweeney, "Monetary Theory and the Great Capitol Hill Baby Sitting Co-op Crisis," *Journal of Money, Credit, and Banking* Vol. 9, No. 1 (February 1977): 86–89.

Tabor, James D., "Religious Discourse and Failed Negotiations," in Stuart A. Wright, *Armageddon in Waco* (Chicago: University of Chicago Press, 1995).

Tabor, James D., "The Waco Tragedy: An Autobiographical Account of One Attempt to Avert Disaster," in James R. Lewis, Ed., *From the Ashes* (Lanham, MD: Rowman & Littlefield Publishers, Inc., 1994).

Tabor, James D., and Eugene V. Gallagher, *Why Waco?* (Berkeley: University of California Press, 1995).

Talbot, Margaret, "The devil in the nursery," *The New York Times Magazine*, January 7, 2001.

Taylor, Arthur R., "Losses to the Public in the Insull Collapse: 1932–1946," *The Business History Review* Vol. 36, No. 2 (Summer 1962): 188–204.

Tetlock, Philip, *Expert Political Judgment* (Princeton, NJ: Princeton University Press, 2005).

Teveth, Shabtai, *Moshe Dayan, The Soldier, the Man, and the Legend*, trans. Leah and David Zinder (Boston: Houghton Mifflin Company, 1973).

Thornton, Nick, "Total retirement assets near $25 trillion mark," http://www.benefitspro.com/2015/06/30/total-retirement-assets-near-25-trillion-mark/?slreturn=20191020151329.

Time, "A Nation Jawed," 106, No. 4 (July 28, 1975): 51.

Tolstoy, Leo, *Anna Karenina*, trans. Constance Garnett (Project Gutenberg, 1998).

Tong, Scott, "Father of modern 401(k) says it fails many Americans," http://www.marketplace.org/2013/06/13/sustainability/consumed/father-modern-401k-says-it-fails-many-americans.

Trimm, James, "David Koresh's Seven Seals Teaching," *Watchman Expositor* Vol. 11 (1994), 7–8, https://www.watchman.org/articles/cults-alternative-religions/david-koreshs-seven-seals-teaching/.

Trivers, Robert L., "The Evolution of Reciprocal Altruism," *The Quarterly Review of Biology* Vol. 46, No. 1 (March 1971): 35–57.

Trivers, Robert, *The Folly of Fools* (New York: Basic Books, 2011).

Trofimov, Yaroslav, *The Siege of Mecca* (New York: Doubleday, 2007).

Trussler, Marc, and Stuart Soroka, "Consumer Demand for Cynical and Negative News Frames," *The International Journal of Press/Politics* Vol. 19, No. 3 (July 2014): 360–379.

Tufekci, Zeynip, "How social media took us from Tahrir Square to Donald Trump," *MIT Technology Review* August 14, 2018, https://www.technologyreview.com/s/611806/how-social-media-took-us-from-tahrir-square-to-donald-trump/.

Turco, R.P., et al., "Nuclear Winter: Global Consequences of Multiple Nuclear Explosions," *Science* Vol. 222, No. 4630 (December 23, 1983): 1283–1292.

Turner, Daniel L., *Standing Without Apology* (Greenville, SC: Bob Jones University Press, 1997).

Tversky, Amos, and Daniel Kahneman, "Availability: A Heuristic for Judging Frequency and Probability," *Cognitive Psychology* Vol. 5 (1973): 207–232,

Tversky, Amos, and Daniel Kahneman, "Belief in the Law of Small Numbers," *Psychological Bulletin* Vol. 76, No. 2 (1971): 105–110.

Tversky, Amos, and Daniel Kahneman, "Judgment under Uncertainty: Heuristics and Biases," *Science* Vol. 185, No. 4157 (September 27, 1974): 1124–1131.

United States Department of Justice, *Report to the Deputy Attorney General on the Events at Waco, Texas February 28 to April 19, 1993* (October 8, 1993), 158–190, https://www.justice.gov/archives/publications/waco/report-deputy-attorney-general-events-waco-texas.

Urofsky, Melvin I., and David W. Levy, Eds., *Letters of Louis D. Brandeis* (Albany: State University of New York Press, 1975).

Vaughn, Robert, Ed., *The Protectorate of Oliver Cromwell and the State of Europe During the Early Part of the Reign of Louis XIV* (London: Henry Colburn, Publisher, 1838).

Velie, Lester, *Countdown in the Holy Land* (New York: Funk & Wagnalls, 1969).

Virginia State Corporation Commission, "Staff Investigation on the Restructuring of the Electric Industry," https://www.scc.virginia.gov/comm/reports/restrct3.pdf.

von Däniken, Erich, *Chariots of the Gods*, trans. Michael Heron (New York: Berkley Books, 1999).

von Hayek, Frederich, "The Use of Knowledge in Society," *American Economic Review* Vol. 35, No. 4 (September 1945): 519–530.

von Kerssenbrock, Hermann, *Narrative of the Anabaptist Madness*, trans. Christopher S. Mackay (Leiden: Brill, Hotei Publishing, 2007).

Vonnegut, Kurt, *Cat's Cradle* (New York: Dial Press Trade Paperback, 2010).

Vosoughi, Soroush, et al., "The spread of true and false news online," *Science* Vol. 359, No. 6380 (March 9, 2018): 1146–1151.

Walker, William Junior, *Memoirs of the Distinguished Men of Science* (London: W. Walker & Son, 1862).

Walvoord, John F., "The Amazing Rise of Israel!," *Moody Monthly* Vol. 68, No. 2 (October 1967): 24–25.

Walvoord, John F., *Armageddon, Oil, and the Middle East Crisis* (Grand Rapids, MI: Zondervan Publishing House, 1990).

Ward, Douglas B., "The Geography of the *Ladies' Home Journal*: An Analysis of a Magazine's Audience, 1911-55," *Journalism History* Vol. 34, No. 1 (Spring 2008): 2.

Ward, Mark, *Authorized* (Bellingham, WA: Lexham Press, 2018).

Warren, Charles, *The Land of Promise* (London: George Bell & Sons, 1875).

Wason, P.C., "On the Failure to Eliminate Hypotheses in a Conceptual Task," *The Quarterly Journal of Experimental Psychology* Vol. 12, Part 3 (1960): 129–140.

Wason, P.C., "Reasoning," in B.M. Foss, Ed., *New Horizons in Psychology* (New York: Penguin, 1966), 145–146.

Watson, Ben, "What the Largest Battle of the Decade Says about the Future of War," *Defense One* (2017), https://www.defenseone.com/feature/mosul-largest-battle-decade-future-of-war/.

Wead, Doug, "The Spirituality of George W. Bush," https://www.pbs.org/wgbh/pages/frontline/shows/jesus/president/spirituality.html.

WGBH, "Betting on the Market," aired January 27, 1997, http://www.pbs.org/wgbh/pages/frontline/shows/betting/etal/script.html.

Whitney, Craig R. "Cult Horror Maims Prominent French Family," *The New York Times*, December 27, 1995.

Wigmore, Barrie, *The Crash and Its Aftermath* (Westport, CT: Greenwood Press, 1985).

Wigmore, Barrie A., "Was the Bank Holiday of 1933 Caused by a Run on the Dollar?" *Journal of Economic History* Vol. 47, No. 3 (September 1987): 739–755.

Williams, George Hunston, *The Radical Reformation* (Philadelphia: The Westminster Press, 1962).

Williams, John Burr, *The Theory of Investment Value* (Cambridge: Harvard University Press, 1938).

Willmington, D.H., *Willmington's Guide to the Bible* (Wheaton, IL: Tyndale House Publishers, Inc., 1984).

Wilson, David Sloan, *Evolution for Everyone* (New York: Delta Trade Paperbacks, 2007).

Wilson, Edmund, *The American Earthquake* (Garden City, NY: Anchor Doubleday Books, 1958).

Wojcik, Daniel, *The End of the World as We Know It* (New York: New York University Press, 1997).

Wolmar, Christian *The Iron Road* (New York: DK, 2014).

Wood, Graeme, "What ISIS Really Wants," *The Atlantic*, March 2015.

Wood, Thomas, and Ethan Porter, "The Elusive Backfire Effect: Mass Attitudes' Steadfast Factual Adherence," *Political Behavior* Vol. 41, No. 1 (March 2019): 135–163.

Wright, G. Frederick, *Charles Grandison Finney* (Boston: Houghton, Mifflin and Company, 1893).

Wright, Lawrence, "Forcing the End," *The New Yorker*, July 20, 1998, 52.

Wright, Lawrence, "Forcing the End," https://www.pbs.org/wgbh/pages/frontline/shows/apocalypse/readings/forcing.html.

Wright, Robert, *The Evolution of God* (New York: Little, Brown and Company, 2009).

Wright, Robert, *The Moral Animal* (New York: Vintage Books, 1994).

Wright, Stuart A., "Davidians and Branch Davidians," in Stuart A. Wright, Ed., *Armageddon at Waco* (Chicago: University of Chicago Press, 1995).

Wyatt, Edward, "Fox to Begin a 'More Business Friendly' News Channel," *The New York Times*, February 9, 2007.

Xin Yi et al., "Sequencing of 50 Human Exomes Reveals Adaptation to High Altitude," *Science* Vol. 329, No. 5987 (July 2, 2010): 75–78.

Yermack, David, "Flights of fancy: Corporate jets, CEO perquisites, and inferior shareholder returns," *Journal of Financial Economics* Vol. 80, No. 1 (April 2006): 211–242.

Yoon, David S., *The Restored Jewish State and the Revived Roman Empire* (Ann Arbor, MI: Proquest/UMI Dissertation Publishing, 2011).

Yourish, Karen, et al., "How Many People Have Been Killed in ISIS Attacks Around the World," *The New York Times*, July 16, 2016.

Zajonc, R.B., "Feeling and Thinking," *American Psychologist* Vol. 35, No. 2 (February 1980).

Zelin, Aaron, "Interpreting the Fall of Islamic State Governance," The Washington Institute, October 16, 2017, http://www.washingtoninstitute.org/policy-analysis/view/interpreting-the-fall-of-islamic-state-governance.

Zimbardo, Philip, *The Lucifer Effect* (New York: Random House, 2007).

Zuckerman, Gregory, and Paul Beckett, "Tiger Makes It Official: Funds Will Shut Down," *The Wall Street Journal*, March 31, 2000.

Zweig, Jason, Introduction to Fred Schwed, *Where Are the Customers' Yachts?* (Hoboken, NJ: John Wiley & Sons Inc., 2006).

NOTES

PRELUDE

1. Charles Mackay, *Memoirs of Extraordinary Popular Delusions* (London: Richard Bentley, 1841), Volumes I–III. All subsequent references to this book, unless otherwise noted, are to this edition.

2. Mackay used the term "tulipomania," later writers omitted the "o."

3. Herodotus, *The Histories* (Baltimore: Penguin Books, 1954), 190–191.

4. Hans C. Breiter and Bruce R. Rosen, "Functional Magnetic Resonance Imaging of the Brain Reward Circuitry in the Human," *Annals of the New York Academy of Sciences* Vol. 877, No. 1 (February 6, 2006): 523–547; John P. O'Doherty et al., "Neural Responses during Anticipation of Primary Taste Reward," *Neuron* Vol. 33, No. 5 (February 28, 2002): 815–826; Gregory S. Berns et al., "Predictability Modulates Human Brain Response to Reward," *The Journal of Neuroscience* Vol. 21, No. 8 (April 15, 2001): 2793–2798; and Wolfram Schultz et al., "A Neural Substrate of Prediction and Reward," *Science* Vol. 275, No. 5307 (March 14, 1997): 1593–1599.

5. Charles P. Kindleberger, *Manias, Panics, and Crashes* (New York: John Wiley & Sons, 2000), 15.

6. David Halberstam, *The Best and the Brightest* (New York: Random House, 1972).

7. Craig R. Whitney, "Cult Horror Maims Prominent French Family," *The New York Times*, December 27, 1995. See also Alan Riding, "Chalets Burn—2 Others Dead in Canada: 48 in Sect Are Killed in Grisly Rituals," *The New York Times*, and Gustav Niebuhr, "Victims in Mass Deaths Linked to Magical Sects," *New York Times*, both October 6, 1994; Alan Riding, "Swiss Examine Conflicting Signs in Cult Deaths," *The New York Times*, October 7, 1994; "18 Sought in 3 Nations; Linked to Doomsday Sect," *The New York Times*, December 22, 1995; Craig R. Whitney, "16 Burned Bodies Found in France; Cult Tie Suspected," *The New York Times*, December 24, 1995; and "French Say 2 Cult Members Shot Others," *The New York Times*, December 28, 1995.

8. David Gelertner, "A Religion of Special Effects," *The New York Times*, March 30, 1997.

9. Todd Bersaglieri et al., "Genetic Signatures of Strong Recent Positive Selection at the Lactase Gene," *American Journal of Human Genetics* Vol. 74, No. 6 (April 2004): 1111–1120; Tatum S. Simonson et al., "Genetic Evidence for High-Altitude Adaptation in Tibet," *Science* Vol. 329, No. 5987 (July 2, 2010): 72–75; and Xin

Yi et al., "Sequencing of 50 Human Exomes Reveals Adaptation to High Altitude," ibid., 75–78.

10. Robert Boyd and Peter J. Richerson, "Culture and the evolution of human cooperation," *Philosophical Transactions of the Royal Society* Vol. 364, No. 1533 (November 12, 2009): 3281–3288.

11. Melanie C. Green and Timothy C. Brock, "The Role of Transportation in the Persuasiveness of Public Narratives," *Journal of Personality and Social Psychology* Vol. 79, No. 5 (2000): 701–721.

12. Robert Trivers, *The Folly of Fools* (New York: Basic Books, 2011), 9–11.

13. Matthew Haag, "Robert Jeffress, Pastor Who Said Jews Are Going to Hell, Led Prayer at Jerusalem Embassy," *The New York Times*, May 14, 2018.

14. Pew Research Center, "Jesus Christ's Return to Earth," July 14, 2010, https://www.pewresearch.org/fact-tank/2010/07/14/jesus-christs-return-to-earth/, accessed August 29, 2019.

15. Jeff Sharlet, "Jesus Killed Mohammed: The Crusade for a Christian Military," *Harpers*, May 2009, 31–43. See also Laurie Goodstein, "Air Force Chaplain Tells of Academy Proselytizing," *The New York Times*, May 12, 2005, and Neela Banerjee, "Religion and Its Role Are in Dispute at the Service Academies, *The New York Times*, June 25, 2008.

16. Daniel Ellsberg, *The Doomsday Machine* (New York: Bloomsbury, 2017), 64–89.

17. Francis Galton, "Vox Populi" *Nature* Vol. 75, No. 1949 (March 7, 1907): 450–451; and Galton, Letters to the Editor, *Nature* Vol. 75, No. 1952 (March 28, 1907): 509–510.

18. The classic modern examples of collective wisdom involve a thermonuclear warhead lost in the Mediterranean in 1966 and the wreck of the USS *Scorpion*, which sank in the Atlantic Ocean in 1968. In both cases, the statistically averaged estimate of their location was off by only 200 meters, which was better than the best individual estimate. See Sherry Sontag and Christopher Drew, *Blind Man's Bluff* (New York: HarperPaperbacks, 1999), 63–65, 96–117.

19. Galton, op. cit., and Galton, "The Ballot-Box," *Nature* Vol. 75, No. 1952 (March 28, 1907): 509; Friedrich von Hayek, "The Use of Knowledge in Society," *American Economic Review* Vol. 35, No. 4 (September 1945): 519–530; and James Surowiecki, *The Wisdom of Crowds* (New York: Anchor, 2005).

20. Joel Greenblatt and Barry Ritholtz, *Masters in Business*, April 20, 2018, https://assets.bwbx.io/av/users/iqjWHBFdfxIU/vcNFFMk_gBGg/v2.mp3.

21. Frederich Nietzsche, *Beyond Good and Evil* (Cambridge, UK: Cambridge University Press, 2001), 70.

22. Charles Mackay, *Memoirs of Extraordinary Popular Delusions*, I:3.

23. F. Scott Fitzgerald, "The Crack-Up," *Esquire* (February 1936), http://www.pbs.org/wnet/americanmasters/f-scott-fitzgerald-essay-the-crack-up/1028/, accessed March 5, 2016.

24. Philip Tetlock, *Expert Political Judgment* (Princeton, NJ: Princeton University Press, 2005).

25. Richard Alfred Davenport, *Sketches of Imposture, Deception, and Credulity* (London: Thomas Tegg and Son, 1837).

26. Ann Goldgar, *Tulipmania* (Chicago: University of Chicago Press, 2007), 5–6.

27. See, for example, Peter Melville Logan, "The Popularity of Popular Delusions: Charles Mackay and Victorian Popular Culture," *Cultural Critique* Vol. 54 (Spring 2003): 213–241.

CHAPTER 1: JOACHIM'S CHILDREN

1. Kurt Vonnegut, *Cat's Cradle* (New York: Dial Press Trade Paperback, 2010), 182.

2. Marjorie Reeves, *Joachim of Fiore & the Prophetic Future* (Stroud, UK: Sutton Publishing, 1999), 8–23.

3. Hesiod, "Works and Days," 640, http://www.theoi.com/Text/HesiodWorksDays .html, accessed March 16, 2016.

4. Ibid., 109–121.

5. Ibid., 170–202.

6. I.E.S. Edwards, Ed., *The Cambridge Ancient History* 3rd Ed. (Cambridge, UK: University Press, 1975), Vol. II, Part 2, 558–605. See also Paul Johnson, *A History of the Jews* (New York: HarperPerennial, 1987), 50–70.

7. A.T. Olmstead, "The Text of Sargon's Annals," *The American Journal of Semitic Languages* Vol. 47, No. 4 (July 1931): 263.

8. II Kings 24:12–14.

9. II Kings 25:7

10. Zedekiah, 1–48, and Paul Boyer, *When Time Shall Be No More*, (Cambridge: Harvard/Belknap Press, 1992), 24–26.

11. Daniel 1:20.

12. Daniel 2:1–35.

13. Mircea Eliade, *Cosmos and History*, trans. Willard R. Trask (New York: Harper Torchbooks, 1959), 124–125.

14. Daniel 2:44.

15. Daniel 2:12. There is controversy about the roles played by Menelaus and Antiochus in the changes in religious practice, especially on whether they were repressive impositions on the part of Antiochus or badly needed reforms favored by enlightened Judeans; see Johnson 104–107; Norman Cohn, *Cosmos, Chaos, and the World to Come* (New Haven, CT: Yale University Press, 1995), 166–175; and John J. Collins, *The Apocalyptic Imagination* (Grand Rapids, MI: William B. Erdmans Publishing Company, 1988), 85–144.

16. R.H. Charles, *Lectures on the Apocalypse* (London: Humphrey Milford, Oxford University Press, 1922), 1, 63. An alternative explanation of Revelation's opacity to the modern audience is that its author/authors were trying to spin a narrative that updates Ezekiel and Daniel to the mainly Jewish audience of the first and second centuries A.D. Personal communication, Christopher S. Mackay.

17. On the difficulties in Revelation's narrative structure, see Robert H. Mounce, *The Book of Revelation* (Cambridge, UK: William B. Eerdmans Publishing Company, 1984), 31–32; and also Charles, 39–51.

18. Cohn, *Cosmos, Chaos, and the World to Come*, 215; Revelation 1:22. For a summary of scholarly interpretation of Revelation, see Charles, *Lectures on the Apocalypse*; and John M. Court, *Myth and History in the Book of Revelation* (Atlanta, GA: John Knox Press, 1979), 16–19, 43–159.

19. Eliade, 123–124.

20. Robert Wright, *The Evolution of God* (New York: Little, Brown and Company, 2009), 193.

21. *Spirit and Power: A 10 Country Survey of Pentecostals* (Washington, DC: The Pew Forum on Religion & Public Life, 2006), 6, 155; see also Pew Research Center, "Jesus Christ's Return to Earth," July 14, 2010, accessed August 29, 2019. Curiously, the study did not look at other developed nations beyond the United States, only developing ones; for example, 88 percent of Nigerians belived the Bible represented the literal word of God.

22. For a detailed discussion of Augustine's views on the millennium and the Second Coming, see http://persweb.wabash.edu/facstaff/royaltyr/augustine.htm.

23. Saint Augustine, *The City Against the Pagans* XVII:53, http://www.loebclassics.com/view/augustine-city_god_pagans/1957/pb_LCL416.79.xml, accessed March 12, 2016, and *City of God* XVIII:30; and Alison McQueen, *Political Realism in Apocalyptic Times* (Cambridge, UK: Cambridge University Press, 2018), 50.

24. Keith E. Stanovich and Richard F. West, "Individual differences in reasoning: Implications for the rationality debate?" *Behavioral and Brain Sciences* Vol. 23 (2000): 645–726.

25. Richard J. Gerrig, *Experiencing Narrative Worlds* (New Haven, CT: Yale University Press, 1993), 10–11. In Gerrig's precise wording,

Someone ("the traveler") is transported

by some means of transportation

as a result of performing certain actions

The traveler goes some distance from his or her world of origin

which makes some aspects of the world of origin inaccessible.

The traveler returns to the world of origin somewhat changed by the journey.
(italics added)

26. Emily Dickinson (Mabel Loomis Todd and T.W. Higginson, Eds.), *The Poems of Emily Dickinson* (Raleigh, NC: Hayes Barton Press, 2007), 1390.

27. Paul Rozin et al., "Operation of the Laws of Sympathetic Magic in Disgust and Other Domains," *Journal of Personality and Social Psychology* Vol. 50, No. 4 (1986): 703–711.

28. "A Nation Jawed," *Time* Vol. 106, Issue 4 (July 28, 1975): 51.

29. Ibid.

30. Clayton H. Lewis and John R. Anderson, "Interference with Real World Knowledge," *Cognitive Psychology* Vol. 8 (1976): 311–335.

31. Gerrig, 223–224.

32. Gerrig, 17.

33. Green and Brock, 701–721.

34. Ibid., 711.

35. Ibid., 719.

36. For the debate interchange, see https://www.youtube.com/watch?v= H1JFGWBAC5c. See also Julie Beck, "Vaccine Skepticism and 'Big Government,'" *The Atlantic*, September 17, 2015.

37. J.E. LeDoux, "The lateral amygdaloid nucleus: sensory interface of the amygdala in fear conditioning," *The Journal of Neuroscience* Vol. 10, No. 4 (April 1990): 1062–1069.

38. George Orwell, *Animal Farm*, 5–6, https://archive.org/details/AnimalFarm -English-GeorgeOrwell, accessed July 20, 2019.

39. Paul Christiansen, *Orchestrating Public Opinion* (Amsterdam: Amsterdam University Press, 2018), 10–30, quote 11. For a detailed discussion of the auditory pathways to Systems 1 and 2, see Jenefer Robinson, *Deeper Than Reason* (Oxford: Clarendon Press, 2005), 47–52.

40. Leo Tolstoy, *Anna Karenina*, trans. Constance Garnett (Project Gutenberg, 1998), ii.

41. Thomas Gilovich, "Biased Evaluation and Persistence in Gambling," *Journal of Personality and Social Psychology* Vol. 44, No. 6 (June, 1983): 1110–1126.

42. For a superb review of this concept, see Roy F. Baumeister et al., "Bad Is Stronger Than Good," *Review of General Psychology* Vol. 5, No. 4 (2001): 323–370. For experimental confirmation of the preference of news stories about negative events over stories about positive events, see Marc Trussler and Stuart Soroka, "Consumer Demand for Cynical and Negative News Frames," *The International Journal of Press/ Politics* Vol. 19, No. 3 (July 2014): 360–379.

43. Soroush Vosoughi et al., "The spread of true and false news online," *Science* Vol. 359, No. 6380 (March 9, 2018): 1146–1151; and Zeynep Tufekci, "How social media took us from Tahrir Square to Donald Trump," *MIT Technology Review* August 14, 2018, https://www.technologyreview.com/s/611806/how-social-media-took-us -from-tahrir-square-to-donald-trump/, accessed May 22, 2019.

44. Bernard McGinn, *Apocalyptic Spirituality* (New York: Paulist Press, 1977), 97–98.

45. McGinn, 104–110.

46. Eric Temple Bell, *The Magic of Numbers* (New York: Dover Publications, Inc., 1991), 11, 77.

47. Francis Bacon, *The New Organon* (New York: The Bobbs-Merrill Company, Inc., 1960), 50.

48. Michael Shermer, "Patternicity," *Scientific American* Vol. 209, No. 6 (December 2008): 48.

49. For a quantitative treatment of this phenomenon, see Kevin R. Foster and Hanna Kokko, "The Evolution of Superstitions and Superstition-like Behaviour," *Proceedings of the Biological Sciences* Vol. 276, No. 1654 (January 7, 2009): 31–37.

50. McGinn, 1979.

51. Quoted in Ruth Kestenberg-Gladstein "The 'Third Reich': A fifteenth-century polemic against Joachim, and its background," *Journal of the Warburg and Courtauld Institutes* Vol. 18, No. 3–4 (July–December, 1955): 246.

52. Ibid., 118–122.

53. 1 Peter 2:13.

54. Elizabeth Eisenstein, *The Printing Press as an Agent of Change* (Cambridge, UK: Cambridge University Press, 1979), 373.

55. George Hunston Williams, *The Radical Reformation* (Philadelphia: The Westminster Press, 1962), 64.

56. For the definitive account of the German Peasants' War, see Peter Blickle, *The Revolution of 1525*, trans. Thomas A. Brady, Jr. and H.C. Erik Midelfort (Baltimore: The Johns Hopkins University Press, 1981).

57. Hans Jürgen-Goertz, *Thomas Müntzer*, trans. Jocelyn Jaquiery (Edinburgh: T&T Clark, 1993), 31–61, quotes 59.

58. Abraham Friesen, *Thomas Muentzer, a Destroyer of the Godless* (Berkeley: University of California Press, 1990), 217–261, quote 261.

59. Jürgen-Goertz, 186.

60. Thomas Müntzer, *The Collected Works of Thomas Müntzer* (Edinburgh: T&T Clark, 1988), 71–72, and Jürgen-Goertz, 61–191.

CHAPTER 2: BELIEVERS AND ROGUES

1. Hermann von Kerssenbrock, *Narrative of the Anabaptist Madness*, trans. Christopher S. Mackay (Leiden: Brill, Hotei Publishing, 2007), I:182.

2. Ibid., II:493.

3. Von Kerssenbrock, I:87–91, 104–138; and Anthony Arthur, *The Tailor-King* (New York: Thomas Dunne Books, 1999), 12.

4. Allan Chibi, *The Wheat and the Tares* (Eugene, OR: Pickwick Publications, 2015).

5. This calculation has also been ascribed to Bernard Rothmann, see Ralf Klötzer, "The Melchoirites and Münster," in John D. Roth and James M. Stayer, Eds., *A Companion to Anabaptism and Spiritualism, 1521–1700* (Leiden: Brill, 2007), 211–212; and von Kerssenbrock, I:12–18. The date of Hoffman's apocalypse has been placed by some in 1534; see Anthony Arthur, *The Tailor-King* (New York: Thomas Dunne Books, 1999), 12.

6. Klötzer, 219–220.

7. Ibid., 220–221; Christopher S. Mackay *False Prophets and Preachers* (Kirksville, MO: Truman State University Press, 2016), 11. This superb volume contains an extensive translator's introduction to Henry Gresbeck's account. Hereafter referred to as Mackay/Gresbeck.

8. Arthur, 12.

9. Arthur, 60–63.

10. Klötzer, 222–224.

11. For a detailed description of the city's premadness social and political structure, see Mackay/Gresbeck, 22–25.

12. Von Kerssenbrock, I:213–214.

13. For further critical discussion of von Kerssenbrock's and Gresbeck's books, see the translator's introduction of both, Mackay/Gresbeck, 1–63.

14. Von Kerssenbrock, I:214.

15. Ibid., I:217.

16. Ibid., I:361.

17. Ibid., I:121, 215, quote 215; Arthur, 15.

18. Christopher S. Mackay, personal communication.

19. Arthur, 16.

20. Klötzer, 225–226; Mackay/Gresbeck, 23.

21. Arthur, 23–24.

22. Cohn, *The Pursuit of the Millennium* (New York: Oxford University Press, 1970), 267–268.

23. Von Kerssenbrock, II:477n23.

24. Klötzer, 226–230, quote 230.

25. Von Kerssenbrock, II:479.

26. Von Kerssenbrock, II:480.

27. Klötzer, 234.

28. Mackay/Gresbeck, 51, 67–68, 77.

29. Christopher S. Mackay, personal communication.

30. Mckay/Gresbeck, 73–77.

31. Mackay/Gresbeck, 208–215.

32. Arthur, 54–58.

33. Mackay/Gresbeck, 89–90.

34. There's some doubt about the date, see ibid., 90, n138.

35. Arthur, 69–72.

36. Ibid., 50–51, 107–108; and Mackay/Gresbeck, 102–110.

37. Mackay/Gresbeck, 114–119, quote 115.

38. Ibid., 120–130. For the precise dating of the marriage proclamation and insurrection, see 124n242.

39. On the political effects of the May and August repulses of the prince-bishop attacks, personal communication Christopher S. Mackay.

40. Mackay/Gresbeck, 140.

41. Ibid., 139.

42. Ibid., 163.

43. Klötzer, 230–246; Arthur, 118–124; and Mackay/Gresbeck, 166–167.

44. Mackay/Gresbeck, 168–169, 205n527.

45. Arthur, 138–142; Mackay/Gresbeck, 285.

46. Klötzer, 246–247.

47. Arthur, 144–146.

48. Mackay/Gresbeck, 237.

49. Ibid., 256.

50. Arthur, 147–149.

51. Ibid., 151–153.

52. Ibid., 156–178; Mackay/Gresbeck, 33–34, 259–265.

53. Mackay/Gresbeck, 281. As to the uncertainty over the queen's death, see 282n895.

54. Von Kerssenbrock, 715.

55. Klötzer, 246–250; Arthur 177–178, 184; von Kerssenbrock, 715–716, 716n9.

56. B.S. Capp, *The Fifth Monarchy Men* (London: Faber and Faber, 1972), 14.

57. Robert Vaughn, Ed., *The Protectorate of Oliver Cromwell and the State of Europe During the Early Part of the Reign of Louis XIV* (London: Henry Colburn, Publisher, 1838), I:156–157.

58. Isaac Newton, *Observations upon the Prophecies of Daniel and the Apocalypse of St. John* (London: J. Darby and P. Browne, 1733).

59. P.G. Rogers, *The Fifth Monarchy Men* (London: Oxford University Press, 1966), 11–13, 136–137; Capp, 23–24; and Henry Archer, *The Personall Reign of Christ Vpon Earth*, Early English Books Online, http://eebo.chadwyck.com, accessed June 16, 2017.

60. For a detailed description of the Fifth Monarchists' theological and political range, see Capp, 131–157.

61. Capp, 105–106.

62. Rogers, 69.

63. C.H. Simpkinson, *Thomas Harrison, Regicide and Major-General* (London: J.M. Dent & Co., 1905), 223–251, quote 251.

64. Samuel Pepys, *The Diary of Samuel Pepys* (London: Macmillan and Co., Ltd., 1905), 51.

65. Ibid. For a discussion of the meaning of "hanged, drawn, and quartered," see Brian P. Block and John Hostettler, *Hanging in the Balance* (Sherfield Gables, UK: Waterside Press, 1997), 19–20; and Ian Mortimer, "Why do we say 'hanged, drawn, and quartered'?," http://www.ianmortimer.com/essays/drawing.pdf, accessed June 19, 2017.

66. Pepys, 64.

67. Rogers, 84–87, 112–122; Capp, 117–118, 199–200.

CHAPTER 3: BRIEFLY RICH

1. William Harrison Ainsworth, *The South Sea Bubble* (Leipzig: Bernhard Tauchnitz, 1868), 48–49.

2. During the late medieval period, bills of exchange also expanded credit. For a lucid description of how the modern system works, see Frederick Lewis Allen, *The Lords of Creation* (Chicago: Quadrangle Paperbacks, 1966), 305–306; and Antoin Murphy, *John Law* (Oxford: Clarendon Press, 1997), 14–16.

3. Montgomery Hyde, *John Law* (London, W. H. Allen: 1969), 9.

4. Hyde, 10–14; see also Malcolm Balen, *The Secret History of the South Sea Bubble* (New York: HarperCollins, 2003), 14. For a detailed account of the machinations surrounding his duel with Wilson and ultimate escape, see Antoin Murphy, *John Law* (Oxford: Clarendon Press, 1997), 24–34.

5. Murphy, 38.

6. Quoted in Murphy, 38.

7. Murphy, 37–40.

8. Ibid., 37.

9. Walter Bagehot, *Lombard Street* (New York: Scribner, Armstrong & Co., 1873), 2–5.

10. Joan Sweeney and Richard James Sweeney, "Monetary Theory and the Great Capitol Hill Baby Sitting Co-op Crisis," *Journal of Money, Credit, and Banking* Vol. 9, No. 1 (February 1977): 86–89. Also see Paul Krugman, "Baby Sitting the Economy," http://www.pkarchive.org/theory/baby.html, accessed April 28, 2017.

11. William Potter, *The Key of Wealth* (London: "Printed by R.A.," 1650), 56. For "barbarous relic," see John Maynard Keynes, *A Tract on Monetary Reform* (London: Macmillan and Co., Limited, 1924), 172.

12. John Law, *Money and Trade Considered* (London: R. & A. Foulis, 1750), 8–14.

13. John Law, *Essay on a Land Bank*, Antoin E. Murphy, Ed. (Dublin: Aeon Publishing, 1994), 67–69.

14. Law, *Money and Trade Considered*, 188.

15. Quoted in Murphy, 93. For a detailed discussion of barter versus the mutual exchange of favors, see David Graeber, *Debt* (New York: Melville House, 2012).

16. Quoted in Murphy, 93, italics Murphy's.

17. Quoted in Murphy, 92.

18. Law, 182–190, quote 190.

19. Hyde, 52–63, Murphy 45–75.

20. Quoted in Murphy, 125.

21. Hyde, 89–90.

22. Murphy, 157–162.

23. In 1717 Law was granted permission to rename it the Company of the West, and in 1719 it was merged with the China Company and renamed the Company of the Indies, but hereafter will be referred to by its original name, the one by which it is known to history: the Mississippi Company.

24. Ibid., 162–183.

25. Hyde, 115; and Murphy, 189–191. The share structure of the company was dizzyingly complex, with several offerings through 1720 and three major share classes, whose ownership rights interlocked; see Murphy 165–166.

26. Mackay, *Memoirs of Extraordinary Popular Delusions*, I:25–26.

27. Ibid., I:30.

28. *Letters of Madame Charlotte Elizabeth de Baviére, Duchess of Orleans*, ii:274, https://archive.org/stream/lettersofmadamec02orluoft/lettersofmadamec02orluoft_djvu.txt, accessed October 31, 2015.

29. Murphy, 205.

30. In 1700, Paris's population was 600,000; see http://www.demographia.com/dm-par90.htm. The Duchess of Orleans estimates that about half that number moved to the city during the boom; see Mackay, *Memoirs of Extraordinary Delusions*, I:40; and Murphy, 213.

31. Murphy, 207.

32. For the precise mechanisms of the scheme's unwinding and the Byzantine politics behind them, see Murphy, 244–311; for the system's serial inflation-adjusted (silver) values, see Table 19.2, 306.

33. Larry Neal, *I Am Not the Master of Events* (New Haven, CT: Yale University Press, 2012), 55–93.

34. Mackay, *Memoirs of Extraordinary Popular Delusions*, I:40; Hyde, 139–210; Murphy, 219–223, 312–333.

35. John Cuevas, *Cat Island* (Jefferson, NC: McFarland & Company, Inc., 2011), 11.

36. Ibid., 10–12.

37. William Lee, *Daniel Defoe: His Life, and Recently Discovered Writings* (London: John Camden Hotten, Piccadilly, 1869), II:189.

38. Barry Eichengreen, *Golden Fetters* (Oxford: Oxford University Press, 1995).

39. Stefano Condorelli, "The 1719 stock euphoria: a pan-European perspective," working paper, 2016, https://mpra.ub.uni-muenchen.de/68652/, accessed April 27, 2016.

40. John Carswell, *The South Sea Bubble* (Gloucestershire, UK: Sutton Publishing, Ltd., 2001), 19.

41. Balen, 23–32. Blunt presented the Company to Parliament in the spring of that year, which approved its charter that fall, subsequent to which Queen Anne awarded the actual charter (personal communication, Andrew Odlyzko).

42. Lee/Defoe, II:180.

43. For a lucid exposition of this phenomenon, see Antti Ilmanen, "Do Financial Markets Reward Buying or Selling Insurance and Lottery Tickets?," *Financial Analysts Journal* Vol. 68, No. 5 (September/October 2012): 26–36. The Kansas state lottery is a good example of the positive skewness/poor payoff phenomenon; see the table in http://www.kslottery.com/games/PWBLOddsDescription.aspx. If one assumes a $100 million payoff for the Powerball, the total expected payout on a single $2 ticket is 66 cents, or 33 cents on the dollar—that is, a loss of 67 percent.

44. Mackay, *Memoirs of Extraordinary Popular Delusions*, I:82.

45. For those interested in the exact mechanisms of both Law's and Blunt's schemes, see Carswell, 82–143; and Edward Chancellor, *Devil Take the Hindmost* (New York: Plume, 2000). On the dates of share purchases and conversions, Andrew Odlyzko, personal communication.

46. Mackay, *Memoirs of Extraordinary Popular Delusions*, I:92–100. In the opinion of Andrew Odlyzko, there is some documentary evidence behind a company "for carrying on an undertaking of great advantage; but nobody to know what it is" (Odlyzko, personal communication).

47. Mackay, *Memoirs of Extraordinary Popular Delusions*, I:112; A. Andréadès, *History of the Bank of England* (London: P.S. King & Son, 1909), n250.

48. Dale, 111–112; Carswell, 128; Balen, 94; quote Kindleberger, 122.

49. Carswell, 131.

50. Ibid., 116.

51. Anonymous, *The South Sea Bubble* (London, Thomas Boys, 1825), 113.

52. Carswell, 131–132, 189, 222.

53. Anonymous, "The Secret History of the South Sea Scheme," in *A Collection of Several Pieces of Mr. John Toland* (London: J. Peele, 1726), 431.

54. Ibid., 442–443.

55. Chancellor, 74.

56. Mackay, *Memoirs of Extraordinary Popular Delusions*, I:112–113.

57. Ibid., I:112.

58. Larry Neal, *The Rise of Financial Capitalism* (Cambridge, UK: Cambridge University Press, 1990), 234. The actual price at the bottom was £100, but this included a 33.3 percent stock dividend, so £150 is closer to the truth (personal communication, Andrew Odlyzko).

59. Carswell, 120; Kindleberger, 208–209.

60. See Helen Paul, *The South Sea Bubble* (Abingdon, UK: Routledge, 2011), 1, 39–42, 59–65. Ms. Paul belongs in the "rational bubble" camp of revisionist modern economic historians who postulate rational behavior during market enthusiasms. Beyond figures on slave offloadings and mentions of experienced slave traders who were connected to the company, there seemed to be no financial data to support the *asiento* as a source of cash flow large enough to justify South Sea's mid-1720 share price; see Carswell, 55–57, 240. A more nuanced modern evaluation of South Sea's intrinsic worth concluded that given the possibility, albeit unrealized, of huge profits, no reasonable estimate could be made; Paul Harrison, "Rational Equity Valuation at the Time of the South Sea Bubble," *History of Political Economy* Vol. 33, No. 2 (Summer 2001): 269–281.

61. The mechanics of South Sea's debt conversions and flotations are highly complex, and well beyond the scope of this volume. For an authoritative description of these, see Richard Dale, *The First Crash* (Princeton: Princeton University Press, 2014), 102–122. For Hutcheson's calculations, see 113–117, quote 114.

62. Ian Cowie, "Oriental risks and rewards for optimistic occidentals," *The Daily Telegraph*, August 7, 2004.

63. Carswell, 221–259. On the brief imprisonments, Andrew Odlyzko, personal communication.

CHAPTER 4: GEORGE HUDSON, CAPITALIST HERO

1. Solomon E. Asch, "Studies of Independence and Conformity: A Minority of One Against a Unanimous Majority," *Psychological Monographs* Vol. 70, No. 9 (1956): 1–70. See also Asch, *Social Psychology* (New York: Prentice-Hall, 1952), 450–501.

2. Asch (1956), 28.

3. See, for example, Ronald Friend et al., "A puzzling misinterpretation of the Asch 'conformity' study," *European Journal of Social Psychology* Vol. 20 (1990): 29–44.

4. Robert R. Provine, "Yawning," *American Scientist* Vol. 93, No. 6 (November/December 2005): 532–539.

5. Boyd and Richerson, 3282.

6. Robert Boyd and Peter J. Richerson, *The Origin and Evolution of Cultures* (Oxford: Oxford University Press, 2005), 8–9.

7. Fritz Heider, "Attitudes and Cognitive Organization," *The Journal of Psychology* Vol. 21 (1946): 107–112. A similar, more formalized model of this was developed in Charles E. Osgood and Percy H. Tannenbaum, "The Principle of Congruity and the Prediction of Attitude Change," *Psychological Review* Vol. 62, No. 1 (1955), 42–55.

8. Keise Izuma and Ralph Adolphs, "Social Manipulation of Preference in the Human Brain," *Neuron Interpersonal Dynamics* Vol. 78 (May 8, 2013): 563–573.

9. Daniel K. Campbell-Meiklejohn et al., "How the Opinion of Others Affects Our Valuation of Objects," *Current Biology* Vol. 20, No. 13 (July 13, 2010): 1165–1170.

10. Mackay, I:137.

11. Stephen E. Ambrose, *Undaunted Courage* (New York: Simon and Shuster, 1996), 52. This statement is not strictly true, since pigeons and the French semaphore signaling system could convey very limited amounts of information faster than a horse.

12. John Francis, *A History of the English Railway* (London: Longman, Brown, Green, & Longmans, 1851), I:4–5.

13. William Walker, Jr., *Memoirs of the Distinguished Men of Science* (London: W. Walker & Son, 1862), 20.

14. Paul Johnson, *The Birth of the Modern* (New York: HarperCollins, 1991), 581.

15. Ibid.

16. Christian Wolmar, *The Iron Road* (New York: DK, 2014), 22–29; and Francis I:140–141.

17. Francis, I:94–102.

18. Francis, I:292.

19. Ibid.

20. Ibid., 288.

21. Sidney Homer and Richard Sylla, *A History of Interest Rates*, 4th Ed. (Hoboken, NJ: John Wiley & Sons, 2005), 188–193.

22. Bagehot, 138–139. Another factor may have been the compensation due wealthy slave owners, the outcome of 1830s emancipation (personal communication, Andrew Odlyzko).

23. Francis, I:290.

24. Ibid., I:293.

25. Ibid., I:289, 293–294.

26. John Herapath, *The Railway Magazine* (London: Wyld and Son, 1836), 33.

27. John Lloyd and John Mitchinson, *If Ignorance Is Bliss, Why Aren't There More Happy People?* (New York: Crown Publishing, 2008), 207.

28. Francis, I:300.

29. Andrew Odlyzko, "This Time Is Different: An Example of a Giant, Wildly Speculative, and Successful Investment Manias," *The B.E. Journal of Economic Analysis & Policy* Vol. 10, No. 1 (2010), 1–26.

30. J.H. Clapham, *An Economic History of Modern Britain: The Early Railway Age 1820–1850* (Cambridge, UK: Cambridge University Press, 1939), 387, 389–390, 391.

31. Richard S. Lambert, *The Railway King* (London: George Allen & Unwin Ltd., 1964), 30–31.

32. Andrew Odlyzko, personal communication.

33. Lambert, 99–107.

34. Ibid., 150–154.

35. Ibid., 156–157.

36. Ibid., 188–189.

37. Frazar Kirkland, *Cyclopedia of Commercial and Business Anecdotes* (New York: D. Appleton and Company, 1868), 379.

38. Lambert, 173–174; Francis II:237.

39. Lambert, 237. See also Clapham, 391.

40. Francis II:175.

41. Lambert, 165.

42. Francis, II:168–169.

43. Anonymous quote in ibid., 144–145.

44. Quoted in Francis, II:174.

45. Lambert, 168–169.

46. Francis, II:183.

47. Alfred Crowquill, "Railway Mania," *The Illustrated London News*, November 1, 1845.

48. Lambert, 207.

49. Lambert, 200–207, 221–240; railway share price index values from W.W. Rostow and Anna Jacobsen Schwartz, *The Growth and Fluctuation of the British Economy 1790–1850* (Oxford: Clarendon Press, 1953), I:437.

50. Francis, II:195–196.

51. Ibid., 275–295; and Andrew Odlyzko, personal communication.

52. John Forster, *The Life of Charles Dickens* (London: Clapman and Hall, 1890), II:176.

53. William Bernstein, *The Birth of Plenty* (New York: McGraw-Hill Inc., 2004), 40–41.

54. Charles Mackay, *Memoirs of Extraordinary Popular Delusions* (London: Office of the National Illustrated Library, 1852), I:84.

55. Andrew Odlyzko, "Charles Mackay's own extraordinary popular delusions and the Railway Mania," http://www.dtc.umn.edu/~odlyzko/doc/mania04.pdf, accessed March 30, 2016.

56. Quotes from the *Glasgow Argus*, October 2, 1845, from Odlyzko, ibid.

57. Andrew Odlyzko, "Newton's financial misadventures during the South Sea Bubble," working paper November 7, 2017. The famous quote is secondhand and undocumented.

CHAPTER 5: MILLER'S RUN

1. Stanley Schacter, "Leon Festinger," *Biographical Memoirs* Vol. 94 (1994): 98–111, and "Doctor Claims World Will Upheave, Not End," *Pittsburgh Post-Gazette*, December 17, 1954.

2. Leon Festinger et al., *When Prophecy Fails* (New York: Harper Torchbooks, 1956), 234.

3. Ibid., 33.

4. Ibid., 33–51.

5. "Doctor Claims World Will Upheave, Not End."

6. Festinger et al., ibid.; and Whet Moser, "Apocalypse Oak Park: Dorothy Martin, the Chicagoan Who Predicted the End of the World and Inspired the Theory of Cognitive Dissonance," *Chicago Magazine*, May 20, 2011.

7. Festinger et al., 28

8. https://www.mtholyoke.edu/acad/intrel/winthrop.htm, accessed August 14, 2017.

9. Frederick Marryat, *A Diary in America* (New York: D. Appleton & Co., 1839), 16.

10. Walter Mann, *The Follies and Frauds of Spiritualism* (London: Watts & Co., 1919), 9–24.

11. Sylvester Bliss, *Memoirs of William Miller* (Boston: Joshua V. Himes, 1853), 8; and David L. Rowe, *Thunder and Trumpets* (Chico, CA: Scholars Press, 1985), 9.

12. Joshua V. Himes, Ed., *Miller's Works* I:8, http://centrowhite.org.br/files/ebooks/apl/all/Miller/Miller%27s%20Works.%20Volume%201.%20Views%20of%20the%20Prophecies%20and%20Prophetic%20Chronology.pdf, accessed August 15, 2017.

13. Joshua V. Himes, *Views of the Prophecies and Prophetic Chronologies, Selected from Manuscripts of William Miller* (Boston: Josuhua V. Himes, 1842), 10.

14. Rowe, *Thunder and Trumpets*, 3–6.

15. Bliss, 47–48, 50.

16. Ibid., 52–53. For a more current interpretation, see Wayne R. Judd, "William Miller: Disappointed Prophet," in Ronald L. Numbers and Jonathan M. Butler, Eds., *The Disappointed* (Bloomington and Indianapolis: Indiana University Press, 1987), 7–19.

17. Martin Gardner, *Fads and Fallacies in the Name of Science* (New York; Dover Publications, 1957), 173–185.

18. Erich von Däniken, *Chariots of the Gods*, trans. Michael Heron (New York: Berkley Books, 1999).

19. T. Rees Shapiro, "Harold Camping, radio evangelist who predicted 2011 doomsday, dies at 92," *The Washington Post*, December 18, 2013.

20. Gardner, 176.

21. Ronald L. Numbers, personal communication.

22. Christopher Hitchens, *God Is Not Great* (New York: Hachette Group, 2007), 60.

23. Leroy Edwin Froom, *The Prophetic Faith of Our Fathers* (Washington, DC: Review and Herald, 1946); for calculations centering on 1843, see especially III:401–413. Those wishing an exhaustive tour down the apocalyptic calculation rabbit hole should consult the full four-volume series, available at http://documents. adventistarchives.org.

24. Absent Wason's laboratory notes, it's not known for sure the experiments were performed in the late 1950s, but since his seminal study was published in 1960, this seems likely; see P.C. Wason, "On the Failure to Eliminate Hypotheses in a Conceptual Task," *The Quarterly Journal of Experimental Psychology* Vol. 12, Part 3 (1960): 129–140.

25. Wason, ibid. It is widely reported in the psychology literature, and elsewhere, that Wason coined the term "confirmation bias" in this paper, when in fact it appears nowhere in it. One later coauthor reports, "That Wason used the phrase 'confirmation bias' seems unlikely. He talked of a 'verifying strategy.' " Philip Johnson-Laird, personal communication. The author can find no mentions of the term before 1977.

26. For a brilliant survey of the psychological research, history, and human significance of confirmation bias, see Raymond S. Nickerson, "Confirmation Bias: A Ubiquitous Phenomenon in Many Guises," *Review of General Psychology* Vol. 2, No. 2 (1998): 175–220.

27. Charles G. Lord et al., "Biased Assimilation and Attitude Polarization: The Effects of Prior Theories on Subsequently Considered Evidence," *Journal of Personality and Social Psychology* Vol. 37, No. 11 (June 1, 1979): 2098–2109. The hardening of opinion by contrary data, known as the "backfire effect," is highly controversial. For a more nuanced view, see Thomas Wood and Ethan Porter, "The Elusive Backfire Effect: Mass Attitudes' Steadfast Factual Adherence," *Political Behavior* Vol. 41, No. 1 (March 2019): 135–163.

28. Rowe, *Thunder and Trumpets*, 11–12; Everett N. Dick, *William Miller and the Advent Crisis 1831–1844* (Berrien Springs, MI: Andrews University Press, 1994), 7–9. Rowe states that Miller settled on 457 B.C. as the date of the fall of the Persian Empire, which did not in fact occur for more than another century.

29. Rowe, *Thunder and Trumpets*, 12–15.

30. Ibid., 14.

31. David L. Rowe, *God's Strange Work* (Grand Rapids, MI: William B. Eerdmans Publishing Company, 2008), 1–2.

32. Thomas Armitage, *A History of Baptists* (New York: Bryan, Taylor & Co., 1887), 769.

33. G. Frederick Wright, *Charles Grandison Finney* (Boston: Houghton, Mifflin and Company, 1893), 61.

34. Rowe, *Thunder and Trumpets*, 17–18, 24.

35. Rowe, *Thunder and Trumpets*, 17, 24, 91–92, quote 92.

36. Bliss, 143.

37. Dick, *William Miller and the Advent Crisis 1831–1844*, 19–20.

38. Rowe, *Thunder and Trumpets*, 17.

39. Ibid., 59–82.

40. Everett N. Dick, "Advent Camp Meetings of the 1840s," *Adventist Heritage* Vol. 4, No. 2 (Winter 1977): 5.

41. Ibid., 3–10.

42. Ibid., 10.

43. Ibid.

44. Whitney R. Cross, *The Burned-over District* (New York: Harper Torchbooks, 1950), 296.

45. Rowe, *Thunder and Trumpets*, 31–40.

46. Dick, *William Miller and the Advent Crisis 1831–1844*, 44–45. On Starkweather, see George R. Knight, *Millennial Fever* (Boise, ID: Pacific Press Publishing Association, 1993), 174–175.

47. William Miller, "A New Year's Address," *The Signs of the Times* Vol. IV, No. 19 (January 25, 1843): 150 (courtesy of Adventist Digital Library).

48. Dick, *Miller and the Advent Crisis 1831–1844*, 121.

49. Ibid., 83–99. For a precise compilation of rabbinical months and years in the mid-nineteenth century, see Isaac Landman, Ed., *The Universal Jewish Encyclopedia* (New York: Universal Jewish Encyclopedia, Inc., 1940), II:636.

50. William Miller, letter, *The Advent Herald* Vol. 7, No. 5 (March 6, 1844): 39.

51. Joshua V. Himes, *The Midnight Cry!* Vol. 6, No. 13 (April 11, 1844), 305 (courtesy of Adventist Digital Library).

52. *The Signs of the Times* Vol. V, No. 16 (June 23, 1843): 123 (courtesy of Adventist Digital Library).

53. Knight, 159–165, quote 163.

54. *The Midnight Cry!* Vol. 7, No. 17 (October 19): 132 (courtesy of Adventist Digital Library).

55. Joseph Bates, *The Biography of Elder Joseph Bates* (Battle Creek, MI: The Steam Press, 1868), 298.

56. Ibid., 167–205. For a description of the Exeter meeting, see *The Advent Herald* Vol. 8, No. 3 (August 21, 1844): 20; and for Snow's exact eschatology, see S.S. Snow, *The True Midnight Cry* Vol. 1, No. 1 (August 22, 1844): 3–4 (courtesy of Adventist Digital Library).

57. William Miller, letter to Joshua Himes, *The Midnight Cry!* Vol. 7, No. 16 (October 12): 121 (courtesy of Adventist Digital Library). For a concise summary of how acceptance of the October 22, 1844 date cascaded through the Adventist leadership, see David L. Rowe, *God's Strange Work*, 186–190.

58. Josiah Litch, letter to Nathaniel Southard, *The Midnight Cry!* Vol. 7, No. 16 (October 12): 125 (courtesy of Adventist Digital Library).

59. William Nicholas, *The Midnight Cry!* Vol. 7, No. 17 (October 19): 133 (courtesy of Adventist Digital Library).

60. Froom, IV:686.

61. Knight, 204–210.

62. Dick, *William Miller and the Advent Crisis 1831–1844*, 149–152.

63. J. Thomas Scharf and Thompson Westcott, *History of Philadelphia* (Philadelphia: L. H. Everts & Co., 1884), II:1448.

64. Rowe, *Thunder and Trumpets*, 137.

65. Ibid., 138.

66. Clara Endicott Sears, *Days of Delusion* (Boston: Houghton Mifflin Company, 1924), 181, 190–191, 195, 203.

67. Francis D. Nichol, *The Midnight Cry!* (Takoma Park, Washington, DC: Review and Herald Publishing Association), 337–426; and Ruth Alden Doan, *The Miller Heresy, Millerism, and American Culture* (Philadelphia: Temple University Press, 1987), 60–61, 158–174; and Dick, *William Miller and the Advent Crisis 1831–1844*, 123–130. The most succinct and compelling modern historical treatment of Millerite excesses, and particularly of ascension robes, is found in Cross, 305–306.

68. *The Signs of the Times* Vol. VI, No. 17 (December 13, 1843): 144 (courtesy of Adventist Digital Library); and Dick, *William Miller and the Advent Crisis 1831–1844*, 121.

69. Knight, 218–219.

70. Louis Boutelle, *Sketch of the Life and Religious Experience of Eld. Louis Boutelle* (Boston: Advent Christian Publication Society, 1891), 67–68.

71. William Lloyd Garrison, *The Letters of William Lloyd Garrison*, Walter M. Merrill, Ed. (Cambridge: Belknap Press of Harvard University Press, 1973), III:137; and Ira V. Brown, "The Millerites and the Boston Press," *The New England Quarterly* Vol. 16, No. 4 (December 1943): 599.

72. Dick, *William Miller and the Advent Crisis 1831–1844*, 161.

73. Rowe, *Thunder and Trumpets*, 141–147.

74. Knight, 219–241.

75. Jonathan M. Butler and Ronald L. Numbers, Introduction, in Ronald L. Numbers and Jonathan M. Butler, Eds., *The Disappointed* (Bloomington and Indianapolis: Indiana University Press, 1987), xv; and Doan, 203–204.

76. For Festinger's discussion of the Millerite episode, see Festinger et al., *When Prophecy Fails*, 11–23.

77. Ernest Sandeen, *The Roots of Fundamentalism* (Grand Rapids, MI: Baker Book House, 1970), 54–55.

CHAPTER 6: WINSTON CHURCHILL'S EXCELLENT ADVENTURE IN MONETARY POLICY

1. Bagehot, 158.

2. Martin Gilbert, *Winston S. Churchill* (Boston: Houghton Mifflin Company, 1977), V:333–351, quote 350.

3. Liaquat Ahamed, *Lords of Finance* (New York: Penguin, 2009), 231.

4. H. Clark Johnson, *Gold, France, and the Great Depression, 1919-1932* (New Haven, CT: Yale University Press, 1997), 141; converted at $4.86/pound sterling, see also Federal Reserve Bulletin, April 1926, 270–271.

5. Benjamin M. Blau et al., "Gambling Preferences, Options Markets, and Volatility," *Journal of Quantitative and Financial Analysis* Vol. 51, No. 2 (April 2016): 515–540.

6. Hyman Minksy, "The financial-instability hypothesis: capitalist processes and the behavior of the economy," in Charles P. Kindleberger and Jean-Pierre Laffargue, Eds., *Financial crises* (Cambridge, UK: Cambridge University Press, 1982), 13–39.

7. William J. Bernstein, *The Birth of Plenty*, 101–106.

8. For a marvelously lucid description of this system, see Frederick Lewis Allen, *The Lords of Creation* (Chicago: Quadrangle Paperbacks, 1966), 305–306.

9. https://fraser.stlouisfed.org/theme/?_escaped_fragment_=32#!32, accessed March 30, 2016.

10. Minsky, 13–39.

11. Floris Heukelom, "Measurement and Decision Making at the University of Michigan in the 1950s and 1960s," Nijmegen Center for Economics, Institute for Management Research, Radboud University, Nijmegen, 2009, http://www.ru.nl/publish/pages/516298/nice_09102.pdf, accessed July 18, 2016.

12. Malcolm Gladwell, *David and Goliath* (New York: Little, Brown and Company, 2013), 103.

13. Daniel Kahneman, *Thinking, Fast and Slow* (New York: Farrar, Straus and Giroux, 2013), 4–7.

14. Amos Tversky and Daniel Kahneman, "Judgment under Uncertainty: Heuristics and Biases," *Science* Vol. 185, No. 4157 (September 27, 1974), 1124.

15. Ibid., 1130.

16. "Judgment under Uncertainty" (vide supra) is Kahneman and Tversky's most widely quoted work. Also see, by the same authors, "Availability: A Heuristic for Judging Frequency and Probability," *Cognitive Psychology* Vol. 5 (1973): 207–232; "Belief in the Law of Small Numbers," *Psychological Bulletin* Vol. 76, No. 2 (1971): 105–110; "Subjective Probability: A Judgment of Representativeness," *Cognitive Psychology* Vol. 3 (1972): 430–454; "On the Psychology of Prediction," *Psychological Review* Vol. 80, No. 4 (July 1973): 237–251; "On the study of statistical intuitions," *Cognition* Vol. 11 (1982): 123–141; and "Intuitive Prediction: Biases and Corrective Procedures," *Advances in Decision Technology*, Defense Advanced Research Projects Agency, 1977.

17. For firearms deaths, see https://www.cdc.gov/nchs/fastats/injury.htm; for motor vehicle deaths, see https://www.cdc.gov/vitalsigns/motor-vehicle-safety/; and for opioid addiction, see https://www.cdc.gov/drugoverdose/.

18. Between 2005 and 2019, terrorists have killed 250 Israelis, about fifteen per year, whereas in 2018, 315 were killed in road accidents; see https://www.jewishvirtuallibrary.org/comprehensive-listing-of-terrorism-victims-in-israel and https://www.timesofisrael.com/cautious-optimism-as-annual-road-deaths-drop-for-the-first-time-in-5-years/.

19. In 1925, there were twenty million automobiles in the United States out of a population of 116 million; see http://www.allcountries.org/uscensus/1027_motor_vehicle_registrations.html, accessed July 18, 2016.

20. Allen, *The Lords of Creation*, 235–236.

21. John Kenneth Galbraith, *A Short History of Financial Euphoria* (Knoxville, TN: Whittle Direct Books, 1990), 16.

22. Galbraith, *The Great Crash 1929* (Boston: Houghton Mifflin Company, 1988), 22.

23. K. Geert Rouwenhorst, "The Origins of Mutual Funds," in *The Origins of Value*, William N. Goetzmann and K. Geert Rouwenhorst, Eds. (Oxford: Oxford University Press, 2005), 249.

24. Galbraith, *The Great Crash 1929*, 47.

25. Amalgamated from Galbraith, *The Great Crash 1929*, 60–63; and J. Bradford De Long and Andrei Schleifer, "The Stock Market Bubble of 1929: Evidence from Closed-end Mutual Funds," *The Journal of Economic History* Vol. 51, No. 3 (September 1991): 678.

26. Galbraith, *The Great Crash 1929*, 58–62; and Barrie Wigmore, *The Crash and Its Aftermath* (Westport, CT: Greenwood Press, 1985), 40, 45, 248–250.

27. From Robert Shiller database, see http://www.econ.yale.edu/~shiller/data/ie_data.xls, accessed July 17, 2016.

28. Robert Shiller database, ibid.

29. Neal, *The Rise of Financial Capitalism*, 232–257. Even these numbers may overstate the degree of price rise, since 1709 was near the end of the debilitating War of the Spanish Succession, and so represented a low starting point upon which to build further price increases.

30. "Radio Declares Dividend," *Ellensburg Daily Record*, November 5, 1937.

31. The canonical form of the technique was laid down in John Burr Williams, *The Theory of Investment Value* (Cambridge: Harvard University Press, 1938). See also Irving Fisher, *The Theory of Interest* (New York: The Macmillan Company, 1930); and Benjamin Graham and David Dodd, *Security Analysis* (New York: Whittlesey House, 1934).

32. Graham and Dodd, 310.

33. Paraphrased in Frederick Lewis Allen, *Only Yesterday* (New York: Perennial Classics, 2000), 265. I am unable to locate a primary source.

Chapter 7: Sunshine Charlie Misses the Point

1. Bernstein, *The Birth of Plenty*, 127–128.

2. *The Bend [OR] Bulletin,* July 16, 1938, 1, 5.

3. Allen, *The Lords of Creation*, 267–269.

4. Quoted in Allen, *The Lords of Creation*, 281–282.

5. Ibid., 266–286.

6. Virginia State Corporation Commission, "Staff Investigation on the Restructuring of the Electric Industry," https://www.scc.virginia.gov/comm/reports/restrct3.pdf, accessed April 17, 2019.

7. Allen, *The Lords of Creation*, 279

8. Ibid.

9. Adolph A. Berle, Jr., and Gardiner C. Means, *The Modern Corporation and Private Property* (New York: The Macmillan Company, 1948), 205n18.

10. Allen, *The Lords of Creation*, 281.

11. Ibid., 286.

12. Arthur R. Taylor, "Losses to the Public in the Insull Collapse: 1932–1946," *The Business History Review* Vol. 36, No. 2 (Summer 1962): 188.

13. "Former Ruler of Utilities Dies in France," *Berkeley Daily Gazette*, July 16, 1938.

14. "Insull Drops Dead in a Paris Station," *The Montreal Gazette* Vol. 167, No. 170 (July 18, 1938): 9.

15. Allen, *The Lords of Creation*, 353–354.

16. Evans Clark, Ed., *The Internal Debts of the United States* (New York: The Macmillan Company, 1933), 14.

17. See, for example, "Reveal Stock Pool Clears 5 Million in Week," *Chicago Tribune* Vol. 91, No. 121 (May 20, 1932): 1.

18. Samuel Crowther, "Everybody Ought to Be Rich: An Interview with John J. Raskob," *Ladies' Home Journal*, August 19, 1929, reprinted in David M.P. Freund, *The Modern American Metropolis* (New York: Wiley-Blackwell, 2015), 157–159. Circulation estimate from Douglas B. Ward, "The Geography of the Ladies' Home Journal: An Analysis of a Magazine's Audience, 1911–55," *Journalism History* Vol. 34, No. 1 (Spring, 2008): 2.

19. Yanek Mieczkowski, *The Routledge Historical Atlas of Presidential Elections* (New York: Routledge, 2001), 94.

20. Galbraith, *The Great Crash 1929*, 139.

21. David Kestenbaum, "What's a Bubble?," http://www.npr.org/sections/money/2013/11/15/245251539/whats-a-bubble, accessed August 1, 2016. For a sample of the academic literature on the nonpersistence of money manager performance, see Michael C. Jensen, "The Performance of Mutual Funds in the Period 1945–64," *Journal of Finance* Vol. 23, No. 2 (May 1968): 389–416; John R. Graham and Campbell R. Harvey, "Grading the Performance of Market Timing Newsletters," *Financial Analysts Journal* Vol. 53, No. 6 (November/December 1997): 54–66; and Mark M. Carhart, "On Persistence in Mutual Fund Performance," *Journal of Finance* Vol. 52, No. 1 (March 1997): 57–82.

22. Robert Shiller, *Market Volatility* (Cambridge: MIT Press, 1992), 56.

23. Anonymous, "Jacobellis v. Ohio," https://www.law.cornell.edu/supremecourt/text/378/184#ZC1-378_US_184fn2/2, accessed August 1, 2016.

24. Allen, *Only Yesterday*, 288.

25. Ibid., 273–274.

26. Chancellor, 210.

27. Alexander Dana Noyes, *The Market Place* (Boston: Little, Brown and Company, 1938), 323–324.

28. Galbraith, *The Great Crash 1929*, 84–85; and *The Wall Street Journal* September 6, 1929.

29. "Fisher Sees Stocks Permanently High," *New York Times*, October 16, 1929, 8.

30. Michael Perino, *The Hellhound of Wall Street* (New York: The Penguin Press, 2010), 197.

31. Bruce Barton, "Is There Anything Here that Other Men Couldn't Do?" *American Magazine* 95 (February 1923): 128, quoted in Susan Estabrook Kennedy, *The Banking Crisis of 1933* (Lexington: The University Press of Kentucky, 1973), 113–114.

32. Quote in Allen, *The Lords of Creation*, 313; also see Edmund Wilson, *The American Earthquake* (Garden City, NY: Anchor Doubleday Books, 1958), 485.

33. Allen, *The Lords of Creation*, 313–319.

34. Edmund Wilson, 485.

35. As measured by the Dow Jones Industrial Average.

36. For longitudinal U.S. stock ownership, see https://www.fdic.gov/about/history/timeline/1920s.html.

37. Benjamin Roth, *The Great Depression: A Diary* (New York: Public Affairs, 2009), 44.

38. Fred Schwed, *Where Are the Customers' Yachts?* (Hoboken, NJ: John Wiley & Sons Inc., 2006), 155.

39. Thomas F. Huertas and Joan L. Silverman, "Charles E. Mitchell: Scapegoat of the Crash?" *The Business History Review* Vol. 60, No. 1 (Spring 1986): 86.

40. Perino, 40–59.

41. Ibid., 135–155.

42. Ibid., 202.

43. "Hearings before a Subcommittee of the Committee on Banking and Currency of the United States Senate, Seventy-Second Congress on S. Res. 84 and S. Res. 239," 2170, http://www.senate.gov/artandhistory/history/common/investigations/pdf/Pecora_EBrown_testimony.pdf, accessed August 17, 2016.

44. Ibid., 2176.

45. Ibid., 2168–2182.

46. Wigmore, *The Crash and Its Aftermath*, 446–447; Barrie A. Wigmore, "Was the Bank Holiday of 1933 Caused by a Run on the Dollar?," *Journal of Economic History* Vol. 47, No. 3 (September 1987): 739–755.

47. William J. Bernstein, *The Four Pillars of Investing* (New York: McGraw-Hill Inc., 2002), 147.

48. Schwed, 54.

49. Allen, *The Lords of Creation*, 225.

CHAPTER 8: APOCALYPSE COW

1. Gershom Gorenberg, *The End of Days* (New York: The Free Press, 2000), 7–8; and "Apocalypse Cow," *The New York Times* (March 30, 1997).

2. Mendy Kaminker, "Meet the Red Heifer," http://www.chabad.org/parshah/article_cdo/aid/2620682/jewish/Meet-the-Red-Heifer.htm, accessed March 11, 2016.

3. Mishneh Torah, Laws of Mikvaot, 11:12.

4. Mishneh Torah, Laws of Parah Adumah 3:4.

5. Gorenberg, 9–10.

6. David Gates, "The Pop Prophets," *Newsweek*, May 24, 2004, 48; and https://news.gallup.com/poll/193271/americans-believe-god.aspx; https://news.gallup.com/poll/210704/record-few-americans-believe-bible-literal-word-god.aspx; and https://www.pewresearch.org/fact-tank/2010/07/14/jesus-christs-return-to-earth/, accessed April 19, 2019.

7. Crawford Gribben, personal communication.

8. 1 Thessalonians 4:16–17.

9. Donald Harman Akenson, *Discovering the End of Time* (Montreal: McGill-Queen's University Press, 2016), 88–90; and J. Gordon Melton, *Encyclopedia of American Religions* (Detroit: Gale Press, 1999), 107–108.

10. David S. Yoon, *The Restored Jewish State and the Revived Roman Empire* (Ann Arbor MI: Proquest/UMI Dissertation Publishing, 2011), 107–113; and Richard Hastings Graves, *The Whole Works of Richard Graves, D.D.* (Dublin: William Curry, Jun. and Company, 1840), II:416–438.

11. Crawford Gribben, personal communication.

12. Isaac Newton, ibid.

13. Joseph Priestly, *Letters to a Philosophical Unbeliever, Part I, Second Ed.,* (Birmingham: Pearson and Rollason, 1787), 192.

14. Yoon, 150, 274; Melton, 109.

15. Stephen Larsen, *The Fundamentalist Mind* (Wheaton IL: Quest Books, 2014), 145–146.

16. David W. Bebbington, *Evangelicalism in Modern Britain* (London: Routledge, 1989), 2–5.

17. C.I. Scofield, *The Holy Bible* (New York: Oxford University Press, American Branch, 1909); and *The New Scofield Reference Bible* (New York: Oxford University Press, 1967); sales estimates, Boyer, 97–98; and Crawford Gribben, personal communication.

18. Sandeen, 273–277, quote 276–277; on adoption year of 1890, see Julie Scott Jones, *Being the Chosen: Exploring a Christian Fundamentalist Worldview* (London: Routledge, 2010), 38.

19. Arthur Posonby Moore-Anderson, *Sir Robert Anderson and Lady Agnes Anderson*, http://www.casebook.org/ripper_media/rps.apmoore.html, accessed December 19, 2017; and Alexander Reese, *The Approaching Advent of Christ*, https://theologue.wordpress.com/2014/10/23/updated-the-approaching-advent-of-christ-by-alexander-reese/, 237 accessed December 19, 2017.

20. B. W. Newton, *Prospects of the Ten Kingdoms Considered* (London: Houlston & Wright, 1863), 42.

21. Ibid.

22. William Kelly, Ed., *The Collected Writings of John Nelson Darby Vol. 11* (London: G. Morrish, 1867–1900), 595–596.

23. Crawford Gribben, personal communication.

24. Daniel 8:14.

25. Robert Anderson, *The Coming Prince* (London: Hodder and Stoughton, 1881), 46–50; and Anderson, *Unfulfilled Prophecy and "The Hope of the Church* (London: Pickering & Inglis, 1923), 7–9, quote 9.

26. Anderson, *The Coming Prince*, 186–187.

27. Ibid., 150.

28. For "king of the east," see ibid., Vol. 2, 359, and Revelation 16:12; and for "king of the south," see ibid., Vol. 2, 519.

29. Ibid., Vol. 2, 517.

30. Ibid, Vol. 2, 518; see also Yoon, 202.

31. Paul Charles Merkley, *The Politics of Christian Zionism 1891–1948* (London: Frank Cass, 1998), 59, 63.

32. D.H. Willmington, *Willmington's Guide to the Bible* (Wheaton, IL: Tyndale House Publishers, Inc., 1984), 563; William E. Blackstone, *Jesus Is Coming* (Chicago: The Moody Bible Institute, 1916); and Matthew Avery Sutton, *American Apocalypse* (Cambridge: Belknap Press, 2014), 210.

33. Merkley, *The Politics of Christian Zionism 1891–1948*, 69.

34. Ibid., 73.

35. Melvin I. Urofsky and David W. Levy, Eds., *Letters of Louis D. Brandeis* (Albany: State University of New York Press, 1975), IV:278; see also Sutton, 73.

36. E.T. Raymond, *A Life of Arthur James Balfour* (Boston: Little, Brown, and Company, 1920), 1.

37. Ibid., 110, 184–197.

38. Jonathan Schneer, *The Balfour Declaration* (London: Bloomsbury, 2010), 134–135.

39. A photographic image of this letter is available at http://i-cias.com/e.o/slides/balfour_declaration01.jpg.

CHAPTER 9: GOD'S SWORD

1. Tom Segev, *One Palestine, Complete*, trans. Hiam Watzman (New York: Holt Paperbacks, 1999), 430.

2. Moshe Dayan, *Story of My Life* (New York: William Morrow and Company, Inc., 1976), 45.

3. Yoon, 233.

4. André Gerolymatos, *Castles Made of Sand* (New York: Thomas Dunne Books, 2010), 71–77.

5. Ralph Sanders, "Orde Wingate: Famed Teacher of the Israeli Military," *Israel: Yishuv History* (Midstream—Summer 2010): 12–14.

6. Anonymous, "Recent Views of the Palestine Conflict," *Journal of Palestine Studies* Vol. 10, No. 3 (Spring, 1981): 175.

7. Lester Velie, *Countdown in the Holy Land* (New York: Funk & Wagnalls, 1969), 105.

8. Simon Anglim, *Orde Wingate and the British Army, 1922–1944* (London: Routledge, 2010), 58.

9. Yoel Cohen, "The Political Role of the Israeli Chief Rabbinate in the Temple Mount Question," *Jewish Political Studies Review* Vol. 11, No. 1 (Spring 1999): 101–105.

10. For the full range of theological discussion on the matter, see, on the pro-rebuilding side, Jerry M. Hullinger, "The Problem of Animal Sacrifices in Ezekiel 40–48," *Bibliotheca Sacra* Vol. 152 (July–September, 1995): 279–289; and on the anti-rebuilding side, Philip A.F. Church, "Dispensational Christian Zionism: A Strange but Acceptable Aberration of Deviant Heresy?," *Westminster Theological Journal* Vol. 71 (2009): 375–398.

11. Chaim Herzog, *The Arab-Israeli Wars* (New York: Random House, 1982), 54–55.

12. Paul Charles Merkley, *Christian Attitudes Towards the State of Israel* (Montreal: McGill-Queen's University Press, 2001), 140.

13. Hertzel Fishman, *American Protestantism and a Jewish State* (Detroit: Wayne State University Press, 1973), 23–24, 83. For oil company opposition to Israel's establishment, see Zohar Segev, "Struggle for Cooperation and Integration: American Zionists and Arab Oil, 1940s," *Middle Eastern Studies* Vol. 42, No. 5 (September 2006): 819–830.

14. Quoted in ibid., 29.

15. Quoted in ibid., 34.

16. Ibid., 53–54.

17. Reinhold Niebuhr, *Love and Justice* (Louisville, KY: Westminster John Knox Press, 1992), 139–141. (Note: the section quoted is reprinted from "Jews After the War," published in 1942.)

18. Ibid., 141.

19. Yoon, 354–365, quote 362.

20. Samuel W. Rushay, Jr., "Harry Truman's History Lessons," *Prologue Magazine* Vol. 41, No. 1 (Spring 2009): https://www.archives.gov/publications/prologue/2009/spring/truman-history.html, accessed January 8, 2018.

21. Merkley, *The Politics of Christian Zionism* (London: Frank Cass, 1998), 187–189, quotes 188.

22. Paul Charles Merkley, *American Presidents, Religion, and Israel* (Westport, CT: Praeger, 2004), 4–5.

23. Merkley, *The Politics of Christian Zionism*, 191.

24. Yoon, 391, 395; and Thomas W. Ennis, "E. Schuyler English, Biblical Scholar, 81" *The New York Times*, March 18, 1981.

25. Shabtai Teveth, *Moshe Dayan, The Soldier, the Man, and the Legend*, trans. Leah and David Zinder (Boston: Houghton Mifflin Company, 1973), 335–336.

26. Dayan, 31, 128–131.

27. Herzog, 156–206; Dayan, 366; and Ron E. Hassner, *War on Sacred Grounds* (Ithaca, NY: Cornell University Press, 2009), 117.

28. Cohen, 120 n3.

29. Dayan, 386.

30. Ibid., 387.

31. Ibid., 388.

32. Gorenberg, 98.

33. Ibid., 387–390; and Rivka Gonen, *Contested Holiness* (Jersey City, KTAV Publishing House, 2003), 153.

34. Gonen, 157; Gorenberg, 107–110; and Abraham Rabinovich, "The Man Who Torched al-Aqsa Mosque," *Jerusalem Post*, September 4, 2014.

35. See, for example, Ronald Siddle et al., "Religious delusions in patients admitted to hospital with schizophrenia," *Social Psychiatry and Psychiatric Epidemiology* Vol. 37, No. 3 (2002): 130–138.

36. Gershom Scholem, *Sabbatai Sevi* (Princeton, NJ: Princeton University Press, 1973), 125–142, 461–602, 672–820.

37. For a masterful history of assassination as an instrument of Israeli/Jewish policy, both before and after independence, see Ronen Bergman, *Rise and Kill First* (New York: Random House, 2018), especially 18–30 for those involving Irgun and Lehi. For the eighteen points, see http://www.saveisrael.com/stern/saveisraelstern.htm.

38. Lawrence Wright, "Forcing the End," *The New Yorker*, July 20, 1998, 52.

39. Gonen, 158–159.

40. Jerold S. Auerbach, *Hebron Jews* (Plymouth, UK: Rowman & Littlefield Publishers, Inc., 2009), 114–116; and Nur Mashala, *Imperial Israel* (London: Pluto Press, 2000), 123–126.

41. Gonen, 161–162.

42. Charles Warren, *The Land of Promise* (London: George Bell & Sons, 1875), 4–6.

43. Nadav Shragai, "Raiders of the Lost Ark," *Haaretz*, April 25, 2003.

44. Serge Schmemann, "50 Are Killed as Clashes Widen from West Bank to Gaza Strip," *The New York Times*, September 17, 1996.

CHAPTER 10: ENTREPENEURS OF THE APOCALYPSE

1. Bruce Lincoln, *Holy Terrors*, 2nd Ed. (Chicago: University of Chicago Press, 2006), 28–31, quote 30.

2. Ted Olson, "Bush's Code Cracked," *Christianity Today*, September 1, 2004, https://www.christianitytoday.com/ct/2004/septemberweb-only/9-20-42.0.html, accessed June 30, 2019.

3. See, for example, Doug Wead, "The Spirituality of George W. Bush," https://www.pbs.org/wgbh/pages/frontline/shows/jesus/president/spirituality.html, accessed June 30, 2019.

4. "Bible Prophecy and the Mid-East Crisis," *Moody Monthly* Vol. 68, No. 1 (July–August 1967): 22.

5. John F. Walvoord, "The Amazing Rise of Israel!," *Moody Monthly* Vol. 68, No. 2 (October 1967): 24–25.

6. See Yoon, 407.

7. Hal Lindsey, "The Pieces Fall Together," *Moody Monthly* Vol. 68, No. 2 (October 1967): 27. For "yellow peril," see Hal Lindsey and C.C. Carlson, *The Late Great Planet Earth* (Grand Rapids, MI: Zondervan Publishing House, 1977), 70.

8. Hal Lindsey, "The Pieces Fall Together," 26–28, quote 27.

9. Ibid., 27.

10. Jonathan Kirsch, "Hal Lindsey," *Publishers Weekly*, March 14, 1977, 30.

11. Stephen R. Graham, "Hal Lindsey," in Charles H. Lippy, Ed., *Twentieth-Century Shapers of American Popular Religion* (New York: Greenwood Press, 1989), 248.

12. Yoon, 411; and ibid., 247–255.

13. Yoon, 31.

14. Paul Boyer, "America's Doom Industry," https://www.pbs.org/wgbh/pages/frontline/shows/apocalypse/explanation/doomindustry.html, accessed September 3, 2019.

15. The quotes from Falwell, Bakker, Robertson, Graham, and Lindsey, are transcribed by the author from an audiocassette recording of a ninety-minute NPR program, Joe Cuomo, *Joe Cuomo and the Prophecy of Armageddon*, 1984 WBAI-FM. On Reagan and *Late Great*, see Crawford Gribben, *Evangelical Millennialism in the Trans-Atlantic World, 1500-2000* (New York: Palgrave Macmillan, 2011), 115.

16. John McCollister, *So Help Me God* (Louisville: Winchester/John Knox Press, 1991), 199.

17. Daniel Schorr, "Reagan Recants: His Path from Armageddon to Détente," *Los Angeles Times*, January 3, 1988.

18. John Herbers, "Religious Leaders Tell of Worry on Armageddon View Ascribed to Reagan," *The New York Times*, October 21, 1984, 32; and Schorr, ibid.

19. Author's transcription of *Joe Cuomo and the Prophecy of Armageddon*.

20. Nancy Gibbs, "Apocalypse Now," *Time* Vol. 160, No. 1 (July 1, 2002): 47.

21. Gribben, *Evangelical Millennialism in the Trans-Atlantic World, 1500–2000*, 115.

22. Loveland, 223, 228.

23. Lou Cannon, *President Reagan: The Role of a Lifetime* (New York: Simon & Schuster, 1991), 156.

24. Ronald Reagan, *An American Life* (New York: Simon and Schuster, 1990), 585.

25. Ibid. For Falwell's threatened boycott, see Carla Hall et al., "The Night of 'The Day After,'" *The Washington Post*, November 21, 1983; and Philip H. Dougherty, "Advertising: Who Bought Time on 'The Day After,'" *The New York Times*, November 22, 1983.

26. R.P. Turco et al., "Nuclear Winter: Global Consequences of Multiple Nuclear Explosions," *Science* Vol. 222, No. 4630 (December 23, 1983): 1283–1292.

27. For a transcript of the October 21, 1984, debate, see http://www.debates.org/index.php?page=october-21-1984-debate-transcript. For Nancy Reagan's reaction, see

Boyer, *When Time Shall Be No More*, 142. For Reagan's backpedaling, see Richard V. Pierard, "Religion and the 1984 Election Campaign," *Review of Religious Research* Vol. 27, No. 2 (December 1985): 98–114.

28. Paul Lettow, *Ronald Reagan and His Quest to Abolish Nuclear Weapons* (New York: Random House, 2005), 133.

29. For a comprehensive survey of Lindsey's literary output, see Stephen R. Graham, 254.

30. Lindsey and Carlson, *The Late Great Planet Earth*, 72.

31. Ibid., 145.

32. Ibid., x, 75, 89, 115, 163.

33. Ibid., 23–23, 78.

34. Ibid., 53.

35. Ibid., 43.

36. Ibid., 104.

37. Ibid., 140–157.

38. Daniel Wojcik, *The End of the World as We Know It* (New York: New York University Press, 1997), 43.

39. Mark A. Kellner, "John F. Walvoord, 92, longtime Dallas President, dies," *Christianity Today* Vol. 47, No. 2 (February 2003): 27.

40. John F. Walvoord, *Armageddon, Oil, and the Middle East Crisis* (Grand Rapids, MI: Zondervan Publishing House, 1990), 182. For the book's salient details, see 53–56, 61–62, 109–146, and 177–184. Pages 201–202 provide an excellent tabulation of the biblical passages underlying the dispensationalist interpretation of current-day events.

41. For a comprehensive overview of Lindsey's oeuvre from the 1970s and 1980s, see Stephen R. Graham.

42. Hal Lindsey, *The 1980's: Countdown to Armageddon* (New York: Bantam Books, 1981).

43. Ibid., 29.

44. Peter M. Shearer and Philip B. Stark, "Global risk of big earthquakes has not recently increased," *Proceedings of the National Academy of Sciences of the United States* Vol. 109, No. 3 (January 2012): 717–721.

45. Lindsey, *The 1980's: Countdown to Armageddon*, 44.

46. Hal Lindsey, *Planet Earth—2000 A.D.* (Palos Verdes, CA: Western Front, Ltd., 1996), 41, 107–124, 175–192, subheading title 114.

47. Deaths from choking: https://www.statista.com/statistics/527321/deaths-due-to-choking-in-the-us/; and lighting, https://www.cdc.gov/disasters/lightning/victimdata.html; and terrorism, https://www.cato.org/blog/terrorism-deaths-ideology-charlottesville-anomaly.

48. See, for example, http://www.who.int/hiv/data/mortality_targets_2016.png?ua=1, accessed February 25, 2018.

49. https://www.hallindsey.com/, accessed February 25, 2018.

50. Peter Applebome, "Jerry Falwell, Moral Majority Founder, Dies at 73," *The New York Times*, May 16, 2007, A1.

51. Susan Friend Harding, *The Book of Falwell* (Princeton, NJ: Princeton University Press, 2000), 195.

52. https://www.upi.com/Archives/1984/08/23/Moral-Majority-founder-Jerry-Falwell-calling-President-Reagan-the/6961462081600/, accessed April 19, 2018.

53. Applebome, ibid.

54. Miles A. Pomper, "Church, Not State, Guides Some Lawmakers on Middle East," *Congressional Quarterly* Vol. 58 (March 23, 2002): 829. For a controversial but thorough critique of the American-Israel lobby, see John Mearsheimer and Stephen M. Walt, *The Israel Lobby and U.S. Foreign Policy* (New York: Farrar, Straus and Giroux, 2007).

55. Pomper, ibid.

56. Ibid., 830.

57. Ibid., 831.

58. Michael Lind, *Up from Conservatism* (New York: Free Press Paperbacks, 1999), 99.

59. Myra MacPherson, "The Pulpit and the Power," *The Washington Post*, October 18, 1985, Friday Style D1.

60. Gregory Palast, "I don't have to be nice to the spirit of the Antichrist," *The Guardian* (May 23, 1999), available at https://www.theguardian.com/business/1999/may/23/columnists.observerbusiness1.

61. David Edwin Harrell Jr., *Pat Robertson* (Grand Rapids, MI: William B. Eerdmans Publishing Company, 2010), 86–124; and Wayne King, "Robertson, Displaying Mail, Says He Will Join '88 Race," *The New York Times*, September 16, 1987, D30.

62. Harrell, 108.

63. Yoon, 551–552.

64. Yoon, 514–515.

65. Harrell, 324.

66. See, respectively, https://www.youtube.com/watch?v=uDT3krve9iE; Richard Kyle, *Apocalyptic Fever* (Eugene, OR: Cascade Books, 2012); https://www.youtube.com/watch?v=W0hWAxJ3_Js; and https://www.youtube.com/watch?v=P6xBo9EijIQ.

67. Bruce Evensen, "Robertson's Credibility Problem," *Chicago Tribune*, February 23, 1988; and Michael Oreskes, "Robertson Comes Under Fire for Asserting That Cuba Holds Soviet Missiles," *The New York Times*, February 16, 1988, 28.

68. Harrell, 326–328; and Gorenberg, 139, 157, 169.

69. Harrell, 103.

70. Tom W. Smith, "Beliefs about God Across Time and Countries," NORC/University of Chicago working paper (2012). One essayist, for example, noted the almost complete absence of apocalyptic belief in Australia, despite the cultural similarities with the United States; see Keith Gordon, "The End of (the Other Side of) the World: Apocalyptic Belief in the Australian Political Structure," *Intersections* Vol. 10, No. 1 (2009): 609–645; while a poll commissioned by Reuters looked at belief in the 2012 "Mayan Calendar" apocalypse across 21 nations; see Ipsos Global Advisor, "Mayan Prophecy: The End of the World?," https://www.ipsos.com/sites/default/files/news_and_polls/2012-05/5610-ppt.pdf, accessed February 17, 2018.

71. https://news.gallup.com/poll/1690/religion.aspx, accessed September 3, 2019.

72. Pippa Norris and Ronald Inglehart, *Sacred and Secular* (Cambridge, UK: Cambridge University Press, 2004), see especially 3–32.

73. Ibid.

74. Pew Research Center, "In America, Does More Education Equal Less Religion?," April 26, 2017, http://www.pewforum.org/2017/04/26/in-america-does-more-education-equal-less-religion/, accessed December 3, 2018.

75. Edward J. Larson and Larry Witham, "Leading scientists still reject God," *Nature* Vol. 344, No. 6691 (July 23, 1998): 313.

76. James H. Leuba, *The Belief in God and Immortality* (Chicago: The Open Court Publishing Company, 1921), 255; and Michael Stirrat and R. Elisabeth Cornwell, "Eminent Scientists Reject the Supernatural: A Survey of Fellows of the Royal Society," *Evolution Education and Outreach* Vol. 6, No. 33 (December 2013): 1–5.

77. See, for example, Marie Cornwall, "The Determinants of Religious Behavior: A Theoretical Model and Empirical Test," *Social Forces* Vol. 66, No. 2 (December 1989): 572–592.

78. The interactive OECD PISA database can be accessed at http://www.oecd.org/pisa/; the 2015 test results, for example, are located at http://www.keepeek.com/Digital-Asset-Management/oecd/education/pisa-2015-results-volume-i_9789264266490-en#page323; a summary can be found at https://en.wikipedia.org/wiki/Programme_for_International_Student_Assessment.

79. Michael A. Dimock and Samuel L. Popkin, "Political Knowledge in Comparative Perspective," in Shanto Iyengar and Richard Reeves, Eds., *Do The Media Govern?* (Thousand Oaks, CA: Sage Publications, 1997), 217–224. For the source of the five-question survey, see Andrew Kohut et al., *Eight Nation, People & The Press Survey* (Washington, DC: Times Mirror Center for People & The Press, 1994), 17, 23.

80. Dimock and Popkin, quote 218.

81. James Curran et al., "Media System, Public Knowledge and Democracy: A Comparative Study," *European Journal of Communications* Vol. 14, No. 1 (2009): 5–26.

82. Ibid.

83. Hal Lindsey and Cliff Ford, *Facing Millennial Midnight* (Beverly Hills, CA: Western Front, Ltd., 1998).

84. Gorenberg, 222.

85. J. Eric Oliver and Thomas J. Wood, "Conspiracy Theories and the Paranoid Style(s) of Mass Opinion," *American Journal of Political Science* Vol. 58, No. 4 (October 2014): 952–966.

86. Hermann Rauschning, *Hitler Speaks* (London: Eyer & Spottiswoode, 1939), 134.

87. For the briefest of samples of this critical research, see Robert L. Trivers, "The Evolution of Reciprocal Altruism," *The Quarterly Review of Biology* Vol. 46, No. 1 (March 1971): 35–57, quote 49; W.D. Hamilton, "The Genetical Evolution of Social Behaviour I," *Journal of Theoretical Biology* Vol. 7, No. 1 (July 1964): 1–16,

and Part II, 17–52; Leda Cosmides and John Tooby, "Cognitive Adaptations for Social Exchange," in Jerome H. Barkow et al., *The Adapted Mind* (New York: Oxford University Press, 1992), 180–206; and Luciano Arcuri and Gün Semin, "Language Use in Intergroup Contexts: The Linguistic Intergroup Bias," *Journal of Personality and Social Psychology* Vol. 57, No. 6 (1989): 981–993. For a general treatment of the subject of the origins of human morality and Manichean thinking, see Robert Wright, *The Moral Animal* (New York: Vintage Books, 1994).

88. See, for example, Rebecca S. Bigler et al., "When Groups Are Not Created Equal: Effects of Group Status on the Formation of Intergroup Attitudes in Children," *Child Development* Vol. 72, No. 4 (July/August 2001): 1151–1162.

89. The experiments, and their theoretical implications, are discussed in Muzafir Sherif et al., *Intergroup Conflict and Cooperation: The Robbers Cave Experiment* (Norman, OK: Institute of Group Relations, 1961), see especially 59–84 and 97–113. Although it's not certain, it appears that this book describes the 1954 experiment; the 1949 one was less detailed, and there also seems to have been an abortive one in 1953.

90. Ibid., 118, 153–183, 187.

91. Paul Boyer, *When Time Shall Be No More*, 265.

92. Lindsey, *The Late Great Planet Earth*, 51–52, 63–64, 71–75, 101–102, 232.

93. Susan Solomon et al., "Emergence of healing in the Antarctic ozone layer," *Science* Vol. 253, No. 6296 (July 16, 2016): 269–274.

94. Lindsey, *The 1980's: Countdown to Armageddon*, 5–6.

95. Ibid., 4–7.

96. Sharlet, "Jesus Killed Mohammed," 38.

97. Anne C. Loveland, *American Evangelicals and the U.S. Military 1942–1993* (Baton Rouge, LA: Lousiana State University Press, 1996), 1–66, 118–164, quote 164.

98. Ibid., 7.

99. Sharlet, 38.

100. Loveland, xi–xii.

101. Goodstein; also, Banerjee.

Chapter 11: Dispensationalist Catastrophes: Potential and Real

1. Ellsberg, 64–65 and 67–89; and Eric Schlosser, *Command and Control* (New York: Penguin Press, 2013), 300. For a superb overview of the risks of accidental nuclear war, see Bruce Blair, *The Logic of Accidental Nuclear War* (Washington, DC: The Brookings Institution, 1993); for the critical concept of "predelegation" of strike authority, see especially 46–51.

2. Schlosser, 245–247

3. William Burr and Thomas S. Blanton, "The Submarines of October," National Security Archive, October 31, 2002, https://www.webcitation.org/67Zh0rqhC?url=http://www.gwu.edu/%7Ensarchiv/NSAEBB/NSAEBB75/, accessed May 8, 2018; and Marion Lloyd, "Soviets Close to Using A-Bomb in 1962 Crisis, Forum is Told," *The Boston Globe*, October 13, 2002.

4. Bruce Blair, *Frontline* interview, https://www.pbs.org/wgbh/pages/frontline/shows/russia/interviews/blair.html, accessed May 9, 2018. See also Blair, 59–167.

5. Peter Schweizer, *Victory* (New York: Atlantic Monthly Press, 1994), 8–9.

6. Robert M. Gates, *From the Shadows* (New York: Simon & Schuster Paperbacks, 1996), 114.

7. Schlosser, 367–368, 371.

8. Charles Perrow, *Normal Accidents* (Princeton, NJ: Princeton University Press), 11.

9. https://jimbakkershow.com/watch/?guid=3465, accessed June 17, 2018, *Dr. Strangelove* (movie).

10. Lindsey, *The 1980's: Countdown to Armageddon*, 77, 85, 107, 122, 134, 138, 153, 212.

11. Ibid., 154.

12. Lindsey, *Planet Earth—2000 A.D.*, 61.

13. Boyer, 146.

14. A.G. Mojtabai, *Blessed Assurance* (Syracuse, NY: Syracuse University Press, 1997), 180–183; and Robert Reinhold, "Author of 'At Home with the Bomb' Settles in City Where Bomb Is Made," *The New York Times*, September 15, 1986, A12.

15. Mojtabai, 164.

16. Gordon D. Kaufman, "Nuclear Eschatology and the Study of Religion," *Journal of the American Academy of Religion* Vol. 51, No. 1 (March 1983): 8.

17. Stuart A. Wright, "Davidians and Branch Davidians," in Stuart A. Wright, *Armageddon at Waco* (Chicago: University of Chicago Press, 1995), 24.

18. James D. Tabor and Eugene V. Gallagher, *Why Waco?* (Berkeley: University of California Press, 1995), 33–35.

19. April 22, 1959, actually fell 1,264 days after November 5, 1955, but apparently the announcement was mailed out on November 9; see https://www.gadsda.com/1959-executive-council-minutes/.

20. Stuart A. Wright, "Davidians and Branch Davidians," 30–32.

21. Edward D. Bromley and Edward G. Silver, "The Davidian Tradition," in Stuart A. Wright, *Armageddon at Waco*, 50.

22. Ibid., 52–53.

23. Tabor and Gallagher, 35–41, quote 41.

24. Charles, 1, 63. An alternative explanation of Revelation's opacity to the modern audience is that its author/authors were trying to spin a narrative that updates Ezekiel and Daniel to the mainly Jewish audience of the first and second centuries A.D. Personal communication, Christopher Mackay.

25. Yair Bar-El et al., "Jerusalem syndrome," *British Journal of Psychiatry* Vol. 176 (2000): 86–90.

26. Ibid.

27. Tabor and Gallagher, 29–30, 61; Jeffrey Goldberg, "Israel's Y2K Problem," *The New York Times*, October 3, 1999; "A date with death," *The Guardian*, October 26, 1999; and Nettanel Slyomovics, "Waco Started With a Divine Revelation in Jerusalem. It Ended With 76 Dying in a Fire on Live TV," *Haaretz*, February 24, 2018.

28. Bromley and Silver, 60.

29. Tabor and Gallagher, 41–43, 52–76, 79, direct quotes 72 and 73, and for apologizing for his lust to partners, see 74; also, Bromley and Silver, 43–72.

30. Bromley and Silver, 52–58, and James Trimm, "David Koresh's Seven Seals Teaching," *Watchman Expositor* Vol. 11 (1994): 7–8, available at https://www.watchman.org/articles/cults-alternative-religions/david-koreshs-seven-seals-teaching/.

31. James D. Tabor, "The Waco Tragedy: An Autobiographical Account of One Attempt to Avert Disaster," in James R. Lewis, Ed., *From the Ashes* (Lanham, MD: Rowman & Littlefield Publishers, Inc., 1994), 14.

32. Tony Ortega, "Hush, Hush, Sweet Charlatans," *Phoenix New Times*, November 30, 1995. In these pages, I've intentionally avoided using the word "cult," a term shunned by most theologians.

33. Associated Press, "Davidian Compound Had Huge Weapon Cache, Ranger Says," *Los Angeles Times*, July 7, 2000; for gun show loophole, see "Gun Show Background Checks State Laws," https://www.governing.com/gov-data/safety-justice/gun-show-firearms-bankground-checks-state-laws-map.html.

34. Tabor and Gallagher, 64–65, 95. This law is still on the books; see https://codes.findlaw.com/tx/penal-code/penal-sect-9-31.html.

35. Mark England and Darlene McCormick, "The Sinful Messiah: Part One," *Waco Tribune-Herald*, February 27, 1993. The entire series can be accessed at http://www.wacotrib.com/news/branch_davidians/sinful-messiah/the-sinful-messiah-part-one/article_eb1b96e9-413c-5bab-ba9f-425b373c5667.html.

36. For a detailed discussion of the child abuse and sex with minors allegations, see Christopher G. Ellison and John P. Bartkowski, "Babies Were Being Beaten," in Stuart A. Wright, *Armageddon in Waco* (Chicago: University of Chicago Press, 1995); 111–149; and Lawrence Lilliston, "Who Committed Child Abuse at Waco," in James R. Lewis, Ed., *From the Ashes* (Lanham, MD: Rowman & Littlefield Publishers, Inc., 1994), 169–173.

37. Moorman Oliver, Jr., "Killed by Semantics: Or Was It a Keystone Kop Kaleidoscope Kaper?" in James R. Lewis, Ed., *From the Ashes*, 75–77.

38. Department of the Treasury, "Report of the Department of the Treasury on the Bureau of Tobacco, Alcohol, and Firearms investigation of Vernon Wayne Howell, also known as David Koresh," September 1993, 95–100, available at https://archive.org/stream/reportofdepartme00unit/reportofdepartme00unit_djvu.txt, accessed June 23, 2018.

39. Federal Bureau of Investigation, "The Megiddo Project," October 20, 1999, 28–29, available at http://www.cesnur.org/testi/FBI_004.htm.

40. Mark England, "9-1-1 records panic, horror," *Waco Tribune-Herald*, June 10, 1993.

41. James R. Lewis, "Showdown at the Waco Corral: ATF Cowboys Shoot Themselves in the Foot"; and Stuart A. Wright, "Misguided Tactics Contributed to Apocalypse in Waco," in *Armageddon in Waco*, 87–98.

42. Tabor, "The Waco Tragedy: An Autobiographical Account of One Attempt to Avert Disaster," 12–21, quote 16. For the CNN transcript, see http://edition.cnn .com/TRANSCRIPTS/1308/25/cotc.01.html.

43. Dean M. Kelly, "The Implosion of Mt. Carmel and Its Aftermath," in Stuart A. Wright, *Armageddon in Waco*, 360–361.

44. For a detailed discussion of how Koresh interpreted the BATF raid and subsequent siege in light of the seals, see Phillip Arnold, "The Davidian Dilemma—To Obey God or Man?," in James R. Lewis, Ed., *From the Ashes*, 23–31.

45. Ibid., 5–17, 100–103, quote 15–16.

46. R.W. Bradford, "Who Started the Fires? Mass Murder, American Style," and "Fanning the Flames of Suspicion: The Case Against Mass Suicide at Waco," in *Armageddon in Waco*, 111–120.

47. For the uncompleted, manuscript, see https://digital.library.txstate.edu/ bitstream/handle/10877/1839/375.pdf.

48. James D. Tabor, "Religious Discourse and Failed Negotiations," in Stuart A. Wright, *Armageddon in Waco*, 265.

49. United States Department of Justice, *Report to the Deputy Attorney General on the Events at Waco, Texas February 28 to April 19, 1993* (October 8, 1993), 158–190, available at https://www.justice.gov/archives/publications/waco/ report-deputy-attorney-general-events-waco-texas.

50. Opinion, "History and Timothy McVeigh," *The New York Times*, June 11, 2011; and Lou Michel and Dan Herbeck, *American Terrorist* (New York: ReganBooks, 2001), 166–168.

CHAPTER 12: RAPTURE FICTION

1. Joseph Birkbeck Burroughs, *Titan, Son of Saturn* (Oberlin, OH: The Emeth Publishers, 1905), 4, 5. Crawford Gribben has identified an even earlier work of Rapture fiction, a brief pamphlet dating to around 1879 by an author identified only as "H.R.K.," *Life in the Future*. Crawford Gribben, "Rethinking the Rise of Prophecy Fiction," unpublished, uncirculated manuscript, kindly provided by its author.

2. Crawford Gribben, *Writing the Rapture* (Oxford: Oxford University Press, 2009), 33.

3. Burroughs, 211, 223, 244–252, 289–324, see especially 304, 319.

4. For the authoritative précis of the genre, see Gribben, vide supra.

5. Frank Peretti, *This Present Darkness* (Wheaton, IL: Crossway, 2003).

6. Hal Lindsey and C. C. Carlson, *Satan Is Alive and Well on Planet Earth* (Grand Rapids, MI: Zondervan Publishing House, 1972), 18–19.

7. Philip Jenkins and Daniel Maier-Katkin, "Satanism: Myth and reality in a contemporary moral panic," *Crime, Law and Social Change* Vol. 17 (1992): 53–75. For the causative role of dispensationalism, see especially 63–64. Quote, Dr. Alan H. Peterson, *The American Focus on Satanic Crime, Volume I* (Milburn, NJ: The American Focus Publishing Company, 1988), foreword, and also see i–iii.

8. Ted L. Gunderson, in *American Focus on Satanic Crime, Volume 1*, 2–4.

9. Jenkins and Maier-Katkin, 57. For the May 16, 1985, *20/20* segment, "The Devil Worshippers," see https://www.youtube.com/watch?v=vG_w-uElGbM, https://www.youtube.com/watch?v=gG0ncaf-jhI, and https://www.youtube.com/watch?v=HwSP3j7RJlU. *NPR Weekend Edition Saturday*, March 12, 1988, courtesy of Jacob J. Goldstein. For a superb overview of the "satanic ritual abuse" moral panic of the 1980s, see Philip Jenkins, *Moral Panic* (New Haven, CT: Yale University Press, 1998), 145–188 and 275–277n1–10.

10. Margaret Talbot, "The devil in the nursery," *The New York Times Magazine*, January 7, 2001.

11. Ibid.

12. Daniel L. Turner, *Standing Without Apology* (Greenville, SC: Bob Jones University Press, 1997), 19.

13. Randall Balmer, *Encyclopedia of Evangelism* (Waco, TX: Baylor University Press, 2004), 391–392.

14. Tim LaHaye, Jerry B. Jenkins, and Sandi L. Swanson, *The Authorized Left Behind Handbook* (Wheaton, IL: Tyndale House Publishers, 2005), 7.

15. Gribben, 136 and 210n55. See Salem Kirban, *666* (Wheaton, IL: Tyndale House Publishers, 1970); the James essay is available at http://www.raptureready1.com/terry/james22.html.

16. Gribben, 8. From Amy Johnson Fryckholm, *Rapture Culture* (Oxford: Oxford University Press, 2004), 175: "Although LaHaye is listed as an author of the series, he himself has not written a word of the text." See also Bruce David Forbes "How Popular Are the Left Behind Books . . . and Why?," in Jeanne Halgren Kilde and Bruce David Forbes, Eds., *Rapture, Revelation, and the End Times* (New York: Palgrave Macmillan, 2004), 6.

17. Tim LaHaye and Jerry B. Jenkins, *Left Behind* (Wheaton, IL: Tyndale House Publishers, 1995), 1.

18. Ibid., 19.

19. Ibid., book summation.

20. Gribben, 129.

21. Forbes, 6–10.

22. David D. Kirkpatrick, "A Best-Selling Formula in Religious Thrillers," *The New York Times*, February 11, 2002, C2.

23. Nicholas D. Kristof, "Apocalypse (Almost) Now," *The New York Times*, November 24, 2004, A23.

24. Mike Madden, "Mike Huckabee hearts Israel," https://www.salon.com/2008/01/18/huckabee2_4/, accessed March 25, 2018.

25. David Gates.

26. Mark Ward, *Authorized* (Bellingham, WA: Lexham Press, 2018), 61.

27. David Gates.

28. Ibid.

29. Stuart A. Wright, 42–43; and Anonymous, "Christian evangelicals from the US flock to Holy Land in Israeli tourism boom," *Independent*, April 6, 2018.

30. Lawrence Wright, *Forcing the End*, https://www.pbs.org/wgbh/pages/front-line/shows/apocalypse/readings/forcing.html, accessed September 4, 2019.

31. Ibid.

32. Louis Sahagun, "The End of the world is near to their hearts," *Seattle Times*, June 27, 2006.

33. Gorenberg, 173.

CHAPTER 13: CAPITALISM'S PHILANTROPISTS

1. Jason Zweig, Introduction to Schwed, xiii; and Zweig, personal communication.

2. Maggie Mahar, *Bull!* (New York: HarperBusiness, 2003), 333–334. A Vanguard Group study demonstrated that by 2002, 70 percent of their 401(k)s had lost at least 20 percent of their value; Vanguard investors were, in general, more conservative than usual, and the firm offered no internet fund; for a better sense of how the dot-com bubble devastated small investors, see the "Bill's Barber Shop" section of Chapter 14.

3. In a narrow, semantic sense, though, this was untrue: the word "internet" refers to the fiber optic backbone that connects high-powered computers and servers. The ubiquitous "www" of modern discourse is the gateway to access documents or websites over that backbone with a system of digital addresses—uniform resource locators (URLs)—through browsers such as Chrome, Safari, and Internet Explorer. Technically "http" and "https" are the ways or protocols for accessing web pages. URLs are shortcuts that redirect traffic to the document at a web server computer's location, "IP address" in web argot.

4. William J. Bernstein, *Masters of the Word* (New York: Grove/Atlantic, 2013), 309–310; and Tim Berners-Lee, *Weaving the Web* (San Francisco: HarperSanFrancisco, 1999), 7–51.

5. Jim Clark, *Netscape Time* (New York: St. Martin's Press, 1999), 20–32, quote 32.

6. *The Economist*, "William Martin," August 6, 1998.

7. Robert L. Hetzel, *The Monetary Policy of the Federal Reserve* (New York: Cambridge University Press, 2008), 208–224, see especially Chairman Greenspan's remarks, 221; and Sebastian Mallaby, *The Man Who Knew* (New York: Penguin Press, 2016), 514–521, 536–542.

8. https://www.fdic.gov/about/history/timeline/1920s.html, accessed June 24, 2017.

9. Burton G. Malkiel, *A Random Walk down Wall Street* (New York: W. W. Norton & Company, Inc., 1999), 57–61.

10. Personal communication, Burton Malkiel, Richard Sylla, and John Bogle.

11. For 1929 PE ratios and dividend yields, see Wigmore, 35–85.

12. John Cassidy, *dot-con* (New York: Penguin Press, 2002), 348–363; and Roger Lowenstein, *Origins of the Crash* (New York: The Penguin Press, 2004), 101.

13. Thomas Easton and Scott Wooley, "The $20 Billion Crumb," *Forbes*, April 19, 1999.

14. Ibid.

15. Personal communication, Alan Mauldin, TeleGeography, Inc.

16. Simon Romero, "In Another Big Bankruptcy, a Fiber Optic Venture Fails," *The New York Times*, January 29, 2002.

17. Timothy L. O'Brien, "A New Legal Chapter for a 90's Flameout," *The New York Times*, August 15, 2004.

18. Steven Lipin et al., "Deals & Deal Makers: Bids & Offers," *The Wall Street Journal*, December 10, 1999.

19. Randall E. Stross, *eBoys* (New York: Crown Business, 2000), 30, 36.

20. Linda Himmelstein, "Can You Sell Groceries Like Books?," Bloomberg News, July 25, 1999, http://www.bloomberg.com/news/articles/1999-07-25/can-you-sell-groceries-like-books, accessed October 26, 2016.

21. Mary Dejevsky, "Totally Bananas," *The Independent*, November 9, 1999.

22. William Aspray et al., *Food in the Internet Age* (New York: Springer Science & Business Media, 2013), 25–35; and Mylene Mangalindan, "Webvan Shuts Down Operations, Will Seek Chapter 11 Protection," *The Wall Street Journal*, July 10, 2001.

23. Mangalindan, ibid.; and John Cook and Marni Leff, "Webvan is gone, but HomeGrocer.com may return," *Seattle Post-Intelligencer*, July 9, 2001.

24. Bethany McLean and Peter Eklind, *The Smartest Guys in the Room* (New York: Penguin Group, 2003).

25. Ibid., 4–13.

26. Alexi Barrionuevo, "Did Ken Lay Demonstrate Credibility?" *The New York Times*, May 3, 2006. For Ken Lay's salary, see Thomas S. Mulligan and Nancy Rivera Brooks, "Enron Paid Senior Execs Millions," *Los Angeles Times*, June 28, 2002.

27. David Yermack, "Flights of fancy: Corporate jets, CEO perquisites, and inferior shareholder returns," *Journal of Financial Economics* Vol. 80, No. 1 (April 2006): 211–242.

28. McLean and Elkind, 89–90, 97–98, 338; and Robert Bryce, "Flying High," *Boston Globe Magazine*, September 29, 2002.

29. Ibid., 89–90, 97–98; and Bryce.

30. Elkind and McLean, 225.

31. Ibid., 28–33.

32. Ibid., 183, 184–185, 254.

33. John R. Emshwiller and Rebecca Smith, "Murky Waters: A Primer On the Enron Partnerships," *The Wall Street Journal*, January 21, 2001.

34. Cassel Bryan-Low and Suzanne McGee, "Enron Short Seller Detected Red Flags in Regulatory Filings," *The Wall Street Journal*, November 5, 2001.

35. Elkind and McLean, 405.

36. Chris Axtman, "How Enron awards do, or don't, trickle down," *Christian Science Monitor*, June 20, 2005.

37. Rebecca Smith, "New SEC Filing Aids Case Against Enron," *The Wall Street Journal*, May 15, 2003; Ellen E. Schultz, "Enron Employees' Massive Losses Suddenly Highlight 'Lockdowns,'" *The Wall Street Journal*, January 16, 2002; and Elkind and McLean, 297–398.

38. Lowenstein, 58–60.

39. Clark, 12–15, 19; Joshua Quittner and Michelle Slatalla, *Speeding the Net* (New York: Atlantic Monthly Press, 1998), 242–248.

40. Richard Karlgaard, "The Ghost of Netscape," *The Wall Street Journal*, August 9, 2005, A10.

CHAPTER 14: HUCKSTERS OF THE DIGITAL AGE

1. Edward Wyatt, "Fox to Begin a 'More Business Friendly' News Channel," *The New York Times*, February 9, 2007.

2. Peter Elkind et al., "The Trouble With Frank Quattrone was the top investment banker in Silicon Valley. Now his firm is exhibit A in a probe of shady IPO deals," *Fortune*, September 3, 2001, http://archive.fortune.com/magazines/fortune/fortune_archive/2001/09/03/309270/index.htm, accessed November 17, 2016.

3. McLean and Elkind, 234.

4. John Schwartz, "Enron's Collapse: The Analyst: Man Who Doubted Enron Enjoys New Recognition," *The New York Times*, January 21, 2002.

5. Ibid.

6. Richard A. Oppel, Jr., "Merrill Replaced Research Analyst Who Upset Enron," *The New York Times*, July 30, 2002.

7. Howard Kurtz, *The Fortune Tellers* (New York: The Free Press, 2000), 32.

8. Scott Tong, "Father of modern 401(k) says it fails many Americans," http://www.marketplace.org/2013/06/13/sustainability/consumed/father-modern-401k-says-it-fails-many-americans, accessed November 1, 2016.

9. Jeremy Olsham, "The inventor of the 401(k) says he created a 'monster,'" http://www.marketwatch.com/story/the-inventor-of-the-401k-says-he-created-a-monster-2016-05-16; and Nick Thornton, "Total retirement assets near $25 trillion mark," http://www.benefitspro.com/2015/06/30/total-retirement-assets-near-25-trillion-mark accessed November 11, 2016.

10. The most easily available current report on the gap between IRR and fund returns is Morningstar's annual "Mind the Gap" report, available at https://www.morningstar.com/lp/mind-the-gap?cid=CON_RES0022; on average, investors lose about 1 percent of return per year of return from poor timing; this is on top of fund expenses, which also average around 1 percent.

11. Aaron Heresco, *Shaping the Market: CNBC and the Discourses of Financialization* (Ph.D. thesis, Pennsylvania State University, 2014), 81.

12. Gabriel Sherman, *The Loudest Voice in the Room* (New York: Random House, 2014), 5–9.

13. Joe McGinnis, *The Selling of the President, 1968* (New York: Trident Press, 1969), 64–65.

14. Cassidy, 166.

15. Sherman, 146–147.

16. Heresco, 88–115; and Mahar, 156–157.

17. Heresco, 151–152.

18. Ekaterina V. Karniouchina et al., "Impact of *Mad Money* Stock Recommendations: Merging Financial and Marketing Perspectives," *Journal of Marketing* Vol. 73 (November 2009): 244–266; and J. Felix Meshcke, "CEO Appearances on CNBC," working paper, http://citeseerx.ist.psu.edu/viewdoc/download?doi=10.1.1 .203.566&rep=rep1&type=pdf, accessed November 12, 2016; and for Cramer /Bartiromo, see Kurtz, 207.

19. Kurtz, 117–118.

20. Heresco, 232.

21. James K. Glassman, "Is Government Strangling the New Economy?," *The Wall Street Journal*, April 6, 2000. (In the interest of full disclosure, the *Journal* published a dyspeptic letter to the editor by this author in response to Mr. Glassman's editorial, "The Market Villain: It's Not Your Uncle," April 19, 2000.)

22. George Gilder, "The Faith of a Futurist," *The Wall Street Journal*, January 1, 2000.

23. Shane Frederick, "Cognitive Reflection and Decision Making," *Journal of Economic Perspectives* Vol. 19, No. 4 (Fall 2005): 25–42. For the Four Card Task, see P. C. Wason, "Reasoning," in B.M. Foss, Ed., *New Horizons in Psychology* (New York: Penguin, 1966), 145–146.

24. David L. Hull, *Science and Selection* (Cambridge, UK: Cambridge University Press, 2001), 37.

25. Keith E. Stanovich et al., *The Rationality Quotient* (Cambridge: MIT Press, 2016), 25–27. For an extensive sample of CART questions and scoring, see ibid., 331–368. Quote from Keith E. Stanovich, "The Comprehensive Assessment of Rational Thinking," *Educational Psychologist* Vol. 51, No. 1 (February 2016): 30–31.

26. R.B. Zajonc, "Feeling and Thinking," *American Psychologist* Vol. 35, No. 2 (February 1980): 155, 169–170.

27. Daniel Kahneman, slide show for *Thinking Fast and Slow*, thinking-fast-and-slow-oscar-trial.ppt.

28. Isaiah Berlin, *The Proper Study of Mankind* (New York: Farrar, Straus and Giroux, 1998), 436–498, quote 436.

29. Tetlock, 15, quote 56.

30. Dan Gardner and Philip Tetlock, "What's Wrong with Expert Predictions," https://www.cato-unbound.org/2011/07/11/dan-gardner-philip-tetlock/ overcoming-our-aversion-acknowledging-our-ignorance.

31. Tetlock, 138.

32. Tetlock, 42–88, 98, 125–141, quote 63.

33. Susan Pulliam, "At Bill's Barber Shop, 'In Like Flynn' Is A Cut Above the Rest—Owner's Tech-Stock Chit-Chat Enriches Cape Cod Locals; The Maytag Dealer Is Wary," *The Wall Street Journal*, March 13, 2000, A1.

34. Personal communication, Susan Pulliam.

35. Pulliam, "At Bill's Barber Shop, 'In Like Flynn' Is A Cut Above the Rest—Owner's Tech-Stock Chit-Chat Enriches Cape Cod Locals; The Maytag Dealer Is Wary."

36. Susan Pulliam and Ruth Simon, "Nasdaq Believers Keep the Faith To Recoup Losses in Rebound," *The Wall Street Journal*, June 21, 2000, C1.

37. Susan Pulliam, "Hair Today, Gone Tomorrow: Tech Ills Shave Barber," *The Wall Street Journal*, March 7, 2001, C1.

38. Jonathan Cheng, "A Barber Misses Market's New Buzz," *The Wall Street Journal*, March 8, 2013, and Pulliam, "Hair Today, Gone Tomorrow: Tech Ills Shave Barber."

39. Source: Investment Company Institute 2016 Fact Book from ici.org for U.S. equity fund holdings, and total market cap from http://data.worldbank.org/indicator/CM.MKT.LCAP.CD?end=2000&start=1990, both accessed December 17, 2017.

40. Van Wagoner clip: https://www.youtube.com/watch?v=i9uR6WQNDn4.

41. From transcript of "Betting on the Market," aired January 27, 1997, http://www.pbs.org/wgbh/pages/frontline/shows/betting/etal/script.html, accessed December 17, 2016.

42. Diya Gullapalli, "Van Wagoner to Step Down As Manager of Growth Fund," *The Wall Street Journal*, August 4, 2008; total returns calculated from annualized returns. See also Jonathan Burton, "From Fame, Fortune to Flamed-Out Star," *The Wall Street Journal*, March 10, 2010.

43. Clifford Asness, "Bubble Logic: Or, How to Learn to Stop Worrying and Love the Bull," working paper, 45–46, https://ssrn.com/abstract=240371, accessed on November 12, 2016.

44. Mike Snow, "Day-Trade Believers Teach High-Risk Investing," *The Washington Post*, July 6, 1998.

45. Arthur Levitt, testimony before Senate Permanent Subcommittee on Investigations, Committee on Governmental Affairs, September 16, 1999, https://www.sec.gov/news/testimony/testarchive/1999/tsty2199.htm, accessed December 29, 2019.

46. Mark Gongloff, "Where Are They Now: The Beardstown Ladies," *The Wall Street Journal*, May 1, 2006.

47. Calmetta Y. Coleman, "Beardstown Ladies Add Disclaimer That Makes Returns Look 'Hooey,'" *The Wall Street Journal*, February 27, 1998.

48. Cassidy, 119.

49. Mahar, 262–263, 306–309, quote 307; for Bond sentencing, see "Ex-Money Manager Gets 12 Years in Scheme," *Los Angeles Times*, February 12, 2003.

50. Gregory Zuckerman and Paul Beckett, "Tiger Makes It Official: Funds Will Shut Down," *The Wall Street Journal*, March 31, 2000. During the late 1990s, the author personally experienced a milder version of this kind of pushback on a few occasions at little cost, but quickly learned to keep his opinions about tech stocks to himself. The reader might also reasonably wonder how well he, forewarned by *Extraordinary Popular Delusions*, and given the failure of Mackay to appreciate the railway mania that occurred shortly following its publication, interpreted the late 1990s tech bubble as it unfolded. By happy coincidence, he published a personal finance title in 2000, at the bubble's height, *The Intelligent Asset Allocator* (New York: McGraw-Hill, Inc., 2000). The ongoing bubble, as yet un-burst, was discussed at length on pages 124–132; see especially the brief mention of *Extraordinary Popular Delusions* on page 178.

These extracts are available with the very kind permission of McGraw-Hill, Inc., at http://www.efficientfrontier.com/files/TIAA-extract.pdf.

51. Charles W. Kadlec, *Dow 100,000* (Upper Saddle River, NJ: Prentice Hall Press, 1999).

52. James K. Glassman and Kevin A. Hassett, *Dow 36,000* (New York: Times Business, 1999); and Charles W. Kadlec, *Dow 100,000 Fact or Fiction* (New York: Prentice Hall Press, 1999).

53. Schwed, 54.

CHAPTER 15: MAHDIS AND CALIPHS

1. "Dabiq: Why is Syrian town so important for IS?" *BBC News* (October 4, 2016), http://www.bbc.com/news/world-middle-east-30083303, accessed May 30, 2018.

2. David Cook, *Studies in Muslim Apocalyptic* (Princeton, NJ: The Darwin Press, Inc., 2002), 8.

3. David Cook, *Contemporary Muslim Apocalyptic Literature* (Syracuse, NY: Syracuse University Press, 2005), 84.

4. Samuel P. Huntington, *The Clash of Civilizations and the Remaking of the World Order* (New York: Simon & Shuster, 1996), 257–258.

5. 'Arif, Muhammad 'Izzat, *Hal al-Dajjal yahkum al-'alam al-an?* (Cairo: Dar al-I'tisam, 1997), 85, quoted in Cook, *Contemporary Muslim Apocalyptic Literature*, 220.

6. Jean-Pierre Filiu, *Apocalypse in Islam*, trans. M.B. Devoise (Berkeley: University of California Press, 2011), 14; and Cook, *Contemporary Muslim Apocalyptic Literature*, 16.

7. Cook, *Studies in Muslim Apocalyptic*, 6–13.

8. William McCants, *The ISIS Apocalypse* (New York: St Martin's Press, 2015), 23.

9. Ibid., 26.

10. Cook, *Contemporary Muslim Apocalyptic Literature*, 7.

11. Cook, *Studies in Muslim Apocalyptic*, 95–97.

12. Thomas Lippman, *Inside the Mirage* (Boulder, CO: Westview Press, 2004), 220; Bruce Riedel, *Kings and Presidents* (Washington, DC: Brookings Institution Press, 2018), 50; and Cook, *Contemporary Muslim Apocalyptic Literature*, 23, 33.

13. Cook, *Contemporary Muslim Apocalyptic Literature*, 117.

14. Filiu, 14; and Cook, *Contemporary Muslim Apocalyptic Literature*, 8, 50–52.

15. Cook, *Contemporary Muslim Apocalyptic Literature*, 8–11; Filiu, xi, 11–18.

16. Cook, *Contemporary Muslim Apocalyptic Literature*, 232–233.

17. Quoted in Gorenberg, 188.

18. Ibid., 191.

19. Filiu, 83–94, quote 86; and Cook, *Contemporary Muslim Apocalyptic Literature*, 64, 68.

20. Personal communication, Jean-Pierre Filiu.

21. Filiu, 140.

22. Filiu, 62–63.

23. Edward Mortimer, *Faith and Power* (New York: Vintage Books, 1982), 76–79.

24. Hilaire Belloc, *The Modern Traveler* (London: Edward Arnold, 1898), 41.

25. Robert Lacey, *Inside the Kingdom* (New York: Viking Press, 2009), 15–16.

26. Ibid., 3.

27. Thomas Hegghammer and Stéphane Lacroix, "Rejectionist Islamism in Saudi Arabia: The Story of Juyahman al-'Utaybi Revisited," *International Journal of Middle East Studies* Vol. 39 (2007): 104–106; and Yaroslav Trofimov, *The Siege of Mecca* (New York: Doubleday, 2007), 11–28.

28. Hegghammer and Lacroix, 106–109.

29. Trofimov, 20–49.

30. Hegghammer and Lacroix, 108–110.

31. Filiu, 16.

32. Lacey, 21.

33. Trofimov, 51.

34. For a detailed description of the letters, see Joseph A. Kechichian, "Islamic Revivalism and Change in Saudi Arabia: Juhaymān Al'Utaybī's 'Letters' to the Saudi People," *The Muslim World* Vol. 80, No. 1 (January 1990): 9–15. The author plays down the importance of the letters' eschatological content, and describes their aim as at the corruption of the Saudi regime and *ulema* (the high religious council), particularly bin Baz. He also states that Qahtani was not declared Mahdi at the Mosque uprising, which contradicts most other observers.

35. Lacey, 22–23.

36. Trofimov, 170–172.

37. Trofimov, 68–255; and Kechichian, 1–8.

38. Hegghammer and Lacroix, 109–112.

39. Ibid., 114.

40. Ibid., 29, 248–249.

41. McCants, *The ISIS Apocalypse*, 50–51, 196n12.

42. David Cook, "Abu Musa'b al-Suri and Abu Musa'b al-Zarqawi: The Apocalyptic Theorist and the Apocalyptic Practitioner," private working paper, cited with permission from the author. Quote from hadith of Thawban from Cook, "Fighting to Create a Just State: Apocalypticism in Radical Muslim Discourse," in Sohail H. Hashimi, Ed., *Just Wars, Holy Wars, and Jihads* (Oxford: Oxford University Press, 2012), 374.

43. Dexter Filkins et al., "How Surveillance and Betrayal Led to a Hunt's End," *The New York Times*, June 9, 2006.

44. Steve Coll, *The Bin Ladens* (New York: The Penguin Press, 2008), 12–15, 137–152, 252–256.

45. McCants, *The ISIS Apocalypse*, 66.

46. Trofimov, 161.

47. McCants, *The ISIS Apocalypse*, 10–22.

48. Pew Research Center, "The World's Muslims: Unity and Diversity," 57, http://assets.pewresearch.org/wp-content/uploads/sites/11/2012/08/the-worlds -muslims-full-report.pdf.

49. Ibid.

50. McCants, *The ISIS Apocalypse*, 32.

51. Ibid., 32–42.

52. Cole Bunzel, *From Paper State to Caliphate: The Ideology of the Islamic State* (Washington, DC: Center for Middle East Policy at Brookings, 2015), 22–23.

53. Daniel Kimmage and Kathleen Ridolfo, *Iraqi Insurgent Media* (Washington, DC: Radio Free Europe/Radio Liberty, 2007), 4–5.

54. Ibid., 27–29, 70–71.

55. Anwar al-Awlaki, Full text of "Anwar Nasser Aulaqi" from FBI files, available at https://archive.org/stream/AnwarNasserAulaqi/Anwar%20Nasser%20 Aulaqi%2010_djvu.txt, accessed June 6, 2018.

56. The FBI's transliteration of Alwan's name varies from his more commonly used one.

57. Hugh Macleod, "YouTube Islamist: how Anwar al-Awlaki became al-Qaeda's link to local terror," *The Guardian*, May 7, 2010.

58. Eric Schmitt, "U.S. Commando Killed in Yemen in Trump's First Counter-terrorism Operation," *The New York Times*, January 29, 2017; Charlie Savage, "Court Releases Large Parts of Memo Approving Killing of American in Yemen," *The New York Times*, June 23, 2014; Mark Mazetti et al., "Two-Year Manhunt Led to Killing of Awlaki in Yemen, *The New York Times*, September 30, 2011; and McCants, *The ISIS Apocalypse*, 60.

59. Martin Chulov, "ISIS: the inside story," *The Guardian*, December 11, 2014; Janine di Giovanni, "Who Is ISIS Leader Abu Bakr Baghdadi?," *Newsweek*, December 8, 2014; and William McCants, "The Believer," *Brookings Essay* (September 1, 2015), http://csweb.brookings.edu/content/research/essays/2015/thebeliever.html, accessed June 8, 2018.

60. McCants, *The ISIS Apocalypse*, 85–98.

61. David Remnick, "Going the Distance: On and off the road with Barack Obama," *The New Yorker*, January 27, 2014.

62. http://www.jihadica.com/the-caliphate%E2%80%99s-scholar-in-arms/, accessed September 6, 2019.

63. Cole Bunzel, "The Caliphate's Scholar-in-Arms," http://www.jihadica.com/ the-caliphate%E2%80%99s-scholar-in-arms/, accessed June 10, 2018.

64. Amar Benaziz and Nick Thompson, "Is ISIS leader Abu Bakr Baghdadi's bling timepiece a Rolex or an 'Islamic watch'?," CNN, July 10, 2014, http://www .cnn.com/2014/07/10/world/meast/iraq-baghdadi-watch/index.html, accessed June 12, 2018.

65. The English language issues of *Dabiq* are available from wide variety of sources, ranging from Islamist to Islamophobic to public policy sites. For the last issue,

for example, see "The Return of the Khilafah," https://jihadology.net/2016/07/31/new-issue-of-the-islamic-states-magazine-dabiq-15/, then follow the "previous issue" links back to Issue 1. The magazine was also published in Arabic, French, and German.

66. The Soufan Group, "Foreign Fighters: An Updated Assessment of the Flow of Foreign Fighters into Syria and Iraq," December 2015.

67. *Dabiq*, "The Return of the Khilafah," 4–5, 26.

68. Ibid., 8.

69. Ibid., 10.

70. Ibid., 32–33.

71. McCants, *The ISIS Apocalypse*, 142–143.

72. Robert Mackey, "The Case for ISIS, Made in a British Accent," *The New York Times*, June 20, 2014.

73. Nelly Lahoud and Jonathan Pieslak, "Music of the Islamic State," *Survival* Vol. 61, No. 1 (2018): 153–168, quote 155.

74. Richard Barrett, "Foreign Fighters in Syria," The Soufan Group, June 2014.

75. Mariam Karouny, "Apocalyptic prophecies drive both sides to Syrian battle for end of time," Reuters, April 1, 2014, https://www.reuters.com/article/us-syria-crisis-prophecy-insight/apocalyptic-prophecies-drive-both-sides-to-syrian-battle-for-end-of-time-idUSBREA3013420140401, accessed June 12, 2018.

76. Anonymous, "The Revival of Slavery before the Hour," *Dabiq* No. 4 (September 2014), 17.

77. Nick Cumming-Bruce, "ISIS Committed Genocide Against Yazidis in Syria and Iraq, U.N. Panel Says," *The New York Times*, June 16, 2018; and Valeria Cetorelli, "Mortality and kidnapping estimates for the Yazidi population in the area of Mount Sinjar, Iraq, in August 2014: A retrospective household survey," *PLOS Medicine* May 9, 2017, https://doi.org/10.1371/journal.pmed.1002297, accessed June 12, 2018.

78. For a tabulation of IS-directed and -inspired attacks as of early 2018, see Tim Lister et al., "ISIS goes global: 143 attacks in 29 countries have killed 2,043," CNN, February 12, 2018, https://www.cnn.com/2015/12/17/world/mapping-isis-attacks-around-the-world/index.html, accessed June 12, 2018. The estimate of 3,800 deaths as of August 2019 is tabulated from Karen Yourish et al., "How Many People Have Been Killed in ISIS Attacks Around the World," *The New York Times*, July 16, 2016; and https://en.wikipedia.org/wiki/List_of_terrorist_incidents_linked_to_ISIL, accessed September 6, 2019.

79. Ben Watson, "What the Largest Battle of the Decade Says about the Future of War," *Defense One* (2017), https://www.defenseone.com/feature/mosul-largest-battle-decade-future-of-war/, accessed July 19, 2019; and Rukmini Callimachi and Eric Schmitt, "ISIS Names New Leader and Confirms al-Baghdadi's Death," *The New York Times*, October 31, 2019.

80. See, for example, Graeme Wood, "What ISIS Really Wants," *The Atlantic*, March 2015.

81. Janine di Giovanni, "The Militias of Baghdad," *Newsweek*, November 26, 2014.

82. Jason Burke, "Rise and fall of Isis: its dream of a caliphate is over, so what now?," *The Guardian*, October 21, 2018, https://www.theguardian.com/world/2017/oct/21/isis-caliphate-islamic-state-raqqa-iraq-islamist, accessed June 12, 2018; and Aaron Y. Zelin, "Interpreting the Fall of Islamic State Governance," Washington Institute, October 16, 2017, http://www.washingtoninstitute.org/policy-analysis/view/interpreting-the-fall-of-islamic-state-governance, accessed June 12, 2018; and Sune Engel Rasmussen, "U.S.-Led Coalition Captures Last ISIS Bastion in Syria, Ending Caliphate," *The Wall Street Journal*, March 23, 2019.

EPILOGUE

1. Richard Dawkins, *The Selfish Gene* (New York: Oxford University Press, 2009), vii.

2. David Sloan Wilson, *Evolution for Everyone* (New York: Delta Trade Paperbacks, 2007), 70.

3. Stanley Milgram, "Behavioral Study of Obedience," *Journal of Abnormal and Social Psychology* Vol. 67, No. 4 (1963): 371–378; and Milgram, "Some Conditions of Obedience and Disobedience to Authority," *Human Relations* Vol. 18, No. 1 (February, 1965): 57–76.

4. C. Haney et al., "Interpersonal Dynamics in a Simulated Prison," *International Journal of Criminology and Penology* Vol. 1 (1973): 69–97.

5. For a detailed and scathing analysis of the Stanford Prison Experiment, see Ben Blum, "The Lifespan of a Lie," https://medium.com/s/trustissues/the-lifespan-of-a-lie-d869212b1f62.

6. Laurence Rees, *Auschwitz: A New History* (New York: Public Affairs, 2005).

7. Ibid. On channel island deportations, see 135–139; killing at Belźec, 149–150, quote 203.

8. Lionel Laurent, "What Bitcoin Is Really Worth May No Longer Be Such a Mystery," https://www.bloomberg.com/news/features/2018-04-19/what-bitcoin-is-really-worth-may-no-longer-be-such-a-mystery, accessed July 25, 2018.

INDEX

Note: Page numbers starting with "P–" indicate illustrations/photos in photo insert.